THE FLUTE BOOK

ALSO BY NANCY TOFF

THE DEVELOPMENT OF THE MODERN FLUTE

GEORGES BARRÈRE AND THE FLUTE IN AMERICA

THE FLUTE BOOK

A COMPLETE GUIDE FOR STUDENTS AND PERFORMERS

Second Edition

NANCY TOFF

New York Oxford
Oxford University Press
1996

Oxford University Press

Oxford New York
Athens Auckland Bangkok Bogota Bombay
Buenos Aires Calcutta Cape Town Dar es Salaam
Delhi Florence Hong Kong Istanbul Karachi
Kuala Lumpur Madras Madrid Melbourne
Mexico City Nairobi Paris Singapore
Taipei Tokyo Toronto

and associated companies in
Berlin Ibadan

Original cloth edition published by Charles Scribner's Sons, 1985

Published by Oxford University Press, Inc.,
198 Madison Avenue, New York, New York 10016

Library of Congress Cataloging-in-Publication Data
Toff, Nancy.
The flute book : a complete guide for students and performers /
Nancy Toff. — 2nd ed.
p. cm.
Includes bibliographical references and index.
ISBN 13 978-0-19-510502-5 (pbk.)

1. Flute. 1. Title.
ML935.T65 1996
788.3–dc20 96-23178

19 18 17

Printed in the United States of America
on acid-free paper

TO MY PARENTS

CONTENTS

Figures *x*
Plates *xi*
Terminology Used in This Book *xiii*
Preface to the Second Edition *xvi*
Preface *xvii*
Acknowledgments *xix*

THE INSTRUMENT

1. The Flute Today *3*
   What Is a Flute? • Manufacturing: The State of the Art
2. How to Choose an Instrument *14*
   To Rent or To Buy • Setting Priorities • Materials • Open or Closed Holes • C or B Footjoint • Mechanical Options • Testing an Instrument
3. Care and Maintenance of the Flute *31*
   Preventive Maintenance: Assembling the Instrument • Daily Cleaning • Storage • Polishing • Replating • Lubrication • The Headjoint Cork • Mechanical Problems
4. A Brief History of the Flute *42*
   Old System Flutes • The Boehm Flute • Other Nineteenth Century Flutes • Minor Modifications to the Boehm System
5. The Flute Family *63*
   The Piccolo • The Alto Flute • The Bass Flute • The Flute Choir

PERFORMANCE

6. Breathing *81*
   Posture • Inhalation • Suspension • Exhalation • The Diaphragm • Exercises • Breathing and Phrasing • Circular Breathing

7. Tone *89*
The Acoustical Basis • Tone Production • Focus and Projection • Homogeneity of Sound • Interpretation through Tone Development • Intonation • National Styles of Flute Playing

8. Vibrato *106*
What Is Vibrato? • The History of Vibrato • The Uses of Vibrato

9. Articulation 116
The Bowing Analogy • Single-Tonguing • Double-Tonguing • Triple-Tonguing • Flutter-Tonguing • Tongueless Attack • Legato • Note Endings • Practice

10. Technique *124*
Position • Practice • Fingering • Harmonics • The B♭ Thumb Key • Three Fingering Tricks

11. Style *142*
Virtuosity and Interpretation • The Theoretical Background: Basic Musicianship • Analysis • Phrasing • Performance Practice • The Early Music Movement and Questions of Authenticity

12. Performance *161*
Opportunities for Performance • Planning a Recital Program • Accompanists and Assisting Artists • Choosing a Recital Hall • The Printed Program • Publicity • Preparation and Rehearsal • Stage Protocol • The Entrance • Playing the Program • Memorization • Breaks between Pieces • Encores

13. Recordings *178*
Building a Recording Collection • How to Listen • Playing Along • Making Your Own Recordings

THE MUSIC

14. The Baroque Era *187*
Flute Versus Recorder • Musical Forms • France • Italy • England • Germany

15. The Classic Era *216*
Musical Forms • Paris • Germany • Spain • England • Vienna

16. The Romantic Era *241*
Music by Nonflutists • Music by Flutists

17. The Modern Era *255*
France • Great Britain • Elsewhere in Western Europe • Eastern Europe • The United States • The Avant-Garde • The Flute and Electronics

REPERTOIRE CATALOG

Introduction 285
A. The Baroque Era 289
B. The Classic Era 327
C. The Romantic Era 354
D. The Modern Era 375
E. Study Materials 433

APPENDICES

A. Fingering Chart for the Boehm Flute 445
B. Flute Manufacturers 452
C. Repair Shops 457
D. Sources for Music and Books 460
E. Useful Periodicals 462
F. Flute Clubs and Related Organizations 464

Selected Bibliography 471
Index 481

FIGURES

Joints of the Boehm flute *6*
Headjoint cork and O-Ring *7*
Hand-keys correspondence *8*
Clutch *9*
Boehm flute mechanism *10*
Rib- and post-mounted rods *16*
Closed-hole and open-hole pads *22*
Mechanical options—composite diagram *23*
Joint alignment *32*
Headjoint cork position *36*
Adjusting screws *38*
Pivot screw *39*
Needle spring *40*
Hotteterre's one-key flute *44*
Eight-key flute *48*
Pillars and plates *49*
Nolan's ring keys *50*
Boehm's 1831 flute *51*
Boehm's 1832 flute *52*
Boehm and Briccialdi B♭ thumb keys *56*
Boehm's Alt-Flöte mechanism *72*
Hand position *126*

PLATES

Following page 78

1. One-key flute (DCM 140)
2. Tuning register (detail of Plate 1)
3. Quantz two-key flute with corps de réchange (DCM 916)
4. Four-key flute (DCM 611)
5. Six-key flute (DCM 1406)
6. Eight-key flute (DCM 26)
7. Boehm 1831 model flute (photo courtesy Michael Zadro)
8. Boehm 1832 model flute (DCM 974)
9. Boehm 1847 model flute (DCM 1398)
10. Ward flute (DCM 43)
11. Carte 1851 system flute (DCM 43)
12. Clinton 1863 patent flute (DCM 109)
13. Carte 1867 system flute (DCM 14)
14. Siccama diatonic flute (DCM 1136)
15. Schwedler Reform flute (DCM 1584)
16. Borne-Julliot system flute (DCM 193)
17. Murray flute—Armstrong Prototype I (DCM Collection)
18. French model Boehm flute
19. Boehm piccolo
20. The flute family (photo courtesy W. T. Armstrong Co.)

All photographs are by the author unless otherwise noted.

DCM numbers refer to the accession numbers of the Dayton C. Miller Flute Collection, Music Division, Library of Congress, Washington, D.C.

Instruments without DCM numbers are privately owned.

TERMINOLOGY USED IN THIS BOOK

In general references, notes or keys of the flute are referred to by capital letters, but specific octave references are denoted by the following alphabetic notation:

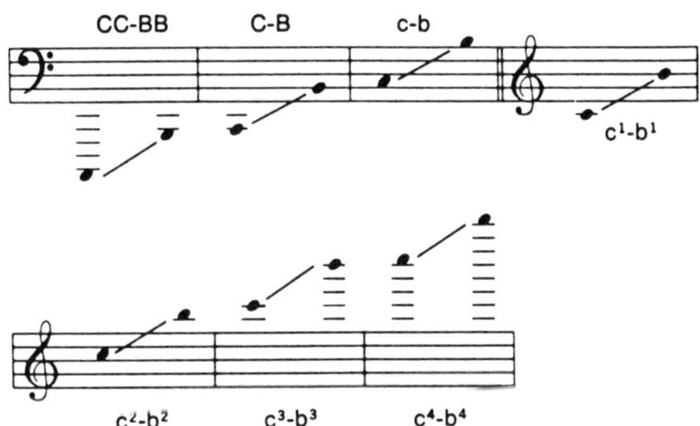

In the repertoire catalog, major keys are denoted by capital letters, minor keys by lower case letters. Thus *F* signifies F major and *f* signifies F minor.

In the text and on the mechanical diagrams, each hole is labeled according to the note that it vents; that is, the note that sounds when that hole is the lowest one open. Keys are named for the notes that are produced when they are depressed. Closed keys, therefore, have the same names as the holes they cover. The names of open keys, however, differ from the names of the holes they cover; thus, on the Boehm flute, the F hole is covered by the E key.

Fingers are numbered and labeled as follows:

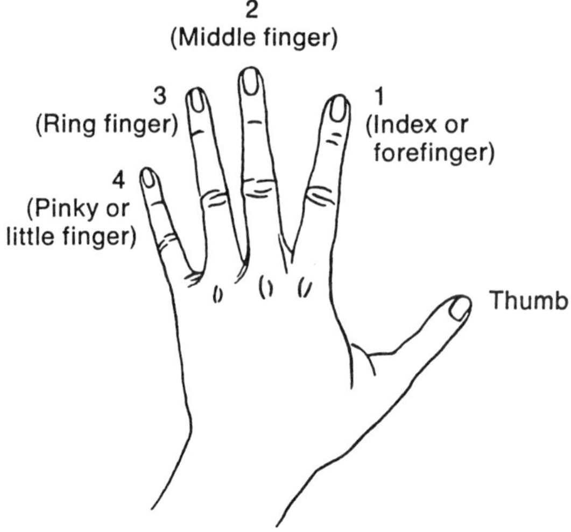

Flutist or Flautist?

On an average of once a week, someone asks me, "Are you a flutist or a flautist?" My answer is always a vehemently declaimed "Flutist!" Ascribe my insistence either to a modest lack of pretension or to etymological evidence; the result is the same.

Less decisive people may call me a fluteplayer. Or even fluter, a term coined by Samuel Pepys. His diary entry for June 21, 1666 notes, "I saw . . . a picture of a fluter playing on his flute." But please, don't call me a flautist. Consider the negative connotation of that pronunciation: The verb *flaut* (to jeer or mock) is related to the Middle English spelling of flute, and apparently derives its meaning from the practice of playing a flute to ridicule.

The word *flute* is derived from the Provençal *flauta,* which in Middle English and Old French became *flaute, flahute,* or *flahuste.* The modern Spanish *flauta* and Italian *flauto* are direct descendants of the Provencal, while modern French took a divergent path toward *flûte.* The earliest English spellings of the modern *flute* are *flowte* and *floute* (Chaucer, 1384), pronounced *fluut, floyte* (Caxton, 1483), pronounced *floo-eet,* as in *Louis;* and *flutes* (Eden, 1555).

Since the English term *flute* is obviously related to the modern French *flûte,* it follows therefore that the player of that instrument would be a *flutist.* The *Oxford English Dictionary* dates the first appearance of the latter term as 1603, when John Florio used it in his translation of Montaigne's essays ("When some commended him to be an excellent flutist. . . ."). *Flautist,* according to the *O.E.D.,* did not appear in English until 1860, when Nathaniel Hawthorne used it in *The Marble Faun.* ("The flautist poured his breath in quick puffs of jollity.") The frequent use of the word *flautist* is probably inspired by the Italian terminology—including *flauto*—that pervades musical scores. Significantly, Hawthorne had lived in Italy for a year and a half before he wrote *The Marble Faun*.

Several experts on English usage have taken on this weighty issue. H. W. Fowler, in *A Dictionary of Modern Usage* (1926), came down on the side of *flutist:* "It is a comfort to learn from the OED that *flutist* (1603) is a much older established word than *flautist* (1860). With three centuries behind us we can face it out against PRIDE OF KNOWLEDGE." Yet in the second edition (1957), Fowler was forced to acknowledge that *flautist* had attained predominance.

But Bergen and Cornelia Evans, in their *Dictionary of Contemporary American Usage* (1957), judged that "The 'proper' word for one who plays a flute is not *flautist,* as the overknowing sometimes insist. *Flautist* is an acceptable word, but it is a fairly recent importation (1860). The more sensible *flutist* had been in use for centuries before the Italianate variation appeared and has remained in use ever since." And Ray Copperud, in *American Usage and Style: The Consensus* (1970), agrees: "Fowler says *flautist* has displaced *flutist,* but in the United States it is something of an affectation, only occasionally met. *Flutist* greatly predominates."

In my own experience, however, I find that *flautist* stubbornly persists, particularly among non-fluteplayers trying to sound knowledgeable and among press agents who, as Copperud suggests, consider the term "a charming antique." Potential charm notwithstanding, I prefer *flutist,* a preference based not only on an aversion to affectation, but also on simple linguistic logic: I play the *flute*, not the *flaut;* therefore I am a *flutist*, not a *flautist*.

PREFACE TO THE SECOND EDITION

In the twelve years since I turned in the manuscript of the first edition, the changes in the flute world may best be described in one word: *more.* More flutists, more instruments (available for more money), more flute makers, and most of all, more music. Similarly, the number of flute clubs and organizations has grown considerably, reflecting the continuing popularity of our instrument. Whether all of these changes are good I leave to the judgment of individual flutists.

In chapter 2, How to Choose an Instrument, prices have been updated (upwards, of course). Though various individual manufacturers offer some new options of keywork or scale, these represent relatively minor changes, and information about them is best found in up-to-date literature available from the flute makers themselves. What is fascinating is the change in the industry: the number of small shops that have spun off from some of the larger companies and the amalgamation of some old and respected names into large corporations.

Most of the revisions affect the Repertoire Catalog and the Appendices. I have added to the Repertoire Catalog several hundred new entries (including many of the winners of the National Flute Association's Newly Published Music competition), have added new information about old editions, and have updated the necrology. These changes are most evident in the Modern Era section. As in the first edition, however, the catalog is intentionally selective.

In the bibliography, there is a new subsection for Historical Flute Methods and Treatises, reflecting increasing interest in authentic performance practice, and a new section of biographies and autobiographies. New entries have been added in all categories.

I would once again like to thank those colleagues who generously contributed repertoire suggestions and other information: Jan Boland, Roberta Brokaw, Leone Buyse, Paula Elliott, Ann Fairbanks, Kathy Borst Jones, Wendy Rolfe, Pat Spencer, Sue Waller, Trevor Wye, and Karen Yonovitz. I would also like to thank Maribeth Payne, executive editor of the Oxford University Press music department, for taking on this project, and Valerie Sauers, for designing the revised appendices.

Finally, I wish to thank all those readers who asked so persistently for a second edition. I hope they find this book useful for many years to come.

PREFACE

This book is intended to supplement basic flute methods and instruction by providing the theoretical and historical background for the techniques presented by most teachers and in most published study materials. I have been luckier than most students not only in the excellence of my teachers but also in the variety of their approaches. As a consequence, this book reflects my experience as a student of various persuasions of the Franco-American school of flute playing. Specifically, my experience derives from the traditions of Georges Barrère (via Arthur Lora), Georges Laurent (via James Pappoutsakis), William Kincaid (via Harold Skinner and Glennis Stout), and Marcel Moyse (via Max Schoenfeld).

Some major characteristics of each teacher stand out in my memory: Harold Skinner sought a big sound, as did Kincaid, and worked on a measured, consciously controlled vibrato. He also used two favorite Kincaid tone-building devices: whistle tones and difference tones. Max Schoenfeld introduced me to Moyse's *Tone Development Through Interpretation,* which uses operatic themes to develop a flexible, singing tone. Arthur Lora, while not ignoring the technical aspects of performance, stressed conscientious scholarship in performance practice. He lent me the books of C. P. E. Bach, Adam Carse, and others, showed me how to evaluate variant editions of a given work, and gave me a solid grounding in baroque ornamentation. Perhaps because he was no longer performing by the time I studied with him, his lessons were generally verbal critiques and discussions, rather than demonstrations. James Pappoutsakis, on the other hand, taught by example, and befitting his longtime position in the Boston Symphony, placed considerable emphasis on the orchestral literature. Though his tonal ideal was much the same as Arthur Lora's, he was emphatic in concentrating on the instrument itself, and rather looked down on the musicological perspective. Thus my educational genealogy represents the convergence of a number of diverse philosophies, sounds, and pedagogical techniques. In this book I will attempt to convey a synthesis of these that reflects my own choices yet presents alternative approaches to various aspects of performance.

Added to this flute training is my education in music theory and history at Harvard, particularly Luise Vosgerchian's keyboard harmony class—a trial by fire in applied theory and musical style, and full immersion in score reading. No one could emerge from those classes without understanding the fundamental nature of musical pulse in the Boulanger tradition.

This book also reflects my lifelong interest in music history, especially in the history of musical performance. As such it includes more theoretical, philosophical, and historical perspectives than does the traditional treatise or how-to method. Moreover, my sources are not limited to flute treatises; I have drawn from a broad spectrum of musicological and theoretical literature and instructional works for a variety of instruments.

Because of this historical orientation, I have organized the catalog of flute repertoire at the end of the book not by level of technical difficulty, as in most pedagogically oriented catalogs, nor solely in alphabetical order by composer, but by historical era. The catalog is designed to be used in conjunction with the other parts of the book. I hope that the flutist will assimilate from the text an overall concept of musical history in a given period and a perception of how the flute fits into that history; that he will use the bibliography to find supplementary information on pertinent performance practice; and that he will then apply this knowledge to the performance of the music listed for each historical period.

ACKNOWLEDGMENTS

A project of this scope entails many debts that I am happy to acknowledge. First, to Jacques Barzun, who suggested that I write the book and helped define its scope and organization; to Susanne Kirk, my editor; and to Remmel Nunn, who saw the manuscript through the rest of the editorial process. The ever-helpful reference staff of the Library of Congress Music Division was absolutely invaluable in expediting my research, particularly for the repertoire catalog. They were never too busy to undertake special searches for seemingly missing scores or to accept vast quantities of call slips–not only without complaint but with enthusiasm. Their constant encouragement and that of the Music Division's "Saturday regulars" is greatly appreciated.

Sarah McKee read most of the text and served as a judicious adviser on matters of organization, style, and language; Penelope Fischer and Carol Kniebusch reviewed the repertoire catalog and made many valuable sugges-tions. I also wish to thank Myrna Brown, executive coordinator of the National Flute Association, for supplying a variety of information; Nancy A. Faigh of the W. T. Armstrong Company, for providing pictures and technical data; Elizabeth Kiehl of the Arlington County (Va.) Public Library, for arranging interlibrary loans of many dissertations; my father, Ira N. Toff, for printing the photographs; my mother, Ruth B. Toff, for proofreading the galleys; Jerry Voorhees, for permitting me to reproduce one of his elegant mechanical diagrams; and Trevor Wye, for providing information on British flute-playing traditions. My thanks also to Eugene Anderson, Henry F. Graff, Greco/Emmi Inc., Vicki Leemon, and Lelia Washburn for their contributions.

THE INSTRUMENT

1

THE FLUTE TODAY

"A flute," wrote an early nineteenth century British critic, "is a musical weed which springs up everywhere."[1] It's still true today. The same lament could as easily be expressed by a high school band director trying to balance eighteen flutes, twelve trumpets, six clarinets, and a lone bassoon, or by one of the legion of young flutists now swelling those ranks. But why the popularity of the flute? Another British critic wrote in 1834, "The preference of our amateurs for this instrument, can only be accounted for by the easiness of attaining to a certain point of proficiency upon it."[2] Indeed, it is among the easiest of instruments to master at a rudimentary level. But, as the second critic cautioned, "to play well, and in tune, even a simple melody, is a degree of merit not reached by one out of twenty who attempt it." The current situation differs from that described by our British friend, for within the last twenty-five years performance standards have risen to an unparalleled extent.

The flute is immensely popular among the younger generation. While there is a long tradition of local and community bands—organizations that have often included flutes, though not as universally as brass and percussion instruments—it was with the growth of public school music in the early part of the twentieth century that the flute and the other woodwinds became so popular. Not surprisingly, perhaps, the growth of instrumental music in the schools was a by-product of expanding athletic programs. Football teams, then as now, needed music to rouse the fans. The first school bands in the United States were formed just before World War I. Soon thereafter, a number of summer music camps were founded, two of the oldest being Eastern Music Camp, renamed New England Music Camp in 1923; and Interlochen (the National Music Camp), founded in 1928. Universities, too, began instrumental music programs and formed student orchestras. The University of Kansas offered the first flute major in 1891; other midwestern universities followed suit in the first decades of this century.

An immediate effect of this burgeoning flutist population was the development of the student flute, an instrument inexpensive enough to be acesssible and durable enough to withstand amateur handling. At first, American musical instrument dealers had to import such instruments. Mass production of musical instruments got a much earlier start in Europe than in the U.S., principally in Mantes and La Couture in France and the German cities of Markneukirchen and Graslitz. A British wind player noted in 1931 that "the making of inexpensive instruments has been for many years a traditional, highly developed peasant industry."[3] But by the 1920s Elkhart, Indiana, had become the center for a new breed of American mass-producers who seized the opportunities offered by public music education. Instrument manufacturing, sheet music publishing, and other educational programs such as traveling clinics and contest sponsorship grew rapidly.

Contests, indeed, are another twentieth century development that promote high-quality flute playing. Contests, of course, are nothing new to the musical world. In 1781, for instance, Mozart and Muzio Clementi engaged in a one-on-one piano contest under the sponsorship of Emperor Joseph II. Today, there is a wide range of flute playing competitions. The National Flute Association began its Young Artist Competition in 1976, and the prestigious Naumburg Foundation, which since its founding in 1927 had limited itself to pianists, string players, and singers, held its first flute competition in 1978.

As in scholarship and athletics, collegiality is an important impetus to musical growth and excellence. In the case of flute players, clubs are a long tradition. The London Flute Players Club was an active organization in the nineteenth century, and the British Flute Society, founded in 1983, enrolled 1,000 members in its first year. In this country, the oldest continuously operating flute club, the New York Flute Club, was founded by Georges Barrère in 1920; the Boston Flute Players Club was established by Georges Laurent the following year. Mark Thomas organized the National Flute Association in 1972, and under that national umbrella there are local clubs nationwide (see Appendix F). The National Flute Association, largely made up of professionals, adult amateurs, and college students, has 5,000 members in 1996. In addition, the memberships of local flute clubs include many young, high school members who are not members of the national organization.

Flute players, like everyone else, learn by example. In the eighteenth century, the models were Michel Blavet in Paris and Andrew Ashe in London, followed in the next generation by Charles Nicholson in London, Louis Drouet and Jean-Louis Tulou in France, Theobald Boehm and the Fürstenau and Doppler families in Germany. In the late nineteenth century, the torch passed to Paul Taffanel and Philippe Gaubert in Paris, Joachim Andersen in Denmark and Germany, and John Lemmone and Eli Hudson in England, to name a small selection of top artists. There has certainly been no shortage of virtuosi in the history of the flute. But in their day all of these men, however distinguished, exercised their influence primarily on a local level, supplemented to a relatively limited extent by European concert tours. In the United States, Georges Barrère toured extensively as soloist with his own chamber orchestra and with several chamber groups during the 1920s and 1930s. But he never appeared as guest soloist with regional orchestras, nor did he present many solo recitals except in New York.

Today, however, as a consequence of improved transportation, communications, and especially of broadcast and recording technology, the situation has changed drastically. It was not until the middle of this century that a Jean-Pierre Rampal, no matter how great his talents, could become a one-man roadshow for his instrument. Beginning a solo concert career in France just after World War II, he soon went on to worldwide concert tours, recordings, and an expansion of the "standard" repertory through archival research in both Europe and the United States. His success has inspired thousands of amateur players and has proved to aspiring young professional flutists that a solo career is possible. A small group of talented and successful professionals has followed his example—James Galway, Paula Robison, Carol Wincenc, Ransom Wilson, Eugenia Zukerman and more. In regard to the number of soloists, flutists are well ahead of other wind players. Until about 1960, the number of flute concertos programmed each year by all the major orchestras combined could be counted on the fingers of one hand. Today, Rampal, Galway, and the others are frequent and welcome guests, and principal players are making solo appearances with their own orchestras.

The contribution of the recording industry to the flute cannot be overstated; the recordings of Rampal and his colleagues have been of inestimable value in expanding the literature, raising technical standards of performance, and giving flute players star status in the entertainment industry. The recording industry has also contributed in large part to the creation of an International Style of flute playing, the pros and cons of which are discussed in further detail in chapter 7, "Tone."

Flutists now revel in a new Golden Age: technical standards are higher than ever, thanks to competition on all levels and to the increased opportunities to hear the world's best performers in public performances, broadcasts, and recordings. The technology of the microphone has also contributed to the rise in technical standards since it is unforgiving in matters of tone and attack. Musicians must now compete not only with their local colleagues but with performances of the top artists on the radio and in the concert hall. James Pappoutsakis, looking back in 1978 over some forty years of teaching, noted, "Material that we used to give to graduate students ten or fifteen years ago, is now given to high school students."[4]

Often, too, contemporary flutists are required to be extremely versatile. There is, of course, historical precedent. In centuries past, private music masters taught a bit of everything. Studio musicians have always been quick-change artists, and school music teachers have long been required to teach at least the rudiments of all the band and orchestra instruments. Today, full-time professional flutists are often expected to have expertise on flute, alto flute, bass flute, piccolo, and even historical instruments, particularly the one-keyed baroque flute. The challenges and opportunities for the flutist have never been greater.

The availability of music for the flute—not to mention instructional materials and historical treatises—is unprecedented in the history of the instrument. The photo offset process has allowed publishers to reprint out-of-print editions without going to the expense of new typography or music calligraphy. Similarly, facsimile editions of important historical treatises on music are readily available.

Periodical literature is also substantial—though certainly not of uniform quality. Today we have the National Flute Association's *The Flutist Quarterly* (formerly *The National Flute Association Newsletter*); *Pan*, the house organ of the British Flute Society; *Flute Network; Flute Talk,* published by *The Instrumentalist; Tibia*; and *Traverso*. There is also flute coverage in *Chamber Music, The Instrumentalist, and Windplayer,* and frequent historical articles in the *Galpin Society Journal, The American Musical Instrument Society Journal and Newsletter*, and *Early Music*.

What Is a Flute?

Physically, the modern flute is relatively easy to describe, because the silver Boehm system instrument is now used almost worldwide. There are, of course, many variations on the standard model (see chapter 2, "How to Choose an Instrument"), but those variations do not impair the flutist's ability to switch from instrument to instrument because the variations do not affect the fingering system.

The Boehm system is simply the application of acoustical principles to the design of a woodwind instrument, and the design of a mechanical system to accommodate those principles to human hands. Beginning with Boehm's truly revolutionary 1832 flute, the position of the holes was no longer determined by the physical size and shape of the human hand, but rather, by the principles of physics and acoustics.

Like Gaul, the Boehm flute is divided into three parts: the headjoint, body or middle joint, and footjoint. They are connected to each other by tenon-and-socket joints, which are integral to the flute tube. The headjoint contains the crown

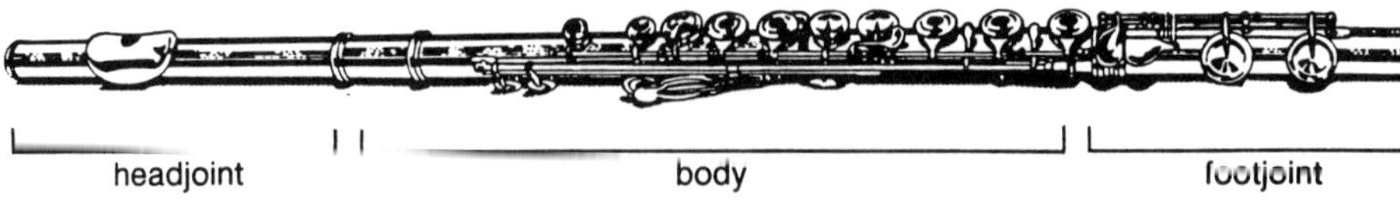

assembly, including a cork or other stopper that determines the total length of the tube; the embouchure hole, which on metal flutes is cov- ered by an embouchure plate; and the tuning slide, which is the tenon of a tenon-and-socket joint by which the headjoint is inserted into the body. The body of the instrument contains the socket portion of that joint, as well as most of the tone holes and mechanism. At its bottom, the body is the socket for another joint that connects it to the footjoint. The footjoint contains the tone holes controlled by the mechanism that the little finger of the right hand operates. The number of keys on the footjoint may vary; the "standard" foot descends to middle C, but many flutes go down to B. The total length of the modern Boehm flute is 26⁵⁄₁₆ inches (66.8 centimeters) for a flute with a C foot; 27¾ inches (70.5 centimeters) with a B foot.

At the top of the headjoint is the crown, a more or less decorative metal cap that protects the tuning mechanism of the headjoint. On its inner side a screw mechanism permits adjustment of the total length of the flute tube, thereby allowing the player to make small adjustments in the internal tuning of the instrument. The distance between the center of the embouchure hole and the bottom of the cork is 17.3 millimeters (0.681 inches). The crown screw allows the player to adjust this distance, using as a guide a tick mark on the cleaning rod conveniently provided by most manufacturers.

At the end of the screw is a stopper of one variety or another; originally cork, it is often, today, fashioned of neoprene, a synthetic rubber that, unlike cork, is not prone to shrinkage, warpage, or other atmospherically induced changes in shape or size. Traditionally, the cork has had a flat internal surface; some configurations of the neoprene version, patented as the O-Ring, have a concave surface.

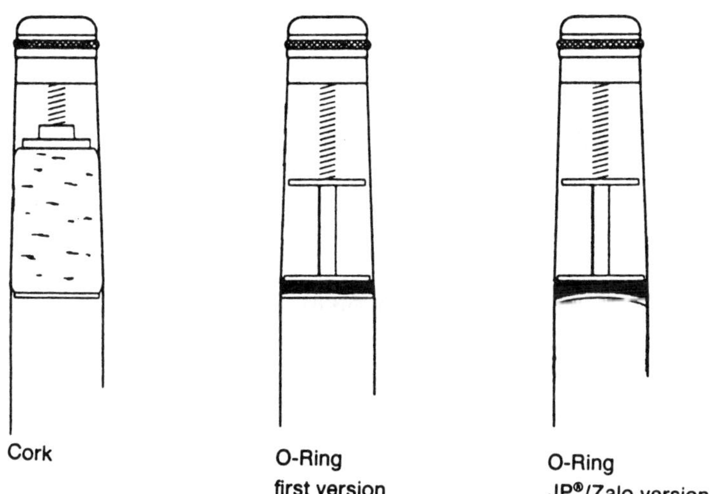

The most important part of the headjoint is the embouchure, or mouth hole. On the metal flute, it is surmounted by an embouchure plate or lip plate whose far side is called the chimney. The hole comes in a variety of shapes, ranging from a long oval to a rounded rectangle. In general, an oval shape makes the upper register more responsive, whereas a rounded rectangle boosts the lower. Similarly, a large embouchure improves the low register, while a small one helps the middle and high registers. Professional flutes usually have the more rectangular shape, student flutes a rounder shape. The tone is produced when the flutist directs the airstream across the embouchure hole so that the airstream is bisected by the far wall of the chimney. The velocity and angle with which the air is directed determines the quality of the tone as well as its intonation.

The embouchure plate is available in a number of different configurations—flat, curved (parallel to the curve of the flute tube), or cusped. The cusped or winged embouchure is a vestige of the nineteenth century reform flute; flutists who use it feel that it directs the airstream more accurately and reliably into the flute. But the curved plate is by far the most frequent variety.

The headjoint is constructed according to what Boehm dubbed a "parabolic curve," though in reality the shape is not a true parabola. The headjoint tube tapers very slightly as it approaches the crown. For some manufacturers, the design of the headjoint is a closely guarded secret that is itself a point of pride, not to mention a potent marketing tool.

The tenon-and-socket joint that connects the headjoint with the body also functions as the tuning slide, thus allowing the player to make adjustments in the overall pitch of the instrument. Pulling the tenon (headjoint) out flattens the pitch; pushing the tenon in sharpens the pitch. Most flutes today are constructed on the basis of A-440 (meaning that the frequency of a^1 is 440 vibrations per second), but they have a tolerance of two vibrations per second. This means that the flute will remain in tune at pitch levels ranging from A-438 to A-442, and that small adjustments of the headjoint tenon within that tolerance will not seriously affect the internal intonational balance of the instrument. Most flutes come equipped with a line etched around the circumference of the headjoint that indicates the optimal in-tune setting for the insertion of the head. In addition, many instruments have longitudinal notches in head and body, parallel to the length of the tube, that indicate the alignment of those two sections.

The body of the flute is more complicated. It is perfectly cylindrical in shape, with a uniform diameter of 19 millimeters (0.748 inches). It normally contains fifteen tone holes, including two holes for trill keys (but not counting the duplicate G♯), all of which are controlled, via the Boehm system mechanism, by eight fingers: all five fingers of the left hand and the first, second

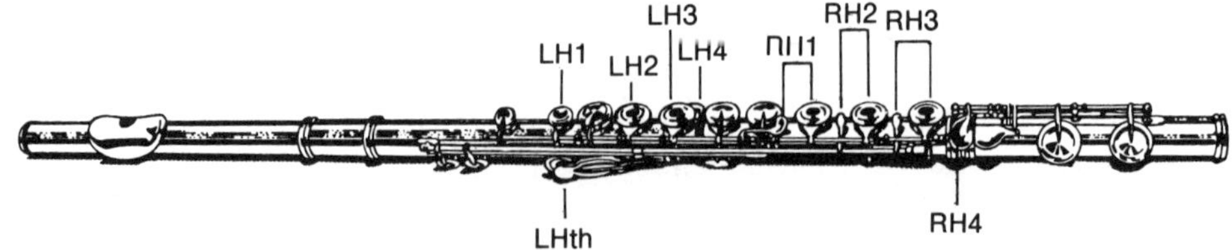

and third fingers of the right. The diagram shows the correspondence between the keys and fingers. The right thumb is employed solely in balancing and supporting the flute; the right pinky controls the footjoint keys.

The distribution of the tone holes along the tube is determined by acoustical formula, summarized on a chart that Boehm called a *Schema*. He published several versions, and each contemporary manufacturer has its own version. Theoretically, the holes should be as large as possible in order to enhance the instrument's acoustical properties; on some flutes, they are graduated in size; on others, equal (with the exception of the small trill holes).

A prime aspect of the Boehm system is that it is an open key system: the holes immediately below the sounding hole (for example, the G and G♯ holes if the player is fingering A) should be open in order to prevent the note being played from going flat or not projecting to the maximum extent possible.

Because nine human fingers are incapable, without mechanical assistance, of controlling fifteen holes, Boehm devised an entirely new fingering system. It is based on two fundamental devices: ring keys and horizontal rod-axles. The ring keys surmount a tone hole and allow a single finger to close both that hole and at least one more. As a result, the fingers do not have to move from their natural or rest position except to operate the trill keys and for small, sliding motions of the right hand pinky.

The first, second, and third fingers of the right hand control the F, E and D keys (F♯, F, and E holes), respectively. On the left hand, the first finger controls the touchpiece for C; the second and third fingers cover the A and B♭ holes, and the fourth finger controls the closed G♯ key. The left hand thumb controls an open key for B on the near side of the flute.

Motion is communicated between the keys by means of the rod-axles and by needle springs, which are made of gold or steel. Each key cover is attached to its own rod; the rods are mounted in a loose sleeve on the side of the flute tube closest to the player. Interconnected keys are linked by clutches (overlapping lugs or pins): one lug is soldered to the sleeve; another to the axle at the top end, above the sleeve; and a third lug is placed atop the other two.

In addition to the ring keys, there are a few levers: the left pinky lever for the closed G♯ key; the trill levers for the right hand, which control far-distant holes at the top end of the flute; and the levers for the little finger of the

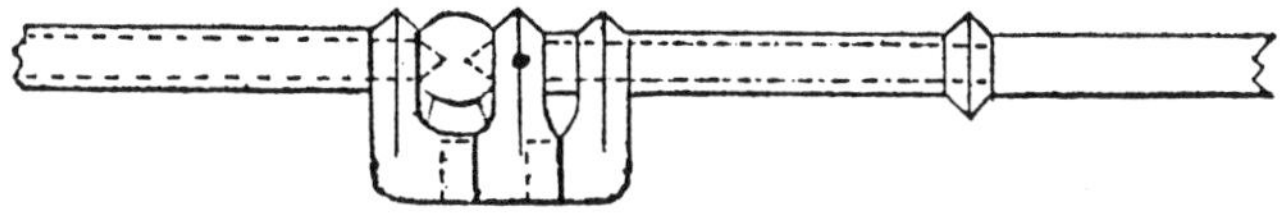

The 'clutch' devised by Buffet
A. Lug attached to sleeve carrying B♭ ring, etc.
B. Lug pinned to axle carrying G cup and E and F rings
C. Lug attached to loose sleeve carrying F♯ ring

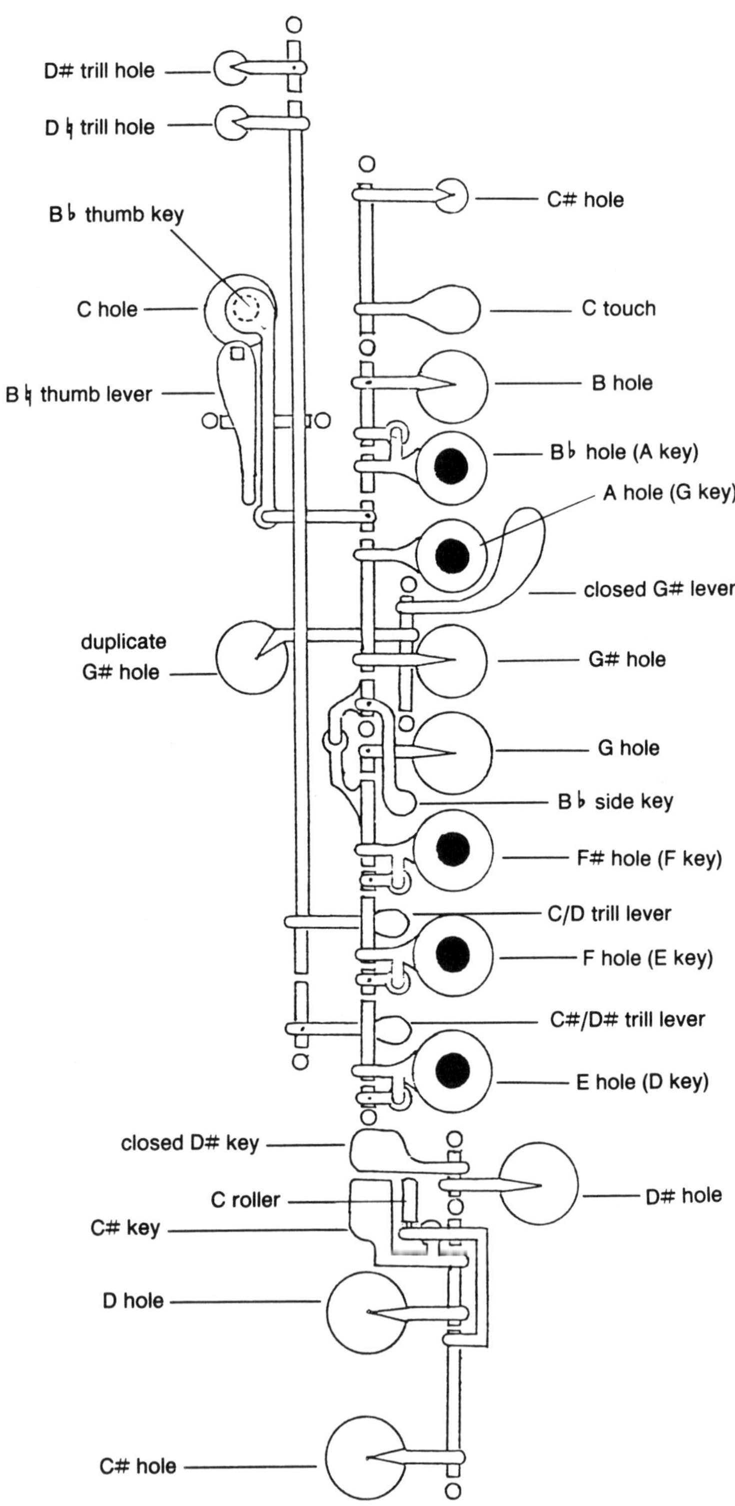

D# trill hole
D ♮ trill hole
C# hole
B♭ thumb key
C hole
C touch
B hole
B ♮ thumb lever
B♭ hole (A key)
A hole (G key)
closed G# lever
duplicate
G# hole
G# hole
G hole
B♭ side key
F# hole (F key)
C/D trill lever
F hole (E key)
C#/D# trill lever
E hole (D key)
closed D# key
C roller
D# hole
C# key
D hole
C# hole

right hand, which control the D♯, D, C♯, C, and B keys of the footjoint (the latter is found on B footjoints only). In contradiction to Boehm's open-hole theory, two of these levers control closed keys: the G♯ key (which Boehm originally designed as an open key) is provided with a duplicate hole to provide the venting that Boehm specified. The low D♯—a Boehm original—is also a closed key. Because the little finger must be almost constantly depressed in order to keep the low D♯ open, the flute is balanced automatically and effortlessly.

In order to stop the holes completely, the inner surface of each key is equipped with a pad, made either of animal skin, felt, or frequently, a durable synthetic material (even plastic). The pads are held in the key cups by a combination of screws and glue.

Manufacturing: The State of the Art

During this century, the Boehm system has been universally adopted, and manufacturers have not been concerned with building a new instrument. They have focused, instead, on making minor improvements on the design of the Boehm system. In recent years, for instance, there has been considerable reevaluation of Boehm's *Schema*. The best-known attempts are the Cooper scale, designed by Londoner Albert Cooper, versions of which are used by Verne Q. Powell Flutes and Brannen Brothers, among other companies; the Armstrong scale of W. T. Armstrong Company; the William Bennett scale, used by Jack Moore, and the Haynes Company's Deveau scale.

Another recent development is the Fajardo Wedgehead, an adjustable wedge inserted in the headjoint with the aim of improving the attack. But this is just one example of the experimentation being done on the headjoint. Acoustician Arthur Benade, flutist-headjoint maker Trevor Wye, Albert Cooper, and many others are constantly experimenting with the fine points of the design in order to make the instrument more responsive. Some direct their efforts at general purpose playing, others toward more specific goals, such as the execution of avant-garde techniques, for which Cooper has recently considered expanding the bore of the headjoint.

In recent years, manufacturers have made relatively few mechanical alterations, though there are of course exceptions to this rule. In 1977, John Coltman, a flutist and an engineer with Westinghouse, developed a new C♯ mechanism, known, logically, as the Coltman C♯, to improve the quality and intonation of that ever-troublesome note. It is quite similar to R. S. Rockstro's "vented D" of 1877, which was itself a modification of an 1842 design of Cornelius Ward.

In the 1970s, Muramatsu introduced the option of a manually operated locking clutch on the split-E mechanism, which allows the player to engage or disengage the mechanism at will. In 1981 the Wm. S. Haynes Company introduced a new B♭-F♯ mechanism, designed by Walter Haedrich and Dennis

Lawson, which makes it possible to play f^{3}♯ and b^{3} without the usual awkward slide from the B♭ thumb lever to the B-natural thumb key. Actually, this device is nearly identical to the Gage Articulated B-F ♯ device patented in 1926.

Emerson offers the RF Modification™, a change in the G/G♯ mechanism patented by Raymond Fabrizio, which Emerson claims improves the high E, G♯, and A. Brannen Brothers offers the Brögger™ Mekanik, based on the patent of Johan Brögger. As the literature describes it, "motion is transferred from one key to another by means of bridge rods rather than through rotating axles, hence keys are no longer pinned to the axles. Second, keys are coupled together using full-sized clutches, rather than the traditional lug and kicker arrangement." In addition, Brannen offers the Brögger™ Acoustic, the use of conical rather than cylindrical tone holes. One of the most interesting recent developments in flute making is the pioneering work on a quarter-tone flute by the Dutch flutemaker Eva Kingma in collaboration with the American maker Bickford Brannen. The Oston-Brannen Kingma system uses a "key-on- key" mechanism to permit both quarter tones and multiphonic production.

Though relatively few new mechanical options have been developed over the last few decades, research has continued with regard to materials. Platinum flutes became a reality in 1933. Some high-end flutemakers are using new alloys: Powell, for instance, has developed an Aurumite™ tube, in which a 14-karat rose gold inner tube is fused to an outer layer of sterling silver.

In the mid-1990s Matit Flutebrothers of Finland introduced a carbon fibre (graphite) flute with square, metal-plastic composite keys. The keys are operated by a magnet-spring system rather than by the traditional needle springs. Synthetic "elastomer" rings take the place of pads.

New alloys for plated flutes are constantly being tested, with the aim of making the instruments less expensive and more durable. Plastics are now used for piccolo bodies, various synthetics for key pads, and so on. With the increasing prices of precious metals it seems likely that such research will become increasingly important.

The greatest changes in the flute-making industry concern its economic and business aspects. Two seemingly disparate trends are evident. Some previously independent middle-size firms have combined (Armstrong and Artley into United Musical Instruments). At the same time, a significant number of workmen have left large companies to set up shop for themselves: Jack Moore (formerly foreman of Armstrong's Heritage Division), David Wimberley (formerly of Armstrong), Dana Sheridan (formerly of Powell), and many others. Of course this trend is nothing new; Verne Q. Powell was an emigrant from Haynes.

Another important development in flute making is internationalization. French performance traditions, in particular, have spread not only throughout the Western hemisphere but to the Orient as well. As a result, Japanese competition has become a major factor; Japanese firms now build not only radios and fuel-efficient automobiles, but musical instruments, too. Muramatsu, the first manufacturer of Boehm flutes in Japan, was founded in 1923.

The East-West cultural traffic has not, however, been one-way: Muramatsu began exporting flutes to the United States in 1974, and three years later the *Wall Street Journal* noted with chauvinistic alarm its inroad into the American market. Other Japanese firms, notably Miyazawa, Prima Sankyo, and Yamaha, have followed Muramatsu's lead. Similarly, E. F. Dean Flutes, whose American office is in Michigan, are actually made in Taiwan at a very competitive price. Yamaha's promotional literature proclaims all the virtues that Americans have come to expect from Japanese automobiles, including computer-assisted design and special assembly-line tooling that make possible the mass production of durable, economical instruments.

(An interesting aside: just as Japanese instruments have come to the West, so too have Japanese educational methods. An adaptation of the Suzuki violin method was introduced to American flute students in the late 1970s. It combines the educational philosophy of Shin'ichi Suzuki and Takeo Takahashi with the Franco-American flute-playing precepts of Marcel Moyse.)

As a result of flute manufacturers' increasing corporate strength and the pressures of foreign competition, marketing musical instruments has become big business. Some flute makers are branching out—expanding what were once modest public relations activities such as clinician programs into largescale educational organizations that encompass publishing, recording, and teaching activities. Others, however, such as Haynes and Powell, remain fiercely independent. Both business philosophies—custom service and mass marketing—seem to have room to thrive amid the flute "boom" that shows no signs of abating.

Notes

1. *Atheneum* 5 (1834): 23; quoted in David William Eagle, "A Constant Passion and a Constant Pursuit: A Social History of Flute-Playing in England from 1800 to 1851" (Ph.D. diss., University of Minnesota,1977), p. 35.
2. Ibid.
3. F. G. Rendall, "English and Foreign Wood-Wind Players and Makers," *Music and Letters* 12 (Apr. 1931): 155.
4. Eleanor Lawrence, "Interview with James Pappoutsakis," *National Flute Association Newsletter* 3, no. 2 (1978): 17.

2

HOW TO CHOOSE AN INSTRUMENT

Selecting an instrument is an important decision, but it should not be a frightening one. It does not require the wisdom of Solomon, but it may require the patience of Job. It requires some research, an ability to wade through the jargon of manufacturers' catalogs, and decisiveness about what you want (as opposed to what a salesman is promoting) in terms of quality, price, and availability.

On the following pages, I'll discuss setting a budget, how to distinguish necessary features from optional ones, and how to test potential instruments. In Appendix B, you'll find a list of flute manufacturers and their addresses, should you want to get information on particular brands. In general, I will not recommend particular manufacturers, though I will discuss various aspects of their product lines. Keep in mind that different players have different needs. So I'll supply the information, but you'll have to make the decisions.

To Rent or To Buy

Many children decide that they want to play the flute in the school band, but the school does not provide the instrument. The prudent parent, unsure whether the child will stick with the instrument or decide in six months or a year to trade it in for a trumpet or a football, may hesitate to invest several hundred dollars in a new instrument. There are two alternatives.

Many musical instrument dealers offer rental instruments. However, *caveat renter* is the order of the day. Unfortunately, many instruments designated for rental are inferior models. Moreover, many beginning players, particularly young ones, are apt to handle their instruments clumsily and/or carelessly—storing the instrument improperly, allowing tarnish to build up on joints, not drying sticky pads, bending keys out of alignment, and so on. Dealers often compound the problem by not investing much time in repairing instruments when they are returned to the store; extensive repairs to very inexpensive instruments are simply not cost-effective. The problem for the next renter, then, is an instrument that will not function satisfactorily even in the hands of an experienced player. Imagine how frustrated a beginner can become with such an instrument.

There are, of course, some decent instruments offered for rental. If you do decide to rent, a few guidelines are in order. Have an experienced flutist, a music teacher or friend, try out the instrument, testing it thoroughly as outlined later in this chapter. Inquire whether there is a repair warranty at the dealership. Many stores offer rental/purchase options, whereby you can rent for a given period, often six months to a year, with the option to apply the rental payments toward the purchase price if you decide to buy that particular instrument. If at all possible, and especially if there's a rental/purchase option, rent a new instrument; you've immediately eliminated the hazard of the previous owner.

Rent a brand-name flute, perhaps from a list suggested by your music teacher. It will be worth any small increment in price to get a responsive instrument. House brands or no-names are not a good gamble.

A good alternative to renting a flute is to buy one secondhand. You do run the risk of previous ownership, but often you can get a better-grade instrument than those available for rental for little or no increment in total price. Generally the owner of a better instrument is a more experienced player who has taken better care of the instrument than a beginner may have.

Many dealers, both woodwind specialists and general instrument dealers, carry reconditioned flutes. Classified advertisements in magazines and newspapers, particularly in newsletters of local flute clubs or the National Flute Association, are another good source. The instruments listed there are often being sold by flutists who have taken good care of them, but are trading up to a more expensive model. As with any instrument, have it checked by a reputable mechanic and tested by an experienced flutist whom you trust. (A list of flute repair shops is in Appendix C.)

Setting Priorities

Today, the price range of flutes is enormous. The least expensive student flute, a nickel-plated, plateau model, lists for about $530. A gold Powell or Brannen with a B foot, in contrast, sells for $22,000 or more. In between, however, there are a large number of choices.

The simplest decision is whether to choose a student or professional model. Student flutes cost about $550 to $3,600; sterling silver professional models (Haynes, Powell, Brannen Brothers, Muramatsu, and those of many other smaller makers) range from $3,000 to $9,000. Logically, most flutists begin with student models and work their way up. Haynes and Powell no longer have the five-year waiting lists that were a rite of passage for several generations of flutists, but there may be a more informal wait for the most popular handmade brands.

The principal difference between student and professional models is the materials of which they are made. This is also the number one determinant of price. The second factor is the amount of machine tooling or mass production versus hand craftsmanship.

Let's assume that you decide on a middle-grade student instrument, in the $800 to $1,500 price range. How best should you spend your money? Top priority, I believe, should be given to the materials. Solid or sterling silver construction throughout is ideal, but hardly possible in the midline price range. The next best choice is a sterling silver headjoint on a silver-plated body—a good compromise, because most flute makers and players believe that the headjoint is the prime determinant of the tone quality. Finally, there are fully plated instruments; silver plating is more expensive than nickel plating, whether on the headjoint or the entire flute. Springs should be gold, if possible, rather than steel.

Next in priority is the quality of the design and the workmanship. Just as solid materials are preferable to plated ones, forged keys are preferable to cast ones. Rods mounted on ribs are preferable to rods mounted merely on posts.

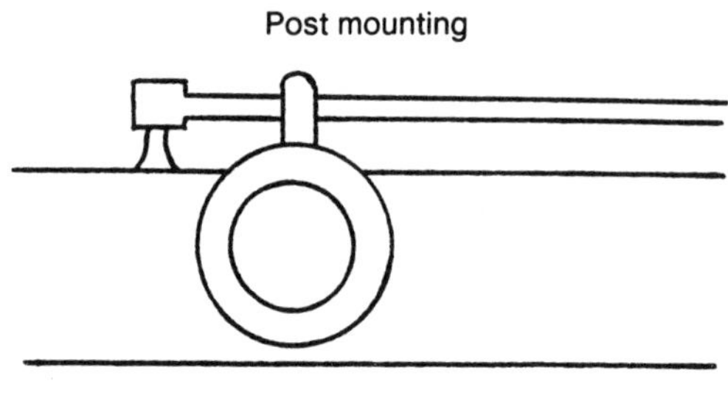

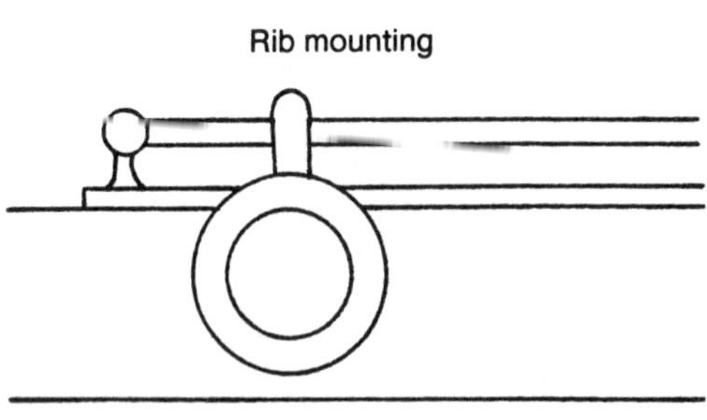

And an instrument should meet all the tests for quality construction outlined in the following pages.

Mechanical options take a definite backseat to both materials and workmanship. The added cost of a B foot over a C foot (typically $100 to $200 on a student flute, $400 to $600 on a professional model) is probably not a worth-while investment for the average student; among professionals, the choice is an aesthetic and technical one, a hotly debated matter of personal preference. Similarly, the standard key mechanism is adequate for most purposes; options such as Split E and extra trill keys may each add $50 to $700 to the cost and are easily dispensable.

Within any given price range, certain characteristics can be compared only by actual hands-on trial: the feel of an instrument, which varies from player to player depending on the size of player and instrument (a small player may be unable to balance a gold flute properly, for instance); the ease of response; whether trill keys are within easy reach of the fingers; and whether the embouchure plate construction is comfortable. These characteristics defy quantification or even description. For this reason it is probably best not to order an instrument by mail unless you have first compared a variety of instruments in a dealer's shop or showroom.

Materials

Almost nothing can start an argument among flutists faster than a discussion of the relative merits of various materials for constructing flutes. Physicist John Backus once hypothesized:

> For many years, there has been discussion and argument on the question of the influence of the wall material of a woodwind instrument on its tone quality. These arguments probably started in early Stone-Age musical circles with assertions that a flute made of a human thigh bone had a better tone than one fashioned from the rib of a sabre-tooth tiger.[1]

Or, as flutist Israel Borouchoff says, "Discussing materials for flute tubing can be compared to swimming in deep water with little hope of getting to shore safely."[2]

There are several aspects to this issue: the effect of the material on responsiveness (perceptible only to the player); its effect on tone quality (evident to both player and listener); and the more concrete questions of ease of fabrication, durability, and dimensional stability. Added to these is the long arm of tradition, a powerful force in the musical world and one that in this case carries strong nationalistic overtones.

The scientific arguments are too lengthy and technical to be of much interest or assistance to the flutist. Factors that scientists consider include hardness, density, thermal mass, and resonant frequency (the rate at which a vibrating body resonates). To cite just one example, acousticians prefer as dense a metal as possible to produce optimal low tones; their order of preference would be gold, platinum, and then silver.

Among players, not surprisingly, the choices between materials are largely unscientific, a matter of tradition and intangible personal preference. These preferences are often factors perceptible only to the player, not to the audience. About fifteen years ago, I participated in a trial of two Lamberson flutes, one gold, one sterling silver, a scene undoubtedly repeated at many times in many places. With backs turned, a group of students listened to our teacher, Harold Skinner, alternate between the two instruments, noting which one we thought we had heard. Our accuracy record was notably poor and the results were, perhaps predictably, inconclusive. When we each played the two instruments ourselves, however, we had strong personal preferences. Being the smallest person in the group, I found the gold flute too breath-resistant and too heavy to hold properly for any length of time.

National tradition plays a large part in choice of material. In the United States, Belgium, and other countries where the French school prevails, the silver flute is the overwhelming choice. In England, Germany, and eastern Europe, however, the wooden flute tradition still persists to some degree. Some flutists, however, strike a compromise by using wooden headjoints on silver bodies or by lining wooden headjoints with metal.

For the average player, the choice will be between a solid silver tube and various types of silver plating. The highest quality flutes are either sterling silver (92.5 percent pure) or coin silver (90 percent pure), between which the difference is negligible. Silver flutes have the greatest immediacy of response; that is, they speak most easily and permit light and tripping articulation. Other advantages include their relative adaptability, in contrast to wood, to imperfectly formed embouchures, and the most responsiveness to changes in tonal coloring. "To me," said William Kincaid, "a fine metal instrument has a sound which floats and is pliant."[3] Says Israel Borouchoff,

> The ability to tolerate a great variety of embouchures makes it an instru- ment capable of a wide range of shading. Its brilliance is remarkable, with no sacrifice in roundness, thus its popularity among symphony players. The silver flute is truly a flute for all seasons.[4]

The only drawback to sterling silver is its price: on 1995 price lists, Sankyo's least expensive all-sterling (body and keys) flute costs $2,485, Miyazawa's, $3,695. A small compromise is to choose a sterling silver body with silver-plated keys, where the material will have less effect on the tone. It will, however, affect durability, so you may consider it a good investment to put an additional few hundred dollars into solid keys, which will never need replating, to protect the rest of your investment.

Most student flutes are made of silver-plated metals such as yellow brass or German silver, which are chosen for durability and low cost. Yellow brass is 70 percent copper, 30 percent zinc; German silver, also known as nickel silver, is a similar alloy that includes 10 percent to 20 percent nickel. The plating is either nickel or silver. Silver plating tends to impart a more mellow sound, the next best thing to solid-silver construction. It does, however, tarnish easily, just as sterling does. Nickel, on the other hand, is shinier in appearance, more durable and resistant to corrosion (and better able to stand minimal care by the young player); however, the very shininess that makes it attractive may also make it slippery to hold.

As a general rule, plated instruments will have a harder, brighter sound than solid-silver ones, because the number of overtones is greater. And the heavier tubing, though more durable, may make the sound unpleasantly rough or shrill.

All in all, a plated flute is the best choice for a young student because of its price and durability. The prospective purchaser should be sure to examine the quality of the plating job carefully. It should be smooth and even, with no "fish scales" or rough spots. At the same time, check for imperfect metalwork such as sloppy soldering and stray tool marks. The condition of the plating is often a good indication of the overall quality of the workmanship.

The more advanced player may want to consider a sterling headjoint on a plated body as a midrange alternative to the solid silver flute. Yamaha student flutes, for instance, come in a variety of grades (those listed here all have C footjoints); the firm also sells three tiers of professional-level flutes.

Standard flute, plateau model, nickel- or silver-plated nickel silver	$610
Standard flute, French model, silver-plated nickel silver	730
Intermediate flute, plateau model, sterling silver headjoint, silver-plated nickel silver body	890
Intermediate flute, French model, sterling silver headjoint, silver-plated nickel silver body	1,030
Intermediate flute, plateau model, sterling silver headjoint and body	1,450
Intermediate flute, French model, sterling silver headjoint and body	1,590

At the other end of the price scale are the so-called precious metal flutes, principally gold and platinum. Gold is the more common of the two, and is offered by a wide variety of flute makers. The gold used is generally 9-karat or 14-karat red or yellow, or sometimes white, but not 18-karat, since William S. Haynes concluded early in this century that 18-karat gold was too soft to be practical.

Yellow or red gold produces a tone with a strong fundamental, and thus a powerful low register, though it may lack some of the brilliance of the silver flute. Many players, such as Israel Borouchoff, prefer it for its "mellow warmth" and "solid core"; he finds it more responsive to dynamic variations and more consistent in pitch, particularly in the face of temperature and dynamic fluctuations. However, he cautions, gold is less forgiving of variations in embouchure, and can easily sound too tubby or hissy. White gold is closer in tone quality to silver, that is, more brilliant, but it is a comparatively inflexible instrument, with a tendency to produce a brittle sound.[5] Gold is the choice of such modern virtuosi as Rampal, Galway, and Gazzelloni. The public relations value of the moniker "The Man with the Golden Flute" is undeniable.

Less common than gold is platinum, the preference of Philadelphia Orchestra legend William Kincaid, and for many years of Chicago Symphony principal Donald Peck. Platinum is a malleable metal, and is often alloyed with irridium. The resulting alloy emits a powerful sound, but requires a correspondingly powerful input of air and accuracy of embouchure. Orchestra players particularly enjoy its projection and wide dynamic range, but many other flutists find its timbral flexibility limited. Platinum flutes are frequently fitted with silver keys because the heaviness of an all-platinum instrument can make it difficult to support. They are available, with silver keys, from Muramatsu and Armstrong Heritage. Palladium, a metallic element of the nickel family, is also used in flute making and has properties very similar to those of platinum.

Very few flutists today play wooden Boehm instruments, though there are some exceptions, notably Felix Skowronek of Seattle. In a 1979 address to the Music Teachers National Association, Skowronek argued that the thicker mass of the wooden instrument and its greater total weight present greater resistance to blowing. If the resistance is sufficiently and properly met by the player, which requires superior embouchure conditioning, says Skowronek, "the resulting tone is usually described as a round, full, dark, and broad sonority." Skowronek disputes the conventional wisdom, as do many British players, that the wooden flute is not sufficiently loud to project from the orchestral sound; he dubs it "a husky treble rather than a shrill or cutting edge." Also, he maintains, the wooden flute blends more easily with the other winds than does a metal instrument.[6]

What led to the decline of the wooden flute was its relatively slow response—the silver flute is more agile and quicker-speaking—which disqualified it from the solo arena, where flexibility and response were paramount. Compromises sprang up—the British thin-walled wooden flute, metal headjoints or metal-lined wooden headjoints on wooden bodies—but in the United States the wooden flute passed into oblivion by World War I. With the immigration of several exemplars of the French school, notably Barrère and Laurent, in the first decade of the century, the wooden flute came to quite a speedy demise.

Skowronek suggests that what is needed is modernization of the wooden flute—based on research like that already undertaken with vigor in regard to the metal flute. This would include research on headjoint bore and the embouchure hole and the redesign of tone hole placement and proportions. To this end, Skowronek himself has collaborated with a young flute maker in Seattle, and his own performances are indeed impressive. He has also experimented with nontraditional hardwoods. Today, wooden Boehm flutes are available only from a few specialist makers, notably Abell Flute Company in the United States and Robert Bigio and the Flutemakers Guild in England. The wooden Boehm's appeal is largely to players with antiquarian interests who wish to approximate an eighteenth- or nineteenth-century wood-flute sound while retaining the convenience of Boehm system fingering.

Open or Closed Holes

The most obvious choice in flutes is between the closed-hole (also called plateau or American) and open-hole (French) models. On the closed-hole or plateau model, all the keys have solid, continuous surfaces, though the "plateaus" are not necessarily absolutely flat. French model flutes, in contrast, have open centers or perforations in the five key covers directly under the fingers—the A, G, F, E, and D keys for the second and third fingers of the left hand and the first, second, and third fingers of the right hand, respectively (see page 8).

For the beginning player, the plateau model is often preferable because the keys will cover the holes no matter how small the player's fingers. In addition, the beginner, who probably has enough trouble mastering basic fingering and embouchure control, is spared the additional complications of the open holes. (The counter argument, however, is that the perforated holes demand proper finger positions, and the initial inconvenience is worth the effort.) Professional studio doublers often find the plateau model more convenient when making frequent switches between flute and other woodwinds.

Most professionals and advanced students today do, however, favor the French model, in part for the sake of a tradition that began in the 1840s with Clair Godfroy and Louis Lot. The open holes also offer a variety of alternate fingerings that enhance technique, by simplifying certain fingerbenders, and extend the tonal palette by offering the option of shading (partially uncovering a perforated key while pressing the rim of the key). Finally, the French model is essential for producing a number of avant-garde effects such as multiphonics, quarter tones, and glissandos.

There has been some resistance to the French model for a long time, however, and it is growing. Marcel Moyse, for instance, alone among the great names of the French School, always played a plateau model. And many acousticians—Dayton C. Miller and Arthur Benade are perhaps the most prominent of them—consider the plateau model acoustically superior. They brand the open holes a significant flaw, "the one acoustical crime that has been perpetrated against the Boehm flute," in Miller's words.[7] Flute maker Albert Cooper considers the French model's scale inherently less accurate because it overcompensates for the sharpening effect of the perforations. Further, he says, the closed keys are more stable; they cover the holes better because their washer-screw construction is more reliable than the friction snap used on perforated keys. The plateau pads are easier to install and repair.[8]

Closed key

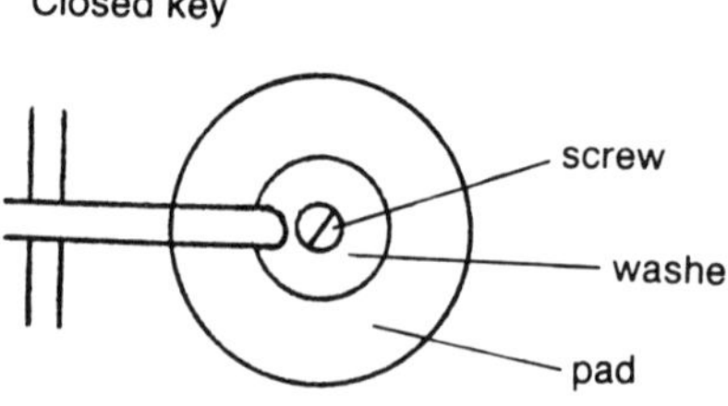

Open (perforated) key

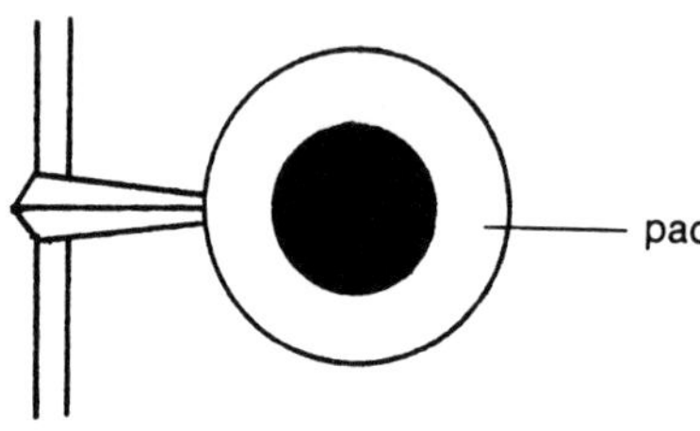

C or B Footjoint

Boehm flutes are customarily equipped with a footjoint to c^1 (middle C on the piano), but a B foot is regularly offered as an option. C versus B is not a life or death decision; you can always buy a new or extra footjoint for your old flute. For the beginner, the extra length is probably not worth considering because of the extra expense (typically \$100 to \$200 on a student flute, \$400 to \$600 a professional model). For more advanced players, however, there are definite pros and cons to be considered.

The most obvious argument for the B foot is that various compositions in the solo and orchestral repertoire call for the low B. Indeed, there are a few such cases: one of Friedrich Kuhlau's op. 39 duets, the flute solo in Rossini's *William Tell Overture,* Verdi's *Il Trovatore,* Bartok's *Concerto for Orchestra*. An increasing number of avant-garde compositions also extend to low B. However, these relatively infrequent cases do not in themselves make a sufficiently strong case for the low B.

Advocates of the C foot believe that it permits an easier response on high notes. The longer tube of the B foot slightly increases the weight of the flute, which may foster a sloppy right hand position, particularly for small players. The B foot may also cause some flatness in the lower register, and it requires a bit more time to warm up. Distinguished professionals such as Rampal insist that the B foot makes notes above c^3 and those in the lowest register hard to produce. He remains faithful to the C foot, as were Laurent, Marcel Moyse, and Gazzelloni.

Other influential flutists--notably Kincaid, Barrère, Wummer, and Lora—were strong advocates of the B foot, and it has become the preference of most

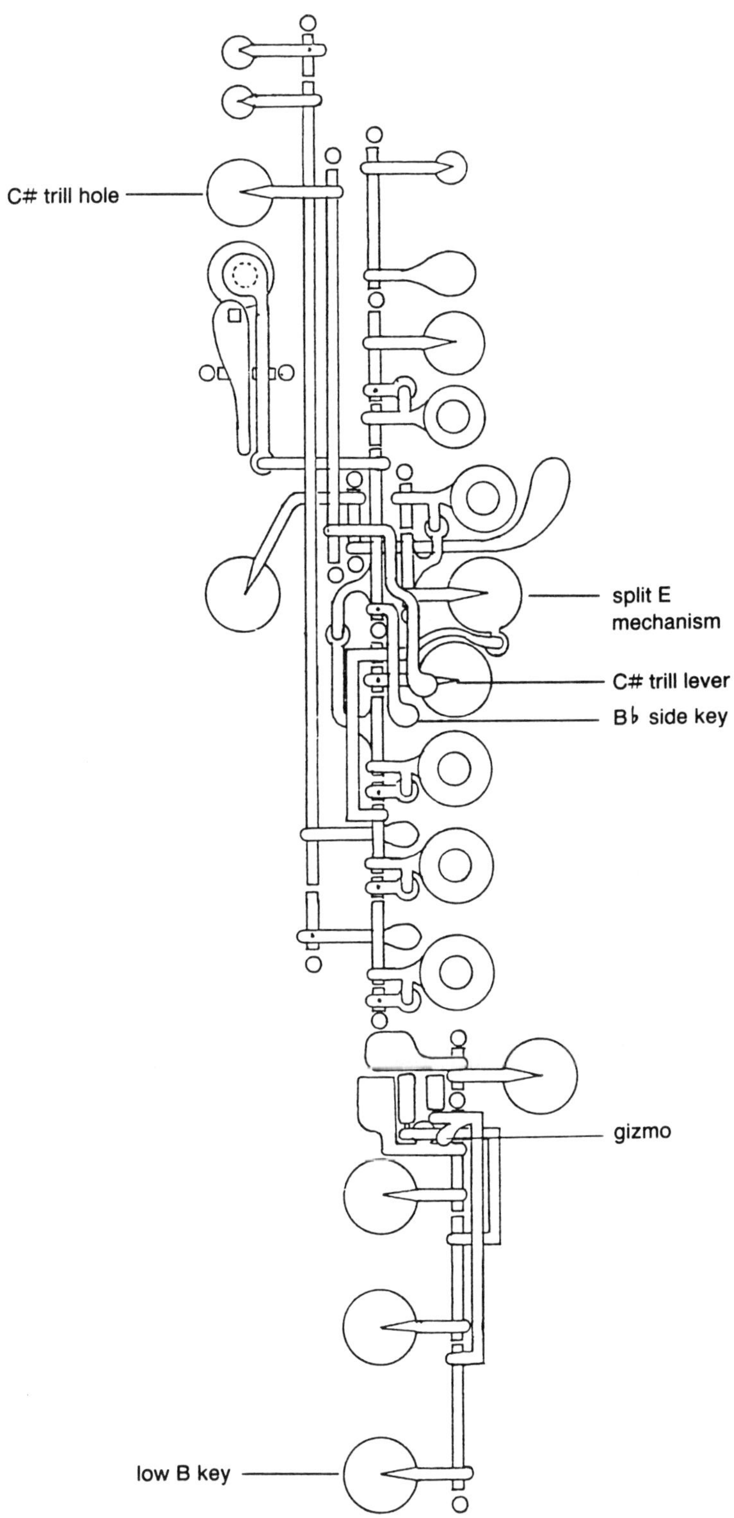
C# trill hole
split E
mechanism
C# trill lever
B♭ side key
gizmo
low B key

professionals and a large proportion of students in the U.S. today. In 1956, Verne Q. Powell made a persuasive argument for the B foot: "In my opinion, a low B improves the timbre of the flute throughout, and it has no effect on the blowing or intonation, with the exception of the high C, which comes a little harder with the low B but has less tendency to be sharp."[9] However, the gizmo key (see page 32), first manufactured by Powell and now a universal option with all manufacturers' B feet, solves the "speaking" problem of the high C by closing the low B key independently of C and C♯.

In general, most players feel that the B foot gives a fuller, darker sound, improves the intonation of the upper register, and particularly improves the response of the high F♯. An investigation conducted under the supervision of Dr. George Bradley of the Western Michigan University physics department in 1976 confirmed these empirical, nonscientific opinions. On the lowest notes of the flute, from c^1 to a^1, the C foot gives the flute tone a richer quality because it has more harmonic content. But the B foot creates a richer sound over the remainder of the flute's compass, some two and a half octaves.[10]

In sum, I recommend the C foot for beginners and the B foot for everyone else.

Mechanical Options

There are a number of optional gadgets, devices, and keys available in current manufacturers' catalogs. The purchaser should consult a variety of those catalogs, as the options offered are constantly changing. As a general guide, however, I have included an approximate price range compiled from the major flute makers' 1995 literature. Keep in mind that almost any gadget can be requested on special order, at a negotiated price, from the custom flute makers.

B♭ Shake Key: Usually offered as a standard feature, this lever for the right hand index finger is also known as a side key. It duplicates the action of the Briccialdi B♭ lever for the left thumb, providing an alternative fingering for the B♭-B trill. It also may be used for A♯ in G♯ -A♯ trills, and it simplifies fingerings for alternations of B-G-B♭-G and of G-A♯-B-A♯. In the latter case, the side key can be held down while G is fingered.

B-C Trill Key: A frequent feature of English flutes, this key is an alternative to the B♭ side key and is likewise operated by the right index finger. It replaces the left thumb trills for b^1-c^2, b^2-c^3, and f^3♯ -g^3. It is much less useful, however, than the B♭ side key. (Price range: $85 to $130)

C♯ Trill Key: This key is offered by many flute makers. Although it is operated by the right index finger, it may be installed in addition to any of the above keys, adjacent to the other side key. This lever controls a large C♯ vent placed just above the thumb keys, below the regular trill holes. It improves the quality of C♯, and also improves several difficult trills: b^1-c^2♯, b^2-c^3♯, and g^3-a^3♭. It eliminates the need for the simultaneous thumb and index finger trill for f^3♯-g^3. And, in combination with the C-D (upper) trill key, it permits the otherwise impossible g^3-a^3 trill. (Price range: $265 to $700)

Split E Mechanism: This device, a reasonably common add-on, remedies the principal defect of the closed-G♯ flute, the troublesome e^3 that is both sharp and difficult to produce. Ideally, for e^3, the A hole (G key) should be open and the G hole (duplicate G♯ vent) closed. But in the usual configuration of the closed G♯ the two are irrevocably linked; because the A hole remains open for e^3, so must the G♯ vent. The Split E separates the action of these two keys; the A key still closes the G♯ vent for G, as usual, but they operate independently for e^3. The duplicate G♯ vent is attached to the E key (right-hand second finger), so that when the E key is depressed for e^3 it closes the duplicate G♯ vent but the A hole (G key) remains open. The Split E thereby enhances the response of e^3 with no change in fingering. It also permits rapid slurs between a^3 and e^3, and in general makes large intervals approaching e^3 speak more easily. (Price range: $175 to $670)

C♯ Roller: The touch for the right-hand pinky to control low C♯ is made as a roller, rather than as a flat key. (Customarily, the low C touch is a roller.) It facilitates quick fingering in the lower register. (Price range: $60 to $125)

D♯ Roller: A roller is added to the lower right corner of the D♯ or E touch of the principal right pinky key. It facilitates transitions to low C, C♯, or B. (Price range: $55 to $125)

Left-hand Levers for Footjoint Keys: A lever for the left pinky may be constructed to control the low E♭ key or C♯ key on the footjoint. The E♭ key permits smoother slurs or trills between low B, C, C♯ and E♭. The C♯ lever makes possible the otherwise impossible c^1-c^1♯ trill. The complication, of course, is that the mechanism must be carefully aligned when the footjoint is connected to the body, and it can easily get out of whack.

Brossa F♯: This lever, for the right-hand third finger, next to the lower trill key, duplicates the distant action of the third-finger key but not its local action; in other words, it closes the F♯ hole without also closing the E hole. It thus allows the player to produce F♯ without depressing either the D or the E key. It improves both F♯ and the E-F♯ trill. However, the Brossa F♯ is superfluous on an open-hole flute, on which the identical effect can be obtained by depressing only the rim of the key. (Price: about $70)

Coltman C♯: Invented by physicist John Coltman in 1976 and currently available only from Jack Moore and David Wimberley, the Coltman C♯ is designed to remedy the poor intonation of C♯ in the second and third octaves, probably the least satisfactory notes on the Boehm flute. Because the usual C♯ hole is not only the tone hole for C♯ but also the vent for six other notes, Boehm moved it up from its ideal position and made it smaller. The Coltman C♯ design has the advantage that it does not require any change in fingering. It consists of a new, full-size hole, added between the regular C♯ vent hole and the C (left-thumb) hole, and is used in combination with the regular vent to produce c^2♯ and c^3♯; the regular vent is used alone for d^2, e^2♭, d^3, g^3♯, a^3, and b^3. (Price: $200)

***Open* G♯:** The standard Boehm flute today has a closed G♯ mechanism, unlike the open G♯ of Boehm's design. A few older players still play old open-G♯ instruments, and some of their protégés also believe that the open G♯ is acoustically superior. This option is, therefore, available on special order from a few flute makers, including Jack Moore and Emerson. However, it should be noted that standard fingering charts in print today are for closed G♯; open G♯ charts are out of print and available only in libraries. There are no open-G♯ fingering charts for avant-garde extended techniques. (Price: $60 to $480)

Reversed thumb keys: Another option is the reversal of the thumb keys, again a restoration of Boehm's original design. In a certain sense more logical than the Briccialdi thumb keys in general use today, this configuration of the thumb keys places the B above B♭, closer to the embouchure. (Price: $60 to $230)

Testing an Instrument

After reading the manufacturers' catalogs and soliciting advice from teachers and colleagues, the best way to select an instrument is to try it yourself. Or, as mentioned earlier, a beginning or intermediate player may want to have a teacher or other more experienced flutist help make the decision.

The place to try out flutes, most often, is a large, well-stocked musical instrument store that carries a variety of brands. Other good testing grounds are the exhibit halls of major conventions, such as the Music Teachers National Association or American Bandmasters Association. The most comprehensive array of flute lines is exhibited at the annual convention of the National Flute Association, held in a different city each August.

There are three categories that should be checked for each flute: response, construction, and physical condition.

Response: A responsive instrument will react to breath and embouchure easily, quickly, and evenly in all registers. Particular trouble spots tend to be the extreme low and high registers; many student flutes have nearly impossible low C's. The instrument should have good intonation not only throughout the melodic range but also throughout the dynamic range. The sound should be pure, with no hiss or growl.

Acoustician and flutist Arthur Benade suggests the following test. It is applicable to all flutes regardless of fingering system or materials of construction:

1. Warm the flute. Then play g^1, mezzo forte, with the fullest sound possible. Try to make a smooth "sneak" to g^2 by overblowing.
2. Repeat this exercise starting on d^1.
3. Play b^1 and try to sneak to b^2. If the sneaks on these three notes are difficult or impossible, the player or the instrument may be at fault. But on these relatively responsive notes, odds are that the instrument is at fault. You might use a flute to which you are accustomed as a "control."
4. A truly fine instrument, says Benade, will sneak or overblow to the third or even the fourth harmonic. Having passed these tests, a flute should allow broad dynamic range and control, have a clear, ringing tone and good intonation, and respond obediently to small modifications of the embouchure.
5. Remove the headjoint from the body of the flute. Set your lips in normal playing position. Then "smite" the flute with the most abrupt, fortissimo attack possible. A poorly cut embouchure hole will cough, hesitate, break the tone, or start the tone slowly; a well-cut one will respond with alacrity.[11]

Construction: The following is a checklist of features to look for. For some items, it may be necessary to research the manufacturers' catalogs.

1. The posts that support the longitudinal axles (on which the keys are mounted) should be mounted on ribs, rather than directly on the flute. This type of construction is more durable.
2. Keys should be forged, rather than cast; forged keys are stronger and less apt to break off.
3. The needle springs, whether gold, silver, bronze, or stainless steel, should not be too short. Ideally, they should extend about $\frac{1}{32}$ inch behind the spring's hook. If they are too short, they will detach themselves from the mechanism.
4. The mechanism should work lightly and smoothly, and the springs should be evenly balanced. There should be no play or excess horizontal motion in the keys, nor should they be sprung too high. They should move silently, with no clicks, clunks, or extraneous noise from the pads.

5. Trill keys should not project too far above the level of the regular keys, nor should they be too pointed or angled upward too sharply. Any of these factors may make them difficult to reach and control.
6. Similarly, the D♯ (E♭) lever for the right-hand pinky should not have pointed corners, and should be aligned so that the pinky can slide easily to the other footjoint levers. A roller on the lower side of the lever can make such motion easier.
7. Student flutes should be equipped with adjusting screws, which regulate the height and closure of the keys.
8. On student flutes, the tone holes should be drawn, rather than soldered, so that they cannot detach themselves from the flute tube. The edges should be rolled, not sharp, so they will not cut into the pads, and they should be even, to permit a hermetic seal.
9. Wooden flutes and piccolos should be reinforced at the tenons, where moisture tends to collect.

Condition: The following checklist applies not only to used instruments, but also to new ones. New instruments can have problems that are not caught by the factory testers. If an instrument has been handled by many people in a showroom, it requires extra careful inspection.

1. On plated instruments, the plating should be evenly applied, with no rough spots, indentations, or thin spots.
2. Check the seal of the headjoint cork or stopper. It should not rattle when you shake the head gently. Rotate the crown or nut inward a bit. The cork should not move freely; if it does, it should be replaced. Then pull straight out on the crown; the cork should still not move.
3. The pads should not be torn, excessively yellowed, or dried out. They must close the tone holes completely. To check for leakage, slowly play a scale, using normal finger pressure; uneven response may indicate an improperly seated pad. Another method, which must be executed with extreme care, is to direct smoke (from a safety match) into the flute tube while holding the keys closed. Look for smoke escaping from the tone holes.
4. The keys should be sprung evenly, and springs should be sufficiently strong to return the keys to their rest position smoothly, with no mechanical interference.
5. The action or keywork should move freely. There should be no lateral motion, nor should there be any clicks or blockages in the normal vertical motion. A click may indicate a sluggishly functioning mechanism or simply the need for oiling; the inside of the rods (of a used flute) may be dirty or rusted.

6. The adjusting screws should not turn too easily, or the mechanism will quickly fall out of adjustment. Neither the threads of the screws nor the grooves in the heads should be worn.

7. The tenons between the joints should be clean and should fit snugly, but not so tightly that they cannot be easily assembled and disassembled.

8. Check the instrument carefully for dents. On the body, small surface scratches or mini-dents on the exterior of the tube will cause no problems, but on the headjoint they may have an effect on intonation. The surface of the tube's interior must be perfectly smooth. It is especially important to check the condition of the embouchure hole and lip plate. Any alteration of the edge of the hole, such as a small nick, is potentially disastrous and should be carefully evaluated. Merely sanding or planing such an imperfection will probably not solve the problem and may make it worse.

9. On wooden instruments, the tube should be straight, not warped; warpage cannot be remedied. Check that the wood has been seasoned and treated and that there are no cracks, inside or out. A pocket flashlight is a good tool for such inspections. In a darkened room, close all the keys and shine the flashlight inside the tube. No light should be visible on the outside. Crack repairing is a hazardous business and should be avoided at all costs.

It is advisable to make sure that the instrument dealer provides a service warranty for at least several months, as minor mechanical problems often surface in new flutes during the breaking-in period. In the case of factory-bought flutes from such companies as Haynes and Powell, this sort of repair is never a problem (these two manufacturers willingly undertake repairs of their own instruments). When dealing with mass-produced flutes purchased through a dealer, however, it is much easier to have the problem corrected locally than at the factory. So purchase your flute from a dealer with his own repair facilities and a reputation for quality service.

Notes

1. John Backus, "Effect of Wall Material on the Steady-State Tone Quality of Woodwind Instruments," *Journal of the Acoustical Society of America* 36 (1964): 1881.
2. Israel Borouchoff, "Effect of Flute Tube Materials on Sonority," *National Flute Association Newsletter* 3, no. 3 (1978): 9.
3. Paul Henry Giroux, "The History of the Flute and Its Music in the United States" (M.A. thesis, School of Music, University of Washington, 1952), p. 105.
4. Borouchoff, p. 10.
5. Ibid.

6. Felix Skowronek, "Whither the wooden flute?" *American Music Teacher* 29, no. 5 (1980): 22–23.
7. Dayton C. Miller, letter to William S. Haynes, 10 June 1925, pp. 1–2.
8. Ray Fabrizio, "The French Model Flute: A Dissenting View," *National Flute Association Newsletter* 6, no. 4 (1980): 3.
9. Dale Higbee, "Needed: A Gold Flute or a Gold Lip," *Woodwind World* 13, no. 3 (June 1974): 22.
10. Charles Osborne, "Concerning the Foot Joint," *NACWPI Journal* 24, no. 4 (1976): 36–37.
11. Nancy Toff, "The Boehm Centenary Lectures," *National Flute Association Newsletter* 7, no. 1 (1981): 3.

3

CARE AND MAINTENANCE OF THE FLUTE

Your instrument is your voice, and how you feel about making music should be expressed in how you care for and handle your instrument. The logic is simple: keep your instrument in the best possible working order, and it will yield the best results that you can coax from it. A clean and well-adjusted instrument will respond best to your technique, no matter what the level of your playing. It is a machine, and like any machine it must have proper maintenance. Remember that the more attractive the instrument is to the lips, fingers, and eyes, the more you will want to play it!

Preventive Maintenance: Assembling the Instrument

The first step in caring for your flute is assembling it properly. Always handle the joints of the flute by the nonkeyed parts. For the body of the flute, this means that you should hold it at the top, above the keywork, where the manufacturer's name is engraved. Hold the footjoint at the very bottom, below the keywork. Attach the footjoint to the body of the flute with a gentle twisting and pushing motion. Align the center rod of the footjoint with the center of the majority of the body keys. To attach the headjoint to the body, the same principle applies. Grasp the headjoint below the embouchure plate and the body at its top, and gently rotate the headjoint into the body's socket. The embouchure should also line up with the body keys.

Never force a joint; if it is stiff, wipe each half with a damp cloth. The cloth should be damp, not wet, to avoid damaging the keys and pads. Often the literal sticking point is merely a small amount of tarnish or dirt that will wipe off easily. Be sure to dry the joint completely before again attemping to

assemble the instrument. If you still have difficulty connecting the joint, check for bent or dented parts. If this is the problem, consult a qualified repairman; without the proper tools, you will probably do more damage than good in trying to reshape the metal. Another caveat: never apply cork grease or any other lubricant to the joints of a metal flute.

Daily Cleaning

When you are finished playing, always clean your flute thoroughly, even if you are planning to play again in a short while. Condensation on the inside of the flute, which results from the difference in temperature between the air inside and outside the flute tube, should be wiped out. Saliva may also accumulate in the headjoint and may even run down into the body. If left inside the flute, such moisture can mix with dust and tarnish, forming a thin sort of mud that may interfere with the mechanism and key pads and harm the metal of the body.

Most flute cases come equipped with a cleaning rod, a long wood or metal stick with a hole or eye at one end. Thread a soft, nonlinting cloth (I use one of my grandfather's old linen handkerchiefs) through the hole and wrap it around the rod completely, so that no metal or wood is visible. Thorough wrapping will prevent the rod from scratching the flute. Carefully insert the wrapped rod into each of the three joints of the flute, swabbing it around to absorb any lingering moisture.

Next, unwrap the rag and wipe the tenons and sockets of each joint (both the inserted and receiving ends) to remove moisture and dirt. Finally, wipe the outside of the flute to remove fingermarks, saliva, and other stray moisture and dirt. For this purpose, you may want to use a soft flannel or chamois cloth or a treated silver-polishing cloth, sold under such brand names as Goddard's, Hagerty's, Herco, and Selvyt.

Periodically, you should also clean the mechanism—a delicate operation that requires a steady hand, good light, and plenty of patience. Every so often, you will notice that dust has accumulated underneath the rods and keys. The easiest solution is to blow gently at close range. If the dust remains, try dusting with a small, soft brush such as a watercolor brush. Or, thread a thin cloth underneath the rod, sliding it gently back and forth and being extremely careful not to dislodge the thin needle springs that control the keys. Do not use a Q-tip or other cotton swab here; the cotton tends to get caught in the mechanism and shed, leaving behind more debris than it removes.

The Gemeinhardt Company now offers an excellent flute cleaning kit, which consists of a polishing cloth, a flannel cloth, swab cloths, and small dusting brushes. It retails for about $5.00.

Storage

Replacing the flute in its case correctly is just as important as assembling it properly. If your flute comes equipped with end caps for the joints, by all means use them. They protect the joints from dirt and damage. Lay the flute carefully into the case in the contoured sections; never force a part to fit.

Storing the cleaning rod may be a problem, particularly if it is quite damp. If you have only the standard hard case, don't fold the cleaning rag into the case until it dries. It is best to use an outer case, usually made of naugahyde or similar plastic and lined with a synthetic wool. You can then store the rag (and other useful items, such as a pencil, and cigarette paper for drying pads) between the inner and outer cases. The naugahyde case also helps to protect your instrument from extremes of hot and cold. Most importantly, it is waterproof.

If you intend to play your flute again in a short time, you may not want to put it back in its case. Never leave your flute on a table that it can roll off, on a bed or chair where someone can sit on it, or anywhere it can be disturbed by a careless child or animal. And *never* rest the flute on the ledge of a music stand. If you do place it on a table or other horizontal surface, make sure that the keys are facing up, so that there is no pressure on the mechanism.

Often, flutists use a flute peg for temporary storage. This is a short dowel, about six inches high, imbedded in a heavy base; the flute is placed on it vertically. If you leave the flute on a peg for any substantial period of time, cover it with a fitted cloth bag (preferably Pacific silvercloth) to keep it dust-free and to protect it from tarnish.

Polishing

If you follow the cleaning and storage regimen outlined above, you should have little need to polish your flute. However, despite your best efforts, perspiration and saliva may discolor parts of your instrument, particularly the embouchure plate and the underside of the body. Light tarnish will often rub off with a slightly moistened rag or a treated silver-polishing cloth. Some teachers recommend using an ammonia solution, but I believe this should be avoided. Not only is ammonia toxic, but if it comes in contact with the steel parts of the mechanism it will cause rapid rusting. Stick with silver polish.

Most instruction books caution you never to polish your flute. If your flute does, however, become highly discolored, or you want to add that extra bit of sparkle to a special performance, you can use silver polish—very carefully. Select a nonabrasive, scentless brand; otherwise it may make the flute unpleasant to play.

Apply the polish with a small cloth, natural sponge, or the tip of a cotton swab. The headjoint, since it has no mechanism, is the easiest section to polish. Nevertheless, use restraint, polishing only a small area at a time. Let the polish sit on the metal briefly; then wipe it off with a clean, damp cloth. Never rinse the headjoint under the tap as you would a fork or a piece of jewelry. The cork or stopper at the headjoint must not get wet under any circumstances.

The body and footjoint are much trickier to polish, and here you would do well to use a cotton swab in order to stay clear of the keywork. Again, polish only a small section at a time, making absolutely certain that no polish or water gets anywhere near the keys or pads. Lingering polish can not only gum up the pads, but can also obstruct the efficient operation of the springs and keys.

When you have finished polishing and drying the flute, buff it very lightly with a soft piece of flannel or a commercial silver-polishing cloth to give it a fine gloss. After polishing, periodic re-buffing with this type of cloth should eliminate the necessity for further polishing for quite a while.

Never try to polish the keys; the danger of dribbling polish and water into the mechanism and onto the pads is just too great. If the indentations in the cups do become tarnished, try running a scarcely damp thin cloth around them with your fingernail. Playing with clean hands and wiping the keys after playing should preclude the necessity for polishing the tops of the keys, but if they do become extremely black, entrust the cleaning to a qualified professional.

Replating

If your flute is silver-plated (most student flutes are), you may find that the plating wears through—particularly on the embouchure plate, which is in constant contact with the chin, and at the points on the body with the greatest finger contact. Such signs of wear begin with an almost imperceptible pitting of the metal surface; eventually, the tiny pits may expand to the point where they are quite noticeable. At this stage, the instrument needs to be replated by a professional repairman, who will have to buff the surface and resilver it. Be sure to get an accurate estimate of the cost before commissioning such a procedure; for inexpensive instruments, the repair may not be worth the investment. This might be the time to consider upgrading the quality of your instrument.

Because of the tendency of plated instruments to corrode, many players choose a flute with a plated body and a solid-silver headjoint, or at least a solid-silver embouchure plate. Some teachers recommend that their students apply a thin coating of clear nail polish to the embouchure plate, particularly if the student has very oily skin, in order to protect the metal. The danger of this procedure is that an uneven coating may interfere with the cutting edge of the embouchure plate, thereby affecting its acoustical properties. A better solution is to use a small piece of adhesive or masking tape on the near side of the embouchure plate. The tape will also help to keep the flute from slipping off the lower lip in hot weather. Some players use a postage stamp, but its glue is harder to remove than that of either kind of tape, and solvents may harm the metal even more than contact with the skin.

Lubrication

Under normal circumstances, the flute mechanism should be oiled about twice a year. In particularly humid areas, or in regions with salty air, however, oiling may be required as often as every three or four months. A metallic clacking in the key action is a strong indication of the need for lubrication. The crucial precept for this procedure is: less is better. Indeed, many repair experts advise that no oiling should be undertaken without completely disassembling the mechanism, in order to avoid gumming up the keywork and thereby doing more harm than good.

The only acceptable type of oil is sold commercially as "key oil" and is available in music stores; occasionally it is called "polished oil." Do *not* use household mineral oils such as sewing machine oil, watch oil, or any sort of all-purpose oil. Apply the oil with the tip of a toothpick, pin, or needle so that only a tiny amount reaches any given surface.

Apply the oil to each junction in the mechanism: between hinges and posts and at the contact points between springs and hooks. Drop the oil into the mechanism, and then operate the appropriate key to spread it around. Have a tissue or cloth handy to mop up any excess oil so that it does not leak onto the pads.

The Headjoint Cork

The only mechanical device for tuning the flute on a daily basis is the tuning slide—that is, the tenon that connects the headjoint and the body. The headjoint cork is not a tuning device, although its placement has a direct effect on the internal tuning of the instrument. Every so often, check the placement of the cork. Its inner end should be exactly 17.3 millimeters from the center of the embouchure hole. There is an easy test: the cleaning rod is equipped with a notch 17.3 millimeters from its end; insert it carefully into the headjoint and check that the notch appears in the exact center of the hole.

If the plug is too high—too far toward the closed end of the tube—unscrew the crown and push the plug down until the guideline on the cleaning rod is centered. If, on the other hand, the plug is too far down toward the open end of the flute tube, tighten the crown screw slowly so that it pulls the stopper up into place.

In many cases, the reason that the cork has moved is that it has dried out and shrunk; eventually, it may have to be replaced. Many new flutes, how-

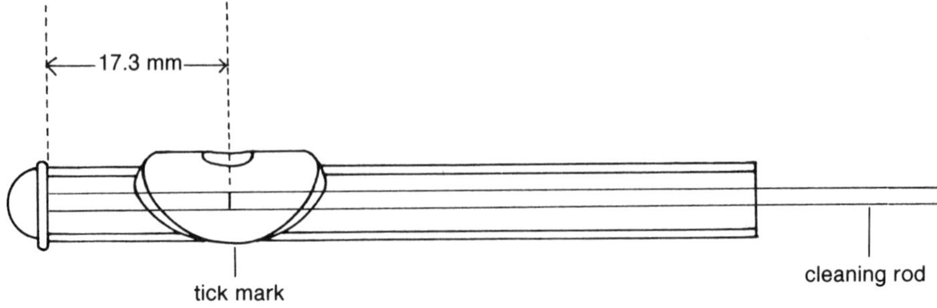

ever, use a synthetic rubber plug in place of the traditional cork. It is far less likely than cork to shrink or warp, but it may nevertheless slide a bit from time to time, so the same position-checking procedure applies.

Mechanical Problems

Mechanical breakdowns of the instrument should not occur frequently, but student flutes, which have more accessible adjusting screws and are generally played by less experienced players, may need periodic adjustment. Uneven finger pressure, characteristic of many student players, may have deleterious effects on pad seating as well as on the mechanism itself. Student instruments, by the very nature of their mass production, may not be as carefully regulated to start out with as handmade models are.

Perhaps the most frequent problem—also, fortunately, the easiest to remedy—is sticky pads. The causes of this problem are basically twofold: atmospheric humidity, which affects all the keys on an instrument more or less equally, and saliva or condensation within the flute, which may affect only one key at a time. The cure is simple. Place a piece of cigarette paper between the pad and the rim of the tone hole. Depress the key and gently slide the cigarette paper out. Repeat the procedure several times, in each instance pulling the paper in a different direction.

Be sure to select a brand of cigarette paper that is not gummed; if you can obtain only the gummed type, tear off the adhesive edge so that there is no chance of the glue sticking to the pad. If you cannot obtain cigarette paper use any sort of porous paper—a coffee filter, for instance, will do. In a crunch, a dollar bill works nicely—but use a clean one.

Pad stickiness may also be caused by the presence of a foreign substance on the pad. Cigarette paper will often cure this problem, too, but if it fails, moisten the paper slightly with water to remove the foreign substance; then dry the pad with a fresh piece of paper. In more difficult cases, the paper may be moistened with alcohol, benzene, or cleaning fluid, but the use of such chemical solvents should be a last resort—not least because those substances are flammable and smelly. Some repair shops apply talcum powder to stubbornly sticky pads in an attempt to absorb excess liquid, but I do not recommend this procedure because the powder can infiltrate the mechanism and cause even worse difficulties.

As they age, pads may also develop the opposite problem, hardness or brittleness. If this is a problem, they should be replaced. Often, only a single pad will need replacement, usually because of uneven finger pressure or moisture absorption. If several keys need repadding simultaneously, and others appear to be hardening, consider having the entire instrument done at once. You may save time and expense in the long run, and the fingering or touch will tend to be more even with pads of equal age and wear. A pad may also need to be replaced if excessive wear causes its surface to tear. This is not likely to happen to plastic pads (a feature of newer models of student flutes), but occurs on the traditional bladder-type pads, which are made of felt covered with a layer of fish skin. It is the fish skin that may tear and cause the pad to seat unevenly. It is possible to change the pads yourself (consult the repair manuals listed in the bibliography), but in most cases repadding should be entrusted to a professional.

A related problem, more difficult to pinpoint, is the case of leaky pads. A frequent warning signal is difficulty in producing low tones. A leaky pad can also reduce responsiveness throughout the flute's compass, diminish the power of the tone, and impair its quality. The first test to locate a leak is the playing test. Play a matching tone exercise: beginning at the top of the second octave, play descending groups of three chromatic notes without changing anything but your fingers: c^2-b^1-$b^1\flat$, then b^1-$b^1\flat$-a^1, and so on. Listen carefully for changes in tone quality or power. However, because your embouchure may instinctively compensate for what you hear, this method of detection is not foolproof. Proceed to the visual test.

Disassemble the flute and test the body and footjoint separately. The visual test is best done in a closet or dark room. Close off one end of the flute tube completely, either with a cork, by resting it firmly on your knee, or with the assistance of another person. Using normal finger pressure, close all the keys; then shine a light—a penlight flashlight works well—into the flute tube. An assistant will be of enormous help. Look for light leaks on the outside of the tube. Conversely, close all the keys and shine the light sequentially at the outside of each key. If light shows through to the inside of the tube, you have found the leak.

Another visual test involves smoke, and should be a last resort. The principle is the same as that of the interior light test. Direct the smoke from an extinguished safety match into the flute tube. If, with all the keys depressed, smoke emerges from a tone hole, there is a leak. Never use cigarette smoke: not only should no woodwind player smoke for obvious health reasons, but the contaminants in the smoke may stick to the pads or the mechanism.

Still another leaky-pad test is the tactile method, using cigarette paper. Insert the cigarette paper under each pad, between the pad and the tone hole rim; close the key and pull the paper out slowly, keeping the tension as even as possible. There should be some resistance if the key is depressed with nor-

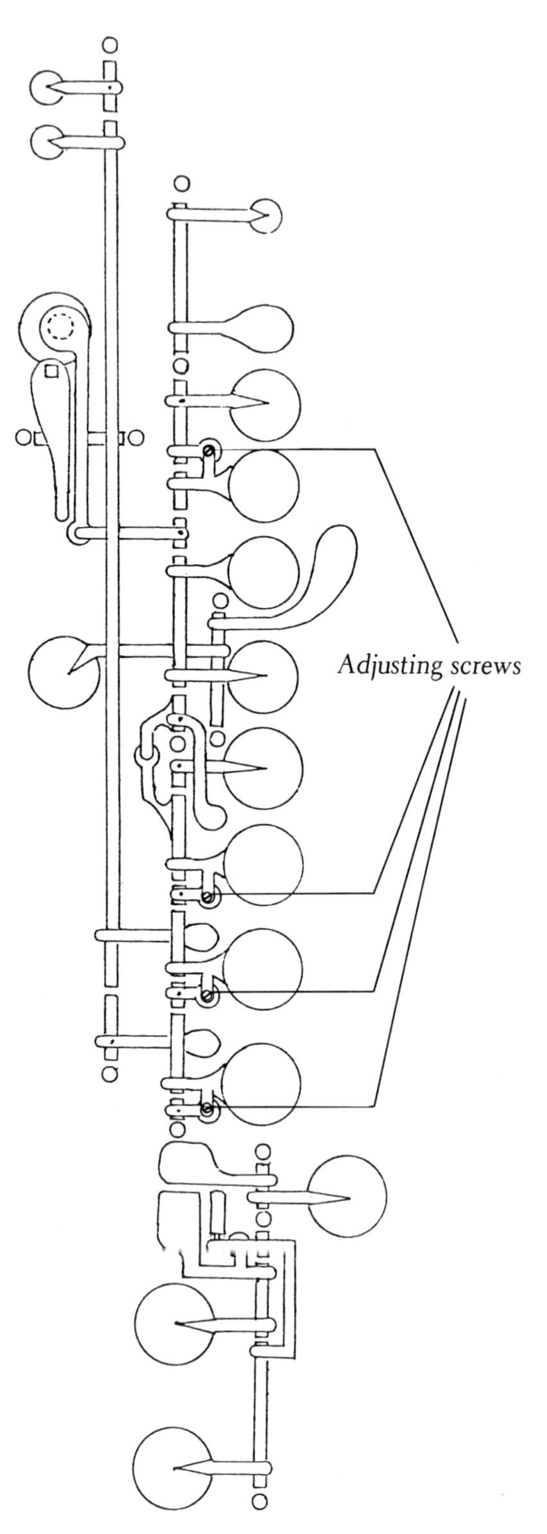
Adjusting screws

mal playing pressure; if the paper slides out quickly or unevenly, it may indicate a leak. This test is subtle, and like the playing test, not foolproof, but can be quite effective once you get the knack of it.

Once you have located the faulty pad, you must determine the exact cause of the leak. First, check the condition of the pad itself; if it is torn, shrunken, or hardened, it may require replacement or the application of shims (paper washers), which are inserted on the inner surface of the pad, between the pad and the key cup.

If the problem is not within the pad itself, the connecting mechanism is probably the culprit. Look for bent rods or keys, which may cause the pad to seat unevenly. If this is the problem, do not try to bend the misaligned part yourself. Such repairs require special tools, sometimes including a heat source.

If you play a student model flute, the adjusting screws may be the cause of the problem. There are four of these—on the A, F, E, and D keys—and they control the linkages between those keys and the F♯ and B♭ keys. Principally, they are responsible for the regulation of key height (the distance between the key pad and the tone hole rim). A quick turn of a jeweler's screwdriver is frequently all that is required to adjust the key height and cure the pad leakage.

Pads are not the only potential trouble spots in the flute mechanism; indeed, the mechanism is far more complicated than a visual inspection might lead you to believe. Each rod, for instance, contains numerous internal working parts. Visible and invisible mechanical components work in tandem to control a delicately regulated mechanism. Let's consider some potential problems.

Clicking keys are a great bother to the performer's ear and may be symptoms of mechanical obstructions that slow down fingering. Fortunately, they can usually be eliminated rather simply. Pinpoint the exact location of the click, and then apply a drop of oil to the corresponding moving part—usually the pivot screw in the appropriate rod.

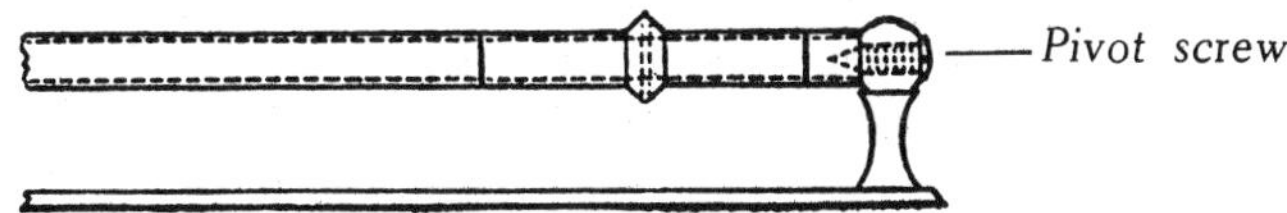

Sometimes, a key or keys will fail to rise rapidly or evenly when finger pressure is released. The most likely cause of such sluggish key action is a malfunction of the springs underneath the rods. Often, you will find that a needle spring has slipped out of its slot. It can easily be reattached using either a spring hook or a thin jeweler's screwdriver to direct it into the slot. Touch the spring with the screwdriver or the hook as far away from its originating end and as close to the dangling end as possible. That way, if it should break, the piece to be removed from the mechanism is longer and thus easier to get at.

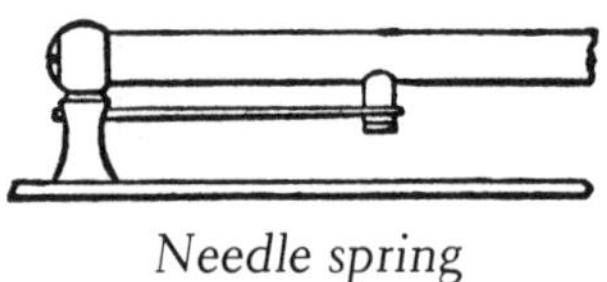

Needle spring

Another hindrance to proper key tension is more subtle: the spring may be attached, but improperly adjusted. The solution is to bend the spring, again using a spring hook. But this procedure requires great delicacy, and probably professional expertise.

Still another potential cause of improperly rising keys is the adjustment of the hinges and rod screws. First check the pivot screws in the end posts; they should be fully screwed in. If they're not, the entire bank of keys controlled by that particular rod may not function efficiently. The solution is to rotate the screw fully back into the rod.

Next, look to see whether the pivot screws are dirty or rusted. If so, unscrew the pivot screw about a quarter turn and test the key action; if the key now operates freely, place a drop of oil on the contact points and retighten the screw. If the problem persists, the screw may have to be removed entirely for a thorough cleaning and oiling.

We have already seen that loose adjusting screws on student flutes may be a cause of pad leakage. However, if they are tightened too much, they may unbalance the key tension, causing the keys to close too tightly and consequently to fail to rise adequately. If a tension problem on your flute involves indirectly controlled keys, gradually rotate the corresponding adjusting screw, and test for improvement with each turn.

Another possible cause of malfunctioning keys, as of leaking pads, is overt physical damage to the mechanism. Such problems as bent keys or rods, twisted posts, broken springs, and the like require expert repair, and an amateur lacking the proper tools should not even attempt to correct them.

Nevertheless, mechanical emergencies will inevitably occur at inconvenient times, and you should be prepared to deal with minor crises on your own. A makeshift solution to a mechanical problem need not be long-lasting or elegant, but it may tide you over until you can seek the services of a professional.

What if a spring breaks in midrehearsal or midperformance? If it is an open key, you are out of luck; the only solution is to replace the spring. But if the broken spring is on either of the two closed keys, D♯ or G♯, there is a temporary remedy. Wrap a rubber band around the flute tube and the affected key, making sure that it does not touch any adjacent keywork. This will hold the key closed, just as the spring normally does; the key can thus be opened by its lever in the usual way. As soon as you are done playing, however, remove the elastic, because the sulfur in the rubber will rapidly corrode the silver.

If a small pad (as on a trill key, or any key on a piccolo) should come loose, hold a match near it (but not too near!) to melt the glue underneath; press the pad back in and maintain the pressure for a few minutes. This procedure should keep the pad in place at least temporarily. If the cork under a key hinge comes loose, cellophane or masking tape, a postage stamp, or almost any type of paper can be used as a temporary shim to hold the cork in place.

To learn more advanced repair techniques, consult the repair manuals listed in the Selected Bibliography, particularly Jonathon Landell's *Flute Tune-Up Manual* and James Phelan and Mitchell Brody's *Complete Guide to the Flute*. Both volumes provide excellent, well-illustrated instructions in major repairs and maintenance. Mr. Landell also offers workshops and apprenticeships in flute repair and flute making through his nonprofit Vermont Guild of Flute Making in Vergennes, Vermont.

As a general rule, the extent and complexity of repairs that you will want to undertake yourself is in inverse proportion to your proximity to a good repair shop. If you use the procedures outlined on the preceding pages, your instrument should remain relatively trouble-free. But should your flute develop mechanical problems, your common sense, your dexterity, and your access to appropriate tools and supplies will help you determine how big a repair job you can tackle. Just as it is a necessity to be able to deal competently with minor emergency repairs, it is also imperative that you introduce yourself to a qualified professional repairman before you need his services.

4

A BRIEF HISTORY OF THE FLUTE

The history of music for the flute and the history of the instrument itself are intimately related. For the modern flutist, therefore, familiarity with the history of the instrument helps in understanding how its physical characteristics determined the technical content and stylistic features of the music. Particularly since 1700, the structural and mechanical development of the flute correlates quite closely with developments in musical composition and performance practice. Needless to say, the correlation is not coincidental.

The history of the flute naturally divides itself into two distinct, though chronologically overlapping, phases, that of the "German" or "old system" flute and that of the Boehm flute. What would seem obvious designations, A.B. and P.B. (Ante Boehm and Post Boehm), do not strictly apply, however, because the Boehm flute, like most new inventions, did not gain immediate public acceptance.

Old System Flutes

The transverse flute of the Middle Ages was constructed of a single piece of wood; cylindrical in shape and just under two feet in length, it sounded a primary scale of D major. It was known as a fife and was used, along with a small drum, to accompany infantry marches. Sebastian Virdung's *Musica getuscht und auszgezogen*, published in 1511, depicts this instrument, called a *Zwerchpfeiff*, as a narrow tube with six unusually closely spaced finger holes.

Although, during the Renaissance, instrumental music achieved an identity distinct from its role as accompaniment to or doubling of singers, the construction of instruments continued to follow the vocal model. Thus each type of instrument was made in a variety of sizes corresponding to the various voice types: soprano, alto, tenor, and bass. And so Martin Agricola's *Musica instrumentalis deudsch*, published in 1529, showed four flutes, called *Schweizer Pfeiffen*, and labeled Discantus, Altus, Tenor, and Bassus. Michael Praetorius's *Syntagma Musicum* (1619–20) was the first work to recognize a family of transverse flutes with musical values distinct from the military function of the fife. Each of the three sizes of flutes in Praetorius's plates has a two-octave range and four additional "falset" notes available only to the most skilled performers. The flute designated alto or tenor is pitched in D major, like all pre-Boehm concert flutes. The bass flute was the first flute divided into two pieces in order to regulate the tuning of the ensemble.

Marin Mersenne, in his *Harmonie Universelle* of 1636, showed two transverse flutes, called *Flûtes Allemands* and pitched in D and G. The former had a two-octave diatonic D major scale (d^1 to d^3), which could be extended upward to a^3. There were six tone holes or finger holes spaced evenly on the cylindrical tube. Cross-fingerings made it possible to play chromatically within the two octave range with the exception of d^1♯ and d^2♯, which could be obtained only by half uncovering the sixth (lowest) hole. Preliminary instructions for playing on such an instrument were available both in Mersenne's treatise and in Jambe de Ferre's *Epitome Musical* (1556).

Although these flutes had no keys, the farsighted Mersenne called attention to their absence and explained that the flute could be made fully chromatic precisely by the addition of keys. He even provided a sketch of what such keys might look like. Nevertheless, it was more than fifty years before the instrument acquired its first key.

In the baroque period, the new expressiveness of the monodic style, with its contrasts in dynamics and expansion of melodic range, required increasingly flexible instruments. The recorder became less and less suitable, and the transverse flute, with its more brilliant tone and third octave range, eventually supplanted it. But the transverse flute itself underwent considerable modification in order to be equal to the specifications of the new music.

The early baroque transverse flute, like its Renaissance predecessors, had six holes, but they were spaced on the flute tube in two groups of three holes each. Within each group, the lowest, and to some extent the second, hole was smaller to help compensate for smaller spacing between the holes. These holes were arranged to correspond to the configuration of the human hands rather than to acoustical specifications. As a result, the first and second octaves tended to be flat. And the excessive spacing between the third and fourth holes made F♯ especially difficult to produce and in some cases nearly a semitone flat. It was necessary, therefore, for flutists to resort to awkward fork-fingering, that is, fingering F with the first and third fingers of the right hand.

Jean Hotteterre (1605–1690/92), a member of a distinguished family of French musical instrument makers, was the principal figure in the redesign of the baroque flute. His major contribution, the addition of the D♯ key, is generally dated about 1660; such a flute was used in Lully's orchestra in Paris in 1670. The closed D♯ key (so-called because its rest position was closed), operated by the fourth finger of the right hand, controlled a new, seventh hole bored just below the E hole. Hotteterre published the first tutor for his one-keyed flute, *Principes de la Flute Traversiere,* in 1707.

Hotteterre's 1-key flute

Hotteterre's instrument was based on the D major scale and was divided into three sections: a head, containing the mouth hole or embouchure; the middle, containing the six finger holes; and the foot, which housed the lone key. The sections were attached to each other by means of tenon and socket joints. To eliminate the shrillness common to earlier instruments, Hotteterre changed the bore of the instrument from cylindrical to what he called conical. Actually, the headjoint remained cylindrical, while the remainder of the tube tapered toward the foot. The flattening effect of the conical bore allowed the finger holes to be placed closer together, which made fingering more natural. Acoustically, the taper prevented the formation of strong first, second, and most even-numbered partials or overtones, resulting in the light tone still typical of French woodwind playing today. Hotteterre also reduced the size of the finger holes, which together with the conical bore increased the brightness of the tone, although it also increased the tendency for flatness of intonation.

The compass of Hotteterre's one-keyed flute was "two octaves and some notes," d^1 to d^3 plus "forced notes" that took the compass up to g^3. His fingering chart noted, however, that "the notes above e^3 are forced notes, and cannot enter naturally in any piece. However, as you sometimes find them in Preludes, I will put here those I could discover." He further qualified his chart with the warning that f^3 "can almost never be done on the flute" (and so he omitted it).[1] Johann Joachim Quantz's *Versuch einer Anweisung die Flöte zu spielen* (1752), for the two-keyed flute, provided scales ranging from d^1 to a^3, but the top notes, from e^3 up, required cross-fingering. Quantz also divided his chart into three sections—the D minor diatonic scale, a flat scale, and a sharp scale—with fingerings that corresponded to each note's context within the mean-tone temperament.[2] (In mean-tone temperament, there is a discrepancy between sharp and flat notes, such as D♯ and E♭. This tuning is acoustically pleasing in tonalities or keys with only a few sharps or flats, but unsatisfactory for more complex harmonies and modulations.)

About 1722, there were several attempts to extend the lower range of the flute down to c^1. Even Quantz owned such a flute, but he attributed its weak tone and faulty intonation to the additional tubing.

The headjoint of the baroque flute was stopped at its upper end by an ordinary cork plug, which could be pushed or pulled by the performer to adjust the instrument's intonation. However, this relatively minor adjustment was not sufficient to compensate for major differences in pitch standards in various cities and provinces (whereas today, the international standard is A-440). This is why Hotteterre had divided the instrument into sections, but now even more drastic steps were needed. The solution devised about 1720 was called *corps de réchange*. The flute was divided into four joints: upper, upper-middle, lower-middle, and lower; the former body joint was subdivided between the finger holes for the left and right hands. Each instrument was provided with a set of alternative upper-middle joints, in three to six lengths, to be chosen on the basis of the prevailing pitch. In this manner, the response of the left-hand cross-fingerings was left undisturbed.

A device called the register, generally credited to Quantz's teacher, Pierre Gabriel Buffardin, appeared shortly after the *corps de réchange*. Designed to regulate the internal tuning of the lower body and footjoint, it consisted of a two-part footjoint, the length of which could be varied by about half an inch by sliding the telescopic metal tubes that lined the internal joint. Quantz criticized it severely, branding it another cause of false intonation. He suggested an alternative: the division of the head into two pieces. The tenon of the lower part would be longer than that of the upper, and when inserted, could be adjusted to improve the intonation. This invention ultimately became the modern tuning slide.

Yet another device introduced by Quantz was a second footjoint key, this one for E♭. Added in 1726, it was designed to distinguish D♯ from E♭ within the mean tone system of tuning. It did not, however, win public acceptance, a fact that Quantz acknowledged in his 1752 *Versuch*.

Even Quantz's elaborate fingering system was not sufficient to compensate for the flute's inherently poor intonation. The $b^1\flat$, $g^1\sharp$, $g^2\sharp$, f^1, and f^2 were particular trouble spots. And thus, though F♯ was far from perfect, the best keys for the flute were G and D major. The favorite keys for the recorder, on the other hand, were B♭ and F. The tonal limitation of the transverse flute thus provides a useful device for musicologists to ascertain whether a particular piece marked merely "flute" or "flauto" was intended for transverse flute or recorder. Johann Georg Tromlitz wrote, at the end of the eighteenth century, that keys with more than three sharps or flats were "difficult and unsuitable" for the flute,[3] and for the most part, composers were wary of dangerous keys.

Despite its poor intonation, the flute enjoyed great popularity in the eighteenth century. A succession of printed instruction books, beginning with Hotteterre's in 1707, promoted the instrument's popularity among amateurs. Composers obliged this growing market with increasingly difficult music, so that the defects of the instrument became progressively more obvious and bothersome. Composers as well as performers became disenchanted. Alessandro Scarlatti reportedly said, "I cannot endure wind-instrument players; they all blow out of tune,"[4] and Luigi Cherubini commented similarly that "the only thing worse than one flute is two."[5] It was only the attractive tone of the eighteenth century flute that saved its reputation.

At midcentury, the introduction of equal temperament (the division of the octave into twelve equal semitones) eliminated the need for Quantz's numerous chromatic cross-fingerings. At the same time, it permitted the possibility of developing a chromatic key mechanism for the woodwind instruments—the beginning of the mechanical approach to intonational remedies.

The flute, holding the dubious honor of possessing the worst cross-fingerings, thus became the first orchestral woodwind to acquire additional chromatic keywork. (Chromatic keys had been used on the bagpipes since the early seventeenth century.) Just before 1760, three London flute makers, Pietro Florio (about 1730–95), Caleb Gedney (1754–69), and Richard Potter (1728–1806), began adding three additional keys—for G♯, B♭, and F—to the existing one-keyed flute. Two of the new keys were assigned to fingers that previously had no mechanical function. The G♯ key, a closed key lying lengthwise down the side of the flute, controlled the G♯ hole bored below the A hole on the far side of the lower end of the upper-middle joint, and was controlled by the little finger of the left hand. A B♭ key, also lying lengthwise on the tube, governed a hole bored on the near side of the tube below the B-natural hole and was played by the left-hand thumb. There was no finger free to play the added F key, so the third finger of the right hand, which already covered the E hole, also operated a closed cross key for F natural whose hole was bored on the back of the tube between the E and F♯ holes. The touch curved over the top of the flute.

The new keys made the production of f^3 thoroughly reliable; more important, the only remaining cross-fingered chromatic note in the D scale was C natural, but its quality was acceptable. Thus the new keys gave composers unprecedented freedom of tonality, and therefore greater opportunities for harmonic modulation, an advance evident, for instance, in the works of Haydn and Mozart.

Acceptance of the new keys was slow, however. Some professionals were insulted; they considered the very suggestion of the need for keys to be a reflection on their technical ability. Lew Granom wrote in his *Plain and Easy Instructions for Playing on the German-Flute*, published in London in 1766, that the only reason for adding more keys was to draw more public attention to the instrument. Furthermore, he said, they would not improve the intonation.

> Blowing in tune does not depend so much upon the Flute as upon the Player; for a Performer, who has a good Ear, will play in Tune, even on a very indifferent Instrument, so soon as he has found its defects; which is not hard to conceive, since every Note on the flute may be blown either Sharper or Flatter at the will of the Performer.[6]

Secondly, performers were skeptical of the mechanical reliability of the new keys. Indeed, the springs were frequently sluggish and the hole closure far from hermetic. Finally, players objected to the change of fingering. As a result, at first they used the new keys only for shakes or other awkward ornaments, rather than to improve the quality of the forked sounds, the primary purpose for which they were designed. By 1785 or 1790, however, the four-keyed flute had become the instrument of choice.

In 1774, notwithstanding players' objections to the three new keys, Florio, Gedney, and Potter revived the earlier eighteenth century idea of the C footjoint. They lengthened the flute by two inches, and the two new holes bored in the footjoint were controlled by open keys operated by the fourth finger of the right hand. And again the first reaction was negative. Wrote W. N. James in 1826, "These notes are excrescences and are grafted most artificially on the tube of the natural flute."[7] But eventually, these keys, like their predecessors, caught on.

The extension of range and technical facility afforded by the four- and six-keyed flutes had a profound effect on musical composition, which may be seen, for example, in a comparison of the works of Haydn and Mozart. The flute begins to appear regularly in Haydn's symphonies only after 1780. The range was conservative at first, but it grew to d^1 to g^3. Haydn's works foreshadowed the flute's coming role as an integral member of the orchestra, as it appears in Mozart's late symphonies.

Eighteenth century organological development culminated in the development of the eight-keyed flute, later referred to as the "German," "ordinary," "old system," "simple system," or "Meyer system" flute. In 1782, Dr. J. H. Ribock began to promote a closed key for c^2 to control a hole bored on the near side of the tube between the B and C♯ holes. The key was operated by the first finger of the right hand by means of a finger plate connected to the key by a long shank.

Four years later, in 1786, Tromlitz introduced the duplicate F-natural key. On the four- and six-keyed models, it was extremely difficult to move the right-hand third finger sideways from the E hole to the F-natural cross key; thus it was almost impossible to slur from F to D or D♯ without involuntarily sounding a "grace note" F between them. Tromlitz's solution was to bore another F-natural hole on the far side of the instrument, covered by a closed key operated by the fourth finger of the left hand. Because of its shape, the new key became known as the "long F."

Though the eight-keyed flute is generally considered to be the standard instrument of the late eighteenth and nineteenth centuries, the flute was, in fact, far from standardized. The one-keyed flute prospered well into the nineteenth century, side by side with the four-, six-, and eight-keyed models. Several tutors of the era treat the one-keyed model as the norm, appending supplementary information for "additional" keys. One reason for the survival of the one-keyed flute was its lower cost.

At the other extreme, the flute was not limited to eight keys. The nineteenth century, a period of intense mechanical invention in many fields, witnessed great mechanical elaboration upon the "simple system" flute. Some instruments had as many as seventeen keys and compasses extending to low G.

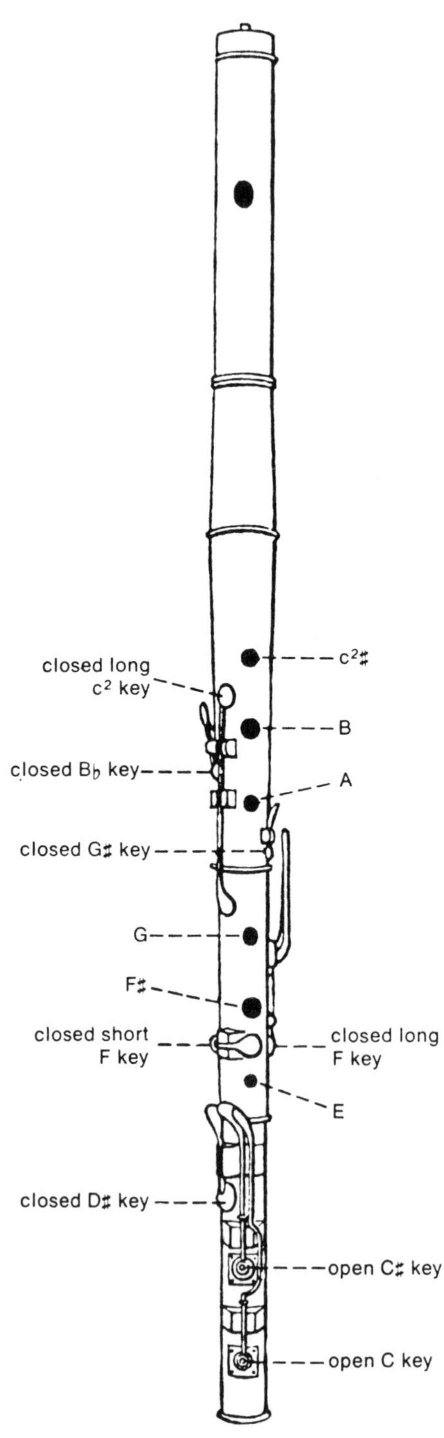

Eight-key flute by Rudall & Rose, London, about 1827

The end of the classic period signaled the end of woodwind players' complacency about their instruments. Bigger orchestras demanded greater volume and projection. Composers were more aware of the possibilities of contrasting tone colors. And so, though the woodwinds were played less often, their passages became exposed and soloistic rather than reinforcements of the string texture. Moreover, composers became more adventurous in their use of key signatures, branching out into multiple sharps and flats. The defects of cross-fingering on the woodwind instruments became increasingly obvious. And so flute makers added more holes and designed the requisite mechanisms to control them.

The early nineteenth century saw several other modifications to the flute's construction that were to have profound, if delayed, effects on the future course of flute making. The most obvious feature of the 1806 patent registered to Paris flute maker Claude Laurent was the use of glass for the construction of the flute tube. In itself, this was neither new nor terribly important. What was significant about the patent, however, was the set of

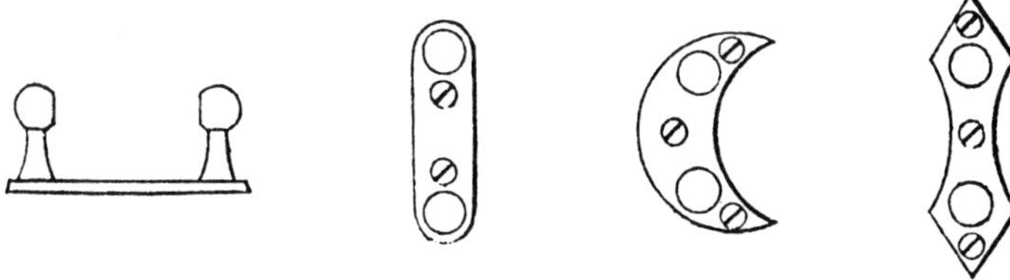

Pillars and plates

mechanical contrivances that the glass necessitated: silver tenons and sockets for the joints; lengthened springs for increased resilience; and the revolutionary design of the key mountings. Previously, the small woodwinds had used metal "saddles"; the key rotated on a screw-headed pin held in a metal bearing. Laurent attached the keys to the glass tube by mounting the keys in silver posts that were then attached to metal plates screwed to the glass tube. Makers of wood flutes soon adopted the idea because it prevented hitherto troublesome lateral play in the keys.

In November 1808, the Reverend Frederick Nolan took out a British patent for a device designed to effect greater evenness of intonation. It consisted of open-standing keys, either a single lever or a linked pair, whose touchpieces were rings that surrounded the finger holes. This is the first known contrivance for simultaneously closing both an open key and a regular hole with the same finger, a principle fundamental to the highly mechanized instruments developed later in the century. A further application was the possibility of closing a connected key while the immediate hole remained open; this was done by sliding the finger off the key, but keeping it on the shank.

A patent registered in 1810 to London flute maker George Miller provided for a cylindrical metal bore. Though intended principally for the military fife,

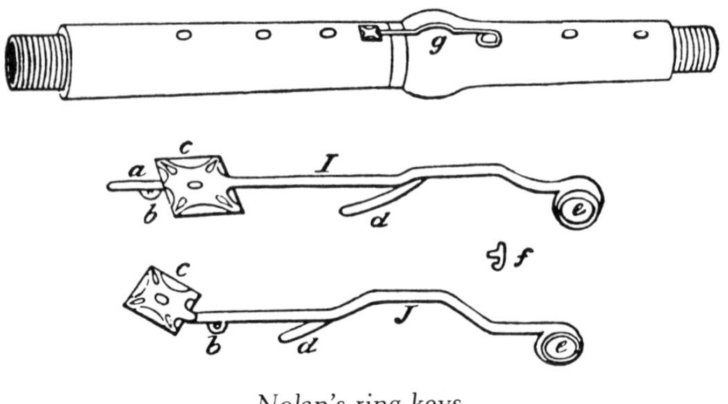

Nolan's ring keys

the patent specification also mentioned concert flutes; this was the first patent for a metal flute, which was to become the norm later in the century.

The Boehm Flute

When it came to fingering systems, there were two schools of thought in the nineteenth century. The first wanted to preserve the traditional systems, adding to them as necessary. The second preferred to start afresh, to drill a hole for each semitone, each in its acoustically correct position, and then to devise a mechanism and fingering system capable of controlling those holes. The leading figure in the second group was, of course, Theobald Boehm.

Boehm, a Munich flutist and goldsmith, began making flutes as a sideline in the 1820s. In 1828 he opened a flute-making factory, where he made the typical simple system instruments of the day. He did, however, make several original modifications to the usual designs, including tuning slides, hardened gold springs, and the mounting of keys on screwed-in pillars. By about 1829, he had begun to experiment with using longitudinal rod-axles to connect the keys.

Meanwhile, Boehm toured Europe as a flutist, in 1831 presenting several concerts in London. Though the critics were complimentary, Boehm was not pleased with his own performances in comparison to those of the exceptional English virtuoso Charles Nicholson, whose tone far exceeded Boehm's in both strength and volume. Even taking into account the enlarged finger holes on Nicholson's flute, Boehm concluded that the vast majority of the defects inherent in the flute's construction were not remediable by the normal flutist population. Wrote Boehm,

> There is no doubt that many artists have carried perfection to its last limits on the old flute, but there are also unavoidable difficulties, originating in the construction of these flutes, which can neither be conquered by talent nor by the most persevering practice.[8]

Boehm concluded that the principal defect of the simple system flute was its indifference to acoustical principles; the finger holes were placed where the fingers could reach them, not where acoustical theory demanded. The addition of keys could not solve this fundamental problem. Moreover, Boehm believed, the tone holes were not large enough to ensure sufficiently easy and in-tune high notes.

Boehm drew on three earlier inventions in redesigning the flute: large tone holes, as on Nicholson's flute; covering the holes with keys to enable the fingers to control distant holes; and ring keys like those invented by Reverend Nolan. Boehm's distinctive contribution was not mechanical, then, but acoustical; he used the mechanisms of others to execute his own acoustical theories.

Boehm's first redesign was built by the London firm of Gerock and Wolf in 1831. It embodied only two changes from the usual eight-keyed model. The left-hand fingering remained the same, but the A hole was brought down to its acoustically correct position and an open key for the left-hand third finger

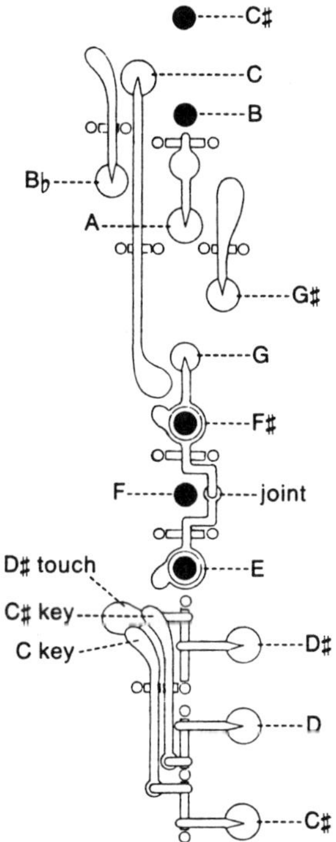

Boehm's 1831 flute

used to reach it. On the right hand, the E, F, F , and G keys were respaced farther down the tube (an idea advanced in 1803 by H. W. Pottgiesser), and controlled by double-jointed ring keys. These keys allowed the first finger of the right hand to stop two holes, rather than the customary one, thereby producing F-natural rather than the old flute's F♯. F♯ was now produced by the right hand third finger by means of another ring key. The new F-F♯

device destroyed the primary D major scale of the simple system flute; as such, it represents the first phase of modern flute construction.

In 1832, Boehm began a series of experiments to determine the proper proportions of tone hole measurements. His aim was to make the holes as large as possible and to place them in their acoustically correct positions in order to enhance the formation of the requisite nodes of vibration. For the same reason, Boehm chose to use an open-keyed system, which would allow full venting of the holes. Boehm explained,

> It is necessary, for obtaining a clear and strong tone, that the holes immediately below the one sounding should remain open, for the air confined in the lower end of the tube tends to flatten the notes, and renders them less free.[9]

The open-keyed system required some rearrangement of the holes.

In order to control the fourteen holes of his flute with only nine fingers (the right-hand thumb was used only to support the instrument), Boehm used

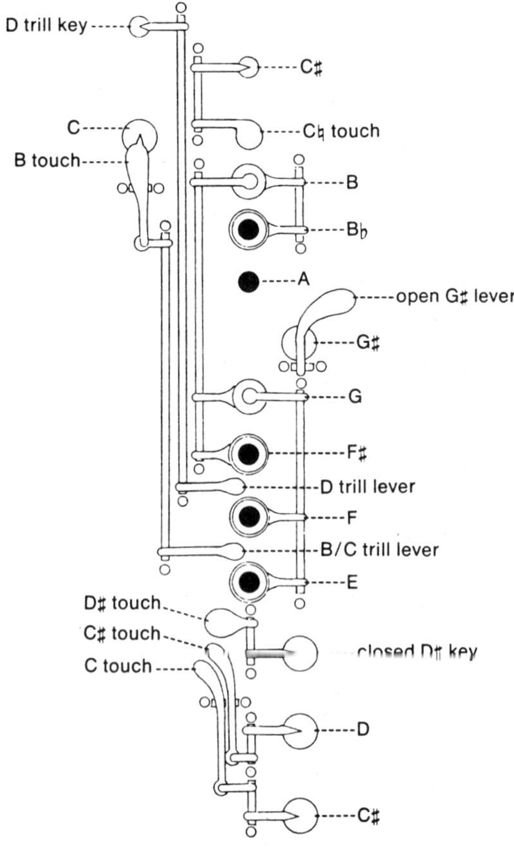

Boehm's 1832 flute

Nolan's ring keys and his own horizontal rod-axles. Under the new system, the fingers were not required to move out of their natural positions for any notes between d^1 and b^3, with the only exception being the right-hand little finger. In this way, Boehm aimed to retain as much as possible of the old system of fingering.

On the body of the flute, the first, second, and third keys of the right hand controlled the F♯, F, and E holes, respectively. The G hole was covered with a padded cup, attached by a horizontal rod-axle to the ring keys for the E and F holes. So the G hole could be closed by either the second or third finger of the right hand, or both. A ring key over the F♯ hole was attached to the end of another axle that extended up to the B hole; an arm projected from that axle over the G hole-cover so that the G hole would also be closed when the F♯ ring was pressed down. Thus, the three fingers of the right hand could control four holes.

On the left hand, the second and third fingers covered the B♭ and A holes, and the fourth finger controlled the open G♯ key. A ring key over the B♭ hole and a key cover for the B hole were attached to a common axle so that depressing the former would also close the latter. In addition, the B cup was connected by a lateral arm to the long axle that carried the F♯ ring, so that the B hole could also be closed by the right-hand first finger; otherwise, opening the B♭ hole would sound B-natural. Because the C♯ hole was too high on the tube to be reached by the left-hand first finger, it was covered by a padded cup and controlled by a finger plate attached to a short axle. The left thumb controlled an open key for the C hole on the near side of the flute. In addition to the basic mechanism, Boehm provided shake keys for the B-C and C-D trills.

Boehm introduced his new flute to the public in Munich concerts beginning in November 1832, and subsequently in Paris and London. By 1833, however, Boehm had sold only one of his flutes in London, primarily because of the natural reluctance of players to relearn the fingering. In Germany, there was similar reluctance, but the new instrument's more "open" tone provided yet another obstacle. Paul Camus, first flutist of the Opéra Italien, introduced the Boehm flute to Paris in 1837, and with the help of several colleagues, it began to catch on in the French capital.

Those colleagues made several significant mechanical changes to the Boehm flute that made it more practical to build and to play, but preserved the essence of Boehm's invention. Paris instrument maker Auguste Buffet objected to Boehm's placement of axles on both sides of the flute, and decided to move them all to the inner side. In order to avoid crowding the rod connecting the F♯ ring with the G and B hole covers, he attached the E and F rings and the G cup to a single axle, with the F♯ ring mounted in a loose sleeve through which the axle passed. A lug was soldered to the sleeve; a similar lug was pinned to the axle above the sleeve. On the left-hand portion of the tube, the B♭ ring–B cup mechanism and the C♯ cup and touchpiece were attached to loose sleeves threaded on a fixed rod. The B-B♭ sleeve carried a third lug that lay on top of the other two, together forming a clutch. Buffet also applied the rod and sleeve device to the footjoint keys. In addition, he used needle springs rather than flat leaf springs to enhance the mechanical action.

Flutist Victor Coche, working with Buffet, suggested a number of other changes that were incorporated into Buffet's 1839 patent. There had been considerable objection among players to Boehm's open G♯. Though Boehm felt strongly that the open G♯ was acoustically superior and mechanically logical, players were uncomfortable with it. Coche, therefore, reinstated the closed G♯ mechanism of the old system flute. However, it did not survive. Coche's greatest contribution was the addition of a trill key for C♯-D♯ in the second and third octaves. Operated by the right-hand third finger, it governed a small hole above the d^2 hole at the top of the flute. Buffet joined Coche's D♯ trill key and Boehm's D trill key in a common sleeve.

Vincent Dorus, flute professor at the Paris Conservatoire and solo flutist of the Opéra, responded to the widespread objections to the open G♯ key with a better solution than Coche's. Dorus designed a new type of closed G♯ key. He added a ring key to the A hole and attached it to the open G♯ key with a divided sleeve and clutch. When the ring key was depressed, the G♯ key closed, but it could be opened independently by a lever for the little finger attached to the part of the sleeve that supported the G♯ key. The defect of Dorus's device was its dependence on two opposing springs of unequal strength, which complicated a number of fingerings. Despite its awkwardness, though, it was important in easing the transition of hesitant players to the Boehm flute.

These modifications succeeded in attracting a good deal of attention to the Boehm flute; by 1838 it was officially introduced to the Paris Conservatoire. The following year, the London flutists Cornelius Ward and Signor Folz adopted the Boehm flute, probably influenced by the performances of their French colleagues. Ward became the first London manufacturer of Boehm flutes. John Clinton, professor of flute at the Royal Academy of Music in London, claimed to have adopted the Boehm flute in 1841, and Richard Carte and George Rudall did so two years later. At this time, Boehm, having closed his own factory in 1839 in order to pursue interests in the steel industry (Boehm invented the modern smelting process), made official arrangements for his flute to be manufactured by Rudall & Rose in London and Clair Godfroy, *ainé*, in Paris.

In 1846 and 1847, Boehm studied classical acoustics with Dr. Carl von Schafhäutl at the University of Munich in preparation for further work on the bore of his flute. The experiments that Boehm undertook at this time confirmed his growing doubts about the conical bore of the flute. He concluded that a cylindrical tube was far more conducive to the production of the harmonic components or partials of the flute tone, and further, that the tube ought to contract in a curve toward the embouchure. Boehm constructed his 1847 flute in accordance with these principles.

The bore of the flute body had an internal bore of 19 millimeters. The headjoint gradually decreased in diameter so that the bore measured 17 millimeters at the cork. Boehm described the curve of the headjoint as "parabolic," though in fact the curve had only a superficial resemblance, not a mathematical one, to that geometrical figure. The redesign of the bore dimensions necessitated fine tuning of the tone hole placement and size, particularly for the c^2♯ hole.

Boehm also reconsidered the size and shape of the embouchure hole. He concluded that not only should the hole be as large as possible, but also, that a rectangular shape with rounded corners was preferable to the traditional oval or round hole. As for the tone holes, Boehm had originally intended to increase their size from the bottom to the top of the flute, but ultimately he discontinued this design because of the difficulty of manufacturing it.

Boehm recorded his conclusions regarding the relationship between bore and tone holes on a geometrical diagram called a Schema. These dimensions could be adapted for various lengths of flute tubing, depending upon the pitch standard to which a given instrument was built.

The large tone holes, while acoustically advantageous, fostered a mechanical problem: they could not be closed directly by the fingers. Boehm therefore replaced both ring keys and open holes with padded hole covers, similar to those already used for the G and B holes on his 1832 model. Each key had to be capable of opening independently yet be attached to other keys in accordance with Boehm's fingering system. He therefore adopted the sleeves and rods of Buffet, attaching each key cover to its own sleeve and springing each one open with a light needle spring. Interconnected keys were linked by clutches (overlapping lugs or pins). Boehm was explicit about the construction of the pads in order to avoid the unreliable stoppage that had plagued old system flutes: he specified fine wool disks, covered with a fine membrane or skin of double thickness. The pads were to be covered on the back with sheets of card, with a hole punched in the center, so that they could be screwed securely into the key cups. A silver washer under the screw head ensured a tight fit.

Another crucial feature of the 1847 flute was the choice of materials for the body. Boehm began to experiment with metal tubes in 1846, and concluded that silver and brass tubes produced the best tone. Furthermore, he found that thin, hard-drawn tubes increased the metal's capacity for vibration and therefore produced a more resonant tone. Boehm concluded that his new silver flute was clearly superior to his earlier wood ones: it was impervious to splitting, the bore was dimensionally stable and less affected by temperature, and it was more suitable for tone modulation. Boehm wrote that it had "unsurpassed brilliancy and sonourousness of tone. I could produce effects on my silver flute, which I could never afterwards produce on wooden flutes."[10]

In 1847, Boehm sold the British rights to his latest model to Rudall & Rose of London and the French rights to Clair Godfroy and his son-in-law Louis Lot of Paris. At first, both firms manufactured Boehm flutes in metal; in 1848, however, Godfroy and Lot made some cocoawood instruments at the behest of Dorus. The Frenchmen also reintroduced perforated keys, opening the centers of the A, G, F♯, E, and D keys, which are played directly by the fingers, to allow increased venting. This model became known as the "open hole" or "French model" flute.

The only mechanical alteration to the 1847 Boehm flute that permanently affected its fingering system was made in 1850 by Giulio Briccialdi (1818–81), an Italian flutist living in London. Boehm's original design had only one thumb lever, which governed an open key for B. B♭ was produced by using the first finger of the right hand. Briccialdi's aim was to provide an alternate B♭ fingering for the left thumb for added convenience in flat keys. And so he added a second thumb lever, placed above the B lever, which was sprung so that pressing it would close the B hole. Thus B♭ could be fingered simply by the first finger and thumb of the left hand.

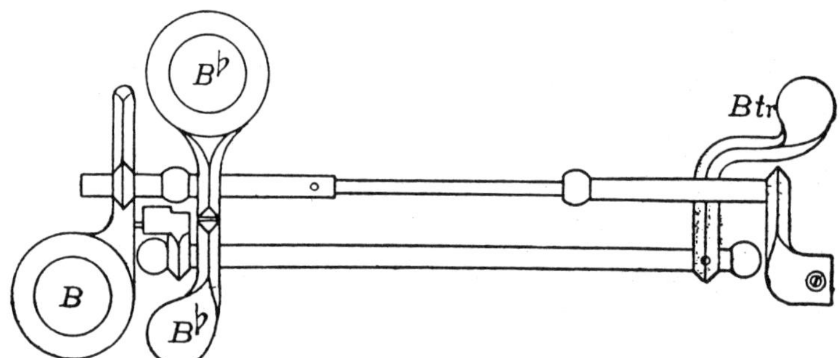

Boehm's B♭ thumb lever

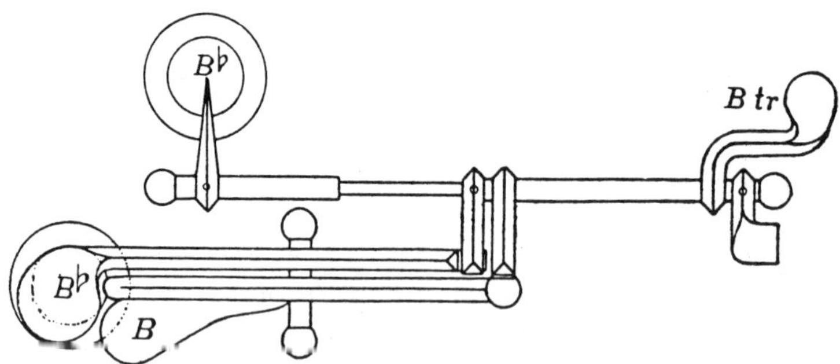

Briccialdi's B♭ thumb lever

Boehm later devised his own B♭ thumb device, which he considered logically superior in that the B♭ lever was below the B lever. On the Briccialdi version, in contrast, the thumb moved upward to produce the lower tone. Nevertheless, Briccialdi's design prevailed.

The Boehm flute quickly became popular with professional players in both France and England. The same was true in the United States; it was first manufactured in the U.S. in 1851. The Boehm flute took first prize in the Industrial Exhibition of All Nations in London in 1851, the gold medal at the Paris Exhibition in 1855, and first prize at the General German Industrial Exhibition in 1855. Ironically, though, the Boehm flute was slow to gain acceptance in the inventor's native Germany. The reasons: its inconsistency with aesthetic standards that demanded a wooden flute in the traditional woodwind choir, and more tangibly, the lack of qualified teachers—two of Boehm's most talented students emigrated to the United States. By the first decade of the twentieth century, the Boehm flute was still not common in Germany, Italy, or Russia, the prime objection still being the new fingering system.

Other Nineteenth Century Flutes

While the French were quite quick to take up the Boehm flute, making only minor (and worthwhile) mechanical changes, flutists in other parts of Europe took other approaches to remedying the defects of the old system flute. In Germany, work continued on the traditional cone system flute; in England, there were several entirely new designs as well as substantive modifications to the Boehm flute. Though only one of these models is used today (the 1867 Guards' model is still used by a few British players), they are of sufficient historical interest to warrant a brief summary.

Most variations on the simple system flute maintained the conical bore—many flutists considered the subtlety of its tone and original fingering scheme great virtues. Designers merely added more keys—and their own names—to create "new" models. One of the best-known modifications was the work of Jean Louis Tulou, whose 1851 model adopted a footjoint similar to Boehm's 1832 model. In Germany, many manufacturers added a *brille* (spectacles). This device consisted of two rings and a vent on the upper joint, designed to improve the intonation of c^2 and $c^2\sharp$. Rudall & Rose later adopted this device.

By the late nineteenth century, the German cone flute evolved into the "reform flute," the work of Leipzig flutist Maximilian Schwedler and manufacturer Friedrich Kruspe. Its footjoint was built on axles and it had an extra side trill key and various other minor mechanical additions. The reform flute was further mechanized by the Mönnig family of Leipzig, who installed plates over some holes, rings for certain automated devices, and rollers between keys. The reform flute's most striking feature was the addition of raised bosses or cusps above and below the embouchure hole, with the aim of expediting the entrance of the airstream into the flute.

Other flutists rejected both the old system and Boehm's and set out to devise their own solutions. Competition was fierce, leading one contemporary observer to refer sarcastically to "the Noble Army of Patentees."[11] In 1842, Cornelius Ward secured a patent for no fewer than seven different conical flutes, each with a distinctive fingering system. All seven, however, had a device called a "Terminator and Indicator," a graduated metal tuning slide coordinated with a silver head stopper. The final Ward model was built on the open-keyed system, with silver ring keys controlled by wires and cranks. It was the first English flute to use needle springs.

John Clinton, one of the earliest English proponents of the Boehm flute, patented two devices in 1848, an event that reflected his growing disenchantment with the open-key system on which the Boehm flute was based. He replaced the three rings that Boehm used to close the G hole with a single bar. More importantly, he restored the old-system fingering for c^2 by covering the B♭ and G♯ holes with closed keys.

Further research culminated in his 1855 Equisonant Flute, a dubious improvement. Said one Boehm partisan, "What is the meaning of 'equisonant,' Mr. Clinton, does it mean equally bad all over?" Answered historian R. S. Rockstro, "Unfortunately, the flute had not even that negative merit, for it was unequally bad."[12] Indeed, by 1862 Clinton had resumed manufacture of the Boehm flute, taking out a patent for graduated holes—a claim whose originality Boehm disputed.

There were also several truly regressive proposals for keyless flutes—intended to obviate the confusion among players regarding the many, many rival key systems then on the market. Londoner Dr. Burghley's various models actually evidenced progressively increasing numbers of keys. Abel Siccama patented a one-keyed "Chromatic Flute" in 1845—the closest he ever came to his keyless ideal. Siccama's 1846 "Diatonic Flute," the flute now generally known as the Siccama flute, reverted almost entirely to the old system of fingering, with the exception of high E, F, G, and A. The firm of Mahillon & Company of Brussels and London was one of several prominent makers who manufactured the Siccama model; its partisans included the leading English players Joseph Richardson (1814–62) and Robert Sydney Pratten (1824–68). A more exotic attempt to design a keyless flute was the work of Carlo Giorgi in 1888. Made of ebonite, the Giorgi flute had eleven finger holes and was held vertically; the embouchure hole and plate were at the top end of the flute. Significantly, Giorgi's patent shows options for adding keys.

And then, there were a number of compromise and combination models—principally the adaptation of a single feature of the Boehm flute to the old system conical flute. William Card of London, for instance, took the Boehm system's right-hand mechanism. The Card flute's fingering was identical to the old system except for the open-standing F♯ key.

In 1850, Richard Carte attempted to restore the old F♯ fingering and free the left hand pinky and thumb, while retaining Boehm's cylinder bore, open-key principle, and large, equally spaced holes. In 1852, Richard S. Rockstro brought out a conical adaptation of the Boehm flute; the lowest four notes were fingered under the old system, all the rest à la Boehm. Rockstro also modified the position and size of the tone holes. Most importantly, he added an extra F♯ lever for the right-hand third finger to remove objections to the Boehm flute's right-hand fingering.

In the same year, Robert Sydney Pratten introduced his "Perfected Flute," an old-system flute with a revised bore design and finger plate mechanism. He expanded the lower portion of the bore, which allowed him to use larger holes for the lower notes than had previously been possible. The Pratten flute was manufactured for many years by Boosey & Company of London.

Rockstro introduced a new cylinder flute in 1858, another in 1864, and yet another in 1877. In 1866, Richard Carte obtained a patent for the "Carte and Boehm Systems Combined," subsequently known as the Carte 1867 system. Its aim was to simplify the fingering of B♭, F, and F♯. It permitted a wealth of alternate fingerings, and in some ways was technically superior to the Boehm flute. It remained popular in Great Britain well into this century. A slight variation, the Guards' Model, had a closed G♯ key.

In 1870, John Radcliff made still another attempt to reconcile Boehm's arrangement of the tone holes with the old system of fingering. In fact, it was a simplification of the Carte 1851 model, and was based almost entirely on simple system fingering. Among its partisans was the great Australian flutist John Amadio, accompanist to Nellie Melba.

Two other minor inventions are also characteristic of the middle nineteenth century: Jean Firmin Brossa (born 1839) added an F♯ device similar to that of Carte and Rockstro, a small touch for the right-hand third finger that duplicated the F♯ action of the finger's regular key; it was useful in moving between E and F♯.

The second invention, contrived by Christopher Welch, consisted of a modification of the closed key reversions of Carte (for F), Buffet (for B♭), and Radcliff (for G♯). In order to retain the advantages of Boehm's open-keyed system, Welch added duplicate vent holes.

Minor Modifications to the Boehm System

The end of the nineteenth century witnessed a significant change of orientation among flute makers; they acknowledged that the Boehm flute was there to stay, and contented themselves and their customers with minor mechanical modifications that required little or no conscious adaptation by the player. Those keys that were added were supplementary keys intended to solve specific technical problems; they did not affect the basic mechanism in any way. Other modifications had to do with materials and techniques of construction designed for the benefit of the player, but primarily of concern to the manufacturers, not the least of whose motives was economical production.

Indicative of the Boehm flute's new, secure status was a cartoon that appeared in a 1920 issue of *The Flutist* magazine. With typical literary pretension, the caption read, "Breathes there a man with soul so low/Who in preference to a Boehm a Meyer would blow?"[13]

One of the most extensive variations on the Boehm system was the Borne-Julliot flute, the work of French manufacturer Djalma Julliot and François Borne, a professor at the Toulouse Conservatory. It began its long and anguished evolution in 1889. The twosome came up with so many gadgets, in fact, that they could not fit them all on one flute. It was the last gasp of nineteenth century overinvention. The one Borne-Julliot device that survives to any significant degree in modern manufacture is the split-E or split-G device, to remedy the sharpness and problematic production of e^3.

The Murray flute, the work of Alexander Murray, is another extensive variation on the Boehm design that has gone through myriad incarnations. Beginning in 1948, Murray, then a flutist with the Royal Air Force Band in England, reinstituted open G♯, soon followed by open D♯. He moved on to a split-A mechanism, analogous in construction to the split-E; various reversals (and re-reversals) of the thumb keys; more modifications of the footjoint; the addition of roller keys; and experiments with rectangular keys. Meanwhile, Murray came to the United States. In 1967, while teaching at Michigan State University, Murray arranged to have the W. T. Armstrong Company of Elkhart, Indiana, build a prototype of his latest model. In 1972, Armstrong produced fifty production model Murray flutes and six Murray piccolos. Murray has since made several other modifications to his design, one called the "Multiple Option" flute. Today, it is available only on a custom basis from Jack Moore, an independent flute maker who had worked closely with Murray when he was foreman of Armstrong's Heritage Division. The changes in fingering, and most of all, the complications inherent in most of the Murray mechanisms, make it seem unlikely that the Murray flute will ever see full-scale commercial availability.

More typical of twentieth century research and development efforts are several French patents from the early part of the century. The 1902 patent issued to J. Thibouville-Lamy & Cie. covered three trill keys, facilitating c^1-c^1♯, B-C, and B♭-B. The 1909 patent granted to Mme. Cornélie Villedieu Laubé added a new trill key that improved several existing trills and permitted a new trill, g^3-a^3, when operated in conjunction with the upper (C-D) trill key.

Louis-Fernand Vigué's 1913 patent reversed the right-hand pinky touches for the c^1♯ and c^1 keys in order to facilitate the c^1-d^1 trill. It also added a second lever for the left pinky, which controlled the c^1♯ key, and created c^1-d^1♭ and c^1♯-d^1♯ trills, hitherto impossible on the Boehm system. Two other trill mechanisms facilitated several difficult third-register trills.

The Gage Articulated B-F♯ device, patented by Charles B. Gage in 1926, was designed to eliminate the difficulty of sliding the left thumb between the Briccialdi B♭ lever and the B-natural lever. The device never saw widespread adoption, but in 1981 the Haynes Company introduced a nearly identical device (see chapter 1, "The Flute Today").

More recently, manufacturers have given significant attention not to the mechanism but to the acoustical properties of the flute. In recent years, a number of new, "named" scales have come out. The Cooper scale, designed by Albert Cooper, is probably the most famous. Various Cooper scales are available on Powell and Brannen Brothers flutes as well as from Cooper himself. W. T. Armstrong offers its own "Armstrong scale," Jack Moore lists the William Bennett scale as an option, and Haynes has the Deveau scale.

On the headjoint, the biggest development in recent years is the O-Ring, the result of dissatisfaction with the mercurial cork stopper, which was prone to shrinkage and thus a potential cause of air leakage and faulty intonation. The O-Ring is made of a synthetic rubber called neoprene; it makes a tighter seal than cork and does not require periodic replacement. The O-Ring was originally used by Rudall, Carte & Company early in this century, altered by English headjoint-maker Leslie Eggs to suit the silver flute, and imported to the U.S. by James Pellerite, professor of flute at Indiana University and proprietor of Zalo Publications and Services, which owns the U.S. patent.

Other research has centered on the size and shape of the embouchure, materials of tube construction, and manufacturing techniques. Developments in manufacturing have permitted production of flutes on a vast scale and have made student model instruments more durable—for example, new synthetic pads made by David Straubinger and others are much more abuse-resistant than the traditional skin-covered felt pads.

I predict that in coming years the trend toward improving manufacturing capability, instrument durability, and intonation and timbral flexibility will continue. It is extremely unlikely that significant work will be done to the mechanism. Even Alex Murray, perhaps the greatest gadgeteer of the present generation, says that the Boehm flute is "98 percent perfect."

Notes

1. Jacques Hotteterre le Romain, *Principles of the Flute, Recorder and Oboe*, trans. and ed. David Lasocki (1707; New York: Praeger Publishers, 1968), pp. 45–46.
2. Johann Joachim Quantz, *On Playing the Flute*, trans. Edward R. Reilly (1752; London: Faber and Faber, 1966), pp. 42–43.
3. Adam Carse, *Musical Wind Instruments* (1939; reprint, New York: Da Capo Press, 1965), p. 87.
4. Richard Shepard Rockstro, A *Treatise on the Construction the History and the Practice of the Flute*, 2nd ed., rev. (1928; reprint, London: Musica Rara, 1967), p. 543.
5. H. Macaulay Fitzgibbon, *The Story of the Flute*, 2nd ed., rev. (London: William Reeves Bookseller; New York: Charles Scribner's Sons, 1928), p. 135.
6. Lew Granom, *Plain and Easy Instructions for Playing on the German-Flute* (London: T. Bennett, 1766), p. 10; quoted in Carol Reglin Farrar, *Michel Cor-*

rette and Flute-Playing in the Eighteenth Century (Brooklyn, N.Y.: Institute of Mediaeval Music, 1970), p. 5.

7. W. N. James, "Essay on Fingering," *Flutonicon* 13 (Feb. 1846): 3–4; quoted in Farrar, pp. 3–4.
8. Theobald Boehm, *An Essay on the Construction of Flutes*, ed. W. S. Broadwood (London: Rudall, Carte & Co., 1882), p. 17.
9. Ibid., p. 20.
10. Ibid., p. 61.
11. Henry Clay Wysham, *The Evolution of the Boehm Flute* (New York: C. G. Conn, 1898), p. 9.
12. Rockstro, p. 390.
13. *The Flutist* 1 (1920): 42.

5

THE FLUTE FAMILY

Flutes come in a variety of sizes, each with its own distinctive tone, character, idiosyncracies, and musical potential. Variety in flutes is not a modern development; it has been a fact of musical life for centuries. Although the evolution of the flute family is often traced to the sixteenth century recorder consort, transverse flutes, too, have been described and illustrated in works on organology since the Renaissance.

Martin Agricola's *Musica instrumentalis deudsch* of 1529, one of the earliest sources on musical instruments, shows four sizes of *Schweitzer Pfeiffen*, which were descendants of the military fife. Michael Praetorius's *Syntagma Musicum* (1619–20) shows three sizes of *Querflöten* or *Querpfeiffen*, which were similar keyless instruments. Their range was as follows:

Discant: natural compass a^1-a^3, falset b^3-e^4

Alto or tenor: natural compass d^1-d^3, falset e^3-a^3

Bass: natural compass g-g^2, falset a^2-d^3

In 1636, Marin Mersenne's *Harmonie Universelle* illustrated two flutes, one in D and one in G. Although recorders of that time often came in sets of eight different sizes—Praetorius wrote that eight comprised a full "chest"—flutes have generally come in more limited assortments.

In more recent times, the history of large and small flutes has basically paralleled that of the standard-sized flute. Their technical improvement has always lagged somewhat behind, however, in line with the smaller demand in the literature for those instruments. In other words, as more keys were added to the flute, more keys were added to the piccolo, which underwent the same process of evolution from fife to Boehm system. Today, piccolos have reached a level of technical achievement close to that of the C or "concert" flute because of their frequent use in the modern symphony orchestra and band. The alto flute has in general not reached the same level of technical accomplishment, although there are a few excellent manufacturers. Bass flutes are a comparative rarity, and are inherently less elegant instruments.

In addition to the piccolo, C flute, alto flute in G, and bass flute in C, there is one other member of the modern Boehm-system flute family that deserves brief mention. The E♭ soprano flute is built a minor third higher than the concert flute. A descendant of the nineteenth century *terzflöte*, which was scored in such works as Mozart's *The Abduction from the Seraglio* and the obbligato to Sir Henry Bishop's famous air, "Lo! Hear the Gentle Lark!," the modern soprano flute is a real rarity. Its principal use today is as a starting instrument for young children who are too small to hold a C flute. In addition, it can when necessary substitute for the E♭ clarinet in the concert band, and it appears occasionally in a flute quartet made up of soprano flute, two C flutes, and alto flute.

The exception to this discussion of the flute family is the traditional British flute band, which to this day uses old-system flutes in eight sizes.

The Piccolo

French: *petite flûte (pte. fl.)*

German: *kleine flöte (kl. fl.)*

Italian: *flauto piccolo, ottavino*

The piccolo may be, with the possible exceptions of the tuba and contrabassoon, the most maligned instrument in the orchestra. It has been criticized by musical theorists, composers, instrument builders, and adult listeners. No one would contest that it is as beautiful or as useful an instrument as the flute, but its unqualified notoriety is equally undeserved.

The history of the piccolo roughly parallels that of the D flute (the standard flute, named after its "open" note; technically, the modern Boehm flute is a D flute, though it is generally referred to as a C flute because it is a non-transposing instrument). Its immediate progenitor was the military fife of the Middle Ages, from which the flute, of course, also descends. Like the flute, it gradually acquired more keys, though it never adopted the two footkeys (or the separate footjoint) that the flute did. It is essentially a structural product of the eighteenth century, but it did not achieve orchestral prominence until the following century.

The modern Boehm piccolo has a compass from d^2 to c^5, notated an octave lower, although the optimum performance range is generally considered to be g^2 to g^4. The lowest notes have low volume; in the extreme upper range, the frequencies are so close together that after a point the notes become indistinguishable from one another. The modern instrument is 32 centimeters (about 12½ inches) in length; the diameter of the embouchure hole is 10 millimeters; the finger hole diameter is 6 millimeters—about half the corresponding dimensions of the C flute.

Today the Boehm flute is constructed exclusively with cylindrical bore and a "parabolic" headjoint, whereas modern piccolos may have either cylindrical or conical bore, the former on silver instruments, the latter on wood and plastic ones. Early piccolos had cylindrical headjoints and conical bodies that narrowed toward the bottom end. Modern instruments, however, generally make a firm choice between conical and cylindrical, with no such compromise. The conical bore produces a more full-bodied, pleasing tone, clearly fuller in the low register, better balanced throughout the compass, and in general more flutelike. Cylindrical bore, in contrast, tends to give the instrument a thin, shrill tone quality, and makes the low register weak and often faulty in intonation. But the cylindrical bore makes the high register somewhat easier to play.

Modern piccolos are available in a choice of materials—wood, silver, and plastic, or some combination of these. The wood version is, obviously, the oldest model; it is fitted with a silver mechanism. It is preferable for orchestral playing because it is less shrill than the metal instrument and has a rounder sonority, which enables it to cut through the massed sound of a large orchestra. However, wood piccolos have a number of disadvantages. First, good ones are hard to find. Powell stopped manufacturing piccolos for many years during the 1960s and 1970s, but begun making them again in the 1980s. Although several of the major mass manufacturers, including Armstrong, Artley, Gemeinhardt, and Selmer, produce wood piccolos, as do a number of independent flute makers, the quality varies widely. Moreover, used instruments that come on the market are often in poor condition, or have been maintained so poorly that they are prone to cracking.

Some players believe that the difficulty of switching between flute and piccolo is exacerbated by the transition from silver flute to wood piccolo, the lack of an embouchure plate being one of the obvious differences between metal and wood piccolos. Also, the wooden piccolo demands a tighter embouchure, which is more tiring and may adversely affect a player's flute tone. For these reasons, some players compromise with a hybrid piccolo: silver head and wood body. The wooden instrument is unsuitable for use on "football occasions," in marching bands or other outdoor performances, where moisture and temperature are apt to damage the instrument. This is the overriding reason why most high school and college players use silver instruments.

The most recent innovation in piccolo manufacture is the use of plastic for the body. Its visual appearance is similar to that of wood, and it sounds woodlike, rounder and less shrill than a silver piccolo. And, of course, it is relatively impervious to the elements, though no woodwind instrument should be exposed to direct precipitation. A plastic piccolo is a very good choice for students and even for professionals. Another argument in its favor is price, as the price list in the 1995 Gemeinhardt catalog demonstrates:

Plastic head and body, silver-plated keys	$565
Silver-plated metal head, plastic body, silver-plated keys	600
Solid silver head, plastic body, silver-plated keys	660
Silver-plated head and body	605–660
Solid silver head, silver-plated body	700
Solid silver head and body, silver-plated keys	780–790
Solid silver head, body, and keys, gold springs	1,300
Grenadilla wood head and body, silver-plated keys	1,325
Grenadilla wood head and body, solid silver keys, gold springs	1,550

I prefer the wood instrument because of the superior quality of its tone. For orchestral and solo work, I believe the wood piccolo must be used. Since most professional players will use their piccolos in an orchestra, the wood instrument is a far wiser long-range investment.

In addition to being the smallest orchestral instrument, the piccolo also has the dubious honor of being one of the most difficult to play well. The small mouth hole demands that the player use a tighter embouchure in order to direct the airstream accurately. And the piccolo demands more breath pressure and airspeed than the flute does. This is a physically exhausting combination, particularly when the instrument is played for extended periods of time. Forte passages in the upper register, which occur rather more frequently than in other orchestral parts, are particularly demanding. Most critically, the tuning of the piccolo is problematic. Because of the forceful airstream required to produce a full-bodied sound, it tends to go sharp. More significantly, the piccolo's small dimensions make its intonational tolerances correspondingly small. It is a supersensitive instrument whose intonation will be affected by even the slightest alteration of airstream pressure or lip position. The acoustical explanation is simple: the higher the register, the smaller the difference in frequencies between notes. In other words, there is progressively less margin for error. Finally, as former Philadelphia Orchestra piccoloist John Krell cautions, the orchestral or band piccolo part is by its very nature exposed: "There's no place to hide."[1]

Experienced piccolo players develop automatic compensations for these difficulties. For instance, many players begin with a "more formed" embouchure, more carefully prepared than on the flute. When playing silver piccolos, many players place the embouchure plate higher on the lower lip than they place the flute. Other players have developed alternate fingerings to correct intonational problems and to play more softly in particular passages. Walfrid Kujala, longtime Chicago Symphony piccoloist, uses a number of special fingerings for B♭, B, C, and C♯ in the second octave, which he finds lack sweetness when played with the regular fingerings.

The modern piccolo is a C, or nontransposing, instrument (though technically, it transposes an octave). However, early Boehm system instruments were also made in D♭, for band use. Because most band arrangements are in flat keys, B♭, E♭, A♭, and D♭, transposing the piccolo part down to A, D, G, and C, the respective written keys for the D♭ piccolo, avoids the difficult high A♭ and in general simplifies the technical demands of the music. Kujala applies this convenience in the orchestra: he uses a D♭ piccolo for the solos in the scherzo of Tchaikovsky's Fourth Symphony in F minor, transposing the music down a half step to simplify the fingering.

The piccolo's prime characteristic, of course, is its high register, and its use in extending the instrumental range is therefore obvious. But one of its outstanding characteristics, though little appreciated, is its extreme variety of tone color within that acoustical range. It is a common and incorrect assumption that the piccolo's only capacity is for loud, high notes—in other words, that it is a range extender and a range extender only. Most commonly, it is used in its middle range, which is sufficiently high to extend the instrumental range of a composition without becoming offensive.

Within its overall written compass, d^1 to b^3♭ or c^4, the piccolo's range divides itself into several distinctive ranges. The following diagram shows the divisions outlined by two typical orchestration textbooks, Th. Dureau's *Cours Théorique et Pratique d'Instrumentation et d'Orchestration* (1905) and George McKay's *Creative Orchestration* (1963):

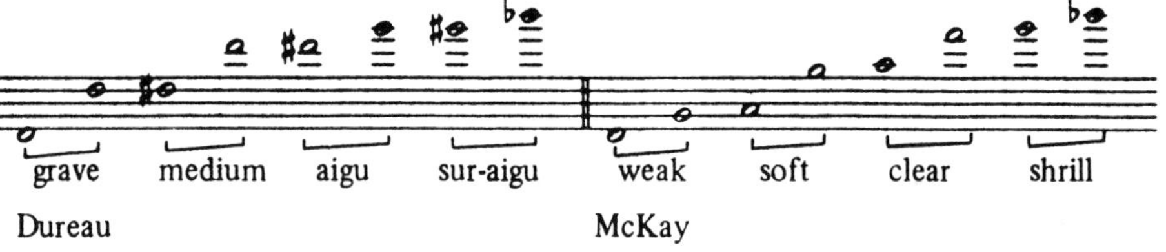

McKay's terminology is perhaps the more helpful of the two because tone color is the major consideration of composers' scoring for the piccolo. Despite these differences in nomenclature, a few generalizations are applicable: the lowest octave is relatively soft and weak in projection. Though not as colorless as some orchestrators allege, its lack of projection severely limits its effect in the orchestral context. But in chamber works, it is not only audible but a useful alternative tone color to the comparable flute register.

The middle register of the piccolo, which contains the most frequently scored notes, is appropriately piercing and colorful. Broad-minded orchestrators set the optimum range from g^1 to g^3, while narrow constructionists limit it to the d^2 to e^3 area.

In the upper register, from about d^3 up, the piccolo tone is, inarguably, shrill. As George McKay so diplomatically put it, the piccolo is "interestingly shrill in its high register, shockingly so in its very highest notes."[2] Inexpertly played, as unfortunately it often is, the piccolo can indeed "scream" at the top of the scale. A less tactful writer termed it "insupportable on the top notes."[3] Moreover, lacking the vocal identification that makes the concert flute so attractive to composers and listeners alike, it can sound like a tin whistle.

Just as the piccolo lagged somewhat behind the flute in sophistication of design, so it was somewhat slower in finding its way into the orchestra. Indeed, it did not achieve any prominence in the orchestra until the early nineteenth century, whereas the flute had been an orchestral regular for more than a century. Some modern researchers disagree vociferously about whether the well-known *flautino* concertos by Vivaldi were intended for sopranino recorder or a one-keyed transverse piccolo. Similarly, scholars now believe that the piccolo parts in Mozart's works, such as *Idomeneo,* were played in the composer's time on a small recorder or flageolet.[4]

When the piccolo first made its debut in the symphony orchestra in the early nineteenth century, it had two rather straightforward functions. The primary one was to extend the upper range of the woodwind choir, and specifically that of the flute. And so the piccolo, which was able to cut through the sound of the entire orchestra, was often given the melody, while the flute played harmony in a lower octave. Beethoven was the first major composer to use the piccolo in a symphony—the Fifth (1809). From that time on, orchestral use of the piccolo became increasingly frequent and increasingly innovative.

The piccolo's second function was to decorate the melodic line with "noodles" of various sorts—thus its reputation as an ornamental rather than a melodic instrument. A good example is the part for two piccolos in Weber's *Der Freischütz:*

Gluck, in the score for *Iphigenie en Tauride* (1779) had been the first composer to use double trills for two piccolos. Meyerbeer and Wagner adopted this technique, and it became a stock device in nineteenth century opera.

The piccolo has other useful functions in nineteenth century orchestral and opera music. It can provide a substitute timbre, because it can play more softly in the upper register than the flute can. A passage from Dvorak's *New World Symphony* illustrates this use:

It can add brilliance or "punch" to fortissimo tutti passages, as in Mozart's overture to *The Abduction from the Seraglio* and Beethoven's Symphony no. 9 and *Egmont* Overture. Typically, the piccolo will double the flute an octave above, functioning as a sort of gilt edge to the flute tone.

The piccolo has a particular aptitude for characterization and the establishment of mood. Its programmatic potential is most evident in martial themes. In "Marcel's War Song" from Meyerbeer's *Les Huguenots,* for instance, piccolo noodles imitate the military fife. The piccolo part is pure decoration and has no independent identity. Other familiar examples include the Racoczy March from Berlioz's *The Damnation of Faust* and the obbligato in the trio of Sousa's *The Stars and Stripes Forever.*

Second only, perhaps, to fife imitation is the piccolo's role as a pseudo-bird. A none-too-subtle example occurs in the first act of Johann Strauss's *Die Fledermaus:* as Frank describes the pleasures of prison, comparing the jail to a birdhouse, the piccolo doubles the melody three octaves above.

A common programmatic use is in storm scenes, as in Beethoven's Symphony no. 6 *(Pastoral)* and particularly in opera—for example, Wagner's overture to *The Flying Dutchman.* Similarly evocative uses of the piccolo occur in the "Magic Fire Scene" and the "Ride of the Valkyries" in *Die Walküre.* In the latter, the piccolo enhances the visual image of shooting sparks, supported elsewhere in the orchestra by small bells, a triangle, and other percussion instruments.

On the other hand, the piccolo can contribute to an atmosphere of serenity. In Mendelssohn's overture *Calm Sea and Pleasant Voyage,* the open octaves between the piccolo part and the unison flute and violins signify clarity and tranquillity. The lower register of the piccolo, too, has programmatic connotations. Two well-known examples occur in the second section of Debussy's *La Mer* and the "Ballet of the Sylphs" from *The Damnation of Faust.*

Certainly not to be ignored are the many solo orchestral passages for piccolo without programmatic connections: Tchaikovsky's Symphony no. 4, the Ravel piano concerto, Brahms's *Variations on a Theme of Haydn,* and so on.

It may surprise most nonflutists and probably most flutists, too, to learn that the piccolo also has a legitimate role as a chamber and solo instrument. The Vivaldi *flautino* concerti appear fairly often on concert programs, so this really should be no surprise. I must say, however, that the three Vivaldi concerti are probably the finest pieces of music of this type for the piccolo.

Piccolo solos were a standby of late nineteenth and early twentieth century band concerts because the instrument is well adapted to the fireworks and pseudo-bird genres. An example currently in print is the *Fantasia on Mexican Airs,* by Fred Lax. More contemporary literature, such as Heinz Benker's *Concertino* for piccolo and orchestra (1958), has been written with the specific tonal characteristics of the instrument in mind. Later works, such as Gordon Jacob's *The Pied Piper* (1959), take advantage of other programmatic associations. And modern composers, with their keen interest in timbre as a compositional element, are incorporating the piccolo into solo and chamber works. To cite only a few examples: Charles Koechlin's *Stèle funeraire* (1950) for flute, piccolo, and alto flute; Arthur Honegger's *Trois Contrepoints* (1930) for piccolo, oboe alternating with English horn, violin, and cello; and Bruno Bartolozzi's *Sinaulodia* (1973) for four flutes, in which three of the players double on piccolo.

The piccolo has strong devotees, chief among them Laurence Trott of Buffalo, New York. In 1977, he presented what was billed as the first piccolo recital in New York, sponsored by the New York Flute Club. Trott played similar recitals in other American cities, including Boston, Cleveland, and Buffalo. Critic Robert Finn of the *Cleveland Plain Dealer* condescended to write, "The piccolo can indeed function in respectable musical society."[5]

In 1978, following the example of the numerous flute clubs and societies around the country, Trott organized The Piccolo Society, with the aim of sponsoring concerts, recordings, and workshops and commissioning new pieces for piccolo. Its most important commission to date, of a total of about twenty, is Morton Subotnick's *Parallel Lines*. Another is *Sonata Piccola*, S. 8va, by P. D. Q. Bach, "history's most justifiably neglected composer."[6]

The piccolo began its orchestral life as an alternative instrument for the second flute player. As it gained prevalence in the orchestral repertory, it warranted its own specialist. Debussy's *La Mer* (1905) and Ravel's *Daphnis et Chloë* (1909–12) each require two flutists and a piccoloist. Arnold Schoenberg's *Gurrelieder* (1901–3) calls for four flutes and four piccolos. As a result, the flute complement of most contemporary orchestras includes two flutists and a piccoloist.

The implication is clear: the piccolo is not only a desirable but an essential part of the Compleat Flutist's musical equipment. And owning an orchestral-quality instrument is nearly as important as possessing the skills to play it.

Another implication is that the flutist who can handle the piccolo with skill has yet another opportunity for performance. Often, being able to play the piccolo becomes a superb entrée into an ensemble whose flute section is otherwise full. Eventually, you may be able to move "up" to one of the flute positions. Just because the piccolo player is traditionally seated at the "bottom" or "wrong end" of the flute section does not mean that you should consider playing the piccolo an insult. Piccolo playing is a specialty. It is not a lower rung on the flute ladder. There is no reason to treat the solo piccolo part in Brahms's *Variations on a Theme by Haydn* with any less respect than you do the solo flute part in Brahms's Fourth Symphony.

The Alto Flute

English: flute in G

French: *flûte alto, flûte en sol, flûte contralto en sol*

German: *Altflöte*

One must assume from this comment that Boehm was referring to the mellow sound of the French horn in a favorable light. Alto flute technique is just a little different from that of the C flute. There is a very slight increase in the finger spread, which is really noticeable only for c^1 and c^1♯, and greater distance between the hands, but both factors may be easily accommodated. However, the large size of the keys makes it relatively unsuited for very rapid, "technical" passages, a fact Boehm recognized when he lauded its *cantabile* virtues. And of course, the size and weight of the alto flute make it awkward or impossible for young or small flutists to play.

The alto flute requires a slightly more relaxed embouchure and gentler blowing than the C flute. In the first octave, especially, the alto flute requires a greater volume of air directed with less velocity; too great an airspeed will cause the tone to break or crack. Because of its larger dimensions, the speech or articulation tends to be somewhat slower than that of the C flute. On poorly made instruments, this reaches the point of heaviness and inflexibility.

There are a number of special fingerings that clear the speech of the alto flute, particularly in passages with octave skips. Many of these fingerings involve the use of the D♯ (lower) trill lever, which provides extra venting at the top of the air column. (Its use is comparable to raising the left index finger on the C flute for d^2 and d^2♯). Although use of this key may sharpen the pitch a bit, the effect is relatively insignificant, and the player can easily and automatically compensate by modifying the airstream direction and/or speed with the embouchure.

As Boehm suggested, the alto flute has enjoyed considerable popularity among recitalists. Its mysterious, picturesque effects have an attractive charm, and the lack of upper harmonics gives it a languid upper register. Boehm considered vocal accompaniment a major use for his alto flute:

> Because of the great facility for modulation of the full, sonorous tones of this flute, it is adapted to music in the song style, and for accompanying a solo voice. A player will, after a very little practice, be in a position to bring out *genre* effects which are impossible upon the C flute.[10]

The Australian flutist John Amadio, who for many years accompanied Nellie Melba on her concert tours, regularly used an alto flute in recital.

In the nineteenth century, most if not all of the alto flute's solo repertoire consisted of arrangements of vocal music or C flute music. Boehm himself contributed copiously to this literature, with a variety of arrangements for what was in fact his favorite instrument: Beethoven's Sonata for Horn and Piano, op. 17; Haydn's Variations on "God Preserve the Emperor" (from the String Quartet, op. 76, no. 3); the adagio from Mozart's Clarinet Quintet; and several Schubert songs. Though believed lost for many years, the manuscripts for many of these compositions have recently resurfaced in the Dayton C. Miller Collection at the Library of Congress.

Like the piccolo, the alto flute has benefited from twentieth century composers' interest in tone color, and its solo and chamber literature is growing.

Examples include Kazuo Fukushima's *Mei* (1966), an avant-garde work for unaccompanied alto flute; Vincent Persichetti's *Parable*, op. 100 (1966), also for solo alto flute; Pierre Boulez's *Le Marteau sans Maítre* (1952–54, revised 1957); and Donald Martino's *Notturno*, in which a single player performs on piccolo, C flute, and alto flute.

Equally significant is the alto flute's growing role in the symphony orchestra. Perhaps the first such use was in Rimsky-Korsakov's 1890 opera-ballet *Mlada*, though Richard Strauss incorrectly assigned pride of place to Felix Weingartner's *Gefilde der Seligen* of 1897. Better known examples from the standard repertoire, which have been influential in promoting the alto flute's potential, are Stravinsky's *Le Sacre du Printemps* (1911), Ravel's *Daphnis et Chloë* (1909–12), and Holst's *The Planets* (1916).

It is interesting that in the early part of this century, when this literature first began appearing on concert programs, even the leading orchestral flutists did not possess the necessary instruments. When the Boston Symphony programmed the second suite from *Daphnis* in the autumn of 1917, the orchestra had to borrow an instrument from Dayton Miller, who had bought one in London in 1900. But four years later, when the orchestra again asked Miller for a loan, he was out of town and could not send the flute, so the management was finally forced to buy its own G flute. And Boston was not alone; in 1922 Miller loaned his alto to the Minneapolis, Cincinnati, and Cleveland symphonies.

Today, with the increase in orchestral, chamber, and solo scoring for the alto flute, there are a number of manufacturers—W. T. Armstrong, Gemeinhardt, and Ostroff-Sagerman, among others—who make the instrument. The 1995 cost of these instruments ranges from about $1,800 for a silver-plated model to about $11,000 for a sterling silver instrument.

The Bass Flute

The bass flute is the poor relation of the flute family, little known, seldom made, and seldom played. Like its smaller cousins, it has a long and rather interesting history, although flutes of this size have always been novelties. Wrote Adam Carse, a distinguished collector and chronicler of musical instruments, "a real bass flute in D [that is, C], an octave below the ordinary flute, has turned up like a rare sea monster at intervals during the last two centuries."[11] The modern bass flute measures approximately 57⅝ inches (146.4 centimeters) in length.

Agricola (1528) and Mersenne (1637) both described true bass flutes, an octave below the regular C flute. There are extant early eighteenth century bass flutes with three keys (made by J. Beuker of Amsterdam) whose length was 48.2 inches (122.4 centimeters). This model was known in its time as "une flûte de 5 pieds" (five-foot flute), using an old definition of the foot, the Hesse Darmstadt foot, five of which equal 49.214 inches (125.0 centimeters).

There are several extant bass flutes dating from the mid-eighteenth century. Thomas Lot, a Paris instrument maker, equipped his bass flute, which measured 102.5 centimeters in length, with five keys. But unlike the more common four-keyed flutes of the period, on which the keys cover finger holes one, three, four, and six, four of Lot's keys were hinged levers that merely extended the reach of the fingers so that they could control the respective holes comfortably. The fifth key was the conventional E♭ key. The head was recurved to make the instrument more manageable.

Around 1760, the French flutist, flute maker, and treatise writer Charles Delusse made an instrument somewhat longer than the Beuker flute. Its bore measured 50 inches (127.0 centimeters) in length, with a smaller diameter than Beuker's; however, the bore flares slightly at the open end.

In 1810, an English instrument maker named Malcolm MacGregor patented a bass flute in C that was similar to the one made by Delusse about a half century earlier. It had eight keys, five open (à la Delusse) and three closed. Its full interior length was 43.52 inches (110.5 centimeters); the distances between the finger holes were approximately twice those on a normal flute. The main tube of the flute was constructed of boxwood, but the curved headjoint tube was made of brass. The patent specification offered an alternative: the double tube of the curved head could be cut from a solid block of wood.

Four bass flutes to low C were displayed at the Paris Exhibition of 1900. One of these was supported at the lower end by a metal tripod; all used long extension rods to make the tone holes accessible to the fingers, but the control was not too effective. Dayton Miller tried these instruments and concluded that "none of these flutes was practicable for musical performance."[12]

Ten years later, Professor Abelardo Albisi of Milan, first flutist at La Scala, invented an instrument he dubbed the Albisiphone. With a compass of two and a half octaves, its lowest note was B (an octave and a note below middle C). In order to put the Boehm system mechanism within practical reach, the instrument was designed to be held vertically, and the metal tube was bent twice near the embouchure. The embouchure itself was a short horizontal tube, blown transversely as on a regular flute, and connected to the body by a double U-tube. The total length of the air column was about 50 inches (127.0 centimeters), with an internal bore diameter of about one and a half inches.

Evidently the Albisiphone was relatively successful, sufficiently so for several composers to include it in their scores: the operas *Melenis* (1912) and *Francesca da Rimini* (1914) by Zandonai and *Parisina* (1913) by Mascagni; a symphonic piece, *Der Sonne-Geist* (1919) by Friedrich Klosé, and even an Adagio for Albisiphone and string quartet by Giannetti. In the Klosé work, one incredulous curator of musical instruments remarked, "the effect was astonishing. The tone is particularly round and full, almost horn-like, yet possessing its own distinct character."[13] Dutch virtuoso Ary van Leeuwen was one of the flutists who played the Albisiphone.

Further work on the bass flute continued in England. In 1922, Rudall, Carte built a B♭ bass flute on special request. Known as the Contra Bass FF Flute, built on the Guards' Model, it was used in flute bands. It was an allmetal instrument, with two continuous semicircular crooks between the headjoint and body to absorb some of the length. In the playing position, the body joint was slightly forward and below, though parallel to, the headjoint. It did not double back.

In 1925, the *Irish Flute News* announced a "Profundo" Bass Flute in F. Also intended for use in flute bands, it was available with either Boehm or Guards' Model fingering system. The same year, Gino Bartoli of Milan produced a "contrabass" Boehm flute, merely an overgrown concert flute.

In 1932, Rudall, Carte introduced a bass C flute. Like the earlier Rudall, Carte model, it had a transverse head, but the tube bent so that the straight body of the instrument was held diagonally downward. A projecting crutch, fitted over the player's thigh, took the weight off the player's arms.

The modern bass flute has not become any lighter or easier to play, and as a result it is still a rarity. It is scored primarily in flute ensembles or special commercial orchestrations. Its usefulness is enhanced in situations where it can be electronically amplified to increase its projection. Bass flutes are currently made by Altus, Artley, Emerson, Yamaha, and others; 1995 prices range from $3,900 to $6,300.

The Flute Choir

The flute choir is an ensemble with a problematic reputation. Perhaps it is an overstatement to say that the flute choir has a sound that only a flutist could love, but there is some truth to it nevertheless.

Historically, the flute choir may be traced to the recorder consort of the sixteenth and seventeenth centuries. In the eighteenth century, Joseph Bodin de Boismortier adapted this type of grouping to the transverse flute, writing six concertos for five flutes (all the same size). What is even more astonishing is that he evidently intended to have them performed by a flute ensemble of more than five members, because the parts are marked solo and tutti.

In Britain, flute bands have a long and rich tradition. Descended from the fife and drum corps that have existed since the Middle Ages, they received more recent impetus from the civilian band movement of the nineteenth century and from such organizations as the Scouts. The flute bands consist of a full range of flutes from piccolos to bass flutes, in a whole assortment of different keys. Even today, most of these bands use five- or six-keyed old-system instruments rather than the Boehm system. Some use intermediate models such as the Pratten, Radcliff, or Carte Guards' Model.

A fully instrumented flute band consists of the following: one E♭ piccolo, one solo B♭ flute, two first B♭ flutes, three second B♭ flutes, three third B♭ flutes, three F flutes (scored first, second, and third), three E♭ flutes, three B♭

bass flutes, two F bass flutes, one E♭ bass flute, and four percussionists. Boismortier seems mild by comparison! Today much of the flute band repertoire consists of arrangements of the orchestral literature.

In the United States, the flute ensemble is rapidly becoming a fixture in music education, simply to give the many, many flutists chamber music experience. The concept first took hold in the 1930s, when Leonardo De Lorenzo introduced the flute ensemble to the curriculum at the Eastman School of Music. Since that time, flute teachers have used the flute ensemble to help their students improve their intonation (particularly at intervals of fourths and fifths and in unison passages) and tone quality (by matching each flutist's tone to that of the other players). Moreover, playing alto or bass flute may help a student with a tense embouchure to relax the facial muscles.

The flute choir literature, like that of the flute band, started out with arrangements. In recent years, however, a good deal of original music has been written for flute choir. The most famous example is Henry Brant's *Angels and Devils, Concerto for Eleven Flutes* (1931, revised 1956), whose latest version is scored for solo flute, three piccolos, five C flutes, and two alto flutes.

The flute club of James Madison University, in Harrisonburg, Virginia, directed by Professor Carol Kniebusch, has since 1979 sponsored an annual competition for a new work for flute choir. The British Flute Society sponsors a similar competition.

Flute choirs have been staple features of flute clubs for many years, both for sight-reading programs and for actual performance. A frequent stunt—one that surely only a flutist could love—is the performance of the Kuhlau *Grand Quartet*, op. 103, with five flutists to a part. The National Flute Association traditionally closes its annual convention with a group reading of the Bach *Air on the G String*, played by as many flutists as wish to participate.

As the number of flutists increases, it is likely that flute choir literature will continue to grow.

Notes

1. Lawrence Trott, "Why Not the Piccolo?" *Woodwind World—Brass and Percussion* 19, no. 3 (1980): 17.
2. George Frederick McKay, *Creative Orchestration* (Boston: Allyn and Bacon, 1963), p. 14.
3. F. Corder, *The Orchestra and How to Write for It* (London: Robert Cocks, 1896), p. 38.
4. Jeremy Montagu, *The World of Baroque & Classical Musical Instruments* (Woodstock, N.Y.: Overlook Press, 1979), p. 41.
5. Piccolo Society Inc. membership invitation, 27 April 1979.
6. P. D. Q. Bach (1807–1742?) is the fictional youngest son of Johann Sebastian Bach. He is the creation of Professor Peter Schickele. See Peter Schickele, *The Definitive Biography of P. D. Q. Bach* (New York: Random House, 1976).

7. Dayton C. Miller, "Modern Alto, Tenor, and Bass Flutes," *American Musicological Society Papers*, 1938, p. 9.
8. Theobald Boehm, *The Flute and Flute-Playing*, trans. and rev. Dayton C. Miller, 2nd ed., rev. (1922; reprint, New York: Dover Publications, 1964), p. 120.
9. Ibid., pp. 122–23.
10. Ibid., p. 120.
11. Adam Carse, *Musical Wind Instruments* (1939; reprint, New York: Da Capo Press, 1965), p. 105.
12. Miller, p. 12.
13. Julius Schlosser of Kunsthistorisches Museum, Vienna; quoted in Miller, p. 13.

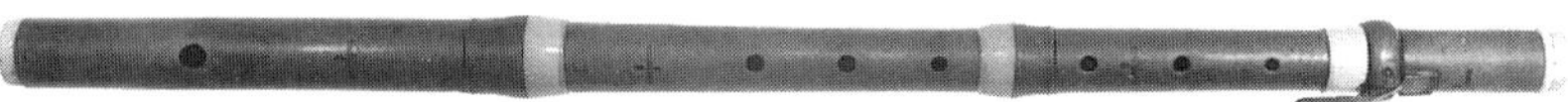

1. One-key flute. August Grenser, Dresden, mid-eighteenth century. Boxwood with ivory fittings, brass key (DCM 140)

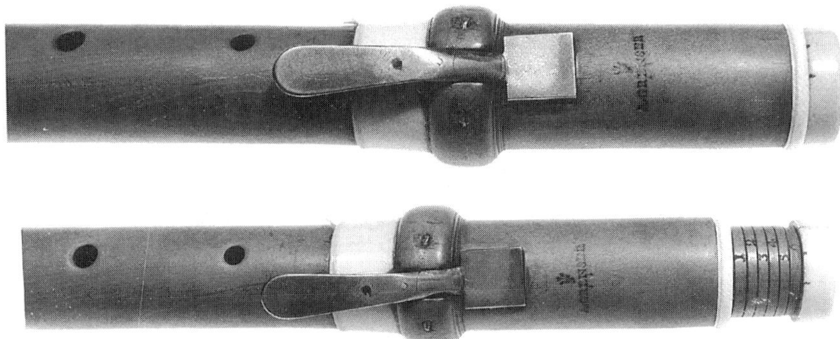

2. Tuning register from one-key flute (detail of Plate 1)

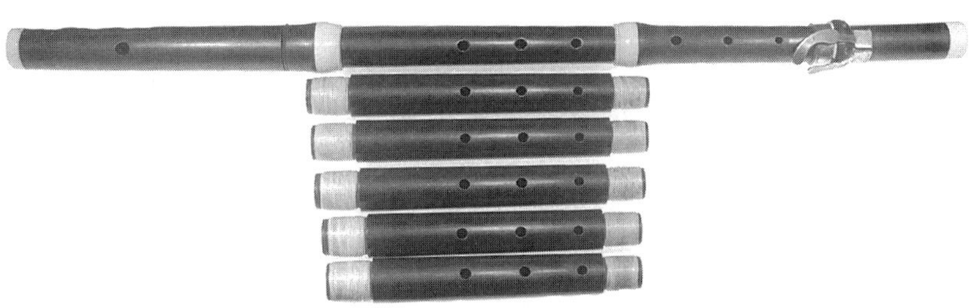

3. Two-key flute with six corps de réchange. Johann Joachim Quantz, Potsdam, about 1750. Ebony with silver keys, ivory rings (DCM 916)

4. Four-key flute. Claude Laurent, Paris, 1818. Crystal glass; interior surface cut in concave, diamond-shaped facets. Silver tenons, sockets, and keys (DCM 611)

5. Six-key flute. Clementi & Co., London, about 1802–21. Ivory with silver ferrules (DCM 1406)

6. *Eight-key flute. Rudall & Rose, London, about 1827–37. Boxwood with silver rings and keys, inlaid ivory embouchure ring (DCM 26)*

7. *Boehm 1831 model flute. Gerock & Wolf, London*

8. *Boehm 1832 model flute. Th. Boehm, Munich. Cocus with silver rings and keys (DCM 974)*

9. *Boehm 1847 model flute. Th. Boehm, Munich, 1849. Silver with gold lip plate (DCM 1398)*

10. *Ward flute. Cornelius Ward, London, about 1842–60. Cocus with silver rings, cap, and keys. "Terminator and indicator" at top; "bell-crank" action (DCM 44)*

11. *Carte 1851 system flute. Rudall, Rose, Carte & Co., London, about 1857–71. Silver. Barrel mouthpiece (DCM 43)*

12. *Clinton 1863 patent flute. Clinton & Co., London, about 1863. Silver. "Equisonant" system (DCM 109)*

13. Carte 1867 system flute. Rudall, Rose, Carte & Co., London, about 1867. Silver (DCM 14)

14. Siccama diatonic flute. Abel Siccama, London, about 1845–62. Cocus with silver keys (DCM 1136)

15. Schwedler Reform flute. Moritz Max Mönnig, Leipzig, ca. 1930. Ebony with silver head and fittings (DCM 1584)

16. Borne-Julliot system flute. Djalma Julliot, La Couture Boussey, 1900. Silver with gold springs. Split E, left-hand F# key, C# trill key. Side keys for duplicate G# hole and C hole; extra right-hand levers for left-hand keys (DCM 193)

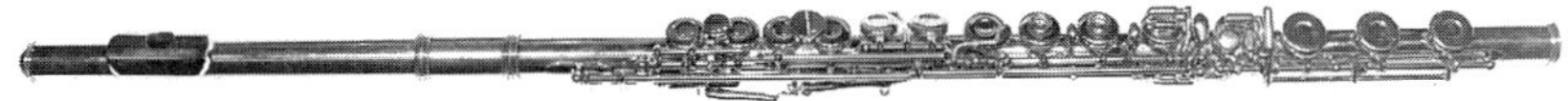

17. Murray flute—Armstrong Prototype I. W. T. Armstrong Co., Elkhart, Ind. (built by Jack Moore), 1971. Silver-plated metal (DCM Collection, unnumbered)

18. French model Boehm flute. Verne Q. Powell Flutes, Arlington Heights, Mass., 1971. Sterling silver

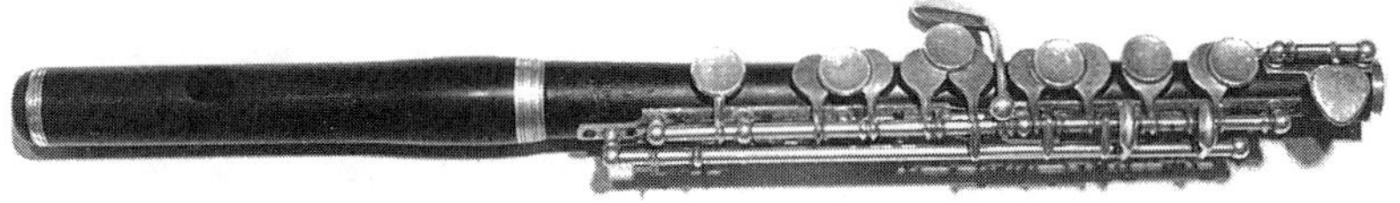

19. Boehm piccolo. Philipp Hämmig, Markneukirchen, about 1971. Grenadilla with silver keys

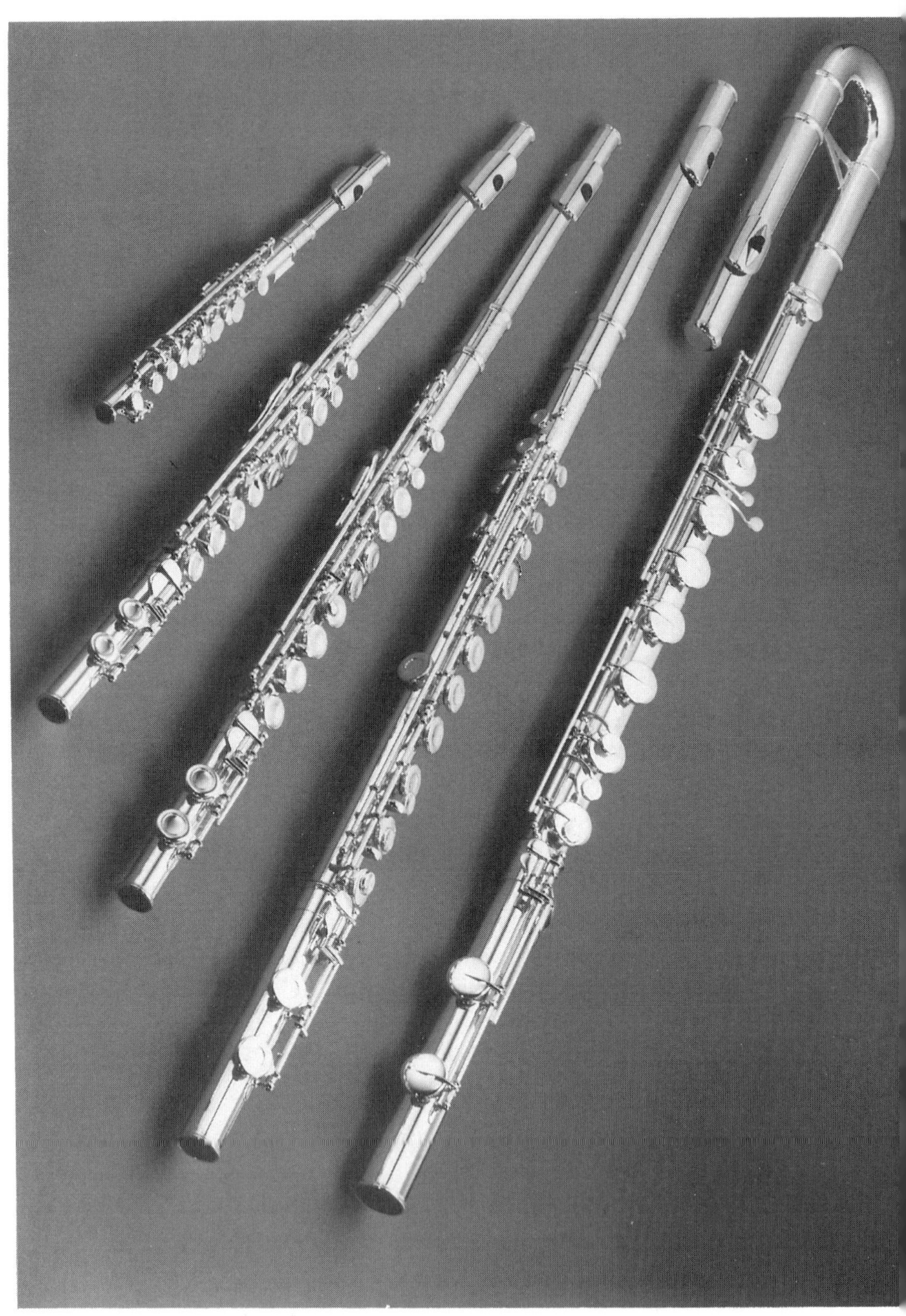

20. *The flute family.* From left: *C piccolo, E♭ soprano flute, C flute, alto flute, bass flute. W. T.* Armstrong *Co., Elkhart, Ind.*

PERFORMANCE

6

BREATHING

Breathing is the foundation of good flute playing, because it is the first step in the generation of tone. When most people think of breathing, they think only of drawing in air; they take the expulsion of breath for granted. That's probably because respiratory congestion usually is noticeable when one tries to inhale; exhalation is generally not a problem. For wind instrument players, in contrast, breathing is a three-step process: inhalation (inspiration), suspension, and exhalation (expiration), of which the third stage is by far the most important. For it is exhalation that activates the air column in the flute and thereby generates the tone. The ability to control that exhalation with the lungs and abdominal muscles before the airstream ever reaches the embouchure, much less the inside of the flute, is essential. Moreover, breathing is a musical tool, because breath functions as the line of demarcation between phrases.

Posture

Good posture assures that the body is in the position most conducive to breathing and thus to the production of the best possible tone. It allows the air to proceed unimpeded. When standing, you should be erect, relaxed but without letting your shoulders droop. Your upper body may be tilted just slightly forward. Your chin should be parallel to the ground to keep the top of the air passage fully open. You should adjust your music stand according to your posture, not the other way around. One foot should be a bit in front of the other to ensure balance. When sitting, the procedure is similar. Your hips should lean slightly forward, and one foot should be placed slightly in front of the other, soles flat on the floor. Under no circumstances should you cross your legs; constriction of the abdominal muscles would result.

The next step in good posture is to maintain this efficient starting position while actually playing. Standing or sitting still helps conserve the air supply; don't squander your breath on unnecessary motion. For the same reason, when Houdini was bound in ropes while in an underwater box, he moved as little as possible while making his escape. Discipline and breath control are essential.

Inhalation

Relax your abdomen, open your mouth and throat, and inhale through your mouth. Open your mouth as if saying "ah" in order to allow the air to pass through it quickly. Allow the air to fill your abdominal cavity so that the middle torso expands at both front and back. All other parts of your body—particularly the shoulders and the chest—should remain stationary. Do not pull in your "stomach." In effect, you are making an exaggerated, extended yawn. Try to take in as much air as you can, as quickly and with as little extraneous noise as possible.

What happens when you inhale is that the diaphragm—the dome-shaped muscle just below the rib cage, which separates the chest and abdominal cavity—moves downward, causing the lower ribs to move upward and outward. This reduces the air pressure in the lungs, so that the pressure outside them exceeds that inside and air rushes in. In effect, the lungs vacuum air in.

Practice breathing in front of a mirror; this will help you avoid several common errors: opening the mouth too wide and gasping for air, and an even more common mistake, lifting the shoulders.

Suspension

The second and shortest step in breathing is suspension. Though brief, it is all-important, because it is the preparation for exhalation. When you have filled your lungs to capacity, hold the "full" position momentarily; the torso should remain expanded and the throat open while you set the diaphragm and abdominal-wall muscles for exhalation. Failure to wait this requisite microsecond may result not only in hyperventilation and dizziness but also a breathy tone, sharp in pitch, which quickly loses resonance and becomes softer and flatter. The brief suspension provides the muscular support that must last for the full duration of the tone.

Exhalation

Exhalation is generally the passive phase of breathing, not only involuntary but also unimportant. For wind instrument players, however, it is the active phase, the phase that requires the most control and finesse. This control is provided by tension between the diaphragm and the muscles of the abdominal wall and chest cavity. Try to keep your rib cage wall expanded while simultaneously allowing the abdominal wall to contract toward its rest position. As the abdominal muscles press against the base of the lungs, the air is forced out. Only when the air in the abdominal cavity is totally expended should you contract the rib cage muscles. Think of the chest as a reserve tank, to be used only for emergencies. Remember that muscular control is the key to breath support and that it takes more abdominal tension to play softly than it does to play loudly.

Do not tighten the throat, even if you're running low on air and feel that throat pressure will expel the last remaining vestiges of air. Actually, constricting the throat muscles will do just the opposite, restricting the airstream rather than propelling it out.

The Diaphragm

There is probably not a flute student alive who has not been instructed to "breathe with your diaphragm." It's not bad advice; in fact it's good advice, but you should know what it does and does not mean. When teachers speak of your diaphragm they are generally referring to the abdominal muscles. The diaphragm cannot actually push air out of the lungs. Its role in inhalation, as explained above, is to contract downward to create a partial vacuum in the lungs. In exhalation, it does the opposite: it relaxes upward, toward its starting position. Thus the diaphragm does not push the air out of the lungs; the abdominal muscles do.

Nor can the diaphragm "support the air column"—that being the job of the abdominal-wall and rib cage (intercostal) muscles. Support is the isometric action of tension between the diaphragm and abdominal muscles, which controls the rate and pressure of air release. The faster the airspeed, the higher the pitch and the more edge or pointedness to the tone quality. By contrast, the slower the airspeed, the lower the pitch and the more diffuse the quality of tone. Thus, for advanced players, a technique known as diaphragm flexing (but actually a diaphragm-abdominal isometric exercise) is an auxiliary method of varying tone color and dynamics. It is, however, as advocate Roger Mather points out, no substitute for a flexible embouchure in creating nuances of register change and color.

Exercises

There are many useful exercises to help you develop the requisite physical skills for effective breathing. As a precursor to good breath control, aerobic exercise of any sort—jogging, swimming, calisthenics, basketball, and so on—will put you several steps ahead. Swimming is perhaps best because, like flute playing, it is a rhythmic exercise in which breathing must be carefully synchronized with several other physical activities. Indeed, the great flutist William Kincaid, who grew up in Hawaii, was a swimming protégé of Olympic swimming champion Duke Kahamamoku. You can also do isometric exercises, flexing the abdominal muscles even while doing something else, such as riding a bus or doing paperwork at your desk.

The simplest exercise is straight breathing, with no complications, not even a flute. Stand erect, with your feet apart, and take a slow, deep draft of air through your mouth, expanding your waist as you do so. Then slowly exhale, also through your mouth. Gradually increase the frequency of the breaths and decrease their duration until you are, essentially, panting. Place your hands on your hips, with your fingers spread so they can feel both front and back abdominal expansion, as a check on your abdominal technique. You should feel the expansion and contraction with each breath.

A particularly good exercise for flutists who play seated is called The Thinker by noted teacher Sarah Baird Fouse. While sitting in an armless chair, place your elbows on your knees and support your jaw with your upwardly cupped hands. This position causes precisely the kind of abdominal constriction you normally try to avoid. But it forces you to breathe deeply because abdominal expansion can occur only at waist level. As you breathe in, your waistline should expand palpably and visibly.

Another exercise is variously known as The Balloon or The Accordion. It is done in a standing position. Hold the palm of one hand about an inch in front of your lower abdomen. Breathe in slowly—take about five seconds—until your abdomen expands to reach your outstretched hand. Then relax and exhale slowly—again, in about five seconds—so that the abdomen falls away from your hand.

Kincaid prescribed two variations on traditional calisthenics, which he labeled push-ups and pull-backs. Kincaid push-ups are just like the ones your gym teacher taught you, except that you inhale deeply before pushing up and arching the back; then you exhale and return to the starting position on the floor. In the second cycle, inhale, do two push-ups, and then exhale; increase the number of push-ups per breath until you can do six.

Pull-backs are actually vertical push-ups. Stand with your legs apart and lift your arms straight up over your head. Inhale, hold your breath, and then lower your arms rapidly to your sides, bending your elbows as you do so. Arch your back and try to touch your elbows to your waist behind your back. Exhale and relax; repeat several times.

The next two exercises simulate flute playing more nearly than what you've done so far, but still do not involve the instrument. For the first, which I'll call The Hiss, place your thumbs and fingers around your waist as you did before. Form your lips into a flute embouchure, inhale, and make a snakelike hiss as you exhale. The hiss, in combination with the abdominal muscles, restrains the airflow and helps you develop the supporting muscles.

Kincaid's candle exercise is similar to one advocated by Taffanel for controlling embouchure shape. Hold a lighted candle about a foot in front of you, at shoulder level, using both hands to keep it steady. Inhale through your mouth, form your lips into a flute embouchure, and slowly exhale. Try to make the flame flicker; it should neither remain still nor go out. This exercise will build breath support for sustained phrases.

Finally, for the last exercise you will need to play your flute. You will find this same exercise useful for developing tone quality, but here the concentration will be on duration (always with a good tone, of course). Take any middle register note between c^2 and a^2. Play it as long as possible and time yourself. (The easiest way is to set the metronome at sixty beats per second and count the clicks.) Do this each day, on a variety of notes, and keep a written record of your progress.

Breathing and Phrasing

The flutist, unlike the violinist or cellist, cannot sustain a melody line indefinitely, because he or she must breathe. Finding a good place to breathe in a piece of music is often difficult, but more often than not, the flutist can make a virtue out of physiological necessity. He can make breathing a function of the music, and conversely, make the musical expression a function of well-placed breathing.

Breath type and placement are functions of their musical context. By breath type, I mean depth and duration of inhalation. Breaths come in three basic lengths. Long breaths, used for sustained and/or highly intense phrases, require the greatest time of the three in order to achieve full expansion of the lungs. Medium breaths are the normal type. Both long and medium breaths separate phrases at the same time as they replenish the air in the lungs.

Short or reinforcement breaths are quick openings of the lungs in midphrase. They are clavicular—that is, they involve only the upper torso, not the abdomen—and are very, very rapid. Save them for emergencies, with one exception: if you are approaching a phrase that calls for a long breath that you know you will not have time to take, take several medium breaths as you approach it from the preceding phrases. Leave enough air in the lungs so that when you reach the long phrase a quick reinforcement breath will be sufficient to top off the air supply. Thus several normal breaths plus one quick one can equal one long breath in total usefulness.

Just as important as knowing how to breathe is deciding where to breathe. Sometimes it's obvious: it's notated in the music by an apostrophe (’), a check (✓), a downbow (V), or simply by a rest. Most of the time, however, breath is at the sole discretion of the performer. Always try to breathe between whole phrases; overly frequent breaths interrupt the melodic line and are distracting to the listener. If you must breathe in midphrase, steal time from the note preceding the breath, rather than the one following it. For this reason, in passages with mixed rhythmic values, it is generally preferable to breathe after the longest note values. In a rapid, "black" passage (one with lots of notes), try to find a set of repeated notes; breathe between them or, if necessary, omit the second one so you have time to breathe. For example, in the Mozart G Major Concerto:

In a running passage with no breaks, breathe after a change of direction.

In duple rhythms, you will generally want to avoid breathing on the bar line except at the ends of sections; instead, breathe after the point of arrival, which is often the downbeat of the bar. In triple rhythm, however, you may breathe between bars.

Keep in mind, also, that even when you have the opportunity to breathe at a rest, you may not want to exercise that option. Particularly if the rests are closely spaced, it is often preferable to make a slight break without a breath in the interest of variety and articulation. On the other hand, there will be times when it is not physically necessary to take a breath, but the musical articulation requires just such a firm, strong demarcation between phrases. By all means breathe!

When beginning a piece (or even a phrase, if there's time), take the initial breath in tempo so that the breath forms the upbeat to the first note. Don't squander the breath on the first few notes of the phrase, because if you start to run out of breath the natural tendency is to rush to the end of the phrase and possibly even to cut off the last note in the rush to breathe again. Breathe as quickly, quietly, and inconspicuously as possible. (Listening to recordings of your performances will quickly tell you if you breathe noisily.)

On the other hand, you may (and usually should) have some left-over breath as you approach the end of a phrase. Don't feel that you have to expel it; if you do, the phrase won't taper properly and the sound will be disproportionately strong. Instead, use the remaining air in the lungs as the base on which to build the next breath.

Circular Breathing

Circular breathing is a rather magical technique designed to help wind instrument players perform long passages without taking a noticeable breath.

The technique is actually several thousand years old, having been used by aulos players in ancient Greece and by performers on the Chinese oboe and the Malaysian seru-nai (a shawm, ancestor of the oboe).

But only recently has circular breathing been adopted by flutists. Czech flutist Antonin Mach was reportedly the first, playing the Allemande from Bach's unaccompanied partita with no audible breaths at the 1959 International Competition of Wind Instruments at Prague. Zdenek Bruderhans used circular breathing in a 1977 recording of *The Flight of the Bumble-Bee* and Paganini's *Moto Perpetuo*. Today, it is becoming indispensable for some of the avant-garde literature.

Simply defined, circular breathing is the seemingly impossible simultaneous combination of inhalation and exhalation. It is accomplished by inhaling through the nose while expelling air from the mouth into the instrument, thereby producing a continuous, uninterrupted sound.

On all woodwind instruments except for the flute, the air to be exhaled during the cycle is stored in the cheeks, which may be puffed for the purpose. For the flute, however, this is impractical because of the role of the lips and the facial muscles in controlling the airstream. The alternative is for the flutist to expand the throat to store the reserve air. The air is then released by the back of the tongue, with the aid of the contracting muscles in the larynx and pharynx. Needless to say, this requirement makes the flutist's challenge greater than the reed or brass player's. Not only is the throat smaller than the cheeks, which means that it can store less air, but the flute requires more air than any other instrument because only a part of the airstream actually enters the instrument. Moreover, the flutist must have an especially well-developed embouchure and focused tone in order to compensate for the requisite tightening of the throat muscles.

Several preliminary exercises, suggested by Bruderhans and by Swiss flutist Aurèle Nicolet (in his book of avant-garde etudes, *Pro Musica Nova*), may be helpful:

- To practice not using the cheeks, expand the back of your throat and blow out using only the back of your tongue to propel the air. Be sure to fix your lips firmly in one position.
- Place a soda straw in a glass of water. Take a deep breath and begin to exhale through the straw, blowing bubbles in the water. Then begin inhaling through your nose while using air stored in the throat to continue blowing bubbles.
- Do the same with an oboe or bassoon reed.
- Transfer the same procedure to the flute, keeping your embouchure firmly fixed. Start with the headjoint alone, which takes relatively little air.
- Attach the body and footjoint to the head and repeat the exercise. The easiest notes to begin with are a^1, $b^1\flat$, and b^1 because they require the

> least air and embouchure movement. When you have mastered a continuous tone on a single note, expand to neighboring tones in groups of two, three, or four notes. Gradually expand the melodic and dynamic range. Ultimately the changing of notes (involving both fingers and embouchure) should operate completely independently of the circular breathing process.[1]

It should be obvious that tonguing and circular breathing are mutually exclusive, since the tongue is otherwise engaged in directing the airstream. The procedure can be used only in sustained, slurred passages. However, Bruderhans does not recommend it for particularly lyrical passages—those with a high emotional content—because circular breathing, while a useful physical tool, obscures the articulative function of breathing in defining phrases. He also cautions that it is difficult to do circular breathing if you blow out too much air before the nasal inhalation. Therefore, he suggests, do not wait until you are down to your last gasp; in circular breathing, inhale *more* often than you would normally.

Two useful etudes for circular breathing are included in Nicolet's *Pro Musica Nova:* No. 4, Konrad Lechner's *Drei Stücke* (III: "Continuum") and No. 11, oboist Heinz Holliger's *Lied.*

Notes

1. Aurèle Nicolet, ed., *Pro Musica Nova: Studien zum Spielen Neuer Musik* (Köln: Musikverlag Hans Gerig; New York: MCA Music, 1974), p. 45.

7

TONE

"The tone is the voice without which one cannot even begin to sing," wrote Theobald Boehm in *The Flute and Flute-Playing.*[1] One needs no higher authority to assert the status of flute tone as the most important element of flute playing. It is the flute's tone that gives the instrument its distinctive quality. Historically, tone has been the reason for the flute's popularity among players and listeners alike. Tone, wrote the great English flutist Charles Nicholson, is "the proudest boast of the instrument."[2]

The production of flute tone is part science and part art. There is no one formula of physical actions that will create a good tone—because there is no consensus on exactly what constitutes the ideal tone. Nevertheless, there are a few general goals, shared by all flute players, for what I'll call a basic sound.

The sound should be full and round, not thin and wispy. It should be clear, focused, and centered, not fuzzy or breathy. It must have resonance and projection. There should be continuity of sound between the registers. Yet the tone should be flexible, capable of a variety of color shadings and dynamic changes so that the tone becomes a vehicle of expression as well as of technique.

Put in the simplest possible terms, the tone is the result of the action of a human-generated airstream in relation to the flute, or in acoustical terms, a duct and an airflow control system. Player and instrument work in tandem to determine the character or quality of the tone.

The flute community is divided on what constitutes the ideal flute—thick or thin wall; silver plate, sterling silver, gold, or wood; open or closed holes; size and shape of bore and embouchure; placement and dimensions of the tone holes, and so on. These choices (see chapter 2, "How to Choose an Instrument") are highly personal, individual, and idiosyncratic; their effect on flute tone, singly or in combination, cannot be condensed into a scientific formula.

Certain playing techniques, however, are applicable no matter what the instrument. Said Verne Q. Powell, one of this century's finest flute makers—and a man with a vested interest in saying otherwise: "As far as tone is concerned, I contend that 90 percent of it is in the man behind the flute."[3] In other words, given a decent-quality flute, the instrument is no excuse for a poor tone.

The Acoustical Basis

The flute tone is governed by an air reed. The airstream is emitted from the player's lips and propelled across the embouchure hole of the flute. It sets up an oscillation in the air column defined by the internal bore of the flute. Modifications in the size, pressure, and direction of the air column produce changes in the sound. Opening and closing the tone holes shortens or lengthens the airstream—on the Boehm flute, by manipulation of the mechanism—thus determining the pitch of the tone.

A given vibration is composed of several frequencies. The lowest is called the fundamental; the higher ones are called partials, overtones, or harmonics.

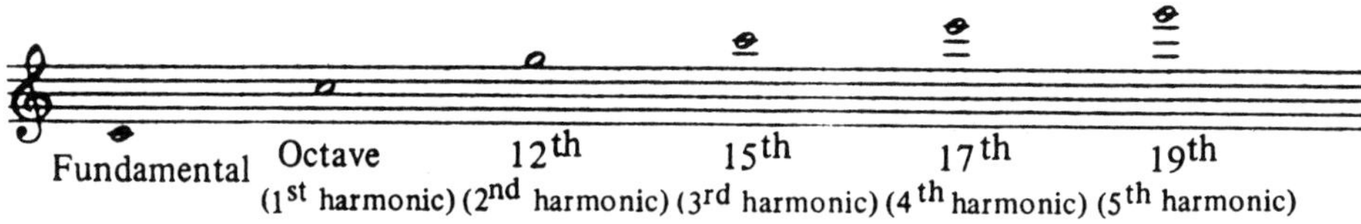

The quality of the sound is determined by the presence and relative strength of those partials. In general, the greater the harmonic content, the richer the sound and the greater its projection.

Many flutists have heard of something called an "edge-tone behavior system" (detailed in Philip Bate's book *The Flute*, for example) as another contributor to flute tone. Edge tone is an acoustical phenomenon in which an air jet that is projected across a slit (as the airstream is projected across the flute's embouchure) breaks up the airstream into eddies or curls. These eddies, along with the air jet itself, form part of the tone generator. The frequency of the air jet is determined by its velocity and by the distance from the edge to the slit. However, recent research suggests that the edge tone effect is not applicable to the flute in any measurable degree. Acoustician Arthur Benade explains the reason: although the flute configuration meets all the acoustical definitions of an edge-tone system, the edge-tone frequencies generated at ordinary musical blowing pressure are so high as to make them inaudible.

Tone Production

Control of the air column may be divided into three elements: speed, size (both width and length), and direction. The physical determinants of these elements are the breathing mechanism; the head-body relationship, which affects the position of the embouchure in relation to the flute; the formation of the embouchure itself (lip position); the position of the jaw and tongue; and the shape of the oral cavity.

The body must be relaxed, with the arms held sufficiently away from the body so that the air can travel from lungs to flute without obstruction. The head should be held up, with the bottom of the chin more or less parallel to the floor. Lowering the head too much will crimp the neck muscles and constrict the throat, and raising it is impractical. Whether the flute should be parallel to the floor or tilted slightly downward is a matter of personal preference and comfort.

In either case, however, the flute should rest lightly against the chin in order to leave the lips free and flexible. And the flute tube should be parallel to the lips; in other words, it should not be pushed forward or back. The head-to-foot line of the flute should be parallel to the line between the player's shoulders. Like every rule, this one has some exceptions. There are a number of prominent players who use a so-called offset embouchure, in which the flute is pushed slightly forward, but for most flutists this is not usually successful.

Tone quality is affected by the position of the tongue within the mouth, not only on attacking a note but also while sustaining it; the relative inflation of the cheeks; and other variations in the size of the oral cavity. The flutist cannot do anything about the maximum size of his or her mouth, but he should take full advantage of that capacity. And the flutist should also be able to make the mouth selectively smaller. Holding the tongue in mid-mouth blocks the air flow; lowering it to the base of the mouth allows freer intraoral air vibration. Similarly, a slight inflation of the cheeks has been shown to enhance tonal resonance. In this regard, action of the jaw, which affects both mouth shape and lip position, is also a factor in tone production.

Unlike stringed or keyboard instruments, wind instruments are shrouded in mystery when it comes to analyzing tone production because it is difficult, if not impossible, to document most of the techniques visually. (University experiments with fluorographs of vibrato production are the exception, but these are neither safe nor practicable for normal use.) You can observe external embouchure shape, but you can't see the airstream either in the mouth or as it crosses the embouchure hole of the flute. For this reason, flute tone pedagogy is inconsistent. This situation by no means implies a lack of analysis—indeed, tone production has been analyzed frequently by dissertation writers. Simply, lacking quantitative tools, flutists must rely on qualitative preference and the imprecision of verbal description.

There is a variety of techniques from which the flutist can choose. The Taffanel-Gaubert method, for instance, states firmly that the airstream should be controlled only by the lips, while Marcel Moyse's book on tone, *De la Sonorité*, advocates the combined use of jaws and lips. Judging from the magnificent playing of the authors, who can say that either Taffanel and Gaubert or Moyse was wrong? The solution is to try all the techniques and then choose those that work for you.

It is fairly safe to say, however, that the most important determinant of flute tone is the embouchure, or lip formation, because the embouchure influences all four factors of tone production: air jet speed or pressure, airstream size, distance from lip opening to flute edge, and air jet angle.

When the flute is placed on the lips, how much of the embouchure hole should the lips cover? The Taffanel-Gaubert method suggests, and I agree, that as a general rule the lips should cover about a quarter of the hole. The amount of coverage will vary in the course of actual performance according to register, tone quality desired, intonational correction, and the thickness of the individual player's lips. If the lips cover too much of the hole, the tone may become thin, weak, muffled, dull, or undesirably metallic, and the pitch tends to go flat. On the other hand, if the lips do not cover enough of the hole, the tone may sound heavy, hollow, shrill, or breathy, and the pitch will tend to be sharp.

It is much harder to define the proper shape of the lip aperture than it is to measure embouchure coverage. Traditionally, teachers have started beginning students with a soda or other narrow-necked bottle; the student blows across the neck until he can produce whistle tones and finally a true tone. Only then does the student move to the flute headjoint and finally to the fully assembled flute.

To form the lip aperture, the Taffanel-Gaubert method instructs, open the mouth halfway, to separate the teeth about a quarter to a half inch. Bring the lips together so that they meet without pressing (they should remain perfectly relaxed). Then stretch them so that they rest lightly against the teeth, with a small space between the lips. Frederick Wilkins, who advocated a particularly firm embouchure, described the position as a "sardonic smile or grimace." William Kincaid called it "simultaneous stretch and pucker." The interior of the mouth should be as large as possible, to allow maximum resonance. The Stokes and Condon method recommends imagining the beginning of a yawn (which, after reading enough flute methods, you will probably not find difficult). The upper lip should remain firm; when the lips are drawn back, they should not turn the corners down in a pout or up into a true smile, nor should they be pursed. The slit between the lips that results will be roughly elliptical in shape; Stokes and Condon liken the shape to saying the word "pure."[4]

It may seem contradictory, but the corners of the mouth, like the rest of the face and breathing apparatus, must remain as relaxed as possible. If the corners are too tight, the upper lip will also be too tight, which usually results in a hard, tight, even coarse sound.

Having established the basic embouchure, you must learn how to use it to affect tone production. The first use of the embouchure is to control the pressure of the airstream; the size of the embouchure is in inverse proportion to the pressure of the air jet. Assuming constant breath pressure, the smaller the opening between the lips, then the greater the speed or force of the airstream. The greater the airspeed, in turn, the higher the pitch, because higher air pressure increases the ease of emitting the harmonics of a fundamental note. Thus the lip aperture is smaller to play c^3 than it is to play c^2, which uses the same fingering. A larger aperture, in contrast, makes the pitch lower and the dynamics louder and is necessary for lower notes.

The second use of the embouchure is to control the angle of the airstream. Again, as with lip position, take a norm: the basic rule is that the airstream functions best in terms of tone quality and projection when the flute wall divides it into two equal parts. Since you cannot see the airstream, how do you find this happy medium? One gimmick is to place a lighted candle on a table, then blow across the flute embouchure in the direction of the candle so that it stops flickering. A less gimmicky, more direct method is to play a long tone in the middle register, adjusting the embouchure until you obtain the best sound. Having found the norm, you can make variations to compensate for changes in register. For lower notes, the airstream must strike the lower part of the opposite edge of the flute wall; for higher notes, direct the airstream higher against the opposite edge.

The embouchure also controls the distance from lips to opposite edge. This is the matter of where to place the flute on the lips and how to modify that basic position. As the lips move closer to the opposite edge, the pitch drops slightly, and then jumps to a higher harmonic of the original note. Therefore, higher notes demand a smaller lip-to-edge distance than do low notes. Movement of the lower lip determines the amount of coverage.

Far more problematic than the role of the lips is that of the jaw. As I mentioned earlier, Taffanel and Gaubert decry the use of the jaw to control the airstream. There are two good reasons for not using it: it tends to tense the facial muscles and throat, and it discourages concentration on lip flexibility. Nevertheless, many prominent flutists, Marcel Moyse particularly, do use jaw techniques to supplement lip action. The important point to remember is that the jaw is merely an auxiliary tool; it should not be regarded as a substitute for embouchure control.

The action of the lower jaw affects the axis of the flute in relation to the lips. The reason that Moyse advocates use of the lower jaw to modify this relationship, rather than using the lips themselves, is precisely because it leaves the lips free to vibrate and to obtain different colorings. The jaw, says Moyse, determines the larger proportions of the tone, leaving the lips free to add nuance and subtlety. The jaw acts much as the lips do to control the airstream. When the jaw is tightened, or brought back, the air column is directed further down into the embouchure hole. This lowers the pitch and makes the lower register speak better. In contrast, projecting the jaw forward raises the pitch and helps produce high notes more easily. Thus, Moyse suggests, the jaw should be slightly tense for soft passages and quite slack in loud ones, just as the lips should be slightly tighter for softer passages, less for fortes.

A more visually obvious way of controlling airstream direction is effected not by the mouth, but by the hands and arms. Rolling the flute by rolling the wrists will do the same things that the lips and jaw do. However, this technique is a remedy of last resort, and is useful, for instance, in adjusting your pitch to an out-of-tune colleague in an ensemble. Flute rolling must be used with extreme caution: rolling too far in will smother the tone, flatten the pitch, and cause you to lose control over dynamics and tone color. Conversely, rolling too far out will jack the pitch way up and will also unfocus the tone. (By the same token, rolling is a useful device for obtaining these results intentionally for variety of tone color.)

Focus and Projection

The ideal flute tone is clear and focused; it has a hard, firm core, modified by qualities of sweetness and beauty. It should not have fuzzy edges. There are several factors that can make the tone fuzzy: misdirection of the air, especially if it is too high over the far edge of the embouchure; too much or too little coverage of the embouchure hole; too small a lip aperture for the desired register and dynamic level, which produces excess air pressure; too large or loose an aperture; or incorrect airstream shape. An asymmetrical aperture tends to make the airstream diffuse, though some excellent players do have a naturally off-center embouchure because of the shape of their mouths. Finally, the flute itself may cause diffusion of the tone, particularly if the pads do not cover the holes properly and thus cause air leakage.

Projection, the delivery of tone from flute to listener, is in large part the result of focus. Even a *pianissimo* sound, if clear and centered, will travel far. Part of a tone's projection capacity is determined by transient sounds, the attack and ending tones of a note, or, in acoustical terms, momentary changes of wave form. These are achieved by a combination of breath, tongue, and lips, which starts the air column inside the flute in motion. The second phase of projection is the maintenance of a full tone throughout the duration of the sound.

From a practical perspective, projection is an intuitive and psychological phenomenon as much as a physical one; at the very least, psychological preparation is a prerequisite for the projection of a focused sound. Georges Barrère suggested imagining "setting the air around the player into vibration,"[5] an acoustical overstatement but an effective ploy. You can either think of driving the tone through the audience, like driving a stake into the ground—particularly if you want to project a penetrating tone with a hard edge to it—or you may want a warmer sound, propelled by its size, richness, and beauty. Whichever sound quality you choose in a given situation, remember that the sound must be intense in order to travel well.

Always imagine, even if you're playing in a four-by-six-foot practice room, that you're playing to the last row in Carnegie Hall. When I studied with

Arthur Lora, he told me to aim my tone at the stern-visaged portrait of Toscanini at the other end of the room, an intimidating but highly effective tactic. Put as much projecting power (that does not mean dynamics: it means focus and beauty of sound) behind your tone as you possibly can.

Homogeneity of Sound

The tonal ideal of the late-nineteenth century French school of flute playing—an ideal still widely accepted today—was homogeneity of sound. Homogeneity is *not* defined as uniformity. The instrument's acoustical characteristics absolutely preclude strict uniformity of tone quality and production. What the concept of homogeneity of flute tone means, then, is not that all notes should sound alike but that adjacent notes should be congruous with one another—they should be qualitatively as well as quantitatively contiguous. Moreover, there should be an overall concept of tone quality that applies irrespective of register or octave. This is what Philadelphia Orchestra flutist Murray Panitz calls a "tonal match" in all registers.[6]

Perhaps the best explanation of tonal homogeneity comes from Marcel Moyse, in his book *De la Sonorité*. In descending the chromatic scale from b^1 to c^1, he explains, you will hear a clear difference in color between the B and the C, yet you should be unable to say just where the change takes place. There is no "break," as on a clarinet. Each note has a slightly different coloring, but the change between contiguous half-steps (minor seconds) is so small that it is impossible to draw a dividing line. Ascending and descending matching tone exercises, working outward from the middle register in progressively larger intervals (see chapter 10, "Technique"), are the surest route to obtaining tonal homogeneity. Once you have attained this goal, says Moyse, you will not be hampered by the instrument in executing your interpretation. In other words, you will make automatic physical compensations for the acoustical characteristics of the instrument's different registers and notes. You will be free to concentrate on nuance, on intentional variations of the basic sound for interpretive purposes.

Interpretation through Tone Development

Moyse entitled one of his best-known study books *Tone Development Through Interpretation;* in it he adapted melodies from opera and song and used the vocal model of flowing melody to help students develop a singing tone and interpretive intuition. But Moyse's subtitle, "The study of expression, vibrato, color, suppleness and their application to different styles," implies the converse of the title: that interpretation is achieved by judicious use of tonal modification. Tone and interpretation are in truth symbiotic, and so it follows that the larger the flutist's palette of tone colors, the greater the range of interpretation. Indeed, variety of tone color is one of the chief glories of modern flute playing.

The mastery of tonal variety is not unlike the mastery of English composition. Once you've mastered the rules of grammar you may break them—by using contractions and sentence fragments, for instance—for good and sufficient reasons of rhythm and style. The same is true in academic music. Composition students must master the rules of strict tonal counterpoint before they are unleashed to use hitherto taboo parallel fifths and the like. The same goes for flute playing. You must have a good basic tone capable of sounding and projecting in all registers. When you have established this you are ready to vary and embellish it.

Once again we're in an area both of semantics and of personal taste. Describing flute tone, beyond the basics, is at best an imprecise art. As Verne Powell once said, "Everyone . . . speaks of dark and bright tone, and I'm never quite sure what they mean. Tell me, when you speak of a dark tone, what is it you are looking for—pea green, cerulean blue, or black magic?"[7] Benevolent black magic—magic of some kind, anyway—is probably closest.

In 1826, W. N. James described three basic types of tone; although he was writing about a wooden flute, the categories still apply in general terms. James likened the first type, achieved by a tight upper lip and a rapid, high-pressure airstream, to the tone of the oboe or clarinet. The second type uses a more relaxed upper lip and a greater volume of air, achieving a "mellow and plaintive" sound suitable for the *dolce* execution that was the norm of nineteenth century flute playing. James considered it the "natural tone of the instrument, as beginners always produce it," slightly unfocused but useful in contrast to the first type of tone.[8] A contemporary use might be the ethereal opening phrase of Debussy's *Prélude à l'Après-midi d'une faune*. "Natural tone" could, if not properly controlled, become rough and harsh as a consequence of the relaxed upper lip. The third type of tone, in James's analysis, was the most difficult but "by far the most beautiful"—the one most flutists strive for today—of "metallic and liquid character, its clearness unrivalled."[9] But these three types are merely guidelines; there are infinite gradations that it would be useless to attempt to quantify or further describe in words.

James's categories illustrate how styles change. In his day, the second type was the ideal; today, the third type is preferred. One flutist wrote in 1953, "I can remember when a tone in the lower register that sounded like a cornet or oboe was considered to be the best tone. Probably Georges Barrère [perhaps unrivalled as a tonal colorist] did more to change this idea than any other artist."[10] Murray Panitz concurs: although many players do aim to create a trumpetlike low register, he considers it "an interesting color of sound and should be in the control of the player, but I feel a quality that joins and matches the second octave is more desirable."[11] A counter example is equally instructive: in playing Enesco's *Cantabile et Presto*, Rampal (who studied it with the composer) begins with a cellolike sound, then brightens the tone as the music ascends to the upper register.

Tonal ideals are greatly dependent on the style of a particular piece of music. Mozart and Haydn demand a clarity and brightness like that of the four-key flute, while Varèse's *Density 21.5,* to take an extreme example, demands something much more astringent. Similarly, ensemble context plays a role in determining appropriate tone quality. The intimacy of a chamber composition—a Bach sonata, for instance, or the Debussy *Sonata for Flute, Viola, and Harp*—does not require a large sound. But a Brahms symphony, in which the flute is in competition with a full romantic brass section, demands power, richness, and fullness of tone. The very essence of ensemble playing is the ability to vary one's tone quality to blend with the other instruments (or to rise above them as needed). Oboist Robert Bloom tells a story of Toscanini rehearsing the third movement of Debussy's *Iberia:* "No, my dears, I am conscious of a flute and a bassoon. That's not what I want. I want to hear a third instrument, the result of a happy marriage between the two."[12]

Some basic technical rules apply to tone modification: to make the sound brighter, bring the lips closer to the opposite edge of the embouchure hole, tighten the lips a bit, and contract the mouth. If, on the other hand, you want a mellower sound, relax the lips but do not enlarge the airstream, blow more gently, and open the throat and mouth (in a semiyawn). Experiment with variations in air speed, quantity, and direction, using lips, jaw, tongue, and teeth, to achieve a variety of combinations. Building a repertoire of tone colors enlarges your musical vocabulary. Add special effects, such as harmonics (see chapter 10, "Technique") and vibrato (see chapter 8), and you are capable of boundless musical expression.

Intonation

Intonation is not, as is often assumed, an independent element of musicianship—it is an integral part of tone production. A flutist with a weak, unfocused tone will generally be out of tune; conversely, a flutist with a beautiful, singing, centered tone will also be centered securely on the correct pitch. The reason is that tone and intonation are products of the same physiological mechanisms.

Nevertheless, good intonation is not automatic, nor are pitch standards absolute. There is no single correct pitch for F♯, for instance; when used as a leading tone to a harmonic resolution in G major, it should be slightly higher than if it functions as the mediant (third degree) of the D major scale. Moreover, as you play, you must constantly make small adjustments to conform with the ensemble. Fortunately, today we need not worry about the large deviations in pitch that plagued eighteenth century flutists (who had to carry interchangeable midsections for their flutes because regional differences in customary pitch were so great), or even early twentieth century players. International standards are now set at A-440, and though some orchestras, such as the Boston Symphony, have traditionally chosen a pitch closer to A-

442 because of the brighter sound that the higher pitch creates, most flutists can compensate easily for these slight deviations.

One thing we cannot legislate, however, is the weather. And so all flutists—everywhere and at all times—must contend with climatic influences on their instruments. This is more of a problem with wooden flutes and piccolos than with metal ones. Air temperature affects the pitch of a wind instrument because of the difference in air weight that it causes: cold air is heavier than warm air. As temperature rises, the rate of molecular motion increases within the flute tube material, and so its density decreases and the pitch rises. The rise and fall of wind instrument pitch is thus parallel to that of the temperature—it rises as temperature rises and falls as temperature falls. Such deviations in pitch make it important for you to warm up your flute before a performance, in order to bring it to "room" temperature.

To warm up the flute, first cover the flute embouchure completely with your mouth. Close all the keys and then blow gently. You will feel the warm air traveling down the flute tube. To warm the very bottom, you can take a clean cloth and rub it vigorously on the unkeyed side of the tube. Be careful not to touch the mechanism. Once the flute is at room temperature, you are ready to tune to the first oboe, if you're playing in an orchestra, or to the accompanying piano, or to a tuning fork or electronic tuner. It is a good idea to tune to a tuning fork or electronic tuner even for private practice, so that your ear becomes accustomed to the correct pitch for the instrument. Most flutes are made with guide marks to assist you in lining up the headjoint with the body of the flute; you will quickly learn how accurate the marks are and how to compensate for any inaccuracy. As you play, your flute will continue to heat up, so later you may need to pull the headjoint out farther.

The flute is not a perfect acoustical specimen; many compromises inherent in its design prevent it from having absolutely just intonation. For example, on most modern flutes the majority of the tone holes are equal in size, whereas in purely acoustical terms they should be graduated. Characteristics of the mechanism, such as the coupling of the F and B♭ keys and the duplicate G♯ arrangement prevent proper venting of certain notes. It is useful, therefore, to be aware of the potential trouble spots, of notes that typically are slightly off—so you can compensate for their small defects automatically.

In the lower register, b (below middle C), c^1, $c^1\sharp$, and f^1 tend to be low. In the middle register, $c^2\sharp$ tends to be high, while f^2 is low. In the top register, d^3 tends to be low, while $e^3\flat$, e^3, $f^3\sharp$, $g^3\sharp$, b^3, and c^4 tend to be high.

British flutist Trevor Wye labels e^3 and $f^3\sharp$ as the "gnomes" of the top register because they are so much sharper and more difficult to play than the neighboring notes. The reason is that they are the only notes between $e^3\flat$ and $b^3\flat$ for which two holes are open. They would be much easier to produce and closer to pitch if one hole were closed—that's what the split-E mechanism does—but it is possible to compensate for the problem with lips and breath alone.

There are several methods of modifying the pitch of a note, all of which affect the direction and pressure of the airstream, the amount of embouchure hole coverage, or the lip aperture size. The easiest and most common method is to change the direction of the airstream. To lower the pitch, drop the lower jaw and lower the head; roll the flute inward; pull the corners of the mouth back slightly; cover the embouchure hole with the lower lip; and pull the upper lip down to direct the airstream lower into the flute. To lower the pitch by decreasing the air pressure, blow more softly, and decrease diaphragm and lip pressure. By so increasing the aperture between the lips, the airstream will become more diffuse and less strongly directed into the flute and the pitch will be lower.

To raise the pitch, do exactly the opposite: raise the head, project the lower jaw outward, blow across the hole at a higher angle (so less air enters the flute), increase breath pressure, increase lip pressure, and decrease lip aperture. In most cases, you will use a combination of these techniques; experiment to determine which ones work best for you in a given situation.

Another solution to continual, built-in intonation problems is to use alternate fingerings, often ignominiously known as "fake" fingerings. Their use as technical facilitators is described in chapter 10, "Technique." But they can occasionally be useful to correct intonation as well. On open-hole (French model) flutes, it is possible to raise the pitch of some notes by rolling the appropriate finger to the lower side of the hole just below the open vent. This is a variation of "half-holing," used on the recorder and pre-Boehm flutes, where the fingers have direct contact with the tone holes. Obviously, the technique is impossible on closed-hole flutes.

Other alternate fingerings are possible on both closed and open-hole flutes; they provide additional venting or muffling as needed, generally by the addition of extra keys to the normal fingerings. For instance, the ever-troublesome C♯ in the second and third octaves can be brought down from its typically stratospheric level by adding the first, second, and third keys of the right hand. This fingering may be helpful, for instance, in the opening measures of Debussy's *Prélude à l'Après-Midi d'une faune.*

The most complete list of alternate fingerings is James Pellerite's *A Modern Guide to Fingerings for the Flute,* second edition (1972).

While the pitch discrepancies inherent in the flute's construction are in general a nuisance, they can be turned to advantage. That same sharp C♯ that is too high to open *Daphnis* and is almost always too high when written as the enharmonic equivalent, D♭, is properly pitched as the leading tone to a tonic D. Indeed, a good flutist instinctively increases lip pressure when approaching D via C♯. Similarly, if he is approaching C by way of D♭, he will instinctively lower the D♭ leading tone.

Making such intonational compensations allows the flute to become a true melody instrument, and not, as baroque flute and recorder virtuoso Frans Brueggen puts it, "a frustrated harmony instrument." Melody instruments have a great advantage, Brueggen explains, because their ability to modify pitch—something a pianist cannot do—gives them an extra means of modifying tone color, and thus another vehicle of expression. He reasons that

> the modern ear is almost crazily attached to playing in tune. . . . That's a 19th century ideal. Of course, one should play in tune within a certain limit. But, as a melody instrument player, you have the obligation to play and to colour with a tone—and this also involves colouring and playing with the pitch a little.[13]

I believe that Brueggen goes overboard, both in writing and playing, in his freedom of pitch. If anything, twentieth century pitch standards, because of the accuracy of recordings, higher performance standards in general, and electronic developments, are even more stringent than they were a century ago. So I recommend that Brueggen's advice be taken with extreme caution. Taste and judgment must be the arbiters of pitch and color. As Paul Taffanel and Louis Fleury put it, "The quality of a good musician is inseparable from that of a good flutist, and the lips must obey the ears.[14]

National Styles of Flute Playing

Today, if there can be said to be an International Style of flute playing, it is an outgrowth of the French style. Indeed, the supremacy of French woodwind playing has been acknowledged for hundreds of years, but it was not until this century that the style achieved worldwide predominance.

What is the qualitative effect of this growing uniformity? Frans Vester sees it as a negative development—evidence of a lack of character and originality. But Geoffrey Gilbert is more sanguine: because such uniformity has caused a concomitant elevation of standards, he views the change as a very positive thing. He notes that in the past it was possible "to recognize by certain weaknesses rather than virtues the origin or source of a particular performer or performers." For instance, Gilbert recalls the "Mengelbergian bulges in the winds" that distinguished Amsterdam's Concertgebouw, the "smoothness but lack of warmth in the woodwinds and the thickness of sound in the brass" of the Berlin Philharmonic, and "the unevenness of the woodwind tuning and the vibrato in the horns and trumpets" in many French orchestras.[15]

The essence of the French style is its tone—silvery, pure, sweet, and above all, refined. It is not necessarily a large tone; its carrying power results from quality rather than quantity. Its simple elegance, often described by such metaphors as "shimmering silk," evokes logical comparisons to the music of Debussy.[16] And indeed, Debussy articulated these very ideas in a 1904 interview: "French music is clearness, elegance, simple and natural declamation. French music wishes first of all to give pleasure."[17]

But the French flute tradition dates from long before Debussy. The root of the French style is evident as far back, in fact, as Hotteterre. His *Principes de la flute traversiere,* published in 1707, laid the groundwork for the French flute school with its presentation of the expressive uses of varied articulations and vibrato. Hotteterre's work as an instrument maker demonstrates the same principles: when he introduced the conical bore and reduced the size of the mouth hole and the finger holes from previous models, he increased the dynamic and color range, thereby making the instrument more expressive.

As Hotteterre suggested, articulation is and was another important component of the French style, an extension, no doubt, of the French language. The traditional French method of tonguing brings the tongue far forward in the mouth, so that tonguing takes place between the teeth. By not requiring the tongue to travel very far, this method enhances clear and rapid enunciation both in speech and flute playing. The French pronunciation of *la flûte* is the perfect example of the national tongue position. The French emphasis on articulation is coupled with emphasis on phrasing, an equally important component of the characteristic *raffinement.*

At the very end of the eighteenth century, the French flute school acquired a school in the institutional sense: the Paris Conservatoire, founded in 1795, became home to several generations of fine and influential flutists. From the first professor, Devienne, through Schnietzhoefer, Hugot, Duverger, Wunderlich, Guillou, Tulou, Coche, Dorus, and Altès, to Taffanel, Hennebains, Gaubert, Moyse, Crunelle, and Rampal, the standards of the Conservatoire have become the standards of the world.

The pure, silvery tone of the modern French school implies the use of the silver flute, and indeed, the silver flute became popular in France before anywhere else. The tone produced by the silver flute is light and limpid and an appropriate top voice to the light-textured French woodwind choir. It responds well to the light, front-of-the-mouth attack and to *pianissimo,* particularly in the upper register and over wide intervals. The silver flute permits a looser embouchure than does wood, which allows the player to make the nuances of timbre and pitch that are the hallmarks of the French style.

Another typically French preference—indeed a French invention—is the open-hole flute, familiarly and logically known as the French model. It was first introduced on the Boehm flute by Clair Godfroy, Boehm's French licensee and the predecessor of Louis Lot. Gaubert was the first major player to adopt the open-hole flute, and its popularity became contagious.

The French school found a second home in the United States in the early part of this century, when a whole generation of Gaubert students emigrated to the New World: the brothers André and Daniel Maquarre, principal flutists in the Boston and Philadelphia orchestras, respectively; René Rateau, solo flute of the Chicago Symphony; Georges Barrère, first flute of the New York Symphony Orchestra; and Georges Laurent, principal with the Boston Symphony. These men brought with them to the U.S. the tonal ideals of the French school, learned firsthand at the Paris Conservatoire from Taffanel, Hennebains, and Gaubert—the concepts of tonal homogeneity (of which Moyse later became the standard-bearer), of the famous "sensitive" timbral control, and of vibrato. And they brought their silver flutes with open holes, which became so popular that by about 1917 the Wm. S. Haynes Company had ceased making wooden flutes altogether.

Yet the French emigrés did not preserve the Taffanel style in a museum case; they endowed it with their own personalities. When Moyse first arrived in this country—rather later than the others, in 1949—he said in an interview with *Woodwind Magazine* that his aim was to develop "an American school of woodwind playing that will challenge the best anywhere in the world." "His secret ambition," the magazine reported, "is to forge a woodwind ensemble that will excel most string quartets. Each instrument can and must learn to express the colors of others in the group.[18]

Even before Moyse's arrival, though, a distinctly American school of flute playing had begun to take shape. One manifestation was evident in the flute itself. Both Barrère and Kincaid played platinum flutes, which enhance the fullness and mellowness of the sound. Barrère debuted his platinum Haynes in 1935. Another American preference was the extension of the footjoint to low B, a feature that today is still found much more frequently in the United States than in France.

The true American style appeared with the first generation of American-born orchestra principals, led by William Kincaid, revered elder statesman of the school. Kincaid's tone was rich and robust, with great projection. Sometimes described as "virile,"[19] it was heavier and darker than the traditional French sound. Like Barrère, Kincaid had a magnificent repertory of tone colors at his disposal, and he was an extremely careful but devoted and effective partisan of vibrato.

In the American generations after Kincaid, little has changed in terms of basic tonal ideals, with the exception that vibrato commands a good deal of pedagogical attention. The Barrère generation, in contrast, considered it a natural or instinctive technique, to be assimilated, not studied. And in the last twenty years, a new avant-garde school of flutists has expanded the concept of timbral variety far beyond what Taffanel could have dreamed of. Robert Cantrick, Robert Dick, Otto Luening, Harvey Sollberger, and their colleagues have introduced entirely new techniques to the flutist's tonal and technical repertoire: buzzing, multiphonics, whistle tones, percussive effects such as key clicks and tongue slaps, and many more.

In England, the tradition has been quite different. It may be traced most clearly to Charles Nicholson (1795–1837), whose powerful tone inspired Boehm's redesign of the flute. Said one of Nicholson's students, W. N. James, his tone was "not only clear, metallic and brilliant, but possesses a volume that is almost incredible."[20] Nicholson's self-confessed goal was to make his tone "as reedy as possible, embodying the round mellowness of the clarinet."[21] He did so on a seven-key old-system wooden flute.

The English, in fact, remained partial to the wooden flute well into the twentieth century; even today, a few British players use wooden instruments. The wooden flute creates a denser, more overtly powerful sound than does silver; the tone of such nineteenth century French virtuosi as Tulou and Drouet seemed weak to the English. The bore, embouchure, and tone holes of the typical English wooden flute were also much larger than on comparable French models.

As with the French, the typical English tone ideal correlates with the vowel sounds of the language. Compare the English pronunciation of *the flute* with the French *la flûte*: The mouth is more open and relaxed, the sound looser. The English flute sound requires more air pressure in blowing and a harder attack, a tighter embouchure, often with the flute pressed rather hard against the lips. The result, typically, is a very, very rich sound, reedy, like Nicholson's in the lowest register. Trevor Wye, one of the finest flutists in Britain today, suggests that the traditional English flute tone is like the typical English weather forecast: "Heavy rain with occasional showers and thick fog with mist patches."[22]

The Old English style reached its apogee in the playing of Robert Murchie (1884–1949), perhaps the premier London flutist between the two world wars, and Eli Hudson (1877–1919), principal flutist of the London Symphony Orchestra and renowned piccolo soloist. Gareth Morris, a pupil of Murchie and later the first flutist of the Philharmonia Orchestra, played a wooden flute with a thinned head, a compromise between English and French styles, yet his playing remained firmly in the British tradition.

The French style has, however, penetrated England as well as America. Albert Fransella (1866–1935), soloist of the Queen's Hall Orchestra, brought the Belgian style, a lighter version of the French, to England in the last decades of the nineteenth century. The modern breed of French virtuosi—chief among them Louis Fleury (1878–1926), Philippe Gaubert (1879–1941), and René Le Roy (1898–1985)—toured England in the early twentieth century, and were well received by the public, though the professional flutists in England did not begin their Francophile conversion until the mid-1930s.

It was at that time that the young Geoffrey Gilbert, then principal flutist of the London Philharmonic, switched to a metal flute—a stainless steel Rudall Carte instrument with a gold head. Gilbert had become convinced that traditional British flute playing was frowned upon in international circles; producer Fred Gaisberg told him that the Gramophone Company refused to record English flutists. When Gilbert heard Marcel Moyse and René Le Roy, he made the difficult decision to change his style in midcareer. He soon began studying with Le Roy, who converted him to the silver flute (he got Gilbert a Louis Lot); to light, front-of-the-mouth articulation; and to the French concepts of tonal coloring. In the next generation, Gilbert's own student James Galway went to Paris for further instruction from Crunelle, Rampal, and Moyse.

German, Russian, and eastern European traditions are much the same as the English, though the typical sound tends to be duller and thicker. It is almost entirely *senza vibrato*. In Vienna, the Boehm flute achieved acceptance only in the early twentieth century. As in Germany, it was slow to catch on; when Boehm introduced the instrument, the conservative Franz Doppler was first flutist of the Imperial Opera and professor at the Vienna Conservatory, and his loyalty to the old-system flute was contagious. When Gustav Mahler hired Dutch flute virtuoso Ary van Leeuwen in 1903 to be first flutist of the Vienna Opera, van Leeuwen became the first musician to bring a silver flute to Austria. Hailing from Arnheim, Holland, he was typical of his countrymen in combining aspects of the French and German styles. He emigrated to the United States in 1922, where he then edited a large quantity of music, much of it still in print.

Japan, too, has adopted the International (French plus American) Style. The first Boehm flute was imported in 1921, a silver Haynes purchased by Masao Okamura, who, while a student in Los Angeles, had been impressed by the beautiful tone of Barrère. In the mid-1930s, the recordings of Marcel Moyse began circulating in Japan. Meanwhile, in 1923 Koichi Muramatsu had begun manufacturing silver Boehm flutes there. A parade of Western flute soloists, beginning with Arthur Lora (1957), Phillip Kaplan (1960), Samuel Baron (1961), Julius Baker (1963), Jean-Pierre Rampal (1964), Severino Gazzelloni (1971), Marcel Moyse (1973), and Paula Robison (1981) helped to spur continued interest in the tradition.

Today, as the result of decades of international cultural exchange, the basic concepts of flute playing are consistent worldwide. Yet each true virtuoso has his or her own individual style, which may or may not conform to what were once exclusively national characteristics.

Notes

1. Theobald Boehm, *The Flute and Flute-Playing*, trans. and rev. Dayton C. Miller, 2nd ed., rev. (1922; reprint, New York: Dover Publications, 1964), p. 140.
2. C[harles] Nicholson, *A School for the Flute* (New York: Firth & Hall, ca. 1830), p. 1.
3. Dale Higbee, "Needed: A Gold Flute or a Gold Lip," *Woodwind World* 13, no. 3 (1974): 22.
4. Wanda Sue Swilley, "A Comprehensive Performance Project in Flute Literature with an Essay on Flute Embouchure Pedagogy in the United States from ca 1925–1977 as Described in Selected Writings" (D.M.A. diss., University of Iowa, 1978), pp. 59–60.
5. Roger S. Stevens, *Artistic Flute Technique and Study*, ed. Ruth N. Zwissler (Hollywood, Calif.: Highland Music Co., 1967), p. 38.
6. Murray Panitz, "Tone and Musicality" (Elkhart, Ind.: W. T. Armstrong Co., 1974), p. [2].
7. Ray Fabrizio, "The French Model Flute: A Dissenting View," *National Flute Association Newsletter* 6, no. 4 (1980), p. 3.

8. W. N. James, *A Word or Two on the Flute* (Edinburgh: Charles Smith & Co.; London: Cocks & Co., 1826), pp. 147–48.
9. Ibid., p. 148.
10. E. C. Moore, *The Flute Book* (Kenosha, Wis.: G. Leblanc Co., 1953), p. 10.
11. Panitz, p. [2].
12. Robert Bloom, "Variety in Tonal Color," *Symphony* 7, no. 5 (1953): 11.
13. Frans Brueggen and Keith Horner, "Frans Brueggen on the baroque recorder," *Early Music* 2, no. 2 (1974), p. 103.
14. Paul Taffanel and Louis Fleury, "La Flûte," *Encyclopédie de la Musique et Dictionnaire du Conservatoire* (Paris: Delagrave, 1926), vol. 3, p. 1523.
15. Eleanor Lawrence, "Interview with Geoffrey Gilbert," *National Flute Association Newsletter* 7, no. 2 (1982), p. 5.
16. George M. Bundy, "The Flute of To-Day," *The Flutist* 9, no. 7 (1928): 199.
17. Edward Burlingame Hill, *Modern French Music* (1924; reprint, New York: Da Capo Press, 1969), p. 197.
18. "Marcel Moyse Profiled," *Woodwind Magazine* 2, no. 5 (1950), p. 1.
19. James A. MacGillivray, "The Woodwind," in *Musical Instruments Through the Ages*, ed. Anthony Baines (London: Faber and Faber, 1961), p. 243.
20. Anthony Baines, *Woodwind Instruments and Their History* (New York: W. W. Norton, 1962), p. 317.
21. C[harles] Nicholson, *A School for the Flute* (London and New York: Wm. Hall & Sons, 1836), p. 3.
22. Trevor Wye, "Boehm in England and Germany" (Paper delivered at National Flute Association convention, Detroit, Mich., 22 Aug. 1981), p. 4.

8

VIBRATO

What Is Vibrato?

Vibrato is a measured fluctuation in the sound or tone effected by a change in air pressure. The effect is of pulsation or vibration, but because what we hear is not exactly what actually happens, it is not easy to define. For one thing, many people find it difficult if not impossible to distinguish the vibrato component from the tone as a whole. (This is actually a good sign, because the vibrato should be an integral, though not omnipresent, part of the sound.) There are three basic types of vibrato: pitch, intensity (dynamic), and timbre.

In pitch vibrato, the pitch fluctuates both above and below the starting note; on A-440, for instance, it varies between 438 and 442 frequencies per second. (Some players, however, advise that the pitch should vary upward only, to avoid the impression of flatness. Also, the higher the pitch, the more brilliant the sound.) Intensity vibrato is a fluctuation in the dynamic level or strength of a note; as a practical matter, it is not totally separable from pitch vibrato. The combination of pitch vibrato and intensity vibrato result in timbre vibrato. The reason is that when the dynamic level of a tone changes, the overtone composition of the tone changes correspondingly; and it is the overtone composition that determines timbre.

Pitch vibrato may be varied by changing either the amplitude of the fluctuation (how far it varies from the "home" pitch) or its speed. The pitch should vary no more than a quarter tone in either direction (as opposed to vocal vibrato, which may swing as much as a half step); within that limit, further variety is possible. In general, the pulsations should occur four to six times per second. If the pulsation is too slow, the vibrato will resemble a wobble rather than a shimmer on the edge of the tone; if it is too fast, the sound will be the infamous "nanny goat" or "billy goat" vibrato, which the French call *chevrotement*.

To summarize the interrelationship of the three forms of vibrato: when airstream velocity increases, the tone becomes louder; the pitch becomes higher; the overtone quotient increases; and so the color becomes brighter. Conversely, when the airspeed decreases, the dynamic level also decreases;

the pitch goes down; and the timbre becomes duller because there are fewer overtones.

Flute vibrato is often compared with violin vibrato because it is so easy to visualize the motion of the violinist's left hand in creating the vibrato on the string. The violinist's right arm, the bow arm, creates the basic tone; the left hand, on the strings, supplies the vibrato independently. The analogy is a good one in that the vibrato is an adjunct to the tone, separate from its basic production; it may be used or not used. So far so good. But the analogy stops here, because in modern practice, violin vibrato is nearly continuous; on the flute it should not be.

For this reason, some flute teachers, Marcel Moyse for one, prefer to compare flute vibrato with vocal vibrato. Partly, this is because their concept of flute playing in general is based on the vocal model, though again flutists should use vibrato with much more restraint than singers generally do. Moyse points out several important distinctions between string and wind vibrato: while string tone is produced by the right arm, vibrato by the left, wind tone and vibrato depend on the same air column. If the dynamic is *fortissimo*, vibrato will be accented and intense; if *pianissimo*, the vibrato will be light and discreet. Also, string vibrato speed is subject to almost limitless variation; the wind range is far more limited. And finally, string vibrato has only a minimal influence on the pitch, whereas on the flute, pitch and vibrato are intimately related.

The production of flute vibrato is a subject of much discussion.There are three basic schools of thought. The first postulates that vibrato is a natural part of tone production, which cannot and should not be taught. The second school believes that because vibrato must be carefully controlled, it must be taught. The third school takes a safe middle position: some players have natural vibrato, but others must be taught, and even those with a natural vibrato can be taught to improve and control it.

Typical of the natural school is Marcel Moyse, who did not teach vibrato as such; instead, he asked for a warm, singing tone, from which vibrato naturally proceeds. A measured vibrato, Moyse wrote,

> which is the last straw, is not vibrating, it is undulating—better yet, it is panting. This is no longer emotion, it is organized agitation. This pseudo-vibrato, measured at 3, 4, 5, even 7 per second is unquestionably destined to disturb, to blindly destroy the expressive significance of a musical phrase, since the notes which it comprises do not all have the same length and the same expressive importance.[1]

John Wummer summarized the view of natural vibrato partisans in a 1948 article: "Taffanel, Gaubert, Maquarre and Barrère have all concurred in the idea that the vibrato is not 'produced' but is the resulting phenomenon of the naturally 'breathed' tone—and is, in fact, not to be thought of as something produced but as something resulting from one's own musical feeling."[2] Violinist and musicologist Sol Babitz concurs:

> A naturally developed vibrato has something which is lacking in the trained vibrato. It is a more faithful presentation of the player's individuality as expressed in his tone. It is his personal voice, whereas the trained vibrato sometimes lacks personality, and is merely correct. . . . [3]

A taught vibrato is far more likely than a natural vibrato to lapse into *chevrotement.*

Typical of the third, compromise school is oboist Robert Sprenkle's warning that

> as soon as one concentrates on the mechanics of production this tone quality appears to deteriorate or become more artificial. In listening specifically for vibrato pulses, one *temporarily* loses the sum total effect of the tone. This psychological but very real tendency is one reason why many wind players are discouraged from trying to evaluate and control the production of their vibrato.[4]

William Kincaid also falls into the third school. In one of his method books, *The Advanced Flutist,* he wrote that "in most cases, [the student] has already produced a haphazard vibrato without realizing it."[5] He goes on to explain the specific physical techniques for controlling vibrato.

Assuming that the physical mechanisms of vibrato production are the same whether instinctive or learned—what are these mechanisms?

Diaphragm: This is one of the muscles that controls breathing, and, in controlling vibrato, it works the same way. As in breathing in general, diaphragm vibrato is misnamed, or at least only partially named, because it involves both diaphragm and abdominal-wall muscles. Diaphragm vibrato, then, is produced by the isometric action of the abdominal muscles and diaphragm pushing against each other. This causes a very slight undulation of the air column as it is propelled out of the lungs. As the pressure increases, it raises the pitch and dynamic level. Diaphragm vibrato has the effect of rapid, unarticulated (untongued) accents. Although it is the overwhelming favorite of flutists, it does have the tendency to be too wide and slow.

Throat: Throat vibrato is produced by action of the rearmost portion of the tongue against the throat. It is similar to the repetition of the syllable "ah" without voice, accompanied by a definite closing of the throat at the end of each such syllable. It is a variation in the constriction of the trachea or windpipe as the air passes through it. Throat vibrato is a potentially dangerous technique, however, because it is a major cause of tension in the throat. And tension is something to be avoided at all costs because it usually results in a smaller sound. Moreover, it is easy to overdo throat vibrato, and it may be audible as physical action—particularly the vocalization of "ah." Throat vibrato is the type most likely to turn into a goat imitation.

Jaw and Lip: Jaw vibrato is used on the reed instruments, especially the saxophone, but should be avoided by flutists. It is not very flexible, and often causes unwanted changes in tone quality, because as the jaw moves it upsets the angle of the airstream entering the embouchure hole. Lip vibrato has the same problem and should also be avoided.

If vibrato can indeed be taught, what are the methods? For diaphragm vibrato, the first step is diaphragm pushes. Attack each note of a quarter- or eighth-note exercise with forceful contractions of the abdominal muscles. Do not articulate the notes with the tongue—use just the abdominal muscles. Only later add the tongue. In other words, "tongue with the breath." Next, play a long tone, slowly punctuating or pulsing it with diaphragm pushes. Using a metronome to monitor your progress, gradually speed up the tempo until the sound appears continuous. At this point, the frequency of the pushes will be greater, but their intensity will diminish.

For throat vibrato, as for breathing, the first exercise does not use the flute. Say *who* or cough lightly at four counts per second, increasing the speed to six and then to eight counts per second. Then do the same with the instrument, playing a single note and gradually increasing the frequency of the *whos* or coughs.

The History of Vibrato

Contrary to popular legend, vibrato is not a modern invention. It began as an ornament—usually produced by the fingers, only occasionally by the breath. The more continuous form did not emerge until the late nineteenth century. Modern flutists should consider the roots of the technique.

In his *Musica instrumentalis deudsch* (1528), Agricola lists "trembling breath" as a "special grace." Praetorius (1619) discusses vibrato created by diaphragm action. Mersenne (1636) talks of "certain tremolos which intoxicate the soul" and specifies that organ tremolo has a frequency of four vibrations per second, which he suggests as a model for wind players.[6] Hotteterre, in his *Principes de la Flute* (1707), discusses a finger vibrato, called a *flattement*,[7] which also appears in the methods of Corrette (about 1735) and Mahaut (1759). Quantz's *Versuch* (1752) defines a *messa di voce*, a swelling and diminishing of volume within a single note, produced by a finger *flattement* on the nearest open hole. (Because this procedure also lowers the pitch, Quantz advised flutists to compensate with the embouchure.)[8] Delusse (about 1761) speaks of a breath vibrato, used in imitation of the organ tremulant, as a measured expression of "solemnity and terror."[9] And Tromlitz (1791) discusses the *Bebung*, a finger vibrato.

In the nineteenth century, flute pedagogues continued to be interested in the matter of vibrato. British flutist and publisher W. N. James, writing in 1826, said that "vibrations on the flute, . . . when introduced judiciously and sparingly, . . . have an exceeding fine effect. The beat of a violin is justly considered one of its chief beauties; and the vibration of the flute, particularly in its lower tones, is very similar." He warned, however, that "great caution should be taken that the beginning of the note shall be neither flatter nor sharper than the middle or ending of it"; in other words, James advocated an intensity vibrato but not a pitch vibrato.[10]

Virtuoso Charles Nicholson, James's contemporary, used an ornament called a "vibration" and notated 𝅘𝅥. He described the vibration as an embellishment that should resemble the beats or pulsations of a bell or glass; it should be slow at first, increasing in rapidity as the sound diminished. It could be produced by

> breath—by a tremulous motion of the Flute, and by the Shake. If by the breath; the moment the note is forced, subdue the tone, and on each succeeding pulsation, let the tone be less vigorous. When the Vibration becomes too rapid to continue the effect with the breath, a tremulous motion must be given to the Flute with the right hand, the lips being perfectly relaxed, and tone subdued to a mere whisper.[11]

Vibration was most effective, Nicholson felt, between e^1 and b^2.

Victor Coche, writing in 1838, stated that flute vibration was practically identical to that of the voice. He called it *le chevron*, notated 𝅗𝅥. It consisted of a forceful attack, followed by a less forceful sound. Thus, he explained, a half note with a chevron would be played as a series of tied eighth notes:[12]

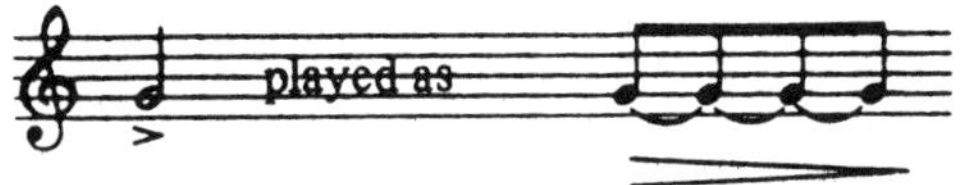

Richard Carte, in his mid-nineteenth century method, described the *tremolo* as

> a grace that consists in the wavering of a note. It is produced on the Flute either by giving a tremendous impulse to the breath, or by tremulously holding the Instrument. It is used in passages of pathos, and is indicated by the word tremolo, or is introduced at the fancy of the Performer.[13]

A *vibration*, wrote Carte, was different from a tremolo "by its greater delicacy." A vibration was a finger vibrato, which should be slow on a loud note, faster on a soft one. It might be indicated in the score by the shake sign (𝅘𝅥); thus the player must distinguish based on the musical context whether a shake or vibration is intended. But this is not as great a problem as it seems, Carte said; a shake is generally intended in rapid passages, a vibration on sustained notes.[14] Carte's colleague, John Clinton, pointed out, however, that vibration is not a realistic possibility on the four lowest notes of the flute (c^1 to d^1♯), because of the lack of lower holes on which to perform the vibration; thus it can only be effected by manipulation of the flute at the embouchure.[15]

J. Harrington Young, in his 1892 method, specified the identical notation and terminology, but cautioned that

> it should only be used in very pathetic movements—such as Adagios, Andantes &c. where great pathos is desired; but, if too frequently used, this effect becomes vulgarized and unpleasant. Some players produce the effect by a tremulous motion of the breath, which is inadvisable, as by its frequent use it endangers the production of a steady tone, which is far more desirable than any artificial effect.[16]

Vibration should, therefore, be produced only by finger movement.

Keep in mind that at that time vibration was an ornament, not an omnipresent element of tone. This was equally true of violin playing. A possibly apocryphal story is illustrative: the great Fritz Kreisler auditioned for the Royal Opera House orchestra in Vienna, but was turned down because of his "restaurant vibrato." Yet later, his "Golden Tone" became the ideal to be copied by all other violinists.[17] And so taste changes.

Vibrato as we know it today—a more or less continuous pulsation or shimmer in the tone—originated in the late nineteenth century in Paris. Paul Taffanel and oboist Fernand Gillet were two of the instigators. This may seem surprising in view of the statement in the Taffanel-Gaubert method:

> There should be no vibrato or any form of quaver, an artifice used by inferior instrumentalists and musicians [an interesting distinction!]. It is with the tone that the player conveys the music to the listener. Vibrato distorts the natural character of the instrument and spoils the interpretation, fatiguing quickly the sensitive ear. It is a serious error and shows unpardonable lack of taste to use these vulgar methods to interpret the great composers. The rules for their interpretation are strict: It is only by purity of line, by charm, deep feeling and heartfelt sincerity that the greatest heights of style may be reached. All true artists should work toward this goal.[18]

Taffanel wrote elsewhere that

> the search for timbre, the utilization towards this end of a light, almost imperceptible vibrato . . . all this derives more from an intelligent empiricism (practical experience) than from precise rules. It is very difficult, besides, to define with certainty what to call a beautiful sound. It is easier to describe faults than to avoid them.[19]

Adolphe Hennebains, Taffanel's student and successor as flute professor at the Paris Conservatoire, provides the key to understanding Taffanel's apparent inconsistency. "When he spoke to us of notes with vibrato or expression, he told us with a mysterious air that these notes, forte or piano, seemed to come from within himself. One had the impression that they came directly from the heart or the soul."[20] In other words, it was intuitive, "natural," not mechanical or premeditated. Similarly, Marcel Moyse recalls, in Philippe Gaubert's classes there was no talk of vibrato per se, but Gaubert spent many hours on musical expression, the idea being to "speak with the music."[21] Yet Gaubert's recording of Bach's fifth Brandenburg Concerto has a shallow, fairly rapid vibrato.

The advent of vibrato in France, around 1905, was the fuel for a great debate. Because it was new, it was often not done very well and was used indiscriminately, and so it got a bad name. Furthermore, "talented instrumentalists had sought for too long, not without difficulty, to find good tone in all registers that was pure, stable and flexible, not to conceive of this perfection as the height of their art."[22] Or as Moyse concluded, "Vibrato? It was worse than cholera. Young vibrato partisans were referred to as criminals. Judgments were final with no appeal. It was ruthless."[23] Some critics, Moyse continued, labelled vibrato "*cache-misère* (literally misery hider, something to hide behind when faced with problems of intonation and tone quality)."[24]

Woodwind vibrato was brought to the United States by Georges Barrère, Georges Laurent, and oboists Marcel Tabuteau (longtime principal of the Philadelphia Orchestra) and Gillet (who joined the Boston Symphony). By 1940 it had become an accepted part of American orchestral woodwind performance. At the same time Moyse, newly arrived in the United States, despaired that, in France, "vibrato is used so excessively that all music is distorted by its constant waver."[25]

Elsewhere, however, vibrato was slower to catch on. Henry Welsh, for instance, wrote in the British periodical *Music and Letters* in 1951:

> As for the woodwinds, I fail to see any aesthetical or technical reason why they should trespass on the noble and intimate qualities which belong so inseparably and essentially to the strings. A plea that vibrato-playing enhances the quality of tone cannot therefore be upheld. Wind instruments should be played with a tone that is as steady as a rock and as pure as crystal.[26]

This was the Viennese as well as the British ideal, and it perturbed foreign critics, who accused the English of coldness and lack of feeling. More recently, vibrato has infiltrated British flute style, though the technique is nowhere near as pervasive as in the United States and France.

The vibrato as first imported to the United States was, true to its roots, both rapid and naturally produced. Barrère's was reportedly very rapid indeed. In a 1944 article Barrère explained: "It being settled that expression in music *must* be a love message, music has to be performed with a quiver in the tone, much as the histrionic lover's lines must be spoken with a *tremolo* in the voice."[27] But Barrère qualified this typically Gallic statement:

> *Vibrato!!* That is the strong word, firmly established in reputation and popularity; recognized, 'patented,' and the only allowed designation for anything expressive . . . The notion has its starting-point in that brand of instruction which teaches our future virtuosos to cater to the masses and to use 'sure-fire' means first . . . music with permanent *vibrato* is bound to win and hold a permanent business. For the fifty years I had been tooting my instrument, my daily care was to *avoid* the *vibrato*. Once I literally scared an audience by asserting that *vibrato* was produced by taking a pure tone and moving it above and below correct pitch at a certain rate of speed, thus indulging in playing more or less out of

tune! Today . . . to declare that Expression might sometimes be achieved just by the *absence* of *vibrato*, would, in most quarters, only earn an incredulous frown. Isn't it still possible to express Beauty by pure lines, such as we find in ancient Greek marbles?[28]

One of Barrère's last students, Pittsburgh Symphony principal Bernard Goldberg, quotes his teacher as saying, "For three hundred years flutists tried to play in tune. Then they gave up and invented vibrato."[29]

Barrère student John Wummer, longtime solo flutist of the New York Philharmonic, was the last of the fast-vibrato school, though even Wummer's vibrato slowed down in later years. William Kincaid was the pioneer in developing a slower vibrato. Just as he sought a darker, fuller sound than the traditional birdlike sound of his French predecessors, he sought a slower, more intense vibrato. New York Philharmonic flutist Paige Brooke explains, "Kincaid was the one who brought it closer to the way string instruments use it—smoother and more controlled, variable speed vibrato depending on what intensity one wants, and making it an integral part of flute playing."[30]

The Uses of Vibrato

The uses of vibrato are many. It can give warmth or beauty to the tone, a gilt edge or shimmer on the surface of the sound. It can intensify expression by lending emphasis to particular notes (the sense in which it is an ornament). Used selectively within the phrase structure, it can enhance the feeling of motion. It can help to project the tone by adding intensity.

The best use of vibrato is as a means of varying the timbre. First of all, it provides a contrast to straight or white tone—which implies that the player must have a fine basic tone to begin with. Within the vibrato domain, however, still more variety is possible. The physical variables are, thus, presence or absence (either sudden or gradual stopping and starting), speed, and amplitude. Writing for string players, Yehudi Menuhin and William Primrose make an analogy that is equally applicable to flutists:

> Vibrato must be as varied as the weather of England, and always beautiful and sweet. It can be very narrow and fast, producing a gleaming, penetrating sound—as wonderful in pianissimo as in fortissimo; pure, with so little vibration as to be almost a choir-boy sound, or so much as to be like a brilliant light, so intense is its penetrating effect. It can be slow and wide, it can be fast and wide, it can be velvety, it can be burning with passion.[31]

Vibrato can be used most frequently in solo work; in ensemble music it must be carefully coordinated with the other instruments. Since the other woodwinds use less—the clarinet practically none—the orchestral use of flute vibrato must be strictly controlled so that the woodwind choir blends properly. The speed of the vibrato should be coordinated with the speed of the music, faster in allegros, slower in adagios. But short notes should be vibratoless; Altès advises that no vibrato be used if the metronome setting is ♩ = 120 or higher. Roger Stevens suggests a different guideline: in order to avoid destroying the continuity of the tone, never use vibrato in a slurred passage where the number of vibrato pulses is equal to or less than the number of notes per second. Moreover, vibrato should be slower in the lower register, and increase in speed as the register climbs.

A few examples from the symphonic literature illustrate effective use of vibrato. In the last movement of the Brahms First Symphony, the flute must cut through the whole orchestra, which calls for a relatively fast and wide vibrato. At the conclusion of Mendelssohn's *Fingal's Cave Overture,* slowing down and narrowing the vibrato enhances the final cadence. An intensity vibrato in Debussy's *Prelude à l'Après-Midi d'une Faune* enhances the static nature of the C♯ before the chromatic movement downward.

So vibrato can be a potent vehicle for musical expression. It is important to remember that vibrato is not a substitute for a full, beautiful tone. The flutist must be able to play a dolce, cantabile adagio totally without benefit of vibrato. William Kincaid, himself master of the selectively expressive vibrato, put it this way: "To Alice in Wonderland there was a Cheshire cat which grinned. Suddenly the cat disappeared and only the grin was left. Equation—grin, no cat = vibrato, no tone."[32] In other words, vibrato is an ornament; while present, an integral part of the tone, but the tone must be capable of standing on its own without any vibrato enhancement. Vibrato is not a means of disguising faulty intonation or a thin or distorted tone.

Notes

1. Marcel Moyse, *How I Stayed in Shape,* trans. Paul M. Douglas (West Brattleboro, Vt.: Marcel Moyse, 1974), p. 5.
2. Normàn C. Chapman, "The Manner and Practice of Producing Vibrato on the Woodwind Instruments: A Survey of the Solo-Chair Players of 14 Major American Symphony Orchestras" (Ed.D. diss., Columbia University, 1953), pp. 23–24.
3. Sol Babitz, "The problem of vibrato teaching," *International Musician* 52 (March 1954): 28–29; quoted in Lawrence Taylor, "The Vibrato," *The Instrumentalist* 11 (Nov. 1956): 35.
4. Robert Sprenkle, "Wind Instrument Vibrato," *Symphony* (Feb. 1951), p. 9.
5. William Kincaid and Claire Polin, *The Advanced Flutist: a guide to multiple tonguing, vibrato, and sensitive fingering* (Bryn Mawr, Pa.: Elkan-Vogel, 1975), p. 60.
6. Hans-Martin Linde, *The Recorder Player's Handbook,* trans. James C. Haden (New York: Schott, 1974), p. 28.
7. Jacques Hotteterre le Romain, *Principles of the Flute Recorder and Oboe,* trans. and ed. David Lasocki (New York: Praeger Publishers, 1968), pp. 30–33.
8. Johann Joachim Quantz, *On Playing the Flute,* trans. Edward R. Reilly (London: Faber and Faber, 1966), pp. 165-66.

9. Catherine Smith, "Special Expressive Characteristics of the Pre-Boehm Transverse Flute," *Woodwind World, Brass and Percussion* 14, no. 4 (1975): 31.
10. W. N. James, *A Word or Two on the Flute* (Edinburgh: Charles Smith & Co.; London: Cocks & Co., 1826), p. 100.
11. C[harles] Nicholson, *A School for the Flute* (New York: Firth & Hall, ca. 1830), p. 71.
12. V. Coche, *Méthode pour servir à l'enseignement de la nouvelle Flûte Inventée par Gordon, modifiée par Boehm et perfectionée par V. Coche et Buffet Jne.* (Paris: Schonenberger, 1838), p. 82.
13. Richard Carte, *A Complete Course of Instructions for the Boehm Flute* (London: Rudall, Carte & Co., ca. 1880), p. 23.
14. Ibid., p. 24.
15. John Clinton, *A School or Practical Instruction Book for the Boehm Flute* (London: Cramer, Beale & Co. and Rudall & Rose, ca. 1846), p. 72.
16. J. Harrington Young, *Modern Method for Students of the Flute* (Boston: White-Smith Music Publishing Co., 1892), p. 28.
17. Max Rostal, "Studies in interpretation and style," *Canon* 8, no. 10 (1955): 397–98.
18. Paul Taffanel and Philippe Gaubert, *Méthode Complète de la Flûte* (Paris: Alphonse Leduc, 1923), vol. 2, p. 186.
19. Paul Taffanel and Louis Fleury, "La Flûte," *Encyclopédie de la Musique et Dictionnaire du Conservatoire* (Paris: Delagrave, 1926), vol. 3, p. 1523.
20. Marcel Moyse, "The Unsolvable Problem: Considerations on Flute Vibrato," *Woodwind Magazine* 2, no. 7 (1950): 4.
21. Ibid.
22. Moyse, *How I Stayed in Shape*, p. 6.
23. Ibid., p. 7.
24. Ibid., p. 5.
25. "Marcel Moyse Profiled," *Woodwind Magazine* 2, no. 5 (1950): 12.
26. Henry Welsh, "Orchestral Reform," *Music and Letters* 12, no. 2 (1931): 25.
27. Georges Barrère, "Expression Unconfined," *Musical Quarterly* 30 (1944): 192.
28. Ibid., p. 193.
29. Patricia Joan Ahmad, "The Flute Professors of the Paris Conservatoire from Devienne to Taffanel, 1795–1908" (M.A. thesis, North Texas State University, 1980), p. 111.
30. Eleanor Lawrence, "Interview with Paige Brook," *National Flute Association Newsletter* 3, no. 1 (1977): 3.
31. Yehudi Menuhin and William Primrose, *Violin and Viola* (New York: Schirmer Books, 1976), p. 75.
32. Chapman, p. 100.

9
ARTICULATION

Articulation, says the dictionary definition, is "the art or process of speaking." The definition applies to flute playing just as it applies to verbal utterance. The components—breath, rhythm, accent, phrasing, termination, and silence—are the same, as are the tools—the respiratory system, lips, and tongue. The intellectual process, too, is similar, whether it forms verbal syllables into words, phrases, and sentences or joins musical notes into phrases, periods, and movements. Articulation is not just tonguing, as most wind players define it, but something much broader, and more akin to what we generally think of as phrasing. Articulation is a method of joining musical tones, determining their beginnings and ends and the relationships between individual notes and those around them. Therefore, while this chapter will discuss the usual, narrow definition of articulation—the physical motion of the tongue—remember that tonguing, like fingering, is only a tool, which must be informed by a broader musical logic.

The Bowing Analogy

Perhaps the easiest way to explain the musical application of flute articulation is to compare it with violin bowing. Indeed, this analogy is centuries old, having been used by Corrette (about 1735), Quantz (1752), and Devienne (about 1792), among others. One of the advantages of this method is that violin bowing can be seen, whereas flute tonguing cannot. The stringed instrument comparison is particularly apt if one considers articulation to include not just the initial attack, but also the length of the stroke or note group.

Using a wide variety of tongue strokes, the flutist can do almost everything the violinist can do: vary the attack, the length of the stroke, and the inflection. The only violin techniques that are almost impossible on the flute are the nearly infinite legato—though circular breathing can provide a reasonable facsimile in certain cases (see chapter 6, "Breathing")—and pizzicato, which one can approximate by combining a tongued attack with a key slap.

The bowing analogy equates the tongue with the bow arm, and for purposes of simplicity, this discussion will do so too. It is important to keep in mind that the diaphragm and abdominal muscles must support each articulation in some way, either actively or passively; like the tongue, these muscles are in constant motion. For staccatos and marcatos, the muscles can provide an additional punch to the airstream; for détachés, a medium-strength impetus; for lourés, less; for sustained notes they lend constant, uninterrupted suppport to the airstream; and for the light spiccato, they emit a sustained and supported pulse.

Remember that the mental concept is crucial to the bowing analogy, not the names of the strokes. The important elements to consider are the strength and nature of the attack and the length of the note or stroke.

Single-Tonguing

Single-tonguing is most common and is used by flutists in music of slow to medium-fast tempo. Though the technique is governed by a certain number of fairly universal rules, it is flexible and allows for many variations.

Most commonly, single-tonguing consists of initiating a tone with a *T* sound, either *TE, TU, TA*, or even *TI*. It is done, quite simply, by pulling the tongue away from the back of the teeth, just at the point where the tip of the tongue touches the roof of the mouth when the mouth is shut. The closer the tongue is to the front of the mouth, the lighter and more agile the articulation.

The tongue is the only part of the mouth that should move. John Krell says, "Never nibble the articulations with the jaw or lips." To do so may alter the quality of the sound, disturb the placement of the airstream, upset the focus of the tone, and most of all, will probably slow down your playing speed. Krell sums up, "Tongue like a ventriloquist, without moving the lips."[1]

The shortest and most pointed version of single-tonguing is *staccato*. It is a carefully prepared articulation: the actual attack is preceded by the valve-like action of the tongue, which prevents the airstream from entering the instrument. At the beginning of the staccato passage, the air is then released by an equally sharp withdrawal of the tongue from the rear portion (the palatal side) of the teeth. Staccato tonguing is done with the farthest tip of the tongue; in a very rapid passage, using just the tip permits the withdrawal of the tip to be minimal, so that it has to move the shortest possible distance. The violin equivalents include *sautillé* or *spiccato* (a rapid, detached stroke, in which the bow bounces off the string) or the regular *staccato*. All are notated with a dot above or below the notehead (♩̣ ♩̇).

Normal, everyday single-tonguing, as described above, is identical to staccato except for the omission of the initial valve action. It is analogous to the violin *détaché*, which allots one note per bow stroke and has no special notation.

A close relative of normal single-tonguing is mezzo-staccato single-tonguing or the "legato slur," articulated with the syllable *DU, DA, DE*, or *DI*.

Analogous to the violin *louré*, it is notated by a combination of dot and slur. The tip of the tongue is softer and more rounded, and strikes farther back in the mouth. For this reason, it is sometimes known as dorsal or top tonguing. A similar articulation is *portato*, notated with a line above or below the note (𝅘𝅥 𝅘𝅥), which indicates not only a *D* attack but also that each note should be sustained for its full value.

Next in the hierarchy of sharpness is pharyngeal tonguing, or back tonguing, which uses the dorsal or upper middle portion of the tongue. Its initial consonant is *K* or *G*. (This tongue stroke also serves as the auxiliary portion of double- and triple-tonguing.) It is the softest, gentlest form of single-tonguing.

Martellato tonguing, analogous to the violin *martellé* (literal translation: hammered), is a sharp, biting staccato; the embouchure should be adjusted as if you were playing a fifth to an octave lower. It is notated with arrow heads (𝅘𝅥𝅮𝅘𝅥𝅮) or a combination of dots and accents (𝅘𝅥𝅮𝅘𝅥𝅮). Or, when notated like *portato*, with lines above or below the notes, it signifies that the notes should be hammered and then held for their full value.

The pearled staccato or *perlé* presets the tongue for the next note more rapidly than usual, resulting in silence between the notes of the staccato passage. It is initiated with a *T* sound, but closer to the biting edge of the teeth than usual; that is, farther forward in the mouth. Imagine the tongue being pointed.

Normal and mezzo-staccato tonguing may be combined in a *TU-DU* (or *TA-DA* or *TE-DE* or *TI-DI*) alternation, which is roughly equivalent to an obscure violin stroke known as Viotti bowing. The signal for its use is most often the combination of a slur and staccato dots; in his 1827 method, Drouet called this combination stroke "slurred staccato." After much experimentation, he came up with the word *territory* as the best articulation, though he later modified the pronunciation to *TETH-THI-TO-DY*. For this bounced tongue stroke, hit the *T* with a great deal of energy and force, and then bounce back for the gentler *D*. For an exceptionally forceful fortepiano (*fp*), the tongue may emerge beyond the edge of the teeth. This may be useful, for instance, in the first movement of Beethoven's Seventh Symphony:

Remember that *staccato*, indicated by a dot above or below the note, does not necessarily mean that the composer wants the note played as short as possible. All notation—rhythmic, dynamic, or ornamental—must be evaluated in context. Thus the duration of the note is relative to the speed of the music. In a molto allegro, a staccato note should indeed be brief, perhaps as short as one half its written length. But in an adagio, it indicates only a slight space between the notes.

Double-Tonguing

Double-tonguing seems such a natural, logical, and altogether useful part of modern flute technique that it is difficult to realize that it has historically been the subject of some truly creative musical invective. For instance, W. N. James, writing in 1826, labeled double-tonguing "Babylonish gabble," "one of the most disagreeable noises which the ear is subject to. It is, in fact, a complete jumble of notes, which have neither meaning, articulation, nor expression."[2] Elsewhere in his essay, James branded double-tonguing "a trick of execution" and "a quackery." But he did make several useful points: if not articulated cleanly, double-tonguing can indeed obscure the musical structure of a composition. The second, weaker syllable of the articulation, James pointed out, is prone to be "ill defined and obscure."[3]

Nevertheless, the pragmatic wave of the future was indicated by Charles Nicholson in his *School for the Flute*, published about 1830:

> The difference in difficulty between the single and double tonguing, is something like a person trying to make a shake on the piano-forte with one finger instead of two. Double tonguing is an articulation which has had its full share of abuse and condemnation, but like other innovations on the 'good old style of fluteplaying,' it has carried conviction by its utility.[4]

Today, the most accepted "pronunciation" of double-tonguing uses the syllables *TE-KE* or *TUH-KUH*, with *DUH-GUH* a close third and a frequent alternative in passages where mezzo-staccato or louré articulation is indicated. Other possibilities, though weaker, are *TU-RU*, *TA-KA*, *TOO-KOO*, *DA-GA*, *DOO-GOO*, and *TOO-TLE*. *TOO-TLE* is the weakest of the lot, because the indistinctness of the second syllable prevents the escape of air, rather than propelling it as the initial syllable should. In the nineteenth century, these preferences were highly nationalistic in nature, as contemporary treatises demonstrate.

A variation of double-tonguing is the *TE-RE* articulation, used not for speed but for phrasing purposes. It simulates the down- and up-bows of the violin, used for accented and unaccented notes, respectively.

Triple-Tonguing

Triple-tonguing is based on the same fundamental principle as double-tonguing—the alternation of tonguing with a glottal throat stop. Only the rhythmic pattern of alternations differs; in triple meter, the articulation becomes *TA-KA-TA, TI-KI-TI, TEH-KEH-TEH, TOO-KOO-TOO,* or *DOO-GOO-DOO*. It is somewhat more difficult than double-tonguing to accomplish smoothly, because the tongued notes outnumber the gutterals by a two-to-one margin. Therefore, an extra measure of care must be taken not to swallow the middle syllable.

Flutter-Tonguing

Flutter-tonguing is the newest addition to the flutist's articulatory repertoire, though it may be considered as much a timbral effect as an articulation. It goes by many names: *Flatterzunge, coupe de lange roulé, en roulant la langue, tremolo dental, tremolo avec la langue, tremolo roulé, vibrato linguale, vibrando, colpo di lingua, frulato, frullante, rullato,* and even plain *tremolo.* It was first used by Richard Strauss in *Don Quixote* (1896–97). Unlike double- and triple-tonguing, which are used in place of single-tonguing as necessitated by the speed of the music and at the discretion of the performer, flutter-tonguing is a notated articulation, expressed in any number of ways:

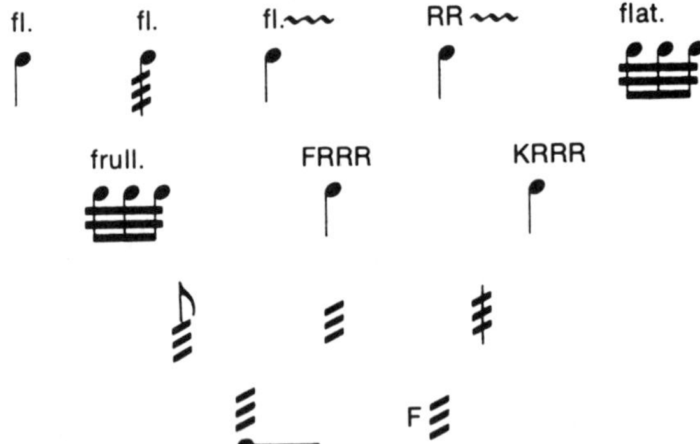

There are two ways of executing flutter-tonguing. The preferred method is to roll the tip of the tongue against the roof of the mouth (the hard palate), as in the sound *B-R-R-R*, creating a rapid tremolo. This technique generally works best with high air pressure in loud or high passages. The alternative is a gutteral *R*—essentially a gargling action—achieved by vibration of the uvula against the back of the throat. Though not technically a flutter, this method is often more comfortable and effective with low air pressure in soft passages. For the many players who are unable to produce a true flutter, this method is invaluable.

Tongueless Attack

The tongueless or breath attack should be used in special instances where the music indicates great subtlety of approach. English flutist William Bennett suggests such an attack, for instance, for the openings of Debussy's *L'après-midi d'une faune* and the *Minuet* from Bizet's *L'Arlésienne.*

The specific articulation that Bennett uses is the "tongue out" technique he learned from Geoffrey Gilbert: he begins the phrase with his tongue outside his mouth, then withdraws it and blows into the flute, using the syllable AW. The same articulation can be used, he suggests, to create brief silences between notes in appropriate passages, much as a violinist lifts the bow off the string in a *martellé* or *sautillé* stroke.

Legato

We cannot leave the subject of articulation without touching on legato. In part, it is a simple term that merely denotes slurring, the absence of tonguing. But legato is something more; it is, as Georges Laurent said, "the smoothest possible passing from one note to another."[5] It must be as cleanly articulated as single-, double-, or triple-tonguing, but it must be accomplished with one less tool—the tongue. In other words, smoothness and continuity of sound must be achieved by a combination of continuous breath and support and flexible embouchure synchronized with finger activity.

Note Endings

Given all the variety possible for starting notes, and all the possibilities for sustaining and coloring them after that (see chapter 7, "Tone"), players often ignore the third ingredient of the phrase—the ending. In modern playing, this is theoretically quite simple, because the basic rule is that the end of any articulation—whether a single syllable or a group of them—must be kept open. In other words, a single-tongued passage should consist of a series of *TU*s, not *TUT*s, as in *TU-TU-TU-TU*, so that there is a distinction made between each note in the pattern. The same is true, in a larger sense, for phrase endings. The tone should not be stopped by either the tongue or the lips, but by an abrupt or gradual cessation of breath, as controlled by the diaphragm. The only exception is that in particularly subtle or sensitive releases, the lips may assist in "feathering off" the tone.

For early music, played on original instruments, different rules may apply. For such situations, consult the original treatises or such modern compilations as Betty Bang Mather's *Interpretation of French Music from 1675 to 1775 for Woodwind and Other Performers*.

Practice

The first stop in practicing any technique—tone, fingering, or articulation—is to isolate it. For tonguing, that means that at first you should vary only the tonguing, keeping fingering and tone color constant. Next add melodic complications within a small range (requiring no substantive change of embouchure). Then vary both articulation and register, first in conjunct (scalar) motion, and then with progressively larger intervals.

Begin in the middle register. Play a single note with single-tonguing. When you can do so evenly and cleanly, gradually expand the range of notes in scale patterns or simple melodies. Move toward the upper register first, then to the bottom of the compass. Next, play octave jumps with no change of fingering in the first and second octaves; this will help you combine tongue and lips. Then, you are ready to combine more complicated melodic patterns, changes of register, and tonguing. The same procedure applies to double-, triple-, and flutter-tonguing and to legato practice. It will solve the three basic problems of articulation: clarity, speed, and tone.

For double- and triple-tonguing, the gutteral syllable (*K* or *G*) usually "limps" because the consonant is softer than *T* or *D*. So reverse the syllables in exercises; play *K-T-K-T* instead of *T-K-T-K*, *G-D-G-D* instead of *D-G-D-G*. Pianist Dinu Lipatti once said that a good musician should concentrate on the weak beats; the strong ones can look after themselves.[6]

Practice all articulation exercises with a metronome. It will help you achieve evenness of execution and will also help you monitor your progress in gaining speed. If your tongue becomes fatigued during the practice session, as it should if you're working hard, switch to long-tone and legato exercises and exercise your lips while your tongue rests.

For one final exercise, you don't even need the flute, which makes the exercise portable. Practice saying the words *kitty* and *doggy*. To avoid strange looks if you're not a pet owner, try *tick-tock, ticket-ticket,* or *giddy-giddy*. Try to keep the enunciation even, and gradually increase your speed.

Notes

1. John Krell, *Kincaidiana* (Culver City, Calif.: Trio Associates, 1973), p. 19.
2. W. N. James, *A Word or Two on the Flute* (Edinburgh: Charles Smith & Co.; London: Cocks & Co., 1826), pp. 122–23.
3. Ibid., pp. 121–22.
4. C[harles] Nicholson, *A School for the Flute* (New York: Firth & Hall, ca. 1830), p. 65.
5. James Collis, "Playing Legato on Flute" [interview with Georges Laurent], *Symphony* 6, no. 2 (1952): 11.
6. Eva and Paul Badura-Skoda, *Interpreting Mozart on the Keyboard*, trans. Leo Black (London: Barrie and Rockliff, 1962), p. 164.

10

TECHNIQUE

Technique is the control and coordination of all the muscular actions that flute playing comprises. While tone is the first prerequisite for good flute playing, technique, as the vehicle of melodic motion, is also of great importance. Louis Moyse sums this up well: "As a teacher, my main concern is to bring the adequate tools and devices to my pupils, namely—technique. One can have technique without music (all too often, unfortunately), but one cannot express the music without technique."[1] Keeping in mind Moyse's caveat regarding over-emphasis on technique—because it is a means to an end, not an end in itself—let's examine the elements that make up the flutist's technique.

Position

Technique begins with a simple premise: the flute must be positioned so that the appropriate parts of the player's body can control it with maximum efficiency. This concept involves total body posture.

The shoulders and back should be straight; slumping restricts the capacity of the abdomen to expand to take in air. The elbows should be held close to the body, only about six inches away. This is far enough out so that the air flow is not restricted but close enough so that the arm muscles are not extended uncomfortably and the fingers can be positioned properly.

The angle of the flute should be parallel to that of the lips. The embouchure or lip plate of the flute is placed against the chin, with the embouchure hole slightly below the fleshy part of the lips. The lower lip should cover about a quarter of the hole. Theoretically, the head should be straight, that is, with lips parallel to the floor. However, many flutists prefer a slight downward tilt to the right. There is nothing wrong with this position, as long as the axis of the flute is parallel to the lips. However, the head should not lean forward or down. The tilted position has become a habit for many band and orchestra players for a very practical reason—the lack of space between players in the ensemble.

When sitting, the player should never rest the right elbow on the hip, because such a position would place the flute at an extreme downward slant. If one took the converse of the parallel-flute-and-lips rule, the chin would have to point down so sharply that the throat, not to mention the right-hand fingers, would be constricted. The chin should always be slightly forward in order to keep the throat open. Another caveat for seated flutists: both feet should remain on the floor at all times. Never cross your legs. The proper position enhances air flow and reduces muscular tension.

The flute is balanced by a lever system in which there are three points of contact with the body: the right thumb, the right pinky on the D♯ key, and the left index finger. Together, these three points bear the full weight of the instrument, freeing the remaining fingers to execute the music.

On the left hand, the third joint (phalanx) of the index finger, which is the joint closest to the palm, acts as a fulcrum between the chin and the right thumb. The base of the index finger (between the knuckle and the first joint) holds the flute securely even when the right pinky is not holding down the D♯ key. The thumb should be outstretched and slightly curved so that its ball rests lightly on the B-natural lever, but the thumb should not support the weight of the flute. Doing so would immobilize the thumb and prevent it from moving between the B and B♭ levers. The wrist should be squarely under the flute, at a right angle to the instrument. The left index finger makes contact with the flute tube at the base of the finger and half way between the C♯ hole and the C touchplate. The other fingers will align logically with the A, G, and G♯ keys. Thus the left hand functions not as a straight extension of the forearm, but should be at approximately a 120° angle to it.

On the right hand, the first, second, and third fingers are placed on the F, E, and D keys, respectively. The little finger, on the D♯ lever, and the thumb, under the body of the flute, support the weight of the instrument. Of these two fingers, the thumb should carry most of the weight since it is the only nonplaying finger. The thumb should be held at a right angle to the flute, directly underneath the first finger. The right hand is at a 135° angle to the forearm, with the knuckles coming out level with the flute. The wrist should be neither straight, which would require raising the right elbow uncomfortably high, nor at a right angle to the forearm, which would cramp the fingers. The ball of the thumb should not curve under the flute tube, but should remain on the side of the tube closest to the player's body, pushing ever so slightly against the tube. In this way, the light pressure of left index finger and right thumb balance each other and maintain the flute in its proper playing position.

On both hands, the fingers should curve over the keys gently. The palms should be elevated sufficiently so that the fingers are clear of the rods. The fingers should align directly and evenly over their respective key cups, with the fingers over the center of the keys. On the French (open-hole) model, the perforated keys force proper fingertip placement. The fleshy part of the third joint, not the fingertips, should touch the keys for more secure control, and

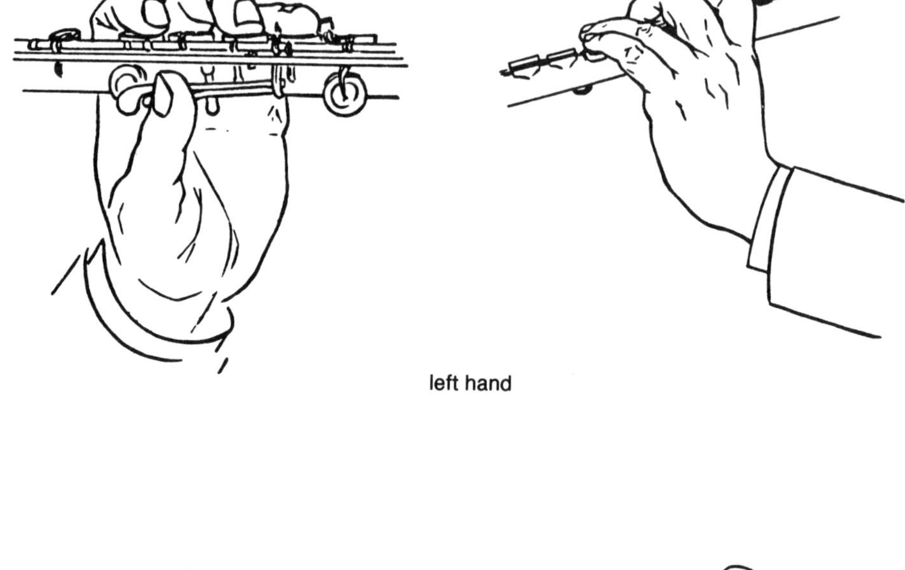

left hand

right hand

in the case of open holes, coverage. The idea is to afford the fingers maximum flexibility and speed while simultaneously enabling the flute's mechanism to function without hindrance by the player's body.

Practice

Practice is necessary to acquire the building blocks of musicianship. Assuming the player has a knowledge of the basic fingerings from c^1 to c^4 (and preferably a bit higher), the next building layer is mastery of diatonic and chromatic scales. Then the student moves on to progressive stages of finger practice: scales, arpeggios, intervals, fingering exercises, and études combining various technical difficulties. Only then is the student prepared to advance to music literature.

A number of conditions not specific to the flute are prerequisites for effective practice. First, the student should find a private practice room, an area free not only of distractions but also of listeners who may make the player self-conscious about errors and repetition. It should have good light and ventilation. The room's acoustics are crucial: too dull or dead a room will be discouraging, and will tend to make the player force the sound. Conversely, too "live" or bright a room will impart a false sense of projection and tone. So, one should avoid both bare rooms and overupholstered or heavily carpeted ones.

The practice room should be equipped with a music stand and chair. Standing during a long session is unnecessarily taxing, and seated practice is good preparation for ensemble work. Other necessary equipment includes a mirror, for checking hand and embouchure position; a tuning fork or electronic tuning device; a metronome; and a pencil.

It is helpful to develop a practice routine, an "order of service" that is observed at least once daily. If you have time for more than one session a day, you may want to use this routine only for the first one of the day, using the others to work on particular problems or pieces. Remember that a musician's practice is not unlike an athlete's: its aim is to develop muscular skills and agility. It is first and foremost a physical learning process, and, admittedly, not necessarily an intellectual challenge. In its basic stages practice is not a creative process, but practice will give you the tools to be creative. It will be most effective—and most rewarding—to concentrate on one small area at any given time. Except when sight-reading, don't gloss over mistakes: tackle them one by one, in isolation, before moving on. Playing through is not practicing.

A good practice routine has four parts:

Warm-up: Begin with long tones, starting in the middle register and working toward the extremes on both ends. This simple exercise will help you develop a straight, even, firm tone without vibrato. As you move from one note to the next, try to match the tone quality of the previous note as closely as possible. To develop breath capacity, play each note with the metronome set at ♩ = 60, and aim to increase your sustaining capacity on a periodic basis.

For tone quality, play a matching tone exercise:

Then do the same ascending:

As with the long tones with which you began, match the tone quality of each note to that of its predecessor. This exercise should help you achieve continuity and homogeneity of tone quality throughout the flute's compass.

The Building Blocks: Scales, Arpeggios, and Intervals: Starting slowly, play all the scales, from C moving chromatically up to B, both diatonically (in major and in both minor modes) and chromatically, and in all octaves. For instance, for the key of C, play:

C major scale

C minor - melodic scale

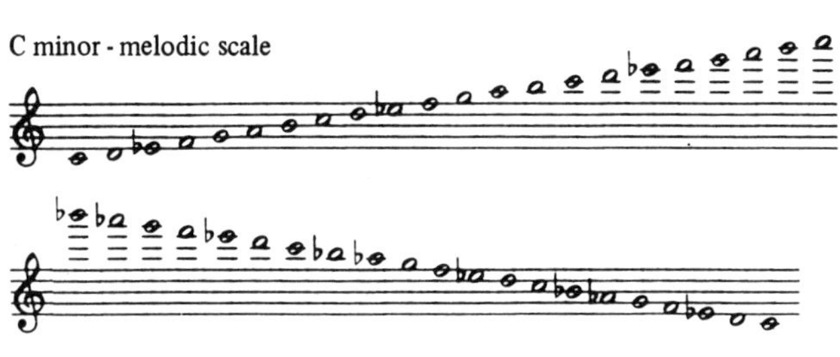

C minor - harmonic scale

C chromatic scale

Practice with the metronome to achieve evenness. Next, do the major and minor arpeggios (broken chords) in all keys, throughout the range. In C, these are:

C major arpeggio

C minor arpeggio

Again, use the metronome to maintain evenness and gradually to increase your speed.

Interval exercises are similar to the matching tone exercise described above. Actually, the matching tone exercise is the simplest interval exercise, using minor seconds. Expand the exercise half-step by half-step. Beginning on a given note, such as a[1], gradually expand the intervals:

Do the same with different starting notes throughout the range. Do the same both ascending and descending.

Another exercise isolates each type of interval—minor third, major third, major fifth, and so on. For example, begin on middle C, and move chromatically up the register playing a sequence of major thirds:

Do the same exercise descending. Vary the articulations on all of these patterns. Slurring will give you the capacity to play any interval *legato* and to make rapid changes of register; tonguing will give you good practice in coordinating your tongue with the movements of the lips necessary to change registers. And of course, eventually you should play the exercises with compound articulations, or mixtures of slurring and tonguing. Varying the articulation will also help relieve the monotony of these very important but admittedly not very "musical" drills. Try to instill them with a sense of style, of phrasing, as if they were real pieces of music and not just exercises.

It is an excellent idea to start with written-out scales, arpeggios, and interval patterns in order to learn them, but as soon as possible, you should perform all of these exercises from memory so that you develop both muscular and intellectual memory of the melodic and harmonic patterns.

To supplement these very basic technical drills, there are a number of excellent technical studies that combine scales, arpeggios, and intervals in progressively more challenging combinations. Some of the best are Taffanel and Gaubert's *17 Daily Exercises*, Marcel Moyse's *Exercices Journaliers (Daily Exercises)*, and Georges Barrère's *The Flutist's Formulae*. Full citations are found in section E of the Repertoire Catalog.

A variation on the above routine—particularly if practice time is limited—is to assign yourself several keys per day, on a regular schedule. Do all the exercises, matching tones, scales, arpeggios, expanding intervals, and sequential intervals in that day's keys or beginning on that day's tonic (starting) notes.

Alternatively, pick particular intervals on which to concentrate in each practice session, and do them in all keys. For instance, on Day One play scales, thirds and fifths; on Day Two, work on fourths, sixths, and octaves. And so on. . . .

You may work on any other combination of exercises you make up, as long as you tackle the full range of keys and registers on a regular schedule. Any system that helps you maintain your concentration and exercise your fingers comprehensively is a good system.

Louis Moyse provides a persuasive and logical argument for this methodical practice routine:

> One should not practice technique only when a difficult section is found in a piece, but to practice scales, arpeggios, any kind of exercises *in advance*, in order to be able to face any difficulties in any pieces. In fact, I do believe that if one would 'store' enough technique in advance, most of the pieces written since the Renaissance period to the beginning of the 20th century could and should almost be played at sight.[2]

Etudes: Having covered scales and intervals and combined them into daily technical exercises, it is time to go a step further. Etudes or studies are longer, more musical versions of technical exercises. They combine a number of technical challenges while setting them in a musical context. Some etudes are designed primarily to attack one technical problem; others concentrate on several areas. Some of the best are by Andersen, Berbiguier, Boehm, and Devienne; there is an extensive list in the Repertoire Catalog.

In any and all of these etudes, play through the entire piece once, slowly. Make a mental note of problem areas; then go back and work on those difficulties individually, reducing each problem to its smallest unit of difficulty—even to two notes, if necessary. Then gradually expand the length of the surrounding phrase on both sides, working out from the nucleus until you can play the particular passage in the context of the extrance and exit notes. Only then should you proceed to the next difficult passage.

Etudes are distinguished from pure exercises by their musical qualities. Once you have tackled the purely technical challenges, and, with the aid of the metronome, have mastered the etude at a reasonable (though not necessarily the final) speed, it is time to consider the musical values. What does the tempo marking tell you about the piece? Is it a dance form, such as a minuet? What does the articulation tell you about its character?

No matter how boring or prosaic an etude may seem on the surface, you should always try to make it sound like a piece of music. The great Paris Conservatoire professor Henri Altès made this point more than a century ago: "An exercise must always be played through as though it belonged to a piece of music with a definite style to it. Conversely, to play indifferently is a waste of time and tires one to no purpose."[3]

Another kind of etude is that designed as much for imbuing technique with the kind of style and expression to which Altès referred as for technical practice. Good examples are Betty Bang Mather's *30 Virtuosic Selections in the Galant Style*, Peter Lindpaintner's *50 Etudes*, Sigfrid Karg-Elert's *30 Caprices*, and Paul Rynearson's *11 Contemporary Flute Etudes*. Again, see the Repertoire Catalog.

A special subset of the style etude is the orchestral excerpt, of which there are many anthologies in print. Orchestral excerpts not only familiarize the student with specific symphonic literature, but also provide more general stylistic orientation.

Solos: Once you've made it through the routine of long tones, scales, arpeggios, intervals, technical exercises, and style etudes, you are ready to tackle the solo literature. If you study with a private teacher, he or she can help you choose appropriate pieces. If you're on your own, there are some published sources that will help you find pieces at an appropriate technical level. The most comprehensive and readily available list is James Pellerite's *A Handbook of Literature for the Flute*, third edition (1978). State music educators' lists, such as that of the New York State School Music Association (NYSSMA), contain graded lists of pieces eligible for use in all-county and all-state auditions. There are similar publications in many other states.

You will not be surprised to read that the method of studying the solo literature is not unlike the method for learning etudes: a slow read-through, followed by analysis and correction of technical difficulties, followed by style analysis and more practice. In isolating technical problems, it is helpful to develop your own exercises, perhaps even writing them out. An excellent example of this procedure is Karl Lenski's *18 Cells for Flute*. What Lenski does is to extract typical technical problems from various works of J. S. Bach, C. P. E. Bach, Mozart, Schubert, and Debussy, and build etudes around them. For instance:

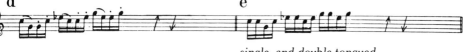

And Lenski suggests taking the principle of isolation one step further: practice the troublesome passages not only as written, but also transposed into other registers and keys and with varied articulations.

Fingering

One of the great advantages of the Boehm system flute, it would seem, is that the fingering is standardized and logical—and so it is, in comparison with the many different kinds of fingering systems that existed during the nineteenth century. But that does not mean that there is only one way to play any given note. It is safe to say that there is one *basic* fingering for each note (with the exception of B♭, which has three basic fingerings), but there are quite a few alternatives available when particular technical situations warrant. These alternative fingerings fall into four categories: those that use trill fingerings in nontrill situations, those that use nonstandard combinations of regular keys, those that use the perforations of the open-holed flute, and harmonics.

The basic fingering chart for the Boehm flute with closed G♯ key, the instrument in almost universal use today, is found in Appendix A. You may also find it useful to refer to James Pellerite's *A Modern Guide to Fingerings for the Flute*, second edition (1972), which gives a number of alternate and multiphonic fingerings.

Alternate fingerings go by many names, from the misnomer "fake fingerings," to the innocuous "special fingerings," to "altered fingerings," which somehow seem reminiscent of a veterinary procedure, to the evocative, and most accurate, "sensitive fingerings." The last was coined by none other than William Kincaid, a master of this art. It derives from the ancient and honorable term *sensible* used in generations of French instruction books. As the term implies, sensitive fingerings must be used judiciously, in the context of the music; moreover, the double meaning of *sensible* implies that the player must be sensitive to the subtleties of each fingering and must compensate appropriately for any inherent defects in intonation, dynamics, or tone quality.

Alternate or sensitive fingerings must be used sparingly. Think of them as a last resort; otherwise, they may not only harm the quality of your tone but may also make your fingers lazy in regular fingering combinations. Their uses are very specific; as Kincaid put it, "to facilitate playing 'sloppy' combinations, or 'unplayable' high, rapid, but smooth phrases, or repeated-note passages which 'click' in normal fingering."[4] In such repeated-note passages, begin with the regular fingering; change to the sensitive fingering only when the passage becomes rapid enough to make the switch inconspicuous.

Alternate Fingerings Using Trill Fingerings for Full-Length Notes: Often, the trill fingering for the auxiliary note is not the most acoustically perfect one; it may lack strength or be defective in intonation. However, in technical passages where the speed is so great that it might as well be a trill, there is no reason not to use the trill fingering. For example, in this passage from Wolf-Ferrari's *Jewels of the Madonna*, use the B♭ side key for the right index finger:

Alternate Fingerings Using Nonstandard Fingerings: The player must be aware of the inherent weaknesses of these fingerings and must be prepared to compensate for them. Often, they will involve leaving extra keys covered at least two holes below the sounding tone hole, in order to make transitions easier. For instance, leaving the right-hand fingers down for C♯ in the second and third octaves will lower its pitch to make it better in tune with its neighbors. Or, alternate fingerings may omit one of the usual keys for a note. For instance, in this passage from the Tchaikovsky Fourth Symphony, not using the D♯ lever will permit e^3 to sound more easily:

In Bach's *Coffee Cantata*, similarly, again omit the D♯ lever for E. Also, use the right middle finger, rather than the third finger, for the high F♯:

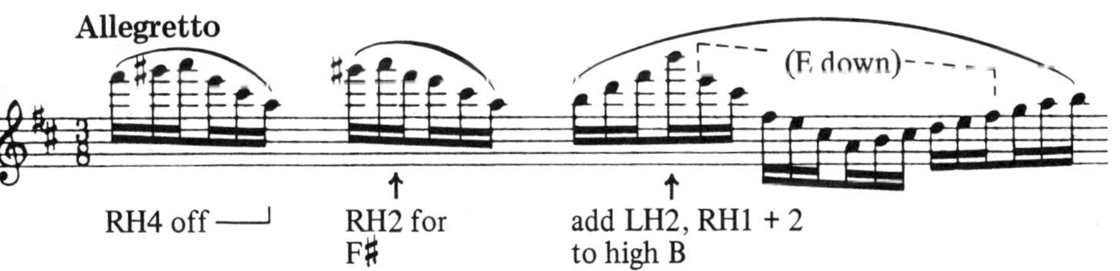

Alternate Fingerings Using the French Model (Open-Holed) Flute: This technique is the descendant of what is a necessity on the keyless recorder: half-holing. It takes two forms on the modern French model flute: depressing the rim of the key while leaving the perforation uncovered, or covering only the upper half of the hole with the finger. For example, in the Mozart D Major Concerto, K. 314, depressing only the rim of the G key will enhance an unobtrusive entrance:

In the Andante from the Molique Concerto in D Minor, the high F is apt to be flat. However, by using the regular fingering but "leaking" or slightly uncovering the F key's hole, the pitch will rise.

Harmonics

Harmonic fingerings come in two varieties. Covert harmonics, like sensitive fingerings, facilitate tricky upper-register fingerings. They are not meant to be noticed, merely to get the flutist out of technical corners. Overt harmonics, in contrast, *are* meant to be noticed. They are employed intentionally to change the timbre for a specific expressive or compositional purpose.

Simply defined, harmonics are the exploitation (in the positive sense) of the overtone or harmonic series. Recall from chapter 7, "Tone," what this looks like:

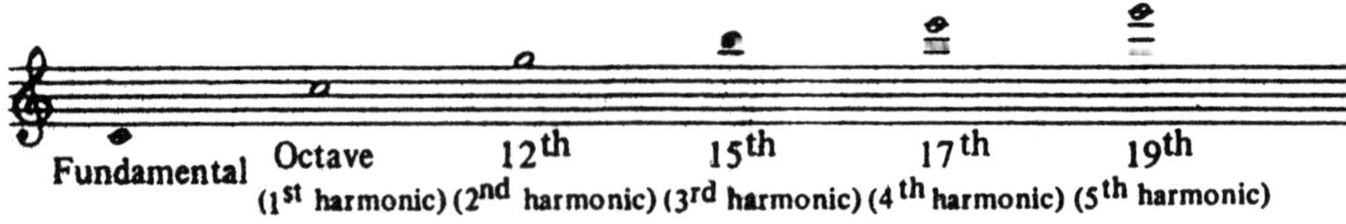

On brass instruments, which have only three valves, regular fingerings require the lip and breath pressure to determine the correct component of the overtone series for every note. On woodwinds, on the other hand, harmonic fingerings are in most cases discretionary.

Covert harmonics, like other sensitive fingerings, are designed to facilitate awkward upper-register technical passages. Indeed, they have been a regular trick of the trade since before Boehm. The great English virtuoso Charles Nicholson was an eloquent advocate of harmonics. Though he played an old-system flute, not a Boehm, his philosophy still holds: the study of harmonics gives flexibility to the lips and enhances technical capability in rapid melodic passages.

Nicholson's student W. N. James made the case for covert harmonics even more strongly in an 1826 essay:

> ... the immense command which a knowledge of them gives you over the instrument is almost incredible. Passages, to perform which, smoothly and in tune, would, without them, be extremely difficult, or, if not impossible, are, by the help of harmonics, rendered not only easy and flexible, but as delicate and liquid as the finest bowing of the violin.[5]

Natural or simple harmonics are produced by overblowing the notes from b to d^2♯. Except for the first harmonics of the notes from e^1 to c^2♯ (the regular fingerings for e^2 to c^3♯), all the octave harmonics will sound slightly flat. This is because only the lowest note of the instrument is perfectly vented; for all other notes, the partials are flattened in relation to the fundamental.

The following chart illustrates the range of harmonics available on the flute. The lower (whole) notes are the fundamental (fingered) notes; the upper, dark notes are the available harmonics.

Perhaps the first published instructions for harmonics on the Boehm flute were contained in John Clinton's *Essay on the Boehm Flute* (about 1843–46). One of his examples is the flute solo from Rossini's Overture to *La Gazza*

Ladra. Here, the smaller, lower notes are the fingered notes; the upper, full-size notes are the pitches that are heard.

Let me reiterate that overt harmonics are intended to be heard. They come in two varieties: unwritten and written. Unwritten overt harmonics were devised by flutists themselves, chief among them Nicholson, as a means of varying tone color. In other words, they are a category of sensitive fingering in its literal sense: a choice based on sensitivity to the tonal and expressive context. For instance, in Ibert's *Pièce* for unaccompanied flute, harmonic fingerings give the last measures an ethereal quality:

Written overt harmonics, in contrast, began as the province of the composer. Composers quickly caught on to what the virtuosi were doing and began writing harmonics into their scores as intentional, nondiscretionary special effects. Not surprisingly, the first composers to do so were flutists themselves. One of the earliest and most famous examples is from Franz Doppler's *Fantaisie Pastorale Hongroise:*

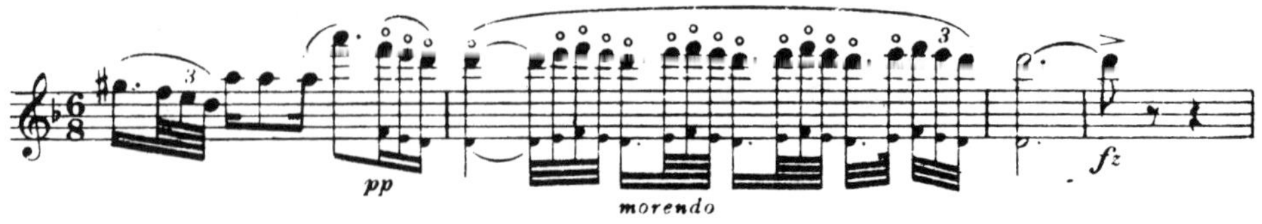

Maurice Ravel used the device in a typically impressionistic mannner in his children's opera *L'Enfant et les Sortilèges*; the flute harmonics imitate the toads in the garden:

Similarly, Ravel used harmonics in *Daphnis et Chloë*:

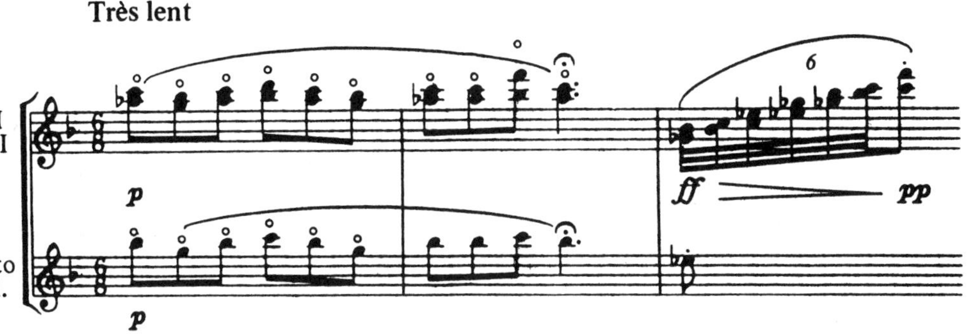

Observe, however, that while the composers notate their desire for harmonics with small circles above the relevant notes, they do not supply the fingered notes. For this reason, it is important to memorize the most-used harmonic fingerings. The most complete catalog of harmonics is Arthur Brooke's *Harmonic Fingerings for the Flute*. Pellerite's *A Modern Guide to Fingerings for the Flute* also contains a section on harmonics.

The B♭ Thumb Key

B♭, in the first two octaves, is the only note that has three "legal," absolutely standard, unquestionable fingerings. The flutist can use either the Briccialdi B♭ lever for the left thumb or the B-natural thumb key in combination with the F key or the B♭ side key (both of which are played by the right index finger). Technically, the B♭ thumb lever and the B♭ side key are the most correct acoustically, because they close only the B♭ hole. Playing B♭ with the thumb and the right index finger on its regular F key also closes two lower holes (F♯ and G). Because of the three intervening open holes, however, the effect is essentially unnoticeable.

The choice becomes a matter of convenience—each fingering has its useful aspects. In a chromatic scale or other passage in which B♭ is adjacent to B-natural, either of the right-hand fingerings is preferable because the thumb slide between B and B♭ is awkward and often uneven. Conversely, the B♭ thumb lever is preferable in passages where B♭ (or A♯) is adjacent to G♭ (F♯), G, or A♭ (G♯). A general principle, then, is to use the B♭ thumb key in the keys of F, D minor (harmonic scale), B♭, G minor, E♭, A♭, and F minor. The right-hand fingerings are preferable in sharp keys where A♯ is the leading tone to B-natural.

Three Fingering Tricks

The following tricks do not fully qualify for status as sensitive fingerings, but they are nonetheless extremely useful:

- To execute difficult slides with the right pinky—for example, from c^1♯ to d^1♯—moisten the finger with skin oil from the crease in your nose. However, be sure to wipe the mechanism especially carefully after playing.
- To smooth the transition from E to F♯ in all three octaves (using regular fingering), leave the middle finger down ever so slightly longer than the first on the way to F♯. When descending from F♯ to E, raise the middle finger a mite early.
- To make the lowest notes on the flute speak easily, slap down the right-hand fingers as you tongue the note. This procedure is particularly helpful for low C♯, C, and B.

Notes

1. Eleanor Lawrence, "Interview with Louis Moyse," *National Flute Association Newsletter* 2, no. 3 (1977): 8.
2. Ibid.
3. [Joseph-Henri] Altès, *Célèbre Méthode Complète de Flûte*, rev. F. Caratgé (Paris: Alphonse Leduc, 1956), vol. 2, p. 334.
4. William Kincaid and Claire Polin, *The Advanced Flutist: a guide to multiple tonguing, vibrato, and sensitive fingering* (Bryn Mawr, Pa.: Elkan-Vogel, 1975), p. 64.
5. W. N. James, *A Word or Two on the Flute* (Edinburgh: Charles Smith & Co.; London: Cocks & Co., 1826), p. 116.

11

STYLE

"Style," wrote Jean-Jacques Rousseau in his 1768 *Dictionary of Music,* "is the distinctive character of music in execution. This character varies much in respect to country, the taste of the inhabitants, and the genius of the authors. According to the matter, the place, the time, the subjects, and the expressions &c."[1] Today, with the internationalization of culture fostered by the technologies of communication and transportation, the elusive element of style maintains strong affinities with the time and place of its origin, though less so with the place of its performance. Style is, however, no less at the mercy of its interpreters.

It may seem overly simplistic or obvious to say that style is the human element in musical performance. It is the element of performance that lifts it above the merely mechanical, that in essence gives it life. In one respect, it is the most difficult aspect of musical performance, because past a certain point it cannot be quantified; it relies on taste. And to quote Rousseau again, "of all natural gifts, taste is that which is most felt and least explained. It would not be what it is, if it could be defined."[2]

The starting point for musical performance is the written score, but at best, the written music is only a linear road map; it may not indicate the topography. The closest equivalent is a play script. Just as the playwright usually does not give precise instructions for voice inflection, makeup, or gestures, the composer usually does not specify in the score the exact nature of accent or dynamics, the duration of rhythmic alterations such as rubato or ritard, or the timbre. Indeed, the composer may, especially in early music, provide no guidance whatever in these matters. It is a general rule that the more recent a composition, the more explicit it is likely to be with regard to details of performance practice.

Style takes audible form in what is generally described as interpretation. Interpretation represents the coauthorship of composer and performer, the performer's contribution being to discern the overall purpose and organization of the composition and to translate it into audible form for the benefit of an audience. To do so, the singer or instrumentalist calls on knowledge of musical context, both structural and historical; the performer then uses the muscular skills that comprise his or her technique to execute or re-create the intentions of the composer as suggested by the written score.

The problem is that the composer does not always tell us exactly what that intention was. The performer, therefore, is left to be a musical Sherlock Holmes. The clues are basically two: structural analysis and conversance with idiom. The first, using the theoretical techniques of basic musicianship, permits comprehension of overall structure or architecture and of smaller-scale phrasing. The second, attained through the study of music history and performance practice, provides an understanding of musical and historical context. I define performance practice broadly, to include all eras up to the present, whereas the traditional definition sets its concluding limit anywhere from the death of Bach to 1900.

Virtuosity and Interpretation

The term *virtuosity* implies a fruitful and judicious combination of charm—that is, style—and speed. C. P. E. Bach summarized this concept well in his *Essay on Playing Keyboard Instruments* of 1753:

> Keyboardists whose chief asset is mere technique are clearly at a disadvantage. A performer may have the most agile fingers . . . and yet may be something less than a clear, pleasing, or stirring keyboardist. More often than not, one meets technicians, nimble keyboardists by profession, who possess all of these qualifications and indeed astound us with their prowess without ever touching our sensibilities. They overwhelm our hearing without satisfying it and stun the mind without moving it.[3]

Bach's observation is equally applicable to all musicians.

What makes a virtuoso? This term gives rise to almost as much controversy as vibrato does. On the positive side, the virtuoso is a social necessity, an attracter of public interest, a commissioner or dedicatee of new compositions, and potentially, a forger into new territory. However, cautions concerto historian Abraham Veinus, "if the virtuoso is sometimes a liberating force, mostly he is a bore." The uncreative virtuoso, the pure technician, "is content to put his fingers to work and his musicianship to sleep."[4] The musician who does so falls under the rubric of "virtuosoism," to use Marc Pincherle's term.[5]

The ultimate exemplar of virtuosoism was the nineteenth century genius of the violin, Niccolò Paganini (1782–1840). The closest equivalent among flutists would be Charles Nicholson, of whom an 1823 review in the British journal *Harmonicon* opined:

> Mr. Nicholson does . . . a great deal more than ought ever to be attempted, beyond the precincts of the school, by a man of judgment and good taste. His rapidity necessarily injures his tone, and the delicious

> pathos which this instrument is capable of expressing, is thus sacrificed to those tricks that should take any name rather than that of music.[6]

In an 1825 commentary, W. N. James made similar protests against overembellishment:

> There is oftentimes an excess of expression,—a constant straining after it, which is as much to be guarded against as its want is to be deplored. This practice, indeed, comes under the denomination of burlesque and affectation. It proceeds either from a want of genuine feeling in the performer, or from bad judgment in using that which he possesses.[7]

Later in the century, the catalog of virtuosoisms expanded to include excessive rhythmic flexibility—a sort of superrubato—and excessive contrast in dynamics.

The era of Paganini and Nicholson was followed by that of Franz Liszt (1811–86). In 1841 Liszt, no less competent a technician than Paganini, called for a change in the nature of virtuosity:

> May the artist of the future cheerfully renounce the vain, egotistic role which, it is to be hoped, has found in Paganini its last brilliant representative; and may he place his goal within and not without himself, making virtuosity a means, never an end.[8]

Liszt and his fellow Romantics regarded technique as the vehicle of emotional expression; Liszt wrote:

> The virtuoso is not a mason, chiselling his stone conscientiously according to the sketches of the architect. He is not a passive tool for reproducing feelings and thoughts, without adding anything of his own. He is not a more or less experienced "interpreter" of works which leave him no scope for his own comments. . . . For the virtuoso, musical works are in fact nothing but tragic and moving materializations of his emotions; he is called upon to make them speak, weep, sing and sigh, to recreate them in accordance with his own consciousness. In this way he, like the composer, is a creator, for he must have within himself those passions that he wishes to bring so intensely to life.[9]

After World War I, however, a period of reaction to the romantic interpreters and a new era of rationalism began. The pendulum of performance practice swung in the other direction, toward interpretive conformism and literalism. More scientific criteria were applied to the evaluation of musical performance. The individuality that distinguished performers decreased as they became more directly competitive in a technical sense; one theorist has likened the emphasis on skill to that of a juggler's act. In the case of pianists, Harold Schonberg observed in *The Great Pianists*, an "American school" developed:

> Eclectic in approach, clear in outline, metrically a little inflexible, tonally a little hard, they tend to be literalists who try for a direct translation of

> the printed score. . . . The result is a uniformity in playing, where the general level is certainly higher than it was years ago, but where there are few peaks.[10]

Recordings have exacerbated this trend: the ability to create technically "perfect" performances on recordings, through the miracle of tape splicing, has put pressure on performers to replicate these feats in the concert hall.

Another impetus to renewed virtuosoism lies in the fact that audiences have become larger and less elite. Performers are still showy, and so, they have a tendency to play too fast. Both Rampal and Galway, the current idols of the flute world, are guilty on this count. In 1976, the *New York Times* reported with perhaps just a shade of journalistic hyperbole, Rampal "will never hesitate to hurtle ahead of an orchestra or pianist, knowing that even if a minority of critics may scowl, the public is as thrilled by a racing vivace as they are to see a fine thoroughbred not merely hold a lead but break away."[11]

We would do better, therefore, to take as a model Theobald Boehm, of whom the *Harmonicon* wrote in 1831, "his style differs from that of Nicholson and Drouet, inasmuch as he strives to touch the heart rather than to astonish."[12]

The new rationalism of twentieth century performance practice does have its constructive aspects. It has led to renewed study of the theory and history of music, most notably in the so-called Early Music Movement (see below). As the progress of the Early Music Movement demonstrates, research and discussion have produced new views of what constitutes authenticity of performance, and have shown as well that authenticity need not be synonymous with rigidity. More recently, there has been renewed interest in the romantic era, as well, which has gained similar scholarly paraphernalia—in seminars, journals, and so on. Research into literature and performance practice can be only a good omen: as more high-quality literature of all eras comes to light, higher standards for all music should result.

The Theoretical Background: Basic Musicianship

The building blocks of expression (unlike those of technique) are not physical, but theoretical. The flutist, in particular, must make a special effort in this direction, because like the violinist and vocal soloist he is prone to top-voice mentality. Not only does the flutist play a single line, but it is generally the melody line. It is all too easy to see a piece of music only from a horizontal, melodic perspective. However, just because other instruments supply the harmony, tone, and texture does not mean that those elements can be ignored.

The first step of interpretation is to discern the overall purpose and organization of the composition. To do so, every musician must have a basic grounding in solfège or ear training, in harmony, and in score-reading and instrumentation, which are the tools of musical analysis.

Basic musicianship begins with the ability to read in the two most common clefs, treble (G) and bass (F), and familiarity with diatonic and chromatic scales, both major and minor; key signatures; and basic triadic chord structure. Almost any flute method (Taffanel-Gaubert and Altès are just two examples of many) will teach all these elements except for the bass clef.

However, understanding the basic rhythmic and melodic elements of music and musical notation intellectually does not automatically guarantee their perception by the ear. For this reason, it is crucial that from the very beginning the student acquire a solid grounding in ear training, so that these basic musical elements become built-in, and may be applied instinctively to actual performance.

The traditional French and Italian method of ear training is called solfège or solfeggio, the *do-re-mi* system of sight-singing in which solmization or *sol-fa* syllables are applied to each note of the scale. This methodology teaches progressively difficult melodic intervals while combining them with various rhythmic patterns. The idea is that the musician, upon seeing an interval, should be able to hear it instantly in his mind. For the instrumentalist, this skill enables him to conceptualize the note he is about to play. Because he knows instinctively how (and where) it should sound, he should be able to play it in tune.

There are two basic varieties of solfège: fixed *do* and movable *do*. Under the fixed *do* system, the tone of C is always *do*, no matter what key or tonality is the basis of the music. Under the movable *do* system, the tonic or key note of the scale is *do;* in G major, for instance, G is *do;* in A major, A is *do*. The following chart illustrates the difference:

	G	A	B	C	D	E	F♯	G
fixed *do*	*sol*	*la*	*si*	*do*	*re*	*mi*	*fa*	*sol*
movable *do*	*do*	*re*	*mi*	*fa*	*sol*	*la*	*si*	*do*

To my mind, the movable system is superior, because it enables the student to master transposition; no matter what the key, the names of the intervals remain the same. This skill is an absolute necessity for horn players, who must constantly transpose orchestral music at sight. It is also useful to woodwind players, who often are called on to transpose in theater orchestra parts and other studio and commercial music. And band players, who even today are occasionally confronted with a D♭ piccolo part, need to be able to transpose for the C instrument. Transposition is also necessary for score reading in the various clefs (see below).

Perhaps the most widely used books of solfege instruction are A. Dannhäuser's *Solfège des Solfèges*, a three-volume set, and Pasquale Bona's *Rhythmical Articulation*.

A slightly different approach is that taken by Paul Hindemith in his *Elementary Training for Musicians*. Hindemith finds solfège alone to be restrictive and uncreative and therefore eschews the traditional solmization in favor of exercises that progressively escalate rhythmic and melodic difficulties, which he distinguishes as "Action in Time" and "Action in Space." Hindemith's workbook is probably the most comprehensive one-stop guide to basic musicianship.

The next level, one for which Hindemith prepares with his introduction of the bass and tenor clefs, is score reading, the technique of assimilating the separate lines or parts of an ensemble composition into a coherent whole. To be most useful, this skill includes the ability to play at least the outline of the score at the piano. A good introductory text is *Preparatory Exercises in Score Reading* by R. O. Morris and Howard Ferguson. More advanced students will find H. Creuzberg's four-volume *Partiturspiel (Score Playing)* a superb curriculum for learning and practice.

The advantages of score reading ability for the flutist are many. For study purposes, the soloist should be able to play the flute cues off a piano score while keeping track of the piano part below. On the next level of sophistication, the ensemble player will find it useful to read through a full score in order to discern the place of the flute part relative to the other instruments. Such a reading may be silent but is more productive if played at the keyboard.

Score reading is also a good rehearsal tool. Indeed, many string quartets rehearse, at least in the early stages of learning a piece together, using full scores. Of course, page turns will be a problem, but securing the assistance of page turners for a few rehearsals is well worth the trouble. A similar technique is useful for the orchestral flutist. Though it is usually impractical to play from the score in rehearsal, because the large number of parts necessitates constant page turning, it is highly beneficial to read through the orchestral score before the rehearsal—ideally, following along with a recording—in order to hear solo parts in relationship to the ensemble as a whole. This knowledge enables the orchestral soloist to shape phrases so that continuing or repeated solo motives or lines are passed seamlessly from player to player; to gauge balances—which instruments should be more, less, or equally prominent in a given passage; and to make articulation consistent—because matching the light tonguing of an oboe is different from matching the heavier sound of the French horn. There is simply no substitute for the intellectual comprehension and preparation that competent score reading provides.

The training routine outlined by the books mentioned in this section is best acquired in well-taught classes, where an expert can reinforce skills and correct errors. But the books will give you the raw materials.

Analysis

The theoretical skills discussed in the preceding section give the performer the tools to analyze a composition and thus understand its construction, its architecture. Why is this musical macrocosm important? W. N. James tells us what happens if we ignore it:

> The great fault of English musicians is, that they labour . . . to be ridiculously correct with minute particulars, and leave the grand outline feeble, obscure, and unfinished. Thus a particular bar might be executed to admiration, and a painter might give the colour, tie, and creases of a sandal, or a shoe, laboriously precise; but who will pronounce that the one is excellent music, or the other a good painting? The true master, in either case, will bear the *whole meaning* and disposal of his subject in his imagination, and make all niceties and technicalities subordinate to this purpose. He ought not, on the slightest account, to lose sight for a moment of this; for the instant he does, he descends into a complete mechanical automaton, and is not better than an engine or machine. . . . [13]

Traditional musical analysis defines five elements of music, usually presented in the following order: melody, harmony, rhythm, dynamics, and tone color.

Rhythm

The most pragmatic and logical analysis advocated by theorists today sets one element—rhythm—far above the others in priority.

"Music," wrote the famed French pedagogue Nadia Boulanger, "is made of two essential elements (line and rhythm), which are complemented by decorative elements (harmony and orchestration)."[14] By rhythm she meant not "being in time," but "having rhythm, which is quite different; it's an inner pulse."[15] Such an impulse provides the foundation for the structural framework, the *ligne grande*, from which an interpretation is carved, much as the marble sculptor works with the natural striations of his raw material to create a work of art. As one of Boulanger's biographers has expressed the concept, "Time simply goes on, but rhythm has a dynamic impulse."[16] Implicit in that impulse is the contrast between motion and repose.

Similarly, theorist Edward T. Cone of Princeton defines musical form by its rhythmic shape. Specifically, Cone says, general rhythmic principles underlie the common formal units of phrase, period, three-part song form, and so on. On higher levels, he continues, more comprehensive formal sections can explain an entire composition as "one all-embracing rhythmic impulse."[17] Other prominent theorists—Curt Sachs, author of *Rhythm and Tempo*, among them—argue that this last part of Cone's thesis is an overstatement. Sachs adopts the linguists' definition that "rhythm is flow," but expands on it: "It is fluency due to some active, organizing principle."[18] So rhythm is the part of musical structure that governs all forms of musical motion; all other musical elements take rhythm as their point of reference.

Tempo

Tempo is a subset of rhythm and as such strongly enhances the motion/repose concept of pulse and phrasing. It may determine the large formal structure, as in the fast-slow-fast organization of classical concerto movements, or it may take the subtle form of tempo rubato, the use of slight accelerandos and ritardandos within a phrase.

Harmony

As the governing force of musical motion, rhythm is most closely allied with harmony. The harmonic concept of consonance versus dissonance is embodied in the concept of strong versus weak, of "good" versus "bad" beats. The close relationship is evident in questions of whether passing dissonances required unaccented 'passing' beats, whether dissonances demand a strong accent to be resolved on a stressless beat, and so on. In sum, says Sachs, "harmony and rhythm share in the alternation of tension and relaxation which are the essence of our music."[19]

Melody and Dynamics

Similarly tied to the rhythmic structure, though on the next lower level of importance, is melody. Just as the rhythm is aligned with harmonic change, it is coordinated with the rise and fall of the melodic curve, which also contributes to the organization of motion and repose. Similarly, dynamics enhance the musical motion, delineating large formal sections or giving nuance to the smallest phrase element, either by subtle gradation or forceful accent.

Tone Color

The fifth element, tone color, is most often used at the player's discretion for expressive purposes. But it may also function as a structural element. As an element of contrast between instrument families, tone color has always been an organizing principle in orchestral music; in the avant-garde solo flute literature, tone color is not only notated, but may also assume large-scale structural importance.

Composers indicate their basic intentions regarding rhythm, harmony, melody, dynamics, and tone to a greater or lesser extent in the written score. It is the player's job to determine the relative emphasis of each of these elements in relation to each other and to execute them on his or her instrument.

Phrasing

Analysis, as we have seen, helps the performer understand the overall architecture of a piece, which is determined primarily by its rhythmic underpinning or "inner pulse." Phrasing is the application of the same principles and techniques on a smaller scale and is equally important. Wrote Rousseau,

> A Singer who feels his phrases and their accent is a man of good taste. But one who renders only notes, keys, scales, and intervals, without comprehending the meaning of the phrases—even if he be precise otherwise—is nothing but a "note-gobbler."[20]

There are two schools of thought on phrasing, one more intuitive, the other more analytical. The intuitive school uses a verbal model, equating the function of phrasing with that of punctuation in language. Thus, said Chopin to a student, "he who phrases incorrectly is like a man who does not understand the language he speaks."

Theobald Boehm, as stylish as a performer as he was talented as an inventor, urged flutists to study vocal music; the declamation of the text, he explained, would indicate the correct interpretation, articulation, and phrasing. To demonstrate this philosophy in his treatise, *The Flute and Flute-Playing*, Boehm reproduced the aria *"Dies Bildnis ist bezaubernd schön"* from Mozart's *The Magic Flute*. The upper staff is Mozart's original vocal line, complete with words; below it is Boehm's transcription for flute, marked with articulation to match the verbal declamation.[21]

Boehm also transcribed six Schubert songs for flute and piano. The student will benefit immensely from modeling his articulation and phrasing on the poetic cadences of the original songs.

The second school of phrasing pedagogy is an extension of formal analysis. It considers a phrase to be created on several levels: attack, or opening articulation; rhythmic formulas, accents, intensity, dynamics, and color, which propel the phrase from beginning to end; characteristic terminations, and finally, silences, both internal and external. It is important to note that nowhere in this definition is the phrase immutably tied to written bar lines.

One form of analytical phrasing is the tension-release method, which involves analyzing a piece of music to determine variations in the rate of tension or motion—the shape of the melody, the harmonic rhythm (the rate at which the harmony changes), and most importantly, the nature of the rhythm or pulse. The phrase is not a straight line, or even a series of broken lines, but a curve determined by these structural elements. One musician has compared the harmonic aspect of the curve to an elastic band: the more it is stretched, the greater the internal resistance becomes, creating dissonance. When the tension is released, the harmony resolves itself.

Marcel Tabuteau, longtime principal oboist of the Philadelphia Orchestra, subscribed to this theory, expressing the dichotomy between motion and repose by means of articulation, dynamics, and tone color, all controlled by what he labeled "the drive." He divided the motion into a series of arches that reached toward the note of repose—not necessarily to the first or other strong beat of a measure, but to the point where dissonance is resolved and there is some pause, however brief, in the forward motion. Thus the motion might not be 1-2-3-4, with the phrase tapering to the fourth beat, but 2-3-4-1, with the phrase tapering toward its resolution. Tabuteau worked out a numerical system to scale or quantify the motion of the phrase, with the numbers representing relative intensity and dynamics (not necessarily the same thing, it is important to note). For instance, a simple pattern might be phrased like this:[22]

Tabuteau's colleague, William Kincaid, expressed the same idea by a system of square brackets, a literal trademark for Kincaid disciples. The brackets were a visual means of obscuring bar lines, which, aftcr all, arc only a notational and reading convenience, not necessarily a compositional element. Kincaid, like Tabuteau, considered strong beats to be points of arrival or "finishing notes." The character of the beat was conditioned by how it was reached.

John Krell, a longtime Kincaid student and colleague, illustrates in *Kincaidiana*, a compilation of his student notes, just how the bracket system works. An isolated figure—couplet, triplet, quadruplet, sextolet, and so on—is incomplete, unresolved:

But the next strong beat gives it purpose, direction, and meaning:[23]

There is something of an analogy to the famous scientific conundrum: assume that sound is composed of a source, a resonator, and a recipient. If a tree falls in a deserted forest, with no human witness to hear it, does it make a sound? The analogy to the Kincaid bracket system is that without a receiver—a point of arrival—a group of notes makes no meaningful sound.

Based on this concept, Kincaid bracketed notes into groups to show the progression of motion within the phrase:

Within each grouping, the player can then use dynamics, articulation, and intensity, perhaps employing Tabuteau's numerical system, to achieve the desired degree of symmetry or asymmetry. Nuance is accomplished within the note group. However, the procedure should not be taken too literally; Kincaid himself cautioned, "Think the groupings, don't do them."[24] The brackets are a suggestion, not an immutable prescription. The resulting organization of the musical subject matter was, in Kincaid's view, something of a panacea. "There are no technical problems," he said, "only phrasing problems."[25] In other words, if you build a piece of music from its phrase structure, it will organize itself.

Performance Practice

The techniques of analysis and phrasing outlined above help the performer determine the technical musical context and make certain basic decisions regarding the architecture of a musical composition: rhythmic and harmonic emphasis, the handling of repeats, overall dynamic levels, and questions of continuity and contrast. In turn, these large-scale decisions help the performer make smaller-scale decisions such as where and how to ornament the melody. But the most detailed possible analysis cannot provide conversance with idiom, which allows the musician to place the music in historical context. Just as we can often understand another person's point of view best if we know something of his social and economic background, so we can understand a piece of music better if we know when it was written, and how, where, and on what kinds of instruments it was meant to be performed. Such knowledge can also help the player correct mistakes in printed editions, which all too often reflect not the intentions of the composer but those of a modern editor.

This relatively new scholarly discipline is destroying many of the stereotypes of musical interpretation, such conventional notions as: Bach must be played straight, Beethoven with passion, Chopin with rubato, Mozart classically, Schumann romantically. Performance practice is continually surprising us by giving permission to indulge rhythmic license in Bach and Mozart or to play Chopin with less rubato than has been customary.

The immediate predecessor of the formal discipline of "performance practice" was the concept of "poetic context" advanced by French pianist and conductor Alfred Cortot (1877–1963). Cortot set great faith in poetic description of music. He required his students, before learning a new piece, to do historical research on its origin, to study the biography of the composer, and to read his letters and those of his contemporaries. Cortot asked his students to infer from this factual background and the musical character of the piece a verbal description—its imagery, poetic insights, literary analogies, and so on. In this way, Cortot believed, the student would be neither a mere technician, nor a mere historicist, but an imaginative interpreter who used technique and history as tools.[26]

Performance practice as a scholarly endeavor draws on a number of different disciplines. Social history describes the social and economic times in which the music was written and performed, for what purpose it was written, how political events influenced cultural life (making it nationalistic or international, for instance), whether the music was played by the aristocracy or the masses, professionals, students, or amateurs. Organology, the history of musical instruments, tells us the physical characteristics of the instruments on which a piece was originally played and, by extension, what techniques of fingering, articulation, and tone were required to overcome its defects or take advantage of its attributes. One of the most useful tools of both social history and organology is iconography, the study of musical subjects in the visual arts. It clarifies physical details of both instruments and playing technique, shows the size of instrumental forces, the location of performances, and so on.

The study of historical treatises—Hotteterre, Corrette, C. P. E. Bach, Quantz, Leopold Mozart, Tromlitz, Taffanel, Altès, and others—is a valuable means of determining theoretical and practical aspects of performance not discernible except from the written commentaries of performers. Articulation is a prime example. A painting may, if the artist has not used too much license, show us the flutist's embouchure, but it cannot convey to us the syllables of articulation he uses, which an instruction book can do very clearly. Finally, the student of performance practice looks at the music of the period itself, not just the piece under current study, but related ones. For instance, as a clue to how a Bach concerto ought to be ornamented, he can study Bach's Concerto for Four Harpsichords, BWV 1065, which is an arrangement of Vivaldi's Concerto for Four Violins, op. 3, no. 10. Telemann's

Methodical Sonatas are useful not only for the performance of those particular twelve compositions, but also as a guide for ornamenting other sonatas of the same genre by Telemann and his contemporaries. Or for learning how to write a cadenza for a Mozart flute concerto, Mozart's own cadenzas for his piano concertos are a perfect case study.

Each historical era has its own particular concerns in the matter of performance practice. For music of the baroque era, realization of the figured bass is a prime requirement. Equally important is a knowledge of how to achieve the baroque ideal of expressive melody through the application of ornaments, whether realized from abbreviated written notation or freely improvised. Other issues include the differences between French and Italian style, rhythmic alteration, the size of the orchestra, and instrumentation (Bach's *Art of the Fugue*, for instance, did not specify the instrumentation). Performers on original or reproduction instruments must also make decisions regarding pitch and temperament (mean-tone or tempered).

In the late eighteenth century, performers became less concerned with improvising ornamentation as composers became more fastidious about making their intentions known in the written score. The figured bass disappeared, eliminating that complication as well. Emphasis shifted, in the classic era, to achieving melodic elegance and architectural balance. However, the modern performer must still make choices as to type of instrument—harpsichord, fortepiano, or piano, for instance—the composition of cadenzas, the size of performance forces, tempo, execution of the remaining ornaments, and so on.

The music of the romantic era, with its expanded harmony and overall broader proportions, and virtually unlimited range of dynamics, tone color, and articulation, presents a whole new spectrum of interpretative choices. The new emotionalism presented as many challenges as opportunities. Cadenzas, for instance, differ greatly from those of the classic period.

For music of the late nineteenth century, the student of performance practice has another important tool at his disposal: recordings. Ironically, this is the era for which we need them least, because the chain of oral history is intact. The music of the nineteenth century has never totally gone out of fashion, as baroque music did, so there has been a continuous succession of teachers and performers in the nineteenth century tradition. Twentieth century musicians still operate in a basically nineteenth century orientation, as even a cursory look at Big Five orchestra programming will quickly reveal. Nevertheless, piano rolls and acoustic recordings are invaluable aids to the student of late-romantic performance practice.

Even quite modern music, particularly that of the avant-garde, presents problems of performance practice. Notation is far from standard, not because it is so old that it has been forgotten, as is the case with baroque music, but precisely because it is so new, and has not yet been codified or standardized. And with few exceptions, such as written "overt" harmonics or whistle tones, matters of tone color can be communicated only by example; there simply is no notation.

So the study of performance practice is the scholarly activity that endows the musician with "conversance with idiom," that makes him comfortable and familiar with the music of a given historical period. Such "conversance with idiom" enables the musician to recognize almost immediately what makes a piece a product of its era, and what, if anything, distinguishes it from its contemporaries. The study of performance practice, in combination with that elusive element of taste, enables the performer to differentiate, for instance, the staccato of Haydn and that of Debussy. Says piano pedagogue David Barnett, "Research prevents taste from being purely whimsical, and taste prevents research from inducing literalness or pedantry."[27] What a diplomatic resolution of the traditional battle between performers and musicologists!

The Early Music Movement and Questions of Authenticity

The most visible manifestation of interest in performance practice is the so-called Early Music Movement, or as the *New York Times* headlined it, the Early-Music Subculture. Whatever its epithet, the movement dates from the late nineteenth century. One landmark date often given is 1886, when the English keyboardist Alfred Hipkins performed Bach's *Goldberg Variations* on the harpsichord for London's Royal Musical Association. A more famous and influential pioneer was Arnold Dolmetsch (1858–1940), who became fascinated with Renaissance and baroque instruments while working as a piano technician in England in the 1880s. He went on to found a dynasty of early-music performers and instrument makers, still in business in Haslemere, England today. In 1915, he published a seminal work, *The Interpretation of the Music of the Seventeenth and Eighteenth Centuries*. This was a valuable addition to the literature of early music, which already included Edward Dannreuther's ground-breaking *Musical Ornamentation* (1893–95).

Another important figure in the revival of early music was Wanda Landowska, the great Polish keyboardist who did so much to revive the harpsichord in the early part of this century. She summarized her philosophy concisely: "You play Bach your way. I will play him his way."[28] Whether she accomplished this intent, or whether she was instinctively too much of a late nineteenth century musician to do so, is another question, but without a doubt her career gave major impetus to interest in the music and instruments of the baroque.

For woodwind players, however, early music is an especially recent arrival. Consider oboist-editor Josef Marx's observation in 1948:

> Standing on the threshhold of a great new culture of instrumentalism, the modern wind instrument player completely fails to understand the Golden Age of his chosen medium. He looks at the 18th century with

> an utter lack of interest and sympathy. Any addition—re-edition—to the standard stock of Bach and Handel sonatas is received with apathy and boredom.[29]

One of the earliest and most significant achievements of the Early Music Movement was the publication of critical, historical editions of the great masters, beginning with the *Bach Gesellschaft* (1851–99), and the complete works of Handel (1858–1902), Beethoven (1862–88), Mozart (1877–83), Haydn (1907–33), and others. As scholarship in the field progresses, publication of such editions has encompassed many more obscure but historically important composers, as well as revisions of oeuvres previously covered, such as the *Neue Bach Ausgabe* (begun in 1954) and revised editions of Handel (published 1955–), Mozart (1955–), Beethoven (1961–), and Schubert (1964–).

Music publishers have also brought out performing editions of older music; examples in the woodwind field include the *Nagels Musik-Archiv* (1927–), Barenreiter's *Hortus musicus* series (1937–), Breitkopf and Härtel's *Collegium musicum* (edited by Hugo Riemann), Ricordi's *Florilegium Musicum* (edited by Gustav Scheck and Hugo Ruf), and Heinrichshofen's *Pegasus* edition. The term coined for authentic, unedited, undoctored editions was *Urtext*, from the German word *Ur*, meaning original or basic. The ideal critical edition presents the Urtext, with any editorial emendations or additions, such as ornamentation or realization of the figured bass, clearly indicated by differences in typography, printing color, or the like.

For flutists, a significant recent contribution to the literature is the publication of *The Flute Library* by the Dutch publisher Frits Knuf, under the general editorship of Frans Vester. This consists of reprints of the major historical treatises on flute playing by Corrette (about 1735), Mahaut (1759), Delusse (about 1761), Tromlitz (1791 and 1800), Devienne (about 1792), and many others.

Performing groups such as Nikolaus Harnoncourt's Concentus Musicus Wien, the Collegium Aureum, Noah Greenberg's New York Pro Musica, Joel Cohen's Boston Camerata, the Waverly Consort, and the Folger Consort have proliferated and attracted enthusiastic audiences. There are a number of training programs specifically geared toward early music. Modeled on such paragons of the workshop/festival genre as Alexander Schneider's Marlboro Festival, these include the Oberlin Baroque Performance Institute at the Oberlin Conservatory and Albert Fuller's Aston Magna Academy in Great Barrington, Massachusetts.

Along with performance, there is a variety of periodicals, most notably *The American Recorder*, house organ of the American Recorder Society, and the superb British journal *Early Music*. As the advertisements in the latter publication clearly show, makers of reproduction early instruments are extremely numerous, and competition in the field is healthy (as are the prices of the instruments). Another economic indicator is the escalating price of antique woodwind instruments in auction houses such as Sotheby's and Christie's.

The intrinsic value of Stradivarius, Amati, and Guarneri violins has long been recognized, but only in the last decade have harpsichords, lutes, and woodwinds joined the ranks of the hard-to-get.

This escalating interest in early music, complete with its specialist performers and scholars, has spawned lengthy and fascinating debates over questions of authenticity. It is this aspect of the early music movement that makes it a distinctly twentieth century phenomenon; eighteenth century music was revived, at least sporadically, in the nineteenth century. Felix Mendelssohn's 1829 performance of Bach's *Saint Matthew Passion* is the best known example, and there were others. But Mendelssohn and others used the music of Bach and his baroque contemporaries as vehicles for nineteenth century performing forces, the symphony orchestra, the large (or mammoth) chorus, and the grand piano. A typical product was Ferruccio Busoni's transcriptions of Bach organ works in high-romantic grand-piano style. Using familiar vehicles of performance, the first baroque revivers made the old music palatable and even attractive to audiences.

The twentieth century revival, in contrast, has applied scientific analysis to the old music in an attempt to present it as accurately as possible in the style that its composers intended and that its first audiences heard. Modern performers have not altered the music to conform to any preconceived tastes of the audience. Instead, audience tastes have changed in response to the music and style presented, and, in turn, the audience for authentic performance has grown rapidly.

The issue of authenticity raises several questions, which baroque scholar Putnam Aldrich set forth in a 1957 essay. To what extent can we discover the baroque tradition? How definite or dictatorial was that tradition; how much latitude did it allow? And to the extent that we are able to answer the first two questions, how much authenticity is desirable for modern performances?[30]

One might begin with the premise, as Donald J. Grout does, that an ideal performance realizes the composer's intentions.[31] But determining the nature of those intentions is quite difficult, because notation is often frustratingly uninformative or nonexistent. The majority of instrumental music through the eighteenth century gives little indication of embellishments and cadenzas, and figured bass is by definition an incomplete notation. Similarly, nineteenth century piano music does not give specific instructions as to the use of the pedals. Many, many baroque sonatas, especially trio sonatas, give alternative instrumentation, such as two flutes or two oboes or two violins; moreover, they often fail to specify the nature of the continuo forces, which may consist of a variety of bass and/or keyboard instruments.

Circumstantial evidence, such as accounts in contemporary memoirs of performances under the supervision of the composer, may be misleading. Though a composer may have preferred an oboe for a particular sonata, for instance, he may have used a flute for the premiere because a flutist was available and an oboist was not. Second, matters of embellishment and improvisation were transmitted for the most part by aural tradition; examples in written instruction books were intended not as immutable formulae but as suggestions. Moreover, one may quite logically argue that figured bass and unornamented solo notation were intentionally incomplete precisely in order to afford the performer interpretative latitude; therefore there can be no single correct performance. And so, Putnam Aldrich concluded, "true authenticity is a chimera."

The arguments for and against original instruments, though fascinating, are somewhat irrelevant to most modern flutists. Let's limit this discussion, therefore, to performances on the modern flute.

Let's begin by reviewing what we miss by not using the baroque flute. First, the sonic ideal in the baroque was thinner, clearer, and more piercing than the full, vibrant ideal of today. Second, the baroque flute, lacking Boehm-system mechanism, permitted tonal shading (half-holing and vibrato) with the fingers.

Baroque instruments were tuned in mean-tone temperament, whereas modern instruments use a tempered scale. On baroque woodwinds, the finger holes were evenly spaced and equal in diameter; it was up to the player to compensate for variations in intonation by such techniques as cross-fingering and half-holing. But the result was a variation in both quality and quantity of sound. Composers anticipated these by-products and built them into the music; key choice was an important compositional element and particular keys had specific emotional associations. Playing the same music on modern instruments, on which keys are interchangeable in color and intonation, obscures these distinctions.

How, then, can the Boehm-flute player achieve an authentic performance on his "too-perfect" instrument? This is not as hard as it seems. Recall that music is made up of five basic elements—rhythm, melody, harmony, dynamics, and tone color. The first three characteristics of a piece of music remain the same irrespective of the instrument on which it is played.

And so, the modern-instrument player should make the same study of performance practice that original-instrument players do. As a result, he should be able to determine the proper tempo for a piece, its rhythmic organization and mannerisms, the harmonic structure, and the character of the melody. He may want to imitate exactly the syllables of articulation set forth by Hotteterre, Quantz, and other theorists, or he may want to achieve similar nuances with other tools, including breath, combinations of tonguing and slurring, and dynamics. And the modern-instrument player is as obligated as is his original-instrument counterpart to execute embellishments and rhythmic alterations within the customs of the time and place in which a piece was written.

What the modern-instrument player should not do, however, is to introduce anachronisms into the performance of baroque music. The prime example is vibrato. We have seen that the baroque masters made effective use of finger vibrato as an ornamental device, and a simulation of that technique is perfectly in order. But a wide, Brahmsian, orchestral-style vibrato is categorically out of place. *Staccatissimo* articulation is similarly inappropriate.

If the Boehm-flute player follows these guidelines, he should not be chastised for using the modern instrument. The performance will be different, but no less valid. There is so much high-quality baroque and classic music that it would be ludicrous to deny it to players of the modern flute. Even Robert Donington, one of the foremost writers on baroque performance practice, says that while the choice of instrument is important, "the manner of using the instrument once chosen is still more important. It is not the instrument but the imagination which knows what to do."[32]

Notes

1. Louis Drouet, *Drouet's Method of Flute Playing* (London: R. Cocks & Co., 1830), p. 18.
2. Jean-Jacques Rousseau, *A Complete Dictionary of Music*, 2nd ed., trans. William Waring (1779; reprint, New York: AMS Press, 1975), p. 428.
3. Carl Philipp Emanuel Bach, *Essay on the True Art of Playing Keyboard Instruments*, trans. and ed. William J. Mitchell (New York: W. W. Norton, 1949), p. 147.
4. Abraham Veinus, *The Concerto* (New York: Dover Publications, 1964), p. 154.
5. Marc Pincherle, *The World of the Virtuoso*, trans. Lucile H. Brockway (New York: W. W. Norton, 1963), p. 40.
6. *Harmonicon* 1 (1823): 73; quoted in David William Eagle, "A Constant Passion and a Constant Pursuit: A Social History of Flute-Playing in England from 1800 to 1851" (Ph.D. diss., University of Minnesota, 1977), pp. 94–95.
7. W. N. James, *A Word or Two on the Flute* (Edinburgh: Charles Smith & Co.; London: Cocks & Co., 1826), p. 146.
8. Henry T. Finck, *Success in Music and How It Is Won* (New York: Charles Scribner's Sons, 1909), p. 284.
9. Eva and Paul Badura-Skoda, *Interpreting Mozart on the Keyboard*, trans. Leo Black (London: Barrie and Rockliff, 1962), p. 2.
10. Harold C. Schonberg, *The Great Pianists* (New York: Simon and Schuster, 1963), p. 223.
11. Peter Hellman, "The most magic flute," *New York Times Magazine*, 22 Feb. 1976, p. 34.
12. Christopher Welch, *History of the Boehm Flute*, 3rd ed. (1886; reprint, Wakefield, N.H.: Longwood Press, 1977), p. 18.
13. James, pp. 143–44.
14. Alan Kendall, *The Tender Tyrant: Nadia Boulanger: A Life Devoted to Music* (Wilton, Conn.: Lyceum Books, 1977), p. 112.
15. Ibid., p. 106.
16. Ibid., p. 104.
17. Edward T. Cone, *Musical Form and Musical Performance* (New York: W. W. Norton, 1968), pp. 38–39.
18. Curt Sachs, *Rhythm and Tempo* (New York: W. W. Norton, 1953), p. 12.
19. Ibid., p. 268.

20. Frederick Dorian, *The History of Music in Performance* (New York: W. W. Norton, 1942), p. 164.
21. Theobald Boehm, *The Flute and Flute-Playing*, trans. and rev. Dayton C. Miller, 2nd ed. (1922; reprint, New York: Dover Publications, 1964), p. 148.
22. Dominique-René de Lerma, "Toward a Concept of Tabuteau's Phrasing," *The Instrumentalist* (March 1974), pp. 44–45.
23. John Krell, *Kincaidiana* (Culver City, Calif.: Trio Associates, 1973), pp. 32–33.
24. Ibid., p. 36.
25. Don Griffis, "The Bird Sang Maquarre," *National Flute Association Newsletter* 2, no. 3 (1977): 13.
26. David Barnett, *The Performance of Music* (New York: Universe Books, 1972), pp. 37–38.
27. Ibid., p. 208.
28. Edward Rothstein, "Early-Music Subculture, a Modern Phenomenon," *The New York Times*, 30 Dec. 1982, sec. 3, p. 12.
29. Josef Marx, "The Baroque Era and Woodwinds," *Woodwind Magazine* 1, no. 1 (1948): 3.
30. Putnam Aldrich, "The 'Authentic' Performance of Old Music," in *Essays on Music in Honor of Archibald Thompson Davison by his Associates* (Cambridge, Mass.: Department of Music, Harvard University, 1957), pp. 161–71.
31. Donald J. Grout, "On Historical Authenticity in the Performance of Old Music," in *Essays on Music in Honor of Archibald Thompson Davison by his Associates* (Cambridge, Mass.: Department of Music, Harvard University, 1957), p. 341.
32. Robert Donington, *A Performer's Guide to Baroque Music* (New York: Charles Scribner's Sons, 1973), p. 39.

12

PERFORMANCE

Opportunities for Performance

The satisfaction of playing chamber music with friends, and for one's own pleasure, is undeniable. Ultimately, however, you will want to perform in public, for music is also a spectator (or auditor) activity. The opportunites are many and varied.

As a soloist, the first step is to participate in a joint recital. Most music schools and many private teachers hold these regularly. They help students gain confidence and experience in performing for an audience, and they provide experience in playing with accompaniment. They also serve as a reward for a semester or year of hard work, and they enable the participants to judge their progress against that of their peers. For this last reason, larger schools or studios often group students by age or level of ability in order not to discourage or embarrass the less advanced players.

As the flutist becomes more proficient, he is ready to perform in settings outside the school or studio. Many opportunities are available in churches, either your own or others in the area. Many churches, in fact, make a musical selection a regular element of the order of service. Such opportunities are often discovered through word of mouth, but an organized approach to organists and music directors, either by letter or telephone, is a good way to proceed. Even if a church does not use instrumental music in regular services, making your name known to the music director may lead to calls to play for special occasions such as weddings.

In addition to weddings, there are a variety of other occasions where flute music provides an appropriate and lovely touch: postlecture receptions, poetry readings, private parties, and recreational programs at senior citizens' homes. Finding such jobs requires a small amount of entrepreneurship—posting notices on bulletin boards, placing inexpensive classified ads in local newspapers, and so on. And again, use the old standby, word of mouth.

The ultimate in solo performance is the solo recital. Many music schools, conservatories, and colleges made the solo recital a requirement for graduation; others merely encourage their students to play one and often help with the arrangements. For college students, a good first step might be a small, intimate recital in a dorm living room or other common area. Often, various student organizations sponsor concert series, as do the academic music departments. Although such concerts do not always draw large audiences, the first-time recitalist will probably be more comfortable in intimate settings before moving on to the formal recital hall.

Formal recitals, required to fulfill academic requirements, often must follow certain guidelines as to length, program content, accompaniment, printed programs, and so forth. The following pages, however, should prove helpful to potential recitalists responsible for their own arrangements.

There are two variations on the recital theme. The first is the lecture recital, intended for either an academic audience or a general one. Adult education courses, clubs, and hobby groups fall into the latter category. Suitable topics might be a survey history of the flute and its music, using historic instruments ranging from the one-keyed traverso to the modern silver Boehm flute; or the flute family, using piccolo, C flute, alto, and bass flutes. Or you can cover a smaller topic such as baroque flute music.

The second variation is the school program, for elementary or high school students. Such a presentation must be carefully geared to the age level and attention span of the audience. Using overhead slides to illustrate different kinds of flutes, bringing different sizes and kinds of flutes (even if you don't play them all), and distributing printed handouts will help keep your audience's attention. Such programs can often be arranged through school music departments or through PTAs, which frequently sponsor assembly and enrichment programs.

Flutists should not ignore the opportunities for playing in chamber groups. If you do not know other musicians, particularly if you are not in school, a good way to meet other players is through amateur music organizations. The oldest and most famous is the Amateur Chamber Music Players, which publishes a list of avocational musicians interested in playing chamber music. Members are identified in the directory by instrument, level of proficiency, and geographical location.

Flutists are especially fortunate that there are numerous flute clubs around the country. Their activities include recitals by members and visiting artists, workshops, master classes, ensemble sight-reading sessions, chamber music parties, and so on. They are an excellent way of meeting flutists and other musicians who like to play with flutists, as well as the perfect opportunity to talk shop with one's colleagues.

The third major performance opportunity is large ensemble work. There is a vast number of community bands and orchestras, generally conducted by professionals. In the Washington, D.C., metropolitan area, for instance, each of the suburban counties has its own orchestra. Many such organizations are all-amateur; others are composed of a combination of avocational and professional players. Most of these orchestras rehearse in the evenings for the convenience of members who work full-time in other professions. In addition, some colleges and universities (generally not conservatories) fill in gaps in their personnel with accomplished local players from outside the college community. A first-rate wind player may also have the opportunity to perform a concerto with any of these orchestras, or to participate in spin-off chamber groups, either at orchestra-sponsored events or elsewhere.

Planning a Recital Program

In planning a program for a solo recital you should be sure to know your capabilities, your audience, and your repertoire.

Your Technical Capabilities: At the very least, you must be comfortable with every piece on the program. If you are not, technical concerns will direct your attention from interpretation—where it belongs—to merely getting through the notes. And technical mistakes during a performance will disturb your concentration and damage your confidence. In addition, you must judge your endurance. Pace yourself; start with a piece that is not technically challenging but gives the tone time to warm up.

After you are comfortable with your audience, you can then proceed to more difficult music. But you may not want to save the most difficult piece until the end if you think you will be too tired at that point. Don't stretch your technique to its limits; with the pressures of public performance added to the usual difficulties, your concentration and endurance may well be less than in the practice studio.

The Audience: Who will be in the audience? Musicians, nonmusicians, or a combination? Mostly flutists? Children with short attention spans? Chamber music aficionados? The general public? You must gauge your program according to the attention span and musical knowledge of your listeners. As Quantz advised two centuries ago, "To ingratiate yourself with your listeners, it is most advantageous to know their humors."[1]

How does this advice translate into practical terms? If the audience is likely to have a short attention span, either because of age or unfamiliarity with the music, keep the individual selections, as well as the total program, fairly short. Better to play a Telemann sonata, for instance, than the entire *Suite in A Minor*. Try to inject some humor in the program—an air and variations on a familiar theme, such as Drouet's *Variations on "God Save the King,"* for example.

Keep the program varied; for this kind of audience, don't play six baroque sonatas. Play pieces of varying tempos, historical styles, and characters. For instance, contrast the seriousness of a J. S. Bach sonata with a more galant work by his son Johann Christian. For even more variety, include a piece for piccolo, such as Gordon Jacob's *The Pied Piper*, whose first movement is for flute, the second for piccolo. Or, if you play historical flutes, use one or more of them for part of the program. Similarly, vary the size of the performing forces—include a piece for unaccompanied flute or one for a small ensemble.

The same rules of variety apply to a more sophisticated audience; you simply have more choices available. If you're playing for other flutists, try to avoid very familiar pieces. There's not much worse, in spring recital season, than an overdose of the Chaminade *Concertino*.

Repertoire: Once you reach a reasonably advanced level of proficiency, you can choose your repertoire from a large selection of music. Don't be misled by the rather limited lists of "contest solos" published by music teachers' organizations for the use of All-City, All-County, and All-State auditioners. Nor should you limit yourself to the stock of the local music store. There is much, much more music available, and a little digging can make your program distinctive and memorable.

The repertoire list at the back of this book includes a large selection of high-quality music, arranged according to historical period, much of it not particularly well-known. Franz Vester's *Flute Repertoire Catalogue* and James Pellerite's *A Handbook of Literature for the Flute* are also good sources.

If you hear an interesting or beautiful piece in concert or on record or radio, it has probably been or will soon be published. Check with one of the major sources listed in Appendix D. The National Flute Association maintains a library within the University of Arizona Music Library; membership in the NFA entitles you to a printed catalog of the collection, and you can borrow anything in it via interlibrary loan through your public or college library. Flutes International and Fluteworld in Michigan (offshoots of the former Flute Center U.S.A.) publish large catalogs of music in print, updated annually, which make ordering easy.

Effective use of any of these catalogs presupposes a basic knowledge of musical history and specifically of flute history. The literature chapters of this book will give you a good start; the bibliography provides many suggestions for more in-depth research into the periods, styles, and composers of particular interest to you. Attending flute concerts and listening to records will give you ideas for what to include on your own programs, and will perhaps suggest good combinations of pieces.

One function of any program is to entertain—you should keep the audience interested from beginning to end. There are many ways to make a flute recital a pleasurable, entertaining, and even educational event.

Some sixty years ago, Arthur Brooke, the principal flutist of the Boston Symphony, outlined his philosophy of program planning. He began with the premise that "the concert-going public is really ignorant as regards the flute and its capabilities."[2] Today, through the efforts of Rampal, Galway, and many other soloists, this musical ignorance is much less of a factor—although the avant-garde is still a source of mystery and fear to most audiences.

Brooke's advice remains valid: to educate the public, which he saw as part of the flute recitalist's mission, he wrote,

> the only way is to play something that will leave an impression on the mind (or the soul or the heart, call it what you will) not merely to dazzle the audience. Do not play merely to make a "hit." Try to make your playing mean something. A brilliant technical piece is all very well, in fact the audience expects it, but play something also that will reach their hearts, then you will be advancing the cause of flute-playing and promoting a just understanding of its art.[3]

With the possible exception of children's concerts, I believe that the flutist should limit the program to works written for the flute. That includes, of course, baroque trio sonatas in which flutes, recorders, oboes, and violins are more or less interchangeable on the treble lines. As the subtitle of Frans Vester's catalog, *10,000 Titles*, suggests, there is a lot of music from which to choose. Most transcriptions for flute are second-rate, not because the music is bad (it's often superb) but simply because the flute cannot realize the full potential of the composition. The character of the music gets lost in transcription. Some prime examples are Rampal's transcriptions of the Khachaturian Violin Concerto (even though he had the composer's blessing) and Cesar Franck's Violin Sonata, and Galway's transcription of Vivaldi's *The Four Seasons*. In all of these pieces, one misses the power of the violin bow, the strings' facility for double-stopping, and the implicit qualities of string tone for which those pieces were written. The flute does, indeed, have many timbral and expressive capabilities, but it simply is not a violin and should not try to imitate it.

By the same token, I disapprove of popular music transcriptions on serious concerts. Galway's *Annie's Song* is perhaps the most famous (or infamous) example. I feel that if an audience chooses to attend a serious flute concert, it does not expect or want "easy listening." A "pops" concert is another matter—a perfectly respectable and enjoyable type of occasion—but a different one. If you do need or want to include an encore there are many short pieces of high-quality classical music. Even single movements of classical sonatas make excellent encores.

Assuming we're not talking about a specifically billed early music concert, in which the choice of repertoire is rather clearly defined, the biggest choice the flutists must make is how to organize the program. Often, recital programs run the chronological gamut, a typical program including a baroque sonata, a classical concerto, a romantic tearjerker, a nineteenth century showpiece, and a neoclassical twentieth century sonata. There is nothing wrong with this system—it provides both variety of style and a chance for the player to show his versatility. Here are some variations:

- The two-era program. Pick just two historical periods, such as baroque and twentieth century. Do a half-program of each; if possible, relate each half to the other. Match a baroque suite and sonata to a modern suite and sonata. Or a Telemann fantasia for solo flute with the Ibert *Pièce* for solo flute.

- Pick a theme, such as the history of French flute music, which gives the program both stylistic unity and chronological diversity. Select your program from the works of Hotteterre, Chédeville, Leclair, Godard, Huë, Taffanel, Gaubert, Debussy, Ibert, Roussel, and so on.
- Pick one chronological period, but vary the form and instrumentation. For instance, create a program called "Music at the Court of Frederick the Great," as Rampal did for a record album. Draw on the works of Frederick himself, his sister Anna Amalie, Quantz, Graun, Hasse, C. P. E. Bach, and so on. But vary the performing forces from solo flute, to flute and keyboard, to flute quartet or quintet. Or do a program of American music. Or music of the Bach family.
- If you're really adventurous, and you anticipate a sophisticated audience, program works by only one composer. You must be a real expert to pull this off, but it is possible. One could conceivably program Bach's Partita in A Minor for unaccompanied flute, several sonatas for flute and keyboard, and the Suite in B Minor for flute and strings (preferably with string accompaniment, not keyboard reduction).

The possibilities are not endless, but there are more than enough to fill many programs for a long time to come.

Programs are traditionally arranged in chronological order. This is not a bad method, but don't feel you have to stick to it religiously. Continuity is important, so don't put an avant-garde piece between two baroque sonatas. On the other hand, feel free to start with a baroque sonata, move to Saint-Saëns, and then back in time to the classic era. Always be aware of jarring key juxtapositions, particularly if you don't intend to leave the stage between works. It may be uncomfortable to the sensitive ear to move from the key of E♭ major to that of D minor; you don't want to appear to go flat! Again, this is not a rule, simply a friendly warning.

One of Arthur Brooke's contemporaries, Henry T. Finck, wrote in his aptly titled book, *Success in Music,* that concert programs should be arranged in the following order: "first the intellectual, then the emotional, then the sensational."[4] There is a good deal of wisdom in that advice, though some caveats are also in order.

Finck is absolutely correct, for instance, when it comes to the fireworks genre; it should come at or close to the end (or at the end of the first half). It is, quite literally, a hard act to follow. A serious work following immediately thereafter will pale in the memory, no matter how meritorious its musical qualities or yours. On the other hand, an intellectually challenging avant-garde piece should not be at the head of a program, because it will probably scare off the audience, emotionally and/or physically! By all means include adventurous repertoire if you wish, but place it strategically—in the middle of the second half of the program.

Accompanists and Assisting Artists: Music for flute alone is a beautiful genre, all too much neglected, but the majority of the flute literature requires keyboard accompaniment. So the question is how to find a good accompanist. As with finding performing jobs and publicizing concerts, word of mouth is about the best tool there is. If you're not affiliated with a music school, where good pianists usually abound, you can still take advantage of schools in your area. Ask the flute students or teachers for their recommendations; that way, you're likely to find a pianist who is familiar with the flute literature. Or talk to a member of the piano faculty who can recommend colleagues or students. Often, college music departments and music schools have placement offices that can help you, and almost all have that old standby, the bulletin board.

One reason that it's a good idea to get references from other musicians—flutists, ideally—is that you want to find a good accompanist, not just a good pianist. (Purists will say, correctly, that in a true sonata the pianist is not merely an accompanist, but an equal partner. But in the interest of brevity I will use the term *accompanist* in this discussion.) A prima donna virtuoso pianist is someone you do not want. What you need is someone who is a sensitive chamber musician, attentive to balance.

Depending on the music you select, you may also want an accompanist who is able to realize a figured bass. Even if the editor has provided a realization, you will need an accompanist who can ornament the part appropriately and make any needed changes in the realization. You will also want to consider whether to use harpsichord or piano for baroque music; if harpsichord, the player will generally need (and want) to provide his own instrument. For practical purposes, however, most flute recitals use piano throughout, simply because of the logistical problems of using two instruments and possibly two different accompanists.

A few practical matters should be established from the beginning. Will the accompanist charge a fee? If so, are rehearsals included? Or will a student take the assignment free or for a nominal fee in order to get the experience? Remember that when dealing with professionals, you may encounter union-scale fees, which are quite high. Have a tentative concert date and rehearsal schedule in mind, so that you and your accompanist have sufficient time to practice together. The soloist must provide the accompanist with the music—well before the joint rehearsal, so the session is not wasted with a sight-reading run-through. Your accompanist's time, like yours, is valuable; don't waste it. By the same token, you should be fully prepared when you get to the first session together; you must know the program technically and interpretively and have in mind at least a tentative plan regarding repeats, ornaments, and so on. The joint rehearsals can then be productive work sessions, to meld the two parts together.

Often, recitalists decide to include one or more compositions that involve more than just a keyboard accompaniment. For a baroque sonata, for example, you may want to realize the basso continuo not only with keyboard, but also with bassoon, viola da gamba, or cello. Or you may want to include in the program chamber music that involves other instruments—a trio sonata, flute quintet, and so on. Assisting artists may function as accompanists or as full partners. In the former category, you can use a string quartet to accompany a baroque concerto. Or you can program chamber works involving other instruments, such as a woodwind trio, or a quartet or quintet for flute and strings. The list becomes endless, and your program becomes much more interesting.

Choosing a Recital Hall

Let's assume (a) that you are not required to perform in a particular auditorium for a required recital, and (b) that you have a choice of several. What factors should you consider in making your choice?

First, do you need free or nearly free facilities? Or are you prepared to pay commercial rental? If you intend to rent a hall, ask the management to quote a price that includes rehearsal time, security, utilities, and box office services. Find out whether the management will handle stage set-up, ticket collection, program distribution, and piano tuning, and whether those items will cost extra. The cost factor will undoubtedly narrow your choice of halls considerably, unless you're affiliated with a university where you have free access to the facilities.

Assuming the hall is either free or affordable, there are several other considerations. Ask about seating capacity. For the recitalist, particularly for anyone without an all-star reputation, smaller is definitely better. Better a full, small hall than a nearly empty large one. Both performers and audience feel more comfortable and less self-conscious in a well-filled hall. Next, consider the ambience. Is the hall dark and dingy, or does it have comfortable seating? Is it in good repair? The performer is ill served by listeners who trip over torn carpeting on the way to their seats and squirm once they get there.

Find out whether the temperature is controllable. If it isn't, you will find it difficult to play in tune. If the air circulation is poor, everyone will be uncomfortable. Don't even consider playing a summer concert in a hall without air conditioning.

Ask if the hall rental includes a concert-quality grand piano and whether the management guarantees to have it tuned just before the concert. Be sure to have your accompanist try the instrument before you contract for the hall. He or she can check not only for obvious defects, such as a broken pedal or string, a key that doesn't sound, or a missing lid peg, but also for defects in voicing or tone. If you need to bring other instruments such as a harpsichord, check whether there is enough room and security to store them safely.

Does the hall have adequate backstage facilities? Is there a soundproof area to warm up? Is there a dressing room? Is there space backstage or in the lobby for a reception? What arrangements can you make for catering the reception yourself or through the hall management?

Test the acoustics by actual trial. Take along your accompanist and another listener, so you can judge both onstage acoustics and the audience perspective. The hall should be neither too live (an echo chamber) nor a padded cell. Keep in mind, however, that a hall full of people will be less live than an empty one.

The Printed Program

Preparing and printing the program is a minor concern—compared with choosing the repertoire, learning the music, and finding a good accompanist. But it is an important and valuable tool for the recitalist. Not only is it the first thing that the audience sees, it is also the last. Many concert goers keep programs or pass them on to others, and you want to create a good impression of yourself and your performance.

The program may be typed, typeset, or hand lettered by a calligrapher, but it must be legible and accurate. Poor photocopies make a sloppy impression. Offset printing is a much better choice, and in quantities of 100 or more is actually less expensive. Offset also allows you to use paste-up elements, either typographical corrections or decorative art, which would show in the photocopying process.

Be sure to proofread the program. Also ask someone else to proofread for you; you may simply be too familiar with the material to catch errors.

The printed program should provide many kinds of information. Always list the movements in a piece. Otherwise, an audience unfamiliar with the composition will not know when it's over, and will clap after each movement. This rule applies particularly to a suite of dance movements or a four-movement sonata. If at all possible, and it usually is, include the opus number of the composition and/or the catalog number (for example, K. for Mozart or Wq. for C. P. E. Bach). The repertoire lists in this book include these numbers whenever they could be determined, although they may not be indicated on the printed music. Optional program items are the date of composition and the birth and death dates of the composer. These latter elements are particularly useful if you do not include program notes. If there is a cadenza, identify its composer if it was not written by the concerto composer—and especially if you wrote it yourself.

At the top of the program, you should list all the participants in the concert. Your name, as soloist, should of course come first, followed by your accompanist(s). They may be billed, if there are several, as "assisting artists," and then listed alphabetically or by instrument. If the latter, it is traditional to rank them in order of orchestral score position. In other words, the woodwinds come first (piccolo, flute, oboe, clarinet, bassoon), then brass (trumpet, French horn, trombone, tuba), followed by strings (violin, viola, cello, double bass), keyboard, and finally percussion. If the pianist is the primary accompanist, however, and the other instrumentalists play only in part of the program, the pianist should come first.

If the performers on the program differ from selection to selection, their names should be included under the appropriate pieces. The following is a sample program entry:

Concerto in C Major, Op. 7, No. 3 (1737) Jean-Marie Leclair
Allegro (1697–1764)
Adagio
Allegro assai

———, flute
———, violin ———, viola
———, violin ———, cello
———, harpsichord

Other items that you must include on the program are the date (including year), time, and place of the concert. That way, the program can also serve as a publicity flyer and as a permanent record "for the archives." If the concert is sponsored by an organization or institution, be sure to include its name. It may appear at the top, as in "The Flute Society of Washington presents . . . ," or it may go discreetly at the bottom. The latter format is generally used to acknowledge financial assistance from a charitable foundation. College recitals may require special wording, such as, "This recital is presented in partial fulfillment of the requirements for the Bachelor of Music degree." If you are performing such a recital, be sure to check with your music department for exact requirements.

You may also want to provide program notes. Like the program itself, they should be neither exhaustive nor exhausting. The notes might give some indication of when and for what purpose the piece was written, and whether it was commissioned by or dedicated to a well-known virtuoso. When it was first performed, how it was received, and any other historical information that will keep the piece in the audience's mind may also be included. A basic description of the piece may be helpful, but don't bore the reader with a detailed analysis. It would be useful and interesting, for example, to know that a particular Telemann sonata is a typical three-movement chamber sonata whose ornaments were indicated by the composer himself in the 1728 edition of the *Methodical Sonatas*. You might also explain how unusual it was for a baroque composer to provide such detailed embellishment.

You should briefly describe the unusual techniques in an avant garde work—the pioneering key-slaps in Varèse's *Density 21.5*, for instance—because the audience is likely to be unfamiliar with them. But don't belabor harmonic modulations or other constructive devices. Almost everyone finds technical analysis boring. Confine your discussion to that aspect of the piece that makes it distinctive and interesting—the aspect that justifies its inclusion on your program.

Moderation is also important when writing the description. By all means include the literary background of a programmatic work such as Debussy's

Syrinx, but don't use too many adjectives. And whatever you do, don't get maudlin in describing a sentimental work.

Finally, you may want to include biographical information on yourself and your fellow performers. Select the highlights from the following list of categories: academic degrees, musical scholarships or fellowships, prizes in musical competitions, orchestra or chamber group membership, academic affiliation, names of teachers, published articles or compositions, recordings, and musical specialty or particular interest (for example, early music, playing antique flutes). Your age, family history, place of residence, and nonmusical hobbies are not relevant to your performance and should be omitted.

With the exception of the soloist, the biographies of all the musicians should be of approximately equal length; it looks very awkward to see ten lines about the violist and two about the cellist. For assisting artists, in fact, current ensemble, orchestral, or academic affiliations may well suffice.

Publicity

If you're arranging your own recital, a crucial component is attracting your audience. Even if your performance is sponsored by an established organization, a little personal footwork can't hurt. The most obvious method, if you're playing at a university, is to post signs or posters outside the auditorium and on music department and other campus bulletin boards. If you're not playing in a university, take advantage of public notice areas in libraries, tourist information booths, and music stores.

Send copies of your program or poster to radio stations, clearly marked "Please announce." If the station has a regular calendar, direct the mailing to the host of that program. If you send a program, which would not ordinarily list the admission price (or whether the concert will be free), be sure to add that information.

When it comes to newspapers and regional magazines, keep in mind that print deadlines are often much earlier than you would expect, as much as two months for some magazines. Even newspapers have early deadlines for monthly calendar features; they often appear around the first of the month, with the deadline as much as a month before that.

There are three types of newspaper publicity:

1. Paid ads, of which there are two kinds. A display ad is exactly what its name implies, an eye-catcher. The paper may require camera-ready art, which means that you submit typeset and laid-out copy, including any decorative elements. Or the paper may do the typesetting and design. The less expensive alternative to a display ad is to run a classified ad in the performing arts or entertainment section. These may appear on a daily or weekly basis. It's to your advantage to keep classified ads short and simple. List your name, your accompanist (but not all the assisting artists), date, time, place, price, how

to get tickets, and, if there's room, a summary of the program, such as "Works of Bach, Handel, Taffanel, and Ibert" or "Modern French flute music."

2. A public service calendar announcement is another good source of publicity. Many papers run a section listing community events, often with the emphasis on free ones or those sponsored by nonprofit organizations.

3. In a small community, you may be able to arrange for the local newspaper to do a feature article, either on you or on the concert series as a whole, or on local musical events in general. Talk to the features editor and suggest such an angle. Better yet, send a press release, which the editor can print as is or modify at his or her discretion. Be sure to include your phone number on the release in case the editor has any questions. If you have a good current picture of yourself, preferably holding or playing the flute, send along an eight by ten inch glossy black-and-white print, with caption information and photo credit printed on the back. The easier you make it for the editor, the more likely you are to see your name in print.

Preparation and Rehearsal

For the purposes of this discussion, let's assume that you've learned the music technically, developed interpretive ideas about it, decided on embellishments for the pieces that warrant them, and written the cadenza if necessary. You've found an accompanist and/or assisting artists. (I'll discuss the pianist here; the same rules apply for other musicians.)

At your first rehearsal with the pianist, both of you should be prepared to concentrate on combining the parts you have learned on your own. Before you begin, go over obvious questions such as whether to take repeats, how to execute recurrent ornaments, how you wish to begin and end cadenzas, whether you want to ritard at the end of the movement, and so on. Then read all the way through each piece, making mental and then written notes of problem areas. This preliminary reading will enable you to set an agenda for future rehearsals and to budget your time advantageously. Then you can go back and work on details of ensemble work—coordinate phrasing, ornaments, and other interpretive details, and refine tonal and dynamic balances.

You should have at least one rehearsal, and preferably more, in the recital hall, because its acoustics are likely to be very different from those of the practice studio or living room where you ordinarily rehearse. Bring along a third person with a trained ear, who can listen from various parts of the audience for problems in balance. Try standing or sitting in various places on the stage. In most halls, the balance and sightlines are best when the flutist stands slightly in front of the bell of the piano.

Be prepared to modify passages that you may have thought were sufficiently worked out in earlier rehearsals on the basis of the auditorium's acoustics. This is particularly true for solo recitals played in large halls. For this reason it is helpful to know what sort of room particular works were intended for, so that you can gauge your concert repertoire accordingly.

Balance is only the most obvious element subject to alteration. Overall dynamic levels may also require modification depending on how live the hall is. In a large room with a reverberation time to match, you may want to take slightly slower tempos than normal in fast movements in order to allow all the notes to speak clearly. Conversely, if the acoustics result in a less weighty tone than usual, a customary slow tempo may seem unduly ponderous, and you may want to speed up slightly.

Several business days before the concert, check your flute thoroughly to make sure it is in good repair. See that the pads don't stick, the keys don't click, and so on. This is no time for amateur repairs; see a professional at once if there's a problem.

On the day of the concert you will undoubtedly be nervous. In the long run, the more concert experience you have, the more at ease you'll feel. But in the short term, there's no substitute for adequate practice, a good night's sleep, and physical relaxation. Eat lightly before the concert, avoiding alcohol and carbonated beverages. Similarly, stay away from tranquilizers, which will impair muscle control.

When you get to the hall, warm up slowly with long tones and basic technical exercises, such as scales in several articulations. Don't try to play through the recital program; it will tire you out, when you want to be fresh for the performance, and if you make mistakes, they are likely to shake your confidence. Clean your flute thoroughly, checking the pads for moisture bubbles, and dry them if necessary with cigarette paper or a dollar bill. Tune the flute to the piano before the audience arrives; you will want to recheck tuning when you begin the concert, but at least you'll be in the right range. It is painful for the audience and embarrassing for the performers when the soloist's first A is nearly a quarter tone off from the piano's. While you're on stage early, make sure it's set up properly, with enough music stands and chairs, the right music (if you're going to put it out ahead), proper lighting, and so forth.

Stage Protocol

The formal recital or concert setting presupposes a certain amount of respect for both music and performers, and the performers should reciprocate. First, the performer should wear attire appropriate to the occasion. Local custom and time of day should dictate details such as white tie or black, tuxedo or business suit, long dress or short. But relative formality should be the rule. Colors should not be distracting nor style sensational. All performers' outfits should be coordinated.

Let me provide a few hints for comfort. Clothes should not be so tight at neck or waist that they constrict breathing. Sleeves should be sufficiently loose to allow you to hold the flute comfortably. Women often find that skirts and blouses are better than dresses, so that their skirts do not hike up when they raise their flutes. Shoes should be comfortable, with moderate heels. Remember that you will be standing in them for the better part of an hour and a half (excluding the reception). Above all, wear something you will be comfortable in; clothes should not even enter your mind once you walk on stage.

The Entrance

The soloist should walk onstage first, followed by the accompanist or assisting artists and then the page turner, if any. Pianists will need page-turning assistance on most programs; soloists should try to be self-sufficient by hand-copying or photocopying passages that run over a difficult page turn. (Such limited photocopying constitutes "fair use" under the Copyright Law.) That way, you can turn the page at a convenient rest. If necessary, spread out the music over two overlapping music stands.

Carry your flute carefully, hands above the keywork, and with respect. Hold it at your side or slightly in front of you; don't sling it over your shoulder as if it were a rifle. A good strategem is to bow to an imaginary audience at the back wall of the auditorium, thereby looking over the top of the real audience and avoiding eye contact, which would only remind you of the hundreds of pairs of eyes staring at you, watching your every move.

After you and your colleagues bow, you may want to warm the flute. Cover the mouthhole with your mouth and blow gently and as silently as possible. Then turn to the pianist and check your tuning with a^1 and a^2, perhaps with an A minor chord. Do not play warm-up exercises or "noodles"; this is not the time to show off. Now you're ready to turn back to your music stand, open the score, and focus your attention on the music.

Playing the Program

The cardinal rule of public performance is not to distract the audience from the music. This rule applies equally to clothing and to behavior. The worst distraction is foot tapping; not only can it be noisy, but it's a visual annoyance. If you must beat time physically, wiggle your toes inside your shoes. This rules out wearing sandals, however.

Most important, communicate with your music, not with your body. As Theobald Boehm wrote, "If one cannot express his feelings through the style of tone, he surely is not in a position to do so by head or body movements. A calm, firm attitude certainly presents a much more pleasing appearance to the hearer than visible exertions, or affected, sentimental movements."[5] Keep your flute in a constant position, either parallel to the floor or angled down slightly. You will need to use the end of your flute to give your accompanist cues for entrances, ritards, and cutoffs, but you do not need to conduct the piece.

Similarly, don't try to characterize the music with your facial expression. Not only are you likely to harm your embouchure by distorting your facial muscles, but you will annoy the audience. Avoid the theatrics described by a critic for the *Dramatic and Musical Review* in 1845:

> One [musician] contents himself with a grimace, mixing up an occasional frown with an abundance of smiles the most bewitching, and bows the most graceful, enlivened occasionally with a decidedly inspiriting and truly national piping and jigging; one makes himself conspicuous by his lank hair, fixing the appearance of age upon what should be a young man's countenance; another depends upon his luxurious ringlets; one places his hopes upon a delicately formed mustache, another upon the thick underwood that half encircles his face. . . .[6]

The catalog of affectations goes on, but you get the idea.

If you want to provide background information for the audience, it is generally best to do so in the printed program notes. Confine your announcements from the stage to last-minute program changes and encores. Some professionals feel that speaking from the stage makes the music more accessible to the audience, but public speaking is an art in itself, and your main focus should be on your playing.

Memorization

The fear of a memory lapse is an added pressure you don't need during your recital. Solo pianists are just about the only performers who are bound by tradition (and inconvenient page turns) to play from memory. String players, observing the customs of such nineteenth century virtuosi as Paganini, often do, but not always. Lieder singers traditionally carry cue hooks containing the words. And opera singers lean heavily on the prompter. You certainly are not showing any inadequacy by using music.

Breaks between Pieces

The time between numbers is an opportunity first of all to acknowledge the applause of the audience. You must bow graciously even if you're not satisfied with your performance. Remember Quantz's good counsel to "ingratiate yourself with your audience."

The break between pieces is also a time to regroup—you may either remain onstage or adjourn briefly backstage. If there is to be a change in performers, the latter is the better choice. Take time to retune your flute. After you've been playing for a while, the temperature of both hall and instrument may have risen, and so will the pitch. If any of the key pads feel sticky, this is the time to slip in a piece of cigarette paper to dry them out.

If your lips or hands have perspired, wipe them with a handkerchief. This is best done backstage, of course, but if you do remain onstage, be discreet. You might be able to keep the handkerchief in a skirt or jacket pocket, and inconspicuously slip your hand in to dry it.

One final don't is in order: if you remain onstage, do not sip from a glass of water to moisten your lips. Inconspicuous action of the tongue or rolling the lips quickly, as if applying lipstick from upper lip to lower, should do the trick.

Encores

You've completed the program. You're pleased with your performance and so is the audience, which claps and cheers. Should you play an encore? Not necessarily. You're probably tired, and there's a good chance you've reached your limit of endurance. You can't go wrong by quitting while you're ahead, but you can injure the good impression you've made in the regular program by sloppiness in the encore.

If you decline to play an encore, some of history's greatest musicians stand firmly behind you. Joseph Haydn had a note printed in the program for the 1798 premiere of his oratorio *The Creation* requesting that the audience not insist on the repetition of any of the numbers. Quantz advised that when the flutist has finished the announced program, "he should not insist upon playing more . . . , lest we must beg him as many times to cease as we had to beg him to begin, a common reproach made against virtuosos."[7]

If you do decide to play an encore, don't be too hard on yourself. Find a piece that sounds much harder than it really is, a piece that may not astound the audience, but will charm it. Think of the encore as an after-dinner mint, to soothe the palate after a heavy meal.

Notes

1. Johann Joachim Quantz, *On Playing the Flute*, trans. Edward R. Reilly (London: Faber and Faber, 1966), p. 201.
2. Arthur Brooke, "The Ignorance of the Public in Regard to the Flute: How Shall We Remedy It?" *The Flutist* 2, no. 4 (1921), p. 369.
3. Ibid., p. 370.
4. Henry T. Finck, *Success in Music and How It Is Won* (New York: Charles Scribner's Sons, 1909), pp. 446–47.

5. Theobald Boehm, *The Flute and Flute-Playing*, trans. and rev. Dayton C. Miller, 2nd ed. (1922; reprint, New York: Dover Publications, 1964), p. 142.
6. "Affectations of Musicians," *Dramatic and Musical Review* 3 (1845): 45; quoted in David William Eagle, "A Constant Passion and a Constant Pursuit: A Social History of Flute-Playing in England from 1800 to 1851" (Ph.D. diss., University of Minnesota, 1977), p. 134.
7. Quantz, p. 203.

13

RECORDINGS

The flutists of the late twentieth century enjoy a tremendous advantage over their predecessors of even a generation ago: access to recordings and recording technology. Recordings can give you new ideas of interpretation and can widen your knowledge of the repertoire. The availability of inexpensive and easy-to-operate home-recording equipment also enables the student to analyze his own performance and to track his progress.

Building a Recording Collection

This is a task that is getting easier and easier—though admittedly more expensive. Jean-Pierre Rampal was the pioneer in getting flute music on record on a large scale, and many, many grateful flutists have followed his example. The current catalogs show twenty versions of the Mozart G Major Flute Concerto in print, a state of affairs that was unimaginable in the 1960s.

In addition to browsing in record stores' preselected bins, either in the flute category or under particular artists' names, there are several organized tools for finding recordings of particular pieces or by particular musicians. The best all-purpose reference for retail recordings—and the most widely available—is the *Schwann Opus Catalog.*

Schwann Opus is updated quarterly and is available for consultation or purchase in almost every record store. It is also available by mail subscription. Recordings (CD and cassette) are listed by composer, with a special section at the front for the month's new releases. Schwann also publishes an *Artist Issue*, which comes out annually; listings are divided by instrument, then by artist within each section. *Schwann Opus* is a virtual necessity for ordering recordings by mail, because it lists the manufacturer's stock numbers that most mail-order firms require.

The British equivalent of *Schwann Opus* is the *Gramophone Classical Catalogue.* Published four times a year, it is helpfully cross-indexed by artist in every issue. It includes many small European labels, as well as the major British ones, none of which are in *Schwann Opus.*

Information on the very newest recordings is available from a number of sources: reviews in newspapers; music magazines such as *American Record Guide* and *Gramophone;* and, of course, advertisements in those publications and in concert programs. Many classical radio stations have new-release features on a regular basis.

Discography—the bibliography of recorded sound—is a burgeoning field of scholarship, and flute recordings have been a beneficiary. *The National Flute Association Newsletter* and its successor, *The Flutist Quarterly*, have published a number of discographies organized by performer. Dissertations on flute music generally include specialized discographies. Finally, Flute World, a Michigan company, has a fine, in-depth stock of flute recordings, which are listed in its annual catalog.

How to Listen

To get the most out of listening to recordings, you must become a critical listener. Just what is a critical listener? It does not mean that you act like the pedantic Beckmesser in Wagner's *Die Meistersinger*, taking pleasure in chalking up the errors of the performers. Such a procedure may give you perverse pleasure—I remember a fellow flutist exclaiming with a mixture of horror and delight after a Rampal concert, "He made twenty-four mistakes in the Bach A Minor Partita!"—but it doesn't teach you anything.

Instead, you should listen to the interpretation and ask yourself the following questions: What tempo do the performers take? How do they use rubato, ritard, and other rhythmic modifications to express the music? How does the ensemble work together? Which melodic lines are important in various sections of the composition? Does the balance between the parts work well? How is the music phrased? How do phrases pass from instrument to instrument? What types of ornamentation do the players add? Is there too much ornamentation, too little, or the right amount? Can you discern an organized pattern to the use of ornamentation? How do the performers use tonal shading to enhance the phrasing? Is the intonation good? If not, can it flag potential problems in your own playing?

Once you've thought about these questions, you're ready to decide what you like about the performance, and which features you might want to make a part of your interpretation. Of course, you will often identify aspects of the performance that you find unacceptable—awkward phrasing, an unsuccessful transition, and so on. Such constructive criticism will help you avoid the same pitfalls in your own performance.

The most important thing to remember is to listen with discretion. Do not become a slavish imitator; if you adopt the affectations of a well-known recording, knowledgeable listeners will recognize it. Instead, use your imagination. Recordings—particularly those of Rampal, who has almost single-handedly put the basic flute repertoire on records—have been a major force in the worldwide adoption of the elegance and timbral sophistication of the French flute school. Some observers, however, caution that there is a negative aspect to this new International Style, a rather boring, monotonous overall conformity of interpretation.

Such criticism may be a bit alarmist, but the fundamental principle is right on target: each flutist's own personality and musical values must determine his or her style. The flutist should certainly absorb all he or she can from the best contemporary exemplars of all flute-playing traditions and then forge a personal, unique style. Use recordings as a springboard to experimentation and stylistic development. And by all means listen to all kinds of music, not just flute music. "Conversance with idiom," as discussed in chapter 11, "Style," comes from familiarity with all styles of music for all instruments and voice.

Playing Along

When you're learning a new piece or practicing for a concert, you may find it useful to play along with a recording. This is a good way to familiarize yourself with the accompaniment; it allows you to absorb the music aurally as well as through visual perception of the score. Do not feel, however, that you must adopt the tempos and mannerisms of the recording artists in your own interpretation; in fact, you are in danger of doing this if you play along with any one recording too much. Nevertheless, playing along is a good way to check intonation and to keep a constant tempo in early stages of practice.

If you set the volume of your stereo at normal levels, you will probably find it difficult to hear the accompaniment over your own flute playing. You have two choices: either turn the volume up considerably or listen to the recording with headphones. In the latter case, you may actually want to turn the volume down somewhat below normal so that you can still hear yourself.

You may want to minimize the recorded flute track, though on standard commercial recordings you can't eliminate it entirely. If the flute seems to be recorded primarily on one track, left or right, turn that channel down. If the flute appears equally on both channels, however, it can still be reduced by lowering the treble. The relative boost to the bass will give you a stronger harmonic and rhythmic frame of reference.

A crucial element of playing along is adjusting your pitch to that of the recording. If the recording was made on modern instruments, you should not have too much of a problem.

When records (LPs) were the prime recording medium, it was a relatively easy matter to alter the pitch of the recording by adjusting the speed of the turntable when adjusting the flute was not sufficient. If you still have an LP collection, as many of us do, you may want to play along with some of the fine performances of the past. The method is as follows.

Before you begin, check the speed of your turntable with a strobe card, a small paper device. The striations should appear to stand still as the turntable rotates. Many state-of-the-art turntables are equipped with an illuminated strobe on the side of the turntable. Most modern turntables also have a pitch adjustment knob or wheel that will allow you to vary the rotation speed to a slight extent. Typical tolerance is 3 percent in either direction. Increasing the speed will raise the pitch; decreasing the speed will lower it. Be aware that when you alter the pitch, you are also altering the tempo, but minor variations should not be bothersome.

Aligning the strobe device properly will allow your stereo equipment to reproduce accurately the pitch at which the recording was made. However, you may not be in tune with the recording if your flute is tuned to A-440 and the recording used A-442 or A-444, which are typical pitches for some European orchestras. With recordings of early music played on original or reproduction instruments, whose pitch is generally much lower than A-44, you are likely to have the opposite problem. The pitch may, in fact, be as much as a semitone low. (Recall the invention of the *corps de réchange,* interchangeable middle joints, to enable the eighteenth-century flutist to tune to the different pitches used in different cities.) In such cases, you will want to alter or "untune" your turntable. For early music, however, this stratagem may be inadequate, even in combination with pulling out your headjoint significantly. Remember, if the headjoint is extended more than a moderate amount, nodes of vibration in the air column will be disturbed for the entire length of the instrument and internal intonation will be noticeably awry.

Today, all new recordings come on compact discs or cassette tapes. Though the audio quality is arguably higher on CDs, the playback equipment allows no variation of pitch. Similarly, few cassette players (decks or "boom boxes") offer variable pitch. Only a few high-end audiophile devices can do so.

In addition to playing long with regular recordings, there is a fairly extensive series of cassettes put out by a company appropriately called Music Minus One (MMO). These recordings contain only the accompaniment. Some of the interpretations are not musically sophisticated by present standards—the baroque orchestral accompaniments were recorded in the 1950s or early 1960s—but they are useful tools for the student. For compositions in which the flute begins in the first measure, percussive taps indicate the tempo, and there is a tuning note at the beginning of each disc. The packages include sheet music in which recording cues are indicated.

In the mid-1970s, MMO published a variation on the usual theme, called the Laureate Series. There are twelve flute records in this set. The repertoire comprises contest solos at various levels of difficulty. On the A side of the record, a noted professional—Julius Baker, Doriot Anthony Dwyer, Murray Panitz, or Donald Peck—plays the program. The B side is in the usual MMO format of accompaniment only.

Since the 1980s, other companies have adapted the MMO concept. Falls House Press and Practice Tracks offer practice accompaniments to pedagogical literature, and David Williams Accompaniments produces cassettes of accompaniments to major works in the flute repertoire.

Making Your Own Recordings

The only way to improve your playing is to listen to yourself, and one of the best ways to do that is to make recordings, both in rehearsal and in concert. Only when you analyze your performance as you would any other flutist's can you evaluate your work accurately. For one thing, your tone sounds different to you while you are playing and your whole body is involved in the process. What you hear while playing may be very different from what the audience hears, especially in large concert halls.

Whether recording in a studio or concert hall, make sure that the microphones are not set up too close to where you're standing. You don't want to pick up inconsequential key clicks, rattles in the mechanism, breaths, or page turns that would not be heard by the audience because of distance.

If you're making a tape at home or in a studio, choose a room that is medium live. That is, it should be neither an echo chamber, which will unduly inflate the volume of your tone, nor a dead room, which will act as a muffler. If you're in the bad habit of tapping your feet, either take off your shoes or stand on a small swatch of carpet (don't use too big a piece, though, because carpet and upholstery act as sound absorbers). If you are forced to use a room that you know is too live, you can construct makeshift baffles by hanging blankets on the walls or putting a rug on the floor so that the sound can't bounce off hard surfaces.

You should use high-grade tape. The cost differential between the lowest-grade ferric tape cassettes and medium-grade chromium dioxide tape is less than a dollar for a sixty-minute cassette. Use a separate microphone, not the condenser microphone included in some portable recorders. Today, professional-quality recordings, and that includes audition tapes, are generally made on digital audio cassettes (DAT) or on reel-to-reel tapes. However, analog cassettes produce excellent quality recordings, and it is not necessary to invest in your own digital recording equipment.

Making audition tapes is a procedure with some special, very practical rules. Before you do anything else, read the instructions for the audition or competition. Is a particular format or order specified? Is there a minimum or maximum time limit? Is specific repertoire required? Must you announce the selections? How should you identify the tape? When you send in the tape, should you include your written application and/or entry fee in the same package?

Before you send your tape, especially if you're sending a dub, listen to it. Make sure there are no technical glitches, such as radio interference, in the tape. And be sure to make a safety copy for your files. If the original is lost or damaged in transit or if the judges' playback equipment malfunctions and destroys your entry, you want to be ready with a backup, and you certainly don't want to go to the trouble and expense of making a new tape. The file tape will also serve as a barometer of your progress as you become more and more advanced.

It is probably not necessary to hire a professional recording studio to make an audition tape. Obviously, this is very expensive, and you may be able to achieve equally satisfactory results on your own. Many home-audio buffs have superb, quality-recording equipment and would jump at the chance to "produce" the recording session for you. Alternatively, some college and conservatory music departments provide recording facilities for their students, along with personnel to operate them.

THE MUSIC

14

THE BAROQUE ERA

Manfred Bukofzer's often-used chronology divides the baroque into three periods: early, 1580–1630; middle, 1630–80; and late, 1680–1730. In discussing flute literature, however, Bukofzer's first two periods are largely irrelevant. The one-keyed flute was not even invented until the middle of his second period, and did not achieve prominence until nearly twenty years into the third. His colleague Jens Peter Larsen chose 1750, the year of J. S. Bach's death, as a convenient endpoint. For purposes of discussing flute literature, I shall define the baroque era as that period corresponding with the exclusive prominence of the one-keyed flute, from approximately 1660 to 1760, though this definition is not without caveats: pre-1700 flute music is nearly nonexistent. The end of the era is particularly difficult to quantify, more so since the transformations of style occurring in the mid-eighteenth century were not consistent from nation to nation.

Scholars have proposed a number of explanations for the hibernation of the transverse flute during the seventeenth century, the period corresponding to Bukofzer's middle baroque. Perhaps, some historians argue, it was due to the growing role of the transverse flute (fife) in military music, which was to continue until the shawm family superseded the fife during the reign of Louis XIV. After the destruction and devastation of the Thirty Years War (1618–48), those historians reason, an instrument with past military associations would tend to lose favor in the public eye. Moreover, physical modifications to make the instrument more suitable for outdoor use—in particular, making it shriller—would consequently make it less suitable for indoor music. Other historians suggest that the growing complication of musical composition after 1600 forced the cylindrical Renaissance flute into obscurity because the instrument was incompetent to deal with the new technical demands of the music. In any case, seventeenth century scorings for flute are nearly nonexistent; those few that do exist place the flute in the context of large ensembles, primarily as accompaniment to vocal music.

The flute did not reemerge as a solo instrument until after its physical remodeling at the hands of the Hotteterre family, sometime between 1660 and 1670. The new flute took a firm hold in France by the turn of the eighteenth century. Thus began the first Golden Age of the flute.

Flute Versus Recorder

Implicit in the escalating prominence of the transverse flute at the beginning of the eighteenth century was its eventual displacement of the recorder. At first, the newly redesigned transverse flute coexisted with its vertically held predecessor; indeed, alternative instrumentation was a common practice, used as early as 1692, when Marin Marais published his *Pièces en trio*, and as late as 1741, the date of Rameau's *Pièces en concerts*.

By virtue of its acoustical characteristics, however, the baroque flute achieved predominance. The flute's range exceeded that of the recorder by at least half an octave, and it spoke more easily in the upper register, which endowed it with greater agility. Moreover, the recorder's airway was built-in and therefore inflexible. Though capable of producing a clear, well-articulated sound (perhaps even more so than the flute), the recorder did not have the capacity to make significant changes in the tone color by means of the airstream.

On the transverse flute, in contrast, the airstream was formed by the player's lips, which are highly flexible. Though articulation was less well defined than on the recorder, the flutist's control over the quantity and direction of air entering the instrument allowed more subtle shading of tone color, as well as greater control of pitch and dynamics. These physical potentialities were attractive to composers; the "soft complaining flute" of Dryden's "Ode to Saint Cecilia's Day" encouraged them to write in the expressive *cantabile* style.

The transition from recorder to flute took nearly a century. The transverse flute, not surprisingly, in view of its French invention, took hold first in France; Germany was next, by the turn of the eighteenth century. The flute became popular in England only after the accession of George I in 1714. In fact, the baroque flute may owe its frequent appellation "German flute" to its importation to England at this time by the House of Hanover. The flute appeared in Italy still later, around 1715, and took a good decade to really catch on.

Tracing the intertwined histories of flute and recorder in the early eighteenth century is complicated immensely by inconsistent terminology. In general, the recorder was known by the names *flute, flûte douce, flauto, Blockflöte, common flute*, and *English flute*; the transverse flute was referred to as *flûte traversière, traverso, flûte d'Allemagne, Querflöte*, or *German flute*. Although some composers were meticulous about specifying which instrument they intended to play their music, others were maddeningly vague.

Musicologists attempting to come to firm conclusions in particular cases must therefore rely on such factors as range—f^3 on the flute was notoriously unstable, for instance—and on keys or tonalities. The flute did best in sharp keys (G and D, particularly), less well in flat ones. The keys of G, D, A, E minor, and B minor were therefore the most popular ones for the transverse flute; F, C, D minor, and A minor were best for the recorder. But these considerations serve merely as guidelines, not as rules, and one can easily find counter examples to disprove them. Bach, for example, was very specific with regard to instrumentation, yet he scored a nearly impossible high F for flute in the obbligato to the tenor aria in his Cantata no. 78.

Bach's careful attention to instrumentation takes on particular importance in his vocal works, where the accompanying instruments have emotional and programmatic significance. He chose the relatively characterless recorder for such intangible emotions as religious devotion and resignation to death. He preferred the flute, however, for more personal expressions, often combining it with the oboe d'amore, whereas he combined the recorder with the viola.

The other great figure of the high baroque, Handel, is representative of the transition from recorder to flute; he marked many of his early works *flauto ou traverso*. Later, he came to appreciate the coloristic possibilities of the flute, perhaps as a result of hearing Karl Friedrich Wiedemann, flutist at the King's Theatre, London, beginning in 1726.

Vivaldi is a particularly good example of the overlap of flute and recorder during the baroque era. Limited choice of keys, generally unidiomatic writing for wind instruments, limited range, and nonspecific terminology characterize his oeuvre as a whole. Scholars have made highly informed guesses regarding Vivaldi's instrumentation, but these remain hypotheses. The consensus is that Vivaldi came to prefer the flute around 1725–30, perhaps after Quantz's visit to Venice in 1726 convinced him of the instrument's potential.

Alessandro Marcello, writing in the preface to his 1738 concertos, expressed the prevalent Italian opinion when he declared that the full effect of his works could be achieved only with two oboes or two transverse flutes.[1] And by 1761, François A. P. Garsault reported in his *Notionnaire ou Memorial raisonné* that the transverse flute was used for accompaniment, but the recorder merely for amusement.[2] Indeed, the transverse flute had become the unequivocal preference of professional musicians; the recorder was relegated to amateurs, and even among them, to amateurs not sufficiently skilled to master the one-keyed flute.

Musical Forms

Because the transverse flute did not achieve prominence until the very end of the seventeenth century, it was heir to a rich inheritance of musical progress that had taken place in the preceding century. Several basic characteristics had become firmly established. Music was highly functional, and was written specifically for use in either the theater, church, or for entertainment. The acoustical requirements of these settings influenced their respective musical genres: reverberant churches such as Saint Mark's in Venice necessitated relatively slow harmonic rhythm, but they also inspired echo effects and terraced dynamics and ultimately the ripieno-concertino dichotomy in the concerto. Chamber music, in contrast, was designed for more intimate surroundings; dynamics on the whole were less extreme or pronounced; instruments were softer, and the harpsichord, virginal, lute, and clavichord were prominent.

Speech became the model for melody, whether vocal or instrumental. Dance forms of all descriptions characterized baroque instrumental rhythms and forms, providing ceaseless motion and clear organization. The bass grew to occupy a position of great importance, a development that paralleled the deepening of perspective in the visual arts; the basso continuo gave depth to the harmony. The broad chasm between the melody in the treble line and the harmony in the bass, with the harmony filled in, if desired, by other voices or instruments, is perhaps the greatest distinguishing facet of baroque style. Hugo Riemann called this characteristic "the touchstone of the Baroque."[3] It established the harmonic structure and the instrumental balance and permitted sophisticated melodic development, including ornate embellishment. The freedom of the melody line was the very essence of baroque monodic style.

Moreover, by having such a means of establishing a firm, unifying meter, the basso continuo allowed Italian baroque pioneers to introduce variety within individual compositions, and they invented instrumental forms—orchestral canzoni, sonatas, concerti, and overtures—with movements in contrasting tempi. In addition, they began to use the movement titles to express not only the tempo, but also the prevailing mood; *adagio* meant not just slow, but also leisurely; *allegro* was gay as well as quick.

The Italian baroque developed several major instrumental forms that were adopted for the flute. First was the trio sonata, with its two melody lines superimposed on the thorough bass, followed by the two types of solo sonata. The *sonata da camera,* or chamber sonata, grew out of the early opera overtures, and consisted of a succession of dances, varied in tempo and meter but all in the same key. The *sonata da chiesa,* or church sonata, began as an instrumental interlude between vocal pieces in the church service. Its melodies were often folkloric, though not dancelike, and the texture was strongly contrapuntal. Typically it had four movements, with a tempo scheme of slow-fast-slow-fast, the third often in a contrasting key to the others. The outstanding exponent of the Italian baroque sonata was Arcangelo Corelli, whose virtuoso treatments succeeded in elevating instrumental music to an equal footing with vocal genres. An outgrowth of the *sonata da camera* was the large suite, in which nondance movements were interspersed among dance types. In the orchestral arena, the concerto, first the concerto grosso and then the solo concerto, was the most important form of the Italian baroque.

An important facet of the middle baroque, one particularly applicable to woodwind music, is the development of distinct national styles, with a particular dichotomy between France and Italy. In general, the French were partial to the suite and overture forms; they wrote precisely notated ornamentation or *agréments;* they were sensitive to program, emotion, and color. Because of this sensitivity, they were partial to the woodwinds.

The Italians, in contrast, concentrated on the sonata and concerto forms; they confined embellishments to the adagio movements; their music had a more energetic, active orientation; and they were partial to the stringed instruments (witness the excellence of the Cremona violin-making tradition). François Raguenet recorded the result in his *Paralèle des italiens et des français,* first published in 1702:

> The French flatter and tickle the ears. . . . The Italians are interested in everything which sounds unusual, even rough. . . . They understand the passionate emotions and express them better in their works. . . . Next to the instruments which are common to both French and Italians, we French also possess the oboe, which in its simultaneously soft and penetrating tone has a tremendous advantage over the violins in all fast and vivacious movements, and secondly the flute, which, as it is being taught successfully by many of our great artists, knows how to lament in mournful movements movingly and to sigh enamouredly in the tenderly moving sections.[4]

The Germans took a compromise position between the French and Italian styles, aiming for a middle ground between contrapuntal texture and emphasis on harmonic materials; this effort, aided by the travels of musicians for study and performance, culminated, by the mid-eighteenth century, in the *style galant,* which would achieve full flower in the rococo or preclassic period.

This movement away from the baroque began as early as 1720, even while those exemplars of the high baroque, Bach and Handel, were at the height of their powers. Coming after the international union of the Italian *da camera* and *da chiesa* styles, it was, like much of eighteenth century music, initially a French product, but was adopted in name and style—and further developed—by the Germans. Largely identified with the pleasure-loving frivolity of the French court, it brought the elegant style of the theater into the realm of chamber music, in sharp contrast to the learned style *(style travaillé, la musique savante, gearbeitet, gebunden, gelehrt),* of Bach, who represented the last hurrah of the church style in the mid-eighteenth century. Primarily, *galanterie* meant a relaxation of the tightly organized motivic play, of imitation, fugue, canon, and other such academic devices. Other features included the beginnings of bithematicism, use of fully notated ornaments, refinements in articulation and dynamics, and the thinning of texture. Ultimately, this trend culminated in the purely homophonic style of the classic era; but at this early stage, *galanterie* was merely a shift in emphasis from a contrapuntal conception to a more purely harmonic one.

Concomitantly, solo melody assumed greater importance; as the texture was reduced, two-part instrumentation became the norm. To compensate for the loss of polyphonic interest, composers smoothed out the melodic lines, emphasizing their horizontal nature and singable character. Moreover, the short motive stretched laterally into the phrase. Thus Quantz, writing in 1723, defined *galant* as "a melodic style, ornamented with many small figures and fast passages."[5]

But, as befits the time—the first galant began thirty years before Bach's death—it retained many baroque characteristics. The melody was still continuous, growing out of the basic motive and paralleling the bass line by using sequences and transpositions; the harmonic rhythm remained rapid; key areas were closely related; and the drive to the cadence continued to be the prime organizing factor.

In his *Versuch*, written in 1752, Quantz takes up the matter of embellishment, another important galant trait. Baroque embellishments were generally of two types: *agréments* (or *Setzmanieren*), indicated by the composer in symbols; and extempore variations or *Spielmanieren*, which included *notes inégales* and variations of articulation improvised by the performer. As the galant style gained prominence, ornaments increasingly appeared in written form as, for example, in Locatelli's flute sonatas (1732). Galant embellishments took on a new function as pure frills, giving galant and rococo music its frivolous reputation. But although they appeared in notation more frequently, they were shorter, and contributed more substantially to the harmonic content of the music by seriously affecting the balance of dissonance and consonance. Middle, slow movements were subject, logically, to the greatest galanterie because of their resemblance to the operatic aria and their potential for embellishment.

The prevailing mood of lightness manifested itself, in addition to the profusion of fussy ornamentation, in the production of new genres of music: the delicate harpsichord music of the Frenchmen Clerambault, Dandrieu, Couperin, and d'Agincourt; suites of descriptive character pieces for harpsichord, known as *ordres* (similar to the German or Italian suite); and the replacement of baroque dances with the minuet. The minuet, indeed, epitomized the rococo style to come, with its formal, courtly air and its small steps and gestures. Character or genre pieces became highly programmatic.

France

The one-keyed flute first appeared as an orchestral instrument in 1681, in Jean-Baptiste Lully's ballet *Le Triomphe de l'Amour*, and subsequently was used in several operas in the 1690s. Louis XIV took a liking to the instrument, and appointed two flute virtuosi, Philbert Rebillé (about 1650–1712) and René-Pignon Descoteaux (about 1646–1728) to the Chambre and Écurie at his court. It is likely that these early flutists played simple airs, perhaps arranged from opera and ballet music, and dance tunes, either traditional or newly composed by the performers themselves. Their performances, coupled with a desire to imitate royal taste, influenced aristocratic and middle class amateurs to take up the flute as well. The rapid growth of the flute's popularity is evident in the visual arts of the period, where the instrument was no longer confined to pastoral settings.

The amateur market demanded a repertory of music, and French composers were quick to oblige. The most common pieces featured one or two treble instruments over a figured bass. Among the earliest examples for flute were collections of suites and trios by Pierre Gaultier (about 1643–97), also known as Gautier [sic] de Marseille, whose works were published in Paris beginning in the 1690s. Marin Marais (1656–1728), leader of the French school of bass viol performance, published his *Pièces en trio pour les flutes, violin, et dessus de viole* in 1692. Significantly, the composer emphasized that the pieces were suitable for nearly any combination of treble instruments and bass. The sixty-three *pièces* were divided into six suites, each unified by key, opened by a prelude, and followed by seven to twelve additional movements. Michel de La Barre, a pupil of Philbert and Descoteaux who had joined the Chambre in 1705, published a set of *Pièces en trio*, for two violins, flutes, or oboes, with basso continuo, in 1694.

The next step was the development of literature for solo flute with accompaniment; La Barre's *Pièces* for flute and continuo, issued in 1702, were the first pieces for solo transverse flute published in Europe. Considered by his contemporaries the best flutist in Paris, La Barre was widely admired for his charming, nuanced sound and expressive interpretation of even the simplest air. His *pièces* are mostly in suite form (a series of simple dances and character pieces, unified by key). Their simplicity of line, elegance of articulation, and intimacy of feeling were well suited to his own performance style. La Barre's *Pièces pour la flûte traversière*, op. 4 (1703) advised the player on embouchure, articulation, and ornamentation, and were the first such printed instructions to appear in France.

Another new form was the unaccompanied flute duet, which, like the far rarer unaccompanied solo, served both artistic and pedagogical ends. It was either contrapuntal, with the two parts relatively equal throughout, or homophonic, with the parts generally fitted into progressions of parallel thirds and sixths. In the former, the contrapuntal structure was sufficiently well constructed that the inclusion of a separate bass line became superfluous; double counterpoint and the crossing of parts were frequent features. Ultimately, the contrapuntal type gave way to the homophonic, but some compositions used the two textures to provide contrasts between movements. The unaccompanied duet form continued well into the eighteenth century, long after the accompanied suite and sonata had declined. In 1709, La Barre became the first composer in France to publish suites for two flutes without bass.

Jacques Hotteterre *le Romain* (1674–1763), best known for his instrument design, also contributed significantly to the flute literature. His 1708 *Pièces*, op. 2, include not only suites for flute and continuo, but also two duos for unaccompanied flutes (dedicated to Louis XIV). Hotteterre also composed the only music of the era for unaccompanied flute: two short echo movements at the end of his 1708 *Pièces*, the preludes in his *L'art de préluder* of 1719, and some arrangements of airs and brunettes that were published about 1721.

The suite of La Barre and Hotteterre was a flexible form that became a French national trademark. But it soon was supplemented and then superseded by the sonata, a trend emblematic of Italian infiltration of the French style after 1700. Sebastien de Brossard, a French lexicographer, theorist, and cleric, reported that "all the composers of Paris . . . had at that time . . . the craze to compose Sonates à la manière Italienne."[6] And Michel Corrette later recalled, "All concerts took on a different form; scenes and *symphonies* from opera were replaced by sonatas."[7] The op. 5 violin sonatas of Corelli, acknowledged as the paragons of the genre, were first printed in Paris about 1701, but they had already been played in the French capital several years earlier, perhaps as early as 1694.

In the flute literature, La Barre was again the pioneer: his third book (1707) includes sonatas for two flutes and bass, the first such score to be published in Europe. Hotteterre began by arranging for flute sonatas by such Italians as Albinoni and Robert Valentine, then published his first original flute sonatas in 1715. These early sonatas were little different from the suites of the time in terms of the types of dances they comprised. But the number of sonata movements was generally limited to four, and the order became fairly fixed. A slow prelude was followed by a fast second movement (a fugue, gigue, or courante); a slow third movement (La Barre preferred gavottes and rondeaux, Hotteterre, the more Italianate grave); and finally a lively last movement, a fugue or gigue. The French sonata form quickly became less standardized, however, with five or six movements, not unlike the Corellian sonata da chiesa.

Hotteterre was also the father of French flute pedagogy. His *Principes de la Flute Traversière* (1707) was the first tutor designed specifically for flute ever published. Such was its quality and success that it was reprinted continuously until 1765. His second treatise, *L'art de preluder sur la flûte traversière* (1719) provided, in addition to exercises and etudes, important information on meters and rhythmical alteration.

Other than La Barre and Hotteterre, the composers of this first French period were not flutists themselves. Anne Danican Philidor (1681–1728), an oboist at the French court and a member of a distinguished musical family, wrote two books of suites and sonatas for flute and continuo. Michel Pignolet de Montéclair (1667–1737), a bass viol player in the Paris Opéra, published six *Concerts* for two unaccompanied flutes and six for flute and figured bass, about 1720–25. These were unconventional suites: uncommonly long, including such novel movement types as pastourelles, musettes, and vilanelles, and unusual in their juxtaposition of tonalities. In harmonic structure and in general style, Montéclair's works, like Hotteterre's, belied an Italian influence.

The second phase of the French baroque flute, characterized principally by the shift of performances from court to city, began in about 1725 and lasted until 1740. After the death of Louis XIV in 1715, the frequency of court concerts began to decrease. The regent, Philippe d'Orleans, though, ironically, a former pupil of Hotteterre, did not encourage musical activities. When Louis XV acceded to the throne in 1723, he perpetuated his regent's lack of interest in music. The aristocracy assumed the responsibility of patronage; among the most prominent musical sponsors were the Count Egmont (patron of Jacques Christophe Naudot) and Le Riche de la Pouplinière, the tax collector who founded the Concerts Pouplinière and had his portrait painted with two transverse flutes as props.

The virtuoso flutist-composers who were the pacesetters of the period taught and performed primarily for the aristocracy and bourgeois public. They took full advantage of the public concert and the music publishing business, and thus owed their livelihoods to commerce rather than to royal patronage. The new middle-class concert life was exemplified by the 1725 establishment of the Concert Spirituel, a concert series founded by Anne Danican Philidor to provide musical entertainment on days when the Opéra was closed for religious observances.

The Concert Spirituel, forbidden to perform opera excerpts, featured violin and flute soloists. In 1726, Michel Blavet became the first of twenty-eight flutists who appeared there during the concerts' sixty-four-year history. His technical virtuosity, combined with a rich, pure tone, raised flute playing to a new level of brilliance and the flute to an equal level with the solo violin. Blavet played the flute left-handed, possibly as a result of self-instruction. (This was a feat possible only on the one-keyed flute; the single D♯ key had a fontanelle or splayed key that allowed it to be reached from either side.) A contemporary music critic, Hubert le Blanc, concluded upon hearing Blavet:

> The flute can declaim better than the violin and is more of a mistress of swelling [the tone] or of making diminutions. At the end of the concert people were of the opinion that the flute, played by a Blavet, is preferable to the first violin, when it is a question of imitating the voice, which cannot, as everyone knows, sing several tones at once.[8]

Blavet not only wrote music for himself, but also inspired works by other composers, even by nonflutists.

The flute's popularity among amateurs grew by leaps and bounds. By 1727, a Dutch traveler to Paris could report,

> The instruments which are the most popular now in Paris are the harpsichord and the transverse or German flute. The French today play these instruments with an unparalleled *délicatesse*.[9]

The composers Joseph Bodin de Boismortier and Michel Corrette both became wealthy men through sales of music to the amateur market; both wrote flute tutors, though neither man was a flutist.

As the Italian influence grew ever stronger in France, the concerto became a favorite vehicle for orchestral soloists. Emblematic of the Italian influence was the publication of Vivaldi's *L'estro armonico*, op. 3 (Amsterdam, 1711), which achieved huge popularity in Paris, resulting in what one historian terms "snobisme vivaldien."[10] Albinoni's concertos, too, had been known in the French capital since 1723; the Concert Spirituel programmed Vivaldi's *The Four Seasons*, a set of four violin concertos, in 1728. The early French concertos essentially adopted the Vivaldian form: fast–slow–fast movements, the tutti–solo contrasts, the Italianate melodies, tutti ritornellos in the fast movements, powerful unisons, and scalar passages.

The flute played an important role in the acceptance of the concerto form in France. The first French publication to use the title concerto was by Boismortier, the *VI Concertos pour 5 Flutes traversières ou autres instruments sans basse*, op. 15 (1727). Boismortier published still more concertos the following year, quickly followed by a set by Michel Corrette. Corrette reportedly wrote the first solo flute concerto in about 1729 (it has since been lost); Jacques Christophe Naudot published the first complete set of flute concertos in France circa 1735–37. These were only the second such set published anywhere, Vivaldi's op. 10 (1730) having been the first.

The French shift from suite to sonata had been evident even in the works of La Barre and Hotteterre, but in the second quarter of the century the sonata became firmly entrenched in France. But the new generation of sonatas began to evolve in several important ways from the earlier French versions of the form. They often retained the slow–fast–medium-fast tempo plan of the early trio sonata, but they abandoned the first-movement preludes, third-movement gavottes, slow allemandes, and fugues. Of the dance movements, only the fast ones survived, though after about 1732–33 all dance movements became infrequent, and movements were designated by tempo markings alone. Technically, the sonatas changed to reflect the increasing virtuosity of the players; there were longer sixteenth-note runs and arpeggios, faster and more ornate passagework, and larger melodic intervals. Slow movements, too, became more ornate. Around 1733 Naudot introduced the aria as a third-movement type, which lent itself to elaborate extempore ornamentation. Blavet's last book of sonatas, published in 1740, was the first such collection to provide elaborate written ornamentation in the reprises. By the early 1740s many sonatas had shrunk to three movements, with fast–slow–fast the usual configuration, and slow–fast–fast a frequent alternative.

The unaccompanied flute duet continued to enjoy tremendous vogue in the second quarter of the century. It was supplemented by a new form, the unaccompanied flute trio, introduced by Boismortier in 1725.

Michel Blavet (1700–68) began his compositional career in 1728, two years after his first appearance at the Concert Spirituel, with six sonatas for two flutes without bass. His op. 2 sonatas for flute and bass, published four years later, show a definite descent from the French suite and Corellian chamber sonata. The movements feature picturesque and expressive titles in the French suite tradition. The op. 3 sonatas are more progressive, showing elements of galanterie. Blavet's only extant flute concerto, a brilliant piece of virtuosity that also takes full advantage of the transverse flute's tone, dates from the 1740s. Its outer movements are clearly in the Vivaldian tradition, but in place of the usual Italian slow middle movement, Blavet used a pair of elegant Gallic gavottes. In a similar manner, Blavet's duets represent a transition from the highly ornamented types of his immediate predecessor to the Italianate sonatas of his younger colleagues. The op. 1 duets (1728), each in four or five movements, feature extensive imitation, but less ornamentation than the duets of La Barre and Hotteterre; the extent of modulations is limited. In the late, three-movement duet sonatas, the themes are more Italianate, and there is greater rhythmic variety and increased use of nonharmonic tones to create dissonance.

The career of the forward-thinking Joseph Bodin de Boismortier (1689–1755) was in sharp contradiction to his unfortunate surname ("dead wood"). In addition to introducing the term *concerto* to French music (his op. 15 concertos for five flutes of 1727, mentioned above) he wrote the first French solo concerto for any instrument, his op. 26 concerto for cello, viol, or bassoon (1729). For the flute, Boismortier claimed many firsts in terms of instrumental combinations: three flutes with bass, three flutes without bass, five flutes with bass, five flutes without bass. And he was the first French composer to write pieces for flute and harpsichord in which the keyboard part was fully realized (op. 91, about 1741–42). He was responsible in great measure for the eventual supremacy of the sonata over the suite, publishing eight books of sonatas for two flutes and four sets for flute and continuo between 1724 and 1733. They are usually of *da camera* form, consisting of four movements in French dance forms, such as allemandes, courantes, sarabandes, and gigues. Perhaps because Boismortier was not a flutist, his works tend to be less virtuosic than those of Blavet, but they are no less elegant.

Even in the earliest opus, Boismortier's concertos were in the Italian style. Indeed, in those six five-flute concertos, the four upper voices are grouped in pairs, and the lowest voice provides the bass line, thus echoing the texture of the trio sonata. Interestingly, the lowest voice was figured to permit the addition of a harpsichord, if desired. The concertos followed the Italian three-movement form and featured solo-tutti alternation. Yet Boismortier did not entirely escape his native roots; the thematic material seems more French than Italian. His later concertos also demonstrate the uncertain nature of the term as then used, for the traditional Italian ripieno is absent. For example, op. 37 (1732) is scored for flute, violin, oboe, bassoon, and bass; op. 38 (1732) for two flutes; op. 68 (1737), entitled *Noëls en concerto a 4 parties*, is scored for musettes, vielles, violins, flutes, or oboes.

Jacques-Christophe Naudot (about 1690–1762), a Paris flutist contemporary with Blavet and Boismortier, composed profusely between 1726 and 1752. His principal contribution was the publication of the first printed set of solo flute concertos in France (about 1735–37). Appropriately, in view of their Vivaldian antecedents, they were paragons of the Italian style. All six are three-movement compositions (fast–slow–fast) constructed on the ritornello principle. The slow movements are highly embellished, in the French style; the outer, fast movements feature typically Vivaldian scalar runs and vigorous arpeggios.

Naudot's sonatas vary between three and six movements in length. They tend to be simple in character, with few ornaments but with great rhythmic interest. His late works begin to assimilate galant elements, particularly in the slow movements, and the fast movements begin to have a clearer phrase structure. Naudot also wrote a number of duos for flutes without bass and trio sonatas.

The case of the Loeillet family is one that has fascinated musicologists for years. The problem involves two cousins, both born in Ghent and both baptized Jean Baptiste, both of whom became musicians, and both of whom editors have confused from the very beginning of their careers. The younger of the two, born in 1688, worked for the Archbishop of Lyons and adopted the name Loeillet de Gant. His musical output includes four sets of twelve sonatas each for recorder and continuo, published between 1710 and 1717; six trio sonatas for flute, oboe or violin, and continuo (1717); and six unaccompanied sonatas for two flutes. Loeillet de Gant was a contrapuntal master, particularly proficient in fugal movements; he also drew heavily on dance forms for his third and fourth books of solo sonatas. He died about 1720.

His cousin, the Jean Baptiste who lived from 1680 to 1730, was a professional flutist. He moved to London in 1705, where he became principal oboist and flutist in the opera band in Haymarket, at which time he anglicized his name to John Loeillet of London. Like his namesake, he wrote a variety of solo and trio sonatas for flute and recorder, though the Londoner's works are considered more idiomatic to the instruments. Many of his movements were in a rudimentary ternary form, with an embryonic recapitulation; he often used a minuet in place of the older gigue movement. Tradition has it that John Loeillet was in large part responsible for the popularity of the flute in England during the early eighteenth century.

Jacques Loeillet (1685–1748), known during his lifetime as Jacob, was the younger brother of John. In addition to the usual flute duets and solo sonatas, he wrote a solo flute concerto and an interesting quintet for two flutes, two recorders, and continuo, in which both types of instruments are treated equally. Jacques Loeillet was a musician at the court of the Elector of Bavaria in Munich, where he had many contacts with Italian musicians; as a result, his own scores include Italian tempo indications and use the Alberti bass pattern.

François Couperin *le grand* (1668–1733) was organist and court composer to Louis XIV. Imbued with a typically French melodic orientation and influenced by the ballets of Lully, he was also enthusiastic about the Italian trio sonata. His first six such works, published about 1692–95, were the first French sonatas "à la manière Italienne." Couperin's philosophical aim, clearly reflected in the works he wrote for flute, was to effect a union between the French and Italian styles, "*les goûts réunis.*" To do so, he used French melodies, moderate chromaticism, and basic simplicity of design within the Italian sonata mold. From the Italian style he also drew such devices as driving harmonic sequences.

The four *Concerts royaux* in the *Troisième livre de pièces de clavecin* (1722) and the nine *Nouveaux concerts* in *Les goûts-réunis* (1724), many of which had been written in the previous decade for the entertainment of the aging and conservative Louis XIV, are French *ordres* of five to seven pieces, as are most of the *Goûts-réunis*. Contrapuntal two-part texture and allemandes predominate. But only one *concert*, the eleventh, has the typical, aristocratic French allemande; the others are lighter and more Italian in gesture.

The scores for two programmatic sonatas, *Apothéoses* for Corelli (1724) and Lully (1725), do not specify instrumentation, but *Lully* does suggest "flutes or violins" for the *Plainte* movement. *Corelli*, appropriately, is a seven-movement sonata da chiesa; *Lully* consists of twelve descriptive pieces and then a final movement that draw inspiration from Lully's operatic *symphonies*.

Jean-Marie Leclair (1697–1764), best known as the founder of the French violin school, also made substantial contributions to the flute literature, probably as a result of his association with Blavet at the Concert Spirituel. Leclair successfully synthesized Italian and French forms and performance traditions. The sonatas had both French and Italian elements: movements of the *pièce* genre or dances (often en rondeau, à la Couperin and Rameau) were intermingled with movements denoted simply by Italian tempo markings. Leclair adopted the tremendous technical resources of the Italian violin school—double, triple, and quadruple stops, double trills, left-hand tremolo, and a carefully notated variety of bow strokes—but his music demanded the use of the French *notes inégales*. And whereas the Italian violin school was known for its elaborate, improvised ornamentation, Leclair wrote his out in full. In the preface to the op. 9 sonatas (1743), he wrote in self-defense: "An important point upon which one cannot insist too much is to avoid that confusion of notes that people add to melodic and expressive pieces and which serve only to disfigure them."[11]

Following the Italian custom, he specified that nine of the violin sonatas could be performed on the flute. But Leclair took into consideration the limited technical abilities of the amateur flutists of the day (clearly he realized that the excellence of Blavet's technique was atypical). He prefaced op. 2 (about 1728) as follows: "I have taken care to compose sonatas for the capacity of people more or less skilled, since most may be played on the German flute."[12] In fact, the solo part for violin in the edition is more difficult than the flute version.

Leclair also specified that one of his violin concertos, op. 7, no. 3 (1737) could be played on flute, or, for that matter, on oboe. His concertos leave no doubt that he was intimately acquainted with the works of Corelli, Albinoni, and Vivaldi, an influence particularly evident in the presentation and reiteration of the tutti themes of the flute concerto. The middle movement, on the other hand, is a typically French tonal showpiece.

Like Couperin, Michel Corrette (1709–95) was an organist, and like Boismortier, his lack of first-hand acquaintance with the flute did not prevent him from composing prolifically for the instrument nor from publishing a method for it (about 1735). As mentioned above, Corrette wrote the first French solo flute concerto, though the music has since been lost. He incorporated popular airs of his day into many works, including the twenty-five *Concertos comiques* (1732–60). He was a perpetual Santa Claus to flutists, using liturgical themes and Christmas tunes in the *Concertos spirituels* and *Concertos de Noëls* for flute.

Corrette also wrote a considerable number of duets, trios, and sonatilles, which adopt the Italian fast–slow–fast plan and feature virtuoso passage work. Taken as a whole, Corrette's oeuvre displays typical mid-century ambiguity: some solo sonatas include highly contrapuntal movements, and there are fugues in duets and trios. Yet the later sonatas incorporate a number of progressive, preclassic features such as dynamic contrasts and crescendos, repeated-note basses, and syncopated themes.

Jean-Joseph Cassanea de Mondonville (1711–72) was one of the most active musicians in Paris in the mid-eighteenth century. A violinist in the royal chapel and chamber, he performed with Blavet during the 1740s. Three of his trio sonatas are scored specifically for flute and violin, and duly exploit the idioms of the respective instruments.

Nicolas Chédeville (1705–82), a grandnephew of Louis Hotteterre, was a court oboist in Paris. His early works, bearing titles like *Amusements champêtres* and *Les galanteries amusantes*, evoke Gallic joie de vivre and allow for many alternatives of instrumentation, including musettes and hurdy-gurdies. Chédeville's op. 7 (by 1739), however, limits the options to transverse flute, oboe, or violin. It uses Italian tempo markings and a wide variety of keys, also an Italian characteristic.

In the early 1740s, the French flute school entered a third phase, which was the beginning of its end. Concert life continued to be vital, and the flute's portability and dulcet tones continued to endear it to amateurs, who learned their craft by means of private instruction and the use of several published tutors, including those of Hotteterre, Corrette, Boismortier, and Delusse.

But despite popular enthusiasm for the flute, composers' interest in the instrument declined. In part, this situation reflected a growing musical sophistication: composition and performance became separate professions, owing to increasing technical demands on performers, the enrichment of the harmonic framework, the expansion of formal structures, and more refined concepts of orchestration. In addition, the evolution of musical style was more suited in many ways to the expressive capabilities of the violin than it was to the relatively less powerful flute. The flute did, however, assume a new role in the orchestra as that ensemble entered a watershed phase of its development.

At the same time there was a decline in the ranks of the professional flutists in Paris. Blavet retired in 1749. With the exception of P. Evrard Taillart *le cadet*, who already had acquired quite a good reputation and who played at the Concert Spirituel from 1749 to 1755, the other flutists who appeared on the series had one-night stands. The official historian of the Concert, Constantin Pierre, commented snidely that although the Englishman Tacet seemed predestined by his name to silence, his contemporaries fared no better.

The solo sonata suffered the most precipitous decline of any genre of flute music. Most of the sonatas published in Paris were foreign imports—by such writers as Johann Baptist Wendling, Fabio Ursillo, Giovanni Battista Sammartini, and M. F. Cannabich. The long-standing French condescension toward instrumental music found expression in the writings of the mid-eighteenth century *philosophes*. Jean-Jacques Rousseau, in his 1767 *Dictionnaire de Musique*, decried the foreign sonatas then fashionable:

> We owe this miserable taste to those who, wishing to introduce the manner of Italian music to a language which is not susceptible of it, have obliged us to seek to do with instruments that which is impossible for us to do with our voice. . . . Purely instrumental music is of little account.[13]

The form that did hold its own at mid-century, however—a form aptly suited to the flute's adoption by amateurs—was the flute duet. Both Taillarts, *ainé* and *cadet*, made numerous arrangements for two flutes; Telemann published his canonic sonatas, op. 5, in Paris in 1738 and a set of duos for violins, flutes, or oboes in 1752.

Jean-Philippe Rameau (1683–1764) is closely associated with Couperin in the realm of harpsichord music. His *Pièces de clavecin en concerts* (1741), scored for harpsichord accompanied by violin or flute and bass viol or second violin, exhibit an old-fashioned lack of precision in instrumentation. Rameau did, however, make allowances for the flute's limitations in the "Advice to Performers" that preceded the score:

> If chords are found, the note that gives the most beautiful melody, and that is ordinarily the highest, should be chosen. . . . In a rapid passage of several notes, one need only substitute for those that are too low, neighboring notes that belong to the same harmony, or repeat those one deems proper. A note that descends too low by a fourth or fifth may be extended to the upper octave.[14]

Rameau's *Concerts* consist of nineteen pieces arranged into five suites. Thus they are remotely descended from the French harpsichord suite, but more closely related to Mondonville's six sonatas, op. 3 (about 1734) for harpsichord and violin. Within a basically homophonic texture, each instrument has its own part, which is heard nearly continuously. The relationship between the instruments may be symphonic, a juxtaposition of thin versus tutti textures, or a simple accompanied melody. Most of the movements are in binary form, though one is a forward-looking miniature sonata form.

Another new chamber form, the quartet sonata, was also foreign-inspired. Telemann published two sets of quartet sonatas in Paris in 1738; Blavet and

Naudot subscribed to the second set. The French violin virtuoso Louis-Gabriel Guillemain (1705–70) subsequently published two sets of quartets for flute, violin, bass viol, and figured bass. Their title is stylistically revealing: *Six conversations galantes et amusantes*. Guillemain in turn influenced flutist Benoit Guillemant (active in Paris 1746–57) to write six quartets for two flutes, violin, and bass, which were published in 1746. Giovanni Battista Sammartini (1700/01–1775) published a number of similarly scored works beginning in the late 1740s. The form evolved over the next decade or so into the standard rococo-classic flute quartet of flute, violin, viola, and bass, which counted among its champions Gossec, Haydn, and Mozart.

The flute works of mid-eighteenth century France reflected the larger musical trends of the era, as the style known as rococo emerged. Influenced by the new symphonic style, composers tried such devices as triadic themes and melodic arpeggiation and figuration, slower harmonic rhythm, an expansion of range and tonality, and in general, a fussier, more ornate style. And though the solo literature fell into decline, the flute began a new era as an orchestral instrument.

Italy

In Italy, meanwhile, the flute was also a presence, if not as important a factor as in France. Italian use of wind instruments dates back to the fourteenth century, when they were used to augment the string orchestra. This tradition culminated in the orchestral concerto, a form in which Albinoni, Torelli, and others made effective use of oboes, horns, and trumpets. The concerto was the vehicle for the distinctive Italian contribution to the baroque flute literature. In chamber music, however, the Italians were much more leery of winds than were the French; they generally scored their trio sonatas for two violins.

The transverse flute did not appear in Italy until sometime between 1715 and 1720, and did not become popular for another ten years or so. When Quantz traveled to Italy in 1724, he reported that he had met only one worthy Italian woodwind player, the oboist Giuseppe Sammartini. In Naples the following year, Quantz later recounted, he was introduced to Alessandro Scarlatti, who made the oft-quoted remark, "You know that I cannot bear wind instruments because they all blow falsely."[15] Scarlatti was persuaded, however, to accompany his visitor in a solo, and was so impressed that he did write a few sonatas for Quantz.

The flute first appeared in an Italian concerto as a member of the concertino in Scarlatti's twelve *Sinfonie di concerto grosso* (1715). In no. 1, for instance, two flutes function as soloists; the Adagio that precedes the final movement is scored for flutes and cello alone. The second *Symphonie* contains flute and trumpet solos that anticipate the orchestration of Bach's second *Brandenburg Concerto*.

The most significant figure in the history of Italian baroque flute music was without question Antonio Vivaldi (1678–1741). Author of more than five hundred concertos, he scored more than fifty of them with solo flute parts. Though an innovative orchestrator, Vivaldi was not meticulous in his notation; unlike Bach and Handel, he was not careful about specifying *flauto* (recorder) or *traverso* (transverse flute). The ambiguity may have been intentional: at the time he was writing much of his flute music, the recorder remained popular among amateurs, while the flute was becoming the instrument of choice among professional musicians. So it is possible that he intended for some of his flute/recorder works to "change their spots," as one analyst of his music aptly phrased it. Similarly, it is not certain whether the three concerti for which Vivaldi specified *flautino* were intended for the sopranino recorder or for the new, one-keyed transverse piccolo. To simplify the discussion in this text, therefore, I shall refer to all of the flute/recorder works as flute works; in the repertoire list instrumentation is given as it appears in the Ryom *Verzeichnis* as quoted in the *New Grove Dictionary*.

Vivaldi's greatest contribution was the development of the concerto, of which the flute was a fortunate beneficiary. He is generally credited as the inventor of the fast-movement ritornello form, in which a refrain or ritornello, played by the full orchestra, appears in different keys in alternation with free, modulating solo passages. He also stylized the fast-slow-fast format of concerto movement organization.

Instrumental forces vary greatly in Vivaldi's concerto oeuvre, and range from solo concertos (more than 350, 20 of them for flute), to double concertos (about 40, including 1 for two flutes), ensemble concertos for three or more soloists (more than 30, of which 7 include flutes or recorders). In addition, Vivaldi wrote more than 20 chamber concertos, which lack the orchestral ripieno; the combined soloists themselves form the tutti. The flute appears in almost all of them. Within this list, however, is evidence of frequent self-borrowing; witness the old joke, attributed to twentieth century composer Luigi Dallapiccola, that Vivaldi wrote the same concerto 400 times.

Though the joke is not accurate numerically, there is some truth to what it suggests. Vivaldi's style is so markedly individual, and so consistent within the total oeuvre, that one may easily perceive repetition where it does not actually exist. A few characteristics stand out: Lombardic rhythm (which Quantz credits Vivaldi with introducing), syncopation, the formation of melodies from what others would consider mere cadential fragments, juxtapositions of slow and fast harmonic rhythms, abundant seventh chords, and transfer of themes from major to minor mode.

Vivaldi gave many of his concertos programmatic titles, and the listener will perceive that the onomatopoeia is not subtle. From his op. 10 flute concertos of 1730 come no. 1, *La tempesta di mare (Storm at Sea)*, and no. 3, *Il Cardellino (The Goldfinch)*, replete with brilliant trills. In no. 2, *La Notte (The Night)*, the second movement, *Fantasmi (Phantoms)*, includes excited scale and arpeggio figures; the fifth movement, *Il sonno (The Sleep)* evokes the stillness of night by scoring muted strings senza continuo.

Though Vivaldi takes the historical laurels for the Italian baroque, many of his fellow countrymen also made significant contributions to the flute literature. Alessandro Marcello (1684–1750), a Venetian dilettante, wrote a set of six concertos called *La Cetra (The Lyre)*, published in 1738, that are clearly in the Vivaldian mode. Not only did he borrow the title from the master's op. 9 (1727), but in some ways the music is markedly similar, notably the wide-ranging arpeggios throughout the orchestration. Yet Marcello's concertos were notable for unusually free interchange between the solo and ripieno strings and the wind instruments above.

Two concertos formerly attributed to Giovanni Battista Pergolesi (1710–36)—an attribution now quite conclusively disproved—are, like Marcello's, in the Vivaldian mode. The rather playful use of minor-mode motives is one example of this stylistic influence. The D major concerto includes profuse written-out ornamentation, as Vivaldi often provided.

The two flute concertos attributed to Giuseppe Tartini (1692–1770), another northern Italian violinist, are similarly in the Vivaldian form, with standard tutti ritornellos. But the solo passages become more extensive than Vivaldi's. These violinistic works display increasing importance of the upper voices and emphasis on phrases, as opposed to motives, in line with pre-Classic compositional technique.

The Italian flute sonatas written in the 1730s and even into the 1740s were for the most part written by composer-violinists and published outside Italy. The sonata was, of course, an Italian form that in large part owed its early development to Arcangelo Corelli. The Italian flute sonatas of the 1730s and 1740s drew inspiration from vocal and violin technique, particularly the latter, whereas the French were influenced more by their national *clavecin* tradition. This background, coupled with the transverse flute's relative novelty in Italy, led many late baroque Italian composers to handle the flute with caution—Geminiani is a good example—limiting its technical requirements and writing fairly neutral, nonemotional cantabiles. The Italians also used ornaments differently from the French; rather than embellishing the melody to make it beautiful and elegant, they did so to make it more dramatic and rich in contrasts. The technique is in general less agile; articulation is more clearly notated. Locatelli, for instance, wrote fast passages requiring a *portato*; though slurred, the downbeats were to be played very deliberately. The prominence of the Italian flute sonata was rather brief—some twenty years, from 1730 to 1750. It is indicative of this situation that Antonio Lorenzoni's tutor, *Saggio per ben sonare il flautotraverso*, published in 1779, recommends only the works of Corelli (probably transcriptions), "Giuseppe Haydn, Wanhal, Giovanni Battista [probably J. C.] Bach, Giovanni Stamitz, Giuseppe Toeschi, and Artamano Graaff."

Benedetto Marcello (1686–1739), younger brother of Alessandro, though considered by one biographer "more famous than appreciated,"[16] wrote an attractive set of twelve sonatas for recorder and continuo, published in Amsterdam before 1717 as his op. 2. The 1732 London edition, confusingly labeled op. 1, specified flute or violin for the solo part. Though not demanding technically, these are imaginative compositions that make it unfortunate that the younger Marcello confined himself largely to vocal works.

Francesco Geminiani (1687–1762) published a set of six sonatas for flute and basso continuo (with violin or oboe alternatives to the flute) in about 1730. These were conservative in scope, avoiding technical difficulties. The keys were easy—G, C, and E minor—and the range did not rise above c^3. As the interchangeable instrumentation implies, the sonatas sacrifice not only virtuosity, but also emotional content. Geminiani's treatise, *Rules for Playing in a True Taste on the Violin, German Flute, Violoncello and Harpsichord* (about 1745) indicates the author's virtual fear of the flute's technical insufficiency: "I must not however omit to observe that the Excellence of this Instrument consists in the Cantabile, as that gives time to regulate the Breath, and not in swift movements where there are Arpeggios and Jumping Notes."[17]

Pietro Antonio Locatelli (1695–1764), a product of conservative Roman training, began composing in the Vivaldian tradition, but his later works make gestures toward early classic style. While his *Concerti Grossi*, op. 1 (1721) are clearly in the conservative Corellian mode, his op. 2 flute sonatas (1732) combine traditional elements such as canon with more innovative procedures. The usual four movements are sometimes reduced to three. Expressively, they far exceed the sonatas of Geminiani, using idiomatic virtuosic effects to increase emotional content. Like his contemporary Tessarini, Locatelli wrote out the ornamentation for the slow movements in full detail.

Vivaldi's solo and trio sonatas are relatively conservative in comparison with his pioneering concertos. There are eleven solo sonatas for flute, including six published as part of *Il pastor fido*, op. 13 (Paris, about 1737). A composite of church and chamber styles, they lean toward the latter in terms of binary construction. The key signatures are relatively limited, with no more than three sharps or two flats. The melodic range is confined to two octaves within any given work—the composite range is $c^1\sharp$ to f^3—but they do display notable contrasts of register between the end of one phrase and the beginning of the next. They are replete with such expressive devices as notated trills and mordents, slides, and appoggiaturas. As in the concertos, Vivaldi uses syncopation and harmonic suspension to give the music rhythmic impulse.

The sonatas of Giovanni Platti (about 1700–1763) effectively illustrate the change in style in the generation just after Vivaldi. Platti, an oboist at the Würzburg court who also performed on violin, cello, harpsichord, and flute, began writing in true baroque style, with most of his sonatas the *da chiesa* variety. His second set of sonatas, op. 3, scored for flute and cello or harpsichord and published about 1743, are typically baroque in polyphonic technique and relatively fast harmonic rhythm. But at the same time, Platti's sonatas belie galant traits: melodic virtuosity and a greater exploitation of the instrument's expressive capabilities. In these areas, Platti approaches C. P. E. Bach, though at a far lesser level of mastery.

Platti's contemporary, violinist Carlo Tessarini (about 1690–after 1766), composed almost exclusively for strings, but both solo and trio sonatas published in Paris about 1749 specify flute as an alternative to the violin(s). Much influenced by Vivaldi, his works also include forward-looking galant themes, clearly phrased and dancelike in character.

Giovanni Battista Sammartini (1700/01–1775) wrote for flute in a variety of forms: solo sonatas for flute and continuo, flute duos, flute quartets (flute, two violins, and cello), and trio sonatas. Sammartini extended the Vivaldian concept of the chamber concerto, in which the ensemble of solo instruments forms the ripieno or tutti. His six solo concertinos, for instance, which date from the mid-1760s, give the impression of classic chamber music. In some, the flute scoring approximates the instrument's new role in the classic symphony.

Giovanni Bononcini (1670–1747), a prolific opera composer active in Mantua, Rome, and Venice, published eight divertimenti or sonatas for violin or flute and continuo in 1722. Leonardo Vinci (1680–1734) (not to be confused with Leonardo da Vinci) published six sonatas for flute and bass in 1746. Tommaso Albinoni (1674–1745) wrote a number of trio sonatas nominally for strings, but also suitable for flute, and two dubiously attributed flute concertos. Antonio Lotti (1667–1740) contributed some early trio sonatas, Antonio Caldara (1670–1736) some solo church sonatas.

England

In England, as in France and Germany, the flute was favored by amateur musicians. And so the English were, like the French, prolific publishers of woodwind instruction books. Of these, a series entitled the *Modern Musick-Master* was, in its many editions beginning in 1730, the best seller. The flute volume, attributed to Peter Prelleur, is based on a pirated 1729 English translation of Hotteterre's *Principes*, but Prelleur's musical examples were taken from Handel opera arias and dances, which made the book immensely popular with the amateur public.

A number of English composers provided music for both recorder and flute. Daniel Purcell (died 1717), younger brother of the more famous Henry, published both sonatas for flute and bass and duets for two flutes. Some appeared with works of Gottfried Finger (about 1660–1730) at the very end of the seventeenth century. Finger, a Moravian, served the Catholic chapel of James II; he also wrote chamber music and incidental music for the London theatres. He regarded Italian music as "the best in the World,"[18] but also wrote in English style, using hornpipes, jigs, and the like, when appropriate.

Johann Christoph Pepusch (1667–1752) wrote solo and trio sonatas and other chamber combinations including flute(s). An emigrant from the Prussian court, he settled in London in 1704 and became music director to James Brydges, the future Duke of Chandos. Though best known for *The Beggar's Opera* (1728), he was also distinguished as a musical antiquarian: he edited Corelli's sonatas for publication in England and adopted their structure for his own sonatas. Because his patron was a flutist, Pepusch included flute parts in the cantatas he wrote for the Brydges' household.

Oboist Johann Ernest Galliard (about 1687–1749) learned to play the flute and oboe from a French musician in Celle and studied composition with Italian masters in Hanover. He became a court musician to Prince George, consort of Queen Anne, in 1707. His first opus, consisting of six sonatas for recorder (or other treble instrument) and continuo, was published in Amsterdam in about 1710. These sonatas, rich in figuration, are notable for their originality and distinctiveness from each other.

The star of English baroque flute music was George Frideric Handel (1685–1759). Handel represents the summit of Baroque internationalism: a German who emigrated to England, he could write equally well in Italian, German, and English styles. Of his op. 3 *Concerti Grossi* (1734), in the Corellian mode, the third is scored for a concertino of flute or oboe and two violins. In the second movement, the flute line is profusely ornamented with nonharmonic tones; the third is an elegant flute solo; and the fourth is conservatively fugal.

Handel's sonatas are more numerous and more problematic; generations of editors have clouded their dating and attribution. The most recent research, by David Lasocki and Terence Best, credits Handel with only four authentic sonatas for flute and six for recorder. The twelve Handel sonatas published as op. 1 in 1730 include three for flute (in E minor, G, and B minor) and four for recorder (in G minor, A minor, C, and F); these appeared in Friedrich Chrysander's 1879 *Handel-Gesellschaft* edition as nos. lb, 2, 4, 5, 7, 9, and 11. No. la of Chrysander's edition is another E minor sonata, written in 1720, probably for Jean Christian Kytch, flutist to the Duke of Chandos.

Of the three Fitzwilliam sonatas for recorder (so called because the manuscripts are located in Cambridge University's Fitzwilliam Museum), edited by Thurston Dart in 1948, only the first is now considered authentic. The second is an amalgam of two movements taken from op. 1, no. 9, and a minuet culled from another manuscript. The latest edition of the third, edited by Terence Best, terms it a violin work. Three additional sonatas, in A minor, E minor, and B minor, are known as the Halle sonatas because Handel was said to have written them while a student and organist in Halle. Lasocki believes the second to postdate the Halle period (1702–3) and casts doubt on the authorship of the other two.

Handel's trio sonatas were originally issued, during his lifetime, in two sets: six in op. 2 (about 1732–33) and seven in op. 5 (1739). Many adaptations and revised versions have appeared since. There is also an F major sonata for two flutes and continuo, recently discovered and published. The trio sonatas of op. 2 are uniformly *da chiesa*, slow-fast-slow-fast, with the fast movements polyphonic in character. There is often a change of mode for the second movement. The op. 5 sonatas are a mixture of church and chamber styles, with as many as seven movements each. Some end with a suite of dances; in the first sonata, for example, the third movement is in the relative minor; the fourth, marked *Polonaise, Allegro,* is dancelike despite imitative writing; and the fifth is a gavotte.

The set of six sonatas for two unaccompanied flutes, published in Paris about 1771 under Handel's name, are not authentic. They are identical to a set by Johann Christian Schultze (Hamburg, 1729), and it is likely that the unauthorized French publisher printed them under Handel's name to increase sales. Other duets allegedly by Handel, published in London in the mid-1730s, were indeed arranged from his opera and oratorio arias, but they were not arranged by the composer himself.

John Stanley (1712–86), a London organist who succeeded William Boyce as Master of the King's Band of Musicians, is best known today for his organ voluntaries, which are often used as wedding processionals. He wrote fourteen *Solos or sonatas* for flute and bass, published as op. 1 (1740) and op. 4 (1745). Stylistically, Stanley belongs to the generation after Handel; his writing incorporates galant elements that anticipate J. C. Bach, then active in London. Stanley's string concertos, paragons of the Corelli-Handel concerto tradition, were so popular that he quickly arranged them as solos for flute or violin and harpsichord, for harpsichord solo, and for organ and strings.

Germany

In Germany, as in Italy, the transverse flute was relatively slow to attain popularity. Only two tutors were published there before 1750: Joseph Majer's *Museum musicum* (1732) and Johann Philipp Eisel's *Musicus* (1738), both of which include fingering charts for flute and many other instruments. Quantz's *Versuch,* the most important flute tutor of the mid-eighteenth century, did not appear in print until 1752.

Foreign influence was evident in the relatively small output of German flute music in the first half of the eighteenth century. Johann David Heinichen (1683–1729), a court musician, may have studied with Vivaldi; in any case he had contact with his works during his Italian studies. This influence is evident is his unusual Concerto Grosso in C for four flutes and strings. The concertino-ripieno alternation is vintage Vivaldi, as is the syncopation of the thematic material. His trios for two flutes and cello (1715), written while he was working in Italy, include similar chamber group dialogue.

Johann Christian Schickhardt (about 1682–1762) was educated in the Prussian city of Brunswick, but launched his career in the Netherlands, where he was associated with the Amsterdam publishers Estienne and Jeanne Roger and Michel-Charles Le Cène. The first of his many solo and trio sonatas—all designated for recorder, not transverse flute—were published about 1709–10. They attained enormous popularity and were pirated in London shortly after their publication in Amsterdam. Among his most unusual scorings was the op. 19 set of six concertos for four recorders and continuo (about 1713–15). Schickhardt also contracted with Roger to arrange Corelli's op. 6 concerti grossi for strings for two recorders and continuo; a woodwind player himself, he published tutors for recorder and oboe.

Significantly, it was French influence that very likely contributed to the interest of Johann Sebastian Bach (1685–1750) in writing for the flute. The noted French flute virtuoso Pierre-Gabriel Buffardin had taught Bach's youngest brother, Johann Jacob, in Constantinople sometime shortly before 1712. In 1715, Buffardin joined the court orchestra of Augustus II in Dresden, where Bach heard him play, and it is quite likely that Buffardin's expertise inspired a number of Bach's flute compositions.

The Partita in A minor for unaccompanied flute, BWV 1013, dates from Bach's Cöthen period, shortly after he met Buffardin. Sometimes erroneously referred to as a sonata, the work is clearly in suite form; its movements are uniform in key, whereas the sonatas all have at least one movement in a contrasting key. A true suite, that in C minor for flute and keyboard, BWV 997 (about 1737–41), is more problematic historically. Musicologists conjecture from the two surviving manuscript copies (one in the hand of the theorist Kirnberger, the other with a title page penned by C. P. E. Bach) that the work may have been written for lute or keyboard. But its pianistic technical difficulties, the high register of the upper part, and the generally wide range leave a good deal of doubt as to its attribution.

Familiar with the *sonata da chiesa* of Corelli, Bach used this four-movement Italian model for the majority of his solo and trio sonatas for flute. However, the solo sonatas differ from earlier models in an important respect: the harpsichord part is largely elaborated, leaving relatively little to chance—that is, to the keyboard player. In the sonatas BWV 1030 and 1032, in B minor and A major, the harpsichord is a particularly full partner to the solo flute. In modern editions, the Bach sonatas are generally divided into two sets, three for flute and obbligato harpsichord (BWV 1030 to 1032, in B minor, E♭, and E) and three for flute and continuo (BWV 1033 to 1035, in C, E minor, and E).

The Sonata in G Minor, BWV 1020, which is included in some modern editions, was originally for violin and harpsichord and is of doubtful authenticity. Along with the E♭ and C major sonatas, it is omitted from the *Neue Bach Ausgabe*, but recent research by Robert Marshall suggests that although the G minor may have been written by C. P. E. Bach, the other two are authentic. Marshall also hypothesizes that Bach may originally have written the C major sonata in about 1718 for unaccompanied flute. Marshall suggests, too, that Bach may have written BWV 1035 at the time of his first visit to Frederick the Great's court in Potsdam in 1741; it is dedicated to the royal valet, Michael Fredersdorf, like his employer an amateur flutist.

There are also three Bach trio sonatas for flute. In the Sonata in G, BWV 1038, for flute, violin, and continuo, Bach directs the violin to tune its two upper strings down a tone—a procedure called *violino discordato*—presumably because the relaxed tension on those strings would reduce the brightness of their sound, the better to blend with the gentle flute. This instruction is characteristic of Bach's sensitivity to the flute's tone color, yet there is considerable evidence that the piece may be the work of one of Bach's sons or students, very likely C. P. E. Bach. Another Sonata in G, BWV 1039, is scored for two flutes and continuo; Bach wrote it while serving as Kapellmeister to Prince Leopold in Anhalt-Cöthen, about 1720. Much later in his career, Bach wrote a Sonata in E minor for flute, violin, and continuo as part of *The Musical Offering*, BWV 1079, presented to Frederick the Great in 1747. Like the ten canons in the set, it is based on a theme supplied by the monarch himself.

Bach probably wrote the *Brandenburg Concertos*, dedicated to the Marquis of Brandenburg and dated 1721, while he was Konzertmeister at Weimar. While nominally using the relatively old-fashioned concerto grosso form, Bach extended it significantly, treating the form with more variety of texture than had his predecessors. Rather than use the strict Corellian division between the choirs, each indivisible, he adopted Vivaldi's technique of setting solo instruments against each other. In the second concerto, for instance, each instrument has many solos, and trumpet, recorder, violin, and oboe combine in duets and trios. In both the second and the fifth concertos, Bach omits the string ripieno entirely in the slow movements in order to highlight the concertino. Similarly, Brandenburg no. 4 is in effect a hybrid solo violin concerto and concerto grosso for solo violin and two recorders. Only the fifth concerto scores the transverse flute.

In the 1730s, Bach reiterated the instrumentation of the fifth Brandenburg in a Concerto in A minor, BWV 1044, written for Collegium Musicum concerts in Leipzig. The second orchestral suite, BWV 1067, in B minor, for solo flute and strings, dates from the same period.

Johann Melchior Molter (1696–1765) was Kapellmeister to Margrave Karl Wilhelm in Karlsruhe and to other aristocrats. From 1719 to 1722 he studied in Italy, where he became acquainted with the works of Albinoni, Vivaldi, Alessandro Scarlatti, and the Marcellos. He wrote ten traditional concertos for flute and strings, including one for flauto traverso d'amore in A♭, and, in the typical German chamber concerto style, two concertinos for four flutes and continuo. Molter combined Vivaldian fast-slow-fast construction and driving pulse with a typically German interest in the use of wind timbres as a structural element. His twenty-eighth concerto for flute eliminates the basso continuo and has a typically rococo/classical theme, along with such *galantieren* as dotted note motives.

Sebastian Bodinus (about 1700–about 1760), Konzertmeister at the Karlsruhe court beginning in 1728, made several contributions to chamber music for the flute, including trio and quartet sonatas, flute duets, and a concerto for flute and strings. His trio sonatas, many of which were published in two sets of *Musikalischen Divertissements*, were in typical Italian chamber-sonata form, slow-fast-slow-fast, yet they showed progressive tendencies—the use of dancelike intermezzi (menuet, bourrée, and so on) and the beginnings of Mannheim-like expressivity—in addition to contrapuntal passage-work derived from his traditional background. Under the guidance of Molter, Bodinus applied the concerto principles to his chamber music.

Gottfried Heinrich Stölzel (1690–1740) contributed to both chamber and concerto genres. Most unusual in his oeuvre is the Concerto Grosso a Quatro Chori; the four concertinos consist of two groups of three trumpets and timpani each; a woodwind choir of flute, three oboes, and bassoon; and a string contingent of four violins, viola, cello, and bass; plus three harpsichords. More conventionally, Stölzel wrote a double concerto for flute, violin, and strings; solo flute concertos; and some twenty trio sonatas for two flutes and continuo or flute, violin, and continuo.

The other leading figure of the Handel-Bach generation—indeed, the man most admired by their contemporaries—was the exceedingly prolific Georg Philipp Telemann (1681–1767). Though the oldest of the three, he was the most progressive in style, and effectively crossed the boundary between German baroque and rococo. At the same time, he assimilated French influence in both his orchestral and chamber suites, as, for example, in the *Tafelmusik*. His works for flute are both numerous and varied: solo, duet, trio, and quartet sonatas; unaccompanied fantasias; flute duets; and solo and group concertos.

The *Suite in A Minor* for flute and strings, which one writer has called the Mendelssohn violin concerto of the flute, was written for the Count Erdmann von Promitz—whom Telemann served as Kapellmeister—when the Count returned from Paris in 1704, much taken with the French suite. The movements are a double-dotted French *Ouverture; Les Plaisirs;* a Handelian *Air à l'Italien;* and a set of French dances: two menuets, *Réjouissance*, two passepieds, and a polonaise.

Telemann's op. 2 is a set of six sonatas (Hamburg, 1727) for two unaccompanied flutes. Dedicated to a pair of amateur flutists, they quickly became popular and were soon reprinted in Amsterdam and London. Op. 5 is a set of canonic sonatas for two flutes or violins.

The *Methodical Sonatas,* issued in two volumes of six sonatas each in 1728 and 1732, were and are of great pedagogical significance. The score provides two alternative versions of the slow movements, an unornamented top line and an embellished version below. (Corelli had used the same procedure in his op. 5 violin sonatas.) The Book I sonatas each have four movements (slow-fast-slow-fast); those of Book II have five. The *Methodical Sonatas* represent an amalgamation of national styles; several of the third movements in the first set are French *genre* pieces with such Italian titles as *Cortesemente, Cunando,* and *Con tenerezza.*

In 1728, Telemann became one of the founders of the first German music magazine, *Der getreue Music-Meister (The Faithful Music Master),* a biweekly publication that included a four-page lesson. Telemann's own contributions include ten flute sonatas, duets for flute and strings, and a trio sonata for two flutes and viola da gamba.

His twelve fantasias for unaccompanied flute (about 1732–33) are unusual for their time. Light and rococo in style, they are sparsely ornamented and call for considerable elaboration by the performer. There is a wide variety of movement types, all of them very short and idiomatically written to accommodate the inherent breathing problems of the unaccompanied literature.

The *Musique de Table* or *Tafelmusik*, intended, as the title indicates, as background music for dining, was published in three parts or "productions" in 1733. Each production contained an orchestral suite, a quartet, a concerto, a trio, and a solo sonata. Included in the *Tafelmusik* are a Concerto in A for flute, violin, and strings; quartet sonatas for two flutes or violins and two cellos or bassoons; as well as solo flute sonatas. An unusual quartet in D minor for recorder, two transverse flutes, and continuo for the most part ignores the timbral differences between the instruments; only occasionally does the recorder have solo passages accompanied by the flutes. The articulation for the two kinds of instruments is parallel. Telemann also wrote some twenty-one other concertos that employ flute or recorder as a solo instrument or as part of the concertino.

The single most outstanding figure in the history of eighteenth century flute music is Johann Joachim Quantz (1697–1773), flutist, teacher, composer, and flute maker to Frederick the Great of Prussia. Quantz began his professional career as a violinist, took up the oboe in 1719, but when he encountered too much competition from his colleagues, he switched to flute, an instrument on which he was unchallenged. He personified the German "mixed style," the amalgamation of French and Italian musical characters, both in philosophy and practice. Not only did Quantz get to know music of both countries while at the Saxon court at Dresden, he also traveled to Italy, France, and England in the mid-1720s; he heard Blavet play in Paris and met Handel in England. Earlier he had studied flute with the Frenchman Buffardin in Dresden. In 1741, Quantz joined Frederick's musical establishment in Berlin and later moved with the monarch to Potsdam.

Of Quantz's approximately 550 compositions, almost all include the flute in one way or another. The statistics are impressive, if not staggering: 300 concertos for flute and strings; 7 concertos for two flutes and strings; 204 sonatas for flute and continuo; 45 trio sonatas; duets; a variety of capriccios, fantasias, and exercises; and one variation set.

The concertos are the best known part of the oeuvre, perhaps because of their sheer numbers. The first 162 date from before Quantz's employment by Frederick in 1741. Many are grouped in stepwise cycles of keys, from A to G, with major and minor modes intermingled. Quantz modeled his ritornello structure on that of Vivaldi, whose concertos he heard in Pirna in 1714. Almost all of his concertos follow the Vivaldian fast-slow-fast movement form; similarly, the middle movement may be in any one of many related keys. However, the Vivaldian model was not a rigid mold. Quantz varied the number of ritornello appearances (though he consistently presented the first and last in the tonic key), and also provided variety in the solo parts, which might consist either of figuration unrelated to the tutti theme, figuration and expansion of the tutti theme, or entirely new solo ideas. Moreover, Quantz simplified the elaborate counterpoint of his predecessors, though not to a fully classic extent.

Quantz's trio sonatas, which were almost all written in Dresden, are scored primarily for flute and violin (with alternative second flute) or for two flutes; a few others pair the flute with recorder, oboe, or viola d'amore. They show the conservative influence of Quantz's Dresden colleagues Zelenka and Heinichen in that the texture is contrapuntal, even fugal. And they are a synthesis of *da chiesa* and *da camera* styles; taking their slow–fast–slow–fast organization from the former, and their frequent dance movements from the latter. Like his colleagues Hasse and Graun, Quantz did, however, adopt the three-movement form (fast-slow-fast) of the concerto for a few trio sonatas, and approached the more homophonic idiom of the preclassic era.

Quantz's early solo sonatas, published as op. 1 in 1734, are typical late baroque Italianate works in the *da chiesa* form. Other Italian characteristics include lyric slow movements, even sicilianos, and arialike recapitulations of opening themes. Fast movements are in binary form, with frequent minuets and gigues, and are far less imitative than the trio sonatas. The Berlin sonatas are in three movements, slow-fast-fast, in one key throughout, typical of mid-century Italian and German composers. Again, there are progressive tendencies: a variety of dances and free-composed movements; a semblance of sonata form in terms of thematic recapitulation; slower harmonic rhythm; and replacement of counterpoint with more accompanied-melody texture. Yet Quantz is still rooted in the baroque, because even these preclassic elements lack the dramatic harmonic contrasts and the preparation for recapitulation of true classic sonata form.

Quantz probably intended the six duets, op. 2 (first published in Berlin in 1752), to serve as a musical supplement to the *Versuch*. They were apparently modeled on Telemann's op. 2, which had appeared twenty-five years earlier.

Quantz's greatest contribution was his idiomatic writing for his own instrument, for he was innovative in adapting the compositional mannerisms and characteristics of stringed instruments, especially the violin, to the relatively limited range and technical capacity of the one-keyed flute. He effectively employed contrast between the registers of the flute while at the same time avoiding extremes (the upper limit is e^3).

And Quantz's contribution to performance practice is unequaled, for in addition to his musical compositions, he authored a treatise, *Versuch einer Anweisung die Flöte traversière zu spielen (Essay on Playing the Flute)*, published in Berlin in 1752 and translated into French, Dutch, and English soon thereafter. Though nominally intended for flutists, Quantz's *Versuch* is in fact a comprehensive manual of performance practice applicable in various aspects to all musicians of the mid-eighteenth century and to modern performers attempting to recreate those performance traditions.

Quantz's most famous student, Frederick the Great (1712–86), composed four concertos and 121 sonatas in addition to the four books of *Solfeggi* written jointly with his teacher. While their interest is more historical than musical, these works are less strictly baroque than Quantz's. The traditional conjecture is that in many instances Frederick wrote the melodies, leaving Quantz to fill in the lower parts. Not surprisingly, since Frederick was writing for his own use at his soirées, his works are virtuosic in style, even brilliant; the sonatas, in which he was usually accompanied by C. P. E. Bach, are generally in three movements, slow–fast–very fast.

The generation after Quantz was a prolific and rich one for the flute literature. One reason, of course, was the atmosphere provided by Frederick, who employed such men as Benda, C. F. C. Fasch, the Grauns, Graupner, Hasse, Kirnberger, Reichardt, and J. C. Fischer in addition to Quantz. Some of these musicians began their careers writing in the baroque mode, but gradually absorbed galant and then rococo characteristics.

The flute works of Johann Adolf Hasse (1699–1783), one of the foremost opera composers of the day, are typical of the baroque-galant transition. The B minor flute concerto, one of six in his op. 3 (1741), is structurally pure baroque; even the slow movements employ the old-fashioned ritornello structure, which was rapidly becoming obsolete in southern Germany and Italy. But the D major concerto of just a few years later is similar to much preclassic chamber music, with the flute accompanied, at times, only by two violins. Moreover, the key layout of the finale is adventurous; the second tutti is in the dominant, then transposes the main theme into A minor, and ends in C minor; the second solo brings the tonality abruptly back to the tonic, which persists into the third tutti.

Johann Friedrich Fasch (1688–1758) also straddles the line between baroque and rococo. Educated at the Thomasschule in Leipzig, he served from 1722 until his death as Kapellmeister at Zerbst. His son was second harpsichordist at Frederick's court in Potsdam, and thus C. P. E. Bach became familiar with the father's works. Many of them—the canonic trio sonatas, in particular—were fully baroque; the concertos, similarly, retain the three-movement, ritornello-based structure of Vivaldi. Fasch's concertos are far more progressive than their basic architecture may indicate; he sometimes assigned contrasting episodes to wind instruments in mid-ritornello; he paired wind instruments as soloists; and he experimented with bithematicism.

And so the style galant that had begun in the 1720s became a dominant force in the 1740s. At midcentury, contradictions were rampant: Bach wrote his *Art of the Fugue*, the acme of that baroque form, in 1749; simultaneously, Gluck achieved his first successes in Paris; Rameau, too, was at his height in the French capital; Johann Stamitz began publishing his symphonies; and Bach's own sons were already writing in a style far removed from that of their father. And less than a decade later, Haydn wrote his first string quartet—a harbinger of the classic era to come.

Notes

1. William Metcalfe, "Dolce or Traverso? The Flauto Problem in Vivaldi's Music," *The American Recorder* 6, no. 3 (1965): 4.
2. Carol Reglin Farrar, *Michel Corrette and Flute-Playing in the Eighteenth Century* (Brooklyn, N.Y.: Institute of Mediaeval Music, 1970), p. 1.
3. Kurt List, *History of Baroque Music* (New York: Orpheus, 1967), p. 48.
4. Ibid., pp. 50–51.
5. "The Life of Herr Johann Joachim Quantz, as Sketched by Himself," in *Forgotten Musicians*, trans. and ed. Paul Nettl (New York: Philosophical Library, 1951), pp. 294–95.
6. James R. Anthony, *French Baroque Music from Beaujoyeulx to Rameau*, rev. ed. (New York: W. W. Norton, 1978), pp. 320–21.
7. Michel Corrette, preface to *Le Maître de Clavecin pour l'accompagnement* (1753); quoted in Anthony, p. 320.
8. Ruth Halle Rowen, *Early Chamber Music* (1949; reprint, New York: Da Capo Press, 1974), p. 67.
9. Anthony, p. 335.
10. Ibid., p. 321.
11. Neal Alexander Zaslaw, "Materials for the Life and Works of Jean-Marie Leclair l'Ainé" (Ph.D. diss., Columbia University, 1970), p. 220.
12. Rowen, p. 67.
13. Zaslaw, pp. 213–14.
14. Marc Pincherle, "On the Rights of the Interpreter in the Performance of 17th and 18th Century Music," *Musical Quarterly* 44 (1958): 152.
15. Rowen, p. 69.
16. Michael Talbot, "Benedetto Marcello," in *The New Grove Dictionary of Music and Musicians*, ed. Stanley Sadie (London: Macmillan, 1980), vol. 11, pp. 648–49.
17. Mario Castellani, "The Italian Sonata for Transverse Flute and Basso Continuo," *Galpin Society Journal* 19 (1976): 5.
18. Michael Tilmouth, "Gottfried Finger," in *The New Grove Dictionary*, vol. 6, pp. 565–66.

15

THE CLASSIC ERA

The mid-eighteenth century was a period of transition for the flute and for music as a whole. It was a time of sweeping social change, as cities replaced courts and palaces as centers of musical activity. The professional composer began to depend on a larger public, through concert attendance and the purchase of sheet music, for financial livelihood. The rise of the orchestra and the pianoforte reversed the flute's proportional roles in orchestra and chamber music. As with any transformation, the process was gradual; the contrasts of beginning and end are obvious, but setting chronological ends is more difficult.

This chapter will cover the style periods variously known as galant, rococo, preclassic, and High Classic. However inexact their labels, all of these periods share one essential unifying principle: the intentional simplification—even primitivization, in Friedrich Blume's word—of musical composition. Typical was the anti-Bach reaction of theorist Johann Adolf Scheibe, who criticized Bach for artificiality and confusion that obscured the "natural beauty" of musical expression.[1] By simplifying the musical content, preclassic and classic composers aimed to heighten the immediacy of emotional expression, and to make it more accessible.

The other basic factor that differentiates the classic era from the baroque is the pervasive concept of contrast. The single-motive construction of the baroque gave way to bithematicism, ultimately codified in sonata form. And the continuous sweep of baroque melody, growing out of that central head motive, gave way to short phrases (typically but not exclusively of four-measure duration), frequently repeated. Dynamics became further differentiated, and articulation provided still another kind of contrast. Homophonic texture provided contrast between treble and bass that had not been heard in such polarity since the early baroque, having been obscured in the interim by the polyphony of inner voices. Primarily, however, the classic principle of contrast was embodied in sonata form, with its thematic duality; the differentation of exposition, development, and recapitulation; and the clear separation forced by the double bar and repeat device.

In terms of the physical flute itself, the classic era encompasses the full evolution of the old-system flute. The three keys added in 1760 caught on in the last years of the eighteenth century; soon thereafter two more were added; and in 1786 another two, until the flute took the eight-keyed form that became the early nineteenth century norm. These improvements made the flute a fully chromatic instrument, which allowed several important musical advances: chromatic figuration in rapid passages, expanded upper range, and the use of more distant keys. These advances equipped the instrument for its new and expanded role in the classic orchestra.

The roots of the classic era reach back as far as Bach—as we have seen, his style was challenged long before his death, and some of his own works have galant traits. We have seen, too, that the early or first galant style retained many baroque characteristics. What historian William Newman calls the second galant style, in contrast, was an anti-baroque development; it peaked in the 1750s and is frequently labeled rococo. Denoted by the beginning of the end of the figured bass, it gave more and more emphasis to the upper melodic line. Increasingly, the other voices provided harmonic support only. As the melody assumed increased importance, the principal tones were subdivided. The extemporized ornamentation of the baroque became an internalized and integral part of the composition, fully indicated in the notation. The *agréments* joined the melody notes in a smooth progression, analogous to the smooth, gliding motions and dainty steps of the courtly dances, particularly the minuet.

Galant melody was somewhat paradoxical: while the long, continuous line of the baroque was broken up into shorter, simpler segments—though not yet into phrases—the line was so embellished, particularly with sequences of short trills, that it had a surface complexity all its own. It was this latter characteristic that earned galant the negative connotations it acquired toward the end of the eighteenth century.

Closely related to this melodic development was the rhythmic factor, again on a small scale. Principally, galant rhythm was notable for its mannerisms—syncopations, Scotch snaps (♪♩.) and various other dotted figures, sixteenth-note triplets, and above all, the appoggiatura "sigh." Both rhythm and melody were reinforced by new refinements in dynamics and articulation.

Galant harmony was largely confined, in yet another effort at simplification, to the primary triads; it was far less adventurous than that of Bach. Because harmonic rhythm was slower, with harmony persisting on one plateau or another for more extended periods, the drive-to-the-cadence organization was considerably weakened. This procedure resulted in large contrasting sections rather than the sequential harmonic development of the baroque.

The texture was defined primarily by the decline of the figured bass. Rococo texture was overwhelmingly a two-voice texture, often melody and chordal accompaniment, whose extreme form is often described as "watery."

One facet of the galant was *Empfindsamkeit*, the ultrasensitive style epitomized by C. P. E. Bach, which reflected the "age of tears" also evident in the other arts. In some ways, *Empfindsamkeit* was an exaggeration of the galant: melodic lines were even more fragmented; mannered sighing appoggiaturas were intensified by expanding the intervals. Small-scale articulation, strategically placed rests, and accents also heightened the effect. The emphasis on expressive melody meant, however, that ornamentation was simplified; it became a vehicle for expression rather than for display. Harmony was also intensified: sudden shifts of tonality and thus of feeling were the norm, with unusual modulations, deceptive cadences, and surprising key contrasts frequent occurrences.

By the beginning of classicism, about 1760, melody had triumphed as the dominant compositional element, and it remained so until well into the nineteenth century, when harmony gained dominance. As Mozart expressed this principle, in a letter to tenor Michael Kelly, "Melody is the essence of music. I compare a good melodist to a good racer, and counterpointists to hack horses."[2]

Just as melody ruled the composition, the tonic was the overriding point of reference within the harmonic structure. It exerted this influence in one of two ways. In circular or solar organization, forays away from the tonic to V, III, VI, II, or IV return occasionally to the tonic as a unifying factor. Alternatively, in polar or contrasting key organization, the dominant (or, in minor keys, the relative major) is simply contrasted to the tonic. The dominant asserts itself toward the middle of the first section of a movement, and the tonic reappears in mid-second section. This tonal organization predominated in classic sonata form, concertos, arias, and many other musical forms. It is the concentration on the tonic—the absolute insistence that a given movement *must* both begin and end in the tonic—along with the emphasis on key as a whole, that distinguishes the classic period from all others.

The first and most important textural change of the classic era was the final dissolution of the basso continuo. This was the result, in part, of the evolution of the baroque solo sonata. As the solo violin gained predominance in that form, making the top line foremost and all other lines subordinate, the middle voices lost melodic interest. With the lower voices written out in full, the continuo became unnecessary. Second, the use of an obbligato keyboard part in chamber compositions also helped to dissolve the continuo: in transcriptions of trio sonatas for solo sonata forces, the solo instrument assumed the second treble part; the first treble went to the keyboard right hand. And finally, the solo keyboard piece, which achieved predominance in the classic era, was a self-contained concerted composition in which the basso continuo was by definition superfluous.

The overriding importance of the upper melody and the supportive, purely harmonic accompaniment function of the other voices created a homophonic texture. It also implied that without strict polyphonic part-writing requirements the number of voices need not remain constant throughout a composition. Counterpoint remained only in a vestigial form—the passing of a single melody sequentially from one voice to another, creating a sort of filigree—employed only as a special effect or textural variant.

The new emphasis on melody resulted in changes in its ornamentation. The number of *Spielmanieren* (those indicated in a shorthand notation of signs or small notes) declined in both frequency and variety. Only the trill and the appoggiatura were ornamental mainstays in the classic era. The more elaborate ornaments were written out and absorbed into the overall melodic context. This made the score a more concrete embodiment of the composer's wishes, and simultaneously made improvisation by the performer not only unnecessary but also undesirable most of the time. Only repeated sections of slow movements, where a vestigial continuo part might also remain, permitted improvised embellishment. The only officially sanctioned place for improvisation became the fermata or cadenza, inserted between the I^6_4 and V chords that precede the final tonic in the concerto. This ornamental simplification may be seen as a means by which composers could shield their works from the excesses of amateur performers.

With the rise of a new commercial class in the mid-eighteenth century, musical life became more democratized; the individual citizen became both financial supporter and qualitative arbiter of musicians. The musician, though he might still be employed by a church or aristocratic patron, reached out as well to a broader public, both as listeners and as amateur performers. His media were public concerts—such as the Concert Spirituel in Paris, the Bach-Abel subscription concerts in London, the Tonkünstler-Societät in Vienna, and the collegium musicums in Leipzig—and publications for the amateur market.

The implications of this development were multifold. Instrumental performers had to develop public personalities, hitherto required only of prima donnas and castrati, to appeal to the new audiences. As they toured the cities of Europe, musicians had to develop a marketing strategy, of which flamboyant virtuosity was the prime component. In turn, the performing musician made new demands on the composer, whether himself or another writer: the music must first of all put the limelight on the soloist; thus the evolution of the classic homophonic texture in which the soloist dominates and all other parts merely accompany. Second, the soloist required a repertory of attention-getting and attention-maintaining devices—contrast, suspense, special effects, and cadenzas. The mastery of perceived technical difficulties and originality of execution were the principal means of securing public acceptance.

Similarly, composers' growing financial dependence on the proceeds of publications affected their compositional technique. Because publication implied a separation of function between composer and performer and the absence of the composer to provide in-person instructions, such as Quantz could provide to Frederick the Great, the score had to be more precise. As a result, published music needed to include specific indications of tempo, expression, and dynamics. Ornaments were reduced in number and melodic elaboration, where used, was embodied in the written-out notation, but overall the melodic line was simplified from its galant excesses. Simplification affected texture as well: the inability of amateur musicians to deal with the complexities of basso continuo realization led to the decline of that device and its replacement by homophonic accompaniment. Dance and folk elements were also included in "serious" music, again to make it more accessible to the amateur. Finally, the growth of the middle class amateur market created a need for the publication of pedagogical materials—instructional methods, etudes, and simple compositions—a need fulfilled for pianists by Clementi, Vogler, Hummel, and Czerny and for flutists by Quantz, Tromlitz, Devienne, and Hugot.

Musical Forms

The flute was the darling of the rococo; its melodic flexibility and grace, coupled with its ability to create nuances of tone, made it uniquely suited to that precious style. Moreover, its aptitude for conjuring up pastoral images made it useful for programmatic applications. Its color capacity continued to make it a favorite of German composers for many years: the 1817 dictionary by Choron and Fayolle said of the Germans, "[T]hey seek effect in color. That is to say, they like chords which are the most sonorous, such as are produced by wind instruments."[3] The flute's importance as a solo instrument continued until the last third of the eighteenth century, when new idioms, principally the string quartet and the clavier sonata, usurped the place of the solo sonata. But at the same time, the flute, its technical capacity enhanced by late-century mechanical improvements, assumed a new role in the orchestra, which would be its throne of glory for the next century.

In the mid-eighteenth century, the flute played a major role in the context of chamber music, a broad term at the time that encompassed works as large as the concerto, since aristocratic establishments still maintained private chamber orchestras. It was not until late in the century that chamber music became more strictly defined as music scored for one player to a part. Anton Meysel's *Handbuch der musikalischen Litteratur*, published in 1817, at the very end of the classic era, reflects the publication history of the previous decades: it includes nearly nine thousand piano works, nearly four thousand for violin, and more than twenty-five hundred for flute (more than twice the number for any other wind instrument). The flute had more solos and almost as many concertos as the violin, and was second to it in duets.

The amateur player had a significant influence on the development of the classic sonata. This is evident not only in the dedications of published editions, but also in the light, galant style of the writing itself. Making the music technically simple enough for the amateur to play was a major consideration for any businesslike composer. The sonata served as a pedagogical tool as well as a performance vehicle for the amateur. Moreover, it filled out the repertoire of the professional performer for use in public and private concerts, and it was still used to some extent in the church service.

The rococo and classical sonata differed from the baroque version in several respects: the principle of symmetry, as opposed to evolution; the element of contrast in the exposition, as opposed to the evolutionary, monomotivic expansion of the baroque movements; simple cadences based on the three principal triads (tonic, dominant, and subdominant); and easily comprehensible rhythmic structures, including phrases and periods. The dance forms of the baroque survived only in the minuet—the march was used infrequently. Sonata form (exposition-development-recapitulation structure, also known as sonata-allegro form) replaced dance forms in the fast movements.

Moreover, the decline of the basso continuo and the superseding of the harpsichord by the fortepiano, which did not mix as well with the woodwind instruments of the day, presaged the decline of the flute sonata. The violin school of Corelli and Veracini, from which the earlier eighteenth century flute music idiom was derived, successfully adapted itself to the instrument. But the new sonata style was best suited to the keyboard, especially the fortepiano. The lengthy, varied expositions and development sections were ill-suited to the wind instruments; the sonata for flute and trio sonata for two flutes, accompanied by continuo or keyboard, went into rapid decline. None of the major classical composers—Haydn, Mozart, or Beethoven—wrote a flute and piano sonata. (The attribution of a flute sonata to Beethoven is a matter of some doubt.)

In terms of performing forces, the accompanied keyboard sonata was the most closely related replacement for the accompanied wind sonata. But the resemblance is only superficial, because the fortepiano took the primary role, and a violin or flute, often indicated as optional, provided reinforcement or accompaniment. The flute or violin had virtually no independent material, as its *ad lib* designation implies, but its inclusion provided an added market for the music. The simplicity of the accompaniment part could be managed by even a relatively inexperienced amateur player with little technical equipment, and therefore was immensely attractive. The form also evolved for several purely musical reasons. The galant keyboard texture was thin, often in need of filling out. The tones of the early fortepiano were a far cry from the strength of the modern grand piano and could gain from reinforcement in weak registers.

The musical function of the accompaniment part was largely, therefore, textural. It could serve a harmonic function, filling in an extra voice in a chord, especially as an obbligato sustained tone. It could highlight the melody by doubling it, or it could support it harmonically by paralleling it at the interval of a third or sixth. Frequently, it played figuration, such as short imitation of melodic fragments, to supplement the keyboard part. Mozart, as a child, wrote six accompanied keyboard sonatas (K. 10–15); James Hook, Muzio Clementi, Ignace Pleyel, and many, many others wrote countless more. The multiple performance options of the form are epitomized by Abbé

Georg Johann Vogler's *Six pièces de musique dans un genre nouveau*, op. 4, which could be executed by clavier alone; clavier and violin; clavier and flute; clavier, violin, viola, and cello; clavier, flute, violin, viola, and cello; or even flute, violin, viola, and cello, dispensing with the clavier entirely!

Another form that took the place of the flute and keyboard sonata was the sonata or duet for two flutes. Alternatively, the flute might be teamed with another treble instrument, violin or viola, later oboe or clarinet. Again, the amateur market spurred the growth of the genre, both for intimate performance and for pedagogical purposes. The *Breitkopf Thematic Catalogue*, published by that leading Leipzig publisher from 1762 to 1787, lists some three hundred duets for two flutes. The duet texture was a straightforward embodiment of the classic duality of voices; the second part either provided a true bass line or harmonically implied the presence of a bass line. Duets for flute and a bass instrument, such as cello or bassoon, tended to take the former format. The texture was essentially homophonic, with the two instruments alternating melodic and accompaniment functions. In the later duets, the accompaniment includes more figuration and the alternation between these functions becomes more frequent, occurring at phrase or period breaks rather than in the large sections of earlier duets. Since a full triad was not possible with only two instruments, the most frequent intervals were thirds and sixths.

The flute also found a place in many larger ensembles, from the trio on up. The most obvious forebear of the classic trio is the baroque trio sonata; the distinction between them is the disappearance of the figured bass by about 1770. The main forms of classic trio were the string trio (violin, viola, and cello) and violin, cello, and piano, but often the flute was indicated as an alternative to the violin. An emerging variety of trio was that for three unaccompanied flutes. Of the twenty-one trios listed in the flute section of the *Breitkopf Thematic Catalogue*, eighteen are for flute, violin, and bass; three are for three flutes.

One of the greatest achievements of the classic era in general and Joseph Haydn in particular was the string quartet. But the string quartet was not the only four-part form of the period, and before it was firmly established as the norm, effectively superseding many other instrumental combinations, the flute had an active presence in the quartet literature. Once again, its favored status among amateur instrumentalists encouraged the form. Most commonly, the flute was teamed with violin, viola, and cello—in works of Cambini, Cimarosa, Danzi, Haydn, Mozart, and so on—taking much the same function as the first violin of the classic string quartet. Indeed, some classic string quartets indicated that the flute could be substituted for the first violin. Other quartet combinations included flute, oboe, clarinet, and bassoon. Johann Scheibe's *Der critischer Musikus* (1840) considered the combination of flute, viola, viola da gamba, and bass (that is, cello) the best quartet of all,[4] though it was hardly the most common. When the flute was the only wind instrument, it took a role similar to that of the soloist in a classic concerto (just as the first violin did in the early string quartets). Thus the *Allgemeine musikalische Zeitung* considered the quartet with wind or winds inferior to the string quartet because it lacked the textural freedom of the latter form.[5]

The quintet form also used the flute; the quintet for flute and string quartet—notable examples are by Boccherini, Hoffmeister, and Toeschi—was merely a thicker-textured version of the flute-and-string quartet. The combination of flute, oboe, and string trio was another frequent configuration. A new form, pioneered by Franz Danzi and Antoine Reicha, was the wind quintet, consisting of flute, oboe, clarinet, horn, and bassoon.

The flute also took its place in the larger wind ensembles that emerged in the classic era. Derived from the *Harmoniemusik* of the baroque (the large wind band that provided background for outdoor events), the classic wind ensemble had much the same flavor—either rustic, military, or ceremonial—and was primarily a medium of entertainment. Often the winds were grouped in pairs; their clear, crisp sounds and the richness of their concerted tones, coupled with the singing capabilities of the solo instruments within the ensemble, made this grouping particularly appropriate for outdoor events. The wind ensemble took advantage of the growing technical capabilities of all its members—the addition of keys to the woodwinds and valves to the brass—and was spurred as well by the growth of the military band in the era of the French revolution.

Many wind ensemble compositions took the form of divertimentos (also known as cassations or serenades), a form much less stylized than the sonata. The divertimento used both sonata-form allegro movements and dance movements, though not all its sonata forms were fully developed bithematic compositions. It also used rondos, variation sets, and the minuet. Its instrumentation, like its forms, was diverse, ranging in number from one to thirteen instruments. Perhaps the earliest examples, still actually baroque, are the late works of Michel Corrette, such as *Les récréations du berger fortune*, nominally a concerto for musette, vielle, flute, or violin and basso continuo, written about 1737. Others, by Wagenseil, Dittersdorf, and Richter, written a quarter century later, still use the harpsichord. Later composers of divertimentos include Michael and Joseph Haydn, Carlo Toeschi, Mozart, and the Stamitz family.

The decline of the solo flute sonata in the classic era did not imply a decline in the flute as a solo instrument; on the contrary, its role as concerto soloist was increasing. Composers now wrote flute concertos with public performance as the goal, and as such they increasingly considered concertos to be virtuoso vehicles to attract audiences. Not yet in the class of Paganini, the mid-eighteenth century soloist often performed his own compositions. Frequently a member of the accompanying orchestra, he was, nevertheless, *primus inter pares* (first among equals). Moreover, the increasing importance of the concerto is but one manifestation of the growth of the orchestra and orchestral music. The trend had begun with Blavet at the Concert Spirituel in Paris in the second quarter of the century, continuing there after his retirement in 1749 by Tacet, Florio, Wunderlich, and Hugot. In Mannheim, similarly, Johann Baptist Wendling was the resident virtuoso; in London, Andrew Ashe.

The concerto form had been, of course, a mainstay of the baroque; the classic concerto was a further development of that form, not a reaction to it. It preserved the tutti-solo dichotomy, for example, but made it even stronger. In the baroque concerto, the difference between tutti and solo materials is most evident in the elaborateness of the solo part, rather than in thematic distinctiveness or the obvious contrasts of size and volume. In the classic concerto, on the other hand, the length of the solo sections increases; the soloist's opening statement, after the opening orchestral tutti, is far more dramatic and forceful. The differentiation of tonal areas, using the solar model of key organization, also distinguished solo and tutti; the soloist's themes were often associated with the dominant tonality for added individuality. Finally, the cadenza was a crucial factor in exhibiting the personality and technical capability of the soloist.

The classic concerto, particularly that for solo wind instruments, shows a clear derivation from the opera aria in its relation of soloist to orchestra; its lyrical solo passages and the voicelike tone quality of the solo instrument; and its variations of the da capo aria form, in which the soloist introduces new, often contrasting material before the tutti recapitulation. The broader role of wind instruments is also reflected in the orchestration of the accompanying body; there are now winds as well as strings in the orchestra, many of which interact with the solo winds in new and colorful combinations. The classic flute concerto achieved its apogee in Mannheim and Vienna in the last quarter of the eighteenth century.

To a public that loved the exhibitionist aspect of the concerto soloist, if one soloist was good, several were better. And so, in addition to the concerto for solo flute, there were also a number of concertos for two flutes and orchestra, as, for example, by Cimarosa and Joseph Schmitt. Alternatively, the flute might be paired with another instrument to form the concertino, as in Antonio Salieri's double concerto for flute and oboe.

The double concerto was only one version of a new type of composition that emerged in the late eighteenth century; the *symphonie concertante* or *sinfonia concertante*. Very much a derivative form, it combined elements of several preexisting structures: concerto grosso, solo concerto, symphony, and divertimento. In some cases, such as the Mozart Concerto for Flute and Harp, K. 299 (1778), it also exhibited aria characteristics. Though superficially most akin to the concerto grosso, the symphonie concertante was much closer to the solo concerto in terms of formal organization and thematic treatment. It applied the new character of the classic symphony to the concerto in new and expanded ways: the instrumentation was similar in both tutti and concertino, and the winds were increasingly important. Eventually, the winds became the most popular solo instruments, and the technical difficulty of the parts increased as well. From the solo concerto the symphonie concertante drew singing melody and virtuosic display. From the divertimento, it drew on a number of elements: the lightness of texture and rhythm, singable tunes, but most of all the colorful sonorities of the wind ensemble, which were reflected most strongly in the multi-wind concertino sections.

Unlike the typical three movement solo concerto, most symphonies concertantes were in two movements, eliminating the slow movement of the Vivaldian fast–slow–fast movement configuration. However, the slower of the two movements rarely exceeded an allegretto or andante marking. Often the first movement was in sonata form, the second a variation of the rondo. The obligatory cadenzas appeared in both.

Often attributed to the Mannheim school, the symphonie concertante actually traces its ancestry in several directions. Many historians trace it from Tartini to Nardini, then to Locatelli and J. C. Bach, through the Mannheim school and thence to Mozart. Professor Barry Brook has shown, however, that the symphonie concertante got much of its impetus in Paris, where such masters as Devienne and the two younger Stamitzes used the form. In any case, it quickly became an international commodity.

Paris

Paris was the musical capital of Europe from the mid-eighteenth century until the Revolution in 1789. The great German flute virtuoso Johann Baptist Wendling recommended Paris to his admirer, Mozart. Reported the young composer in 1777, "He has been twice to Paris.... He maintains that it is still the only place where one can make money and a great reputation."[6] In 1783, the *Almanach musical* reported that for a population of 500,000, Paris had 194 composers, 63 singing teachers, 93 violin teachers, and 30 flute teachers. There were also 53 luthiers, 18 clavecin makers, 8 fortepiano makers, and 8 woodwind makers.

The Institut National de Musique, founded in 1793, was legally incorporated as the Conservatoire Nationale in 1795. It became The Source for the coming generations of French flutists; the professors of the classic era were François Devienne, Schnietzhoefer, Antoine Hugot, Duverger, and Johann Georg Wunderlich.

Of these, Devienne (1759–1803) was the foremost French flutist of his day. In addition to his teaching duties at the Conservatoire, he wrote a method (1794) that includes valuable information on classic performance practice as well as useful practice duets. Devienne was a prolific composer for the flute and did much to promote composition for wind instruments in the late eighteenth century. His compositions are for a wide variety of instrumental combinations: sonatas for flute and bass, duos for two flutes (with and without keyboard accompaniment), trios, quartets, and most importantly, concertos and symphonies concertantes.

The concertos, usually in the traditional Vivaldian fast-slow-fast structure, are preclassic specimens: though the allegro movements do have a clearly defined middle section with at least two new themes (a second exposition), they do not have the development section of true sonata form. The orchestration was standard for its time: solo instrument accompanied by two violins, viola, cello, bass, and pairs of oboes and horns; a favorite textural device was flute solo accompanied by two violins. The solo parts themselves are technically demanding, designed to be played by the composer himself or by an equally talented colleague; the range is wide for the time, d^1 to a^3; the melodic line contains rapid running passages, arpeggios, and large leaps, and allows for cadenzas; cantabile sections contain unusually long phrases that are equally demanding in their own way. Devienne's seven symphonies concertantes, which were performed at the Concert Spirituel and elsewhere in Paris, are indicative of the form's function as public music: they are dedicated to the performer or a friend of the composer, unlike much of his chamber music and concerto output, which is dedicated to his wealthy patrons.

The symphonie concertante was indeed a mainstay of Parisian concert life, and other composers who included the flute in such scores were Jean-Baptiste Breval, Louis-Gabriel Guillemain (also a pioneer of the quartet sonata), Jean-Louis Tulou, and Ignace Joseph Pleyel.

Pleyel (1757–1831) wrote rather prolifically for the flute, although his primary compositional interest was keyboard music. A student of Haydn in the 1770s, he organized public concert series in Strasbourg and London before settling in Paris in 1795. There he established a music shop and publishing house, and as proprietor he became closely attuned to public demand, which in turn probably prompted his interest in producing music for flute. He considered music a commodity like any other and thus shamelessly rearranged his own works and those of others as the market dictated. He wrote a solo concerto equally suitable for flute, clarinet, or cello; and transcribed a set of piano trios into both flute quartets and string trios, transposing keys and mixing up the movements to disguise the procedure a bit. He also produced a number of duets for flutes and violins that are still used for teaching; they use both sonata and rondo forms, but are conservative in that keys are consistent from movement to movement.

François-Joseph Gossec (1734–1829) was one of the most important forces in French classic instrumental music. He served as the director both of private musical establishments and of the public Concert des Amateurs, which he founded in 1760 and developed into one of the greatest orchestras in Europe. Gossec recruited many fine wind players who had come to Paris from Germany and Bohemia, and commissioned a body of music for that superior ensemble that used the wind choir in ways never before equaled in richness of sound. Gossec's works for flute, in addition to a symphonie concertante for flute and violin, include duets and quartets.

Early in the classic period composers wrote considerable numbers of duets, but they largely neglected solo sonatas. Charles Delusse, descendant of a family of wind instrument makers and author of a leading flute method (about 1761), published two sets of six flute sonatas each in 1751. Though the sonatas do retain the baroque continuo, the influences of the melodic character of the rococo and the Mannheim school are evident. Antoine Hugot (1761–1803), the Conservatoire professor who was also author of one of the leading methods of the nineteenth century (first published in 1804), wrote two sets of flute sonatas in the 1790s. He also wrote an unusual set of *Six sonates faciles* for unaccompanied flute, a nearly unique genre for the time.

A number of Italian and German musicians made Paris their home during the classic period. Giovanni Giuseppe Cambini (1746–1825) wears both white and black hats in the annals of flute literature. As a composer, he made substantial contributions to the repertory. But Cambini's reputation is damaged irreparably by his probable role in suppressing Mozart's symphonie concertante for flute, oboe, clarinet, and bassoon, which Mozart wrote for performance at the Concert Spirituel in 1778. Cambini, allegedly exhibiting paranoia and jealousy because his own symphonie concertante for the same forces had been performed shortly before Mozart delivered his manuscript, managed to prevent the parts from being copied. The Mozart work was never performed, and for want of parts, a potential masterpiece was lost.

Filippo Ruge (about 1725–after 1767), an Italian flutist, settled in Paris in 1753. An active performer in the French capital, both in public concerts and aristocratic salons, he was responsible for importing a large amount of Italian music from Rome. He was thus an important agent of the Italian style in midcentury France; his own symphonies are similar to the contemporaneous preclassic symphonies of Sammartini. In Ruge's many chamber works for flute, the Italian *cantabile* style far outweighs technical virtuosity, despite the composer's intimate knowledge of the instrument.

Ruge's fellow countryman Luigi Gianella (about 1778–1817) was a veteran of the La Scala opera orchestra in Milan who came to Paris about 1800. He earned his living playing in theater orchestras while writing ballets, comic operas, and many, many works for the flute. He had a fresh, Italian style, rather pleasant but lacking in deep emotional content. He did, however, produce some interesting "occasional" pieces, the *Concerto lugubre* in C minor, which was probably written for the funeral of Domenico Cimarosa in 1801, and the *Military* Concerto, his third, which includes an appropriately virtuosic and martial solo part.

Antoine Reicha (1770–1836), though a native of Prague, spent much of his professional life in Paris. His writing shows an international variety of influences: he had studied with Albrechtsberger and Salieri in Vienna, and also was impressed by Gluck, Haydn, Mozart, Gretry, and the Mannheim school. For many years Reicha was first flute in the same Bonn orchestra in which Beethoven played viola. He is best known for his pioneering woodwind quintets, which display a keen appreciation for the possibilities of instrumental color. But Reicha also wrote many other chamber music settings that include flute, all of them highly melodic and many with folk elements. In a break from custom, Reicha considered his six quartets for flute and strings, op. 98 (before 1815) to be true quartets, rather than solos for flute and strings. His interest in timbre had a profound influence on his students, including Hector Berlioz, who went on to author one of the nineteenth century's most important treatises on orchestration.

Germany

The patronage of Frederick the Great made Berlin the musical center of northern Germany. Between 1740 and 1786, fourteen major musical figures graced Frederick's court musical establishment, including Carl Heinrich Graun and Johann Joachim Quantz, who represented the older tradition at the Berlin Opera and in instrumental music, respectively; C. P. E. Bach, Franz Benda, and J. G. Graun, who produced important chamber music; the conductors Agricola, C. F. C. Fasch, and J. F. Reichardt, and theorists F. W. Marpurg and J. P. Kirnberger.

Franz Benda (1709–86), Konzertmeister of Frederick's Royal Band, had studied with Quantz and the brothers Graun. His music also reflected the folk influences of his native Prague, but the prime influence on Benda was his teacher Quantz. Benda downplayed virtuoso figuration in favor of thematic development. Though his sonatas and concertos retain a baroque flavor, they are expressive and melodic. Like Geminiani, Benda usually embellished all movements, whereas Corelli and Telemann had limited such decoration to slow movements.

Johann Gottlieb Graun (1702/3–1771), concertmaster of the Berlin Opera from its opening in 1742, was overshadowed by his brother Carl Heinrich (1703/4–1759), who was the chief composer at the opera. Like Benda, J. G. Graun represents a transitional stage between the contrapuntal density of Bach and the cantabile of Mozart. He wrote far less for flute than his brother did: just five concertos and eight trio sonatas. Overall, however, the trio sonata was a dominant form in his oeuvre, since trio sonatas were often played at royal soirées. Graun's concertos are meticulous in contrasting chamber and orchestral resources.

The most important Berlin composer of Frederick's time was Carl Philipp Emanuel Bach (1714–88), second surviving son of Johann Sebastian. He joined Frederick as harpsichord accompanist in 1738, and one flutistic accomplishment was that he accompanied the monarch's first solo as king in 1740. This experience provided much of the material for Bach's landmark treatise, *Essay on the True Art of Playing Keyboard Instruments,* which, with Quantz's *Versuch,* is a major source on mid-eighteenth century performance practice for all instruments. Bach stayed with Frederick until 1768, when he succeeded Telemann as Kantor of the Johanneum in Hamburg. He was a leader in the movement to counter the baroque complexity of his own father; he was the foremost exponent of the sensitive style *(Empfindsamkeit),* with its sighs, echoes, and overwritten expressiveness.

Bach's concertos were all written originally for harpsichord and strings, but he made numerous arrangements for flute, cello, and oboe. They combined the baroque ritornello structure, even in the late, Hamburg concertos, with more progressive, preclassic elements. There is little new material in the modulating solo episodes; the motivic rhythm is derivative of Vivaldi and of J. S. Bach; sequential dissonance chains are also baroque. But the younger Bach used slower harmonic rhythm and a more homophonic texture than did his predecessors, as well as expressive devices such as extreme ranges and surprising textural contrasts.

Bach's sonatas for flute fall into two periods; the earlier ones were written to order for Frederick and cater to the king's conservative preferences. A number of trio sonatas also date from the Berlin period, though Bach eventually abandoned this form, just as he abandoned the continuo for fully written out keyboard accompaniment. The Trio in E, Wq. 162, for two flutes and continuo, for instance, is typically baroque, largely concerned with contrapuntal detail. The two flutes are nearly equal in importance, and the sonata is replete with imitation and harmonic sequencing. The second movement is an intricate canonic invention more than reminiscent of J. S. Bach.

The flute works of the Hamburg period, intended for the public, are less baroque, lighter and simpler. Some of the Hamburg sonatas were probably inspired by the blind flutist Ludwig Dulon, whom Bach met in 1782/83. Bach's sonatas are important not so much for formal innovation as for expressive innovation: the characteristic sigh motifs; the change in mood within a single movement; the vocal melody, in which ornamentation was an integral (rather than added-on) part; and the extension of range (to g^3 in the Sonata in G, Wq. 133). The slow movements are particularly notable, highly emotional compositions that employ such devices as enharmonic changes, augmented chords, and modulations to remote keys. In this respect, Bach was one of the earliest exponents of romantic *Sturm und Drang*.

The *Zwölf Kleine Stücke*, Wq. 81, for two and three voices, scored for flute or violin and harpsichord, and the *Zwölf zwei- und drei-stimmige Kleine Stücke*, Wq. 82, for the same instruments are typical of the later period. Wq. 81 consists of six trios and six unaccompanied duets. Simple and popular, the opus was published in pocket-size format by the Berlin publisher Winter in 1758 and reprinted the following year. Wq. 82, published in 1770, bears the following preface:

> The publisher of this collection has sincerely attempted to create something pleasing for lovers of music. . . . Persons need not be accomplished musicians to take part in these ensembles.[7]

In accordance with contemporary custom, many of Bach's works, not just the concertos, were published with provisions for alternative instrumentation. For instance, trios for flute, violin, and bass could also be played by two violins and bass. Bach even provided a version of one such trio for a single treble instrument with cembalo obbligato; the second treble part would be assigned to the keyboard right hand. Bach's 1788 quartets, Wq. 93–95, foreshadow in some respects the classic piano quartet of Beethoven. One of his most unusual works is the unaccompanied Sonata for Flute in A Minor, Wq. 132 (1747). Like his father's partita for solo flute, it interrupts the singing melodic line to insert low-register notes, thus creating the illusion of an accompanying bass instrument.

Meanwhile, in the southwest of Germany, there was a musical revolution occurring in the city of Mannheim. Though small in size, the city was under the jurisdiction of the Elector Palatine Carl Theodor, a leading patron of the arts. As a result, the provincial city had the most outstanding orchestra in Europe, and its musicians pioneered the new orchestral style that would come to dominate the nineteenth century.

The expressive effects introduced in Mannheim were in the categories of dynamics and tone color. Contemporary critics raved about what they heard there, reporting "a forte like thunder, a crescendo like a cataract, a diminuendo as gentle as a crystal brook rippling from afar." Wrote German critic C. F. Schubart, "Nowhere in performance were light and shade better marked. Nowhere were the half and whole tints of the orchestral palette more clearly expressed."[8] The most characteristic feature of the Mannheim style was the use of dynamics. Dynamics were now clearly indicated in the score, rather than left to the performer's discretion, and they were dramatic as well. The new device was largely the work of Niccolò Jommelli (1714–74), the orchestra's conductor, who imported the idea from Italy in the early part of the century. Johann Stamitz, Christian Cannabich, and others championed the innovation and established it conclusively as part of the Mannheim tradition.

Second only to dynamic innovation was the Mannheim school's original use of wind instruments, aided by the presence of some of the top wind players in Europe. Again Jommelli was the pioneer, becoming the first composer to use wind instruments in his operas in other than a supporting role; they also appear in solo sections to create contrast and provide color effects.

Although the Mannheim school is best known for its contributions to the symphony, it also contributed substantially to the concerto literature, particularly for the woodwinds. In part this was due to the presence of virtuoso players who wrote concerto vehicles for themselves, but these same players also inspired their colleagues to write for them. Members of the older generation, such as Richter, persisted in using the motivic and ritornello construction of north German baroque concerto forms. But well in advance of their north German colleagues, the Mannheim composers assimilated such preclassic characteristics as broader internal dimensions, slower harmonic rhythm, and differentiated thematic materials into their concertos. Their concertos also have a number of distinctive local mannerisms, including fanfare rhythms and stylized syncopations. Simultaneously, the Mannheim composers produced equivalently progressive chamber music in a variety of configurations.

The principal member of the conservative first generation at Carl Theodor's court was Franz Xaver Richter (1709–89). His early works retain baroque counterpoint, even fugal vestiges. But the flexible, singing melody of his later chamber music approaches the classicism of a later era. Richter produced a fair number of flute works, including eight concertos and numerous sonatas; he was also a much-respected teacher of such Mannheim greats as Carl Stamitz.

Ignaz Holzbauer (1711–83), Kapellmeister to Carl Theodor from 1753 to 1778, also belonged to the first generation of the Mannheim school. He was no star, but composed pleasant, well-crafted "utility music." His flute works include a single concerto and two quintets for flute, keyboard, violin, viola, and bass, in which an old-fashioned trio texture predominates: the flute melody competes with the keyboard right hand, while the strings fill in and strengthen the texture.

Johann Stamitz (1717–57) is the best known composer of the first generation. Primarily a composer of symphonies—a form in which he made important innovations, including experiments with sonata form, sudden harmonic changes, and contrasting melodies—he also wrote concertos for flute, oboe, and violin. His flute concertos are emblematic of preclassic transition, freer in imitation and sequence than Richter's and structurally transitional. They represent an advance from the mannerism of the rococo by stabilizing the repetitive syncopations with a slower harmonic rhythm. The first movements are based on a single theme; the "development" is more a transition (to the relative major or minor) than a true development. There is a typical classic emphasis on the tonic. The slow movements are less operatic than those of baroque concertos and are essentially binary in form; the finales are rondos or a preclassic anticipation of sonata form, containing two themes in the exposition but no development.

The second generation of Mannheim composers included Johann Stamitz's two sons, Carl (1745–1801) and Anton (1750–about 1789–1809). Carl wrote prolifically for flute: seven concertos and a variety of chamber works. His compositions embody the characteristics of the classic period—large dimensions, contrast, and such rhythmic stereotypes as second-beat syncopation and slurred eighth-note appoggiaturas. Typically, he developed a dialogue contrast between a forceful opening theme and a graceful cantabile. His chamber music, too was progressive: the Six Trios, op. 14, for flute, violin, and bass, approach the classic string trio in the differentiation of parts and especially in the unusual scoring for cello, which occasionally crosses above the violin line. Carl Stamitz's Flute Concerto in D, dating from about 1776/77, has a typically galant opening theme; overlapping eight-measure periods extend the rhythmic gesture. The first movement ends with an expressive through-composed solo in which a new idea is introduced in a variation of the dominant, and then repeatedly quoted as it modulates back toward the tonic.

Anton Stamitz, Carl's younger brother, also wrote extensively for flute, though he wrote just one solo concerto. It is nevertheless significant for the bithematic structure of its opening movement and disintegration of motivic construction even more advanced than that of his brother. The overall impression of *Empfindsamkeit* is in the tradition of C. P. E. Bach.

Anton Filtz (1733–60), a cellist who played under Johann Stamitz in the Mannheim orchestra, was a composer in the Stamitz tradition. An original writer, he assimilated folk elements into his melodies and achieved interesting, irregular phrase structures. Filtz left the baroque far behind, though he was sometimes guilty of oversimplified texture and phrasing in an effort at clarification. His Concerto in D is pure Mannheim, with its idiomatic tone colors, steep crescendos and diminuendos, sharp dynamic contrasts, and agogic rhythm.

Christian Cannabich (1731–98) was also a Johann Stamitz disciple, an influence evident in details such as small syncopations and rococo figuration. Cannabich's personal cliché was the so-called Cannabich turn, an ornament that pervaded his symphonic output and was typical of his skill and the attention he devoted to working out smaller compositional dimensions. One of his finest works is a triple concerto for flute, oboe, and bassoon, accompanied by a large orchestra, with fully written-out cadenzas that anticipate the symphonie concertante.

Yet another Johann Stamitz disciple—indeed, he studied with both Stamitz and Filtz—was Carl Joseph Toeschi (1731–88), who became Konzertmeister in Mannheim in 1759. Toeschi succeeded in going beyond the stereotyped mannerisms of the Mannheim style, using his Italianate melodic gift to lift the syncopation to a higher level. He was an eager experimenter with form and contrast, as, for example, by inserting adagio sections in the midst of a minuet finale. Said Toeschi's contemporary, Leipzig critic Johann Adam Hiller, he was capable of invention, fire, and melodic and harmonic beauty, but his love of singularity was so great that he feared Toeschi would soon dismember melody into scrap![9]

Toeschi's concertos feature through-composed solos; transitions are more properly recapitulations. He wrote more chamber music for flute than concertos; his *Quatuors dialogués* (1762–66) were revolutionary in their differentiation of instrumental roles. Critic Carl Ludwig Junker, who used *Empfindsamkeit* as his yardstick, acclaimed Toeschi's compositions for flute as "epoch making" in their departure from baroque style.[10]

Cellist Franz Danzi (1763–1826) was another member of the Mannheim orchestra who composed prolifically for flute. Notable in his oeuvre is the Symphonie Concertante no. 1, which is in the traditional three-movement concerto form, as opposed to the two-movement French symphonie concertante. His D Minor Concerto, op. 42, features interesting juxtapositions of orchestral woodwinds with the solo flute.

The outstanding flutist in the Mannheim orchestra from 1753 to 1778, Johann Baptist Wendling (1723–97), was a competent composer in his own right, supplying himself with sonatas for one or two flutes and bass and for two unaccompanied flutes. They are, not surprisingly, virtuosic. Many were first published in Paris and soon reprinted in Amsterdam and London, where he made frequent concert tours. Wendling's op. 5 sonatas for flute, violin, and continuo are lightweight, unremarkable works in terms of invention, but they demonstrate preclassic traits, including a clear phrase structure and refined, detailed indications of articulation and dynamics. More important than Wendling's own compositional activity, which was rather unexceptional, was his influence on the great composers of his time. Mozart considered him the best flutist he had heard; the two men were well acquainted, and Mozart even orchestrated one of Wendling's flute concertos (listed in the Koechel catalog of Mozart's works as K. 284e).

Mannheim produced a number of composers who, like Wendling, took their talents elsewhere, but on a permanent basis. Father Joseph Schmitt (1734–91), who had studied in Dresden with Carl Friedrich Abel and had absorbed elements of the Mannheim style through him, moved from Germany to Amsterdam. His flute music is filled with elegant melodies and delicate cantabiles.

Antonio Rosetti (1750–92), né Rössler, was a double bass player and Kapellmeister to the prince of Oettingen-Wallerstein. He had at his disposal the Wallerstein *Harmonie* or wind ensemble, reputedly the best in Europe, and he wrote prolifically for those players. Rosetti's contemporaries ranked him on a par with Mozart and Haydn; his style was a transitional one, parallel to the early works of Haydn. Rosetti retains baroque ritornello form as a structural device, and rarely introduces a second subject; instead the first is restated in the dominant. His lyrical slow movements, however, are more classic in nature, with their ternary form and use of Austrian and Bohemian folk melodies.

Friedrich Schwindl (1737–86) was Konzertmeister at a succession of courts in Germany, the Netherlands, and Switzerland. He wrote two flute concertos and miscellaneous chamber music in the *Empfindsam* style, which in his day were very popular among amateurs.

Elsewhere in Germany and the rest of Europe, composers not affiliated with the major musical centers also made important contributions to the rococo and classic flute literature. The eldest of J. S. Bach's sons, Wilhelm Friedemann (1710–84), was the most conservative and least experimental of the four musician sons. He was not interested in combining the old and new styles; instead, he shifted back and forth between the two. Many of his excellent duets for two flutes are extremely conservative; they make extensive use of baroque part-crossing, canon, and true fugue. Yet Friedemann was more daring harmonically than were many of his contemporaries. His Sinfonia in D Minor for two flutes and strings is one of his best known works; there are also four extant trio sonatas.

Bartolomeo Campagnoli (1751–1827), an Italian violinist who became leader of the Gewandhaus Orchestra in Leipzig in 1797, represented a fusion of "German learnedness with Italian soul," in the words of a contemporary observer;[11] he wrote three flute concertos and a number of duos for his own instrument and flute.

August Eberhard Müller (1767–1817), who joined the Gewandhaus Orchestra as first flutist in 1794, had studied harmony and composition with J. C. F. Bach, eldest son of Johann Sebastian and Anna Magdalena Bach. A champion of the works of Mozart and Haydn, his own extensive output for flute shows a clear Mozartean influence. Müller was a particularly prolific writer of flute concertos, which were very well received at the time; his eleventh, op. 39, contains two sets of variations on "God Save the King." Müller also published a tutor for flute, *Elementarbuch für Flötenspieler* (Leipzig, about 1815).

Another virtuoso flutist, Caspar Fürstenau (1772–1819), played in the bishop's orchestra in Münster and made concert tours through Germany with his flutist sons in the 1790s. Not surprisingly, his works and those of his sons are virtuosic showpieces of comparatively little musical value.

Spain

Cellist-composer Luigi Boccherini (1743–1805) was the foremost representative of Latin instrumental music during the high classic period. Born in Italy, he worked in Vienna before settling in Madrid (with time out in Berlin) in 1769. His music synthesized a number of international influences: those of G. B. Sammartini and Nardini from Italy, Wagenseil and Monn from Vienna, Gossec and Schobert from Paris, as well as the Mannheim tradition. Spanish features—expansion by direct repetition and repeated syncopations—also crept into his music. Boccherini's phrasing was idiosyncratic and effective, with slurs from weak to strong beats; by eliminating direct accentuation and using *dolce* markings the melodic shape became less angular. The Flute Concerto in D, op. 27, traditionally credited to Boccherini, is now considered to be of questionable attribution. His quintets and sextets for flute and strings are, however, undeniably authentic and on an equal level with his landmark quintets for strings.

England

More than any nation in Europe during the classic period, England was a melting pot—or salad bowl, as revisionist historians have more correctly labelled the phenomenon—of musical styles. The concerto reflected particular foreign influence. English composers were relatively late to invent or adopt new compositional procedures for the concerto, enamored as they were with the Handelian model; Handelian idolatry served to freeze English concerto style even as the continental composers expanded and changed the form.

As in continental Europe, however, the public concert was superseding private patronage as the source of livelihood for musicians. One of the most important concert series was the Bach-Abel Concerts, organized by Carl Friedrich Abel and Johann Christian Bach. Abel (1723–87) was a gamba player under Hasse in Dresden before moving to London. His compositions had a light and energetic style that combined the refinement of Mannheim with the vocalism of Italy. Though his trios were not far advanced from the baroque trio sonata, with two parallel melody lines over the supporting bass, he wrote idiomatically for his instrumental forces, with broken chords, syncopation, and the characteristic galant appoggiaturas. The melodies in slow movements are lyrical and highly ornamented, while the finales often are minuets or rondos. Abel's harmony is expressive but consistently avoids the minor mode.

Abel's partner, J. C. Bach (1735–82), had studied with his older brother C. P. E. in Berlin. In the last decade of his life he worked in both Mannheim and London; in the latter he performed with flutist J. B. Wendling. His official court duties included accompanying the flute playing of King George III. Bach's appropriately elegant works for flute demonstrate his utter mastery of the galant style; he was the only one of J. S. Bach's sons who wholeheartedly embraced the new style. Bach's op. 8 quartets for flute and strings (1772), composed for Wendling, and three other quartets published in 1776 are unpretentious; those of op. 19 (1784), written for the private concerts of Lord Abingdon, are more Haydnesque and substantial. The six quintets of op. 11 (for flute, oboe, violin, viola, and continuo), dedicated to the Elector Palatine Carl Theodor of Mannheim, are uniquely scored for their time and duly exploit the instrumental colors.

One of J. C. Bach's greatest formal contributions is in the area of the concerted symphony or ensemble concerto. Of his fifteen such concertos, four feature the flute. No. 8 (about 1763) is scored for flute, oboe, and bassoon soli, accompanied by strings, oboe, and two horns; no. 12 (about 1772) is for two clarinets and bassoon obbligato, accompanied by strings and pairs of horns and oboes; however, in the second movement, Larghetto, the first oboist switches to flute and becomes the predominant solo instrument as the horns are *tacet*. These works are not true sinfonies concertantes, though they clearly foreshadow that form, because there is no strict division between the soli and orchestral sections. As the term "concerted symphony" implies, the solo instruments function more as projections from the orchestra than as an accompanied concertino.

One of the performers at the Bach-Abel Concerts, oboist Johann Christian Fischer (1733–1800), a veteran of Frederick the Great's court in Potsdam who had also given concerts in Mannheim and Paris, contributed several works for flute in a definitively rococo style. His works include ten concertos for oboe or flute (about 1768–95), ten flute sonatas (about 1780), and divertimentos for two flutes (1782).

Tommaso Giordani (1733–1806), director of the King's Theatre, Haymarket, at the same time Bach and Abel ran their concert series, wrote prolifically for flute in a galant style much like Christian Bach's. His compositions include duets, sonatas, and trios, idiomatically written for the instrument but with a tendency to be dull.

Vienna

The classic era of popular music history is more properly Viennese classicism, which reached its acme in the works of Haydn and Mozart. But Vienna also served as home to Gluck, Salieri, Cimarosa, and later to Beethoven. When the Electoral Court moved from Mannheim to Munich in 1778, Vienna became the center of the classic concerto and its resident composers adopted many Mannheim traits.

Christoph Willibald von Gluck (1714–87) was one of the foremost opera composers in mid-eighteenth century Vienna. His Flute Concerto in G was long thought to date from a 1746 visit to London or from about 1752, when Gluck served as Kapellmeister to Joseph Friedrich Wilhelm, Prince of Saxe-Hildburghausen, in Vienna. Today, however, the attribution is much in question. Gluck's masterwork for flute is the much-loved "Dance of the Blessed Spirits," the ballet-intermezzo from the opera *Orfeo ed Euridice* (1762); the dolce flute represents Orfeo's love for the lost Euridice. Gluck also wrote a set of eight trios for two violins or flutes and continuo, six of which were among his first publications (1746).

Writers of program notes have long observed the irony that Mozart wrote masterworks for the flute despite the fact that he disliked the instrument. The alleged evidence for this statement is a letter Mozart wrote to his father from Mannheim in February 1778. In the standard translation by Emily Anderson, it reads, "You know that I become quite powerless whenever I am obliged to write for an instrument which I cannot bear."[12] The translation in the Eulenberg score of the D Major Flute Concerto, however, reads, "As you know, I am always 'stuck' if I have to write all the time for one and the same instrument (which I dislike)." The ambiguity of the parentheses, critic Andrew Porter points out, is tantalizing; it is unclear whether Mozart disliked the flute or simply the tedium of a large commission for a single instrument.[13] (He was then in the midst of a commission by one De Jean, as Mozart called him—probably a wealthy Dutch amateur flutist named Willem Britten de Jong—for "three short, simple concertos and a couple of quartets." Ultimately, Mozart completed only two of the concertos and three quartets.)

In view of Mozart's frequent and idiomatic use of the flute in all genres—solo works, chamber music, opera, piano concertos, symphonies—it would be a mistake to take too seriously the letter of a twenty-two-year-old defending his tardiness to his disapproving father. It would be a supreme irony to postulate that the composer of *The Magic Flute* truly hated the eponymous instrument.

The earliest of Mozart's solo works for flute is a set of six sonatas, K. 10–15, scored for piano with the accompaniment of violin or flute. These are pleasant works by an eight-year-old prodigy, typical of their form in the dispensability of the flute part. The mature Mozart produced no flute sonatas.

Mozart composed four flute quartets: K. 285 in D, K. 285a in G, K. 285b in C, and K. 298 in A. The first three were part of the 1777 de Jong commission. Mozart probably wrote the Quartet in A, K. 198, in Vienna in 1786/87, the dating based on the derivation of the rondo theme from a melody of Paisiello, which was composed no earlier than 1786.

While Mozart's flute concertos epitomize the elegance of classicism, they are already somewhat preromantic in their virtuosic solo lines, the power of the orchestral accompaniment, and the interplay of soloist and orchestra. The first concerto, in G major, K. 313, is the more important and expressive of the two, a masterwork on a par with the bassoon concerto. Mozart marked the first movement *Allegro maestoso*, an infrequent designation, emblematic of the power and importance of the piece. The development of the first movement, which is in sonata form, is notable for its extended section in minor mode. It is of sufficient quality to survive a plethora of inappropriate romantic cadenzas in the two centuries since its composition, and has proved once and for all the superiority of Mozart to would-be imitators, expanders, and improvers.

The D Major Concerto, K. 314, is in fact a transposition with quite minor changes of the Oboe Concerto in C, written in 1777 for the Salzburg oboist Giuseppe Ferlendis. It is typical of Mozart's Salzburg style, using a small orchestra and emphasizing clarity and elegance.

The Concerto for Flute and Harp, K. 299, is a less substantial work than either of the solo concertos. Written in April 1778 for the amateur flutist the Comte de Guines (whom Mozart styled the Duc de Guines) and his harpist daughter, it is quintessential salon music, galant and full of beautiful melodies. Its infrequent use of minor mode seems designed less for expression than for variety. The concerto generously calls for cadenzas in all three movements, which tends to prolong this relatively shallow work just a bit too much. The Comte had been French ambassador to London, where he evidently obtained a new six-keyed flute with range to low c^1; Mozart uses that novel note three times in the concerto.

The *Andante in C*, K. 315, is a gem. It was probably written in winter 1777 or spring 1778, but its provenance is uncertain. Musicologist Alfred Einstein suggested that Mozart wrote it as an alternative slow movement to K. 313, because the original version was not easy enough for de Jong. But since the C major tonality would be inconsistent with a G major concerto, other historians suggest that the *Andante* may have been the first step toward the third concerto of the de Jong commission, which Mozart never completed.

Joseph Haydn (1732–1809), though older than Mozart, was influenced by him to write for the flute; indeed, Haydn was well into middle age before he gave the instrument serious attention. It is conjectured that the market for flute music that he discovered in England, as well as the visits to London of such flutists as Wendling, Monzani, and Dulon, encouraged this interest. Late in life, Haydn admitted to a pianist colleague, "I have only just learned in my old age how to use the wind instruments, and now that I understand them I must leave the world."[14]

In 1780, Haydn wrote a concerto for flute and strings, which may have been performed in Paris as late as 1832, but it did not survive. The concerto assigned to Haydn in the *Breitkopf Thematic Catalogue* of 1781, still generally attributed to Haydn in modern editions, is actually one of two flute concertos by Leopold Hofmann (1730–93). Ironically, Hofmann, a popular Viennese composer, was one of Haydn's chief rivals.

Four flute quartets, op. 5, though not listed in Haydn's own manuscript thematic index, are in fact genuine. They were first published in Amsterdam about 1767–68 and soon after were reprinted in London. The overall form of the quartets is presto-adagio-minuet-presto. The fast movements are very much like the divertimentos and cassations of which Haydn was such a master, with repeated-triplet accompaniments, hunting rhythms, syncopated breaks in the minuets, sudden dynamic contrasts, and folklike minuet melodies. The adagios, on the other hand, are in the tradition of Mannheim and C. P. E. Bach, a mixture of preromantic *Sturm und Drang* and sighing sentimentalism. In overall texture, the quartets are not mini-concertos for solo flute with string accompaniment, but true chamber music.

Ironically, Haydn's most famous solo flute works are transcriptions. There are two sonatas, op. 90 (1803), in G and F, for pianoforte with flute or violin accompaniment; the G major is an arrangement of the string quartet, op. 77, no. 1. The account books of the publisher, Breitkopf and Härtel, show that the arrangements were the work of flutist-composer August Eberhard Müller, who accomplished the job for twenty Reichsthaler. The Sonata in C, op. 87, "pour le Clavecin ou Piano-Forte avec Accompagnement d'une Flûte ou Violin obligé" (about 1797) is an arrangement of the string quartet, op. 74, no. 1. This piece, too, may have been the work of Müller.

The flute is also prominent in Haydn's other chamber works—cassations, divertimentos, and trios. Best known are the so-called London Trios, for two flutes and cello. Other combinations include flute, violin, and cello; and flute, cello, and keyboard. There is a vast quantity of flute chamber music, once credited to Haydn, that has in recent years been proven spurious. Nevertheless, Haydn did use the flute frequently in his orchestral writing, perhaps due to the presence of the fine flutist Hirsch in the orchestra at Esterhazy.

In a pattern reminiscent of Mannheim, the second generation of classic composers in Vienna contributed the most to the concerto form. Leopold Hofmann has finally earned credit for the "Haydn" Concerto in D. Carl Ditters von Dittersdorf (1739–99) persisted in the baroque tradition in his 1760 flute concerto, but after extensive travel his style changed radically. One of Dittersdorf's most unusual works is a *Notturno* for four flutes.

Johann Baptist Vanhal (also known as Wanhall) (1739–1813), a Czech composer and teacher, was one of the first independent musicians, unaffiliated with court, church, or any other sort of official music. His flute works first appeared in the Breitkopf catalog in 1775; the concertos exhibit such Mannheim characteristics as small-scale syncopation, slurring, and folk melodies derived from his Czech heritage. Vanhal's works from the 1780s are lighter in character, some programmatic, others consisting of themes and variations—all designed, like his pedagogical works, for relatively unsophisticated amateurs. Michael Haydn (1737–1806), younger brother of Joseph, wrote two flute concertos in D, as well as quartets and other small ensembles.

Jean-Baptiste Krumpholtz (1742–90), solo harpist to Count Esterhazy, studied composition with Haydn. He was the foremost virtuoso on his instrument in the late eighteenth century, and he made substantial contributions to its technique and literature. Many of his compositions include flute. Similarly, Mauro Giuliani (1781–1829), an Italian guitar virtuoso, lived in Vienna from 1806 to 1819. A leader of the classic guitar movement in that city, he, too, included the flute in many of his works.

Franz Anton Hoffmeister (1754–1812), known today primarily as a publisher, got his start in Vienna before setting up his publishing house in Leipzig. He wrote twenty-five solo flute concertos and twenty more multiple concertos, many of which include flute as part of the concertino. Hoffmeister's chamber music output for flute is even more prolific and includes an unusual trio for three flutes, "La gallina, il cucco e l'asino," a musical joke that describes a musical contest between a hen, a cuckoo, and an ass.

Franz Krommer (1759–1831), often known as Krommer-Kramář, held a number of positions in the Viennese musical hierarchy, including service as the last court composer to the Hapsburgs. A woodwind specialist, he wrote two solo flute concertos, the first in 1802; five symphonies concertantes that include flute (1799–1808); nine quartets and nine quintets for flute and strings.

Antonio Salieri (1750–1825), longtime protégé of Gluck, served as a Viennese court musician for more than fifty years. Primarily an opera composer—he conducted the Italian Opera in Vienna—he injected a bit of *Sturm und Drang* into his chamber works, along with galant melodies and classic triadic harmony. He wrote a concertino and concerto for flute and strings, and a double concerto for flute and oboe. Salieri was also an important teacher: his pupils included Beethoven, Schubert, Czerny, Hummel, Liszt, and Moscheles.

Johann Nepomuk Hummel (1778–1837), a student as well of Haydn and Mozart, was one of the best composers of the late classic period. He wrote three sonatas and one variation set for flute and piano, and two trios for flute, cello, and piano. They are quintessential classic works, with clear transitions, tertiary harmonic relationships, consistently homophonic texture, modernized Alberti accompaniments, and above all a gift for melody.

And finally—Beethoven (1770–1827), who in his flute works was still very much a classicist, not yet the revolutionary harbinger of romanticism. The Allegro and Minuet for two flutes (1792); the Serenade in D for flute, violin, and viola, op. 25 (1801)—later published, with Beethoven's consent, in an arrangement for flute or violin and piano, op. 41 (1803)—are minor, tritely phrased works. A sonata dating from about 1790–92, the manuscript of which was found among Beethoven's papers after his death, is of doubtful authenticity.

Two sets of *National Airs with Variations,* scored for piano and flute or violin (op. 105 and op. 107, about 1818), are the result of a request by one George Thomson, an amateur musician in Edinburgh. A collector of folksongs, he asked Beethoven, Pleyel, and other composers of the day to write sonatas using Scottish melodies; Beethoven fulfilled the commission with piano trios and in 1818 wrote the variation sets.

Notes

1. Friedrich Blume, *Classic and Romantic Music*, trans. M. D. Herter Norton (New York: W. W. Norton, 1970), p. 18.
2. Leonard G. Ratner, *Classic Music: Expression, Form, and Style* (New York: Schirmer Books, 1980), p. 81.
3. Ruth Halle Rowen, *Early Chamber Music* (1949; reprint, New York: Da Capo Press, 1974), p. 70.
4. Carleton Sprague Smith, "Haydn's Chamber Music and the Flute," *Musical Quarterly* 19 (1933): 436.
5. Ratner, p. 128.
6. Wolfgang Amadeus Mozart, letter to Leopold Mozart, 3 Dec. 1977, in Emily Anderson, ed., *The Letters of Mozart and His Family*, 2nd ed., prepared by A. Hyatt King and Monica Cawlan, 2 vols. (London: Macmillan, 1966), 1: 401.
7. Richard Morris Jacobs, "The Chamber Ensembles of C. P. E. Bach Using Two or More Wind Instruments" (Ph.D. diss., State University of Iowa, 1964), p. 202.
8. Frederick Dorian, *The History of Music in Performance* (New York: W. W. Norton, 1942), p. 146.
9. Walter Lebermann, ed., *Flöte-Konzerte der Mannheimer Schüle*, Das Erbe deutscher Musik, vol. 51 (Wiesbaden: Breitkopf & Härtel, 1964), p. V.
10. Robert Münster, "Toeschi," in *The New Grove Dictionary of Music and Musicians*, ed. Stanley Sadie (London: Macmillan, 1980), vol. 19, p. 24.
11. Chappell White, "Bartolomeo Campagnoli," in *The New Grove Dictionary*, vol. 3, pp. 652–53.
12. Wolfgang Amadeus Mozart, letter to Leopold Mozart, 14 Feb. 1778, in Anderson, 1:481.
13. Andrew Porter, "Flute," *The New Yorker*, 4 Aug. 1980, p. 58.
14. Smith, p. 341.

16

THE ROMANTIC ERA

The nineteenth century represents a low point in the history of flute music. This fact may seem surprising since the Boehm flute, a technological innovation that was to revolutionize instrumental music, came into being during this period. But the new flute was slow to be accepted, and the difficulties for players of adopting the new fingering system and the competition it provoked among instrument makers had a negative short-term effect on the flute literature.

In addition, general developments in music were not conducive to the growth of the solo flute literature, though the romantic movement adopted the flute and the piccolo as valued members of the symphony orchestra. Quite simply, the flute did not, by itself, have the capacity to produce the power and variety of tone that were the vehicles of romantic musical expression. As a member of a large orchestra, however, the flute was an integral component of a varied texture.

In the nineteenth century the flute basically continued on the course it had begun in the classic period: its role in the orchestra became ever more important (*vide* Beethoven and Brahms), while the solo and chamber literature took a precipitous decline in both quality and quantity. The nineteenth century was, for the flute, not a golden age but an ornithological age, as the flute was reduced to a chirping vehicle for virtuosic display and programmatic symbolism.

The narrowest definition of the romantic era dates it from 1828 to 1880; the widest adds an additional three-quarters of a century, placing the limits at 1789 and 1914. Its general characteristics are perhaps easier to list than its dates: a repudiation of classic restraint, discipline, moderation, and symmetry; the replacement of rational expression by a more emotional or subjective perspective, manifested in musical performance by extremes of personal expression and interpretation; a resurgence of nationalism, with concomitant reliance on the melodies and rhythms of folk traditions.

Compositional structures, even sonata form, became less rigid; lyrical and picturesque objectives spawned such new forms as the tone poem and the *lied*. Action and drama were the prime ideals, fostering emphasis on contrast over unification in all elements of composition and performance—tempo, dynamics, rhythm, thematic material, harmonic progression, orchestration, and mood. As a result, all facets of notation—dynamics, tempo, expressive markings—became more numerous and more complex. But, paradoxically, these increased markings gave rise to greater interpretive license for the performer: rather than being restrictive, they provided the performer with a whole new range of possibilities.

Whereas, in the classic period, melody had been the prime compositional element, in the romantic era harmony took the lead. Indeed, harmony was one of the greatest preoccupations of romantic composers, one indication being the large number of treatises published on the subject during the period. More specifically, there were a number of new developments in harmonic practice. Above all, harmony as a coloristic device replaced functional harmony. Harmonic rhythm lost ground as a structural device; whereas it was generally fast in the baroque, and slow in the classic era, in the romantic it was atmospheric, changing with the mood of the music.

Dissonances became progressively elevated, resulting in what one historian terms a "rising dissonance threshold"; there were new, higher discords, in which chords were built by thirds above the ninth. A frequent procedure was the use of chromatically altered chords, especially enharmonic alterations, and these with minimal preparation or resolution—again, the elements of surprise and contrast. There was increased use of borrowed chords—the transfer of characteristic major or minor devices such as the diminished seventh chord from one mode to the other. This was a favorite device in Beethoven's day, which, in its exaggerated form, was one of the prime components of the saccharine sentimentality known as *kitsch*.

Melody, the star of the classic era, now took a back seat to harmony. It retained the classic phrase structure and periodicity, but lines became freer and longer, commensurate with the expanding dimensions of all musical elements. Wide intervals became expressive vehicles, and composers used unusual intervals such as sixths or sevenths, often diminished ones at that. In line with nationalist interests, romantic melody frequently borrowed from folk themes, often as the basis for variation sets; similarly, composers adopted such folk characteristics as irregular phrase structure and altered scales for their original compositions.

Rhythm, too, felt the influence of folk traditions, and, like melody, it became less confined than in the classic period. New complications included cross-rhythms (duplets versus triplets), hemiola, and compound meters. Like all other elements, rhythm was dynamic, capable of rapid change in the service of expression. At the same time, tempo became more flexible, with rubato, a give-and-take within an overall metric rubric, a common expressive device.

Romantic ideals of tone color or timbre had two major goals. The first was euphony, a rejection of the lean, spare sound of classicism in favor of a full, rich sonority. The result was a preference for dense ensembles, such as the string quintet or sextet, rather than the quartet; the addition of woodwinds and brass to the symphony orchestra; and in piano music, the invention of the sustaining pedal and the use of octave doublings and full, rich chords. Second, the romantics valued timbre as an independent compositional element, one with intrinsic value, not merely a servant of melody and harmony. Again, the publication of treatises on instrumentation, Berlioz's and Richard Strauss's being only the most famous of a large group of books, is an indicator of this trend. Between 1800 and 1910 the standard symphony orchestra nearly tripled in size in quest not only of greater volume but also more variety of sound; the string sections expanded and were subdivided further; new instruments, including piccolo, clarinet and bass clarinet, French and English horns, harp, and a greatly enlarged percussion section expanded the coloristic palette as well as the melodic range.

Music had already, in the classic period, become a public activity as well as a private one, with the establishment of public concert series and music publishing businesses the most important manifestations. The trend toward popularization continued in the nineteenth century as the industrial revolution progressed and the middle class, with its newfound financial resources, became the arbiter of taste. The extension of breadth in the music market brought with it a loss of depth. The middle-class music lovers of the nineteenth century lacked the training and sophistication of their artistocratic eighteenth century predecessors. As a result, the music designed for middle-class consumption was far below the standard of the eighteenth century; although virtuosity reached great heights, enhanced by the increasing sophistication and technical capabilities of remodeled musical instruments, the musical substance was inferior.

For professional musicians, the circumstances of employment changed radically. No longer connected to aristocratic households, performers became free agents, frequently making concert tours across Europe and eventually even to the United States. Such travel brought an awareness of national styles—and concomitant chauvinism.

In the case of the flute, the transition from eighteenth century to nineteenth century virtuosity is evident in a comparison of the careers and compositions of François Devienne, last representative of the former, and Charles Nicholson, the prototype of the latter. Devienne's compositions were musically substantive works, his performance brilliant but conservative. Though he recommended that his students use the new multi-keyed flutes, he continued to perform on the one-keyed instrument. In Nicholson's generation, in contrast, flutists made the most of individual idiosyncracies in the interest of public relations; he used lavish embellishments, a reedy and metallic tone, and gimmicks such as the glide to enliven his performance. Nicholson's own compositions were bravura works in the theme-and-variations mold. His competitors included Drouet and Tulou in France and the Fürstenau family, Boehm, and Tromlitz in Germany.

The eighteenth century aristocrat-virtuoso was replaced by the professional virtuoso whose livelihood was at the mercy of the middle class public, and music felt the effects. Though harmony was richer and technique ever more brilliant, formal design suffered. Composers constructed larger forms not by the development of themes but by the amalgamation of smaller forms. Bravura variations and opera fantasies were the stock in trade of the traveling virtuoso.

Social changes also affected amateur musicians. The middle class, with its rising economic and social status, sought to imitate the eighteenth century gentry in manners as well as wealth. And so the flute continued in the nineteenth century to be the favored gentleman's instrument; only the gentleman had changed. In Manchester, England, for instance, this trend was epitomized by the estabishment, in 1774, of the Gentlemen's Concerts, an organization comprising twenty-six flutists.

Just as young ladies considered mastery of the piano a necessary social grace, flutists—mostly men—used their instrument as a social tool. A reporter for the *British Minstrel* in 1843 explained the possible consequences:

> Wind instrument practice, though improved and improving, is certainly not in a high and palmy state among amateurs. Of flutes, indeed, we may easily muster a regiment. . . . Rarely is the first consideration of the young man, in the choice of instrument, the abstract one of utility or public pleasure, but how it will become him, how he will *look* playing. Thus the flute is seldom taken up but for sinister purposes, if not indeed, to break the peace of families. Armed with this deadly instrument, and accoutred *point device*, the flautist makes his attack upon the principal beauty of the evening party, and happy is the victim if she is made an honest woman of. The flute, however valuable in the orchestra, has therefore, a reputation not entirely musical. It is the Don Giovanni of wind instruments.[1]

The first half of the nineteenth century saw the publication of numerous journals for flute players—*The Flutonicon* (1834–50), *The Flutist's Magazine* (1827), and *The Flutist's Magazine and Piano-Forte Review* (1829) among them. An announcement for the last-named publication in the magazine *Athenaeum* stated that one of ten men played the flute.[2] In addition to its attractiveness to social climbers, the flute displayed several characteristics suitable to the romantic temperament: its capability for nuance and its similarity to the human voice made it a favorite instrument in an atmosphere more suited to emotion than to reason. Though audiences still enjoyed and demanded technical display in public performance, amateur musicians wanted an instrument capable of pathos and elegance.

As opera grew in popularity, the audiences wanted to be able to produce "echoes" of those public performances in their own homes. Lacking radio and recordings, they turned instead to transcriptions suitable for home performance—transcriptions not just for piano, but also for flutes. Whole operas were routinely arranged for two flutes. But the most common form was the *air varié* or fantasia, based on operatic themes of the day or traditional national melodies.

Another prevalent chamber form was the accompanied sonata, introduced in the classic era, an ideal vehicle for enthusiastic but relatively inexperienced amateur players. Other forms used in both the piano and flute literature were the *Albumblatt* ("Album Leaf") and *Morceau characteristique* ("character piece"), short, often programmatic works, suitable either for home performance or the "dessert course" of public concert programs. Finally, there were many semipedagogical pieces that also found their way onto concert programs, *étude* being only one of many titles such compositions took.

At the same time, the flute concerto, in both solo and symphonie concertante configurations, decreased in both quantity and quality. In the eighteenth century, the concerto had been primarily a custom-composed piece, commissioned by private patrons or written for particular virtuosi. The romantics, with their emphasis on self-expression, rejected such made-to-order works as antithetical to compositional creativity and imagination. The composition of showpieces for concert-giving virtuosi was, therefore, not a respected activity, and as a result few nonflutists wrote flute concertos, leaving the task to the virtuosi themselves. Moreover, the virtuoso-composers explored forms other than the concerto—for example, Chopin's polonaises, Schubert's impromptus, and Liszt's *Hungarian Rhapsodies*. Finally, the physical proportions of the nineteenth century orchestra made the concerto a less adaptable form. The enlarged romantic orchestra could not fit into a private home, and so the concerto was no longer a multi-purpose composition; it could be played only in the concert hall. Even professional musicians could not always find or afford the large number of musicians necessary to fill out the accompanying orchestra.

The nineteenth century concerto thus became solely a public form. Its proportions were expanded, its texture enriched, its effect ever more dramatic, but there were drawbacks. As concerto historian Abraham Veinus put it, the concerto resorted to broad, obvious gestures meant to be seen and heard from the cheapest seats. "The soloist now stormed into a fantastic bravura uproar intended to astound the multitude, just as hitherto he had spun a filigree of graces and embellishments to amuse the initiate."[3] The suitability of piano and violin for this function is clear, as is the unsuitability of the flute.

Those few flute concertos that were written were pure entertainment, on the level, says another prominent musicologist, of either beer-garden fare or humorous amusements.[4] In short, the flute was reduced to the status of a bird. This was reflected in the titles of many works for flute and orchestra, as for example, Graening's *Polka for Two Flutes and Orchestra*, subtitled *Two Nightingales at the Millstream*; Henri Kling's double concerto for two piccolos, entitled *The Birds of Passage*; and Wilhelm Popp's *Nightingale Con-*

certo, op. 361. As early as 1812–14, the Gerber encyclopedia singled out J. G. Arnold's symphonie concertante for two flutes for particular approbation because the composer "did not make the persistent effort of climbing up to the giddiest heights and degrading the flute to a bird's whistle," as was the custom.[5]

A notable feature of the romantic concerto—one that carried over into the few true flute concertos that were written in the period—was the evolution of the cadenza. Abraham Veinus explains that the cadenza took its modern form,

> a showpiece pure and simple with little pretense to artistic value. It is now a composed piece, a solo etude comprising a number of routine difficulties, the successful rendition of which is taken by less critical members of the audience as proof that the performer is worth the price of admission.[6]

Music by Nonflutists

The roster of nineteenth century composers who wrote for the flute is distinguished by the absence of many of the century's biggest names. Schumann, Brahms, and Wagner are conspicuous by their absence; of the period's luminaries, only Weber, Schubert, Chopin, and Saint-Saëns make cameo appearances in the flute literature. Most of the other nonflutist composers were either virtuosi on other instruments or prolific producers of salon music.

Jan Ladislav Dussek (1760–1812) was one of the first touring piano virtuosi. Though his early compositions are classic in style, those of his last two decades show such romantic characteristics as modulation to remote keys, copious expressive markings, and chromatic harmony, including altered chords. As such, his music represents a departure from immediate predecessors such as Hummel. A number of Dussek's sonatas for pianoforte accompanied by flute date from this late period.

Johann Baptist Cramer (1771–1858) was another of the great early romantic pianists, considered by Beethoven the finest of his day. A student of Carl Friedrich Abel, he championed Bach, Mozart, and Beethoven in England. Though classically oriented, as a pianist he pioneered an expressive legato touch that later became standard practice. As a composer, his idiomatic, truly pianistic passagework was also progressive. Cramer's accompanied keyboard sonatas, scored for piano with either flute or violin, were in a lighter, more romantic vein than were his serious piano sonatas; indeed Cramer composed prolifically for the dilettante market.

Carl Maria von Weber (1786–1826) was one of the founding fathers of the romantic movement in Germany. Most at home in opera, he wrote very little chamber music. He did, however, make a few important contributions to the flute literature: the *Romanza siciliana* for flute and orchestra (1805, published

1839) and a trio for flute, cello, and piano (1819). The trio is historically significant in its juxtaposition of strict classic form with romantic emotionalism; its extremes of emotion range from the melancholy of the Andante to an ebullient Waltz.

Saverio Mercadante (1795–1870), a contemporary of Bellini and Donizetti, turned almost exclusively to opera after 1820. But as a young man, having studied flute as well as composition, he produced six flute concertos, as well as flute duos and trios and quartets for flute and strings.

Perhaps the best known of the early romantic composers for flute is Friedrich Kuhlau (1786–1832), who is often called "the Beethoven of the flute." Like Dussek and Cramer, he gained fame as a pianist and composer of piano works. Kuhlau studied composition with Christian Schwenke, a pupil of C. P. E. Bach and Johann Philipp Kirnberger; this pedagogical descent from J. S. Bach may have inspired Kuhlau's well-developed contrapuntal technique. Conventional flute lore has it that Kuhlau was a flutist, but, although he did study the flute as a child, he never mastered it. He explained to his publisher, Breitkopf & Härtel, in 1814, "I play this instrument only a little, but I know it exactly," this knowledge derived from the assistance of the flutist in the royal orchestra in Copenhagen.[7]

Kuhlau wrote a total of more than three hundred compositions, of which a quarter included flute. The motivation for this prolific output was simple; wrote Kuhlau in 1829, "Because I cannot live with my family on my small salary, I have to write for my public instrumental works and such things, for which I am well paid."[8] The amateur market was ready and waiting.

Though much of Kuhlau's flute music is salon music, well crafted but musically unsophisticated, his sonatas are on a higher level. Indeed, Brahms wrote in 1854 that he wanted to learn to play the flute so that he could perform the Kuhlau sonatas with Clara Schumann.[9] Kuhlau's duets, written between 1813 and 1829, are fairly conventional works, most in three movements, generally in sonata, ternary, and rondo form, respectively. The range is from c^1 to $b^2\flat$, with the two parts of equal technical difficulty. Much of their interest lies in midmovement key signature changes and the use of imitation in development sections. In their time, the duets won laurels from the critics. In 1814, for instance, the *Allgemeine musikalische Zeitung* wrote of op. 10a:

> If two flutists of considerable skill on their instruments, of refined taste directed more toward the serious, the meaningful, and the artistic than toward the galant, the glittering, and the superficial, and of the inclination also to practice many an exception from the usual treatment of the instrument, and to join one another closely in performance, . . . we can recommend to them from the products of recent years no other compositions as unconditionally as those named here.[10]

Kuhlau's trios, which are roughly contemporaneous with the duets, are structurally similar, but distinguished by novel key relationships and hemiola effects. The first flute part is generally predominant. Kuhlau dedicated the trios to some of the leading flutists of his day, including August Eberhard Müller, Caspar Kummer, Louis Drouet, and Benoit Tranquille Berbiguier. He dedicated his sole quartet for four flutes, written about 1829, to Johann Wilhelm Gabrielski, a flutist at the Royal Chapel in Berlin. It is a dramatic work, making effective use of dotted rhythms and dynamic contrast to achieve a maestoso effect. The outer movements are homophonic, with the upper two parts most active while the lower two give harmonic support; the middle movement is contrapuntal, with equal importance given to the four voices.

Peter Joseph von Lindpaintner (1791–1856) was musical director of Munich's Isarthor Theatre, where the young flutist Theobald Boehm got his professional start in 1812. As a conductor, Lindpaintner won raves from such notables as Mendelssohn, who said, "it is as if he played the whole orchestra with his baton alone."[11] Also active as a composer in many forms, Lindpaintner produced many words for flute—including seven pieces for flute and orchestra, two symphonies concertantes, and a set of variations on a theme of Beethoven—but they are not terribly original and are largely ignored today. His etudes, op. 126, however, remain useful in their characteristically trite way, as excellent practice pieces for romantic expression.

Ignaz Moscheles (1794–1870), yet another pianist, studied counterpoint and composition with Albrechtsberger and Salieri, respectively, before becoming codirector of the Philharmonic Society in London. He also founded a series of "historical soirées" for the purpose of reviving the music of Bach, Handel, Haydn, Scarlatti, and the like. Moscheles's best works are his piano sonatas; Schumann considered him one of the best sonata composers of his generation. They combine classic balance and restraint with the more dynamic aspects of early romanticism. He wrote two sonatas for flute and piano—op. 44 and op. 79 (1819 and 1828)—recently revived in concerts and recordings by Jean-Pierre Rampal, and the Concertante in F for flute, oboe, and orchestra.

Franz Schubert (1797–1828), one of the most important early romantics in the symphonic and vocal areas, wrote only one solo work for flute, a set of variations (1824) on "*Trockne Blümen,*" from his song cycle *Die schöne Müllerin.* The piece was written for Ferdinand Bogner, professor of flute at the Vienna Conservatory.

Frederic Chopin (1810–49) contributed little to the chamber music literature; his main interest was the piano. But at age fourteen, during his first year at the Warsaw Conservatory, he wrote a set of variations on Rossini's *La Cenerentola.*

Bernhard Molique (1802–69) was a virtuoso violinist who made extensive concert tours throughout Europe and Russia, one of them, in 1823–24, with Theobald Boehm. Molique wrote one of his earliest works, a *Fantasy on themes from "Der Freischutz"* for flute and violin, for one of their joint performances. Molique's friendship with Boehm also resulted in his Concerto for Flute, op. 69, from which the Andante is commonly excerpted in modern recitals, and a concertante for flute and violin. Boehm premiered the concerto in Leipzig in 1824, but it was not published until after the composer's death. Molique's quintet for flute and strings dates from 1848 and is dedicated to London flutist-publisher Walter Stewart Broadwood of the firm of Rudall, Carte.

Emile Pessard (1843–1917), not a flutist himself but the son of a flutist, was a respected professor of harmony at the Paris Conservatoire at the end of the nineteenth century. Best known for his songs, he produced rather light instrumental music, including some occasional pieces for flute and piano. *Andalouse* is the most famous today.

Carl Reinecke (1824–1910) taught from 1860 to 1902 at the Leipzig conservatory, where he was a strong advocate of preclassic music, particularly that of Bach. He also conducted the Gewandhaus Orchestra. Reinecke was considered one of the foremost Mozart interpreters of his time—he wrote authoritative books on the performance of Mozart concertos and Beethoven sonatas—and composed three excellent cadenzas for the Mozart flute and harp concerto, K. 299. As a composer Reinecke was stylistically akin to Schumann, and a master of chamber music, which included the programmatic Sonata *Undine*, op. 167 (about 1885) and *From the Cradle to the Grave*, op. 202, both for flute and piano. The four-movement *Undine* is based on the 1811 novel of that name by Friedrich de la Motte Fouqué. The harmony is fully romantic, but the work is not a technical showpiece; it is one of the few true romantic flute sonatas. Reinecke's concerted works, including the *Ballade*, op. 288, for flute and orchestra (1911) and the *Concerto*, op. 283 (1909) display notable skill in orchestration.

Benjamin Godard (1849–95), a French violinist and composer, was one of the pre-eminent writers of salon music, specializing in sentimental music for piano. His *Suite de Trois Morceaux*, op. 116, for flute and piano (originally for flute and orchestra) fits the same mold. The suite is reminiscent of Weber, yet, in one historian's view, anticipates the music hall style of Poulenc more than fifty years later.

Cécile Chaminade (1857–1944), a student of Godard, was known during her lifetime as a pianist; her compositions, too, are quintessential salon music and have been largely forgotten. The one exception is her *Concertino* for flute, op. 107, which in recent years has become a staple of the contest solo repertoire. Written in 1902, it was originally scored for flute and piano, but the composer later orchestrated it for a London performance by her friend Marguerite de Forest Anderson. Most of Chaminade's flute pieces, including the *Serenade to the Stars*, *Pièce Romantique*, and *Gavotte*, were dedicated to Adolphe Hennebains, flute professor at the Paris Conservatoire.

Like Moscheles, Camille Saint-Saëns (1835–1921) was a keen student of music history, basing many of his works on the models of his Viennese predecessors. But he was also a true Frenchman at heart, becoming a founder in 1871 of the Société Nationale de Musique, an organization to promote new music by French composers. Saint-Saëns's preference for the woodwinds became particularly notable around the turn of the twentieth century; his *Odelette* for flute and orchestra dates from about 1920. However, he had written flute works much earlier for Paul Taffanel of the Paris Conservatoire: a *Tarantelle* for flute, clarinet, and orchestra in 1857 and a *Romance* for flute and orchestra in 1871.

Music by Flutists

With the exception of Kuhlau, the greatest contributors to the nineteenth century flute repertoire were, not surprisingly, professional flutists themselves. Unfortunately, quite a few of them were better flutists than composers, but many made indirect contributions to the flute literature as dedicatees and commissioners of works by nonflutist colleagues.

Theobald Boehm (1794–1881) is of course permanently inscribed in the history of the flute by his invention of the modern instrument. But he was also a competent composer and arranger for his beloved instrument; in all he wrote some seventy-two compositions. Many remain unpublished (the manuscripts for many of the alto flute arrangements are in the Dayton C. Miller Collection at the Library of Congress), but others have been revived in recent years. Best known, perhaps, are the op. 4 *Variations on Nel cor più* and the op. 21 *Fantasy on a Theme of Schubert.* Boehm's works are above all the work of a flutist writing gratefully for his instrument. Schilling's *Musik-Lexicon* of 1835 made the following evaluation:

> We find concert pieces containing movements in which the player cannot but acquire sober admiration of his practical mastery; divertissements and potpourris, thoroughly pleasing to the ears, which do nothing more than to amuse pleasantly. Through both, however, he wins the interest of the majority of flutists and amateurs, and he has reached the point where his "La Sentinelle," his Variations on "Nel cor più non mi sento," his "Grande Polonaise," the "Fantaisie Concertante" for flute and piano, composed together with Ogden [an English gentleman-flutist], and other similar masterpieces, cannot fail to find a rather wide circulation, and thus exert an influence on the awakening of understanding of true art.[12]

Jean-Louis Tulou (1786–1865), one of the first flute students at the Paris Conservatoire, epitomized the French ideal of flute playing, with his precise, brilliant technique and tonal perfection. A consummate showman as a performer, he once discovered a crack in his wooden flute just before he was about to begin a concert with the eminent soprano Mme. Catalani. Remaining onstage, he calmly produced wax and cord and repaired the instrument under the watchful gaze of the admiring audience. Similar exhibitionism carried over into his compositions; one of Tulou's five concertos, a large quantity of duets, and several of the fifteen appropriately titled *Grands Solos* remain in print today.

Louis Drouet (1792–1873) was tremendously successful as a flute soloist in Paris, though he was generally ranked second to Tulou. When he visited England in 1817, however, the critics felt that he masked poor intonation with technical brilliance. An early partisan of the eight-keyed flute, Drouet increased his technical command by a novel use of double tonguing, which also drew criticism, much of it probably inspired by professional jealousy. Drouet's flute compositions are appropriately virtuosic but of negligible musical value; some duets and trios remain in print. He also wrote a method for the eight-keyed flute (1827), which is an important document of early nineteenth century performance practice.

Anton Bernhard Fürstenau (1792–1852) was the second of three generations of virtuoso flutists in his family. He made several concert tours of Europe with his father, Caspar; on one such tour to Prague, in 1815, he made the acquaintance of Weber. He then played under Weber as first flutist in Dresden in 1820, and later traveled with him to Paris and London. Anton Fürstenau won praise both for expressiveness, befitting a colleague of Weber, and for technical dexterity. But the British found his tone, as they found Drouet's, inferior to the rich sound of native son Charles Nicholson.

Weber was the dominant influence on Fürstenau's compositional style; not only did his operas provide themes for variation sets, but his overall operatic orientation carries over into other Fürstenau works. Fürstenau's output includes countless such variation sets and fantasies on operatic themes by Meyerbeer, Halevy, and Bellini and a vast quantity of other chamber music. His son Moritz (1824–99) carried on the flute-playing tradition—he toured with Jenny Lind in 1855—but even though he transcribed operatic themes (including some by Wagner!) for flute and piano, his fame rests on his contributions as a music historian and writer rather than as a composer.

Caspar Kummer (1795–1870), who succeeded Drouet as Kapellmeister at Coburg in 1855, was one of the finest German flutists of his day. His many, many compositions won raves from flute historian R. S. Rockstro, and his duets are still frequently played today. Heinrich Soussman (1796–1848), a Berliner who in about 1820 became first flutist at the Grand Opera in Saint Petersburg, is best known today for his pedagogical etudes, but his bona fide music includes the flute in a variety of instrumental combinations, among them three quartets for four flutes.

Giulio Briccialdi (1818–81), a self-taught flutist who gave concerts in both Europe and the United States, is most famous for a mechanical invention: the now universal configuration of the thumb keys on the Boehm flute, which he commissioned from the London firm of Rudall, Carte. Briccialdi composed prolifically for the flute, including the obligatory opera fantasies, but is remembered (and perhaps cursed) today by students who work their way through his very useful exercises and etudes.

The Polish flutist Franz Doppler (1821–83) debuted at age thirteen in Vienna. He toured extensively with his brother Karl (1825–1900), also a flutist, before settling in Pest (later part of Budapest), where the brothers helped found the Philharmonic Society in 1853. Franz later returned permanently to Vienna, where he taught flute at the conservatory beginning in 1865. Both brothers were opera as well as flute composers; their flute works (many composed jointly), like their operas, combine Italian, Russian, Polish, and Hungarian influences. National derivations are often specified in the titles, as in the *Pastorale fantaisie hongroise* and *Souvenir de Prague*.

German flutist Wilhelm Popp (1828–1903) was a prolific producer of potboilers—his *Musikalische Tonbilder*, a set of etudes, have the stratospheric opus number 501. His concert works include a *Nightingale Serenade* for flute and piano; the *Polka di Bravura*, op. 201, a typical air varié; *Fantasy and Variations on an American Air (Yankee Doodle)*; and the fully romantic *Swedish Concerto*, op. 266. Popp's *Bagatelle*, written in 1890 for New York flutist Eugene Weiner, is unique: though scored for flute and piano, it is designed for only one player, who plays flute with the left hand and piano with the right.

Joseph-Henri Altès (1826–95) studied at the Paris Conservatoire with Tulou, though, unlike his teacher, he adopted the Boehm flute. He joined Tulou on the faculty in 1868. Altès represented a new generation, not only in his adoption of the Boehm flute, but also in his pedagogical approach: he required his flute students to study theory as well as technique. His *Méthode*, the oldest French method for the Boehm flute still in use, was progressive for its time in its description of the metronome, charts of alternate fingerings, and theoretical emphasis. Altès's etudes and concert works remain quintessentially romantic compositions.

Jules Demersseman (1833–66) studied with Tulou but never received an appointment to the Conservatoire faculty because he refused to change from the old system to the Boehm flute. He was, however, a prolific composer for his instrument, writing a multitude of virtuosic *airs variés* and *solos de concert*.

Johannes Donjon (1839–about 1912), yet another student of Tulou, was a prominent Paris flutist, performing at the Opéra and the Concerts Pasdeloup, but he was less important as a composer. Only his *Offertoire* remains a staple of the repertoire, though he also wrote numerous other solo pieces and a *Nocturne* for four flutes.

Karl Joachim Andersen (1847–1909), a Dane, learned the old-system flute from his father. He played in the Royal Orchestra in Copenhagen before touring Russia and Germany. In 1881 he became a founding member of the Berlin Philharmonic Orchestra, where he stayed until 1891, when a tongue problem ended his performing career. But he continued to compose—Taffanel commissioned him to write examination pieces for the Paris Conservatoire. His solos are period pieces, but his etudes continue to be pedagogical mainstays.

Paul Taffanel (1844–1908) lived at the end of the romantic era, but he was arguably the most important flutist of the century. He took the Paris Conservatoire's first prizes in flute (1860), theory (1862), and counterpoint (1865) and joined the faculty in 1893 after a distinguished performing career in the leading Paris orchestras. His numerous European concert tours were influential in raising the standards for woodwind playing throughout the continent. As a flutist, Taffanel was without peer; said his student Georges Barrère,

> Taffanel was not only the best flutist in Europe but I doubt if anyone can ever fill his place. Quality as well as quantity of tone and fine technique were only a small part of his splendid characteristics as a flute player. He loathed cheap sentimentality, excessive expression, endless vibrato or shaking of tone, in a word all the cheap tricks which are as undignified as they are unmusical.[13]

When Taffanel took over as professor of flute at the Conservatoire in 1893, he caused a near revolution in flute teaching. Though he retained the traditional master class format, he individualized instruction so that each student could work at his own level. And though he commissioned the annual examination or contest pieces in the prevalent genre of romantic virtuosity—Joachim Andersen's 1895 *Morceau de concert*, for example—he did much to revive baroque and classic works. The Mozart concertos, for instance, had not been heard in Paris in fifty years while Tulou's concertos held sway. Taffanel and his students grew increasingly sophisticated in their taste; significantly, the Taffanel-Gaubert method (1923), especially notable for its concepts of varied tone color, was also the first conservatory method to devote sections to style and orchestral excerpts. The ornamentation of the Bach sonatas and the cadenzas for the Mozart concertos are indeed outmoded in the light of more recent musicological research, but they nevertheless represent an important step in the revival of then-forgotten masterpieces of the flute literature.

Taffanel's compositions for his instrument are disappointing in the context of his exalted reputation as a performer and pedagogue; they are typical salon or contest music, including a fantasia on Weber's *Die Freischütz,* the well-known *Andante Pastorale et Scherzando,* and transcriptions of Chopin piano pieces. One of Taffanel's best works is his delightful woodwind quintet.

Taffanel's contribution to the flute literature was, thus, not as a composer, but as the inspiration for compositions by more original composers. As one of the most respected members of the Paris musical establishment, he exerted considerable influence on the production of new French woodwind music. In 1879 he founded the Société de musique de chambre pour instruments à vent. This organization became an important force in reviving the woodwind quintet, which had lain dormant for nearly half a century, by commissioning new works from such composers as Charles Lefebvre, Gabriel Pierné, and Charles Gounod.

As a composer, Taffanel represents the last phase of the French romantic flute tradition. As a flutist and teacher, however, he initiated a new era, the most golden yet. In the next generation—beginning with Taffanel's protégé, Philippe Gaubert—the flute shed its birdlike reputation and again became an instrument worthy of serious attention.

Notes

1. *British Minstrel* 1 (1843): 54; quoted in David William Eagle, "A Constant Passion and a Constant Pursuit: A Social History of Flute-Playing in England from 1800 to 1851" (Ph.D. diss., University of Minnesota, 1977), pp. 36-37.
2. Eagle, p. 6.
3. Abraham Veinus, *The Concerto* (New York: Dover Publications, 1964), p. 134.
4. Hans Engel, *Das Instrumentalkonzert* (Wiesbaden: Breitkopf & Härtel, 1974), vol. 2, p. 419.
5. Hans Engel, *The Solo Concerto,* trans. Robert Kolben, Anthology of Music, vol. 25 (Cologne: Arno Volk Verlag, 1964), p. 89.
6. Veinus, p. 41.
7. Ann Kozuch Fairbanks, "Music for Two, Three, and Four Flutes by Friedrich Kuhlau" (D.M.A. diss., Ohio State University, 1975), pp. 11-12.
8. Ibid., p. 13.
9. Ibid., pp. 68-9.
10. *Allgemeine musikalische Zeitung,* 27 July 1814, col. 508; quoted in Fairbanks, p. 74.
11. Jennifer Spencer, "Peter Josef von Lindpaintner," in *The New Grove Dictionary of Music and Musicians,* ed. Stanley Sadie (London: Macmillan, 1980), vol. 11, p. 5.
12. Karl Ventzke, "A Lecture on the Life and Works of Theobald Boehm (1794-1881)," trans. Susan Eareckson (Paper delivered at National Flute Association convention, Pittsburgh, Pa., 16-17 Aug. 1974), pp. 14-15.
13. Patricia Jean Ahmad, "The Flute Professors of the Paris Conservatoire from Devienne to Taffanel, 1795-1908" (M.A. thesis, North Texas State University, 1980), p. 91.

17

THE MODERN ERA

The physical evolution of the flute since the turn of the twentieth century has had a direct effect on the music written for the flute ever since. Perhaps the most important factor is stability, for the absence of mechanical change is evidence of the Boehm system's proven excellence and reliability. The stabilization of the flute mechanism has permitted all manner of experimentation with music for the instrument because composers are able to deal with a known quantity.

In other ways, too, the histories of instrument and music are closely related. First, mechanization, which began with methods of manufacture, later influenced the musical employment of the flute. This is reflected not only in the high technical standards of the modern literature but also in such avant-garde techniques as key percussion. Second, just as there is international cross-fertilization in the flute manufacturing industry, there is cross-cultural interchange in musical composition and in music education. Third, composers' interest in smaller and variable pitch intervals parallels manufacturers' interest in microdimensions. Similarly, musical interest in tone and timbre is largely a result of flute makers' earlier attention to this subject. And both groups are concerned with economy. Just as manufacturers aim to maximize production efficiency and cost effectiveness, composers have scaled down instrumental forces, resulting in a renaissance both of small chamber music and the use of the chamber orchestra for concerted accompaniment.

At the same time, flute performance has evolved in a number of important ways. Variety and quality of tone have become the dominant concerns, and vibrato has become a significant factor. Many performers have become specialists in one type of music or another. The overall technical level of flute performance has never been higher. Performance opportunities have increased both in magnitude and scope; although most flutists still maintain orchestral and/or academic bases, more and more are venturing out as soloists, some on a full-time basis. The solo literature has grown correspondingly, in both chamber and concerted forms. In the latter category, the trend has been toward the intimacy of chamber music—in part an antiromantic aesthetic reaction, in part an economic response to the expense of paying large symphony orchestras to accompany a soloist. Most recently, flute music has witnessed the inclusion of electronic media.

Another distinctly twentieth-century development is a division of labor that has resulted in the decline of the flutist-composer. Indeed the role of the flutist-composer has been negligible for most of the twentieth century. Even in the early years, Philippe Gaubert was the only one of any significance, and he was far more respected as a flutist, teacher, and conductor than as a composer. Georges Barrère, emblematic of the succeeding generations, published only two pieces for his instrument. Perhaps very few flutists wrote for their instrument because full-time composers—at last convinced of the flute's potential—were already doing so with such success. Not until the avant-garde revolution did flutists again begin writing for their instrument to any significant extent. When they did, it was a matter of necessity, because the new techniques required such intimate knowledge of the instrument's technical capabilities.

The history of flute music divides into five phases, defined, respectively, by dance, bird imitation, vocal imitation, noise elements, and electronics. In the eighteenth century, dance elements dominated musical composition and tone color was of little importance. Indeed, instruments of similar range were relatively interchangeable: the trio sonata demanded merely two treble voices and basso continuo. Whether the solo lines were carried by flute, oboe, recorder, or violin was of little consequence. The relative unimportance of timbre as a compositional element in the solo literature continued into the classic period.

In the second phase of its history, coinciding with the romantic era, flute music had little independent identity; its literature consisted largely of arrangements and transcriptions, with the air varié and fantasia the predominant forms. Technical gymnastics were intended to glorify the player's technique, but more often, owing to the defects of the pre-Boehm flute, they did just the opposite. Even after the advent of the Boehm flute at midcentury, technical display remained the norm, as composers found it necessary to demonstrate the new instrument's abilities. In sum, the nineteenth century treated the flute as a bird; trills and ornaments predominated.

Only in the last quarter of the nineteenth century did the flute enter its third phase; it evolved from imitating the birds to imitating the human voice. At first the goal was the production of a homogeneous tone throughout the compass of the flute, which would remain constant in spite of anything the fingers might do. But soon the philosophy expanded to encompass sophisticated timbral modification, first as an expressive element, then as a compositional one. Since the modern flute is a product of the mechanical age, it may seem paradoxical that the emphasis of composition and performance shifted away from technical—that is, digital—display. Actually, this is not a paradox at all, because once the fingering capabilities of the Boehm flute ceased to be a novelty, they were taken for granted, and performers (and then composers) became more interested in the new challenges of timbre. Composers did not stop writing fingertwisters; they merely gave this aspect of composition less conscious attention. This is not to say, either, that the subtle techniques of tone production are any easier or require any less virtuosity than "traditional," digitally challenging technical showpieces. On the contrary, they demand not only physical capability, but may require the player to make more of an intellectual contribution, which cannot be learned by rote as fingering can.

Thus the twentieth century flute has gained an independent musical identity and developed an impressively extensive literature that is uniquely geared to its capabilities. Within this corpus of literature, however, there is no single "modern" or "contemporary" style whose characteristics can be concisely enumerated. Instead, twentieth century flute composition encompasses a lengthy list of styles and techniques that, when taken together, can be adequately described by only one adjective: eclectic. Neoromanticism, impressionism, classicism, neoclassicism, contrapuntalism, pointillism, chromaticism, multitonality, polytonality, microtonality, and atonality are just some of the styles and techniques that fall under the twentieth century umbrella.

France

The modern flute school, like its eighteenth century ancestor, was born in France. It actually dates from around 1885, the time of Taffanel's prominence and also a time of significant historical importance in music in general. As historian Roger Shattuck wrote in *The Banquet Years,*

> The fashionable salon declined after a last abortive flourishing. The café came into its own, political unrest encouraged innovation in the arts, and society squandered its last vestiges of aristocracy. The twentieth century could not wait fifteen years for a round number; it was born, yelling, in 1885.[1]

The establishment of the Troisième République in 1871, following the Franco-Prussian War, had far-reaching implications in French musical circles. At the beginning of the nineteenth century, the operas of Rossini, Bellini, and Donizetti had dominated the Paris musical scene, and Germanic influence, particularly Wagnerian, was a significant factor in midcentury. After the Franco-Prussian War, however, there was a chauvinistic reaction against foreign influences, particularly Italian and German. Symptomatic of this development was the establishment of such organizations as Saint-Saëns's Société Nationale de Musique (1871), with its *Ars Gallica* program for the promotion of French music.

At the same time, there was a return to historical sources, with musicological research on the Middle Ages and Renaissance; the founding of the Société des Instruments anciens, the Schola Cantorum, and the Société Bach; and the establishment of a music history class at the Paris Conservatoire in 1871 (though it did not become a required course until 1905).

Music became a more and more democratized, public activity. The number of theaters had been growing steadily, and the number of concerts increased, as did the scope of music education. The dichotomy between amateurs and virtuosos became ever more defined. Music criticism experienced a renaissance, which made the public more demanding in the realm of musical interpretation.

Most importantly for the flute, there was a profusion of research into musical timbre. This trend had begun in the early part of the nineteenth century, with the instrumentation treatises of Kastner (1837, 1839) and Berlioz (1844); now there were new volumes by Widor (1904)—Georges Barrère contributed the flute section—Ernest Guirard (1909), and others. Wind instrument makers, active in research, gave players the tools to exploit timbre more fully, and Taffanel's Société de musique de chambre pour instruments à vent (founded in 1879) spurred composers to write for the newly improved wind instruments.

French music of the modern era—exclusive of the avant-garde—divides, more or less, into four schools: the romanticism of Franck, the classicism of Saint-Saëns and Dubois, the impressionism of Debussy, and the aesthetic of Les Six. None of them, however, is neatly or firmly defined or exclusive; a given composer often was influenced by more than one teacher or philosophy. In general, however, the affinity groups of French composers derive from particular professors of composition in the Paris music schools.

First was the romantic school of Cesar Franck, with its rich harmony, emphasis on chromaticism, purposely obscured or unexpected modulations, ample phrase structure, and beautiful, lyric slow movements. Franck also transmitted a definite German influence and exhibited the historicism of the late nineteenth century.

Vincent d'Indy (1851–1931) advanced Franck's symphonic ideals; he was a champion in France of both classicism and Wagner. He was one of the earliest members of the Société National de Musique, and served as director of the Schola Cantorum in Paris. Under his regime it became a bastion of musical orthodoxy that emphasized antiquarian and musicological interests, as opposed to the progressive tendencies of the Conservatoire. D'Indy's historical interests are reflected, for instance, in his *Suite dans le style ancien* (1886), for trumpet, two flutes, and string quartet. His *Concerto* for flute, cello, and piano (1927) demonstrates his adherence to classical forms.

Among the composers most influenced by d'Indy was Heitor Villa-Lobos (1887–1959), a Brazilian composer who combined the folk influences of his homeland, as in the fourteen *Chôros* of 1920–29, with the historicism of the *Bachianas brasilieras* (1930–45). *Chôros no. 2* (1924) is scored for flute and clarinet; *Bachianas Brasilieras no. 6* (1938) for flute and bassoon. The *Concerto Grosso* (1959) also reflects the influence of d'Indy's historical consciousness. The flute part of *Assobio a jato (The Jet Whistle)* of 1950, however, pioneered the then-radical simulation by the flute of the title sound, accomplished by blowing directly into the embouchure.

A number of Franck's French pupils also wrote for flute. Louis Ganne (1862–1923), music director of the Monte Carlo casino, was best known for his salon pieces and songs, including the *Andante et scherzo* (1905). He also wrote an operetta entitled *Hans, le joueur de flûte* (1906). Gabriel Pierné (1863–1937), who had studied organ with Franck and composition with Massenet at the Conservatoire, succeeded Franck as organist at Sainte Clotilde in 1890. His works are especially notable for their clear textures and balance; they include a *Canzonetta, Nocturne,* and *Sonata* for flute and piano; two works for flute, violin, and cello; and two pieces for flute, string trio, and harp: *Variations libre et finale* (1933) and *Voyage au pays du tendre* (1951).

A second French style, often called the classic style, derives from Saint-Saëns and from Theodore Dubois, director of the Conservatoire from 1896 to 1905. Its major characteristics include short, periodic, overwhelmingly regular phrases, and a carefully restrained lyricism. Saint-Saëns' most famous pupil was Gabriel Fauré (1845–1924), who was a regular at the older man's salon beginning in 1871. Fauré succeeded Dubois as director of the Conservatoire in 1905, serving until 1920. His melodies are as chromatic as Franck's, but are less expansive. Unfortunately, his works for flute are few: the well-known *Fantaisie*, op. 79, written as the contest piece for the Conservatoire in 1898; the *Morceau de concert* of the same year; and a gorgeous transcription of the *Sicilienne* from the incidental music to *Pelléas et Mélisande*.

A number of younger composers were strongly influenced by Fauré's distinctive combination of classic and romantic elements (the classic ultimately predominating): Charles Koechlin, Florent Schmitt, Maurice Ravel, the revered organist-pedagogue Nadia Boulanger, and Georges Enesco.

Charles Koechlin (1867–1950) studied composition with both Massenet and Fauré; in 1909, with Ravel and Schmitt, he founded the Société Musicale Indépendante, an intentional rival to d'Indy's Société Nationale, to promote new music. Koechlin was a prolific composer for flute, both solo and in various chamber combinations. His *Deux Nocturnes*, op. 32b (1904–12) for flute, horn, and keyboard, and *Trois Pièces*, op. 34/2 (1899–1907), for flute, bassoon, and piano, have strong romantic traits, but contain the genesis of his later, more modern style, combining Chopin-Mendelssohn influence with polytonal and bitonal inflections. The flute sonata (1911–13), premiered by Adolphe Hennebains, exhibits the trademarks of his harmonic vocabulary: pure, open fifths and parallel quartal and quintal harmonies. The *Suite en quatour* (1911–15) shows clearly the influence of Fauré; the *Trio* for flute, clarinet, and bassoon (1924) is a pseudofugue that contains a Haydnesque Alberti bass in the third movement. The *Sonate* for two flutes (1918–20) is composed of typically French conjunct melody; it received its premiere in 1922 at the Société des Instruments à vent. *Quatorze Chants* (1936) for flute and piano shows folksong influence.

Florent Schmitt (1870–1958), the most romantic of Fauré's disciples, also studied composition with Massenet and harmony with Dubois. He acquired a taste for German romanticism as well as for the exoticism of the Orient. His forms are conventional, the harmony tonal, and his music has an overriding rhythmic feel. Schmitt's works for flute are numerous; various chamber settings include a quartet for four flutes (1944–49).

Reynaldo Hahn (1875–1947), a harmony student of Dubois, made a limited contribution to flute literature; his *Variations on a Theme of Mozart* (1905) for flute and piano is typical. Georges Enesco (1881–1955) had the same pedagogical pedigree; his *Cantabile et Presto* (1904) was a Paris Conservatoire examination piece.

The third major French style is impressionism, characterized primarily by soft, hazy, broadly defined harmonies, delicate nuances of timbre, and freedom of form and phrase structure. The Expositions Universelles held in Paris in 1878, 1889, and 1900 were instrumental in the impressionist absorption of Oriental influences. Impressionism is personified by Claude Debussy (1862–1915), who was the seminal figure in the development of the truly modern flute literature. His orchestral *Prélude à l'Après-midi d'une faune* (1892–94) and *Syrinx* (1912) for solo flute foreshadowed the course of French music and flute music for many years to come. Debussy's style is above all one of restraint: he achieves maximum emotional effect with minimum musical gesture. Solo lines are constructed of short melodic cells; melodies draw inspiration from plainsong, the whole-tone scale, and Oriental elements. Dynamics are restricted. Germanic chromaticism is replaced by pentatonic modes, symptomatic of Debussy's receptivity to non-Western sources. There is an emphasis on the affinities between chords rather than on the differences between them, a goal achieved by the use of multirelational seventh and ninth chords, diminished and augmented triads, and four-part chords. Concomitantly, the sound impression is of a static nature, with harmony functioning in a nontraditional manner. Lush use of color is the predominant sonic element.

Given these aesthetic aims and techniques, the flute, with its narrow dynamic range, its limitation to relatively short melodic units, its "microscopic focus," its ability to create subtle nuances of color, and its affinities for the conjunct melodic line, made it the ideal vehicle for Debussy. Moreover, Debussy was sensitive in his orchestral scoring when accompanying the flute, using pianissimo strings, muted horns, and harp, and sustained chords or tremolos rather than more rhythmic figures. Against this thin texture, the moving line of the flute stands out in relief.

Debussy wrote the unaccompanied *Syrinx* (1912) as incidental music to Gabriel Mourey's play *Psyche*; it was to be played just before Pan's death. He dedicated the piece to Louis Fleury, who premiered it in 1913; Fleury retained the manuscript, and it was not published until fourteen years later.

Syrinx was the first piece for solo flute by a major twentieth century composer.

Debussy's *Sonata for Flute, Viola, and Harp* (1915) is neoclassical in its melodic emphasis. The harmonies are diatonic and often triadic, and the use of timbre is masterful, particularly in the flute-viola unisons of the *Pastorale* section. (Interestingly, Debussy had originally intended to use oboe, but later opted for the darker sound of the viola.) It is an intimate, tender work, of which the composer wrote, "It is frightfully mournful and I don't know whether one should laugh or cry—perhaps both?"[2]

Albert Roussel (1869–1937) continued the Debussy tradition, though his works also show the influence of his teacher d'Indy. The d'Indy influence is most evident in the *Divertissement* for piano and winds (1906). About 1910, however, Roussel's music began to make increasing use of chromatic alteration and addition, resulting in increasing dissonance; *Krishna*, the third movement of *Les Joueurs de Flûte* (1924), was his last strict application of an altered-scale form. *Les Joueurs de flûte*, comprised of four programmatic movements, is perhaps the most famous of Roussel's many works for flute. The composer dedicated each of its four component pieces to one of the leading flutists of the day: *Pan* to Marcel Moyse, *Tityre* to Gaston Blanquart, *Krishna* to Louis Fleury, and *M^r. de la Péjaudie* to Philippe Gaubert. Other works include a *Serenade* for flute, harp, and string trio (1925) and a trio for flute, viola, and cello (1929).

Many of the same Debussian characteristics apply to Roussel's younger colleague, Maurice Ravel (1875–1937). They had a common literary background; the impressionist character of Ravel's orchestral masterpiece *Daphnis et Chloë* (1909–12) is the prime example. Unfortunately, Ravel did not contribute to the solo flute repertoire except for later arrangements of his *Pavane pour une infante defunte*, though he included the flute in the *Introduction and Allegro* (1905–06), really a chamber concerto for harp.

Philipp Jarnach (1892–) was a protégé of both Debussy and Ravel, both of whom provided him entrée to the publisher Durand. Strongly influenced by the neoclassicism of Ferruccio Busoni, and an editor of baroque works, he wrote a *Sonatine* (1920) for flute and piano.

The works of Jehan Alain (1911–40), an organist killed in World War II, demonstrate the influences of Satie, Debussy, and organist-composer Olivier Messiaen. His *Trois Mouvements* for flute and piano (1935) are also available in a version for flute and organ, rescored by his sister, organ virtuoso Marie-Claire Alain.

Beginning about 1919, French music experienced significant changes. Among the social symptoms were the complete disappearance of the salons and the decline of the piano as "bourgeois furniture." The chamber orchestra was on the rise, partly as a result of the influence of Schoenberg and Stravinsky. It embodied economy of expression, which small jazz ensembles had proved both workable and valuable; it was also an outgrowth of film and radio music, which favored the smaller ensemble because its balance could easily be controlled electronically.

A group of young Paris musicians semiofficially known as *Les Six* epitomized the trend toward economy of expression. Their aims were simplicity, terseness, and clarity, as well as opposition to German romanticism and to impressionism. They were receptive to jazz, and adopted its syncopations and complex rhythms, including quintuple and septuple time interjected into simple 2/4 and 4/4 compositions. Woodwinds and brass were used more than strings, and the piano became a percussive instrument. Harmony was almost always tonal. The *Les Six* aesthetic, at its height from 1917 to 1927, has been described as the "beauty of banality."[3] Ultimately, the movement resulted in neoclassic pastiche, as in the works of Poulenc. *Les Six* included four members who wrote for flute: Arthur Honegger, Germaine Tailleferre, Darius Milhaud, and Francis Poulenc.

Arthur Honegger (1892–1955) varied his instrumental forces from solo flute, in *Danse de la Chèvre* (1932), dedicated to René Le Roy, to chamber orchestra, as in the *Concerto da camera* for flute, English horn, and strings (1949). Many of his works use chorales or choralelike melodies. Germaine Tailleferre (1892–1983), the only woman in the group, contributed several flute works: *Pastorale* for unaccompanied flute; a *Concertino* for flute, piano, and strings (1953); and *Forlane* (1973), for flute and piano. Tailleferre's music is gracious, with both the concision of Couperin and an interest in timbre and sound inherited from Fauré and Ravel.

Darius Milhaud (1892–1974) made extensive use of folk materials derived from his Provençal background, but absorbed German elements as well. He made frequent use of bitonality in melody and harmony, and in this regard exerted a great influence on Honegger. His *Sonata* for flute, oboe, clarinet, and piano (1918) uses triple counterpoint over quartal chords and a double pedal, as well as superimposed seventh chords. The first movement of the *Sonatine* for flute and piano (1922) is in classic sonata form, with a contrapuntal development, followed by a section of birdlike trills and mordents. The second movement is a dance form with jazz, syncopation, hemiola, and a folklike melody. The harmony includes quartal chords, tone clusters, and tritones. Milhaud wrote his *Concerto for Flute, Violin and Orchestra* (1938) for Blanche Honegger and Marcel Moyse, who premiered it with the Radio Suisse Romande, under Ernest Ansermet, in 1940.

Francis Poulenc (1899–1963), was, like Tailleferre, a student of Koechlin. He was a supreme melodist, firmly committed to diatonic harmony. He wrote just one solo work for flute, the classically balanced, urbane, and lyrical *Sonata* (1956). (Poulenc made it a rule never to write more than one piece for any particular instrumental combination.) He dedicated the sonata to that great patron of chamber music, Elizabeth Sprague Coolidge, and he and Jean-Pierre Rampal premiered it at the Strasbourg Festival in 1957.

Vittorio Rieti (1909–), though born in the United States and educated in Italy, was closely associated with *Les Six* from 1925 to 1940, and was one of the founders of La Serenade, a Paris organization for the promotion of modern chamber music. Rieti is a neoclassicist in the Stravinskian tradition—

indeed, he went to Paris because Stravinsky was there—though he had earlier experimented with atonality. He scored flute in a number of important chamber works: the *Sonatina* for flute and piano (1920); the *Partita* for harpsichord, flute, oboe, and string quartet (1945); and a *Concertino* for flute, viola, cello, harp, and harpsichord (1963). The last work is quintessentially neoclassical, using the harpsichord and the concerto grosso principle.

Alexandre Tansman (1897-), who emigrated from Poland to Paris in 1919, was associated with Ravel, Milhaud, and Honegger. By the 1920s, the influences of Ravel and Stravinsky gave way to a more lyric, melancholy style, as in the flute sonata (1925). Like Milhaud, Tansman made use of folk materials. A late work is the *Concertino* for flute and strings (1969).

In the same generation as *Les Six* was Lili Boulanger (1893–1918), the first woman to win the Prix de Rome and the younger sister of the more-famous Nadia. Her music is in the mainstream of the day: contrapuntal and slightly chromatic. In her short lifetime she wrote three works for flute: *Nocturne* (1911), *Cortège* (1914), and *D'un Matin de Printemps* (published posthumously in 1922), all for flute with piano accompaniment.

Others of this generation were, fortunately, more prolific contributors to the flute literature. Jean Rivier (1896-) was one of the most progressive composers of the 1920s and 1930s. The instrumentation of his flute opus is unusual: a quartet for four flutes and three pieces for unaccompanied flute in addition to a concerto (1955), three pieces for flute and piano, and several other chamber works. Russian emigré Alexandre Tcherepnin (1899–1977), who settled in Paris in 1921, combined folk derivations, Chinese and Japanese ideas picked up in travel to the Far East between 1934 and 1937, and the clarity and simple textures of contemporary French music. His *Concerto da camera* (1924) is scored for flute, violin, and strings; there are also a flute trio, a quartet for four flutes, duets, and other chamber works.

Eugène Bozza (1905-) has written nearly thirty works for flute; indeed, his woodwind chamber music forms the basis of his international reputation. The first of these pieces was published in 1936, and Bozza is still composing. Henri Tomasi (1901–71) was not quite as prolific. His interest in writing for flute perhaps grew out of his conducting studies with Philippe Gaubert. A particularly brilliant orchestrator, Bozza includes three concertos among his flute compositions.

Jacques Ibert (1890–1962) retained classical forms, but used them in a uniquely flexible manner. He viewed the conciseness of baroque and classical forms as a means of reaction against nineteenth century German romanticism; the restrained emotions and dancelike rhythms of his music earned him the neoclassical label that he usually bears. Ibert's thematic material generally falls into two categories: quick, clever, witty motivic statements that are subdivided and recombined contrapuntally; and long-breathed lyric lines.

Ibert's orchestral palette is derived from the impressionist colors of Debussy and Ravel. The impressionist influence is also evident in such early chamber works as *Jeux* (1923), for flute and piano. The *Trois Pièces Breves* for woodwind quintet and the *Aria* for flute and piano (both 1930) are exquisitely crafted works from his middle period. Ibert's later works are mainstays of the flute repertory: the masterful *Concerto* (1934); the lyrical *Pièce* for solo flute (1936), with its exquisitely ornamented melodic line; and the beautiful, Iberian-influenced *Entr'acte* for flute and harp (1954). The concerto, premiered by Marcel Moyse with Philippe Gaubert conducting, is evidence of Ibert's total mastery of the flute's technical and expressive potential.

The flute works of Jean Françaix (1912–) are stylistically like those of Ibert, and even more numerous. They, too, are classical in inspiration, elegant, graceful, and idiomatically written for the instrument. In addition to the well-known woodwind quintet (1933), Françaix has written a quintet for flute, harp, and string trio (1934); a charming *Divertimento* for flute and piano; a suite for unaccompanied flute; a quadruple concerto for woodwinds and orchestra; and many other chamber works.

In the next generation, Jacques Castérède (1926–), who had studied analysis with Messiaen, writes in a basically diatonic style reminiscent of Honegger. His works include *Sonate en Forme de Suite* (1957), dedicated to Jean-Pierre Rampal, and *Ciels* (1980), both for flute and piano; and *Flûtes en vacance* for three or four flutes.

Jean-Michel Damase (1928–) is also a product of the Paris Conservatoire; his music embodies the elegance represented by that institution, and is idiomatically written, particularly in the concertante works. His numerous works for flute include a *Quintet* for flute, harp, and string trio (1947); the *Serenade* for flute and strings (1957); a *Sonate* for flute and harp (1964), which was commissioned by Rampal and harpist Lily Laskine for a recording; and a *Double Concerto* for flute, piano, and orchestra (1974).

Pierre-Max Dubois (1930–) has been influenced by Milhaud, Francaix and Prokofiev. In addition to a difficult set of flute etudes, Dubois has written a flute concerto (1958); *Incantation et Danse* for unaccompanied flute (1960); several pieces for flute and piano; *Piccolette*, for piccolo and piano; and a quartet for four flutes (1962).

Great Britain

The most common perceptions of British music are the elegant pomp of Henry Purcell, Handel, and Sir Edward Elgar, and the traditional, folk-derived style of Ralph Vaughan Williams. Twentieth century British flute music has been little affected by the former, but it has absorbed much of the lyricism and tunefulness of the latter. It has also, in recent years, encompassed such international styles as serialism.

The works of Sir Arnold Bax (1883–1953), such as the *Elegiac Trio* for flute, viola, and harp (1926), combine the chromatic interest of late German romanticism with the more subtle approach of Elgar and Debussy. Gustav Holst (1874–1934), well known to many students as a band composer, wrote only one piece of genuine chamber music: a *Terzetto* for flute, oboe, and viola (1925). But his *Fugal Concerto* (1923), for flute, oboe, and strings, is quite chamberlike. Holst's polyphonic interests reflect the clear influence of Vaughan Williams.

Sir Arthur Bliss (1891–1975), who counted both Vaughan Williams and Holst among his mentors, was at first considered the *enfant terrible* of English music. He used brilliant orchestration to separate the parts, as did Stravinsky. His sole work for flute is *Conversations* (1920), for flute (alternating with bass flute), oboe (alternating with English horn), and string trio.

The flute works of Sir Eugene Goossens (1893–1962), at midcentury conductor of the Rochester and Cincinnati orchestras, and brother of oboist Leon Goossens, have today fallen into obscurity. In his time, however, his works were considered equal to those of Bax and Walton. They are technically difficult, and use the flute in a variety of chamber combinations—for example, *Five Impressions of a Holiday* (1914) is scored for flute, cello, and piano; *Pastorale and Harlequinade* (1924) for flute, oboe or violin, and piano; and *Three Pictures* (1935) for flute, strings, and percussion.

Gordon Jacob (1895–) studied with Charles Stanford and Herbert Howells at the Royal Conservatory of Music just after World War I. A consummate craftsman and author of the textbook *Orchestral Technique* (1931), he has a particular talent for wind writing. Jacob was one of the first composers to use the piccolo as a solo instrument—in *The Pied Piper* (1959) for unaccompanied flute and piccolo and the *Trio* (1960) for flute (alternating with piccolo), oboe, and keyboard.

Sir Lennox Berkeley (1903–), a student of Nadia Boulanger from 1927 to 1932, taught at London's Royal Academy of Music for many years. A friend of Poulenc, he drew far more on the influences of Mozart, Chopin, Fauré, and Ravel than from the English national tradition represented by Elgar, Vaughan Williams, and Holst. Berkeley's flute works include an early *Sonatina* (1940), a concerto (1952), and a *Concertino* (1955) for flute, violin, cello, and keyboard.

Benjamin Britten (1913–76), arguably the most important British composer of this century, wrote only one piece for flute. The *Gemini Variations* (1965), based on a theme by Zoltan Kodaly, were composed for a Hungarian flute and violin duo, the Jeney brothers; the two children premiered the variations in Britten's hometown of Aldeburgh in 1965.

Malcolm Arnold (1921–), a composition student of Jacob, is a trumpeter as well as a composer, and has a strong interest in unmixed timbres. He is an apt writer of appealing tunes and an expert orchestrator—a skill derived, he says, from Berlioz. His flute works include two concerti, a sonata, a sonatina, and several chamber pieces. The *Sonatine* (1948) is a stylistic pastiche; Arnold uses the fashionable technique of flutter-tonguing, and its final movement is a bluesy nod to jazz.

Thea Musgrave (1928–), like Berkeley, studied with Boulanger. Her early works were diatonic, but after 1955, they became increasingly chromatic and abstract. Her first important instrumental work was the *Trio* for flute, oboe, and piano (1960), written in relatively orthodox serial technique. An admirer of Ives, Musgrave borrowed from popular music for her second *Chamber Concerto* (1960); the piece is also asynchronous—the parts are fully notated but need not be exactly coordinated with the others. Appropriately, Musgrave dedicated the piece to Ives.

Richard Rodney Bennett (1936–), a student of Berkeley and Pierre Boulez, writes in a variety of styles, from neoromantic serialism like that of Webern, to jazz, to the avant-garde. His *Sonatina* for solo flute dates from 1954; the chamber works, such as the *Conversations* for two flutes (1965), are divertimentolike and elegantly constructed.

Elsewhere in Western Europe

Paul Hindemith (1895–1963) is the outstanding German contributor to twentieth century flute music. From Hindemith's eclectic early output come *Acht Stücke (Eight Pieces)* (1927) for solo flute; *Abendkonzert no. 2* for flute and strings (1927); and *Spielmusik* (1927) for flute, oboe, and strings; the latter two make typical neoclassical use of the concerto grosso format. From Hindemith's neobaroque period, a time when he was concentrating on euphonious compositions for an amateur market, comes the *Canonic Sonata* for two flutes (1924), a tribute to the contrapuntal art of J. S. Bach. And from the fully neoclassic, tonal, sonata style, dating from 1933, come the flute sonata (1936), the *Echo* for flute and piano (1942), and the *Concerto* for flute, oboe, clarinet, bassoon, harp, and orchestra (1949), the finale of which uses Mendelssohn's *Wedding March* as the cantus firmus. Georges Barrère and Jesus Maria Sanroma premiered the flute sonata in Washington, D.C. during Hindemith's first U.S. concert tour. It is part of Hindemith's second sonata cycle, and is less severe than many of his works.

Harald Genzmer (1909–) studied composition with Hindemith and also became a prominent academic. His works are, not surprisingly, much like those of his teacher. Genzmer's earliest pieces are lyrical and clearly constructed—for instance, the two sonatas (1940 and 1945) and the trio for flute, viola and harp (1947). After 1954, they are more rhythmically propulsive, as, for example, the sonata for two flutes (1956), the *Divertimento giocoso* (1961) for two winds and strings, and the *Divertimento* for flute and violin (1962).

Hans Werner Henze (1926–) studied traditional counterpoint with Wolfgang Fortner at the Institute for Church Music in Heidelberg. His earliest acknowledged compositions, written during his student days, are both for flute: the *Kammerkonzert* for piano, flute, and strings (1946) and the *Sonatine* for flute and piano (1947). His music is reminiscent of the neoclassicism of Hindemith and Stravinsky and the rhythm of Bartok. There is little in these flute works to suggest Henze's later interest in avant-garde compositional techniques; though the overall range and individual intervals are wide, the harmony is totally conventional.

The career of Boris Blacher (1903–75) reflects the broad changes inherent in twentieth century musical history. His early works show the influence of Satie, Milhaud, jazz, and Stravinskian rhythm. He wrote tonally until the 1940s, later switching to twelve-note organization and ultimately to fully serial techniques. His flute works include *Dialog* for flute, violin, piano, and strings (1950), the lyrical *Duo* for flute and piano (1972), and a quintet for flute, oboe, and string trio (1973).

In Switzerland, Frank Martin (1890–1974) represents a melding of French and German styles. His overall compositional emphasis was harmonic, but his *Ballade* for flute with piano or strings (1939), one of Martin's many concerted works, is lyrical and melodic. Martin's melodies use the entire chromatic scale; triads are enharmonically related.

Carl Nielsen (1865–1931) of Denmark is the only major modern composer from that nation to write for flute. His music combines classical structure with contemporary chromaticism and use of tone color; typically, his *Flute Concerto* (1926) begins in one key and ends in another. It is a technical tour de force, dedicated to Holger Gilbert Jesperson, flutist of the Copenhagen Wind Quintet and a devotee of elegant French music.

In Italy, Alfredo Casella (1883–1947) was the most influential figure in the interwar period. Trained at the Paris Conservatoire, his interests were wide-ranging: Debussy, Strauss, Mahler, Bartok, and the Russian nationalists influenced him. He also edited a quantity of baroque music—Vivaldi was a particular favorite—and with Gian-Francesco Malipiero, Ottorino Respighi, and Mario Castelnuovo-Tedesco, founded the Società Nazionale di Musica (renamed the Società Italiana di Musica Moderna) to sponsor concerts of modern music. Casella wrote two pieces for flute, *Barcarolle et Scherzo* (1903) and *Sicilienne et Burlesque* (1914), which are far more accessible than the composer's career might indicate.

Casella's colleague Castelnuovo-Tedesco (1895–1968) was an exceedingly prolific composer, active in the American movie industry in the 1940s and 1950s. His opus, much influenced by Jewish liturgical chant and Spanish folk music, includes elegant, neoclassic works, many of a light character. The *Divertimento* for two flutes (1943) and the *Sonatina* for flute and guitar (1965) are typical.

Eastern Europe

A number of interesting flute works have come out of eastern Europe. Bela Bartok (1881–1945), who with Kodaly was responsible for the renaissance of interest in Hungarian folk music, wrote no original music for flute. But Paul Arma has made two flute-and-piano arrangements from Bartok's *Fifteen Hungarian Peasant Songs* (1914–17) for piano: *Three Popular Hungarian Songs* and *Suite Paysanne Hongroise,* both of which have become standards of the flute repertory.

Hungarian pianist Ernő (Ernst von) Dohnányi (1877–1960) was an ardent champion of the work of Bartok and Kodaly. He wrote masterful chamber music, including the *Aria* and *Passacaglia,* op. 48 (1958 and 1959). The *Aria,* for flute and piano, is short and romantic; the *Passacaglia,* for unaccompanied flute, is, in contrast, angular and includes a flutter-tongued descending chromatic scale.

Bohuslav Martinů (1890–1959), at one time a student of Roussel in Paris, shared his teacher's classic outlook. Martinů was a violinist in the Prague Philharmonic before fleeing the Nazis, subsequently living in Paris (1923–40), the United States (1941–46), and then Switzerland and France. His music combines Czech traditions with Debussy-like timbre. An admirer of the concerti grossi of Corelli and Vivaldi, he adopted a neoclassic outlook that is evident in several works written after 1929, including the *Promenades* for flute, violin, and harpsichord (1939) and the concerto for flute and violin (1936). The American compositions—the *Madrigal Sonata* (1942) and *Sonata* (1945) for flute and piano and the *Trio* (1944) for flute, cello, and piano—in contrast, are more lyrical.

Sergei Prokofiev (1891–1953) had a career similar to Martinů's in that it combined nationalist elements with neoclassicism. His only work for flute, the *Sonata,* premiered in Moscow in 1943. It is a traditional work—its three movements are in sonata, rondo, and ternary form, respectively—but modern at the same time. It calls for a brassy tone quality, which Rampal's edition specifically indicates, for the trumpetlike passage in the first movement.

Jaromir Weinberger (1896–1967), best known for his opera *Schwanda the Bagpiper* (which, incidentally, has a marvelous piccolo part in the overture), incorporated traditional tunes of Czechoslovakia and many other nations in his works. His one flute work is a *Sonatine* (1941).

Nationalism of a different breed is represented by Paul Ben-Haim (1897–), an Israeli refugee from Germany. His music reflects both Eastern and Western traditions, including Jewish and Oriental folk material; among his works are a *Serenade* (1952) for flute and string trio and *Three Songs without Words* (1953) for flute and piano.

The United States

Just as the United States has been the home of the flute's mechanical progress in the twentieth century, so it has been a breeding ground for a large quantity of flute composition. The first distinctive American flute works came from the so-called Boston Classicists: Harvard-educated Arthur Foote (1853–1937) wrote his *Night Piece* for flute and strings in 1923. Amy Marcy Cheney Beach (1867–1944), who preferred to be known as Mrs. H. H. A. Beach, wrote in a similar romantic style; her *Theme and Variations* (1916) for flute and string quartet, like most of her instrumental works, is broadly developed and rather long—twenty minutes—with finely crafted fugato sections.

Flutist Lamar Stringfield (1897–1959) worked in a traditional, distinctly American idiom. In 1932 he organized the institute of folk music at the University of North Carolina, and he drew heavily on Appalachian folk material for such works as the *Indian Sketches* (1922), *Mountain Dawn* (1945), and *To a Star* (1948).

Similarly American in outlook was William Grant Still (1895–1978), whose eclectic background included studies with Varèse and work with Memphis jazzman W. C. Handy. He is remembered for his American nationalist works, such as the 1963 *Miniatures* (based on folk songs of the Americas) for flute, oboe, and piano.

Ruth Crawford Seeger (1901–53) had strong interests in American folk music and music education as well as composition, which she studied with future husband Charles Seeger. She arranged many folk songs for children and transcribed folk recordings in the Library of Congress collections. Her *Diaphonic Suite* (1930) for unaccompanied flute is of another hue entirely; though of only moderate technical difficulty, it is, like many of her original works, atonal. Irregular rhythmic patterns are also a prominent feature of the suite.

The experimental tradition in America has been as strong as the nationalist one. Charles Ives (1874–1954), the quintessential twentieth century American rebel, wrote no solo flute music, but the flute figures prominently in his chamber works. One of these pieces, the second piano sonata, *Concord, Mass., 1840–1860* (1909–15, revised 1947), includes a short obbligato flute passage in the fourth movement, "Thoreau." Philosopher Henry David Thoreau was an enthusiastic amateur flutist, and the flute symbolizes the mist over Walden Pond.

Several of Ives's colleagues, however, did write for solo flute. His collaborator and biographer, Henry Cowell (1897–1965) began his flute oeuvre with the early (1915–17) *Quartet Romantic*, continuing with *Two Bits* for flute and piano (1941); an unpublished quartet for flute, oboe, cello and harpsichord (1954); a *Trio* for flute, violin, and harp (1952); the *Triple Rondo* (1961) for flute and harp; and two concerted works, the 1961 *Duo concertante* for flute, harp, and orchestra and the 1963 *Concerto Grosso*.

Quincy Porter (1897–1966), like Ives, was a student of Horatio Parker at Yale; he also studied with d'Indy and Ernest Bloch. After stint as director of the New England Conservatory, he returned to his alma mater to teach from 1946 to 1965. A violist, he excelled in chamber music composition. His flute works are *Blues lointains* for flute or viola and piano (1928); the *Little Trio* of the same year for flute, violin, and viola; and a quintet for flute and strings (1937).

A stalwart of the American experimental tradition was Juilliard-educated Wallingford Riegger (1885–1961), who studied composition with the exceedingly conservative Percy Goetschius. Along with Edgard Varèse, Ives, and

Cowell, he was active in the Pan-American Association of Composers in New York, an organization dedicated to "ultramodern" music. Riegger's *Suite for Flute Alone* (1929) is a landmark of the flute repertoire. Its final movement ends with a thirty-six-note tone row in which each note in the flute range from d^1 to $c^4\sharp$ is sounded once in staccato sixteenth notes. (The only repeated pitch is a grace note c^3.) The *Suite*'s extended range, chromaticism, and wide melodic leaps were symptomatic of what was to many flutists an uncomfortable leap from their nineteenth century orientation. As such, the piece signaled the beginning of the new virtuosity.

Henry Brant (1913–), a Riegger student during the 1930s, was in the same tradition. An orchestrator and arranger for André Kostelanetz and Benny Goodman and a prolific composer for radio, television, and films, Brant has an intimate knowledge of instrumental capabilities. He is well known to flutists for one of the earliest original flute choir compositions, *Angels and Devils* (1931, revised 1956), which not only introduced the new sonority of the flute choir, but scored a massed flutter-tongued passage. His *Temperamental Mobiles* (1932) for unaccompanied flute was probably the first solo flute work to make substantial use of flutter-tonguing, glissandos, sliding variations of pitch achieved by rolling the flute, and notated variation in vibrato.

Walter Piston (1894–1976) was the first composer of a new Harvard school (class of 1924). Later a student of Nadia Boulanger, he was a key member of the Harvard faculty from 1926 to 1960 and wrote standard textbooks on harmony, harmonic analysis, counterpoint, and orchestration. This disciplined approach is evident in his music. Drawing on influences of Stravinsky, Fauré, and Ravel, Piston adopted typically French clarity, concision, and proportion. After the 1920s his music shows a neobaroque aspect. The harmonic emphasis is on perfect fourths and fifths; later Piston turned to twelve-tone techniques. His most popular work is, without a doubt, the ballet *The Incredible Flutist* (1938); he also wrote an outstanding flute sonata (1930) dedicated to Georges Laurent, a quartet for flute and strings (1942), and a concerto (1971).

Virgil Thomson (1896–), like Piston, studied at Harvard and with Boulanger. Adopting the simplicity and humor of Satie from his French studies, he continues the American nationalist tradition in his use of hymn and popular tunes. His flute works, surprisingly little known in view of his international reputation, are a *Serenade* for flute and violin (1931), an unaccompanied sonata (1943), and a concerto (1954).

Elliott Carter (1908–) studied with Piston at Harvard and with Boulanger. His *Sonata* (1952) for flute, oboe, cello, and harpsichord, commissioned by harpsichordist Sylvia Marlowe, won the Naumburg Prize in 1956. A 1934 flute sonata has never been published.

Aaron Copland (1900–) also studied in Paris with Boulanger after graduation from Harvard, and has intermittently returned to his alma mater to teach. He was for many years chairman of the faculty at the Berkshire Music Center. Copland's flute works, all quite recent, are, unfortunately, few: two threnodies (1971 and 1973); the *Vocalise*, which, at the suggestion of Doriot

Anthony Dwyer, he arranged from a vocal piece in 1972; and the *Duo* for flute and piano. The *Duo,* which bears a striking thematic resemblance to *Appalachian Spring,* was commissioned as a memorial to William Kincaid and premiered in 1971 by Elaine Shaffer, who later recorded it with the composer at the keyboard.

Robert Russell Bennett (1894–1981), best known for his Broadway orchestrations (*Showboat, On Your Toes, Annie Get Your Gun, Kiss Me Kate,* and others) was also a Boulanger student. His orchestrational virtuosity is evident in the scores of the *Concerto Grosso* for woodwind quintet and wind orchestra (1958), written for the American Wind Symphony; and the *Rondo Capriccioso* for four flutes, whose original version was published by the New York Flute Club in 1922.

Another group of American composers is based at Rochester's Eastman School of Music. Howard Hanson (1896–1981), director of Eastman from 1924 to 1964, wrote in a neoromantic style much in the tradition of Sibelius and Grieg. His sole work for flute is the *Serenade* for flute, harp, and strings (1945).

Bernard Rogers (1893–1968) studied with Bloch and with Boulanger and was for many years chairman of Eastman's composition department. He is the author of a standard text on orchestration, and drew inspiration for the colors of his own orchestral composition from Japanese prints (he was an amateur painter). Rogers's *Allegory* (1961) is scored for the unusual combination of two flutes, marimba, and strings; other concertante works are the *Soliloquy no. 1* for flute and strings (1922); *Fantasy* for flute, viola, and strings (1937); and *The Silver World* for flute, oboe, and strings (1950).

Alec Wilder (1907–80), a Hanson student, became active in the New York jazz scene, working as an arranger for the Benny Goodman and Tommy Dorsey bands. His late 1930s arrangements pioneered in introducing woodwinds. Wilder's serious compositions from the 1930s experiment with jazz and unusual ensembles that include harpsichord and woodwinds. Several small chamber works, such as the *Suite for Flute Choir* of 1972, use piccolo, alto flute, and bass flute as well as C flute.

Kent Kennan (1913–), another Hanson-Rogers student (composition and orchestration, respectively), worked largely in a neoclassical metier reminiscent of Hindemith. His *Night Soliloquy* (1938) for flute and orchestra (also available in piano and band arrangements) is a staple of the literature.

Gardner Read (1913–) studied with Copland, Hanson, and Rogers. Author of classic texts on orchestration and notation, his one published solo flute composition is the *Threnody* for flute and strings (1948).

Gail Kubik (1914–84) studied with Rogers, Piston, and with Leo Sowerby, and was also part of the Boulanger circle. A staff composer for NBC during World War II, he works mostly on radio, television, and movie scores. Kubik is above all a melodist; his music is simple, functional, and dramatic. He has written a *Nocturne* (1947) for flute and piano and a *Little Suite* (1948) for flute and two clarinets.

William Bergsma (1921–) also studied with Hanson and Rogers; he served on the faculty of the Juilliard School from 1946 to 1963. Bergsma writes in a tonal and lyrical mode, though recent works explore the avant-garde idiom. His *Pastorale and Scherzo* (1943) is scored for flute or recorder and two violas.

John La Montaine (1920–), yet another Rogers-Hanson-Boulanger product, uses a consonant twelve-note technique. His flute works include a sonata (1958), a concerto (1981), and several "occasional" pieces.

Lou Harrison (1917–) represents the fusion of two distinct traditions: the American experimental tradition and ethnomusicology. In the mid-1930s he studied with Henry Cowell, and in 1947 conducted the first full performance of an Ives symphony, the third. With John Cage, he organized recitals of percussion music during World War II. Then, in the 1960s, Harrison studied Chinese classical music and Korean court music, and joined the East-West Center at the University of Hawaii, where he worked as an instrument builder. In addition to conventionally scored works such as the *Trio* for flute, violin, and viola, Harrison frequently combines the flute with percussion and non-Western instruments, as in *Concerto no. 1* for flute and percussion (1939); *Canticle no. 3* for flute or ocarina, guitar, and percussion (1941); and *Quintal taryung*, for two flutes and chango (1961).

Another American composer with a strong interest in non-Western music is Alan Hovhaness (1911–). After traditional study with Frederick Converse at the New England Conservatory, he came into contact with Indian music in the Boston area. He has formally studied Japanese, Korean, and Indian music. Hovhaness's Armenian ancestry is frequently reflected in the titles of his compositions. Modal but chromatic, they tend to be contrapuntal, using such devices as motivic construction, ostinato rhythms, and pedal tones. The flute occupies an important place in Hovhaness's oeuvre of nearly three hundred compositions.

The United States has become a second home to many important European composers for the flute. Hindemith, for example, fled Nazi Germany in 1937, but most of his flute music predates his arrival in America. Ernest Bloch (1880–1959) emigrated from Switzerland to the United States in 1916 and is known primarily for his works in the Jewish tradition. His orientation became primarily neoclassic, as evidenced in the *Concertino* for flute, viola, and strings (1950); the hauntingly beautiful *Suite Modale* (1956) for flute and orchestra; and the somber *Two Last Poems (Maybe . . .)* (1958). Bloch dedicated the latter two works to Elaine Shaffer.

Igor Stravinsky (1882–1971), the father of neoclassicism, came to this country in 1939. He did not, however, write for flute until very late in his life: an unusual, serial work, the 1959 *Epitaphium* for flute, clarinet and harp "für des Prinzen Max Egon zu Fürstenburg"; its companion piece was a memorial to Raoul Dufy, scored for string quartet. The duration of each is just over a minute.

Ingolf Dahl (1912–70), a Boulanger student, had also studied with Philipp Jarnach in Cologne; he came to the United States in 1938, joined the faculty of the University of Southern California, and became an important member of the American musical establishment. As conductor of the University of Southern California orchestra, he introduced pieces by such American composers as Piston, Ives, Copland, and Foss as well as works of Stravinsky and Schoenberg; he also translated Stravinsky's *Poetics of Music* (the 1939–40 Norton Lectures at Harvard) into English.

Though Dahl's early compositions were dissonant, expressionist pieces, his style mellowed as a result of the combined influences of Stravinsky and his American colleagues, and his interests turned to a more diatonic idiom. Dahl wrote the first version of *Variations on a Swedish Folktune* (1945, revised 1962) while studying with Boulanger. He composed *Variations on an Air by Couperin* (1956), for alto recorder or flute and harpsichord or piano, for Lili Lampl, who taught recorder at U.S.C.; it is based on *Les Grâces Naturelles* from Couperin's eleventh *ordre* for harpsichord. The 1960 *Serenade* for four flutes is a light, entertaining work, in which Dahl makes one of his rare uses of nontraditional notation. He wrote the *Duettino concertino* (1966) for flute and percussion at the request of Boston Symphony flutist Doriot Anthony Dwyer, who wanted a piece that she could record with her orchestra colleague Everett Firth. Despite the serial organization of the flute part, each movement has a different key orientation.

The Avant-Garde

The fourth phase of the flute literature did not begin until after World War I. First influenced and ultimately supplemented by electronic media, its evolution was a direct and logical continuation of the third phase; it expanded and exaggerated the elements of sonic contrast developed in the previous thirty years. At first, contrast had been achieved, in ensemble music, through pointillism, a musical technique analogous to Monet's visual one. One instrument was assigned no more than a few notes, and the sound passed successively to instruments of different timbres. As musical style evolved, broader areas of a composition were assigned to choirs of contrasting tone colors. This concept, labeled *Klangarbenmelodie* (tone-color melodies) by Arnold Schoenberg in his 1911 *Harmonielehre,* was epitomized by his *Five Pieces for Orchestra,* op. 16, which consists of successions of chords, each scored for different combinations of instruments.

Eventually, composers began to exploit the tonal possibilities of single instruments and developed a preference for solo sounds. Tonal contrast took several forms: contrasts between various registers of the instruments, unorthodox and variegated timbres on a single note, extreme dynamic contrast, and innovative articulation. This is when the flute really came into its own, particularly in the unaccompanied solo repertory.

At first, the flute sound was altered within the pitch limits of the traditional literature by means of harmonics, inflected pitches such as hollow or weak tones, whistle tones, specific composed vibrato instructions, and varied articulation, especially flutter-tonguing. Eventually, timbral modification began to affect pitch as well: key vibrato and lip oscillation or smorzato grew into quarter tone trills; then the quarter tone scale, other microtones, and microtonal segments; and finally into glissando. And in addition to the enlargement of pitch choices within the traditional scale, the range of the flute was extended in both directions by means of fingering and new embouchure techniques such as buzzing.

Timbral modification also incorporated percussive effects produced by the flute mechanism—key clicks and key rattling—and human-generated noises such as unpitched air sounds, tongue clicks, and whistling or singing while playing.

The expansion of sonic possibilities to encompass noise elements had its theoretical basis in the proclamations of Italian futurist composers during the second decade of this century. In 1912, Balilla Pratella called for songs of factories, warships, automobiles, and airplanes, incorporating the machine age into contemporary music. The following year, writing in *The Art of Noise,* his colleague Luigi Russolo advocated a new music composed of six types of noise:[4]

1. Bangs, thunderclaps, explosions
2. Whistles, hisses, snorts
3. Whispers, murmurs, rustling, gurgling
4. Screams, shrieks, buzzing, crackling, sounds produced by friction
5. Sounds produced by striking metal, wood, stone, china, and the like
6. Animal and human cries—roars, howls, laughter, sobs, sighs

At first this manifesto was considered a bit extreme, but avant-garde flute music has adopted most of these sounds within the framework of its own technical means.

Composer Edgard Varèse (1883–1965) was one of Russolo's most ardent critics. "Why," he said, "do you merely reproduce the vibrations of our daily life only in their superficial and distressing aspect?"[5] Yet Varèse went on in 1936 to write the landmark *Density 21.5,* which pioneered in the production of previously extramusical sounds by a traditionally nonpercussive musical instrument.

Varèse had studied with Widor, Roussel, and d'Indy, but diverged from his mentors in the extreme. His orchestral work *Amériques* (1921, revised 1927) betokens the influence of Debussy in the use of the alto flute to generate melodic sections, a procedure evocative of Debussy's *Faune.* Varèse made major innovations in rhythmic complexity, the use of unpitched percussion, and nonserial atonality. Debussy's influence is evident, also, in the choice of unaccompanied flute for *Density 21.5,* composed in 1936 for performance by

Georges Barrère on his platinum flute. In contrast to then-traditional flute writing, Varèse used above-normal range (up to d^4), the exploitation of dynamics and rhythm—the juxtaposition of long and short notes and the subtle use of triplets—and the reduction of melody to mere motives. Sharp contrasts, such as shifts from high *fortissimo* to *subito piano* in the middle register, give an effect either of several instruments or of an echo. The differentiation of the timbral characteristics of the flute registers and their use, in combination with note-by-note changes in attack and intensity, became structural elements of the composition. What *Density* is best known for, however, is its key clicks, notated .

Varèse served as unofficial mentor to a new generation of French composers, familiarly known as *La Jeune France*. André Jolivet (1905–74), one of the group's principals, studied with Varèse from 1930 to 1933, concentrating on orchestration and concepts of sound masses. With Olivier Messiaen, in 1936 he founded La Jeune France to stimulate the composition and performance of new music. Jolivet's orchestral music gives the flute an important role, but his solo flute music is particularly significant. His *Cinq Incantations* (1936) contains one of the first extended uses of flutter-tonguing in the solo flute literature. In the first movement, flutter-tonguing in the high register simulates a second instrument, in contrast to the "straight" line in the lower register. The piece also contains numerous instructions regarding expressive techniques, including "comme une grande respiration, quasi Tromba" (like a large breath, like a trumpet) on low D, and "sifflant," a hissing or wheezing. Much of the melodic material is drawn from repetitions of five- or six-note groups evocative of primitive music. The piece also includes pitch slides of a half-step, executed by rolling the flute. Jean-Pierre Rampal premiered Jolivet's flute concerto in February 1950, with the composer conducting.

Jolivet's compatriot Messiaen (1908–) has written only one work for flute, though it has become a standard of the contemporary repertory. *Le Merle Noir* (1951), for flute and piano, gives timbre a functional role and reflects the composer's lifelong fascination with birdsong. It uses flutter-tonguing and improvisatory cadenza sections to imitate the birds.

In 1946, Louis Gesensway, a violinist in the Philadelphia Orchestra, wrote a fiendishly difficult concerto for his colleague William Kincaid. Its upper-register harmonics—a Kincaid pedagogical trademark—Kincaid reported, "had never before been attempted by the flute in public orchestral performance."[6] The concerto was so challenging that it took Kincaid the entire summer preceding the premiere to memorize the work.

Pierre Boulez (1925–) was a member of Messiaen's Paris Conservatoire harmony class in the 1940s; he also studied serial techniques with René Leibowitz, the academic standardbearer of the Second Vienna School of Schoenberg, Berg, and Webern. The *Sonatine* for flute and piano (1946) was one of his earliest published works. Though Jean-Pierre Rampal commissioned it, he declined to perform it; the piece went unheard until Severino Gazzelloni premiered it at Darmstadt in 1954. Its structure is linear and melodic; its pointillism is reminiscent of Webern, and the piece's form is modeled on Schoenberg's *Chamber Symphony*, op. 9 (1906). The slow melodies, however, are in the Debussian impressionist tradition. *Le Marteau sans Maître* (1952–54, revised 1957), scored for the unusual combination of alto flute, guitar, vibraphone, xylorimba, percussion, and viola, is in a circular, improvisatory form.

Bruno Maderna (1920–73) has been closely associated with the summer courses in new music in Darmstadt, West Germany, since 1951. His *Musica su due dimensioni* (published in 1963) was the first composition to combine live instruments (flute and cymbals) with recorded sources. *Honeyrêves* for flute and piano (1963) includes a variety of avant-garde techniques: pizzicatos, harmonics, interior noise in the piano part, and glissandos and key-tapping in the flute part.

Maderna's *Hyperion* supplements the music with stage action. As historian Eric Salzman describes it, the flutist "spends the first ten minutes of the work quietly unpacking piccolo, flute, alto flute, and bass flute; when he finally gets around to the actual act of performance, the sound that gushes forth is in fact an enormously amplified percussive fortissimo (on tape)."[7] In *Hyperion 3* (1965) for flute and orchestra, the melodious flute contrasts with the heavy sound of the orchestra; the organizational scheme is improvised by the performers.

Luigi Nono (1924–), a student of Maderna and son-in-law of Arnold Schoenberg, included the flute in two concertante works with strings before he began to explore electronic composition in the 1960s. *Konzertante Musik* is scored for flute and strings; *Y su sangre ya viene cantando* for flute, strings, and percussion is the second part of the 1952 *Epitaffio per Garcia Lorca*, and is based on Lorca's poetry.

Luciano Berio (1925–), another Maderna student, represents the far avant-garde wing of Italian music. His landmark *Sequenza* (1958) for solo flute includes the first known use of a flute multiphonic—the woodwind equivalent of a double-stop—a perfect C–G fourth. Other avant-garde devices in the piece are flutter-tonguing and a unique trill in which the blown tone makes a diminuendo while the tapping of the trilling keys crescendos. Reflecting the influence of John Cage, *Sequenza* also employs proportional or spatial notation, as does *Tempi Concertati* (1958–59) for chamber ensemble.

Niccolò Castiglioni (1932–) writes in much the same vein as Berio, his aim being the "love of pure sound."[8] *Gymel* (1960) employs tone clusters, the soundboard, and brilliant high notes on the piano; the flute part is agile in the extreme, dynamically flexible, and exploits the instrument's lower range.

The career of Ernst Krenek (1900–) is illustrative of many changes in twentieth century flute music. The early works, such as the *Concertino* for flute, violin, harpsichord, and strings (1927), were much influenced by Stravinskian neoclassicism. Krenek then turned, in the 1930s, to twelve-tone techniques; his *Suite* for flute and strings (1954) is a difficult, atonal piece. In the late 1950s Krenek adopted serial procedures, which he combined with avant-garde flute techniques in the experimental *Flötenstück neunphasig* ("Flute

Piece in Nine Phases") (1959). Scored for flute and piano, its first movement may be played unaccompanied. It uses all the tricks of the advanced modern flute technique: harmonics, whistle tones, flutter-tonguing, and the extreme third octave.

George Perle (1915–), a student of Krenek, was one of the first Americans to become interested in the Second Vienna School, but he did not adopt that style as is. Instead, he built his own "twelve-tone modal system" by superimposing such serial techniques as set inversions onto tonal key centers. *Monody I* (1960) for unaccompanied flute epitomizes this technique; it also employs an assortment of avant-garde devices, including key clicks.

Heinz Holliger (1939–), the Rampal of the oboe, is also a leading composer of the avant-garde school. A composition student of Boulez, he has pioneered using avant-garde effects on the oboe. His *Lied* (1971) for flute (or alto flute or bass flute, amplified ad lib) is in this style and uses such techniques as the trumpet attack, playing while inhaling, key clicks, and most novel of all, required circular breathing.

The flute has a long and honorable tradition in the Far East in the form of the shakuhachi and other nonmechanized instruments. The modern flute has also received much attention in recent years. Yoritsune Matsudaira (1907–) began as an admirer of French music, from Debussy to *Les Six*, and from 1920 on adopted neoclassicism as his own. About 1935 he became interested in the rhythms and modes of *gagaku*, the traditional orchestral music of the Japanese court, whose instruments include the *ryuteki* and *komabue*, seven- and six-holed flutes, respectively. The *gagaku* influence is particularly evident in Matsudaira's *Sonatine* for flute and piano (1936). Matsudaira later turned to serial techniques and aleatory music, with a decided preference for woodwind scoring, especially flute and oboe. His *Rhymes for Gazzelloni* (1966) is dedicated to the Italian virtuoso who did so much to promote avant-garde flute music. It combines the flute sound with percussion and half-spoken, primitive sounds made by the flutist. The score specifies a duration of thirty-six seconds for each of the twenty rhymes, which automatically dictates the tempo; however, the performer determines the order of the rhymes.

Toru Takemitsu (1930–), a self-taught composer, shares with Matsudaira an interest in traditional Japanese music, including the shakuhachi. He has experimented with a broad array of contemporary techniques, including musique concrète and various other types of taped music, free improvisation, aleatory music, and graphic notation. Consistently, however, Takemitsu has been concerned with timbre, texture, and the relationship between sound and silence. His *Ring* (1961), for flute, guitar, and lute, takes its title from the initial letters of its four sections: General theme, Retrograde, Inversion, and Noise. The movements may be performed in any order; there is an interlude between two of them, notated in graphic score.

Kazuo Fukushima (1930–), also self-taught, joined Takemitsu's Experimental Workshop in 1953. *Three Pieces from Chū-U* (1958) employs notably sharp registral contrast. *Ekagura*, for alto flute and piano, won a prize at the

1958 contemporary music festival in Karuizawa, where it was played by Ririko Hayashi. Its Sanskrit title translates as "concentration," which is precisely what is required for the performance of its medley of avant-garde techniques; it is expressionistic, rhapsodic, and extremely intense and virtuosic. *Hi-Kyō (The Flying Mirror)* (1962), for flute, strings, and percussion, a prizewinner at the 1964 ISCM Festival, is dedicated to Severino Gazzelloni. Its second movement, *Mei*, for solo flute, takes its rhythm and sonority from traditional Japanese music; its portamentos, quarter tones, and overblowing are derived from fue and shakuhachi techniques. Most of the titles of Fukushima's works are taken from Buddhist philosophy or other Oriental thought.

Barney Childs (1926–) worked with both Copland and Carter. His *Music for Two Flute Players* (1963) uses throat flutter and has a range up to high E♭. The first flute part alternates with piccolo, and includes several unusual avant-garde effects. In one place, the score instructs the piccoloist to make c^2♯ "gradually as flat as possible." Another instruction is: "Improvised Cadenza: optional length, frantic, stammering, strangled, full of odd sounds and awkward pauses."

Important work in flute composition is centered at Columbia University. First of this "school" is flutist-composer Otto Luening (1900–). A student of Jarnach and Busoni in Europe, he began his career composing chamber music, then moved into the electronic realm, teaming with Vladimir Ussachevsky to set up Columbia's electronic music center. In recent years he has returned to the chamber music idiom.

Chou Wen-Chung (1923–) studied with Martinů and Varèse—he became musical executor for the latter—and with Leuning, and has taught at Columbia since 1972. His music represents a fusion of Western compositional technique with Chinese tradition; many of his pieces are based on the principles of Chinese calligraphy. *Cursive* (1963) uses tiny glissandos, microtonal trills, and a variety of timbres. Like many of his compositions, it takes its title from Chinese calligraphy, and it aptly describes the composition's use of specified but indefinite pitches and rhythms and regulated but variable tempo and dynamics.

Donald Martino (1931–), chairman of the composition department at the New England Conservatory, studied composition with Milton Babbitt at Columbia and with Roger Sessions. Like many of his contemporaries, he has written both for unaccompanied flute (*Quodlibets*, 1954) and for the range of the flute family. In *Notturno* (1973), for flutes, clarinets, strings, percussion, and piano, cadenzalike solo lines emerge out of dense ensemble passages, a typical Martino strategem.

Charles Wuorinen (1938–) studied with both Luening and Ussachevsky and is on the faculty of the Manhattan School of Music. With flutist Harvey Sollberger, he founded the Group for Contemporary Music in New York in 1962. His early compositions are tonal, later ones serial, featuring registral duplication of pitches. He uses the precision of electronic music to control rhythm. *Flute Variations I* (1963) and *Flute Variations II* (1968), both composed for Sollberger, are an extension of twelve-tone technique; they also show Japanese shakuhachi influence.

Sollberger (1939–) is active as a composer and player of avant-garde flute music; he studied composition with Luening. His music is largely dodecaphonic; it includes a *Grand Quartet* (dedicated to Friedrich Kuhlau) for four flutes. His work in the avant-garde idiom grew out of a performance of Berio's *Sequenza* by Gazzeloni in about 1956. Recent compositions, such as *Sunflowers* (1981), specify a variety of new techniques: mandated vibrato and nonvibrato, changing fingerings on a single pitch, key clicks, hisses, and simultaneous playing and singing. In *Riding the Wind I* (1974), the solo flute is amplified.

Roger Reynolds (1934–), an engineer as well as a musician, continues the experimental tradition of Ives, Varèse, and others, using a wide timbral vocabulary. His *Four Etudes* (1961) for piccolo, two flutes, and alto flute make particularly effective use of antiphonal scoring. *Mosaic* (1962), for flute alternating with piccolo and piano, employs harmonics, whistle tones, flutter-tonguing, key slaps and other percussive attacks, and contrasts between straight and vibrato tone. *Ambages* (1965) adds glissandos to the catalog of devices and makes particular use of vibrato-nonvibrato contrasts.

Burt Levy's *Orbs with Flute* (1966) is another example of contemporary supertechnique. Though just three minutes long, its composition involved three consulting flutists at the University of Illinois: Patrick Purswell, one of the originators of the buzz flute technique; Thomas Howell, author of a treatise on the avant-garde flute; and flutist-composer David Gilbert. The score devotes as much space to fingering and tone instructions as to the music itself. After a litany of four kinds of key clicks, multiphonics, harmonics, and glissandos, the piece ends on a high B♭, played successively as part of a multiphonic, as a harmonic, and finally as a whistle tone.

The Flute and Electronics

The fifth and latest stage of flute composition, an extension of the avant-garde, is the association of the flute with electronic music. Most directly, this association has taken the form of amplification or modification of the "standard" flute tone by electronic means. But composers have also found that the flute sound combines well with electronically produced sounds, and the ability to play with preprogrammed recorded sounds adds another dimension to the techniques the modern flutist must master. Electronic music, a post–World War II phenomenon, has become an integral part of the flute literature in the last decade, thanks in large part to such players as Harvey Sollberger and Samuel Baron. Baron, in fact, has labeled tape "a new continuo."[9] Although the medium has not pervaded the literature to so considerable a degree, it is an important new phenomenon.

The *Synchronisms* of Mario Davidovsky (1934–), associate director of the Columbia-Princeton Electronic Music Center, are typical of the flute-and-electronics genre. These virtuoso compositions—no. 1 (1962) is scored for flute and tape, no. 2 (1964) for flute, clarinet, violin, cello, and tape—challenge the performers to match the inventiveness of the electronic parts with an expanded spectrum of playing techniques that include extremes of register and speed. One of the greatest challenges, as the title of the series implies, is the synchronization of rhythm and pitch between flute and prerecorded tape. For this reason, there is an aleatoric element to the pieces.

Karl Korte (1928–), whose teachers at Juilliard included Vincent Persichetti and Luening, wrote *Remembrances* for flute and synthesized sound in 1971 for Samuel Baron. The work features reverberation and the spatial movement of the recorded sounds, while the flute plays quarter tones and uses alternate fingerings for novel timbral effects.

Perhaps the ultimate flute-and-tape composition to date is Meyer Kupferman's *Superflute*, also written for Baron in 1971, in which taped fragments of piccolo and alto flute passages are combined with a live C flute to create the illusion of a single instrument. Baron admitted, once he had completed the painstaking tasks of recording and editing, that "the joke was on me. The final result was not like flute playing at all. It sounded like electronic music."[10]

Baron's skeptical comment about *Superflute* leads us, inevitably, to question whether these recent developments in flute music have been healthy. There is a certain irony implicit in many of the new techniques; as Virgil Thomson wrote some years ago,

> The European effort toward writing atonal music not for noise-making instruments but for those whose design had been perfected over centuries for avoiding tonal obfuscation has been . . . a waste of effort, save possibly for proving it could be done.[11]

Boston Symphony flutist James Pappoutsakis echoed the sentiment; he compared asking a flutist with a beautiful tone to sound like a foghorn to asking a fine portrait artist to paint kitchen walls. Contemporary music, Pappoutsakis warned, should "not distort the tone quality or degrade the player."[12]

There has certainly been an over-emphasis on technique in modern compositional practice; what has been called the flute's "fatal facility" has led to gimmickry.[13] Technical innovation has often been invoked for its own sake, rather than as a vehicle for musical expression, not only because the avant-garde is by definition experimental, but also because novelty is a great temptation to composers. In Thomson's typically acerbic words, "Music has its fashion industry and its novelty trade." But as another critic has written, "Sensationalism will always be with us; fortunately, such music does tend to die a natural death."[14]

So it seems likely that many of the avant-garde works now appearing on concert programs of contemporary music groups will join in well-deserved obscurity such works as Pierre de Breville's *A Flute in the Orchards*, which graced Georges Laurent's recital programs just fifty years ago. The best of the new literature, on the other hand, will survive.

Notes

1. Roger Shattuck, *The Banquet Years* (New York: Harcourt, Brace & Co., 1958), p. 4.
2. Ernestine Whitman, "Analysis and Performance Critique of Debussy's Flute Works" (D.M.A. diss., University of Wisconsin, Madison, 1977), p. 8.
3. Martin Cooper, *French Music from the Death of Berlioz to the Death of Fauré* (London: Oxford University Press, 1951), p. 185.
4. H. H. Stuckenschmidt, *Twentieth Century Music* (New York: McGraw Hill, 1969), pp. 50–51.
5. Virgil Thomson, *A Virgil Thomson Reader* (Boston: Houghton Mifflin, 1981), pp. 41–42.
6. John Krell, *Kincaidiana* (Culver City, Calif.: Trio Associates, 1973), p. 97.
7. Eric Salzman, *Twentieth-Century Music: an Introduction* (Englewood Cliffs, N.J.: Prentice-Hall, 1967), p. 183.
8. Mario Baroni, liner notes, [program by Severino Gazzelloni, flute], CBS S 61256.
9. G. P. Melante, liner notes, *Music for Flute & Tape* (Samuel Baron, flute), Nonesuch H-71289.
10. Ibid.
11. Thomson, p. 11.
12. Eleanor Lawrence, "Interview with James Pappoutsakis," *National Flute Association Newsletter* 3, no. 2 (1978): 18.
13. Paul Henry Giroux, "The History of the Flute and Its Music in the United States" (M.A. thesis, School of Music, University of Washington, 1952), p. 123.
14. Thomson, p. 80.

REPERTOIRE CATALOG

INTRODUCTION

This catalog emphasizes the finest compositions for flute from each historical era, with considerable attention given to works by flutists. In general, this catalog includes "professional" quality literature; that is, music suitable for public performance. It includes very little purely pedagogical material, though some works, such as Kuhlau chamber music, may be of marginal interest to a general audience.

The catalog includes music for piccolo, alto flute, and bass flute as well as for concert C flute. It includes some material originally written for flute choir, but does not include flute ensemble arrangements. (See the Selected Bibliography for other catalogs that do list large ensembles and arrangements.) The list includes both solo literature—accompanied and unaccompanied—and small chamber works. The general criterion for the latter was that the flute be the principal or one of the principal instruments; for this reason, woodwind quartets (flute, oboe, clarinet, and bassoon) and woodwind quintets (flute, oboe, clarinet, bassoon, and horn) are omitted. Very few of the ensemble works require more than five players.

Most but not all of the literature is in print; so much out-of-print literature is available from libraries and even from music stores with extensive stock that it seemed pointless to limit the catalog to in-print items. Many of the works in this catalog are available through interlibrary loan from the National Flute Association library, housed at the University of Arizona. The NFA publishes an annual catalog of its collection that includes instructions for ordering.

The baroque section of this catalog includes works for both recorder and transverse flute. Wherever possible, the instrumentation column indicates the instrumentation of the original score, as well as permissible alternatives—particularly in the case of trio sonatas. Bach's *Brandenburg Concerto no. 4,* for instance, was written for two recorders, but is commonly played today by two flutes. In the case of Vivaldi's flute and recorder works, the intended instrumentation is a matter of informed speculation; this catalog follows the choices of the *New Grove Dictionary.*

This catalog includes very few transcriptions; it concentrates on works written specifically for flute. Although it also omits a large body of classic-era accompanied keyboard sonatas, since the flute merely accompanies the harpsichord or fortepiano, a few examples are included to represent the form. Finally, the catalog omits vocal music with flute obbligato or accompaniment and chamber music that includes voice, since classically trained singers are generally not available to perform with most students and amateur flutists.

Publication information is derived from publishers' catalogs, other printed catalogs (see the Selected Bibliography), the Library of Congress card and computer catalogs, references in dissertations and other literature, and, whenever possible, from examination of the music itself. These data were then collated to cross-match keys, opus numbers, and so on to determine if a *Sonata in D* of Publisher A is the same as the *Sonata in D* of Publisher B. Therefore, if two sonatas in D are listed without opus numbers or other identifying data, they are different sonatas. (There may be some lapses in cases where I was unable to obtain copies of the music itself.)

Format and Terminology

The first column of each entry lists the title of the composition; if a particular work is part of a series, it is listed under the series title. For instance, Telemann's concertos from the *Tafelmusik* are listed under *Tafelmusik* rather than under *Concerto.* Works are listed under their original titles, in the original languages when they are descriptive; generic titles such as *Trio sonata,* however, are listed as such and not, for instance, as *Sonata a tre.* In cases where a single composition is published under several different titles, I have chosen the most frequent or best known one and indicated alternatives in brackets; for example, Bach's *Partita* [*Suite*] *in A minor.* If you do not at first find a particular title, therefore, scan the full entry for the composer for an alternative title. Wherever possible, I have listed keys and opus numbers, even if the publisher does not provide such information. Compositions are listed in alphabetical order by title; within a particular genre, such as concerto, by opus number or catalog number (such as K. for Mozart or Quantz). When there are no opus or catalog numbers, compositions are listed alphabetically by keys and then by size of instrumentation. Comments regarding the authenticity of works follow the title in brackets; for example, Beethoven's Sonata, B♭, K. Anh. 4 [doubtful].

The second column of each entry lists the instrumentation. Whenever possible, this reflects the original edition of the work, though a modern edition may specify fewer alternatives. This is particularly true of listings for baroque sonatas. The use of a plus (+) between instruments indicates that one player plays both instruments; for example, "fl+afl" means that one player plays both flute and alto flute. The use of a slash (/) between instruments indicates alternative instrumentation; for example, "flute/violin, bc" means flute or violin and basso continuo. The presence of a semicolon (;) between instruments separates the concertino (soloists) from the ripieno (accompaniment) in a concerto grosso format; for example, fl, ob; 2vn, va, vc indicates that the work is a double concerto for flute and oboe, accompanied by strings.

The third column contains the name of the publisher(s); the name of the editor, if any, is indicated in parentheses after the publisher's name. In the case of European editions, I have cited the original publisher rather than the American distributor because distribution contracts are subject to frequent change.

Instrument Abbreviations

afl	alto flute
amp	amplified
b	bass (generally equivalent to cello)
bc	basso continuo
bfl	bass flute
bn	bassoon
b viol	bass viol
ch orch	chamber orchestra
cl	clarinet
db	double bass
eh	English horn
fl	flute
gamba	viola da gamba
guit	guitar
hn	French horn
hp	harp
hpd	harpsichord
kbd	keyboard
kbd red	keyboard reduction (from orchestral score)
mar	marimba
ob	oboe
ob d'am	oboe d'amore
orch	orchestra
org	organ
perc	percussion
pf	piano(forte)
pf red	piano reduction (from orchestral score)
pf4h	piano four hands
picc	piccolo
rec	recorder
str	string orchestra
tam	tam tam
trb	trombone
tpt	trumpet
vibr	vibraphone
va	viola
va d'am	viola d'amore
vc	(violon)cello
vn	violin
wind ens	wind ensemble
xyl	xylophone

Publisher Abbreviations

ACE	American Composers Edition (American Composers Alliance)
AMP	Associated Music Publishers
Belwin	Belwin-Mills
Boosey	Boosey & Hawkes
Breitkopf	Breitkopf & Härtel
Broekmans	Broekmans & Van Poppel
Colombo	Franco Colombo
Ed. Musicus	Edition Musicus
EMB	Editio Musica Budapest
EMT	Editions musicales transatlantiques
Fischer	Carl Fischer
IMP	Israel Music Publications
Kalmus	Edwin F. Kalmus-Belwin
Kistner	Kistner & Siegel
Mitteldeutscher	Mitteldeutscher Verlag Halle
Moeck	Hermann Moeck Verlag
Müller	Willy Müller, Süddeutscher Musikverlag
NYPL	New York Public Library
ÖBV	Österreicher Bundesverlag
Ouvrières	Editions Ouvrières
Peer	Peer International
Piper	Piper Press
Presser	Theodore Presser
Spratt	Jack Spratt Music Co.
Trio	Trio Associates
WIM	Western International Music
Zerboni	Edition Suvini Zerboni

A. THE BAROQUE ERA

Work	Instrumentation	Editions
ALBINONI, TOMASO GIOVANNI (1671–1751)		
Concerto, G [doubtful]	fl, str, bc	Ricordi (ed. Scheck & Ruf)
	fl, str/pf red	Sikorski (ed. Brinckmann & Mohr)
Sonata, b, op. 4, no. 6	fl, bc	Ricordi (ed. Scheck & Ruf)
Trattenimenti armonici per camera		
Sonata no. 6, a	fl/ob/vn, bc	Nagel (ed. Schäffler)
ANNA AMALIE, PRINCESS OF PRUSSIA (1723–1787)		
Sonata, F	fl, bc	Kalmus; Vieweg (ed. Lenzewski)
BACH, JOHANN ERNST (1722–1777)		
Sonata, e	fl, hpsd	Zimmermann (ed. Michael)
BACH, JOHANN SEBASTIAN (1685–1750)		
Brandenburg Concerto no. 2, F, BWV 1047	tpt, rec, ob, vn; str, bc	AMP; Bärenreiter (ed. Wenziger); Eulenberg; Heugel
Brandenburg Concerto no. 4, G, BWV 1049	vn, 2 rec; str, bc	Barenreiter (ed. Wenziger); Breitkopf; Eulenberg; Heugel; Möseler
	vn, 2 rec; pf red	Breitkopf (ed. Haverkampf)
Brandenburg Concerto no. 5, D, BWV 1050	fl, vn, hpd; str, bc	Bärenreiter (ed. Dürr)' Breitkopf; Eulenberg; Heugel; Peters (Urtext)
Concerto, a, BWV 1044	fl, vn, hpd; str, bc	Belwin (ed. Applebaum & Gordon); Breitkopf (Urtext); Eulenberg (ed. Schering); Peters (ed. Schulze)
Musical Offering, BWV 1079		
Sonata, c	fl, vn, kbd	Breitkopf (ed. Seiffert); Colombo (ed. Casella); Durand; Henle (ed. Kirnberger); International (ed. Hermann); Kalmus; Peters (ed. Kirnberger); G. Schirmer (ed. L. Moyse)

Partita, a, BWV 1013	fl	Armstrong (ed. Goldberg); Bärenreiter (Urtext); Bärenreiter (ed. Schmitz, from *Neue Bach Ausgabe*); Berben (ed. Gatti); Billaudot; Boonin; Breitkopf; Durand (ed. LeRoy); Galaxy (Urtext); Henle; International (ed. Rampal); Leduc (ed. M. Moyse); Peters (Urtext, ed. List); Piper; G. Schirmer (ed. L. Moyse); Universal (ed. Braun)
Partita [Suite], c, BWV 997	fl, kbd	Billaudot (ed. Marion); Heinrichshofen; International (ed. Rampal); Kalmus; Reinhardt (ed. Bopp); Sikorski (ed. Muller & Berndsen); Universal (ed. Petrenz)
Sonata, g, BWV 1020	fl, hpd	Bärenreiter; Edu-Tainment (ed. Goldberg); Henle (ed. Eppstein); International (ed. Rampal); Leduc (ed. Moyse); Nagel
Sonatas, b, E♭, A, BWV 1030-1032 C, e, E, BWV 1033-1035	fl, hpd fl, bc	Bärenreiter (ed. Schmitz from *Neue Bach Ausgabe*); Billaudot; Boosey; Boston; Breitkopf (ed. Barge, Spiro & Todt); Chester (ed. Bennett); Durand (ed. Fleury); Edu-Tainment (ed. Goldberg); Elkan-Vogel (ed. Kincaid & Polin); Fischer; Henle (ed. Eppstein); International (ed. Rampal, Veyron-Lacroix); Kalmus; Leduc (ed. Moyse); Peters (Urtext); Southern (ed. Wummer & la Tournerie)
Sonatas, B, E♭, A, BWV 1030-1032		Boosey (ed. Roth); Boston (ed. Barrère)
Sonata, E♭, BWV 1031		Bärenreiter (ed. Durr); Universal (ed. Braun)
Sonata, A, BWV 1032 [orig. 1st mvmt. incomplete]		Oxford (ed. Baron)
Sonata, e, BWV 1034		Foetisch (ed. Crussard); Simrock (ed. Gruters)
Sonata, E, BWV 1035		Breitkopf (ed. Kuijken); Simrock (ed. Gruters)
Sonata, G, BWV 1033	fl, vn, bc	Breitkopf; International (ed.Hermann); Peters (Urtext; ed. Hermann; ed. Langhoff); G. Schirmer (ed. L. Moyse)

Sonata, G, BWV 1039	2fl, bc	Bärenreiter (ed. Schmitz, from *Neue Bach Ausgabe*); Billaudot (ed. Marion); Breitkopf; Durand; Foetisch (ed. Crussard); Henle (ed. Eppstein); Peters (Urtext, ed. Landshoff); G. Schirmer (ed. L. Moyse)
Suite, b, BWV 1067	fl, str, bc	AMP; Breitkopf (ed. Reger); Broude Bros.; Dover; Eulenberg (ed. Altmann); Fischer; Heugel (ed. Dufourq); Lea; Leuckart; Peters (ed. Soldan & Landshoff); Ricordi; Universal (ed. von Bülow)
	fl, pf red	Boosey (ed. Sieber); Fischer (ed. Eck); Hinrichsen (ed. Johnson); International (ed. Wummer); Peters (ed. List & Weyrauch); Rudall, Carte; G. Schirmer (ed. L. Moyse); Schott (ed. Callimahos); Southern (ed. Cavally)
BARSANTI, FRANCESCO (1690–1772)		
Sonata, d, op. 1, no. 1	rec/vn, b/bc	Schott (ed. Bergmann)
Sonata, C, op. 1, no. 2	rec/vn, b/bc	Bärenreiter (ed. Ruf); Oxford (ed. Beechey)
Sonata, g, op. 1, no. 3	rec/vn, b/bc	Schott (ed. Bergmann)
Sonata, c, op. 1, no. 4	rec/vn, b/bc	Bärenreiter (ed. Ruf)
Sonata, F, op. 1, no. 5	rec/vn, b/bc	Schott (ed. Bergmann)
Sonata, B♭, op. 1, no. 6	rec/vn, b/bc	Bärenreiter (ed. Ruf)
BLAVET, MICHEL (1700–1768)		
Concerto, a	fl, str, bc/pf red	Broekmans (ed. Vester); International (ed. Rampal); Ricordi (ed. Scheck & Ruf)
15 Duets	2fl	Peters (ed. Nagel)
3e Receuil de pieces: 5 pieces	2 fl	Zurfluh (ed. Cotte & Crunelle)
6 Sonatas, op. 1 (e,a,D,G,d,A)	2fl	Leduc (ed. Patero); Müller (ed. Kolneder); Ricordi (ed. Ruf); Schott (ed. Ruf)
No. 4, G	2fl	Sikorski (ed. Ruf & Zöller)

Sonatas, op. 2 (no. 1, G "L'Henriette"; no. 2, d, "La Vibray"; no. 3, e, "La Dhérouville"; no. 4, g, "La Lumagne"; no. 5, D "La Chauvet"; no. 6, a, "Le Bouget")	fl, bc	Amadeus (ed. Hess); Bärenreiter; Boosey ed. Fleury); Müller (ed. Kolneder; (Sonntag); Peters (ed. Kolneder)
No. 2, "La Vibray"		Heinrichshofen; Leduc (ed. Veilhan & Salzer); Schott (ed. Ruf)
No. 3, "La Dhérouville"		Fischer; Schott (ed. Ruf)
No. 4, "La Lumagne"		Fischer; Sikorski (ed. Ruf)
No. 5, "La Chauvet"		G. Schirmer
No. 6, "Le Bouget"		G. Schirmer
Sonatas, op. 3	fl, bc	Billaudot (ed. Corado); Broekmans (ed. Uittenbosch)
No. 2, b	fl, bc	Bärenreiter (ed. Ruf)
Variations on a Theme by Corelli	2fl	International (ed. Wilson)

BODINUS, SEBASTIAN (ca.1700–ca.1760)

Concerto no. 3, e	fl, str, bc/pf red	Leuckart (ed. Schultz-Hauser)
Musikalischen Divertissements		
Sonata, E♭, vol. 1, no. 2	2ob/2vn/2fl, bc	Möseler (ed. Koch); Vieweg (ed. Fischer)
Sonata, e	2fl	Broekmans (ed. Havelaar); Moeck (ed. Birkner)
Trio, G	fl, 2 bn	Lienau (ed. Delius)

BOISMORTIER, JOSEPH BODIN DE (1689–1755)

6 Concertos, op. 15 (G,a,D,b,A,e)	5fl	Bärenreiter (ed. Harras); Billaudot (ed. Paubon); Piper
Nos. 1–3 (G,a,D)		Hofmeister (ed. Glasenapp)
Nos. 4–6 (b,A,e)		Hofmeister (ed. Spindler); Kalmus
Concerto, G, op. 21, no. 3	rec/fl, bc	Schott (ed. Doflein)
Concerto, a, op. 28, no. 7 "Zampogna"	2rec/2ob/2fl/2vn, bc	Ricordi (ed. Ruf)
Concerto, C, op. 28, no. 8 "Zampogna"	2rec/2ob/2fl/2vn, bc	Ricordi (ed. Ruf)

Concerto, e, op. 37, no. 6	rec/fl, vn, ob, bn, bc	Ricordi (ed. Ruf)
Diverses pièces, op. 22 [as 55 Leichte Stücke]	fl/2fl	Schott (ed. Doflein)
12 Petites Sonates, op. 13	2fl	Broekmans (ed. Bowers); Zimmermann (ed. Delius)
Sonatas, op. 1 (D,g,e,A,b,D)	2fl	Bärenreiter (ed. Fratscher); Müller (ed. Frotscher)
No. 2, g		International (ed. Schlenger)
Sonatas, op. 2	2fl	Möseler (ed. Nagel)
Nos. 3,4 (G,D)		Oxford (ed. Beechey)
Sonatas, op. 6 (G,C,g,D,e,b)	2fl	Müller (ed. Frotscher)
No. 2, C		International; Zimmermann (Schlenger)
No. 3, g		Zimmermann (ed. Schlenger)
No. 6, b		Bärenreiter (ed. Raugel)
6 Sonatas, op.9	fl, bc	Kunzelmann (ed. Mariassy)
No. 1, e	fl, bc	Oxford (ed. Parkinson)
No. 2, G	fl, bc	Oxford (ed. Platt)
No. 6, c	fl, bc	Oxford (ed. Platt)
6 Sonatas [Suites], op. 25	2fl	Schott (ed. Ruf)
2 Sonatas, C,G, op. 27	rec/fl, ob, vn, bc	Schott (ed. Doflein)
Sonata, g, op. 34, no. 1	3fl/3vn/3ob, bc	Bärenreiter (ed. Ruf)
Sonata, G, op. 34, no. 2	3fl, bc	Heinrichshofen (ed. Hiby)
Sonata, e, op. 34, no. 3	3fl/3vn/3ob, bc	Schott (ed. Ruf)
Sonata, a, op. 34, no. 6	3fl/3vn/3ob, bc	Schott (ed. Ruf)
Sonata, G, op. 44, no. 3	fl, bc	Nova (ed. Lasocki)
6 Sonatas, op. 51	fl, vn	Breitkopf (ed. Kubitschek); Nova (ed. Douglas)
Sonatas, op. 91 (D,g,G,e,A,c)	hpd, fl	Heugel (ed. Pincherle); Universal
Nos. 3,6 (G,c)		Billaudot (ed. Paubon)
No. 6 (c)	fl, bc	Musikhaus Pan (ed. Harras)
6 Sonates en trio, op. 7 (D,b,A,d,G,e)	3fl	Schott (ed. Doflein)
No. 1, D		Boosey (ed. Rawski); Breitkopf; Möseler (ed. Koch); Schott (ed. Bergmann)
No. 4, d		Billaudot

No. 5, G		Boosey (ed. Rawski); Breitkopf
Sonate en trio, e, op. 37, no. 2	fl, gamba, bc	Bärenreiter (ed. Ruf)
Sonate en trio, D, op. 37, no. 3	fl/ob/vn, gamba/vn/vc	Schott (ed. Ruf)
Sonate en trio, a, op. 37, no. 5	fl/ob/vn, gamba/bn/vc, bc	Musica Rara; Schott (ed. Ruf)
6 Suites [Duos], op. 1	2fl	Heinrichshofen (ed. Harf)
6 Suites [Duets], op. 17	2rec/2fl/2ob	Schott (ed. Ruf)
No. 1		Billaudot (ed. Paubon)
Nos. 1,4		Augener (ed. Vellekoop)
6 Suites, op. 27	2rec/2fl/2ob	Bärenreiter (ed. Doflein)
Nos. 1–3		Eds. Ouvrieres
6 Suites, op. 35	(fl, bc)/fl	Schott (ed. Ruf)
No. 1, e	fl, bc	Leduc (ed. Veilhan & Salzer)
No. 2, G	fl, bc	Schott (ed. Ruf)
Nos. 1, 2 (e,G)	fl, bc	Billaudot
No. 5, b	fl, bc	Schott (ed. Ruf)
Nos. 5, 6	fl	Billaudot

BON, ANNA, DE VENEZIA (1740–after 1767)

6 Sonates da Camera (C,F,B,D,g,G)	fl, hpsd	Clar/Nan (ed Jackson)

BONONCINI, GIOVANNI (1670–1747)

8 Divertimenti da camera (F,d,a,g,B♭,c,e,G)	vn/fl, bc	Schott (ed. Ruf)

BUCQUET, PIERRE (1700–?)

Suite no. 1, D	2fl	Eschig (ed. Bouvet); Ed. Musicus (ed. Felix)
Suite no. 2, e	2fl	Eschig (ed. Bouvet); Ed. Musicus (ed. Felix)
Suite no. 4, A	2fl	Eschig (ed. Bouvet)

Work	Scoring	Publisher
BUFFARDIN, PIERRE-GABRIEL (c.1690–1768)		
Concerto, e	fl, pf red	Peters (ed. Augsbach/Haupt)
CHÉDEVILLE, NICOLAS (1705–1782)		
Les galanteries amusantes [Pastoral sonatas], op. 8		
Nos. 3, 6 (c,C)	2fl/2vn	Bärereiter (ed. Upmeyer); International (ed. Upmeyer & Wummer); Nagel (ed. Upmeyer)
No. 3, c, "L'Allemande"		Ricordi (ed. Taylor)
Sonata, e, op. 7 no. 1	fl/ob/vn, bc	Schott (ed. Ruf)
Sonata, g, op. 7, no. 6	fl/ob/vn, bc	Richli (ed. Favre)
CORELLI, ARCANGELO (1653–1713)		
La Follia [arr. of Sonata, d, op. 5, no. 12, vn, bc]	rec, bc	Leduc (ed. Veilhan); McGinnis & Marx (ed. Krainis); Schott (ed. Linde—transposed to g)
Sonata, F	rec, bc	Lienau (ed. Delius)
CORRETTE, MICHEL (1709–1795)		
Concerto, A, op. 3, no. 3	2fl/2vn/2ob, bc/hpd	Schott (ed. Ruf)
Concerto, C, op. 4, no. 3	(rec, 2fl)/3fl, bc	Broekmans (ed. Pauler/Hess)
Concerto, e, op. 4, no. 6	3fl/3vn/3ob, bc	Schott (ed. Ruf)
Concerto, d, op. 26, no. 6	hpd, fl ad lib, str	Bärenreiter(ed. Ruf); Nagel (ed. Ruf)
Concerto comique, B♭, op. 8, no. 1	3fl, bc	Amadeus (ed. Pauler/Hess)
Concerto comique, C, op. 8, no. 3	3 rec/fl, bc	Amadeus (ed. Pauler/Hess)
Concerto comique, G, op. 8, no. 6	(rec, 2fl)/3fl, bc	Amadeus (ed. Pauler/Hess)
Concertos de Noel		
No. 4, Concerto Noel suisse	fl/ob/vn, 2vn, bc	Amadeus (ed. Morgan/Hess)
No. 5, Concerto Noel allemand	fl, 2vn, bc	Amadeus (ed. Pauler/Hess)
No. 6, *Lobt Gott ihr Christen allzugleich*	fl/vn, 2vn, bc	Amadeus (ed. Pauler/Hess); Peters (ed. Hofmann); Richli (ed. Guy-Lambert)
6 Sonatas, op. 2 (g,F,B♭,d,B♭,C)	2fl	Nova (ed. Block)

Work	Instrumentation	Publisher
6 Sonatas, op. 13	fl, bc	Kunzelmann (ed. Mariassy)
Nos. 1, 2 (D,e)	fl, bc	Dovehouse (ed. Hadidian)
Sonata, e, op.21, no. 1	2fl	Broekmans (ed. Havelaar)
6 Sonatas, op. 23	2fl	Peters (ed. Nagel)
6 Sonatilles, op. 19	fl/vn, bc	Schott
Sonatille, b, op. 19	fl/vn, bc	EMT (ed. Boulay)
Trio sonatas, op. 14, nos. 1, 3, 5	fl, vn, bc	King's Music
Trio sonata, G, op. 14 no. 5	fl, vn, bc	EMT (ed. Petit)
COUPERIN, FRANÇOIS (1668–1733)		
L'Apothéose de Lully	2fl/2ob/2vn, gamba, bc	Durand; Musica Rara (ed. Higginbottom)
Concerts royaux (G,D,A,e)	fl/2fl, bc	Durand; Musica Rara (ed. Lasocki); l'Oiseau-Lyre (ed. Gilbert & Hanson); Schott
No. 1, G	fl, bc	Billaudot; Heinrichshofen
No. 2, D	fl, bc	Heinrichshofen
No. 3, A	fl, bc	Zimmermann (ed. Eppinger/Michael)
No. 4, e	fl, bc	EMT (ed. Boulay); International (ed. Rampal)
Nouveaux concerts, nos. 5–11, 14 in *Les gouts-réunis* (F,B♭,g,G,E,a c,d)	fl/ob/vn, bc	EMT; Musica Rara
No. 6, B♭		Durand (ed. Dukas); EMT (ed. Boulay); Schott (ed. Ruf)
No. 9, E, "Ritratto dell'amore"	fl, bc	Universal (ed. Vester); Zimmermann (ed. Eppinger/Michael)
No. 13, G	2fl	Bärenreiter (ed. Schmitz); Schott (ed. Ruf); Zimmermann (ed. Michael)

DORNEL, LOUIS-ANTOINE (ca.1680–1756)		
Suite no. 1, D	fl, bc	Richli (ed. Aubert)
1ere Suite en trio, g	2rec/2ob/2fl/2vn, bc	Leduc (ed. Poulteau)
2e Suite en trio, C	2rec/2ob/2fl/2vn, bc	Leduc (ed. Poulteau)
Suite en trio no. 3, d	2rec/2ob/2fl/2vn, bc	Schott (ed. Ruf)
FASCH, JOHANN FRIEDRICH (1688–1758)		
Concerto, D	fl, ob, str, bc	Sikorski (ed. Winschermann)
Concerto, d, FWV L:D8	fl, orch	Möseler (ed. Kuntzel)
Concerto, e	fl, ob, str, bc/pf red	Eulenberg (ed. Braun)
Concerto, G	fl, ob, str, bc	Sikorski
Quartet [Sonata], G	fl, 2rec, bc	Moeck
Sonata [Kanon], e	2vn/2ob/2fl, bc	Möseler (ed. Hoffmann)
Sonata, B♭	rec/fl, ob/vn, bc	Bärenreiter (ed. Woehl)
Sonata, B♭	2ob/2fl/2vn, bc	Nagel (ed. Schäffler)
Sonata, D	fl, vn, bn/vc, bc	Bärenreiter (ed. Gerlach); Sikorski (ed. Wojciechowski)
Sonata, D	fl, vn, bc	Eulenberg (ed. Nagel)
Trio Sonata, G	fl, bn, bc	Sikorski (ed. Grebe)
Sonate a4, B♭	rec, ob, vn, bc	Nagel (ed. Dancker-Langner)
FESCH, WILLEM DE (1687–?1757)		
Concerto, D, op. 10, no. 7	fl, str, bc	AMP (ed. Ruf); Nagel
Concerto, G, op. 10, no. 8	2fl, str/pf red	Schott (ed. Ruf)
Duets (F,C,C)	2rec	Noetzel (ed. Koschinsky)
Sonatas, op. 6, nos. 1,3	vn/fl, org	De Ring
Sonatas, op. 7, nos. 2, 4, 8 (D,g,e)	2fl/2vn, bc	Broekmans; Pegasus (ed. Schroeder)
Sonatas, op. 8, nos. 1–6 (D,c,e,G,A,b)	rec/fl, bc	Bärenreiter (ed. Woehl)
6 Sonatas, op. 9 (D,G,a,D,d,e)	2fl	Müller (ed. Ruf)
Trio Sonatas, op. 12, nos. 1–3 (D,g,G)	2fl/vn, bc	Bärenreiter (ed. Schouwman); Heuwekemeijer (ed. Noske, Schouwman)

Work	Instrumentation	Publisher
FESTING, MICHAEL CHRISTIAN (d. 1752)		
Concerto, D, op. 3, no. 10	2rec/2fl, str, bc	Nagel (ed. Ruf)
Concerto, e, op. 3, no. 11	2rec/2fl, str, bc	Oxford (ed. Platt)
FINGER, GOTTFRIED (ca.1660–1730)		
Collection of Choice Ayres: Sonata, C	2rec	Schott (ed. Bergmann)
Collection of Musick [Leichte Duette] (C/c,G,B♭)	2rec	Pegasus (ed. Harf)
Pastorelle and Sonata	3 rec	Oxford (ed. Platt)
Sonata, F	3 rec	Universal (ed. Marshall)
Sonata, op. 2, nos. 3–6 (C,B♭,g,G)	2rec	Schott (ed. Giesbert)
Sonata, c, op. 3, no. 2	rec, bc	Nova (ed. Marshall)
Sonata, d	fl, bc/hpd	Boosey (ed. Boyle); Schott (ed. Ruf)
Sonata, F	fl, bc/hpd	Boosey (ed. Boyle)
Sonata, G	fl, bc/hpd	Boosey (ed. Hunt); Schott (ed. Ruf)
Tempo di Menuetto, divisions	rec, kbd	Schott (ed. Dinn)
FREDERICK II (THE GREAT) (1712–1786)		
Concertos nos. 1–4 (G,G,C,D)	fl, str, bc	Da Capo
	fl, pf red	Kalmus (ed. Reinecke)
No. 1, G	fl, str, bc	Breitkopf
No. 2, G	fl, str, bc	Breitkopf
No. 3, C	fl, str, bc/pf red	Vieweg (ed. Lenzewski)
No. 4, D	fl, str, bc/pf red	Vieweg (ed. Lenzewski)
Solfeggien [some by Quantz]	fl	Amadeus (ed. Michel & Teske)
[as *Das Flötenbuch Friedrichs des Grossen*]		Breitkopf (ed. Schwarz-Reiflingen)
10 Sonatas	fl, kbd	Breitkopf (ed. Bartuzat); Breitkopf (ed. Braun/Petrenz)
25 Sonatas (C,c,b,B♭,A,g,G,F,e,E♭,d,C,g,E♭,c, C,a,A,e,A,D,g,G,G,g)	fl, kbd	Da Capo; Kalmus

Work	Instrumentation	Publisher
Sonata no. 2, c	fl, kbd	Edu-Tainment (ed. Schanley)
Sonata no. 12 [no. 117], A	fl, kbd	Sikorski (ed. Sonntag)
Sonata [Solo] no. 122, b	fl, kbd	Forberg (ed. Fischer)
Sonatas, g, b	fl, bc	Universal
GALLIARD, JOHN ERNEST (ca.1687–1749)		
Sonatas, op. 1, nos. 1–3 (C,d,e)	rec/fl/ob/vn, bc	Ricordi (ed. Scheck & Ruf)
GALUPPI, BALDASSARE (1706–1785)		
Concerto, D	fl, str, bc	Breitkopf (ed. Schroeder)
Concerto, G	fl, str/pf red	Müller (ed. Brinckmann & Mohr)
Concerto, d	2fl, str, bc/pf red	G. Schirmer (ed. Jenkins)
Concerto, e	2fl, str, bc/pf red	Noetzel (ed. Schroeder)
Triosonata, G	fl, ob, bc	Bärenreiter (ed. Ruf)
GAULTIER, PIERRE (ca.1642–1697)		
Suite, G	fl, bc	Richli (ed. Favre)
GEMINIANI, FRANCESCO (1687–1762)		
Sonata no. 3, e	fl/vn, hpd	Baärenreiter (ed. Ruf)
GUILLEMAIN, LOUIS-GABRIEL (1705–1770)		
6 Sonates en quatuors ou conversations galantes, op. 12	fl, vn, b viol/vc, bc	
Nos. 1, 3, 5 (G,d,F)	fl, vn, vc, bc	Musica Rara
No. 1, G	fl, vn, va/vc, kbd	Breitkopf
No. 2, b	fl, vn, vc, bc	Sikorski (ed. Polnauer)
No. 3, d	fl, vn, vc, bc	EMT (ed. Petit)
No. 4, A	fl, vn, vc, bc	Sikorski (ed. Polnauer)
No. 6, C	fl/ob, vn, gamba, bc	Sikorski (ed. Winschermann)

Work	Scoring	Editions
GUILLEMANT, BENOIT (fl Paris 1746–1757)		
2 Petites Suites	2fl/2rec	Heinrichshofen (ed. Gianini)
HANDEL, GEORGE FRIDERIC (1685–1759)		
Concerto Grosso, G, op. 3, no. 3	fl/ob, 2vn; str, bc	Bärenreiter; Breitkopf (ed. Seiffert); Eulenberg (ed. Sadie)
Fitzwilliam Sonatas (B♭,d,d)	rec, bc	Schott (ed. Dart)
No.1, B♭		Faber (ed. Lasocki & Bergmann)
Halle Sonatas (a,e,b)	fl, bc	Bärenreiter (ed. Schmitz); Kalmus; Litolff; Peters (Urtext); Reinhardt
Sonatas, op. 1		
No. 1a, e; no. 1b, e; no. 5, G; no. 9, b	fl, bc	Bärenreiter (ed. Schmitz); Faber (ed. Lasocki); Reinhardt (ed. Bopp)
Nos. 1b, 5, 9 (e,G,b)		Peters (Urtext); G. Schirmer (ed. L. Moyse)
Nos. 2, g; 4, a; 7, C; 11, F	rec, bc	Bärenreiter (ed. Schmitz); Breitkopf (ed. Seiffert); Faber (ed. Lasocki & Bergmann); Leduc (ed. Poulteau); Peters (Urtext); Reinhardt (ed. Bopp); G. Schirmer (ed. L. Moyse); Schott (ed. Hunt)
Triosonata, b, op. 2, no. 1	fl/vn, vn, bc	Eulenberg (ed. Lam); Schott
Triosonata, F, op. 2, no. 4	fl/rec/vn, vn, bc	Eulenberg (ed. Lam); Nagel (ed. Flesch);Schott (ed. Mönkemeyer)
Triosonata, c	rec/fl, vn, bc	Nagel (ed. Flesch)
Triosonata, e	2fl, bc	Schott (ed. Nagel)
Triosonata, F	2rec, bc	Faber (ed. Hogwood)
HASSE, JOHANN ADOLF (1699–1783)		
Concerto, G, op. 3, no. 5	fl, str, bc	Bärenreiter (ed. Engländer); Nagel (ed. Engländer)
Concerto, D, op. 3 no. 6	fl, str, bc	Eulenberg (ed. Engländer)

Concerto, op. 3, no. 7	fl, hpd red	Kunzelmann (ed. Mariassy)
Concerto, b, op. 3, no. 10	fl, str, bc/pf red	Breitkopf (ed. Walther)
Concerto, A	fl, str, bc/pf red	Müller (ed. Mohr)
Concerto, D	fl, str, bc/pf red	Schott (ed. Sonntag)
Concerto, F	fl, str, bc/pf red	Eulenberg (ed. Jeney & Müller)
Sonatas, op. 1	fl, bc	
D		Nagel
d		Broekmans
G		Hofmeister
6 Sonatas, op. 2	fl, bc	Universal (ed. Braun/Petrenz)
Nos. 2, 6 (G,b)	fl, bc	Forberg (ed. Weyer)
Sonata, D	fl, bc	Kalmus; Nagel (ed. Walther)
Sonata, D, op. 3, no. 6	2fl/vn, bc	Doblinger; ÖBV (ed. Schenk)
6 Sonatas, op. 5 (G,A,G,D,e,D)	fl, bc	Breitkopf (ed. Braun/Petrenz)
Triosonata, D	2fl, bc	Nagel (ed. Frotscher)
Triosonata, E	2fl, bc	Zimmermann
Triosonatas no. 1, e; no. 4, G	2fl/vn, bc	Schott (ed. Ruf)
Triosonata, F	ob/fl, fl, bc	Sikorski (ed. Winschermann)
HERTEL, JOHANN WILHELM (1727–1789)		
Sinfonia a6	2fl, str, bc	Möseler
HOTTETERRE, JACQUES MARTIN (1674–1763)		
L'art de préluder, op. 7 [as 48 Preludes]	rec/fl/ob	Schott (ed. Doflein & Delius)
Echos, op. 2	rec/fl	Schott (ed. Bergmann)
[in 50 *Klassische Studien für Flöte*]		Universal (ed. Vester)
Sonatas, op. 3, nos. 1,2 (g,D)	2fl/2rec/2vn/2ob, bc	Schott (ed. Ruf)
Suites, op. 2	fl, bc	EMB (ed. Mariassy)
No. 1, D	fl/ob/vn, bc	Musica Rara (ed. Smith); Nagel (ed. Schäffler); Nova (ed. Lasocki)

No. 1, F [transposed per composer's instructions]	rec/fl, bc	(Nova (ed. Lasocki); Pelikan (ed. Ruf)
No. 2a and 2b, G	fl, bc	Nova (ed. Lasocki)
Nos. 3a and 3b, e	fl/ob/vn, bc	Nova (ed. Lasocki)
No. 4, e	fl/ob/vn, bc	Bärenreiter (ed. Ruf)
No. 5, g	rec, bc	Moeck (ed. Braun)
Suite, b, op. 4, no. 1	2fl/2rec	Amadeus; Sikorski (ed. Ruf & Zöller)
Suites, op. 5 (b♭,e♭,F,d) [transposed per composer's instructions]	rec/fl/ob, bc	Amadeus; EMB (ed. Mariassy); Eulenberg (ed. Kneihs)
No. 2, e [transposed per composer's instructions]		Bärenreiter (ed. Ruf)
No. 3, D		Ricordi (ed. Scheck & Ruf)
[as Sonate]		Richli (ed. Viollier)
Triosonatas, op. 3, nos. 1–6	2fl/2ob/2vn, bc	Nova (ed. Lasocki)

KIRNBERGER, JOHANN PHILIPP (1721–1783)

Sonata, G	fl, bc	Schott (ed. Weigart)
Sonatas, G,g	fl, bc	Peters (ed. Sonntag)

KREBS, JOHANN LUDWIG (1713–1780)

6 Sonata da camera [Kammersonaten] (A,G,C,e,a,D)	hpd, fl/vn	Peters (ed. Klein)
No. 1, A		Hansen (ed. Höckner)
No. 3, C		Ricordi (ed. Scheck & Ruf)
No. 4, e		Bärenreiter (ed. Ermeler)
No. 6, D		Pegasus (ed. Ermeler)
Sonata, d	fl, vn, bc	Möseler (ed. Nagel)
Trio no. 1, D	2fl/2vn, bc	Breitkopf (ed. Riemann); Schott (ed. Ruf)
Trio no. 2, b	2fl/2vn, bc	Kalmus; Schott (ed. Ruf)
Trio no. 5, G	2fl/2vn, bc	Heinrichshofen (ed. Ruf)

Trio no. 6, a	2fl/2vn, bc	Nagel (ed. Werner)
Trio, D	2fl/2vn, bc	Müller (ed. Nagel)
Trio, e	2fl/2vn, bc	Müller (ed. Nagel)
Trio Sonata, A	2fl, bc	Zimmermann (ed. Kölbel)
LA BARRE, MICHEL DE (ca.1675–1743/44)		
Pièces, op. 4 (Suites in D,G,e,g,d)	fl, bc	Heugel (ed. Bowers & Borgir)
No.1, D		Sikorski (ed. Nagel & Radeke)
1ere livre: Suite, G	2fl	Ricordi (ed. Scheck & Ruf)
2e livre: Suite no. 9, G	fl/ob/vn, bc	Ricordi (ed. Ruf)
[as Sonate dite L'inconnue]	fl/ob/vn, bc	Richli
3e livre des trio: Sonata V, G	2fl, bc	Pegasus (ed. Viollier)
2e Suite de pièces, f	2fl	Schott (ed. Doflein in *Alte frz. Duette)*
3e Suite, e	2fl	Sikorski (ed. Ruf & Zöller)
LECLAIR, JEAN-MARIE (1697–1764)		
Concerto, C, op. 7, no. 3	fl, str, bc/pf red	EMT (ed. Oubradous); Foetisch (ed. Crussard); Leuckart (ed. Redel); Ricordi (ed. Scheck & Ruf); Southern (ed. Wummer)
	fl, pf red	Belwin; International (ed. Rampal)
2e récréation de musique [suite with overture], g, op. 8	2 rec/vn, bc	Bärenreiter (ed. Ruf) Ricordi (ed. Scheck & Ruf)
Sonata, C, op. 1, no. 2	fl, bc	Schott (Ruf)
[as op. 3, no. 2]	fl, bc	Eschig (ed. Guilmant & Debroux)
Sonata, e, op. 1, no. 6 [as op. 3, no. 2]	fl, bc	Eschig (ed. Guilmant & Debroux)
Sonata, e, op. 2, no. 1	vn/fl, bc	Breitkopf; Kalmus; Ricordi; Schott (ed. Bouillard); Zimmermann (ed. Zanke)
Sonata, C, op. 2, no. 3	vn/fl, bc	Breitkopf; Ricordi
Sonata, G, op. 2, no. 5	vn/fl, bc	Bärenreiter (ed. Ruf); Breitkopf; Ricordi
Sonata, D, op. 2, no. 8	vn/fl, gamba, bc	Breitkopf; Foetisch; Schott (ed. Ruf); Sikorski (ed. Höffer von Winterfeld);

Sonata, b, op. 2, no. 11	vn/fl, bc	Breitkopf; Richli (ed. Druilhe)
Sonata, e, op. 9, no. 2	vn/fl, bc	Chester (ed. Polnauer); Eschig; Leduc (ed. Veilhan); Schott (ed. Ruf)
Sonata, G, op. 9, no. 7	vn/fl, bc	Schott (ed. Ruf)
LEFFLOTH, JOHANN MATTHIAS (1705–1731)		
Concerto, D	vn/fl, hpd	Nagel (ed. Ruf)
LOCATELLI, PIETRO ANTONIO (1695–1764)		
12 Sonatas, op. 2 (C,D,B♭,G,D,g,A,F,E,G,D,G)	fl, bc	Zerboni (ed. Zagnoni & Farina)
Nos. 1, 3, 7 (C,B♭,A)		Ricordi (ed. Scheck & Ruf)
No. 2, D		Peters (ed. Feldtkamp)
No. 3, B♭		Schott (ed. Ruf)
Nos. 4–6 (G,d,g)		Bärenreiter (ed. Scheck & Upmeyer); Kalmus
No. 8, F		Hug (ed. Kowatscheff)
6 Sonatas or Duets, op. 4 (e,g,G,d,b,D) [spurious]	2fl/2vn	Ricordi (ed. Ruf)
No. 1, e		International (ed. Wummer); Kalmus; Peters (Urtext)
Nos. 4, 5 (d,b)		Schott (ed. Ruf)
No. 6, D		Sikorski (ed. Ruf & Zöller)
Sonata, G, op. 5, no. 1 [as op. 3, no. [illegible]]	2vn/2fl, bc	Foetisch (ed. Crussard); Kistner (ed. Albrecht) International (ed. Riemann-Lyman); Noetzel (ed. Kölbel); Simrock (ed. Moffat & Mlynarczyk)
Sonata, E, op. 5, no. 3	2vn/2fl, bc	Müller; Schott (ed. Ruf)
Sonata, C, op. 5, no. 4	2vn/2fl, bc	Concordia (ed. Albrecht)
Sonata, d, op. 5, no. 5	2vn/2fl, bc	Concordia (ed. Albrecht)

Work	Instrumentation	Publisher
LOEILLET, JACQUES (1685–1748)		
Concerto, D	fl, str, bc	Bärenreiter
Quintet [attrib.], b	2fl, 2rec, bc	Bärenreiter (ed. Ermeler)
6 Sonatas, op. 5 (e,G,g,D,b,G)	fl/vn, bc	Bärenreiter
LOEILLET, JEAN BAPTISTE "JOHN LOEILLET OF LONDON" (1680–1730)		
Sonata, F, op. 1, no. 1	rec/fl, ob/rec/vn, bc	Moeck (ed. Ruf); Schott (ed. Bergmann & Champion)
	arr. fl, pf	International (ed. Béon); Lemoine (ed. Béon)
Sonata, G, op. 1, no. 2	2fl, bc	Möseler (ed. Schroeder); Schott (ed. Ruf)
Sonata, g, op. 1, no. 3	arr. fl, pf	International (ed. Béon); Lemoine (ed. Béon)
Sonata, D, op. 1, no. 4	2fl, bc	Schott (ed. Ruf)
Sonata, c, op. 1, no. 5	fl, ob, bc	International (ed. Béon); Lemoine (ed. Béon)
Sonata, e, op. 1, no. 6	2fl, bc	International (ed. Béon); Lemoine; Nova; Schott (ed. Ruf)
Sonata, F, op. 2, no. 2	rec, ob, bc	Bärenreiter (ed. Ruf); Heinrichshofen (ed. Ermeler & Kluge); Musica Rara (ed. Sadie); Universal (ed. Ring)
Sonata, d, op. 2, no. 4	rec, ob, bc	Bärenreiter (ed. Ruf); International (ed. Béon); Lemoine (ed. Béon);Music Press (ed. Mann)
Sonata, c, op. 2, no. 6	rec, ob, bc	Bärenreiter (ed. Ruf); International (ed. Béon); Musica Rara (ed. Sadie)
Sonata, b, op. 2, no. 8	2fl, bc	Leduc (ed. Poulteau)
Sonata, G, op. 2, no. 12	2fl, bc	Bärenreiter (ed. Ruf)
12 Sonatas, op. 3		
Nos. 1–6 (C,d,F,a,g,d)	rec, bc	Schott (ed. Ruf)
No. 1, C	rec, bc	E.C. Schirmer (Weiss-Mann)
No. 7, e	fl, bc	Leduc (ed. Poulteau); Musikhaus Pan; Rudall, Carte (ed. Lovering)
No. 8, G	fl, bc	Leduc (ed. Poulteau); Schott (ed. Ruf)
Nos. 9–12 (D,b,D,G)	fl, bc	Leduc (ed. Poulteau)

LOEILLET, JEAN BAPTISTE "LOEILLET DE GANT" (1688–ca.1720)

Work	Instrumentation	Publisher
12 Sonatas, op. 1 (a,d,G F,B♭,C,c,d,g,F,G,e)	rec, bc	
Nos. 1–3 (a,d,G)		Bärenreiter (ed. Hinnenthal)
Nos. 1,4,6,8 (a,G,C,d)		Moeck (ed. Mönkmeyer)
Nos. 1,12 (a,e)		Heugel
No. 10, F		Broekmans (ed. Feltkamp)
12 Sonatas, op. 2 (F,g,d,B♭,c,G,e,F,g,D,g,a)	rec, bc	BMI-Canada (ed. Kasemets)
No. 5, c		Broekmans (ed. Feltkamp); Moeck (ed. Mönkmeyer)
Nos. 5,7 (c,e)		Heugel
12 Sonatas, op. 3	rec, bc	
No. 1, C		Leduc (ed. Fleury); Leduc (ed. Veilhan & Salzer); Schott (ed. Poulteau)
No. 2, B♭		Heugel
Nos. 2–6, 10 (B♭,g,G,c,e,d)		Schott (ed. Scherber & Kutz)
No. 7, E♭		Leduc (ed. Poulteau); Rudall, Carte (ed. Lovering)
No. 8, F		Heugel
No. 9, B♭		Bärenreiter (ed. Hinnenthal); Ricordi (ed. Ruf)
No. 11, A		Hargail (ed. Mirsky); Heinrichshofen (ed. Ruf); Noetzel (ed. Wood)
No. 12, e		Bärenreiter (ed. Hinnenthal)
12 Sonatas, op. 4	rec, bc	EMB
No. 2, a		Zurfluh (ed. Poulteau)
No. 4, G		Leduc (ed. Poulteau)
No. 6, g		Moeck (ed. Mönkmeyer)
Nos. 9, 10 (G,C)		Bärenreiter (ed. Hinnenthal);De Ring (ed. Etsen)
Nos. 11, 12 (f,a)		Bärenreiter (ed. Hinnenthal)

6 Sonatas, op. 5, book 1 (e,b,d,D,G,g)	fl, ob/vn, bc	Musica Rara (ed. Sadie)
6 Sonatas, op. 5, book 2 (D,e,G,g,G,e)	2fl/2ob/2vn	Schott (ed. Ruf)
Nos. 1,4,5 (D,g,G)		Leduc (ed. Poulteau)
Nos. 1,4 (D,g)		Oxford (ed. Beechey)
No. 6, e		Zerfluh (ed. Poulteau)
6 Sonatas of 2 parts, Fitted and Contrived for 2 Flutes (a,G,F,d,B♭,F)—arr. by original pubs.	2fl	
from I/1,3,4; II/3,4,8		Schott (ed. Ruf)
Nos. 1, 3 (a,F)		Moeck (ed. Mönkmeyer)
No. 3, F		Universal (ed. Dolmetsch)
LOTTI, ANTONIO (1667–1740)		
Sonata, G	fl/vn, gamba/vc, hpd	Zimmermann
Trio, A	fl, ob d'am/ob/vn, bc	Ricordi
MARAIS, MARIN (1656–1728)		
Les Folies d'Espagne [arr. of Pièces de viole, livre 2, no. 20]	fl	Bärenreiter (ed. Schmitz)
	rec/fl, gamba, hpd	Leduc (ed. Veilhan)
	fl, kbd	Zimmermann (ed. Eppinger/Michael)
Pièces en trio	2fl/2rec/2ob/2vn, bc	
Suite no. 1, C		Schott (ed. Delius)
Suite no. 2, g		Schott (ed. Delius)
Suite no. 5, e		EMT (ed. Boulay); Moeck (ed. Delius)
Suite, b (1717)	fl, bc	Leduc
MARCELLO, ALESSANDRO (1684–1750)		
La Cetra, 6 Concerti Grossi	2fl/2ob, bn, str, bc	Sikorski

MARCELLO, BENEDETTO (1686–1739)		
12 Sonatas, op. 2 (F,d,g,e,G,C,B♭,d,C,a,g,G)	rec, bc	Amadeus (ed. Hess); De Santis (ed. Tassinari & Toma); EMB (ed. Mariassy)
[also published as op. 1, in different order]	fl/vn, bc	
No. 1, F		Heinrichshofen (ed. Witney International (ed. Wummer); Oxford (ed. Slater)
Nos. 4, 6, 9 (e,C,C)		Sikorski (ed. Höffer von Winterfeld & Stolze)
Nos. 1, 5, 8, 11 (F,G,d,g)		De Santis (ed. Veggetti)
Nos. 1–4, 6–7 (F,d,g,e,C,B♭)		Bärenreiter (ed. Glode)
No. 4, e		Broekmans
No. 5, G		Noetzel (ed. Ermeler)
[as no. 12]		Oxford (ed. Slater)
No. 7, B♭		Oxford (ed. Pearson)
[as op. 1, no. 6]		Noetzel (ed. Ermeler & Kluge)
No. 8, d		Schott (ed. Ruf)
No. 10, a		Schott (ed. Ruf)
[as op. 1, no. 9]		Noetzel (ed. Ermeler & Kluge)
No. 12, G		Noetzel (ed. Ermeler & Kluge); Oxford (ed. Slater); Zimmermann (ed. Zanke)
MATTHESON, JOHANN (1681–1764)		
Der brauchbare Virtuoso: 12 Kammersonaten	fl/vn, hpd	Kalmus; Zimmermann (ed. van Leeuwen)
Sonata, A	fl/vn, bc	Schott (ed. Ruf)
12 Sonatas, op. 1		
Nos. 1,2,11,12 (c,F,B♭,a)	2 rec	Nagel (ed. Giesbert); Schott (ed. Hunt)
Nos. 3–10 (g,c,C,B,G,F,g,f)	3 rec	Nagel (ed. Giesbert); Schott (ed. Hunt)
Nos. 4,7 (c,G)	3 rec	Schott (ed. Hunt)

Work	Instrumentation	Publisher
MOLTER, JOHANN MELCHIOR (1696–1765)		
Concerto, G	fl, orch/pf red	Musica Rara
3 Concerti	4fl, bc	Universal (ed. Imbescheid)
MONDONVILLE, JEAN-JOSEPH CASSANEA DE (1711–1772)		
Sonates en trio, op. 2	2vn/2fl, bc	Heugel (ed. Blanchard)
Sonate, G	2fl, kbd	Salabert (ed. Peyrot & Rebufat)
MONTECLAIR, MICHEL PIGNOLET DE (1667–1737)		
6 Concerts (D/d,e/E,G/g,a,A,b)	2fl	Müller (ed. Frötscher)
Nos. 1–3 (D,e,G)		Pegasus-Heinrichshofen (ed. Viollier)
NAUDOT, JACQUES-CHRISTOPHE (ca.1690–1762)		
6 Babioles, op. 10 [Suites in C,G,C,C,G,C]	2rec/2fl/2ob/2vn	Schott (ed. Ruf)
Concert, C, op. 17, no. 2	rec, 2vn, bc	Schott (ed. Ruf)
Concert, G, op. 17, no. 5	rec/fl/ob, 2vn, bc	Bärenreiter (ed. Ruf)
Concerto, op. 11, no. 4	fl, str, bc	Billaudot
6 Duets, op. 3	2fl	Heinrichshofen
6 Fêtes rustiques, op. 8	rec, ob, bc	
Trio no. 1, C		Richli (ed. Favre); Schott (ed. Ruf)
Trio no. 3, C		Schott (ed. Ruf)
25 Menuets	2fl/2ob/2vn	Pelikan (ed. Schoch & Jaunet)
6 Sonatas, op. 1	fl, bc	Billaudot (ed. Paubon); Peters (ed. Gurgel)
No. 5		Leduc (ed. Fleury)
6 Sonates, Op. 4	fl, kbd	Billaudot (ed. Paubon)
6 Sonatas, op. 6 (b,D,g,A,e,G)	2fl	Billaudot (ed. Paubon); Simrock (ed. Höckner)
No. 1, b		Leduc (ed. Fleury); Ricordi (ed. Taylor)
6 Sonatas, op. 9 (D,b,G,E,G,d)	rec/fl, bc	Billaudot (ed. Paubon)
No. 5, G	rec/fl, bc	Bärenreiter (ed. Ruf)

PEPUSCH, JOHANN CHRISTOPH (1667–1752)

Concertos, F, op. 8, no. 1	2fl, 2rec, bc	Musica Rara
Concerto, G, op. 8, no. 2	2fl, 2ob/2vn, bc	Musica Rara
Concerto, F, op. 8, no. 4	2fl, 2rec, bc	Musica Rara
Concerto, C, op. 8, no. 5	2fl, 2rec, bc	Musica Rara
Concerto, C, op. 8, no. 6	2fl, 2rec, bc	Musica Rara
Quintet, F	2rec, 2vn, hpd	Schott (ed. Dart)
Solos [Sonatas], 2nd set, c, d	rec/fl/ob/vn, bc	Schott (ed. Ruf)
Sonatas, op. 1 (C,d,G,F,E♭,B♭)	rec/fl/ob/vn, bc	Schott (ed. Giesbert)
No. 2, d		Delrieu (ed. Ruyssen)
Sonate, G	fl, bc	Musikhaus Pan
Triosonatas, op. 3, nos. 1,3,5,9,11,12	2vn/2ob/2fl, bc	Breitkopf (ed. Hoffmann-Erbrecht)
Triosonatas, B♭, F	2fl, bc	Schott (ed. Ruf)
Triosonata, C	rec/fl/ob/vn, vn, bc	Schott (ed. Hausswald)
Triosonata, d	fl, va, bc	Bärenreiter (ed. Ruf)
Triosonata, e	fl, va, bc	Schott
Triosonata, F	fl, vn, bc	Heinrichshofen
Triosonata, g	fl, bn, bc	Kalmus
Triosonata, g	fl, vn, bc	Kistner (ed. Hoffmann-Erbrecht)

PERGOLESI, GIOVANNI BATTISTA (1710–1736)

Concerto no. 1, G, P. 33	fl, str, bc/pf red	Billaudot (ed. Paubon); Boosey (ed. Meylan); Sikorski (ed. Brinckmann & Mohr)
	fl, pf red	International (ed. Rampal)
Concerto no. 2, D, P. 34	fl, pf red	International (ed. Rampal)

Work	Instrumentation	Edition
PHILIDOR, ANNE DANICAN (1681–1728)		
1e livre de pièces	fl/rec/vn/ob, bc	Galaxy (ed. Gourrier/Teniere);
Sonata, d		Amadeus (ed. Habert); Bärenreiter (ed. Ruf)
Suite I, g		Schott (ed. Ruf)
2e livre de pièces	fl/rec/vn/ob, bc	Amadeua (ed. Nitz); Moeck (ed. Boullet)
PHILIDOR, FRANÇOIS DANICAN (1689–1717/18)		
Pièces, livre 1 (G,D,A,e)	fl, bc	Schott (ed. Beechey)
No. 3 [transposed], C	rec, bc	Heinrichshofen (ed. Nitz)
PLATTI, GIOVANNI BENEDETTO (ca.1700–1763)		
Concerto, G	fl, str/pf red	Schott (ed. Lebermann)
6 Sonatas, op. 3	fl, vc/bc	
Nos. 1,4,5,6 (D,A,c,G)		Ricordi (ed. Scheck & Ruf)
No. 3, e		Schott (ed. Delius)
Nos. 2,3,4 (G,e,A)		Schott (ed. Jarnach)
No. 6, G		Schott (ed. Ruf)
Triosonata, G	fl, ob, bc	Musica Rara
PORPORA, NICOLA (1686–1768)		
Sinfonia no. 10, d	fl, bc	McGinnis & Marx (ed. Marx & Maynard)
PURCELL, DANIEL (d.1717)		
3 Sonatas, F,d,C	rec, hpd, gamba ad lib	Schott (ed. Giesbert)
Sonata no. 1, F	fl, bc	Oxford (ed. Slater); Ricordi (ed. Fleury); Schott (ed. Jarnach)
Sonata [Sonatina] no. 2, d	fl, bc	Schott (ed. Hunt)
Sonata no. 3, C	fl, bc	Oxford (ed. Slater)
Trio Sonata, d	2fl, bc	Schott (ed. Ruf)

QUANTZ, JOHANN JOACHIM (1697–1773)

Work	Scoring	Publisher
Concerto no. 57, e	fl, str, bc/pf red	Sikorski (ed. Sonntag)
	fl, kbd red	International (ed. Rampal)
Concerto no. 82, D	fl, str, bc	Möseler (ed. Sonntag)
Concerto no. 108, c	fl, str, bc/pf red	Pegasus (ed. Sonntag)
Concerto no. 118, C	fl, pf red	Müller (ed. Sonntag)
Concerto no. 161, G	fl, str, bc	Breitkopf (ed. Weissenborn); Peters (ed. Burmeister)
	fl, str, bc/pf red	Eulenberg (ed. Schroeder); Kalmus
	fl, pf red	Boosey (ed. Nagy); Fischer (ed. Barge); International (ed. Rampal); Peters (ed. Augsbach); G. Schirmer (ed. Blaisdell, Barrère cadenza); Southern (ed. Wummer)
Concerto no. 182, D [as no. 17]	fl, pf red	Forberg (ed. Wittenbecher)
Concerto no. 182, D ["pour Potsdam"]	fl, str, bc/pf red	Baärenreiter (ed. Upmeyer)
	fl, pf red	Bärenreiter (ed. Walther)
Concerto, A	fl, pf red	Eulenberg (ed. Muller & Jeney)
Concerto, C	fl, str, bc	Möseler (ed. Sonntag, Hoffmann)
Concerto, c	fl, pf red	International (ed. Rampal)
Concerto, D	fl, kbd red	Bärenreiter (ed. Walther)
Concerto, d	fl, str, bc/pf red	Musica Rara (ed. Lasocki)
Concerto, e	fl, pf red	International (ed. Rampal)
Concerto, g	fl, str, bc	Peters (ed. Burmeister)
Concertos nos. 1–4 (G,g,D,D)	2fl, str, bc	Musica Rara
Concerto, g	2fl, str/pf red	Musica Rara (ed. Voxman & Block)
6 Duets, op. 2	2fl	Breitkopf (ed. Müller); International (ed. Wummer); Nova; Schirmer (ed. Wittgenstein) Schott (ed. Delius); Sikorski; Simrock
Nos.1-3		Kalmus

Nos.1,2 (G,a)	2fl	Edu-Tainment (ed. Tipton)
No.2, a	2fl	Sikorski (ed. Ruf & Zöller)
6 Duets, op. 5	2fl	Heinrichshofen (ed. Nagel)
Solfeggi	fl	Amadeus (ed. Michel & Teske)
[as *Das Flötenbuch Friedrichs des Grossen*]		Breitkopf (ed. Schwarz-Reiflingen)
Sonata VI, D [no. 3 of Sonates Italiennes, Boivin, 1729; no. 1 of Walsh's op. 2, 1732]	fl, hpd	Forberg (ed. Fischer)
6 Sonatas [5 from lst Walsh vol., 1730, of which no. 3 spurious. no. 5 of this ed. is No. 3 of Walsh's 2nd vol.] (D,G,e,G,D,A)	fl/ob/vn, bc	Müller (ed. Sonntag)
Sonata No. 5, D, [no. 5 of Walsh's lst vol., 1730; orig. pub. as work of Handel]	fl/ob/vn, bc	Bärenreiter (ed. Jarnach)
6 Sonatas, op. 1 (1734)		
No. 1, a	fl, hpd	Breitkopf (ed. Schroeder); Fischer; Forberg (ed. Fischer)
No. 2, B♭ [Fred. no. 102]	fl, hpd	Forberg (ed. Fischer); Heinrichshofen; Nagel
No. 3, c	fl, hpd	Forberg (ed. Fischer); Heinrichshofen (ed. Nagel)
No. 4, D	fl, hpd	Breitkopf (ed. Schroeder); Forberg (ed. Fischer)
No. 5, e	fl, hpd	Forberg (ed. Fischer)
Sonata, D	fl, hpd	Müller (ed. Sonntag)
Sonata [8], D [Fred. no. 219]	fl, hpd	Forberg (ed. Fischer)
Sonata, e [Fred. no. 234]	fl, hpd	Breitkopf (ed. Schreiter)
Sonata, F	fl, hpd, vc ad lib	Breitkopf (ed. Schroeder)
Sonata Andante, K. 47	2fl, bc	Fischer (ed. Fischer)
Triosonata, C, K. 2	rec/fl/vn, fl/vn, bc	Bärenreiter (ed. Birke)
Triosonata, G, K. 5	2fl, bc	Pegasus (ed. Sonntag)
Triosonata, G, K. 8	2fl/2vn/2ob, bc	Bärenreiter (ed. Ruf)
Triosonata, D, K. 11	fl, vn/fl/ob, bc	Breitkopf (ed. Schroeder)
Triosonata, D, K. 12	2fl/2vn/2ob, bc	Kistner (ed. Seiffert); Ricordi (ed. Ruf)
Triosonata, a, K. 21	2fl/2ob, bc	Möseler (ed. Koch)

Triosonata, e, K. 28	2fl, bc	Nova
Triosonata, c, K. 33	2fl, bc	Nova
Triosonata, c, K. 36	fl/vn, ob/fl/vn, bc	Zimmermann (ed. Blumenthal)
Triosonata, F, K. 38	va d'am/vn, fl, hpd, vc ad lib	Zimmermann (ed. Cor. Kint.)
Triosonata, c, K. 39	(fl, vn/va d'amore)/(fl/ob, 2fl,2vn), bc; vc ad lib	Schott (ed. Schultz-Hauser)
Triosonata, D, K. 42	2fl, bc	Pegasus (ed. Sonntag)
Triosonata, C, K. 43	rec/fl, vn/ob/ten rec, bc	Schott (Bergmann & Lefkovitch)
Trio [Sonata], D, K. 46	3fl/3vn	Billaudot; Eulenberg (ed. Delius); Forberg (ed. Fischer); International (ed. Wummer); Nagel (ed. Doflein)
Triosonata, b	fl, vn/fl, bc	Sikorski (ed. Pistorius)
Triosonata, c	fl, ob, bc	Kalmus
Triosonata, G	fl, ob d'am, bc	Heinrichshofen (ed. Ruf); Sikorski (ed. Friedrichsen & Jonsson)
28 Variations on "Ich schlief da träumte mir"	fl, bc	Breitkopf (ed. Nagel, cadenzas: Radeke)

RAMEAU, JEAN-PHILIPPE (1683–1764)

Pièces de clavecin en concerts: No. 1: La Coulicam, E♭; La Livri, c; Le Vezinet, C No. 2: La Laborde, G; La Boucon, g; L'agacante, G; 1er menuet, G; 2e menuet, g No. 3: La Poplinière, A; La timide, 1er rondeau, a; La timide, 2e rondeau, A; 1er tambourin, A; 2e tambourin, a No. 4: La pantomime, B♭; L'indiscrete, B♭; La Rameau, B♭ No. 5: La Forqueray, d; La Marais, D	hpd, vn/fl, viol/vn	Bärenreiter (ed. Jacobi) Bärenreiter (Urtext) Durand EMB (ed. Horusitzky) Salabert (ed. Peyrot & Rebufat)

ROUSSEAU, JEAN-JACQUES (1712–1778)		
Le printemps de Vivaldi [arr.]	fl	McGinnis & Marx (ed. Marx)
No. 1, Primavera		ALRY (ed. Preston)
SAMMARTINI, GIOVANNI BATTISTA (1700/01–1775)		
Concerto No. 1, F	fl, str/pf red	G. Schirmer (ed. Jenkins)
Sonata, A, op. 5, no. 9 [as Notturno a quatro, op. 9]	fl, 2vn, vc	Breitkopf (ed. Rhau)
Sonata, D, op. 5, no. 11	fl, 2vn, bc	Heinrichshofen (ed. Mönkemeyer)
Sonata, G	fl/rec/vn, bc	Noetzel (ed. Peters)
SAMMARTINI, GIUSEPPE (1695–1750)		
Concerto No. 1, F	ob/fl, orch	G. Schirmer (ed. Jenkins)
Concerto, F	rec, str, hpd/pf red	Schott (ed. Brinckmann)
12 Sonatas (F,F,G,F,F,d,F,F,G,F,F,B♭)	2rec/2vn, bc	Schott (ed. Giesbert)
Sonata, G, op. 13, no. 4	fl/vn/ob, bc	Schott (ed. Ruf)
SARRI, DOMENICO (1679–1744)		
Sonata, a	fl, str, bc	Leuckart (ed. Meylan)
SCARLATTI, ALESSANDRO (1660–1725)		
12 Sinfonie di concerto grosso		
No. 1, F	2fl/2rec, str, bc	Bärenreiter (ed. Meylan); Schott
No. 2, D	fl/rec, tpt, str, bc	Bärenreiter (ed. Meylan)
No. 3, d	fl/rec, str, bc	Schott (ed. Ring)
No. 4, e	fl, ob/vn, str, bc	Bärenreiter (ed. Meylan)
No. 5, d	2fl/2rec, str, bc	Bärenreiter (ed. Meylan)
Nos. 6–11 (a,g,G,g,a,c)	fl, str, bc	Peters
No. 6, a		Moeck
No. 12, c	fl, str, bc	Bärenreiter (ed. Meylan)
Sonata, A	2fl, 2vn, bc	Moeck

Sonata [Quartet], F	3fl, vc/bn ad lib	Peters (Urtext); Rieter-Biedermann (ed. Woehl)
Sonata, F	fl, 2vn, bc	Bisping (ed. Fellerer); Peters (ed. Woehl)
7 Sonatas (D,a,c,a,A,C,g)	fl, 2vn, bc	Casa Editrice Nazionalmusic
No. 4, a		Ricordi (ed. Casella)
Suite, F [as Sonata]	fl, bc	Müller (ed. Ewerhart)
Suite, G [as Sonata]	fl, bc	Müller (ed. Ewerhart)

SCHEIBE, JOHANN ADOLF (1708–1776)

Concert a4	fl, 2vn, pf	Moeck
Concerto, B♭	fl/rec/ob, bc	Dimit (ed. Hess)
3 Sonatas, D,b,A	hpd, fl	Moeck

SCHICKHARDT, JOHANN CHRISTIAN (ca.1682–before 1762)

Concerto, g	fl, str, 2ob, bc/pf red	Müller (ed. Brinckmann & Mohr)
6 Concerts (C,d,G,F,e,c)	4rec, bc	Bärenreiter (ed. Knab); Hinrichsen
6 Sonatas, op. 5	rec, 2ob/2vn, gamba, bc	
Nos. 1,3,6 (C,F,d)		Lienau (ed. Peter)
No. 2, D		Oxford (ed. Cooper)
6 Sonatas, op. 14	rec, ob/vn, gamba, bc	Lienau (ed. Peter)
12 Sonatas, op. 17	rec, bc	
No. 2, d		Doblinger (ed. Beechey)
No. 3, a		Oxford (ed. Platt)
Nos. 5,9,10,11 (B♭,g,F,f)		Musica Rara (ed. Everett)
No. 11, f		Galaxy (ed. Lasocki & Block)
No. 12, a		Schott
24 Sonatas, as L'alphabet de la musique, op. 30	rec/fl/vn, bc	Musica Rara (ed. Everett)
Nos. 4,7,16		Pelikan (ed. Erig)

Work	Instrumentation	Publisher
SCHULTZ, C. F.		
Concerto no. 3, G	fl, orch	Breitkopf
Rondo, F	fl, vn, va, vc	Breitkopf
STANLEY, JOHN (1712–1786)		
8 Solos, op. 1 (d,g,G,D,C,D,d,e)	fl/vn, bc	Concordia (ed. Boeringer); Oxford (ed. Caldwell); Peters (ed. Pratt)
6 Solos, op. 4 (a,e,G,b,D,D)	fl/vn, bc	Chester (ed. Pratt); Concordia (ed. Boeringer); Oxford (ed. Caldwell)
STÖLZEL, GOTTFRIED HEINRICH (1690–1749)		
Concerto, e	fl, ob, str	Sikorski (ed. Tessmer)
Concerto, F	vn, ob/fl, str, bc	Möseler (ed. Schroeder)
Concerto, e	fl, str, bc	Sikorski
Triosonata, D	fl, vn, bc	Sikorski (ed. Frotscher)
Triosonata, e	fl, vn, bc	Breitkopf (ed. Frotscher)
Triosonata, G	fl, vn, bc	Müller (ed. Hausswald)
Triosonata, G	2fl, bc	Sikorski (ed. Frotscher)
TARTINI, GIUSEPPE (1692–1770)		
Concerto, F	fl, pf red	International (ed. Rampal)
Concerto no. 1, G	fl, str, bc/kbd red	Sikorski (ed. Brinckmann)
Concerto no. 2, G	fl, str, bc	Sikorski (ed. Nagel)
6 Sonatas	2fl bc?	Zimmermann
2 Triosonatas, D	fl, vn, bc	Ed. Musicus (ed. Maganini)
TELEMANN, GEORG PHILIPP (1681–1767)		
Canonic sonatas, op. 5 (G,g,D,d,A,a)	2fl	Bärenreiter (ed. Hausswald); International (ed. Hermann); Möseler; Peters; Schott (ed. Richert); Weaner-Levant

Work	Scoring	Publisher
Concerto, a	fl, pf red	Bärenreiter
Concerto, C	rec, pf red	Moeck (ed. Hechler)
Concerto, c [MS: Darmstadt 1033/56]	ob/fl/vn, str, bc/pf red	Schott (ed. Schlövogt)
Concerto, D [MS: Schwerin 297]	fl/ob d'amore, str, bc/pf red	Leuckart (ed. Schroeder)
Concerto, D [MS: Stockholm]	fl, pf red	Sikorski (ed. Brinckmann & Mohr)
Concerto, D [MS: Darmstadt 6303]	fl, str, bc/pf red	Leuckart (ed. Hinnenthal)
Concerto, D [MS: Darmstadt 1033/39]	fl, str, bc/pf red	Eulenberg (ed. Schroeder)
Concerto, D	fl, pf red	International (ed. Rampal)
Concerto, e	fl, str, bc/pf red	Eulenberg (ed. Schroeder)
Concerto, e	fl, str, bc	Heinrichshofen
Concerto, F	rec, str	Bärenreiter (ed. Ruetz & Noack)
Concerto, G	fl, str, bc	Bärenreiter
Concerto, G	fl, pf red	International (ed. Rampal)
Concerto, A	2fl, str, bc/pf red	Hug (ed. Kölbel)
Concerto, a	2fl, str	Nagel (ed. Stein)
Concerto, C	2fl, str, bc	Vieweg
Concerto, D	2fl, str, bc	Pegasus (ed. Kölbel)
Concerto, D [MS: Darmstadt 1033/15]	2fl, str, bc	Sikorski (ed. Schroeder)
Concerto, e	2fl, pf red	G. Schirmer (ed. L. Moyse)
Concerto, e [MS: Darmstadt]	rec, fl, str	Bärenreiter (ed. Kölbel)
Concerto, B♭ [MS: Darmstadt]	2rec, str	Möseler (ed. A. Hoffmann)
	2rec, pf red	EMT (ed. Oubradous)
Concerto, e	fl, vn, str	Möseler (ed. A. Hoffmann)
Concerto, G [MS: Rostock]	ob d'am, fl, hpd	Litolff (ed. Havemann)
Concerto, F [MS: Darmstadt]	rec, bn, str	Möseler; Pegasus (ed. Hechler)
Concerto, a [MS: Darmstadt 1033/59]	rec, gamba, pf red	Moeck (ed. Händler)
Concerto, E	fl, ob d'am, va d'am, str/pf red	Peters

Concerto, B♭	2fl, 2ob, str, bc	Breitkopf (ed. Komma)
Concerto, F	rec, ob, 2hn, bn, str, bc	Eulenberg (ed. Schroeder)
Concerto, a	2rec/2fl, 2ob/2vn, 2vn, bc	Schott (ed. Hechler)
Concerto, F	2rec, 2ob, 2vn, bc	Schott (ed. Brüggen)
Concerto, F	ob/rec, vn, bc	Pegasus (ed. Hechler)
Concerto, G	fl, 2vn, bc	Bärenreiter (ed. Upmeyer)
Concerto a4, a [MS: Darmstadt 1033/6]	rec, ob, vn, bc	Moeck (ed. Hechler)
Concerto, a	rec, ob, vn, bc	Sikorski (ed. Töttcher & Grebe)
Concerto, a	fl, ob, vn, bc	International (ed. Rampal)
6 Concerts (D,g,A,e,b,a] and 6 Suites (G,B♭,b,E,a,d)	2fl, bc	Bärenreiter (ed. Hinnenthal)
Corellisierende Sonaten (F,A,b,E,g,D)	2vn/fl, bc	Bärenreiter (ed. Hoffmann); Nagel (ed. Hoffmann)
6 Duets (G,a,G,e,A,E)	2fl	Bärenreiter (ed. Hausswald)
Essercizii musici		
Solo [Sonata] no. 2, D	fl, bc	Nagel (ed. Upmeyer)
Sonatas nos. 4,10, d, C	rec, bc	Peters (ed. Woehl)
Sonata, F	rec, bc	Nagel (ed. Dohrn)
Sonatas, B♭,e,D,G (no. 8, G)	fl/ob/vn, bc	Schott (ed. Ruf)
Trio Sonata no. 4, A	fl, hpd, bc	Schott (ed. Ruf); Sikorski (ed. Scheurich & Braun)
Trio Sonata no. 5, a	rec/fl/vn, vn, bc	Peters (ed. Woehl)
Trio Sonata no. 7, F	fl/rec, gamba, bc	Nagel (ed. Upmeyer)
Trio Sonata no. 8, B♭	rec/fl/vn, hpd, bc	Bärenreiter (ed. Ruetz); Pelikan (ed. Ruf)
Trio Sonata no. 9, E	fl, vn, bc	Nagel (ed. Ermeler)
Trio Sonata no. 11	fl, ob/vn, bc	Bärenreiter (ed. Ruf)
Trio Sonata, a	fl/rec, vn, bc	Mercury (ed. Rikko & Mann)
Trio Sonata, b	fl, gamba, bc	Schott
Trio Sonata, c	rec/fl/vn, ob/vn, bc	Forberg; International; Peters (Urtext)
12 Fantaisies	fl	Bärenreiter (ed. Hausswald); Billaudot (ed. Larrieu); Boonin; International (ed. Rampal); Leduc (ed. Veilhan); Peters (ed. Thiemann); G. Schirmer (ed. L. Moyse); Southern (ed. Cole)

Der Getreue Music-Meister	misc.	Bärenreiter (ed. Degen)
Duet, A	fl, gamba	Schott (ed. Delius)
Duet, G	fl, vn	International; Nagel (ed. Ermeler)
4 Sonatas (F,B♭,f,C)	rec, bc	Amadeus; Bärenreiter (ed. Degen); Musica Rara; Nagel (ed. Degen); Peters (ed. Gerdes); Schott (ed. Bergmann)
Sonatas (B♭,e,D,G)	fl, bc	Schott (ed. Ruf)
Sonata, a	fl, bc	Musikhaus Pan
Sonatas, a, g	vn/fl/ob, bc	Bärenreiter (ed. Degen)
Sonata, b	rec, bc	Bärenreiter (ed. Degen)
Sonata, C	rec, bc	Peters (ed. Degen); Peters (Urtext); Schott (ed. Bergmann & Hunt)
Sonata, F	rec, bc	Broekmans; Hargail (ed. Mirsky); Haslinger (ed. Guericke); Heugel (ed. Sanvoisin); International (ed. Dohrn); Nagel (ed. Dohrn); Reinhardt; G. Schirmer; Schott (ed. Bergmann & Hunt)
Sonata, f	rec, bc	Doblinger (ed. Staeps); Schott (ed. Kneihs)
Sonata, B♭	2fl	Bärenreiter
Sonata, G	fl/ob/vn, vn/va	Bärenreiter (ed. Degen)
Spielstücke: L'hiver, Air Trompette, Niaise, Napolitana	vn/fl/ob, bc	Bärenreiter (ed. Degen)
Spielstücke: Polonoise, Pastourelle, Capriccio, Pastorale	fl/rec, bc	Bärenreiter (ed. Degen)
Triosonata, C	2rec/2vn/2fl, bc	Bärenreiter (ed. Degen)
Heldenmusik	fl, bc	Bärenreiter; Lienau (ed. Pätzold)
Eine Kammermusik, Concerto di camera, F	rec/fl/ob, 2vn, bc	Schott (ed. Friedrich)
Die Kleine Kammer-Music: 6 Partitas (B♭,G,c,g,e,E♭)	vn/fl/ob/rec, bc	Bärenreiter (ed. Woehl); Forberg (Urtext; ed. Lauschmann)
Partita no. 2, G	rec, pf	Schott (ed. Bergmann)

Work	Instrumentation	Publisher
Partita no. 3, c	rec, pf	Faber
Partita no. 4, g	rec, pf	Schott (ed. Bergmann)
12 Methodical Sonatas		
Nos. 1–6 (C,c,D,d,E,e)	vn/fl, bc	Bärenreiter (ed. Seiffert)
No. 2, c	vn/fl, bc	Kistner
Nos. 7–12 (G,g,A,a,b,B♭)	fl/vn, bc	Bärenreiter (ed. Seiffert)
Ouverture [Suite], e	fl, str, bc	Sikorski (ed. Winschermann)
6 Quatuors ou trios (D,e,A,G,a,E)	2fl/2vn, 2vc/2bn	Bärenreiter (ed. Ruhnke)
Quadri [Paris Quartets nos. 1–6]: Concerto no. 1, G; Concerto no. 2, D; Sonata no. 1, A, Sonata no. 2, g; Suite no. 1, e; Suite no. 2, b	vn, fl, gamba/vc, bc	Bärenreiter (ed. Bergmann)
No. 1, G		Sikorski (ed. Grebe)
No. 2, D		Schott (ed. Richter)
No. 3, A		Schott (ed. Richter)
No. 4, b		Nagel (ed. Dohrn)
Nouveau Quatuors [Paris Quartets nos. 7–12] (D,a,G,b,A,e)	fl, vn, vc, bc	Bärenreiter (ed. Bergmann)
Nos. 4,6 (b,e)		Nagel (ed. Dohrn)
Quartet, A	fl, vn, va, bass	Foetisch (ed. Crussard)
Quartet, G [MS: Darmstadt 1042/90]	fl, vn, va, bc	Sikorski (ed. Kölbel & Grebe)
Quartet, G	rec, ob, vn, bc	Peters (ed. Woehl)
Scherzi melodichi	2 insts, bc	Bärenreiter (ed. Hoffmann)
Sinfonia, F	rec, gamba, str	Schott (ed. Hofmann)
Sonatas, op. 2 (G,e,D,b,A,E)	2fl/2vn	Bärenreiter (ed. Hausswald); Billaudot; Broekmans; International (ed. Rampal); Kallmeyer (ed. Budde); Mitteldeutscher (ed. Linde von Winterfeld); Möseler (ed. Budde); G. Schirmer (ed. L. Moyse)
[corrected to Nos. 2,1,4,5,6,3 of orig. ed.]		Weaner-Levant (ed. Rikko)
No. 1, D		Armstrong (ed. Baron in *Duets for Flute*)
No. 5, e [i.e. no. 4]		Sikorski (ed. Ruf)

Sonata, A	2fl, bc	Breitkopf (ed. Schreiter)
Sonata, a	fl, ob, bc	International (ed. Woehl & Lyman)
Sonata, c	fl, gamba, bass	Hänssler (ed. Braun)
Sonata, c	rec, ob, bc	International (ed. Woehl & Lyman)
Sonata, D	fl, vn, va, bass	Foetisch (ed. Crussard)
Suite, a	fl, str	Eulenberg (ed. Büttner)
	fl, str/pf red	G. Schirmer (ed. L. Moyse)
	fl, pf red	EMT (ed. Oubradous); Hinrichsen (ed. Salter); International (ed. Rampal); Schott (ed. Hunt); Southern (ed. Wummer)
Suites, F, c	rec/fl, bc/(3vn, bc); hpd ad lib	Bärenreiter (ed. Mönkemeyer)
Tafelmusik [Musique de Table]		Bärenreiter (ed. Seiffert & Moser)
Prod. 1, no. 1: Suite [Ouverture], e	2fl, str, bc	Chappell (ed. Young); Sikorski (ed. Winschermann)
	2fl, str, bc/pf red	Schott (ed. Nagy)
Prod. 1, no. 2: Quatuor, G	fl, vn, ob, bc	Sikorski (ed. Töttcher & Grebe)
Prod. 1, no. 3: Concerto, A	fl, vn, str	Bärenreiter (ed. Hinnenthal)
Prod. 1, no. 5: Solo, b	fl, bc	Breitkopf (ed. Seiffert); Chester (ed. Silver); International (ed. Rampal)
Prod. 2, no. 2: Quatuor, d	(2fl, rec)/3fl, bc	Breitkopf
Prod. 2, no. 4: Trio, e	fl, ob, bc	Breitkopf (ed. Seiffert)
Prod. 3, no. 2: Quatuor, e	vn, fl, vc	Breitkopf (ed. Seiffert); Eulenberg; Nagel
Prod. 3, no. 4: Trio, D	2fl, bc	Breitkopf (ed. Moser); Breitkopf (ed. Seiffert)
3 Trietti methodici e 3 Scherzi	2insts, bc	Breitkopf (ed. Schneider)
6 Triosonatas, 1718		
No. 2, a	rec, vn, bc	Peters (Urtext, ed. Schultz-Hauser)
No. 3, G	fl, vn, bc	Peters (Urtext, ed. Schultz-Hauser)
Triosonata, a [MS: Darmstadt 1042/84]	rec, ob, bc	Hänssler (ed. Braun); Pegasus (ed. Ruf) Schott (ed. Ruf)

Triosonata, a [MS: Darmstadt 1042/87]	fl, gamba, bc	Pegasus (ed. Ruf)
Triosonata, a	fl, ob, pf	International (ed. Lyman)
Triosonata, B♭	ob/fl, vn, bc	Bärenreiter (ed. Ruf)
Triosonata, b, no. 72 [MS: Darmstadt 1042/72]	vn/fl, va, bc	Amadeus (ed. Drüner)
Triosonata, C	rec, discant viol/rec/fl/ ob/vn, bc	Pelikan (ed. Ruf)
Triosonata, C [MS: Darmstadt]	rec, vn/rec, bc	Breitkopf (ed. A. Hoffmann)
Triosonata, c [MS: Darmstadt 1042/79]	rec, ob, bc	Bärenreiter (ed. K. Hofmann)
Triosonata, c	fl,ob/2vn, pf	International (ed. Lyman)
Triosonata, D [MS: Darmstadt 1042/62]	fl, vn, bc	Ama (ed. Pauler/Hess)
Triosonata, D [MS: Darmstadt 1042/82]	fl, vn, bc	Ama (ed. Pauler/Hess)
Triosonata, d [MS: Brussels V.7117]	rec, vn, bc	Moeck (ed. Hechler)
Triosonata, d [MS: Darmstadt]	rec/fl, vn/ob, bc	Schott (ed. Ruetz)
Triosonata, d	fl, ob/vn, bc	Bärenreiter (ed. Hofmann)
Triosonata, E♭	fl, vn, bc	International
Triosonata, e	fl, ob, bc	Kalmus
Triosonata, e [MS: Darmstadt] number?	fl, vn, bc	Peters (ed. Kölbel)
Triosonata, e	rec/fl/vn, ob/fl/vn, bc	Bärenreiter (ed. Ruetz)
Triosonata, e [MS: Darmstadt 1042/39]	fl, vn,bc	Amadeus
Triosonata, F [MS: Darmstadt 1042/70]	rec, ob/vn, bc	Bärenreiter (ed. K. Hofmann)
Triosonata, F [MS: Darmstadt]	2 rec, bc	Breitkopf (ed. A. Hoffmann)
Triosonata, F, no. 32 [MS: Darmstadt 1042/32]	2rec/2fl, bc	Amadeus (ed. Hess)
Triosonata, F	rec, ob/vn, bc	Pelikan (ed. Ruf)
Triosonata, G [MS: Dresden 2392/Q27]	fl, vn, bc	Sikorski (ed. Grebe)
Triosonata, g [MS: Darmstadt]	rec/fl, vn/ob, bc	Schott (ed. Ruetz)

TESSARINI, CARLO (ca.1690–after 1766)

Sonata, C	fl, bc	Vogel
Sonata, D	fl, bc	Zimmermann
Sonata, F	fl, bc	Bärenreiter

Work	Instrumentation	Publisher
TROTT, LAURENCE (arr.)		
The Bird Fancyer's Delight	picc	Alry
VERACINI, FRANCESCO MARIA (1690–1768)		
12 Sonatas (F,G,d,B♭,C,a,c,F,g,d,F,c)	vn/rec, bc	Peters (ed. Kolneder)
Nos. 1–3 (F,G,d)		Bärenreiter (ed. Bär)
Nos. 1,2 (F,G)		Breitkopf (ed. Paumgartner); Rudall, Carte (ed. Paumgartner)
No. 1, F		Zanibon (ed. Ricci)
No. 2, G		Hargail (ed. Brüggen)
[as Sonata da camera, op. 3, no. 2]		Chester (ed. Polnauer)
VINCI, LEONARDO (ca.1690–1730)		
Sonatas Nos. 1, 2 (D,G)	fl/vn, bc	Bärenreiter (ed. Bopp); Berben; Reinhardt (ed. Bopp)
Sonata, D		Leduc; Oxford
Sonata, G		Billaudot (ed. Paubon); Kalmus
VIVALDI, ANTONIO (1678–1741)		
Chamber concerto, g, P. 402; F. XII,4	rec, ob, bn, bc	EMB (ed. Oubradous); Hargail; International (ed. Rampal); Moeck; Schott (ed. Palfalvi)
Chamber concerto, g, F. XII,5 "La notte"	fl/vn, 2vn, bn, bc	Musica Rara
Chamber concerto, g, P. 360, F. XII,6	fl, ob, vn, bn, bc	Musica Rara
Chamber concerto, D, P. 198; F. XII,7	rec, vn, bn/vc	McGinnis & Marx
Chamber concerto, g, P. 404; F. XII,8	fl, vn, bn, bc	International; Musica Rara
Chamber concerto, D, F. XII,9 "Il Cardellino"	fl/vn, ob/vn, vn, bn/vc/bc	Musica Rara
Chamber concerto, a, P. 77; F. XII,11	rec, 2vn, bc	Moeck (ed. Schroeder); Schott (ed. Ruf)
Chamber concerto, g, P. 403; F. XII,20	rec, ob, vn, bn, bc	International
Chamber concerto, C, P. 82; F. XII,24	fl, ob, vn, bn, bc	Musica Rara
Chamber concerto, D, P. 207; F. XII,25	rec, ob, bn, bc	Musica Rara

Work	Scoring	Publisher
Chamber concerto, F, P. 323; F. XII,26	fl, ob, vn, bn, bc	Musica Rara
Chamber concerto, D, P. 206; F. XII,27	fl, vn, bn, bc	International
Chamber concerto, D, P. 204; F. XII,29	rec/vn, ob/vn, vn, bn/vc, bc	Musica Rara; Noetzel (ed. Schroeder)
Chamber concerto, C, P.81; F.XII,30	rec, ob, 2vn, bc	Musica Rara
Chamber concerto, d, P.6/7; F.XII,42	fl, vn, bn, bc	Musica Rara
Concertos, op. 10		
No. 1, F, P. 261; F. VI,12 "La tempesta da mare"	fl, str, bc	Ricordi
	fl, str, bc/pf red	Schott (ed. Fortner)
	fl, pf red	EMB (ed. Balla); International (ed. Rampal)
No. 2, g, P. 342; F. VI,13 "La notte"	fl, str, bc	Ricordi
	fl, str, bc/pf red	EMT (ed. Oubradous)
	fl, pf red	International (ed. Rampal); Schott
No. 3, D, P. 155; F. VI,14 "Il Cardellino"	fl, str, bc/pf red	Eulenberg (ed. Einstein); Kalmus; Ricordi
	fl, pf red	AMP; Boosey; EMT (ed. Kovacs); International (ed. Rampal); Schott (ed. Fortner & Kolneder)
No. 4, G, P. 104; F. VI,15	fl, str, bc	Ricordi
	fl, pf red	International (ed. Rampal); Schott
No. 5, F, P. 262; F. VI,1	fl, str, bc/pf red	Ricordi (ed. Smith-Kardt)
	fl, pf red	Columbo (ed. Smith); International (ed. Rampal); Schott
No.6, G, P. 105; F. VI,16	fl, str, bc	Ricordi
	fl, pf red	International (ed. Rampal); Schott
Concerto, D, P. 203; F. VI,3	fl, str, pf red	International (ed. Rampal)
Concerto, G, P. 118; F. VI,6	fl, str, bc/pf red	Ricordi (ed. Malipiero)
	fl, pf red	International (ed. Rampal)
Concerto, a, P. 80; F. VI,7	fl, str, bc	Ricordi
	fl, str, pf red	International (ed. Rampal)
Concerto, G, P. 140; F. VI,8	fl, str, bc/pf red	Ricordi (ed. Malipiero)
	fl, pf red	International (ed. Rampal); Schott (ed. Kovacs)

Concerto, D, P. 205; F. VI,10	fl, str, bc/pf red	Eulenberg (ed. Braun); Ricordi
	fl, pf red	Colombo; International (ed. Rampal)
Concerto, c, P. 440; F. VI,11	rec, str, bc/pf red	Eulenberg; Musica Rara
	fl, pf red	EMB (ed. Hartai & Nagy); International (ed. Rampal)
Concerto, C, P. 79; F. VI,4	flautino, str, bc/pf red	Eulenberg (ed. Schroeder & Siefer); Ricordi (ed. Malipiero); Schott (ed. Linde)
	flautino, pf red	Broekmans; Colombo (ed. Baron); International (ed. Rampal)
Concerto, C, P. 78; F. VI,6	flautino, str, bc	Musica Rara; Ricordi
	flautino, str, bc/pf red	EMT (ed. Oubradous)
	flautino, pf red	Billaudot; International (ed. Rampal); McGinnis & Marx (ed. Arbatsky)
Concerto, a, P. 83; F. VI,9	flautino, str, bc	Musica Rara
	flautino, str, bc/pf red	Ricordi (ed. Malipiero)
	flautino, str, pf red	Armstrong (ed. Barone); Billaudot; Boosey (ed. Nagy); EMB (ed. Magy); International (ed. Rampal)
Concerto, C, P. 76; F. VI,2	2fl, str, bc/pf red	EMT (ed. Oubradous); International (ed. Rampal)
	2fl, pf red	Billaudot; Eulenberg
Concerto, F, F.XII,28 "La tempesta da mare"	fl, ob, bn; str, bc	Eulenberg; Schott
Sonatas from "Il pastor fido," op. 13 (no. 1, C, P. 3/9; no. 3, G, P. 4/3; no. 4, A, P. 4/2; no. 5, C, P. 4/3; no. 6, g, P. 4/4; no. 12, C, P. 3/10)	fl/rec/ob/vn, bc	Bärenreiter (ed. Upmeyer); International (ed. Rampal); Southern (ed. Wye)
No. 6, g, P. 4/4		McGinnis & Marx (ed. Marx)
Sonata, C, F. XV,3	fl, bc	Berben; Chester (ed. Silver); International (ed. Rampal); Noetzel (ed. Nagel); Ricordi

Sonata, F, P. 7/11; F. XV,4	rec, bc	Broekmans (ed. Brüggen); Fischer; International (ed. Rampal); Müller (ed. Kolneder); Ricordi; Schott
Sonata, d, P. 7/9; F. XV,5	fl, bc	Harmonia-Uitgrave; International (ed. Rampal); Müller; Noetzel (ed. Nagel); Ricordi; Schott (ed. Nagel)
Sonata, e, F. XV,6 [Stockholm]	fl, bc	Musica Rara (ed. Lasocki)
Sonata, g	fl, bc	McGinnis & Marx; Schott
Triosonata, a, P. 7/8, F. XV,1	rec, bn, bc	Musica Rara; Noetzel
Triosonata, D, P. 6/5; F. XII,43	fl, vn, bc	Möseler (ed. Nagel); Musica Rara; Ricordi; Schott (ed. Fussan)

WOODCOCK, ROBERT (late 17c.–by 1734)

Concerto no. 2, A	fl, vns, vc, hpd	NYPL (ed. Beck & Mann)

B. THE CLASSIC ERA

ABEL, CARL FRIEDRICH (1723–1787)

Concerto, C, K. 51	fl, str, bc/pf red	Pegasus (ed. Peters)
Concerto, C, op. 6, no. 6	fl, orch	Noetzel
6 Easy Sonatas, K.141-146	gamba/vn/fl, bc	
Nos. 1,2,5 (C,A,A)		Bärenreiter (ed. Woehl)
Nos. 3,4,6 (e,D,G)		Bärenreiter (ed. Bacher)
Quartet, G, op. 12, no. 6	fl, vn, va, vc	Schott (ed. Hunt)
Quartet, A, op. 12, no. 2, K. 68	fl, vn, va, vc	International; Musica Rara
Sonata, C, op. 2, no. 1, K. 111	hpd, vn/fl	Pegasus (ed. Sonntag)
Sonata, D, op. 2, no. 3, K. 113	hpd, vn/fl	Pegasus (ed. Sonntag)

Sonata, F, op. 2	hpd, vn/fl	Pegasus (ed. Sonntag)
6 Sonatas, op. 5, K. 117-122	hpd, vn/fl, vc	Heuwekemeijer
Sonatas, op. 6	fl, bc	Amadeus (ed. Pauler/Hess)
No. 1, C	fl, bc	Nova (ed. Beechey)
No. 2, K. 124	fl, bc	Schott (ed. Ruf)
No. 3, e, K. 125	fl, bc	Oxford (ed. Beechey); Schott (ed. Ruf)
No. 6, G, K. 128	fl, bc	Bärenreiter (ed. Beechey)
Trio, G, op. 16, no. 1, K 98	2fl, bc	Pegasus (ed. Sonntag)
Trio, C, op. 16, no. 4, K 101	2fl, bc	Pegasus (ed. Sonntag)
Trio Sonata, c	fl, vn, bc	Zimmerman (ed. Kölbel)

BACH, CARL PHILIFP EMANUEL (1714–1788)

Concerto, d, Wq. 22	fl, str/pf red	International (ed. Rampal); Leuckart (ed. Redel)
	fl, pf red	Musica Rara (ed. Nagy)
Concerto, a, Wq. 166	fl, str	Eulenberg
Concerto, B♭, Wq. 167	fl, str/pf red	International (ed. Rampal); Musica Rara
Concerto, A, Wq. 168	fl, str/pf red	Eulenberg (ed. Kneihs); International (ed. Rampal)
Concerto, G, Wq. 169	fl, str/pf red	International (ed. Rampal); Musica Rara (ed. Lasocki)
Duett, e, Wq. 140	fl, vn	Mercury (ed. Marx); Nagel (ed. Stephan)
Duetto, E, Wq. 84	hpd, fl	Breitkopf (ed. Walther)
12 Kleine Stücke mit 2 und 3 stimmen, Wq. 81	fl/vn, hpd; 2fl/2vn, hpd	Kalmus; Vieweg (ed. Oberdörffer); Zimmermann (ed. Walther)
12 2- und 3-stimmige kleine Stücke, Wq. 82	fl/vn, hpd; 2fl/2vn, hpd	Breslauer (ed. Hohenemser)
	2fl, hpd	Mitteldeutscher (ed. Johnen & Wierejewski); Vieweg
3 Quartets, Wq. 93-95 (a,D,G)	hpd, fl, va, vc	Bärenreiter (ed. Schmid); Nagel (ed. Schmid)
Sonatas, Wq. 83-86 (D,E,G,G)	fl, cemb	Breitkopf (ed. Braun/Petrenz)
Sonata, D, Wq. 83 [with Wq. 84-5]	hpd, fl	Breitkopf (ed. Walther); Ricordi (ed. Scheck & Ruf)

Sonata, G, Wq. 85	hpd, fl	Breitkopf (ed. Walther); Ricordi (ed. Scheck & Ruf)
Sonata, G, Wq. 86	hpd, fl	Breitkopf (ed. Walther)
Sonata, C, Wq. 87	hpd, fl	Fischer; International (ed. Rampal); Ricordi (ed. Scheck & Ruf); Zimmermann (ed. Walther)
7 Sonatas, Wq. 123-129 (G,e,B♭,D,G,a,D)	fl, bc	
Sonatas Wq. 123-125,128,129 (G,e,B♭,a,D)		Edu-Tainment (ed. Baron)
Sonatas, Wq. 123,124,128 (G,e,a)		Bärenreiter (ed. Walther; Kalmus
Sonatas, Wq. 125,126 (B♭,D)		Zimmermann (ed. Walther)
Sonatas, Wq. 125,127,129 (B♭,G,D)		Ricordi (ed. Scheck & Ruf)
Sonatas, Wq. 127,129 (G,D)		Zimmermann (ed. Walther)
Sonata, B♭, Wq. 130	fl, bc	Zimmermann (ed. Walther)
Sonata, D, Wq. 131	fl, bc	Bärenreiter (ed. Walther); Kalmus
Sonata, a, Wq. 132	fl	Amadeus (ed. Teske); Billaudot (ed. Paubon); Edu-Tainment (ed. Baron); Fischer (ed. Wittgenstein); Hofmeister (ed. Niggemann); Hofmeister (ed. Siber); International (ed. Wummer); Ricordi (ed. Scheck & Ruf); G. Schirmer (ed. L. Moyse); Simrock (ed. Kurth); Universal; Zimmermann (ed. Richter)
Sonata, G, Wq. 133 "Hamburger"	fl, bc	Bärenreiter (ed. Schmitz); Ricordi (ed. Ruf); Schott (ed. Walther)
Sonata, G, Wq.134	fl, bc	Zimmermann (ed. Walther)
Sonata, b, Wq.143	fl, vn, bc	Peters (ed. Ermeler); Zimmermann
Sonata, G, Wq.144	fl, vn, bc	Broekmans; Zimmermann (ed. Walther)
Sonata, d, Wq.145	fl, vn, bc	Nagel (ed. Keller)
Sonata, C, Wq.147	fl, vn, bc	Bärenreiter (ed. Ruf); Zimmermann (ed. Richter)
Sonata, a, Wq.148	fl, vn, bc	Zimmermann (ed. Walther)
Sonata, D, Wq.151	fl, vn, bc	Hänssler (ed. Braun); Zimmermann (ed. Walther)
Sonata, B♭, Wq.161/2	fl, bc	Kalmus; Musica Rara; Nova; Zimmermann (ed. Lorenz)
Sonatina I, C, Wq.106	hpd, 2fl, str	Bote & Bock (ed. Dameck); Breitkopf

Sonatina II, d, Wq.107	hpd, 2 fl, str	Bärenreiter (ed. Oberdörffer)
Sonatina, E♭, Wq.105/108	hpd, 2fl, str	Bärenreiter (ed. Oberdörffer)
Trio, E, Wq.162	2fl, bc	Kalmus; Zimmermann (ed. Walther)
BACH, JOHANN CHRISTIAN (1735–1782)		
Concerted symphony, C	fl, ob, vn, vc; orch	Eulenberg; Schott (ed. Maunder)
Concerto, D	fl, 2hn, str/pf red	Universal (ed. Meylan)
6 Quartettos, op. 8 (C,D,E♭,F,G,B♭)	fl, vn, va, vc	
Nos. 1, 3, 5 (C,E♭,G)		Bärenreiter (ed. Küster & Glöder)
No. 1, C		Bote & Bock (ed. Dameck)
No. 2, D		Musica Rara (ed. Sadie)
No. 3, E♭		Müller (ed. Janetsky); Schott (ed. Nagel)
No. 4, F		Nagel (ed. Hillemann)
No. 5, G [as no. 2]		Möseler (ed. Nagel)
No. 6, B♭ [as no. 5]		Möseler (ed. Nagel)
4 Quartettos, op. 19 (C,D,G,C)	2 for 2fl, va, vc; 1 for 2fl, vn,vc; 1 for fl, ob/fl, va, vc	Kistner
No. 1, C	2fl, va, vc	Novello
Nos. 1, 3 (C,G)	2fl, va/vn, vc	Musica Rara (ed. Sadie)
No. 2, D [as op. 20, no. 2]	2fl, va, vc	Bärenreiter (ed. Ermeler)
3 Quartets, D,C,A [nos. 1, 3, 5 in *Six Quartettos ... by Messrs. Bach, Abel and Giardini*, 1776]	fl/vn,vn,va,bc	Musica Rara (ed. Sadie)
6 Quintettos, op. 11 (C,G,F,E♭,A,D)	fl, ob, vn, va, bc	
Nos. 1, 2, 3, 5 (C,G,F,A)		Musica Rara
Nos. 4, 6 (E♭,D)		Nagel
No. 6, D		Nagel (ed. Steglich)
Quintette, D, op. 22, no. 1	fl, ob, vn, bc, hpd/pf	Bärenreiter (ed. Ermeler)

Sonata, F [also attrib. C.P.E. Bach and W.F. Bach]	hpd, fl	Moeck (ed. Maguerre)
Sonata, G, op. 2, no. 3	hpd, vn/fl	Bärenreiter
6 Sonatas, op. 16 (D,G,C,A,D,F)	hpf/pf, vn/fl	Pegasus (facsimile ed.); Zimmermann
No. 5, D		Pegasus (ed. Ermeler)
No. 6, F		Breitkopf (ed. Hinnenthal)
Nos. 1, 2, 4 (D,G,A)		Nagel (ed. Küster)
Sonata, C, op. 18, no. 1	hpd/pf, vn/fl	Hansen
3 Sonatas, op. 19, nos. 1, 2, 6 (C,G,B♭) [doubtful or spurious]	fl, pf	Bärenreiter (ed. Dingfelder)
Triosonata, B♭ [doubtful or spurious]	fl, vn, bc	Hug (ed. Kölbel); Müller (ed. Nagel)
Trio sonata, G	2fl/(fl,vn), bc	Müller (ed. Nagel)
Trio, C	fl, fl/vn, vc/bc	Möseler (ed. Nagel)
BACH, JOHANN CHRISTOPH FRIEDRICH (1732–1795)		
Concerto, D	fl, orch/pf red	Universal (ed. Meylan)
6 Quartets, HW VI (D,G,C,A,F,B♭)	fl, vn, va, b	Zimmermann (ed. Kölbel)
Nos. 1, 4, 6 (D,A,B♭)		Ricordi (ed. Scheck & Ruf)
No. 1, D [as Sonata]	fl, vn, va, vc, hpd	Bärenreiter
Sonata, C	fl/vn, pf	Schott (ed. Ruf)
6 Sonatas (d,D,D,C,A,C)	fl/vn, kbd	Schott (ed. Ruf)
6 Sonatas (D,G,C,A,F,B♭)	fl, hpd	Zimmermann (ed. Schwedler & Wittenbecher)
Sonata no. 1, F [from 8 Sonatas] HW VIII	kbd, fl/vn	Breitkopf (ed. Hinnenthal)
7 Trios, HW VII/1-7		
Sonata, A	fl, vn, bc	Sikorski (ed. Frotscher)
Sonata, C	fl, vn, hpd	Schott (ed. Nagel)
Sonata no. 4, D	hpd, fl/vn, vc	Kistner; Nagel (ed. Ruf)
Sonata no. 7, C	hpd/pf, fl, vn	Kistner

Work	Instrumentation	Editions
BACH, WILHELM FRIEDEMANN (1710–1784)		
6 Duets (e,E♭,E♭,F,f,G), op. 54-59	2fl	Breitkopf (ed. Braun); Breitkopf (ed. Walther); International (ed. Wummer); Kalmus
Sonatas, e,f, op. 54, 58		Bärenreiter (ed. Rodemann)
Sonata, E♭, op. 55		International (ed. Glöder); Nagel (ed. Glöder)
Sinfonia, d	2fl, str	Eulenberg (ed. Lebermann); McGinnis & Marx
[as Adagio und Fuge]		Schott (ed. Lebermann)
4 Trio sonatas (D,D,a[frag],B♭)	2fl, bc	Breitkopf (ed. Seiffert); International (ed. Seiffert); Wünderhorn (ed. Tillmetz & Schittler)
No.1, D		Amadeus; Kalmus; Zimmermann (ed. van Leeuwen)
No. 2, D		Amadeus
No. 3, a		Amadeus; Kalmus
BEETHOVEN, LUDWIG VAN (1770–1827)		
Allegro and Minuet, G, Wo.O. 26	2fl	Breitkopf; EMB; Ed. Musicus (ed. Maganini); International (ed. Wummer); Kalmus; Zimmermann (ed. Walther)
6 National Airs with Variations, op. 105	pf, fl/vn	Breitkopf; EMB (ed. Jeney); Peters (Urtext, ed. Hauschild); Schott & Universal (ed. Jarecki)
Variations on Austrian & Scotch Airs		Southern (ed. Cavally)
10 National Airs with Variations, op. 107	pf, fl/vn	Breitkopf; EMB (ed. Jeney); Kalmus; Peters (Urtext, ed. Hauschild); Schott & Universal (ed. Jarecki)
Variations on Russian & Tyrolean Airs		Southern (ed. Cavally)
Romance cantabile [fragment]	pf, fl, bn, orch	Breitkopf (ed. Hess)
Serenade, D, op. 25	fl, vn, va	Eulenberg; Henle; International; Kalmus; Peters (ed. Hermann); Ricordi
Serenade, D, op. 41 [arr. of op. 25]	pf, fl/vn	Boosey (ed. Roth); Henle (ed. Gerlach); International (ed. Rampal); Peters (ed. Bartuzat)

Sonata, B♭, K. Anh. 4 [doubtful]	fl, pf	Billaudot; Breitkopf (ed. Hess); Fischer (ed. Laube); Henle (ed. Gerlack & Theobald); International (ed. Rampal); Kalmus; G. Schirmer (ed. L. Moyse); Zimmermann (ed. Richter); Zimmermann (ed. van Leeuwen)
Trio, G, Wo. O. 37	pf, fl, bn	Breitkopf (ed. Badura-Skoda); Henle (ed. Klugmann); International
BENDA, FRANZ (1709–1786)		
Concerto, e	fl, str/pf red	Schott (ed. Lebermann)
Sonata, C [by Franz or Georg Benda]	fl, bc	Hofmeister (ed. Janetsky)
Sonata, C	fl, bc	International (ed. Rampal)
Sonata, e	fl, bc	Hofmeister (ed. Janetsky)
Sonata, e	fl, bc	Supraphon/Artia (ed. Schoenbaum)
Sonata, F	fl, bc	International (ed. Munclinger)
Sonata, G, op. 3, no. 1	fl, hpd	Nagel (ed. Ruetz); Schott (ed. Ruf)
Trio, G	2fl, pf	International (ed. Rampal)
BENDA, GEORG (1722–1795)		
Sonatas, C, e	fl, bc	Hofmeister (ed. Janetsky)
Sonata, F	fl, bc	Ed. Musicus
Sonata, G, op. 3, no. 3 [listed as by Franz Benda]	fl, bc	Nagel
BERBIGUIER, BENOIT TRANQUILLE (1782–1838)		
7 Duets, op. 28	2fl	International
3 Duets, op. 32	fl, vn	Heuwekemeijer
6 Duets, op. 59	2fl	Ed. Musicus; International (ed. Boehme); Kalmus
3 Duos Concertants, op. 4	2fl	Heuwekemeijer
3 Duos Concertants, op. 11	2fl	Ed. Musicus
3 Duos Concertants, op. 22 (E,C,D)	2fl	Simrock

3 Duos Concertants, op. 46	2fl	Heuwekemeijer
3 Grands Duos Brillants, op. 38 (e,E♭,A)	2fl	Heuwekemeijer
3 Grands Trios, op. 40 (F,e,D)	3fl	Heuwekemeijer
Melodie Concertante: Les Regrets, op. 104	fl, pf	Heuwekemeijer
2 Petits Duos, op. 149	fl, vn	Ricordi
Souvenir de Tyrol, op. 103	fl, pf	Heuwekemeijer
Trios, op. 110	3fl	Ashdown
3 Trios Concertants, op. 51 (B♭,a,D)	3fl	Southern (ed. Weinandt)

BOCCHERINI, LUIGI (1743–1805)

Concerto, D, op. 27 [attrib. F.X. Pokorny]	fl, orch	Fischer; Nagel (ed. Upmeyer); Ricordi
	fl, orch/pf red	Kalmus;Southern (ed. van Leeuwen)
	fl, pf red	Bärenreiter (ed. Upmeyer); International (ed. Rampal); Leuckart (ed. Redel); Zanibon (ed. Pais)
Quartet, D, op. 5, no. 1	fl, vn, va, vc	International (ed. Rampal)
Quintet, D, op. 21, no. 1	fl, 2vn, va, vc	Benjamin; Musica Rara
Quintet, G, op. 21, no. 5	fl, 2vn, va, vc	Musica Rara
Quintet, E♭, op. 21, no. 6	fl, 2vn, va, vc	International (ed. Rampal); Musica Rara; Novello (ed. Haas)
Quintet, C [doubtful]	fl, ob, vn, va, vc	Musica Rara (ed. Janetsky)
Quintets, op. 45, nos. 1–3 (G,F,D)	fl/ob, 2vn, va, vc	Eulenberg (ed. Lebermann)
Quintets, op. 45, nos. 4–6 (A,E♭,d)	fl/ob, 2vn, va, vc	Sikorski (ed. Giegling)
Sextet (Nocturne), E♭, op. 42, no. 2	fl/ob, vn, va, bn, eh, db	Novello (ed. Haas); Sikorski (ed. Bormann)
Sextet, C, op. 15, no. 6 [G. 466]	fl, 2vn, va, 2vc	Oxford (ed. Solum)

BREVAL, JEAN-BAPTISTE SEBASTIEN (1753–1823)

Symphonie concertante, F, op. 31 [? arr. by Devienne of Breval's op. 30]	fl, bn, orch/pf red	Musica Rara

CAMBINI, GIUSEPPE MARIA (1746–1825)		
Duets, op. 11, nos. 4–6 (e,A,G)	2fl	Schott (ed. Lebermann)
Trio, op. 3, no. 6	2fl/(fl,vn), vc	Eulenberg (ed. Nagel)
3 Trios, op. 32	2fl, va	Schott (ed. Schultz-Hauser)
Trios, op. 45, nos. 1, 2	fl, ob, bn	Eulenberg
Trios nos. 5, 6 (F,A)	2fl/2vn, va	Schott (ed. Schultz-Hauser)
6 Trios concertants, op. 26, nos. 1–6	fl, vn, va	Nova
CAMPAGNOLI, BARTOLOMEO (1751–1827)		
Concerto no. 2, D	fl, orch/pf red	Pegasus (ed. Sonntag)
Duetti, op. 2, nos. 2–4 (A,D,C)	fl, vn	Zanibon (ed. Guglielmo & Carraro)
CANNABICH, CHRISTIAN (1731–1798)		
Concerto, D	fl, orch/pf red	Leuckart (ed. Peters)
Concerto, C	fl, ob, vn, orch	Eulenberg (ed. Päuler)
6 Duettos (G,A,e,C,D,D)	fl/vn, va	Simrock (ed. Höckner & Twarz)
Quartet, G, op. 1, no. 2	vn, fl, va, b	Pegasus (ed. Walther)
CIMAROSA, DOMENICO (1749–1801)		
Concerto, G	2fl, orch/pf red	Bote & Bock (ed. Wollheim); International (ed. Rampal); Southern (ed. L. Moyse)
[as Concertante]		EMT (ed. Oubradous)
Quartets Nos. 1,4,6 (D,F,a)	fl, vn, va, vc	Musica Rara (ed. Lenski)
CLEMENTI, MUZIO (1752–1832)		
3 Sonatas, op. 2, nos. 1,3,5 (D,F,G)	pf/hpd, fl/vn	Heuwekemeijer
No. 3, G		International (ed. Rampal)
Sonata, D, op. 22, no. 1	fl/vn, vc, pf/hpd	Müller (ed. Sauer, Harnest & Meier)

DANZI, FRANZ (1763–1826)		
Concertant, B♭, op. 41	fl, cl, orch	Hieber (ed. Adorjan)
Concerto no. 1, G, op. 30	fl, pf red	Heinrichshofen (ed. Anspacher)
Concerto no. 2, d, op. 31	fl, orch	Eulenberg (ed. Förster)
	fl, orch/pf red	Heinrichshofen (ed. Anspacher)
Concerto no. 3, d, op. 42	fl, orch/pf red	Müller (ed. Sonntag)
Concerto no. 4, D, op. 43	fl, orch/pf red	Eulenberg (ed. Förster)
3 Petits Duos, op. 64	fl, vc	Ama (ed. de Reede); Sikorski (ed. Sonntag)
Quartet, D, op. 56, no. 1	fl, vn, va, vc	Musica Rara
Quartet, d, op. 56, no. 2	fl, vn, va, vc	Pegasus (ed. Sonntag)
Quartet, F, op. 56, no. 3	fl, vn, va, vc	Zimmermann (ed. Eppel)
Sinfonia concertante, E♭	fl, ob, hn, bn, orch	Musica Rara (ed. Block); Schott (ed. Zirnbauer)
Sonatine, D	pf, fl	Hofmeister (ed. Niggemann); Schott (ed. Lebermann)
Sonatine, e, op. 34	pf, fl	Müller (ed. Draheim)
3 Trios, op. 71 (G,e,D)	fl, vn, vc	
No. 1, G		Noetzel
Nos. 1,2 (G,e)		International (ed. Rampal); Kalmus
Nos. 2,3 (e,D)		Müller (ed. Sonntag)
DeLUSSE, CHARLES (ca. 1720–?)		
12 Caprices	fl	Nova (ed. Lasocki)
DEVIENNE, FRANÇOIS (1759–1803)		
Air with [6] Variations, D	2fl	International
Concerto no. 1, D	fl, orch	Heugel (ed. Dudley)
	fl, pf red	Billaudot (ed. Paubon); EMB (ed. Szebenyi & Nagy)
Concerto no. 2, D	fl, orch/pf red	International (ed. Rampal)

Work	Instrumentation	Publisher
Concerto no. 4, G	fl, orch/pf red	Schott (ed. Szebenyi)
	fl, pf red	EMB (ed. Imre)
Concerto no. 5, G	fl, orch	Heugel (ed. Dudley)
Concerto no. 7, e	fl, orch/pf red	EMT (ed. Oubradous); International (ed. Rampal)
Concerto no. 8, G	fl, orch/pf red	Billaudot (ed. Paubon); EMB (ed. Szebenyi & Nagy)
Concerto no. 10, D	fl, orch/pf red	Billaudot (ed. Paubon)
Concerto in D, posthumous	fl, orch/pf red	Billaudot (ed. Paubon)
6 Duos, op. 1 (G,d/D,C,D,B♭,A)	2fl	Heuwekemeijer
3 Duos, op. 5, nos. 3–5	fl, va	Litolff (ed. Drüner)
6 Duos, op. 15 (a,D,G,C,G,F) [as op. 5]	2fl	Heuwekemeijer
6 Easy Duets, op. 18 (D,C,g/G,A,F,G)	2fl	Heinrichshofen
Nos. 4–6 (A,F,G)		Peters (ed. Nagel)
12 Duos, op. 75 (C,G,D,C,G,D,F,G,d,F,B♭,g/G)	2fl	Amadeus (ed. Pauler); Broekmans (ed. Barwahser)
6 Duets, No. [part] 2 (F,G,d,G,B♭,g)	2fl	Bärenreiter (ed. Baum)
6 Duettinos, op. 82 (D,G,D,G,D,D)	2fl	Broekmans; International; Kalmus; Peters (ed. Boehme)
6 Duos Concertants, op. 83 (D,a,D,G,e,D)	2fl	Hug; Kalmus
Quartet, G, op. 2, no. 1 [as op. 11, no. 1]	fl, vn, va, vc	Broekmans; Musica Rara (ed. Janetsky)
Sinfonie concertante, op. 76	2fl, orch/pf red	Musica Rara (ed. Lasocki)
6 Sonatas	fl, pf	Ed. Musicus; Kunzelmann; Southern (ed. Andraud)
Sonata, e, op. 53, no.1	fl, bc	International (ed. Rampal)
Sonatas, op. 58, nos. 1, 6 (e,E♭)	fl, pf	International
Sonatas, op. 68, livre 4 (D,G,C,A,e,D)	fl	Billaudot; Southern
Nos.1, 4, 5 (D,A,e)	fl, pf	International (ed. Rampal)
4 Sonatinas, lst series (D,F,G,d)	2fl, bn/vc ad lib	Heuwekemeijer
6 Trios, op. 1	3fl	Billaudot (ed. Rampal)
No. 2, D	3fl	Eulenberg (ed. Steinbeck); Kneusslin
No. 3, C	3fl	Eulenberg (ed. Steinbeck)
No. 5, g	3fl	Simrock (ed. Koch)
6 Trios, op. 19 [same as op. 66]	3fl	Billaudot; Heuwekemeijer; International (ed. Wummer)

Trios, op. 61, nos. 1–3 (G,B♭,d)	fl, cl, bn	Eulenberg (ed. Balassa)
Nos. 1, 2	fl, cl, bn	Eulenberg (ed. Meerwein)
No. 2, g	fl, cl, bn	Kneusslin (ed. Hess)
No. 3, a	fl, cl/vn, bn/vc	Litolff (ed. Meerwein)
Trio, E♭, op. 63	pf, fl, vc	Kunzelmann (ed. Delius)
Trio, g, op. 66, no. 2	fl, vn, vc	Kneusslin (ed. Hess)
Trio, F, op. 66, no. 5	3fl	Simrock
DITTERSDORF, CARL DITTERS VON (1739–1799)		
Cassation, D	4fl	Doblinger (ed. Steinbeck)
Concerto, e	fl, orch	Möseler (ed. Sonntag & Hoffmann)
Notturno	4fl	Berben (ed. Gatti); Schott (ed. Schültz-Hauser)
DUSSEK, JAN LADISLAV (1760–1812)		
Sonatinas, op. 20, nos. 1–5	pf, vn/fl	Litolff (ed. Köhler & Winkler)
Sonatinas, op. 46	pf, fl	Litolff
Trio, F, op. 65	fl, vc, pf	Musica Rara
EBERWEIN, TRAUGOTT MAXIMILIAN (1775–1831)		
Quartet No. 1, op. 71	fl, vn, va, vc	Hofmeister
FILTZ, ANTON (1733–1760)		
Concerto, D	fl, orch/pf red	Baärenreiter (ed. Kaslik & Suchy); Supraphon/Artia (ed. Kaslik & Suchy))
Sonatas, op. 2, nos. 3, 4 (G,D)	fl, vc, hpd	Pegasus (ed. Sonntag)
Triosonata, E♭	fl, vn, bc	Breitkopf

FISCHER, JOHANN CHRISTIAN (1733–1800)		
3 Divertimenti, op. 2	2fl	Ricordi (ed. Ruf)
FÜRSTENAU, CASPAR (1772–1819)		
3 Duets, op. 2	2fl	Heuwekemeijer
6 Duets, op. 37	fl, guit	Peters
6 Duets, op. 40 [arr. from piano sonatas]	2fl	Heuwekemeijer
12 Original Compositions, op. 35	fl, guit	Bärenreiter; Kalmus; Nagel (ed. Homann)
12 Pieces, op. 16	fl, guit	Breitkopf (ed. Nagel)
12 Pieces, op. 38	fl, guit	Schott (ed. Nagel)
Suite, op. 34	fl, guit	Zimmermann (ed. Behrend)
Suite, op. 35	fl, guit	Zimmermann (ed. Behrend)
GIANELLA, LOUIS (?1778–1817)		
3 Nocturnes, op. 28 (G,F,D)	2fl, vc/bn	Southern (ed. Weinandt)
Quartetto, G, op. 52	4fl	Ashdown; Universal (ed. Imbescheid)
2 Trios, op. 27	3fl	Universal (ed. Imbescheid)
GIORDANI, TOMMASO (ca.1733–1806)		
Quartet, D, op. 2, no. 5	fl, vn, va, vc	Broekmans; Musica Rara
Quartet, G, op. 3, no. 1	fl, vn, vc, pf/hpd	Musica Rara (ed. Sadie); Schott (ed. Ruf)
6 Trios, op. 12	fl, va, vc	Schott (ed. Schultz-Hauser)
GIULIANI, MAURO (1781–1829)		
Divertimento	fl, guit	Zimmermann (ed. Thomatos)
Easy Duo [Duettino facile], op. 77	gui, fl/vn	Schott (ed. Nagel); Simrock (ed. Hill); Zerboni (ed. Saldarelli); Zimmermann (ed. Wensiecki)
Gran duetto concertante, op. 52	gui, fl/vn	Ariel (ed. Noad); Belwin (ed. Segal & Ketchum); Schott (ed. Nagel); Sikorski
Grand Sonata [Grosse Sonate], op. 85	fl/vn, gui	Auriel (ed. Noad); Zimmermann (ed. Albert)

Grosse Serenade, D, op. 82	gui, fl/vn	Breitkopf (ed. Nagel); Sikorski
Qual mesto gemito [Quintet from Rossini's *Semiramide*]	fl/vn, gui	Zerboni (ed. Saldarelli)
Serenata, op. 127	fl/vn, gui	Zerboni (ed. Saldarelli)
Theme, Variations, and Menuet	fl, gui	Billaudot
GLUCK, CHRISTOPH WILLIBALD VON (1714–1787)		
Concerto, G [doubtful]	fl, orch/pf red	Hug (ed. Scherchen; cads. Wanausek)
	fl, pf red	Kalmus
Dance of the Blessed Spirits [Scène d'Orphée aux Champs Elysées from *Orfeo*]	fl, pf red	Breitkopf (ed. Haverkampf & Klengel); Fischer (ed. Brooke); Leduc (ed. Taffanel & Gaubert); Presser (ed. Anthony); Rubank (ed. Voxman); G. Schirmer (ed. Barrère); Schott; Southern (ed. Cavally); Universal (ed. Stolba); Zimmermann
Trio no. 2, g	2fl/2vn, bc	Music Press (ed. Einstein)
GOSSEC, FRANÇOIS-JOSEPH (1734–1829)		
Gavotte et Tambourin	fl, pf/gui	Billaudot
Quartet, D, op. 14, no. 1	fl/vn, vn, va, vc	NYPL (ed. Beck)
Quartet, B♭, op. 14, no. 5	fl/vn, vn, va, vc	NYPL (ed. Beck)
GRAUN, CARL HEINRICH (1703/4–1759)		
Concerto, e	fl, str/pf red	Müller (ed. Brinckmann)
Solo/Sonata, D	fl, bc	Noetzel (ed. Ruf)
Sonata, E♭	2fl/vn, bc	Bärenreiter (ed. Kölbel)
Triosonata, D	2fl, bc	Leuckart (ed. Stadelmann)
Triosonata, F	2fl/vn, bc	Moeck (ed. Gerlach)

GRAUN, JOHANN GOTTLIEB (1702/3–1771)		
Concerto, C	rec, vn, pf red	Moeck (ed. Hechler)
Concerto, C	fl, vn, str, bc	Ricordi (ed. Scheck & Ruf)
Concerto, e	fl, str, bc	Müller
Concerto, F	rec/fl, 2vn, bc	Moeck
Concerto Grosso, G	fl,vn,va,vc; str, bc	Müller (ed. Flattschacher)
Trio sonata, D	2fl, bc	Zimmermann (ed. Kölbel)
Trio sonata, F	fl/vn, vn, vc ad lib	Zimmermann (ed. Fischer)
Trio sonata, F	2fl, bc	Noetzel (ed. Kölbel)
Trio sonata, F	fl/vn, va, bc	Bärenreiter (ed. Kölbel)
Trio sonata, G	fl, vn, bc	Noetzel (ed. Kölbel)
GRAUPNER, CHRISTOPH (1683–1760)		
Canon (Sonata a3), F	2vn/2fl/2ob, vc/gamba, bc	Möseler (ed. Hoffmann)
Concerto, D	fl, str, bc	Möseler (ed. Hoffmann); Ricordi (ed. Scheck & Ruf)
Concerto no. 35, e	2fl, str, bc/pf red	Eulenberg (ed. Braun); Leuckart (ed. Rottler)
Concerto	2fl, 2ob, str, bc	Breitkopf (ed. Schering)
Ouverture, E	fl, str, bc	Bärenreiter
Ouverture, F	rec, str, bc	Nagel (ed. Hofmann)
Sinfonia, D	2fl, str, bc	Bärenreiter
2 Sonatas, g	fl, hpd	Bärenreiter (ed. Hoffmann)
Sonata, C	fl, vn/va d'am, bc	Müller (ed. Flattschacher)
Suite, F	3fl/3rec/3vn	Hinrichsen; Peters (Urtext)
Triosonata, B♭	fl, va d'am, bc	Leuckart (ed. Goebels)
GRÉTRY, ANDRÉ-ERNEST-MODESTE (1741–1813)		
Concerto, C	fl, orch	Kalmus; NYPL (ed. Beck)
	fl, orch/pf red	Noetzel (ed. Sonntag); Southern (ed. van Leeuwen)
	fl, pf red	Bärenreiter; International (ed. Rampal)

HAYDN, JOSEPH (1732–1809)

Work	Instrumentation	Publisher
Cassation, D, H. IV:D2 [doubtful]	fl, vn, bc	Litolff (ed. Nagel); Peters (ed. Nagel)
Concerto, D, H. VIIf:D1 [attrib: L. Hofmann]	fl, str/pf red	Leuckart (ed. Kowatscheff); Lengnick (ed. Zanke); Simrock (ed. Zanke); Southern (ed. L. Moyse)
	fl, pf red	Armstrong (ed. Kniebusch); International (ed. Philipp); Peters (ed. Burmeister-Tast)
Cadenzas only: Feltkamp	fl	Broekmans
Divertimento, D, H. II:D8 [doubtful/spurious]	fl, 2vn, va, vc/pf red	Hug (ed. Graf)
Divertimento, A, H. IV:A1	fl, vn, vc	Möseler (ed. Nagel)
Divertimento da camera, G, H. IV:G1	vn/fl, vn, vc	Möseler (ed. Nagel)
Divertimento da camera, A, H. IV:A1	fl, vn, vc	Möseler (ed. Nagel)
20 Flötenuhrstücke aus Hob. XIX	3 fl	Breitkopf (ed. Imbescheid)
London Trios, H. IV:1-4 (C,G,G,G)	2fl, vc	International; Kalmus ; Nagel (ed. Balet); Southern (ed. L. Moyse)
6 Quartets, op. 5 (D,D,D,G,D,C)	fl, vn, va, vc	International (ed. Rampal)
Nos. 1, 2 (D,D)		Musica Rara; G. Schirmer
No. 4		Doblinger (ed. Scheit-Brojer); Nagel (ed. Upmeyer)
Quartet, D, H. II:D9 [doubtful/spurious]	fl, vn, va, vc	Musica Rara
Quartet, G, H. II:G4 [doubtful/spurious]	fl, vn, va, vc	Musica Rara
Quartet, C [doubtful or spurious]	fl, vn, va, vc	Hug (ed. Kölbel)
Sonata, C [arr. from String quartet, op. 74, no. 1; H. III:72]	fl, pf	Bote & Bock; International (ed. Rampal); Universal (ed. Lenski)
Sonata, E♭ [arr. from String quartet, op. 76, no. 6; H. III:80]	fl, pf	Bote & Bock; International (ed. Rampal)
Sonata, G [arr. by A. E. Müller from String quartet, op. 77, no. 1; H. III:81]	fl, pf	Boosey (ed. Perry); International (ed. Rampal); Kalmus; Peters; Rudall, Carte
Sonatas [Trios], op. 11, nos. 4–6 (F,C,D)	fl, vn, vc	Broekmans; Musica Rara
No. 4, F		Schott

6 Trios, op. 100, H. IV:6–11 (D,G,C,G,A,D)	vn/fl, vn, vc	Zimmermann (ed. Dittrich)
Trios, H. XV:15	pf, fl/vn, vc	Breitkopf (ed. David); Doblinger (ed. Landon); Fischer; Henle; Heugel; International (ed. Rampal); Peters
HAYDN, MICHAEL (1737–1806)		
Concerto, D (1766)	fl, orch/pf red	EMB (ed. Vecsey)
	fl, pf red	Presser (ed. Byrns); Schirmer (ed. Boehm)
Concerto, D (ca.1771)	fl, orch/pf red	Haydn-Mozart Presse (ed. Landon)
Quartet, D	fl, vn, va, vc	Lienau (ed. Sonntag)
Quartet, F	fl, vn, va, vc	Doblinger (ed. Rainer)
Sonata [Divertimento], G	hpd, fl, vc	Eulenberg (ed. Beyer)
HOFFMEISTER, FRANZ ANTON (1754–1812)		
Concertante sonate	2fl	Boosey (ed. Muller)
Concertos nos. 4, 18, 23, 34 (D,D,G,G)	fl, orch/pf red	Billaudot (ed. Paubon)
Concerto no. 18, D	fl, orch/pf red	EMB (ed. Szebenyi); Schott (ed. Szebenyi)
Concerto no. 6, D, op. 20	fl, orch/pf red	Sikorski (ed. Sonntag)
Concerto, G	fl, pf red	International (ed. Rampal)
3 Duette op. 20	2fl	Broekmans (ed. Vester)
Duets, op. 24, nos. 1–3	2fl	Heuwekemeijer
3 Duets, op. 31	2fl	International (ed. Rampal)
3 Duos, op. 30	2fl	Amadeus (ed. Pauler); Eulenberg (ed. Pauler)
Duo, F	fl, va	Peters (ed. Drüner)
3 Duos Concertants (G,D,F)	fl, va	Amadeus (ed. Bonnet)
Quartet, c, op. 16, no. 2	fl, vn, va, vc	Pegasus (ed. Ermeler)
Quartet, G	fl, vn, va, vc	Sikorski (ed. Sonntag)
Sonata, A, op. 17	fl, pf	Universal
Sonata, C, op. 13	fl/vn, pf	Nagel (ed. Schmitz)
Sonata, G, op. 14	fl, pf	Musica Rara (ed. Cox)
Sonata concertante no. 1	2fl	Leach
Trio no. 3, D	fl, vc, pf	Boosey (ed. Müller)

Trio, D, op. 16, no. 6 "La gallina, il cucco e l'asino" ("The hen, the cuckoo, and the ass")	3fl	Doblinger (ed. Biba); Hänssler (ed. Gümbel); Marbot (ed. Höckner); Pegasus (ed. Höckner)
HOLZBAUER, IGNAZ (1711–1783)		
Concerto, D	fl, orch/pf red	Leuckart (ed. Gronefeld)
	fl, pf red	Bärenreiter
Quintets, G, B♭	hpd, fl, vn, va, vc	Bärenreiter
Quintet, G	hpd, fl, vn, va, vc	Breitkopf (ed. Schroeder)
HOOK, JAMES (1746–1827)		
Sonata, F, op. 54, no. 1	hpd/pf, vn/fl	Schott (ed. Salkeld)
Sonata, C, op. 54, no. 2	hpd/pf, vn/fl	Schott (ed. Salkeld)
Sonata, G, op. 54, no. 6	rec/fl, pf	Schott (ed. Goodyear)
6 Trios, op. 83 (G,F,D,C,D,G)	3fl	Rubank (ed. Voxman)
No. 2, F		Schott (ed. Colwell)
No. 4, G		Boosey
HUGOT, ANTOINE (1761–1803)		
Duets, op. 9, nos. 1–3	2fl	Heuwekemeijer
HUMMEL, JOHANN NEPOMUK (1778–1837)		
Grand Rondeau Brillant, op. 126	pf, vn/fl	Billaudot; EMB; Schott; Universal (ed. Guthmann)
Sonata, G, op. 2, no. 2	pf/hpd, vn/fl	Doblinger (ed. Riessberger)
Sonata, D, op. 50	pf, vn/fl	Doblinger (ed. Riessberger); Pegasus (ed. Sonntag)
Sonata, A, op. 62	pf, fl/vn	Doblinger (ed. Riessberger)
Trio, A, op. 78 [Adagio, Variations, and Rondo on "Schöne Minka"]	fl, vc, pf	Eulenberg (ed. Päuler); Musica Rara

JOMMELLI, NICCOLÒ (1714–1774)		
Sonata, D	2fl, bc	Hofmeister (ed. Niggemann)
KROMMER, FRANZ (1759–1831)		
Concertante	fl, ob, vn, orch/pf red	Hofmeister
Concerto no. 1, G, op. 30	fl, pf red	Zimmermann (ed. Anspacher)
Concerto no. 2, e, op. 86	fl, orch	Artia; Bärenreiter
Quartet, op. 94	fl, vn, va, vc	Hofmeister
Sinfonia Concertante, B♭, op. 70	fl, cl, vn, orch/pf red	Musica Rara
Sinfonia Concertante, D, op. 80	fl, cl, vn, orch/pf red	Musica Rara
KRUMPHOLTZ, JEAN-BAPTISTE (1742–1790)		
Sonata, F, op. 8	fl/vn, harp	Nagel (ed. Zingel)
LINIKE, JOHANN GEORG (ca.1680–after 1737)		
Concerto, G	rec/fl, str, bc/pf red	Pegasus (ed. Schroeder)
Ouverture, C	2rec/2fl, bc	Vieweg (ed. Fischer)
2 Suites (g,C)	2fl, bc	Mitteldeuscher (ed. Rücker)
Suite, g		Vieweg (ed. Fischer)
MAHAUT, ANTOINE (ca.1720–ca.1785)		
6 Sonatas, op. 1	fl, bc	Heuwekemeijer
No. 6, G		Bärenreiter (ed. Schmitz)
6 Sonate da Camera	2fl/2vn	Heuwekemeijer
MERCADANTE, SAVERIO (1795–1870)		
10 Arias	fl, pf	Billaudot (ed. Larrieu)
Arie variate	fl	Billaudot (ed. Larrieu)
Concerto no. 2, e, op. 57	fl, orch/pf red	Boccacini e Spada (ed. Spada); Little Piper (ed. Monroe); Zerboni (ed. Girard)

Work		Instrumentation	Publisher
Serenatas No. 1, F; No 2, G, No. 3, C		3fl	Belwin; Boccaccini & Spada; Ricordi; Zerboni (ed. Fabbriciani)
Variazioni		fl, pf	Boccaccini & Spada/Presse
MOZART, FRANZ XAVER WOLFGANG (1791–1844)			
Rondo (Sonate), e		fl, pf	Pegasus (ed. Ermeler); G. Schirmer (ed. L. Moyse)
MOZART, WOLFGANG AMADEUS (1756–1791)			
Adagio and Rondo, c, K 617		armonica, fl, ob, va, vc	Breitkopf; Eulenberg (ed. Salter); Kalmus; Zimmermann (ed. Schwedler)
Andante, C, K. 315		fl, orch/pf red	Breitkopf (ed. Wolff)
		fl, pf red	Armstrong (ed. Peck); Fischer (ed. Voxman); International (ed. Rampal); Kalmus; Leduc (ed. Caratgé); Novello (ed. Wye); Presser (ed. Cole); Rubank (ed. Voxman); Rudall, Carte (ed. Wolff); Schott (ed. Lutz); Southern (ed. Peck); Zimmermann (ed. Walther)
Cadenzas only:	Andersen & Tillmetz	fl	Fischer
	Flothuis		Broekmans
	Solum		McGinnis & Marx
Concerto no. 1, G, K. 313		fl, orch	Eulenberg (ed. Gerber); Kneusslin (cads: Bopp)
		fl, orch/pf red	Breitkopf (ed., cads.: Horn)
		fl, pf red	Billaudot (ed. & cads.: Le Roy); Fischer; International (ed. Rampal); Kalmus; Leduc; Novello (ed. Wye); Peters (ed. List) ; Rudall, Carte (ed. Weissmann); G. Schirmer; Southern (ed. van Leeuwen)
Cadenzas only:	Andersen & Tillmetz		Fischer
	Barrère		Galaxy

	Bopp		Kneusslin
	Bozza		Leduc
	Flothuis		Broekmans
	Solum		McGinnis & Marx
Concerto no. 2, D, K. 314		fl, orch	Boosey (ed. Paumgartner); Eulenberg (ed. Gerber)
		fl, pf red	Armstrong (ed. Peck); Billaudot (ed, cads: LeRoy); Boosey (ed. Roth); Breitkopf (ed. Burchard); Fischer; International (ed. Rampal); Kalmus; Leduc (ed. Caratgé; cads. Taffanel, Gaubert, Bozza); Novello (ed. Wye); Peters (ed., cads: List); Rudall, Carte (ed. Roth); G. Schirmer; Southern
Cadenzas only:	Andersen & Tillmetz		Fischer
	Barrère		Galaxy
	Bopp		Kneusslin
	Donjon & Anderson		Southern
	Flothuis		Broekmans
	Karg-Elert		Zimmermann
	Reizenstein		Boosey
	Solum		McGinnis & Marx
Concerto, C, K. 299		fl, hp, orch	Eulenberg (ed. Gerber)
		fl, pf red	G. Schirmer (ed. L. Moyse); Universal (ed. Kontarsky/Braun)
Cadenzas only:	Houdy		Leduc
	Jamet		Leduc
	Müller		Hug
	Pillney		Zimmermann
	Previn		Hansen
	Reinecke		Breitkopf
	Rota		Salvi

Quartet, D, K. 285	fl, vn, va, vc	Bärenreiter (ed. Pohanka); Breitkopf; Fischer; International (ed. Rampal); Peters; G. Schirmer (ed. L. Moyse); Zimmermann (ed. Eppel)
Quartet, G, K. 285a	fl, vn, va, vc	Bärenreiter (ed. Pohanka); Hinrichsen (ed. Einstein); International (ed. Rampal);Zimmermann (ed. Eppel)
Quartet, C, K. 285b	fl, vn, va, vc	Bärenreiter (ed. Pohanka); Fischer; International (ed. Rampal); Peters; G. Schirmer (ed. L. Moyse)
Quartet, A, K. 298	fl, vn, va, vc	Bärenreiter (ed. Pohanka); Breitkopf; Fischer; International; (ed. Rampal); Peters; G. Schirmer (ed. L. Moyse)
6 Sonatas, K. 10–15 (B♭,G,A,F,C,B♭)	kbd, vn/f	Bärenreiter (ed. Plath & Rehm, from *Neue Mozart Ausgabe*); Kalmus; Reinhardt (ed. Bopp); G. Schirmer (ed. L. Moyse)
Zauberflöte Duets	arr. 2fl	Universal
NARDINI, PIETRO (1722–1793)		
Triosonata, C	2fl, bc	Bärenreiter (ed. Gümbel)
Triosonata, C	2fl, bc	Müller
NEUBAUER, FRANZ CHRISTOPH (1760–1795)		
Trio, C, op. 3, no. 3	fl, vn, va	Sikorski (ed. Bormann)
PAISIELLO, GIOVANNI (1740–1816)		
6 Divertimenti	fl, vn, va, vc	Eulenberg (ed. Päuler)
Quartet, G, op. 23, no. 3		Eulenberg (ed. Delius)
PLEYEL, IGNACE JOSEPH (1757–1831)		
Concerto, C, op. 60 Ben 106	fl, pf red	International (ed. Rampal); Zimmermann (ed. Richter)

12 Duette (D,F,G,e,D,G,C,C,C,C,G,A) [from various opp.]	2fl	Doblinger (ed. Steinbeck)
Quartet, F, op. 17, no. 2	fl/vn, vn, va, vc	Musica Rara
Quartet, G, op. 20, no. 1, Ben 384	fl/vn, vn, va, vc	Kistner (ed. Albrecht)
Quartet, B♭, op. 20, no. 2, Ben 385	fl/vn, vn, va, vc	Kistner (ed. Albrecht)
Quartet, C, op. 20, no. 3, Ben 386	fl/vn, vn, va, vc	Kistner (ed. Albrecht)
Quartets, op. 41 (D,F,A), Ben 387-389	fl, vn, va, vc	International (ed. Rampal)
Quartet, E♭, Ben 395	fl, 2cl, bn	Musica Rara (ed. Meerwein)
Quintet, E♭, op. 10, no. 3, Ben 282	fl, ob, vn, va, vc	Doblinger (ed. Steinbeck)
Sonatas, op. 16		
Nos. 1, 2, 5 (C,G,e)	fl/vn, pf	Kistner (ed. Albrecht)
No. 2 (G)	fl, pf, vc	McGinnis & Marx (ed. Hoover/Lincoln)
Nos. 3, 4, 6 (B♭,A,D)	fl, pf	Eulenberg (ed. Alberti)
Symphonie Concertante no. 5, F, Ben 115	fl, ob/cl, hn, bn, orch/pf red	EMT (ed. Oubradous)
	fl, ob/cl, hn, bn, pf red	Musica Rara (ed. Lasocki)

REICHA, ANTOINE (1770–1836)

Grand Duo Concertant [Sonata], D, op. 103	fl, pf	Schott (ed. Lebermann)
Grand Trio, G	fl, vn, vc	Eulenberg (ed. Päuler)
Quartet [Sinfonico], D, op. 12	4fl	Ashdown; Billaudot (ed. Rampal); Cranz; Fischer; Hofmeister; Jobert; Kalmus
[as Menuett]		Zimmermann
Quartets, op. 98, nos. 4–6 (g,C,G)	fl, vn, va, vc	Artia
3 Romances, op. 21 (e,G,D)	2fl	Edu-Tainment (ed. Poor); International (ed. Moyse); Schott (ed. Polnauer)
Sonata [Quatuor], op. 19	4fl	Billaudot (ed. Rampal)
Sonata, G, op. 54	fl, pf	Eulenberg (ed. Päuler)
Sonata, D, op. 103	fl, pf	Schott
Trio, D, op. 26	3fl	Broekmans; McGinnis & Marx
Variations, op. 20	2fl	Amadeus (ed. de Reede); Peters (ed. Polnauer)

REICHARDT, JOHANN FRIEDRICH (1752–1814)		
Sonata, C	fl, kbd	Breitkopf (ed. Wiltberger)
RICHTER, FRANZ XAVER (1709–1789)		
Concerto, D	fl, pf red	Müller (ed. Sonntag)
Concerto, e	fl, str, bc/pf red	Leuckart (ed. Gronefeld)
Divertimento, G	fl, ob/vn/fl, bc	Müller (ed. Nagel)
Kammersonaten, op. 2	hpd, vn/fl, vc	
lst set, nos. 2,6 (D,A)		Bärenreiter (ed. Upmeyer)
2nd set, no. 3, G		Bärenreiter (ed. Upmeyer); Schott (ed. Zirnbauer)
2nd set, Sonata da camera, A		Breitkopf (ed. Riemann)
Sonata, G	fl, bc	Schott (ed. Ruf)
Trio, G	fl, ob/vn/fl, bc	Müller (ed. Nagel)
ROMBERG, ANDREAS JACOB (1767–1821)		
Duo concertant, b, op. 62, no. 2	2fl	Eulenberg (ed. Steinbeck)
Trio Intermezzo Concertant, op. 7	fl, vn, vc	Eulenberg
ROSETTI, ANTONIO (ca.1750–1792)		
Concerto, D	fl, orch/pf red	EMB (ed. Szebenyi); Schott (ed. Szebenyi)
Concerto, G	fl, orch/pf red	EMB (ed. Szebenyi); Schott (ed. Szebenyi)
RUGE, FILIPPO (ca.1725–after 1767)		
Sonata, G, op. 2, no. 5	3fl	Piper
SALIERI, ANTONIO (1750–1825)		
Concertino, G	fl, pf red	Zerboni (ed. Ballola)

Work	Instrumentation	Publisher
Concerto, C	fl, ob, orch	Doblinger (ed. Sabatini)
	fl, ob, orch/pf red	Peters (ed. Wojciechowski)
SCHMITT, JOSEPH (1734–1791)		
Concerto, G, op. 15	2fl, pf red	Mitteldeutscher (ed. Gottron); Müller (ed. Gottron)
Trio, G, op. 13, no. 4	fl, vn, vc	Hansen (ed. Höckner)
SCHUBERT, FRANZ (1797–1828)		
Introduction and Variations on "Trockne Blumen" from *Die schöne Müllerin*, e, op. 160, D. 802	fl, pf	Bärenreiter (ed. Wirth, from *Neuen Schubert Ausgabe*); Breitkopf (ed. Delius); Henle; International (ed. Rampal); Kalmus; Novello; Peters (ed. Richter); Schott (Urtext)
Trio, G, D. 96 [added to Schubert's arr. of W. Mateigka's Notturno, op. 21] [pub. as Quartett]	fl, va, vc, guit	Bote & Bock; Peters
SCHWINDL, FRIEDRICH (1737–1786)		
Concerto, D	fl, pf red	Breitkopf (ed. Meylan)
STAMITZ, ANTON (1750–ca.1789-1809)		
8 Capricien	fl	Litolff (ed. Lebermann)
Capriccio-Sonata, A	fl	Breitkopf (ed. Gradenwitz)
Concerto, C	fl, pf red	International (ed. Rampal)
Concerto, D	fl, orch/pf red	Breitkopf (ed. Lebermann); Haverkampf
Rondo Capriccioso, G	fl	Breitkopf (ed. Gradenwitz)
Symphonie concertante, G	2fl, str/pf red	Schott (ed. Lebermann)
STAMITZ, CARL (1745–1801)		
Concerto no. 3, D	fl, orch/pf red	Breitkopf (ed., cad. Lebermann); Haverkampf

Concerto, D	fl, orch/pf red	Sikorski (ed. Sonntag)
Concerto, D	fl, pf red	Breitkopf (ed. Gradenwitz)
Concerto, D	fl, pf red	International
Concerto, D	fl, pf red	Kalmus
Concerto, D	fl, pf red	L'Oiseau Lyre
Concerto, G, op. 29	fl, orch/pf red	Schott (ed. Lebermann)
	fl, pf red	Amadeus; International (ed. Rampal)
Concerto, G	fl, str/pf red	Leuckart (ed. Gronefeld)
Concerto, G	fl, pf red	L'Oiseau Lyre
Concerto, G	fl, pf red	Peters
Concerto, G	fl, str, bc	Ricordi (ed. Scheck & Ruf)
Concerto, G	fl, pf red	Zimmermann (ed. Bodart)
Sinfonia Concertante	fl, ob, cl, 2hn, vn, vc, orch	Universal
6 Duets, op. 27	2fl	Broekmans (ed. Bonsel)
Nos. 1–3 (D,A,G)	2fl	Nagel (ed. Glöder)
Nos. 4–6 (F,C,G)	2fl	Nagel (ed. Bormann)
Quartet, D, op. 4, no. 3	rec/fl/vn, 2vn, vc [arr.]	Schott (ed. Mönkemeyer)
[as op. 14, no.1]	cl/fl/ob, vn, va, vc	McGinnis & Marx (ed. Marx)
Quartet, A, op. 4, no. 6	fl/ob/cl, vn, va, vc	Leuckart (ed. Ott)
[as op. 14, no. 2]	cl/fl/ob, vn, va, vc	McGinnis & Marx (ed. Marx)
Quartet, D, op. 8, no. 1	fl/ob, vn, va/hn, vc	Bärenreiter (ed. Upmeyer)
Quartet, E♭, op. 8, no. 4	fl/cl/ob, vn, va, vc	Bote & Bock
Trio, G, op. 14, no. 1	fl, vn, vc/bc	Nagel (ed. Upmeyer)
	fl, vn, pf	International
Trio, g, op. 14, no. 4	fl, vn, vc/bc	Moöseler (ed. Nagel)
Trio, F, op. 14, no. 5	fl, vn, vc, kbd	Breitkopf (ed. Hillemann)
Trio, G	fl, fl/vn, vc	Bärenreiter (ed. Schnapp)
Trio, G	2fl, vc	Eulenberg (ed. Nagel)

STAMITZ, JOHANN (1717–1757)		
Concerto, C	fl, str/pf red	Hug (ed. Kölbel)
Concerto, D	fl, orch/pf red	Breitkopf (ed. Gradenwitz)
Concerto, D	fl, orch	Peters
Concerto, G	fl, str/pf red	Breitkopf (ed. Lebermann)
SÜSSMAYR, FRANZ XAVER (1766–1803)		
Quintet, D	fl, ob, vn, va, vc	Doblinger (ed. Steinbeck)
TOESCHI, CARL JOSEPH (1731–1788)		
Concerto, G	fl, orch/pf red	Leuckart (ed. Münster)
6 Duets [Sonatas], op. 11 (C,G,D,A,e,F)	2fl	Schott (Lebermann)
TROMLITZ, JOHANN GEORG (1726–1805)		
6 Partitas	fl	Litolff (ed. Lebermann)
Sonata, G	fl, hpd	Noetzel (ed. Ruf)
VIOTTI, GIOVANNI BATTISTA (1755–1824)		
Concerto, A	2fl, pf red	International (ed. Rampal)
Quartet, B♭, op. 22, no. 1	fl, vn, va, vc	Musica Rara
VOGLER, GEORG JOSEPH (1749–1814)		
Quartet No. 1, B♭	fl, vn, va, vc	Sikorski (ed. Zöller)
WAGENSEIL, GEORG CHRISTOPH (1715–1777)		
Concerto, G	fl, str/pf red	Hug (ed. Kölbel)
Sonata, D	fl, bc	Doblinger (ed. Scholz, cad. Kapun)
WANHALL, JOHANN BAPTIST (1739–1813)		
6 Duets	2fl	Universal (ed. Bryan)

3 Leichte Sonaten [Petites pieces faciles]	fl, kbd	Universal (ed. Imbescheid)
Notturno, C	fl, 2va/(vn,va), bc	Lienau (ed. Schroeder)
Sonata, B♭	fl, kbd	McGinnis & Marx (ed. Tuthill)
Sonata no. 2, G	fl, kbd	Artia (ed. Klement)
6 Variations on the Theme "Nel cor più non mi sento," op. 42	fl/vn, guit	Schott (ed. Nagel)

WENDLING, JOHANN BAPTIST (1723–1797)

Concerto, C	fl, pf red	Hug (ed. Anspacher)
6 Duets, op. 4	2fl	Heuwekemeijer
Quartet, G, op. 10, no. 4	fl, vn, va, vc	Nagel (ed. Bopp)
Sonata, G, op. 1	fl, bc	Ichthys (ed. Ade)

C. THE ROMANTIC ERA

ALTÈS, HENRI (1826–1895)

L'Helvétienne, op. 5	fl, pf	Billaudot
5e Solo de Concours, g, op. 24	fl, pf	Billaudot
6e Solo de Concours, B♭, op. 25	fl, pf	Billaudot
La Venitienne, op. 4	fl, pf	Billaudot

ANDERSEN, JOACHIM (1847–1909)

Allegro militaire, op. 48	fl, pf red	Billaudot (ed. Adorjan); Southern (ed. Cavally)
Ballade et Danse des Sylphes, op. 5	fl, pf	Billaudot (ed. Adorjan); Jobert; Southern

Canzone, op. 53, no. 1	fl, pf	Fischer
Concertsttück [Morceau de Concert] no. 2, op. 61	fl, orch	Hansen
Fantaisies Nationales, op. 59: no. 2, Ecossais; No.3, Russe; no. 4, Suedois, no. 5, Italien	fl, pf	Hansen
Intermezzo, op. 51, no. 2	fl, pf	Fischer
Introduction et Caprice, op. 58	fl, pf	Hansen
Leichtere Stücke, op. 56: No. 1, Im Herbst; No.2, Die Blumen; no. 4, Abendlied	fl, pf	Southern (ed. Cavally)
Morceau de concert no. 2, op. 61	fl, pf	Hansen
6 Morceaux de Salon, Suites I & I, op. 241	fl, pf	Little Piper
Moto Perpetuo, op. 8	fl, pf	Billaudot (ed. Rampal); Zimmermann (ed. Richter)
Opera Fantasies, op. 45: no. 2, Norma; No. 4, The Merry Wives of Windsor	fl, pf	Hansen
10 Pieces, op. 62: no. 2, Intermezzo; no. 3, Dans la Gondole; no. 4, Serenade d'Amour	fl, pf	Hansen
5 Songs Without Words: Reverie, 2 Berceuses, Melodie, Au bord de de la Mer	fl, pf	Oxford (ed. Solum)
Le Tourbillon, op. 57, no. 3	fl, pf	Hansen; Southern (ed. Cavally)
Variations drolatiques sur un air suédois, op. 26	fl, pf red	Billaudot (ed. Rampal); Fischer
Variations Elegiaques, op. 27	fl, pf	Billaudot (ed. Rampal); Fischer
8 Vortragsstücke, op. 55	fl, pf	
Nos. 1–5, 7–8 [as Miniaturen]		Zimmermann (ed. Richter)
No. 1, Elegie		Rubank (ed. Voxman)
No. 4, The Mill		Southern (ed. Cavally)
No. 5, Legende		Southern (ed. Cavally)
No. 6, Scherzino		Belwin; Fischer; Rubank (ed. Voxman); Southern (ed. Cavally); Zimmermann

BAYR, GEORG (1773–1833)

2 Caprices, op. 8	fl	Ed. Musicus; Heuwekemeijer

BAZZINI, ANTONIO (1818–1897)		
La Ronde des Lutins	fl, pf	Billaudot (ed. Paubon)
BERLIOZ, HECTOR (1803–1869)		
Trio of the Young Ishmaelites, op. 25 [from *L'Enfance du Christ*]	2fl, hp	Chappell (ed. Butterworth); Ed. Musicus (ed. Maganini); Kalmus; Universal (ed. Imbescheid); Zimmermann (ed. Richter)
BIZET, GEORGES (1838–1875)		
Three Pieces from *L'Arlésienne*	fl, pf	Southern; Zimmermann (ed. Walther)
BOEHM, THEOBALD (1794–1881)		
Air suisse, Op. 20	fl, pf	Billaudot
Concerto G, op. 1	fl, pf red	International (ed. Rampal)
3 Duets [arr. Boehm]: Rossini, Duett, D, op. 66; Weber: Pieces Faciles, no. 3, C, op. 67; Weber: Romanze, F, op. 68	fl, altofl, pf	Zalo (ed. Pellerite)
Elegie, A♭, op. 47	fl, pf red	Billaudot (ed. Adorjan); Schott (ed. Delius); Southern (ed. Thomas)
Etude-Landler, op. 26	fl, pf	Southern (ed. Wummer & Ephross)
Fantasy on a Theme of Schubert, "Le Desir," A♭, op. 21	fl, pf red	Billaudot; Universal (ed. Braun)
Grande Polonaise, D, op 16	fl, pf red	Billaudot (ed. Heriché); International (ed. Rampal)
Introduction and Variations on a Theme from "Freischutz," op. 9	fl, pf	Zimmermann (ed. Eppel)
6 Lieder von F. Schubert, op. 52	fl, pf	Universal (ed. Meerwein)
Nel cor più non mi sentc: Thème favori variée, op. 4	fl, pf red	Armstrong (ed. Robison); Billaudot (ed. Heriché); Zimmermann (ed. Eppel)

Souvenir des Alpes, 6 Morceaux de Salon	fl, pf	
No. 1, Andante Cantabile, E♭, op. 27		Fischer
No. 5, Andante Pastorale, G, op. 31		Edu-Tainment (ed. Cole); Fischer; Southern (ed. Cavally)
Thèmes Suisses variés, C,G, op. 11	fl, pf	Amadeus (ed. Burkhard)
Variations sur un Air Allemand, E, op. 22 [Variations on a German air, "Du, du liegst mir im Herzen"]	fl, pf	Billaudot; Southern (ed. Cavally)
Variations sur un Air Tyrolien, C, op. 20 [Air Suisse. Variations Brillantes]	fl, pf red	Billaudot
BORNE, FRANÇOIS (1840–1920)		
Carmen Fantaisie	fl, pf	Billaudot (ed. Rampal); International (ed. Stallman); Little Piper; Presser (ed., arr. Wilson); G. Schirmer (ed. Galway); Southern (ed. Ephross)
BRICCIALDI, GIULIO (1818–1881)		
Carnival of Venice, op. 77	fl, pf	Fischer (ed. De Lorenzo)
	fl, pf/band	Ludwig (ed. Wilkins)
Concertino no. 2, G, op. 48	fl, pf red	International (ed. Rampal)
Duetto [Duo concertant] no. 1, op. 100,	2fl	International (ed. Wummer); Kalmus
16 Duets [Dialogues], op. 132	2fl	Belwin; International (ed. Wummer)
Quartetto, A	4fl	Zanibon (ed. Petrucci)
Rigoletto Fantaisie, op. 106	fl, pf	Zimmermann (ed. Eppel)
Il Vento [The Wind], op. 112	fl, pf	Fischer
CARULLI, FERDINANDO (1770–1841)		
Nocturne, op. 190	fl, guit	Breitkopf (ed. Nagel/Meunier)

CHAMINADE, CéCILE (1857–1944)		
Air de ballet, op. 30	fl, pf	Masters Music
Concertino, D, op. 107	fl, orch/pf	Enoch; Kalmus
	fl, band	Fischer (ed. Wilkins & Wilson)
	fl, pf	Armstrong (ed. Peck); Boosey (ed. Vraz); Fischer; International (ed. M. Moyse); G. Schirmer (ed. L. Moyse); Southern
Sérénade aux Etoiles, op. 142	fl, pf	Belwin; Enoch; Masters Music
CHOPIN, FREDERIC (1810–1849)		
Variations, E, on "Non più mesta" from Rossini's *La Cenerentola*	fl, pf	International (ed. Rampal); E. B. Marks
CIARDI, CESARE		
Le Carnevale Russe	fl, pf red	Bote & Bock
Nocturnes, op. 133, nos 1, 3	fl, pf	Fischer
COSTE, NAPOLEON (1806–1883)		
4 Pieces	fl, guit	Chanterelle
CUI, CESAR (1835–1918)		
Bagatelle	fl, pf	Belwin (ed. Taylor)
Cantabile (Andante), op. 36	fl, pf	Fischer
5 Little Duets [Pieces], op. 56	fl, vn	International
Orientale, op. 50, no. 9	fl, pf	Fischer
Scherzetto	fl, pf	Heugel

CZERNY, CARL (1791–1857)		
Duo Concertant, G, op. 129	fl, pf	Eulenberg (ed. Förster); Universal (ed. Vester)
Fantasia Concertante, op. 256	fl, vc, pf	Eulenberg (ed. Förster)
DAMARÉ, EUGÈNE (1840–1919)		
L'Alouette	picc, pf	Billaudot
Les Amours d'un Rossignol	picc, pf	Billaudot
Le Bouquet de roses, op. 408	picc, pf	Billaudot
Caprice, op. 174	picc, pf	Billaudot (ed. Beaumadier)
La Cracovienne, op. 224	picc, pf	Billaudot
Le Merle blanc, op. 161	picc, pf	Billaudot (ed. Beaumadier)
L'Oiseau et les Roses, op. 153	picc, pf	Billaudot
Tarantelle, op. 391	picc, pf	Billaudot
Le Tourbillon, op. 212	picc, pf	Billaudot (ed. Beaumadier)
La Tourterelle, op. 119	picc, pf	Billaudot (ed. Beaumadier)
DELIBES, LEO (1836–1891) **& JULES MASSENET** (1842–1912)		
3 Original Pieces for Sight-Reading Examinations at Paris Conservatoire	fl, pf	Oxford (ed. Solum)
DEMERSSEMAN, JULES AUGUSTE (1833–1866)		
Air Varié et Polonaise, op. 8	fl, pf	Billaudot; Leduc (ed. M. Moyse)
Duet, A♭, op. 25, no. 1	fl, pf	Billaudot
Evening Echoes	fl, pf	Southern (ed. Ephross)
Fantaisie Brillante sur "La Déesse et le Berger" de Duprato, E, op. 130	fl, pf	Leduc (ed. M. Moyse)
Fantaisie concertante, op. 36	2fl/(fl, ob), pf	Billaudot
6 Fantaisies, op. 28: no. 1, Balladine; no. 2, Simplicité	fl, pf	Billaudot
Fantasia on a Chopin Melody, op. 29	fl, pf	Fischer

Grand Air Varié: Le Trémolo, op. 3	fl, pf	Billaudot; Leduc (ed. M. Moyse); Zimmermann (ed. Richter)
Grande Fantaisie Musicale sur *Oberon* de Weber, op. 52	fl, pf	Leduc (ed. M. Moyse)
Hommage à Tulou, op. 43	fl, pf	Leduc (ed. M. Moyse)
Introduction and Variations on "The Carnival of Venice," op. 7	fl, pf	Billaudot; Costallat; Universal (ed. Braun)
6 Petites Pièces, op. 2: no. 1, Fantaisie; No. 2, Bolero; no. 6, Ballade	fl, pf	Billaudot
Polonaise, op. 9, no. 1	fl, pf	Costallat
Serenade Espagnole, op. 9, no. 3	fl, pf	Billaudot
Solo de Concert no. 1, c, op. 19	fl, pf	Broekmans (ed. Roorda); Costallat
Solo de Concert no. 2, E♭, op. 20	fl, pf	Billaudot; Costallat
Solo de Concert no. 3, e, op. 21	fl, pf	Costallat
Solo de Concert no. 4, e, op. 80	fl, pf	Costallat
Solo de Concert no. 5, C, op. 81	fl, pf	Costallat
Solo de Concert no. 6, F, op. 82	fl, orch/pf	Billaudot (ed. Heriché)
	fl, pf	Leduc (ed. M. Moyse); Southern (ed. Cavally)
Sonata no. 1, E♭, op. 22	fl, pf	Costallat
Sonata no. 2, A, op. 23	fl, pf	Costallat
Sonata no. 3, c, op. 24	fl, pf	Costallat
Souvenir de Bayonne, op. 5	fl, pf	Billaudot
Sur l'Albaicin	fl, pf	Lemoine

DIABELLI, ANTON (1781–1858)

Serenade, d, op. 95	fl, va, guit	OBV
Serenade, G	fl, guit	Simrock (ed. Domandl)

Serenata Concertante, op. 105	fl, va, guit	Zerboni (ed. Chiesa)
3 Stücke	fl/vn, guit	Breitkopf (ed. Nagel)
Trio	fl, va, guit/hp	EMT; OBV (ed. Schindler)
DONIZETTI, GAETANO (1797–1848)		
Larghetto [Trio]	fl, bn, pf	Litolff (ed. Päuler)
Sonata, C [orch. version as Concertino]	fl, orch/pf	Litolff (ed. Meylan)
Sonata, F	fl, pf	Zimmermann (ed. Schmalfuss)
DONJON, JOHANNES (1839–ca.1912)		
Adagio Nobile	fl, pf	Broekmans (ed. Roorda); Fischer (ed. Medicus)
8 Etudes de Salon	fl, pf	Billaudot
Invocation	fl, pf	Broekmans (ed. Roorda); Fischer (ed. Medicus); Southern (ed. Guertin)
Offertoire, op. 12	fl, pf/org	Billaudot; Broekmans (ed. Roorda); Fischer; Galaxy; Southern
Pan! Pastorale	fl, pf	Fischer (ed. Medicus); Southern
Pipeaux Pastorale	fl, pf	Fischer (ed. Medicus)
Rossignolet [Nightingale], op. 8	fl, pf	Broekmans (ed. Roorda); Fischer (ed. Gould)
2 Short Pieces: Shepherd's Lament, Minuet	fl, pf	Southern (ed. Perkins)
Spirale: scherzo-valse	fl, pf	Fischer (ed. Medicus)
DOPPLER, FRANZ (1821–1883)		
Airs Valaques (Fantaisie), e, op. 10	fl, pf	Belwin (ed. Eck); Billaudot (ed. Rampal); EMB (ed. Laszlo); Emerson (ed. Wye); Little Piper
Andante et Rondo, C, op. 252	fl, pf	Billaudot; International (ed. Rampal); Musica Rara; Southern (ed. Ephross)
The Bird of the Forest, op. 21	fl, 4hn	McGinnis & Marx
Chanson d'amour, op. 20	fl, pf	Billaudot; Emerson (ed. Wye); Fischer

Concerto, d	2fl, orch/pf red	Billaudot (ed. Adorjan)
Duettino Americain, op. 37	fl, vn/fl, pf	Billaudot
Duettino Hongrois, op. 362	fl, pf	Billaudot
Fantaisie pastorale hongroise, op. 26	fl, pf	Billaudot; Chester (ed. Wye); Fischer (ed. Brooke); G. Schirmer (ed. L. Moyse); Schott
3 Morceaux, opp. 15-17 (Berceuse, op. 15; Mazurka de Salon, op. 16; Nocturne, op. 17)	fl, pf	Billaudot; Zimmermann (ed. von Herner)
Berceuse, op. 15		Southern (ed. Cavally); Zimmermann (ed. Eppel)
Nocturne, op. 17		Cranz; Southern
Nocturne, op. 19	fl, vn, hn/vc, pf	International (ed. Rampal); Masters Music
L'oiseau des bois, Idylle, op. 21	fl, pf	Billaudot
La Sonnambula: paraphrase en souvenir de Adelina Patti, Op. 42	2fl, pf	Billaudot (ed. Adorján)
Souvenir du Rigi, Idylle, op. 34	fl, hn, pf	Fischer

DOPPLER, FRANZ (1821–1883), **with KARL DOPPLER** (1825–1900)

Fantaisie sur des motif hongroises [Duettino hongroise], op. 352	fl, orch/pf	Musica Rara (ed. Adorjan)
	2fl, pf	Billaudot (ed. Adorjan)
Rigoletto Fantaisie, op. 38	3fl, pf	Billaudot (ed. Adorjan)
Souvenir de Prague, op. 242	fl, pf	Billaudot; Musica Rara
Valse di Bravura	2fl, pf	Southern (ed. Ephross)

DROUET, LOUIS (1792–1873)

2 Airs Variés	2fl	Broekmans
Duets, op. 74, nos. 1–3 (C,G,A)	2fl	Heuwekemeijer
3 Fantaisies très faciles, op. 38	fl, pf	EMT (ed. Artaud)
3 Trios, op. 33	3fl	Heuwekemeijer

DUVERNOY, VICTOR ALPHONSE (1842–1907)		
Concertino, op. 45	fl, pf	G. Schirmer
DVORAK, ANTONIN (1841–1904)		
Sonatine in G, Op. 100	fl, pf	Billaudot (ed. Marion)
FARRENC, LOUISE (1804–1875)		
Trio, e, op. 45	fl/vn, vc, pf	Da Capo (ed. Gideon)
FRANSELLA, ALBERT (ca. 1866–1935)		
Concert Etude, F	fl, pf	Galaxy
FÜRSTENAU, ANTON BERNHARD (1792–1852)		
3 bekannte varierte Themen, op. 71	fl	Broekmans (ed. De Reede)
Caprices, op. 30	fl	Universal (ed. Hunteler)
Concertino no. 2, op. 87	2fl, orch	Heuwekemeijer
Concertino, op. 119	fl, pf	Belwin (ed. Eck)
Concerto no. 6, op. 58	fl, pf	Heuwekemeijer
Concerto no. 8, D, op. 84	fl, orch/pf red	Zimmermann (ed. Richter)
6 Duets, op. 137	2fl	Amadeus (ed. Pauler); International; Kalmus; Litolff
Grand Quartet, F, op. 88	4fl	Ashdown; Broekmans (ed. Münster); Presto; Southern; Zimmermann (ed. Richter)
3 Grands Duos Concertants, op. 36 (F,E,g)	2fl	Eulenberg (ed. Steinbeck); Heuwekemeijer
Grand Trio, C, op. 66, no. 1	3fl	Heinrichshofen (ed. Engelsberg)
Grand Trio, F, op. 66, no. 2	3fl	Heinrichshofen
L'Illusion: Adagio with Variations, op. 133	fl, pf	International (ed. Rampal)
Introduction and Variations, op. 72	fl, pf	Billaudot (ed. Rampal)
Rondo Brillant, op. 102	2fl, pf	Ed. Musicus (ed. Maganini); Litolff
3 Trios, op. 14 (D,F,G)	3fl	Breitkopf
Trio, F, op. 118	3fl	International (ed. Wummer)

24 Übungen, Capricien, und Praeludien, op. 125	fl	Litolff (ed. Boehme)
L'Union: Introduction and rondo brillant on themes from *Norma* (Bellini), D, op. 115	2fl, pf red	Musica Rara (ed. Adorjan)
FÜRSTENAU, CASPAR (1772–1819)		
12 Stücke, op. 16	fl, guit	Breitkopf (ed. Nagel/Meunier)
GABRIELSKI, JOHANN WILHELM (1795–1846)		
Trois Duos Concertants, Op. 40	2fl	Falls House
Trois Duos Concertants, Op. 85	2fl	Falls House
GARIBOLDI, GIUSEPPE (1833–1905)		
6 Easy Duets, op. 145a	2fl	Leduc
6 Easy Duets, op. 145b	2fl	Fischer
6 Easy Melodic Duets, op. 145c	2fl	Fischer
Grand Fantasy on an Arabic Theme	fl, pf	Southern (ed. Cavally)
GENIN, PAUL AGRICOLE (1832–1903)		
Air Napolitain, Fantaisie Avec Variations, op. 8	fl, pf	ALRY; Billaudot; Costallat
Berceuse, op. 6	fl, pf	Costallat
Carnival of Venice Variations, op. 14	fl, pf	Billaudot; Chester (ed. Wye)
Fantaisie sur La Traviata	fl, pf	Billaudot
Grand Air Varié, op. 5	fl, pf	Costallat
Grand Duo Concertant A, op. 51	fl, fl/vn/ob, pf	Billaudot
	fl, cl, pf	Billaudot
Meditation, op. 49	fl, pf	Billaudot
Mélodie, op. 7	fl, pf	Billaudot

Petite Fantaisie Concertante, op. 4	fl, pf	Billaudot
Sur la Terrasse, op. 62	fl, pf	Costallat
GODARD, BENJAMIN (1849–1895)		
Suite de 3 Morceaux: Allegretto, Idylle, Valse, op. 116	fl, pf red	Chester (ed. Wye); Durand; Fischer; Southern; Zimmermann (ed. Anspacher)
No. 1, Allegretto		Edu-Tainment (ed. Thomas); Kalmus
GOUNOD, CHARLES (1818–1893)		
Souvenir d'un Bal	fl/2fl, str	Choudens
HOFMANN, HEINRICH KARL JOHANN (1842–1902)		
Konzertstück [Concert Piece], op. 98	fl, pf red	Breitkopf; Fischer; Southern (ed. Cavally)
JADASSOHN, SALOMON (1831–1902)		
Elegiefl, pf	Falls House (ed. Worthen)	
JONGEN, JOSEPH (1873–1953)		
Danse lente	fl, pf/hp ck hp in LC	Chester
KÖHLER, ERNESTO (1849–1907)		
Au vol d'oiseau, op. 98	fl,vn, vc ad lib, hp/pf	Zimmermann
Blümen Walzer, op. 87	2fl, pf	EMB; Emerson (ed. Wye); Kunzelmann; Zimmermann
Concert Fantasie on the Russian Song "Moskwa" op. 62	fl, pf	Fischer (ed. Cochrane)
Grand Quartet, D, op. 92	4fl	Fischer (ed. Cochrane); Southern
Morceaux, op. 30	fl, pf	
No. 2, Berceuse		Fischer; Southern (ed. Cavally)
No. 4, Papillon		Fischer; Southern (ed. Cavally); Zimmermann
Nightingale Polka	fl/picc, pf	Fischer (ed. Dole)

Papillon—Souvenir Russe, op. 60	fl, pf	Zimmermann
40 Progressive Duets, op. 55	2fl	Fischer; Kalmus; Salabert; Zimmermann
Serenade, op. 59	fl, pf	Zimmermann
6 Sonatinas, op. 96	2fl	Kalmus; Southern

KUHLAU, FRIEDRICH (1786–1832)

12 Caprices, op. 10a [as op. 10bis]	fl	Billaudot (ed. Heriché)
6 Divertimentos, op. 68	fl, pf ad lib	Armstrong (ed. McGinty); Billaudot (ed. Rampal); Fischer; International (ed. Taffanel); Kalmus
3 Duos, op. 80 (G,C,e)	2fl	Billaudot; Fischer; International; Kalmus; Litolff; Peters; Ricordi (ed. Veggetti)
No. 1, G		Armstrong (ed. Baron)
3 Duos, op. 81 (D,F,g)	2fl	Billaudot; Costallat; Fischer; International; Kalmus; Peters
3 Duos brillants, op. 102 (D,E/e,A)	2fl	Belwin; Billaudot; Fischer; International; Kalmus; Peters; Ricordi
3 Duos brillants, op. 110 (B♭,e,D)	fl, pf	Billaudot (ed. Rampal); Spratt
3 Duos concertants, op. 10b (e,D,G)	2fl	Billaudot; Edu-Tainment (ed. Baker); Fischer; International; Kalmus; Peters; Ricordi (ed. Veggetti)
3 Fantasias, op. 38 (D,g,C)	fl	Billaudot (ed. Heriché); Universal (ed. Vester)
No. 1, D		Bärenreiter (ed. Gümbel)
Nos.1, 2 (D,g)		Heuwekemeijer
3 Fantasias, op. 95 (G,e,D)	fl, pf ad lib	Billaudot (ed. Heriché); Zimmermann (ed. Richter)
3 Grand Duos, op. 39 (e,B♭,D)	2fl	Billaudot; Breitkopf; Costallat; Fischer; Edu-Tainment (ed. Baker); International; Litolff; G. Schirmer (ed. L. Moyse)

3 Grand Duos, op. 87 (A,g,D)	2fl	Billaudot; Fischer; International; Kalmus; Litolff; McGinnis & Marx (ed. Harper); Schott (ed. Delius)
Grand Quartet, e, op. 103	4fl	Ashdown; Billaudot; Costallat; Kalmus; Peters (ed. Nagel); Southern (ed. Andraud)
3 Grand Solos, op. 57 (F,a,G)	fl, pf ad lib	Billaudot (ed. Rampal); Costallat; Fischer; Peters
No. 1, F		Edu-Tainment (ed. Robison)
3 Grand Trios, op. 13 (D,g,F)	3fl	Billaudot; Breitkopf; International (ed. Rampal); Kalmus
3 Grand Trios, op. 86 (e,D,E♭)	3fl	Billaudot; Kalmus
No. 1, G		International (ed. Rampal)
Grand Trio, b, op. 90	3fl	Billaudot; International (ed. Rampal); Kalmus; Schott (ed. Delius)
Grand Trio, G, op. 119	(2fl,pf)/(fl,vn,pf)/(fl,vc,pf)	Billaudot; International (ed. Rampal); Zimmermann (ed. Eppel)
Introduction and Rondo on "Ah! quand il gêle" from Onslow's *Le colporteur*, op. 98	afl, pf	Billaudot (ed. Rampal)
Introduction und Variationen, op. 101 [on "Schönes Mädchen, wirst mich hassen" from Spohr's *Jessonda*]	fl, pf	Zimmermann (ed. Eppel)
3 Quintets, op. 51 (D,E/e,A)	fl, vn, 2va, vc	
No. 1, D		Kunzelmann
Nos. 2, 3 (E,A)		Musica Rara
No. 3, A		Kunzelmann
Sonata, E♭, op. 64	fl, pf	Billaudot; Fischer
Sonata, G, op. 69 [as Grand duo]	fl, pf	Billaudot (ed. Heriché)
Sonata, e, op. 71 [as Grand duo]	fl, pf	Billaudot (ed. Rampal)
3 Sonatas, op. 83 (G,C,g)	fl, pf	Fischer (ed. Tillmetz)
Nos. 1, 2 (G,C)		Müller (ed. Sonntag)
No. 3, g		Billaudot (ed. Rampal)

Sonata, a, op. 85 [Grande sonate concertante]	fl, pf	Billaudot (ed. Rampal); Schott (ed. Delius)
Trio, G, op. 119	2fl, pf	Zimmermann (ed. Eppel)
Variations on an Irish Folksong ("The Last Rose of Summer"), op. 105	fl, pf	Billaudot (ed. Rampal); Universal (ed. Braun)
Variations on a Scottish Folksong, op. 104	fl, pf	Billaudot (ed. Rampal)
Variations on a theme from Weber's *Euryanthe*, op. 63	fl, pf	Bärenreiter (ed. Schmitz); Billaudot (ed. Rampal)
3 Virtuoso Duets, op. 102	2fl	McGinnis & Marx (ed. Harper)
KUMMER, CASPAR (1795–1870)		
Carnival of Venice, op. 157, no. 3	fl, pf	Fischer
Concertino, G, op. 42	fl, orch	Heuwekemeijer
3 Duets, op. 25	2fl	Costallat
3 Duets, op. 1322	fl	International; Kalmus
2 Duos Concertants, op. 46	fl, cl	Billaudot (ed. Lancelot); Fischer
3 Duos Faciles, op. 74 (C,G,D)	2fl	Billaudot (ed. Heriché)
Grand Duet [Sonatina], F, op. 36, no. 32	fl	Ed. Musicus
3 Grands Duos Concertants, op. 92	fl	Heuwekemeijer
3 Petits Duos Faciles, op. 20 (D,G,C)	2fl	Billaudot; Kalmus
Trio, G, op. 24	3fl	Ed. Musicus; Fischer; Heuwekemeijer; International (ed. Doppler)
Trio, D, op. 30	3fl	Heuwekemeijer; International (ed. Wilson); Kunzelmann
Trio, F, op. 32	fl, cl, bn	Rubank
Trio, C, op. 53	3fl	Fischer
Trio, D, op. 58	3fl	Broekmans (ed. Vester); Fischer; Heuwekemeijer
Trio A, op. 59, no. 6	3fl	Fischer; Kalmus; Zimmermann

LALO, EDOUARD (1823–1892)		
Introduction et Allegretto	fl, pf	Hamelle; Musica Rara
MOLIQUE, WILHELM BERNARD (1802–1869)		
Concertante [Duo Concertante], g	fl, vn	International (ed. Rampal & Gingold); Zimmermann (ed. Eppel)
Concerto, d, op. 69	fl, pf red	Billaudot (ed. Marion); Bote & Bock; Southern
Andante		Fischer (ed. Maganini); Fischer (ed. Medicus); Southern
Impromptu	fl, pf	Southern
Introduction, Andante and Polonaise, op. 43	fl, pf	Zimmermann (ed. Richter)
3 Musikalische Skizzen	fl, pf	Zimmermann (ed. Anspacher)
MOSCHELES, IGNAZ (1794–1870)		
Concertino, F	fl, ob, orch/pf red	Kunzelmann (ed. Forster); Litolff (ed. Wojciechowski)
4 Divertimenti, op. 82	fl, pf	Kunzelmann (ed. Forster)
Duo Concertante, G, op. 79	fl, pf	Schott (ed. Delius)
Grand Sonate Concertante, A, op. 44	fl, pf	Billaudot (ed. Adorjan); Universal (ed. Pinschof)
Trio Concertante, F	fl, ob, pf	Nova
Variations in d, op. 21	fl, pf	Eulenberg (ed. Forster); Kunzelmann
MOUQUET, JULES (1867–1946)		
Berceuse, op. 22	fl, str/pf red	Lemoine
Danse Grecque, op. 14	fl, hp/pf	Lemoine
Divertissement Grec, op. 23	fl, hp/pf	Lemoine
Eglogue, op. 29	fl, pf	Lemoine
La Flûte de Pan (Sonata), op. 15	fl, orch/pf red	Lemoine
	fl, pf red	International (ed. Wummer); Kalmus; Southern (ed. Cavally)

5 Pièces Brèves, op. 39	fl, pf	Lemoine; Southern (ed. Cavally)
PAGANINI, NICOLÒ (1782–1840)		
24th Caprice	fl	Zalo (arr. Pellerite)
	fl, pf	Schott (arr. Callimahos); Southern (ed. Cavally)
PESSARD, ÉMILE (1843–1917)		
Andalouse, op. 20	fl, pf	Fischer (ed. Brooke); Kjos (ed. Buchtel); Leduc; Rubank (ed. Voxman); Southern (ed. Cavally)
Bolero, op. 28, no. 2	fl, pf	Fischer; Southern
4 Pieces, op. 75	fl, pf	Leduc
POPP, WILHELM (1818–1903)		
Bagatelle	fl, pf (1 player: fl, LH; pf, RH)	Oxford (ed. Solum)
Birdsong [Chanson de Oiseau], op. 324	fl, pf	Billaudot (ed. Verroust); Fischer (ed. Medicus)
La Chasse Galop Brillant, op. 250, no. 6	fl, pf	ALRY (ed. Pope)
Concert Fantaisie, op. 382	fl, pf	Cranz
Concert-Stück, op. 237	fl, pf	Cranz
Decoy Bird, op. 410, no. 5	fl, pf	Fischer
Fantaisie Brillante	fl, pf	Southern (ed. Cavally)
Fantasy and variations on an American Air	fl, pf	Southern (ed. Ephross)
Hungarian Rhapsody, op. 385	fl, pf	Zimmermann (ed. Eppel)
Kleine Angangübungen	fl, pf	Zimmermann (ed. Richter)
Melodic Suite, op. 281	2fl	Ed. Musicus
Nightingale Serenade, op. 447	fl, pf	Fischer; Presser (ed. Pellerite)
2 Pieces: Rattenfanger von Hameln, Brillante Concert-Fantasie	fl, pf	ALRY

Polka de Bravura, op. 201	fl, pf	Cranz
Staccato fantaisie	fl, pf	Billaudot
Swedish Concerto, op. 266	fl, pf	Cranz
Valse Gracieuse, op. 261, no. 2	fl, pf	Rubank (ed. Voxman); Southern (ed. Cavally)
RACHMANINOFF, SERGEI (1873–1943)		
Vocalise, op. 34, no. 14	fl, pf	Ed Musicus; Fentone (arr. DeSmet); Fischer (ed. Amans)
REINECKE, CARL (1824–1910)		
Ballade, op. 288	fl, orch/pf red	Ludwig (ed. Rager); Zimmermann
Concerto, D, op. 283	fl, orch/pf red	Breitkopf
Sonata "Undine," e, op. 167	fl, pf	International; Kalmus; Rudall, Carte; Universal
Von der Wiege bis zum Grabe [From the Cradle to the Grave], op. 202	fl, pf	Zimmermann
REISSIGER, CARL GOTTLIEB (1798–1859)		
Concertino, D, op. 60	fl, orch	Kunzelmann (ed. Forster)
Sonata, b, op. 45	fl, pf	Zimmermann (ed. Delius)
RHEINBERGER, JOSEF (1839–1901)		
Rhapsodie, B, op. 27	fl, pf	Kunzelmann; Zimmermann (ed. Pinschof)
RIES, FERDINAND (1784–1838)		
Fantasia, op. 113, no. 2	fl, pf	Kunzelmann (ed. Forster)
Introduction and Polonaise, F, op. 119	fl, pf	Eulenberg (ed. Meerwein)
Quartet no. 2, e, op. 145	fl,vn,va,vc	Falls House
Sonata, G, op. 87	fl, pf	Musica Rara (ed. Hill)
Sonate sentimentale, E♭, op. 169	fl, pf	Bärenreiter (ed. Schmitz); Musica Rara
Trio, E♭, op. 63	fl, vc, pf	Musica Rara

RIETZ, JULIUS (1812–1877)		
Sonata, g, op. 42	fl, pf	Breitkopf
ROMBERG, BERNHARD HEINRICH (1767–1841)		
Concerto, b, op. 17	fl, pf red	Kunzelmann; Wion (ed. Wion)
Concerto, b op. 30 (i.e., 17)	fl, orch/pf red	Eulenberg (ed. Forster)
SAINT-SAËNS, CAMILLE (1835–1921)		
Airs de ballet from *Ascanio*	fl, pf	Durand; Galaxy (ed. Barrère); Piper; Southern
Caprice sur des Airs Dancis et Russes, op. 79	fl, ob, cl, pf	Durand; International
Le Cygne	fl, pf	Durand; Schirmer (ed. Barrère)
Odelette, D, op. 162	fl, orch/pf red	Durand; Zimmermann (ed. Richter)
Romance, D♭, op. 37	fl, orch/pf	Durand; Southern
Tarantelle, a, op. 6	fl, cl, orch/pf red	Durand
	fl, cl, pf red	Fischer; International; Kalmus
SOUSSMAN, HEINRICH (1796–1848)		
Concertino, op. 19	fl, pf red	Southern
12 Easy Duets, op. 53	2fl	Edu-Tainment (ed. Goldberg); International (ed. Tillmetz)
12 Easy Pieces, op. 47	2fl	Ed. Musicus; Fischer; International; Kalmus (ed. Doppler)
Quartet, G, op. 27, no. 1	4fl	Southern (ed. Porter)
TAFFANEL, PAUL (1844–1908)		
Andante Pastorale and Scherzettino	fl, pf	Enoch; International; Kalmus; G. Schirmer; Southern (ed. Cavally)
Fantasia on *Freyschütz*	fl, pf	Southern (ed. Ephross)

Work	Scoring	Publisher
TERSCHAK, ADOLF (1832–1901)		
12 Characteristic Duets [Pieces], op. 69	2fl	Ed. Musicus
The Chatterer [Le Babillard], op. 23	fl, pf	Fischer (ed. Brooke); Rudall, Carte
L'Esperance, op. 26, no. 1	fl, pf	Southern (ed. Cavally)
A Little Gem	fl, pf	Rubank (ed. Haas)
Mélancolie Hongroise, op. 149	fl, pf	Fischer (ed. Medicus)
40 Progressive Duets, op. 55	2fl	Fischer
Progressive Duets, op. 70a	2fl	Fischer
Reproche, op. 19, no. 1	fl, pf	Southern (ed. Cavally)
Russian Rhapsody, op. 176	fl, pf	Zimmermann
TILLMETZ, RUDOLF (1847–1915)		
Fantasia, op. 34	fl, orch	Zimmermann
Konzertetude, D, op. 22	fl, orch	Zimmermann
Rhapsodie Croatique, op. 56	fl, orch	Zimmermann
	fl, pf red	Fischer
Roumanian Pastorale Fantaisie	fl, pf red	Fischer
TULOU, JEAN LOUIS (1786–1865)		
Concerto no. 3, D, op. 10	fl, pf red	International (ed. Rampal)
3 Duos, op. 8	2fl	Lemoine
3 Duos concertants, op. 34	2fl	Zimmermann (ed. Grünenthal)
3 Duos Difficiles, op. 12	2fl	Heuwekemeijer
3 Duos Difficiles, op. 15	2fl	Heuwekemeijer
3 Duos Elementaires, op. 102	2fl	International; Kalmus
3 Duos Faciles, op. 14 (D,e,A)	2fl	Heuwekemeijer; Universal (ed. Braun)
3 Duos Très Faciles, op. 103	2fl	Breitkopf; International; Kalmus; Lemoine
3 Duos Très Faciles, op. 104	2fl	International; Kalmus; Lemoine
3 Grand Duos, op. 72	2fl	International (ed. Rampal)
3e Grand Solo, D, op. 74	fl, pf red	Billaudot (ed. Rampal)

5e Grand Solo, op. 79	fl, pf	Billaudot (ed. Rampal); International (ed. Rampal)
6e Grand Solo, A, op. 82	fl, pf	Billaudot (ed. Heriché)
11e Grand Solo, op. 93	fl, pf	Billaudot (ed. Heriché)
12e Grand Solo, b, op. 94	fl, pf red	Billaudot (ed. Rampal)
13e Grand Solo, a, op. 96	fl, pf	Billaudot (ed. Heriché)
14e Grand Solo, op. 97	fl, pf	Southern (ed. de Wetter-Smith)
Souvenir anglais, op. 51	3fl	Broekmans (ed. de Reede)
Trio, op. 65	3fl	International (ed. Rampal)
WALCKIERS, EUGÈNE (1793–1866)		
Grand quartet no. 1, f, op 46	4fl	Zimmermann
Quartet no. 2, op. 70	4fl	Broekmans (ed. van Munster)
WEBER, CARL MARIA VON (1786–1826)		
Menuet & Trio, A (from *Donna Diana*)	fl, vn/va, guit	Bote & Bock (ed. Behrend); Noetzel
Romanza siciliana, g, op. post. no. 2	fl, pf red	Hänssler (ed. Thalheimer); Lienau
6 Sonatas, op. 10	pf, fl	Eulenberg; Universal (ed. Braun)
Trio, g, op. 63	fl, vc, pf	Eulenberg (ed. Fiske); International; Lienau (ed. Wackernagel); Peters; G. Schirmer (ed. L. Moyse)
WIDOR, CHARLES-MARIE (1844–1937)		
Serenade, op. 10	pf, fl, vn, vc, harmonium/pf red	Hamelle
Suite, op. 34 (Romance and Scherzo)	fl, pf	Hamelle; Heugel; International (ed. Wummer); Piper; Southern
No. 1, Romance		Armstrong (ed. Borouchoff)
No. 2, Scherzo		Ed. Musicus (ed. Maganini); Fischer
Suite florentine	pf, fl/vn	Hamelle

D. THE MODERN ERA

ADLER, SAM (1928–)		
Concerto	fl, pf red	Southern
Flaunting	fl+optional picc, afl	Presser
Sonata	fl, pf	Southern
AITKEN, HUGH (1924–)		
Pastiche	fl	Oxford/NFA
AITKEN, ROBERT (1939–)		
Plainsong	fl	Universal
ALAIN, JEHAN (1911–1940)		
Aria	fl, org	Leduc
3 Mouvements	fl, pf	Leduc; Salabert
	fl, org	Leduc (arr. Marie-Claire Alain)
ALBISI, ABELARDO (1872–1939)		
Miniature Suites nos. 1, 2	3fl	Fischer
ALWYN, WILLIAM (1905–)		
Naiades	fl, hp	Lengnick
AMLIN, MARTIN (1953–)		
Sonata	fl, pf	Meridian
AMRAM, DAVID (1930–)		
Discussion	fl, pf, perc, vc	Peters

Overture & Allegro	fl	Peters
Zohar fl/rec	Peters	
ANDRIESSEN, JURRIAAN (1925–)		
Pastorale d'ete	fl	Broekmans
Plain-chant	fl, hp	Broekmans
Trio no. 2	fl, va, pf	Donemus
Trio No. 4	fl, ob, bn	Donemus
ANTHEIL, GEORGE (1900–1959)		
Sonata	fl, pf	Weintraub
ARNELL, RICHARD (1917–)		
Andante and Allegro, op. 58	fl, pf	Schott
5 Inventions	2fl	Hinrichsen
Music for Harp	fl, vn, va, hp	Peer
Trio	fl, vc, pf	Hinrichsen
ARNOLD, MALCOLM (1921–)		
Concerto no. 1, op. 45	fl, str/pf red	Paterson
Concerto no. 2, op. 111	fl, ch orch/pf red	Faber
Divertimento, op. 37	fl, ob, cl	Paterson
Duets, op. 10	fl, va	Faber, G. Schirmer
Fantasy, op. 89	fl	Faber
Quintet	fl, vn, va, bn, hn	Paterson
Sonata, op. 121	fl, pf	Faber
Sonatina, op. 19	fl, pf	Lengnick

Trio, op. 6	fl, bn, va	Paterson
Trio	fl, cl, bn	Paterson
AVSHALOMOV, AARON (1894–1965)		
Concerto	fl, orch	ACE
AVSHALOMOV, JACOB (1919–)		
Disconsolate Muse	fl, pf	AMP
BABBITT, MILTON (1916–)		
Composition for Four Instruments	fl, vn, cl, vc	Presser
Soli e duettini	fl, guit	Oxford/NFA
BADINGS, HENK (1907–1987)		
Ballade	fl, hp	Donemus
Capriccio	fl, pf	Donemus
Cavatina	(fl, pf)/(afl,hp)	Donemus
Concerto	fl, wind orch	Peters
Dialogues	fl, org	Donemus
Sonata	fl, guit	Schott
Trio no. 9	fl, va, gui	Donemus
BAKER, DAVID N. (1931–)		
Inspiration	fl, pf	Oxford/NFA
BAKSA, ROBERT (1938–)		
Monologue	fl	Composers Library Eds.
Sonata	fl, pf	Composers Library Eds.; Presser

BARBER, SAMUEL (1910–1981)		
Canzone, [transcribed by Barber from his Piano Concerto, op. 38, 2nd mvmt.]	fl, pf	G. Schirmer
Capricorn Concerto, op. 21	fl, ob, tpt, str	G. Schirmer
BARRAUD, HENRY (1900–)		
Concertino	pf, fl, cl, bn, hn	Soc. d'Eds. Mus. Intl.; Marbot
Concerto	fl, str/pf red	Boosey
BARRÈRE, GEORGES (1876–1944)		
The Barrère Album (Nocturne and 17 arrangements)	fl, pf	G. Schirmer (ed. Blaisdell)
Nocturne	fl, pf	G. Schirmer
2 Pièces Brèves (Preludiettino, Verlainade)	3fl	C. Fischer
BARTOK, BELA (1881–1945)		
3 Popular Hungarian Songs (arr. Arma)	fl, pf	Boosey (ed. Szebenyi) EMB (ed. Szebenyi)
Suite Paysanne Hongroise (arr. Arma)	fl, pf	Boosey; Universal
BARTOLOZZI, BRUNO (1911–1980)		
Cantilena	afl	Zerboni
The Hollow Man	fl	Zerboni
Per Olga	fl	Zerboni
Repitu	fl, va, guit, perc	Zerboni
Sinaulodia	4fl (lst-3rd: fl+picc; 4th: fl+afl)	Zerboni

BAX, ARNOLD (1883–1953)		
Elegiac Trio	fl, va, hp	Chester
4 Pieces	fl, pf	Chappell
BEACH, AMY MARCY CHENEY (1867–1944)		
Theme and Variations, a, op. 80	fl, 2vn, va, vc	G. Schirmer
BEASER, ROBERT (1954—)		
Il est né, le Divin Enfant	fl, guit	Helicon
Mountain Songs	fl, guit	Helicon (ed. Fisk)
The Old Men Admiring Themselves in the Water	fl, pf	Helicon
Song of the Bells	fl, orch	Helicon
Variations	fl, pf	Helicon
BEN-HAIM, PAUL (1897–1984)		
Serenade	fl, vn, va, vc	IMP
3 Songs Without Words	fl, pf	A. Broude; IMP/Presser [Israeli Music Pubs.]
BENKER, HEINZ (1921–)		
Der Abreiss-Kalendar: Miniature Suite	fl, pf	Breitkopf
Concertino	picc, orch	Breitkopf
Rondo Scherzando	fl, str	Breitkopf
BENNETT, RICHARD RODNEY (1936–)		
Commedia II	fl, vc, pf	Novello
Conversations	2fl	Universal
Memento	fl, str/pf red	Novello
Sonatina	fl	Universal
Summer Music	fl, pf	Novello
Trio	fl, ob, cl	Universal

Trio	fl, ob, pf	Mills
Winter Music	fl, pf	Mills
BENNETT, ROBERT RUSSELL (1894–1981)		
Concerto Grosso	fl, ob, cl, bn, hn; wind orch	Henmar
A Flute at Dusk	fl	Chappell
Rondo Capriccioso	4fl	Chappell
Suite	fl, cl	Warner
BERGSMA, WILLIAM (1921–)		
Pastorale and Scherzo	rec/fl, 2 va	Hug
Quintet	fl, str qt	Galaxy
BERIO, LUCIANO (1925–)		
Sequenza I	fl	Zerboni
Serenata I	fl, 14 insts	Zerboni
BERKELEY, LENNOX (1903–1989)		
Concertino, op. 49	rec/fl, vn, vc, hpd/pf	Chester
Concerto, op. 36	fl, orch/pf red	Chester
Piece	fl, cl, bn	Chester
Sonata, op. 97	fl, pf	Chester
Sonatina, op. 13	rec/fl, pf	Schott
BERLINSKI, HERMAN (1910–)		
Sonata	fl, pf	Southern

BERNSTEIN, LEONARD (1918–1990)		
Halil	fl, str, perc	Boosey
BIGGS, JOHN (1932–)		
Invention	fl, tape	Consort
BITSCH, MARCEL (1921–)		
3 Sonatines	fl, pf	Leduc
BLACHER, BORIS (1903–1975)		
Dialog	fl, vn, pf, str	Universal
Divertimento, op. 38	fl, ob, cl, bn	Bote & Bock
Duo	fl, pf	Bote & Bock; AMP
Quintet	fl, ob, vn, va, vc	AMP
Sonata, op. 15	fl, pf	Bote & Bock/AMP
BLISS, ARTHUR (1891–1975)		
Conversations, op. 15	fl+bfl, ob+eh, vn, va, vc	Curwen; Goodwin & Tabb
BLISS, MARILYN (1954–)		
Rima	picc, pf	Pan
BLOCH, ERNEST (1880–1959)		
Concertino	fl, va/cl, str/pf red	G. Schirmer
Suite Modale	fl, str/pf red	Broude Bros.
2 Last Poems (Maybe...)	fl, orch/pf red	Broude Bros.
BONET, NARCIS (1933–)		
Tricorde	fl, pf	Southern

BOTTJE, WILL GAY (1925–)		
Concertino	picc, orch	ACE
	picc, orch/wind ens/pf red	Zalo
Concerto	2fl, small orch	Zalo
BOULANGER, LILI (1893–1918)		
Cortège	vn/fl, pf	Ricordi
D'un Matin de Printemps	vn/fl, pf	Durand
Nocturne	fl, pf	Ricordi
BOULEZ, PIERRE (1925–)		
Le Marteau sans Maître	afl, gui, vib, xylorimba, perc, va	Universal
Sonatine	fl, pf	Amphion
BOZZA, EUGÈNE (1905–1991)		
Agrestide, op. 44	fl, pf	Leduc
Air de vielle	fl/ob, pf	Leduc
Air pastoral	fl/ob, pf	Leduc
Aria	fl, pf	Leduc
Atmospheres	4fl, ch orch	Leduc
Berceuse	fl/ob, pf	Leduc
Berceuse et sérénade	fl, guit	Leduc
5 Chansons sur les thèmes japonais	fl, pf	Leduc
Concertino da camera	fl, str/pf red	Leduc
Contrastes I	fl, bn	Leduc
2 Esquisses	4fl	Leduc

Dialogue	fl, pf	Billaudot
Fantaisie Italienne	fl, pf	Leduc
Image, op. 38	fl	Leduc
2 Impressions	fl, hp	Leduc
3 Impressions	fl, pf	Leduc
Interlude	fl/rec	Leduc
Jour d'été à la montagne	4fl	Leduc
3 Mouvements	fl, cl	Leduc
Phorbéia	fl	Leduc
3 Pièces	fl, guit	Leduc
3 Pièces	fl, ob	Leduc
3 Pièces	4fl	Leduc
4 Pièces faciles	fl, pf	Leduc
Polydiaphonie	fl, guit	Leduc
Serenade en trio	fl, cl, bn	Leduc
Soir dans les montagnes	fl, pf	Leduc
Sonatine	fl, bn	Leduc
BRANT, HENRY (1913–)		
Angels and Devils	solo fl; 3picc, 5fl, 2afl	MCA
Colloquy	fl, str/pf red	Spratt
Mobiles	fl	MCA
Temperamental Mobiles	fl	Spratt
BRIEF, TODD (1953–)		
Canto fl	Universal	
BRITTEN, BENJAMIN (1913–1976)		
Gemini Variations, op. 73	fl, vn, pf4h	Faber

BROUGHTON, BRUCE (1945–)		
Concerto	picc, pf red	Meridian
BROWN, ELIZABETH (1953–)		
Augury (1987)	fl, guit	Quetzal
The Memory Palace	fl, vc, pf	Quetzal
The Secret Life of Birds	fl, koto	Quetzal
BROWN, NEWEL KAY (1932–)		
Lyric	fl, hp	Little Piper
BURTON, ELDIN (1913–1981)		
Concerto	fl, pf red	Fischer
Sonatina	fl, pf	Fischer
BUSONI, FERRUCCIO (1866–1924)		
Albumblatt	fl, pf	Breitkopf
Divertimento, B♭, op. 52	fl, orch/pf red [by Kurt Weill]	Breitkopf
CAGE, JOHN (1912–1992)		
3 Pieces	2fl	Henmar/Peters
Two (April 1987)	fl, pf	Peters
CAPLET, ANDRÉ (1878–1925)		
Reverie et Petite Valse	fl, pf	International, Southern

CARTER, ELLIOTT (1908–)		
Esprit Rude/Esprit Doux	fl, cl	Hendon/Boosey
Scrivo in vento	fl	Hendon/Boosey
Sonata	fl, ob, vc, hpd	AMP
CASADESUS, ROBERT (1899–1972)		
Concerto, op. 35	fl, orch/pf red	Southern (ed. Cavally)
Fantaisie, op. 59	fl, pf	Durand
Sonata, op. 18	fl, pf	Durand
CASELLA, ALFREDO (1883–1947)		
Barcarolle et Scherzo, op. 4	fl, pf	Salabert
Sicilienne et Burlesque, op. 23	fl, pf	Leduc
CASTELNUOVO-TEDESCO, MARIO (1895–1968)		
Divertimento	2fl	Weaner-Levant
Eclogues	fl, eh, guit	General
Sonatina, op. 205	fl, gui	Eschig
CASTÉRÈDE, JACQUES (1926–)		
Ciels	fl, pf	Leduc
Flûtes en vacance	3fl (4th fl ad lib)	Leduc
Sonate en forme de Suite	fl, pf	Leduc
CASTIGLIONI, NICCOLO (1932–)		
Consonante	fl, ch orch	Schott
Gymel	fl, pf	Zerboni
CHASALOW, ERIC (1955–)		
Over the Edge	fl, tape	McGinnis & Marx

CHAVEZ, CARLOS (1899–1978)		
Vocalizacion Aguda	fl, pf	Carlanita (G. Schirmer)
CHILDS, BARNEY (1926–)		
Duo	fl, bn	ACE
The Location of Music	fl, db	Pembroke
Music for One Player	fl	ACE
Music for Two Flute Players	fl+picc, fl+afl	Merion
Quartet	fl, ob, db, perc	ACE
Sonata	fl, pf	ACE
Stances for Flute and Silence	fl	Seesaw
CHOU WEN-CHUNG (1923–)		
Cursive	fl, pf	Peters
3 Folk Songs	hp, fl	Peters
COLQUHOUN, MICHAEL (1953–)		
Charanga	fl	Colquhoun
COPLAND, AARON (1900–1990)		
Duo	fl, pf	Boosey
Threnody I: Igor Stravinsky, in memoriam	fl, vn, va, vc	Boosey
Threnody II: Beatrice Cunningham, in memoriam	afl, vn, va, vc	Boosey
Vocalise [arr. Copland]	fl, pf	Boosey
CORIGLIANO, JOHN (1938–)		
Pied Piper Fantasy	fl, orch/pf red	G. Schirmer
Voyage	fl, str/pf red/hp	G. Schirmer

COWELL, HENRY (1897–1965)		
2 Bits	fl, pf	Fischer
Duo Concertante	fl, hp, orch	AMP
Quartet Romantic	2fl, vn, va	Peters
Trio	fl, vn, hp	Peters
Triple Rondo	fl, hp	Hendon
CRAWFORD-SEEGER, RUTH (1901–1953)		
Diaphonic Suite no. 1	fl	A. Broude; Continuo; Merion
CRESTON, PAUL (1906–1985)		
Partita, op. 12	fl, vn, str/pf red	Belwin; Leeds
	fl, vn, str	Pro-Art
Suite, op. 56	fl, va, pf	Shawnee
CROLEY, RANDALL (1946–)		
Concerto for Flute and Metal Orchestra	fl, 4trb, tuba, pf, perc	Boonin
CRUMB, GEORGE (1929–)		
An Idyll for the Misbegotten	amp fl, perc	Peters
DAHL, INGOLF (1912–1970)		
Duettino concertante	fl, perc	A. Broude
Serenade	4fl	Boosey
Variations on a French Folk Tune	fl, pf	Boonin
Variations on an Air by Couperin	rec/fl, hpd/pf	Boonin
Variations on a Swedish Folktune	fl	Presser
	fl+afl	Boonin

DAMASE, JEAN-MICHEL (1928–)		
Divertissements	fl, pf	Billaudot
Double Concerto	fl, hp/hpd, str	
	(red: fl, hp/hpd)	EMT
Nocturne	fl, pf	Mondia
Quatuor de flûtes	4fl	Billaudot
Quintet, op. 2	fl, hp, vn, va, vc	Lemoine
Scherzo	fl, pf	Lemoine
Serenade, op. 36	fl, str/pf red	Lemoine
Sonate	fl, hp	Lemoine
Sonate	fl/vn, pf	Lemoine
Sonate en concert	fl, pf, vc ad lib	Lemoine
Suite pastorale	3fl	Billaudot
Trio	fl, hp, vc	Lemoine
Trio	fl, ob, pf	Lemoine
Variations on "Early One Morning"	fl, hp	Lemoine
DANIELS, MABEL WHEELER (1878–1971)		
3 Observations, op. 41	ob/fl, cl, bn	C. Fischer
Pastoral Ode, op. 40	fl, str	J. Fischer
DAVIDOVSKY, MARIO (1934–)		
Synchronisms no. 1	fl, tape	McGinnis & Marx
Synchronisms no. 2	fl, cl, vn, vc, tape	McGinnis & Marx

DAVIES, PETER MAXWELL (1934–)		
Two Pieces:		Boosey
The Kestrel Paced Round the Sun	fl	
Solita	fl, opt. musical box	
DEBUSSY, CLAUDE (1862–1918)		
Sonata	fl, va, hp	Durand
Syrinx	fl	Broekmans; Chester (ed. Wye); Jobert; Novello (with text)
DELANEY, CHARLES (1925–)		
"... and the strange unknown flowers"	fl	Southern
Hymn of Pan	fl	Little Piper
DELLO JOIO, NORMAN (1913–)		
Concertino	fl, str	G. Schirmer
The Developing Flutist	fl, pf	E.B. Marks
Trio	fl, vc, pf	Fischer
Trio	fl, vn, pf	Fischer
DENISOV, EDISON (1929–)		
Concerto fl, pf, ob, perc	Universal	
Duo	fl, va	Leduc
4 Pièces	fl, pf	Leduc
Prélude et Air	fl, pf	Leduc
Sonata	fl	Leduc
Sonata	fl, guit	Sikorski
Sonata	fl, hp	Leduc
Sonata	fl, pf	Peters

DIAMOND, DAVID (1915–)		
Elegies	fl, eh, str	Peer
Quintet, b	fl, vn, va, vc, pf	Peer; G. Schirmer
DICK, ROBERT		
Afterlight	fl	Dick; Multiple Breath
Flying Lessons I & II	fl	Dick; Multiple Breath
Lookout	fl	Multiple Breath
DIEMER, EMMA LOU (1927–)		
"A Certain Slant of Light..."	fl, guit	Diemer
Concerto	fl, pf red	Southern
Quartet	fl, va, vc, hpd, tape	Seesaw
Sonata	fl, pf	Southern
Suite "Homage à Hindemith"	fl, pf	Oxford/NFA
Trio	fl, marimba, vc	Seesaw
DIERCKS, JOHN (1929–)		
3 Diversions	fl, pf	Shawnee
DOHNÁNYI, ERNÓ (1877–1960)		
Aria, op. 48, no. 1	fl, pf	AMP
Passacaglia, op. 48, no. 2	fl	Broude Bros.
DOMINUTTI, FRANCO		
Specchi; Comme dans un miroir	fl, optional tape	Leduc

DORAN, MATT (1921–)		
Andante and Allegro	fl, vc, pf	WIM
Poem	fl, pf	WIM
4 Short Pieces	fl	WIM
Sonatina	2fl	WIM
Sonatina	fl, vc	WIM
DUBOIS, PIERRE MAX (1930–)		
A Tempo Classico	fl, pf	Rideau Rouge
Berceuse et Rondo Capriccioso	2fl	Leduc
La Capricieuse	fl, pf	Rideau Rouge
Classiquement Votre	fl, guit	Billaudot
Concerto	fl, orch/pf red	Leduc
Incantation et Danse	fl	Leduc
Novelette	fl, pf	Leduc
Petite Suite	fl, bn	Leduc
Piccolette	picc, pf	Rideau Rouge
Pop Variations	fl, pf	Leduc
9 Preludes Faciles	fl, pf	Choudens
Quatuor	4fl	Leduc
Slowly and Swingy	fl, pf	Rideau Rouge
Sonate	fl, pf	Leduc
DU BOIS, ROB		
Bewegingen	picc, pf	Donemus
DUBOIS, THEODORE (1837–1924)		
Terzettino	fl, va, hp	Heugel
Vergiliens	fl, pf	Heugel

DUKAS, PAUL (1865–1935)		
La plainte, au loin, du Faune	fl, pf	Durand (arr. Samazeuilh)
DURUFLÉ, MAURICE (1902–1971)		
Prélude, Recitatif et Variations, op. 3	fl, va, pf	Durand
DUTILLEUX, HENRI (1916–)		
Sonatine	fl, pf	Leduc
ENESCO, GEORGES (1881–1955)		
Cantabile et Presto	fl, pf	Boosey; Enoch; International; Kalmus; Southern
Introduction et Variations	fl, pf	Enoch
ERB, DONALD (1927–)		
Drawing Down the Moon	picc, perc	Merion
Music for Mother Bear	afl/fl	Merion
ETLER, ALVIN (1913–1973)		
Duo	fl, cl/va	New Valley
Suite	fl, ob, cl	AMP
FAURÉ, GABRIEL (1845–1924)		
Fantaisie, op. 79	fl, pf	Armstrong (ed. McGinty); Belwin; Chester (ed. Wye); EMB (ed. Jeney); Hamelle; International; Kalmus; Peters (ed. Burmeister); Southern
Morceau de concert	fl, pf	Bourne (ed. Brieff)
Pavane	fl, pf	A. Broude; Hamelle (ed. Büsser); Southern (ed. Ephross)

Pièce	fl/ob/vn, pf	Broekmans (ed. de Reede); Leduc
Sicilienne, op. 78 [trans. from *Pélleas et Meliscnde*]	fl, pf	Chester (ed. Biglio); EMB (ed. Palfalvi & Jeney); Hamelle (ed. Busser); International (ed. Büsser); Kalmus; Southern (ed. Cavally)
FELD, JINDRICH (1925–)		
2 Danses	fl, guit	Leduc
Duo Concertant	2fl	Leduc
Fantaisie Concertante	fl, (str, perc)/pf red	Leduc
5 Inventions	2fl	Leduc
Petit Caprice	fl, pf	Leduc
Petit Divertissement	3fl	Leduc
4 Pièces	fl	Leduc
Sonate	fl, pf	Leduc
Sonatine	fl, hp	Leduc
FENNELLY, BRIAN (1937–)		
For Solo Flute	fl	Margun
FERNEYHOUGH, BRIAN (1943–)		
Cassandra's Dream Song	fl	Peters
Four Miniatures	fl, pf	Peters
Superscriptio	picc	Peters
Unity Capsule	fl	Peters
FERROUD, P. O. (1900–1936)		
3 Pièces	fl	Salabert
FINE, VIVIAN (1913–)		
Emily's Images	fl, pf	Margun; Oxford/NFA
The Flicker	fl	Margun

FINZI, GERALD (1901–1956)		
5 Bagatelles	fl, pf [arr. from cl, pf]	Boosey (arr. Albright)
FLAGELLO, NICOLAS (1928–)		
Burlesca, op. 34	fl, gui	General
Concerto Antoniano, op. 12	fl, orch/pf	General
Furann	fl	General
FLOTHIUS, MARIUS (1914–)		
Sonate da camera, op. 27	fl, pf	Donemus
FOOTE, ARTHUR (1853–1937)		
A Night Piece	fl, 2vn, va, vc/pf red	Southern
3 Pieces, op. 31	ob/fl, pf	Schott
Scherzo	fl, 2vn, va, vc	Southern
FOSS, LUKAS (1922–)		
3 American Pieces	fl, pf	C. Fischer
Renaissance Concerto	fl, orch/pf red	C. Fischer
FRANÇAIX, JEAN (1912–)		
A Cinq	fl, vn, va, vc, hp	Schott
A Quatre	fl, ob, cl, bn	Schott
Le Colloque des deux Perruches	fl/altofl ck abbrev	Schott
Concerto	fl, pf red	Schott
Concerto	fl, pf red	Schott
Divertimento	fl, pf	Schott

Duo Concertante	fl, vn, orch	Schott
Impromptu	fl, pf	Schott
7 Impromptus	fl, bn	Schott
Musique de cour	fl, vn, orch/pf red	Schott
5 Piccoli Duetti	fl, hp	Schott
Quadruple Concerto	fl, ob, cl, bn, orch	Schott
Quintet no. 2	fl, vn, va, vc, hp	Schott
Suite	fl	Schott
Trio	fl, vc, hp	Schott
FUERSTNER, CARL (1912–)		
Nocturne & Dance, op. 36	fl, pf	Zalo
FUKUSHIMA, KAZUO (1930–)		
Deux Kadha	fl	Zerboni
Ekagura	afl, pf	Zerboni
Hi-kyo [The Flying Mirror]	fl, perc, pf, str	Zerboni
	afl, orch	Zerboni
Mei [2nd mvmt. of Hi-kyo]	fl	Zerboni
Kadha karuna [Poem of Compassion]	fl, pf	Zerboni
3 Pieces from Chu-U	fl, pf	Peters
Requiem	fl	Zerboni
GABER, HARLEY (1943–)		
Chimyakyu	fl/afl	ACE
Fantasy	fl	ACE
Koku	fl	ACE (ed. Sollberger)
Scambio	fl, pf	ACE

GANNE, LOUIS (1862–1923)		
Andante et Scherzo	fl, pf	Belwin; Billaudot; Fischer; Southern
GAUBERT, PHILIPPE (1879–1941)		
3 Aquarelles	fl, vc, pf	Bornemann
Serenade		Southern (ed. Cavally)
Ballade	fl, pf	Heugel
Berceuse	fl/vn, pf	Enoch; Eschig; Little Piper; Southern (ed. Cavally)
Divertissement grec	fl/2fl, hp/pf	Leduc; Music Masters
2 Esquisses: Soir sur la Plaine, Orientale	fl, pf	Heugel
Fantaisie	fl, pf	International (ed. Wummer); Salabert; Southern (ed. Ephross)
Madrigal	fl, pf	Belwin; Enoch; International (ed. Wummer); Little Piper
Nocturne and Allegro Scherzando	fl, pf	Enoch; International; Kalmus; Southern
Piece Romantique	fl, vc, pf	Bornemann
Romance	fl, pf	Enoch; Leduc; Little Piper
Sicilienne	fl, small orch/pf red	Heugel
	fl, pf red	Leduc; Little Piper
Sonata no. 1, A	fl, pf	Durand
Sonata no. 2, C	fl, pf	Heugel
Sonata no. 3, G	fl, pf	Heugel
Sonatine	fl, pf	Heugel
Suite	fl, pf	Heugel; Meridian
Sur l'eau	fl, pf	Lemoine; Little Piper
Tarantelle	fl, ob, pf	Enoch

GENZMER, HARALD (1909–)		
Concertino no. 1	pf, fl/vn, str	Schott
Concerto	fl, orch/pf red	Schott
Divertimento giocoso	2fl/2rec/(fl,ob), str	Schott
Divertissement	fl, pf	Peters
Divertissement	fl, vn	Litolff
Pan	fl/afl	Litolff
Quartet	4fl	Litolff
Sonata	fl	Peters
Sonata	fl, ob	Schott
Sonata no. 1	fl, pf	Ries & Erlers; Schott
Sonata no. 2, e	fl, pf	Schott
Sonata, f♯	2fl	Schott
Sonata no. 2	2fl	Litolff
Sonata no. 3	2fl	Peters
Trio	3fl	Schott
Trio	fl, bn/vc, kbd	Litolff
Trio	fl, va, hp	Litolff
GESENSWAY, LOUIS		
Concerto	fl, 2pf red	Horowitz
GIESEKING, WALTER (1895–1956)		
Sonatine	fl, pf	Little Piper
Variations on a Theme by Edward Grieg	fl, pf	Little Piper
GINASTERA, ALBERTO (1916–1983)		
Duo, op. 13	fl, ob	Billaudot; Mercury; Music Press
Impressions of Puna	fl, 2vn, va, vc	Peer

GLASS, PHILIP (1937–)		
Diversions	2fl, trb	UMI
Divertimento	fl, cl, bn	UMI
Fantasy	fl	UMI
Serenade	fl, pf ck insts	Elkan-Vogel
GOLDMAN, RICHARD FRANKO (1910–1980)		
Divertimento	fl, pf	Shawnee
Two Monochromes	fl	Shawnee
GOOSSENS, EUGENE (1893–1962)		
5 Impressions of a Holiday, op. 7	fl/vn, vc, pf	Chester
Pastoral and Harlequinade, op. 41	fl/vn, ob/vn, pf	Curwen; Leduc
3 Pictures, op. 55	fl, str, perc/pf red	Chester
Scherzo fantasque	fl, pf	Leduc
4 Sketches	fl, vn, pf	Chester
Suite, op. 6	fl/vn, vn, hp/pf	Chester
GORDELI, OTAR (1928–)		
Concerto	fl, pf red	Progress Press (ed. Kujala)
GRETCHANINOV, ALEXANDER (1864–1956)		
Bachkiria, op. 125	fl, hp	Schott
Brimborions, op. 138	fl, pf	Augener; Galaxy
Concertino, op. 171	2fl, pf	Hargail
2 Miniatures, op. 145	fl, pf	Leduc
12 Short Pieces	fl, pf	Presto

GRIFFES, CHARLES TOMLINSON (1884–1920)		
Poem	fl, orch	G. Schirmer
	fl, pf red	G. Schirmer (arr. Barrère)
	fl, band	G. Schirmer (ed. Thornton)
GROFÉ, FERDE (1892–1972)		
Table d'Hôte	fl, vn, va	General; Kjos
GROVLEZ, GABRIEL (1879–1944)		
Romance and Scherzo	fl, pf	Masters Music; Southern
GRYČ, STEPHEN M. (1949–)		
5 Préludes	fl	Leduc
GUBAIDULINA, SOFIA (1931–)		
Allegro Rustico: Sounds of the Forest	fl, pf	Sikorski
HAHN, REYNALDO (1875–1947)		
Danse pour une déesse	fl, pf	Heugel
L'Enchanteuse	fl, pf	Heugel
2 Pieces	fl, pf	Heugel
Romanesque	fl, va, pf	Heugel
Variations on a Theme of Mozart	fl, pf	Heugel; International; Kalmus
HANSON, HOWARD (1896–1981)		
Serenade, op. 35	fl, hp str/pf red	Fischer
HARBISON, JOHN (1938–)		
Duo	fl, pf	AMP

HARRIS, ROY (1898–1979)		
Four Minutes and Twenty Seconds	fl, 2vn, va, vc	Belwin; G. Schirmer
HARRISON, LOU (1917–)		
Canticle no. 3	fl/ocarina, gui, perc	Music for Percussion
Concerto no. 1	fl, perc	Peters
Trio	fl, vn, va	Peters
HARTLEY, WALTER S. (1927–)		
Duet	fl, tuba	Tritone/Presser
4 Sketches	fl, pf	Tenuto/Presser
Sonata	fl, pf	Tenuto/Presser
Sonatina	fl	FEMA
HEIDEN, BERNHARD (1910–)		
5 Short Pieces	fl, pf	Southern
Sonatina	fl, pf	AMP
HEISS, HERMANN (1897–1966)		
Concerto	fl, str, perc	Breitkopf
Konzertante Suite	fl, str, pf	Môseler
Modi	fl	Breitkopf
Sonata	fl, pf	Müller
HEISS, JOHN (1938–)		
Capriccio	fl, cl, perc	E.C. Schirmer
Chorale; Multiples	fl	Oxford/NFA
6 Etudes, op. 20	fl	J.B. Elkus

4 Lyric Pieces	fl	Southern
Mosaics I	fl choir	MMB Music
4 Movements	3fl	Boosey
5 Pieces	fl, vc	E.C. Schirmer
Sonata Appasionata	fl	J.B. Elkus
HENZE, HANS WERNER (1926–)		
Kammerkonzert	pf, fl, str	Schott
Sonatine	fl, pf	Schott
HETU, JACQUES (1938–)		
Aria, op. 27	fl, pf	Doberman
Concerto, op. 51	fl, orch/pf red	Doberman-Yppan
Serenade, op. 45	fl, str qt	Doberman-Yppan
HIGDON, JENNIFER (1962–)		
The Hefrey Mode	fl, pf	Lawdon
Steely Pause	4 fl	Lawdon
HINDEMITH, PAUL (1895–1963)		
Abendkonzert no. 2 [from Plöner Musiktag]	fl, vn, va, vc	Schott
Concerto	fl, ob, cl, bn, hp, orch	Schott
Echo	fl, pf	Schott
3 Kanonische Sonatine, op. 31 no. 3?	2fl	Schott
8 Pieces	fl	Schott
Sonata	fl, pf	Schott
Spielmusik, op. 43, no. 1	fl, ob, str	Schott
HOLLIGER, HEINZ (1939–)		
Lied	fl/afl/bfl	Breitkopf

HOLST, GUSTAV (1874–1934)

A Fugal Concerto, op. 40, no. 2	fl, ob, str/pf red	Novello
Terzetto, op. 44	fl, ob, va/cl	Chester

HONEGGER, ARTHUR (1892–1955)

Concerto da camera	fl, eh, str/pf red	Salabert
3 Contrepoints	picc, ob+eh, vn, vc	Hansen
Danse de la chevre	fl	Salabert
Petite suite no. 2	2fl, pf	Philharmusica; Salabert
Rapsodie	2fl, cl, pf	Salabert
Romance	fl, pf	International
Suite	fl, vn, pf	Senart

HOOVER, KATHERINE (1937–)

Canyon Echos	fl, guit	Papagena
Divertimento	fl, vn, va, vc	Papagena
Kokopeli	fl	Papagena
Lyric Trio, op. 27	fl, vc, pf	Papagena
Medieval Suite, op. 18	fl, pf	Presser
Reflections	fl	Papagena
Sound Bytes	2fl	Papagena
Summer Night	fl, hn, str/pf red	Presser

HORWOOD, MICHAEL (1947–)

Birds	picc, pf	ALRY

HOSMER, JAMES (19[illegible]1–)

4 Duos	2fl	McGinnis & Marx

HOVHANESS, ALAN (1911–)		
Elibris, op. 50	fl, str	Peer
The Garden of Adonis, op. 245	fl, hp	Peters
7 Love Songs of Saris, op. 252/3	vn/fl, pf	Peters
Pastoral and Fugue, op. 271	2fl	AMP
Prelude and Fugue, op. 13	fl/ob, bn	Peters
Quartet no. 1, op. 97	fl, ob, vc, hpd/pf	Peters
Quartet no. 2, op. 112	fl, ob, vc, pf	Peters
Sonata, op. 118	fl	Peters
Sonata for Ryuteki & Sho, op. 121	fl, org	Peters
The Spirit of Ink, op. 230	3fl	Peters
Symphony No. 17 (for Metal Orch.), op. 203	6fl, 3trb, perc	Peters
Tzaikerk (Evening Song)	fl, vn, timp, str	Peer
Upon Enchanted Ground, op. 90, no. 1	fl, hp, tam, vc	Peters
HÜE, GEORGES (1858–1948)		
Fantaisie	fl, pf red	Billaudot; Leduc
Nocturne et Gigue	fl, orch/pf red	Leduc
Gigue	fl, pf red	Fischer; Southern (ed. Ephross)
Petite Pièce, G	fl, pf	Leduc
Serenade	fl, pf	Fischer; Leduc; Southern (ed. Cavally)
HURD, MICHAEL (1928–)		
Sonatina	fl, pf	Novello
IBERT, JACQUES (1890–1962)		
Allegro scherzando [from Concerto]	fl, orch/pf red	Leduc
Aria	fl, vn/cl, pf	Leduc
	fl, pf	Leduc
Concerto	fl, orch/pf red	Leduc

Entr'acte	fl/vn, hp/gui	Leduc
Histoires [arr. by Ibert of nos. 1,2,5, 8-10 of piano work]: no. 1, La Meneuse de tortues d'or; no. 2, Le petit âne blanc; no. 5, Dans la maison triste; no. 8, La cage du cristal; no. 9, La marchande d'eau fraiche; no. 10, Le cortège de Balkis	fl, pf	Leduc
2 Interludes, from *Le Burlador*	fl, vn, hpd/hp	Leduc
Jeux	fl/vn, pf	Leduc
2 Mouvements	2fl, cl, bn	Leduc
Paraboles	fl, guit	Leduc (arr. Starr)
Pièce	fl	Leduc
Quartet	2fl, cl, bn	Leduc

D'INDY, VINCENT (1851–1931)

Concerto, op. 89	fl, vc, pf, str	Rouart; Salabert
Suite dans le style ancien, D, op. 24	tpt, 2fl, 2vn, va, vc	Hamelle; International
Suite en parties, A, op. 91	fl, vn, va, vc, hp	Heugel
Trio	fl, vc, pf	Heugel

INGELBRECHT, D. E.

Sonatine	fl, hp/pf	Leduc

JACOB, GORDON (1895–1984)

Concerto	fl, orch/pf red	Galaxy; Williams
Concerto no. 2	fl, orch/pf red	Boosey
3 Inventions	fl, ob	Williams
The Pied Piper	fl+picc	Oxford

Suite	fl/rec, str/pf red	Oxford
	fl/rec, pf red	Reinhardt
Trio	fl+picc, ob, hpd/pf	Oxford
JACOBI, FREDERICK (1891–1952)		
Night Piece and Dance	fl, pf	Boosey
JAFFE, GERARD		
Three Figures and a Ground	fl, pf	Merion
Pastoral Suite	fl, pf	Southern
JARNACH, PHILIPP (1892–)		
Sonatine, op. 12	fl, pf	Lienau
JEANJEAN, PAUL (1929–)		
Heureux Temps	fl, pf	Billaudot
Reverie de Printemps	fl, pf	Billaudot
JOLIVET, ANDRÉ (1905–1974)		
Alla rustica	fl/2fl, hp	Boosey
Ascèses, 5 pieces	fl/afl/altocl/cl	Billaudot (ed. Rampal)
Cabrioles [Capers]	fl, pf	International; Noël
Chant de Linos	fl, pf/(vn,va,vc,hp)	Costallat; Leduc
Concerto	fl, str/pf red	Heugel
Fantaisie-caprice	fl, pf	Leduc
Incantation "Pour que l'image devienne symbole"	vn/fl/ondes martenot	Billaudot
5 Incantations	fl	Boosey
Pastorales de Noël	fl/vn, bn/va/vc, hp	Heugel
Petite suite	fl, va, hp	EMT
Sonate	fl, pf	Heugel

Sonatine	fl, cl	Boosey
Suite en concert	fl, perc	Billaudot
JONES, CHARLES (1910–)		
Sonata Piccola	picc, hpd/fl	Zalo
KARG-ELERT, SIGFRID (1877–1933)		
Impressions exotiques, op. 134	fl, pf	Falls House (ed. Worthen); Zimmermann
Jugend, op. 139	fl, pf	Falls House (ed. Worthen)
Kolibris	picc, pf	PWM Edition
Sinfonische Kanzone, E♭, op. 114	fl, pf	Zimmermann
Sonata, B♭, op. 121	fl, pf	Zimmermann
Sonata appassionata, f♯, op. 140	fl	Southern (ed. Levy); Zimmermann
Suite pointillistique, op. 135	fl, pf	Zimmermann
KAY, ULYSSES (1917–)		
Aulos fl, ch orch/pf red	Pembroke	
Prelude	fl	Pembroke
Suite	fl, ob	Leeds
KENNAN, KENT WHEELER (1913–)		
Night Soliloquy	fl, str/band/pf red	Fischer
Threnody	fl, pf	Presser
KERNIS, AARON JAY (1960–)		
Delicate Songs	fl, vn, vc	AMP

KHACHATURIAN, ARAM (1903–1978)		
Concerto [arr. of Violin Concerto]	fl, pf red	International (ed. Rampal)
KOECHLIN, CHARLES (1867–1950)		
L'album de Lilian, première serie, op. 139		Eschig
No. 4, Les yeux clairs	fl, pf	
No. 6, Skating-smiling	fl, sop, pf	
No. 7, En route vers le bonheur	fl, sop/cl, pf	
No. 8, Pleurs	fl, pf	
L'album de Lilian, deuxième serie, op. 149		
4 Pièces: Serenade à l'étoile errante, Swimming, Le voyage chimerique, Les jeux du clown	fl, pf	Eschig
14 Chants [Pieces], op. 157/2	fl, pf	Salabert
Les Chants de nectaire, op. 198	fl	Billaudot
3 Divertissements, op. 90	2fl, afl/cl	Schneider
Epitaphe de Jean Harlow, op. 164 (op. post.)	fl, sax, pf	Eschig
Morceau de lecture, op. 218	fl, pf	Billaudot
2 Nocturnes, op. 32 bis	hn, fl, pf	Billaudot
Pastorales, op. 75 bis	fl, cl, pf	Billaudot
Quintet "Primaver," op. 156	fl, hp, vn, va, vc	Senart; L'Oiseau Lyre; Eschig
Sonata, op. 52	fl, pf	Senart; Salabert
Sonata, op. 75	2fl	Senart; Salabert
3 Sonatines, op. 184	fl	Salabert; Ricordi
Sonatine modale, op. 155	fl, cl	Eschig
Stele funéraire, op. 224	fl+picc+afl	Eschig
Suite en quatuor, op. 55	fl, vn, va, pf	Eschig
Trio, op. 92	ob/fl, cl, bn	Salabert

KOLB, BARBARA (1940–)

Figments	fl, pf	Fischer
Homage to Keith Jarrett & Gary Burton	fl, vibra	Boosey
Musique pour un vernissage	vn, fl, va, guit	Boosey

KORDE, SHIRISH (1945–)

Tenderness of Cranes	fl	Neuma

KORTE, KARL (1928–)

Colloquy	fl, computer processed tape	K Note Press
Remembrances	fl+afl+picc, tape	Elkan-Vogel

KRENEK, ERNST (1900–1991)

Concertino, op. 27	fl, vn, hpd/pf, str	Universal
Flôtenstück neunphasig [Flute Piece in Nine Phases]	fl, pf	Bärenreiter; Rongwen
Fluteplayers Serenade	4fl	Belwin
Sonatina, op. 92, no. 2b	fl, cl	Bärenreiter
Suite	fl, str/pf	Bärenreiter; Rongwen

KUBIK, GAIL T. (1914–1984)

Little Suite	fl, 2cl	Hargail
Nocturne	fl, pf	G. Schirmer

KUPFERMAN, MEYER (1926–)

4 Charades	fl, cl	General
4 Constellations	fl, cl	General
Infinities One	fl	General

Line Fantasy	fl	General
Music from Hallelujah the Hills	fl, pf/hpd	General
Quiet Piece	fl, pf	General
Short Shrift	picc, cl	General
Superflute	fl, tape	General
LADERMAN, EZRA (1924–)		
Celestial Bodies	fl, str/pf red	Oxford
Concerto	fl, orch/pf red	G. Schirmer
Duet	fl, dancer	Broude
Double Helix	fl, ob, orch	Oxford
MBL Suite	2fl, str qt	G. Schirmer
Sonata	fl, pf	Oxford
LA MONTAINE, JOHN (1920–)		
Canonic Variations	fl, cl	Fana
Come into my garden	fl, pf	Fredonia
Concerto, op. 48	fl, pf red	Fredonia
Conversations, op. 44	fl, pf	Fredonia
Sonata, op. 24	fl	Broude Bros.
Sonata, op. 61	picc, pf	Fredonia
LANGLAIS, JEAN (1907–1991)		
Mouvement	fl/ob/vn, pf/hpsd/org	Pro Organo
LARSEN, LIBBY (1950–)		
Aubade	fl	E.C. Schirmer
Fantasy on Slane	fl, pf	E.C. Schirmer
Ulloa's ring	fl, pf	E.C. Schirmer

LEES, BENJAMIN (1924–)		
Duo	2fl	Boosey
3 Duos	fl, cl	Boosey
Evocation	fl	Carlvi
Soliloquy Music from King Lear	fl	Boosey
LENNON, JOHN ANTHONY (1950–)		
Echolalia	fl	Oxford/NFA
LEVY, BURT (1936–)		
Orbs with Flute	fl	Apogee
LIEBERMANN, LOWELL (1961–)		
Concerto, op. 39	fl, orch/pf red	Presser
Soliloquy, op. 44	fl	Presser
Sonata, op. 23	fl, pf	Presser
Sonata, op. 25	fl, guit	Presser
LIGETI, GYÔRGY (1923–)		
Double Concerto	fl, ob, orch	Schott
LOEB, DAVID (1939–)		
Nocturnes and Meditations	picc	ALRY
4 Preludes, Vol. II	picc	ALRY
6 Preludes	picc	ALRY
Sonata No. 3	fl	ALRY

LUENING, OTTO (1900–)		
10 Canons	2fl	ACE
Concertino	fl, hp, str, cel	Peters
3 Duets	2fl	New Valley
Fantasia brevis	fl, pf	Galaxy; Highgate
Lyric Scene	fl, orch	Peters
2 Pieces	fl, pf	ACE
Serenade	fl, pf	Oxford/NFA
Short Sonata	fl, hpd/pf	ACE; Galaxy; New Valley
2nd Short Sonata	fl, pf	ACE; New Valley
3rd Short Sonata	fl, pf	New Valley
Sonatina	fl, pf	ACE; New Valley
Song, Poem & Dance	fl, str qt	ACE; Galaxy
Sonority Canon	2-37fl	Galaxy; Highgate
5 Suites	fl	E.B. Marks
No. 1		Galaxy; Highgate
Nos. 1–4		ACE
Nos. 3–5		Joshua/G. Schirmer
Suite	2fl, pf	General; Joshua/G. Schirmer
Suite	fl, cl, bn	Galaxy
Suite	fl, ob, bn	Galaxy
Suite	fl, ob, vc	Galaxy
Trio	fl, vn, pf	Galaxy; Highgate
Trio	fl, vc, pf	Peters
Trio	3fl	Galaxy

MADERNA, BRUNO (1920–1973)		
Concerto	fl, orch	Ars Viva; Schott
Dialodia	2fl/2rec/2ob	Ricordi
Dimensioni III	fl, orch	Zerboni

Grande aulodia	fl, ob, orch	Ricordi
Honeyrêves	fl, pf	Zerboni
Musica su due dimensioni (Dimensioni no. 1)	fl, optional tape	Zerboni
Le Rire	fl, mar, tape	Zerboni
MALIPIERO, GIAN FRANCESCO (1882–1973)		
Concerto	fl, orch/pf red	Ricordi
MARTIN, FRANK (1890–1974)		
Ballade	fl, pf	Universal
	fl, str, pf	Universal (orch. Ansermet)
Pièce Brève	fl, ob, hp	Hug
Sonata da chiesa	fl, org/str	Universal
MARTINO, DONALD (1931–)		
Notturno	picc+fl+afl, cl+bcl, vn+va, vc, pf, perc	E.C. Schirmer
Quodlibets	fl	McGinnis & Marx
Quodlibets II	fl	Dantalion
MARTINON, JEAN (1910–1976)		
Concerto	fl, orch/pf red	Billaudot
Sonatine, op. 19b	fl, pf	Billaudot (ed. Rampal)
MARTINŮ, BOHUSLAV (1890–1959)		
Concerto	fl, vn, ch orch	Bärenreiter
Divertimento	2fl	Eschig

Madrigal Sonata	fl, vn, pf	AMP
Promenades	fl, vn, hpd	Bärenreiter
Scherzo	fl, pf	Artia; Bärenreiter
Sonata	fl, vn, pf	Bärenreiter
Sonata	fl, pf	AMP; Schott
Trio	fl, vc, pf	AMP
MASON, THOM (1941–)		
Thoughts	fl	Zalo
MATSUDAIRA, YORITSUNE (1907–)		
Orbits I,II,III	fl, cl, pf	Zerboni
Rhymes for Gazzelloni	fl	Zerboni
Somaksah	fl	Zerboni
Sonatine	fl, pf	Shawnee
MAW, NICHOLAS (1935–)		
Night Thoughts	fl	Faber
Quartet	fl, vn, va, vc	Faber; G. Schirmer
Sonatina	fl, pf	Chester
MEKEEL, JOYCE (1931–)		
Rune	fl, perc	Oxford/NFA
The Shape of Silence	fl	Peters
MENNIN, PETER (1923–1983)		
Concertino	fl, str, perc	Hargail
Concerto	fl, pf red	Fischer

MESSIAEN, OLIVIER (1908–1992)

Le merle noir	fl, pf	Leduc

MIGOT, GEORGES (1891–1976)

Fantasie No. 1	fl, pf	Galaxy
26 Monodies Permodales	fl	SEDIM
Trio	fl, vn, hpd	EMT

MIHALOVICI, MARCEL (1898–)

Miroir des Songes	fl, pf	Eschig

MILHAUD, DARIUS (1892–1974)

Concerto, op. 197	fl, vn, orch/pf red	Salabert
Quintet, Op. 443	ww qnt	Eschig
Sonate, B♭, op. 47	pf, fl, cl, ob	Durand
Sonatine, op. 76	fl, pf	Durand

MISURELL–MITCHELL, JANICE (1946–)

Mobius Trip	fl	ACA
On Thin Ice	fl, guit	ACA
Uncommon Time	fl	ACA

MIYAGI, MICHIO (1894–1956)

Haru No Umi (The Sea in Springtime)	fl, guit	Pierrot (trans. Ketchum & Siegel)

MOLS, ROBERT (1921–)

Music for Two Flutes	2fl	Edu-Tainment

Sonata	fl, pf	Edu-Tainment
Three Miniatures and Coda	5fl	JP
MOYSE, LOUIS (1911–)		
7 Caprice-Etudes	fl; fl, pf	Costallat
4 Dances	fl, vn	McGinnis & Marx
30 Easy Duets in all keys	2fl	McGinnis & Marx
Fantaisie	fl, pf	Leduc
Improvisation on harmonics	fl	Leeds (Canada)
Introduction, Theme & Variations	fl, pf	G. Schirmer
Kojo no Tsuki (The Castle by Moonlight)	fl, pf	McGinnis & Marx
3 Pieces Faciles	fl, pf	Leduc
Suite, C	2fl, cl, va	Southern
MUCZYNSKI, ROBERT (1929–)		
Duos, op. 34	2fl	G. Schirmer
Duos	fl, cl	G. Schirmer
Fragments	fl, cl, bn	Shawnee
Moments	fl, pf	Presser
3 Preludes, op. 18	fl	G. Schirmer
Sonata, op. 14	fl, pf	G. Schirmer
MUSGRAVE, THEA (1928–)		
Chamber Concerto no. 2 "in homage to Charles Ives"	picc+fl+afl, cl+bcl, vn+va, vc, pf	Chester
Impromptu no. 1	fl, ob	Chester
Impromptu no. 2	fl, ob, cl	Chester
Narcissus	fl, digital delay	Novello
Orfeo II	fl, str	Novello
Piccolo Play	picc, pf	Novello

Serenade	fl, cl, va, vc, hp	Chester
Sonata for three	fl, vn, guit	Novello
Trio	fl, ob, pf	Chester
NELHYBEL, VACLAV (1919–)		
Concert Etudes	fl	General
4 Duets	2fl	General
Short Stories	2fl	J. Christopher
Suite	fl, pf	General
NEWMAN, ANTHONY (1941–)		
Introduction and Toccata	fl, pf	G. Schirmer
NIELSEN, CARL (1865–1931)		
Concerto	fl, orch/pf red	Chester; Dan Fog
Faith and Hope are Playing [Tro og hab spiller]	fl, va	Hansen
The Mother [Moderen]		
The Children are Playing [Børnene spiller]	fl	Hansen
The Fog is Lifting [Taagen letter], op. 41	fl, pf/hp	Hansen
NIXON, ROGER (1921–)		
Duo	fl, afl	Galaxy
2 Duos	picc, fl/E♭ clar	Galaxy
NONO, LUIGI (1924–)		
Konzertante Musik	fl, str	Schott
Y su sangre ya viene cantando	fl, str, perc	Ars Viva; Schott

OFFERMANS, WIL (1957–)		
Honami	fl	Zimmermann
Just a Short Version	picc, 2fl, afl	Zimmermann
PEETERS, FLOR (1903–1974)		
Trio, op. 80	fl, cl, bn	Peters
PÉRILHOU, ARMAND (1846–1936)		
Ballade	fl/vn, pf	Heugel; G. Schirmer
PERLE, GEORGE (1915–)		
Monody I, op. 43	fl	Merion
PERSICHETTI, VINCENT (1915–1987)		
Parable, op. 100	fl	Elkan-Vogel
Parable XII, op. 125	picc	Elkan-Vogel
Serenade no. 10, op. 79	fl, hp	Elkan-Vogel
PETRASSI, GOFFREDO (1904–)		
Dialogo Angelico	2fl	Zerboni
PIAZZOLLA, ASTOR (1921–)		
Histoire du Tango	fl, guit	Lemoine
Tango Etudes	fl	Lemoine
PIERNÉ, GABRIEL (1863–1937)		
Canzonetta, op. 19	fl, pf	Leduc
Nocturne en forme de Valse, op. 40, no. 2	fl, pf	Hamelle
Sérénade, op. 7	fl, vc, pf	Leduc
	fl, pf	Leduc; Williams

Sonata, op. 36 [arr. by Pierné from his violin sonata]	fl, pf	Durand
Sonata da camera, op. 48	fl, vc, pf	Durand
Variations au Clair de Lune	fl, vn, va, vc, hp	Lemoine
Variations libres et finale	fl, vn, va, vc, hp	Salabert
Voyage au pays du tendre	fl, vn, va, vc, hp	Leduc
PIJPER, WILLEM (1894–1947)		
Sonata	fl, pf	Donemus
PINKHAM, DANIEL (1923–)		
Eclogue	fl, hpd, off-stage hand-bells (2 players)	E.C. Schirmer
Miracles	fl, org	E.C. Schirmer
Prelude	fl, vn, va, vc	ACE
PISTON, WALTER (1894–1976)		
Concerto	fl, orch/pf red	AMP
3 Pieces	fl, cl, bn	AMP
Quintet	fl, 2vn, va, vc	AMP
Sonata	fl, pf	AMP
POLIN, CLAIRE C. J. (1926–)		
The Death of Procris	fl, tuba	Seesaw
Margoa	fl	Seesaw
O, Aderyn Pur	fl	Seesaw
1st Flute Sonata	fl, pf	Southern
Structures	fl	Elkan-Vogel

POOT, MARCEL (1901–1988)		
Ballade	fl, pf	Eschig
Berceuse	fl, pf	Leduc
Fantasietta	fl, pf	Leduc
3 Pièces	fl, pf	Leduc
Scherzetto	fl, pf	Leduc
Sicilienne	fl, pf	Leduc
PORTER, QUINCY (1897–1966)		
Blues lointains	fl/vn, pf	ACE; Oxford/NFA
Little Trio	fl, vn, va	New Valley
Quintet in 1 Movement on a Childhood Theme	fl, 2vn, va, vc	ACE
POULENC, FRANCIS (1899–1963)		
Mouvements Perpetuels	fl, guit	Chester (arr. Levering)
Sonata	fl, pf	Chester
POWELL, MEL (1923–)		
Three Madrigals	fl/afl	Oxford/NFA; G. Schirmer
PRESSER, WILLIAM (1916–)		
Partitafl	Tenuto	
Rondo	picc, pf	Tenuto
Sonatina	fl, pf	Tenuto
PROKOFIEV, SERGEI (1891–1953)		
Sonata, D, op. 94	fl, pf	International (ed. Rampal); Kalmus; Leeds; Peters; Sikorski
RAN, SHULAMIT (1947–)		
East Wind	fl	Presser

RAVEL, MAURICE (1875–1937)		
Pavane pour une infante défunte	fl, pf	Eschig (ed. Fleury); Eschig (ed. Kochanski); Fischer (ed. Bettoney); Ed. Musicus; Rubank (ed. Walters); Schott
READ, GARDNER (1913–)		
Threnody, op. 66	fl, hp, str/pf red	Seesaw
REGER, MAX (1873–1916)		
Allegretto grazioso, A	fl, pf	Junne; Musica Rara
Romance, G	fl, pf	Breitkopf (ed. Schwedler)
Serenade, D, op. 77a	fl, vn, va	Bote & Bock (ed. Schnirlin); Eulenberg; International; Kalmus
Serenade, G, op. 141a	fl/vn, vn, va	Peters
6 Vortragsstücke [Suite], a, op. 103a:		
Nos. 4–6: Burleske, Menuett, Gigue	fl, pf	Bote & Bock
REIF, PAUL (1910–1978)		
Banter	fl, pf	Seesaw
Trio	picc, fl, afl	Seesaw
Trio	fl, vc, pf/hpd	Seesaw
REYNOLDS, ROGER (1934–)		
Acquaintances	fl, db, pf	Peters
Ambages	fl	Peters
4 Etudes	picc, 2fl, afl	Peters
Mosaic	fl, pf	Peters

REYNOLDS, VERNE (1926–)		
Sonata	fl, pf	Fischer
Xenoliths	fl, pf4h	Zalo
RIEGGER, WALLINGFORD (1885–1961)		
Canons for Woodwinds, op. 9	fl, ob, cl, bn	Presser
Duos for Three Woodwinds, op. 35	fl, ob, cl (no. 1: fl,ob; no. 3: fl,cl)	Presser
Suite, op. 8	fl	Presser
RIETI, VITTORIO (1898–1994)		
Concertino	fl, va, vc, hp, hpd	General
Partitah	pd, fl, ob, 2vn, va, vc	Broude Bros.
Pastorale and Fughetta	fl, va, pf	General
Sonata	fl, ob, bn, pf	Universal
Sonata a5	fl, ob, cl, bn, pf	General
Sonatina	fl, pf	Bongiovanni
Variations on "When, From My Love" by John Bartlett (1606)	fl, cl, vn, vc	General
RIVIER, JEAN (1896–1987)		
Ballade	fl, pf	EMT
Concerto	fl, str/pf red	Billaudot; Noël
Duo	fl, cl	Billaudot
Oiseaux tendres	fl	Salabert
3 Pastorales	fl, vn, pf	Salabert
3 Silhouettes	fl, pf	Salabert
Sonatine	fl, pf	EMT
Virevoltes	fl	Billaudot (ed. Rampal)
Voltige	fl	De Santis; Salabert

ROCHBERG, GEORGE (1918–)		
Contra Mortem et Tempus	fl,cl,vn,pf	Presser
Music of Fire	fl, guit	Presser (ed. Fisk)
Ora Pro Nobis (Nach Bach I)	fl, guit	Presser (ed. Fisk)
Slow Fires of Autumn (Ukiyo-e II)	fl, hp	Presser
Between two worlds : Ukiyo-e III : five images	fl, pf	Presser
ROGERS, BERNARD (1893–1968)		
Allegory	2fl, mar, str	Presser
Fantasy	fl, va, str	Kalmus
The Silver World	fl, ob, str	Peer
Soliloquy no. 1	fl, str/pf red	Fischer
Study fl	Accura; Rochester	
ROREM, NED (1923–		
Books of Hours	fl, hp	Boosey
Mountain Song	fl/ob/vn/vc, pf	Peer
Romeo and Juliet	fl, gui	Boosey
Trio	fl, vc, pf	Henmar
RÓZSA, MIKLÓS (1907–)		
Sonata, op. 39	fl	Faber
ROUSSEL, ALBERT (1869–1937)		
Andante et Scherzo, op. 51	fl, pf	Broekmans (ed. Boorda); Durand
Aria	fl, orch/pf red	Broekmans (ed. Boorda); Leduc
Joueurs de flûte, op. 27: Pan, Tityre,		

Krishna, Monsieur de la Péjaudie	fl, pf	Broekmans; Durand
Serenade, op. 30	fl, vn, va, vc, hp	Durand
Trio, F, op. 40	fl, va, vc	Durand
RUTTER, JOHN (1945–)		
Suite Antique	fl, hpd, str/pf red	Oxford
SANCAN, PIERRE (1916–)		
Sonatine	fl, pf	Durand
SCHICKELE, PETER (1935–)		
The Boston Wonder	fl, pf, narr	Elkan-Vogel/Presser
Dream Dances	fl,ob,vc	Presser
A Little Welcome Serenade	fl,vn	Presser
Monochrome I	8fl	Presser
Monochrome V	8fl	Presser
Music for Mary	fl/alto rec, pf	Elkan-Vogel/Presser
Spring Serenade	fl, pf	Presser
Summer Trio	fl,vc,pf	Presser
Trio Serenade	2fl,pf	Presser
Two Pleasant Songs	fl/sop, pf	Elkan-Vogel/Presser
SCHMITT, FLORENT (1870–1958)		
Pour presque tous les temps, op. 134	fl, vn, vc, pf	Durand
Quartet, op. 106	4fl	Durand
Scherzo-pastorale, op. 17	fl, pf	Durand; Hamelle; International
Sonatine en trio, op. 85	fl, cl, pf/hpd	Durand
Suite, op. 129	fl, pf	Durand
Suite en rocaille, op. 84	fl, vn, va, vc, hp	Durand

SCHOCKER, GARY (1959–)		
Airborne	fl, pf	Presser
Conversations	fl, pf	Zalo
Gilded and Bronzed	fl, pf	JP
Green Places	fl, pf red	Presser
In Memoriam	fl, hp	JP
Regrets and Resolutions	fl, pf	Presser
Three Dances	2fl, pf	Zalo
SCHULHOFF, ERWIN (1894–1942)		
Sonata	fl, pf	Chester
SCHULLER, GUNTHER (1925–)		
Adagio	fl, vn, va, vc	Margun; Oxford/NFA
Aphorisms	fl, vn, va, vc	AMP
SCHWANTNER, JOSEPH (1943–)		
A Play of Shadows	fl, orch	Helicon
Soaring	fl, pf	Helicon; Oxford/NFA
SCOTT, CYRIL (1879–1970)		
The Ecstatic Shepherd	fl, pf	Schott
Lotus Land	fl, pf	Galaxy (arr. Wummer)
Scotch Pastoral	fl, pf	Masters Music
SEARLE, HUMPHREY (1915–1983)		
Divertimento, op. 26	fl, str/pf	Schott

SEIBER, MATYAS (1905–1960)		
Pastorale and Burlesque	fl, str/pf red	Schott
SHATIN, JUDITH (1949–)		
Fasting Heart	fl	ACA
Ruah	fl, pf	J.S. Allen
SHAWN, ALLEN		
Summer Pages	fl, ob hpsd/pf	Galaxy
SHINOHARA, MAKOTO (1931–)		
Kassouga	fl, pf	Leduc
SIEGMEISTER, ELIE (1909–)		
Concerto	fl, orch/pf red	MCA
Nocturne	fl/ob, pf	Fischer/MCA
SLONIMSKY, NICOLAS (1895–1995)		
Piccolo Divertimento	fl, ob, cl, perc	Cambria
SOLLBERGER, HARVEY (1939–)		
Divertimento	fl, vc, pf	ACE
Duo	fl, pf	ACE
Grand Quartet, In Memoriam Friedrich Kuhlau	4fl	McGinnis & Marx
Met him pike hoses	fl, vn	ACE
Music	fl, pf	ACE
2 Pieces	2fl	McGinnis & Marx
Quodlibetudes	fl	McGinnis & Marx
Riding the Wind I	amp fl, cl, vn, vc, pf	ACE

Riding the Wind II, III, IV	fl	ACE
Sunflowers	picc+fl+afl, vibra	McGinnis & Marx
SOMERS, HARRY (1925–)		
Etching	fl	Ricordi
STAEPS, HANS ULRICH (1909–)		
Sonata, E♭	rec/fl/ob/vn, pf	Universal
STARER, ROBERT (1924–)		
Cadenza	4fl	MCA
Colloquies	fl, pf	MCA
Recitation	fl, pf	Peer
STEVENS, HALSEY (1908–)		
6 Canons	2fl	ACE
5 Duos	fl, cl	Peer
Quintet	fl, vn, va, vc, pf	G. Schirmer
Sonatina Piacevole	fl, pf	Peer
Sonatina	fl, pf	Broude Bros.
Trio	fl/vn, cl/va, bn/vc	ACE
STILL, WILLIAM GRANT (1895–1978)		
Miniatures (based on Folksongs of the Americas)	fl, ob, pf	Oxford
STINE, ROBERT		
The Heaventree	fl, tape	Zalo

STOCKHAUSEN, KARLHEINZ (1928–)		
Kathinkas Gesang als Luzifers Requiem	fl	Stockhausen
Licht. Montag. Montags-Gruss. XI	fl	Stockhausen
Licht. Samstag. Luzifers Tanz. Zugenspirtentanz	picc, 2 euph/synthesizer, perc, dancer	Stockhausen
Zungenspitzentanz vom Samstag aus Licht	picc/fl	Stockhausen
STOUT, ALAN (1932–)		
3 Canons	fl, vc	ACE
Music fl, hpd	Peters	
Ostinato, op. 59, no. 3	fl, orch	ACE
Velut Umbra, op. 35a	fl, va, orch	ACE
STRAVINSKY, IGOR (1882–1971)		
Epitaphium für das Grabmal des Prinzen Max Egon zu Fürstenburg	fl, cl, hp	Boosey
STRINGFIELD, LAMAR (1897–1959)		
Indian Sketches: Serenade	fl, pf red	Fischer
Morning	fl, vc, pf	Ed. Musicus
Mountain Dawn	fl, str/pf red	Ed. Musicus
Pastoral Scene	fl	Leeds
To a Star	fl, pf	Ed. Musicus
SUBOTNICK, MORTON (1933–)		
Parallel Lines	picc, 8 players, electronics	Presser
TAILLEFERRE, GERMAINE (1892–1983)		
Forlane	fl, pf	Lemoine
Pastorale	fl	Presser

TAKEMITSU, TORU (1930–1996)		
Ame no jumon (Rain spell)	fl, cl, hp, pf, vibr	Schott
Eucalypts ck spelling	fl, ob, hp, str	Salabert
Eucalypts II	fl, ob, hp	Salabert
Itinerant	fl	Schott Japan
Koe [Voice]	fl	Salabert
Masque	2fl	Salabert
Masque, Incidental II	2fl	Salabert
Ring	fl, guit, lute	Slabaert
Sacrifice	afl, lute, vib	Ongaku-no-Tomo Sha
Toward the Sea	afl, guit	Schott Japan
TAKTAKISHVILI, OTAR (1924–)		
Sonata	fl, pf	Lib Soviet Music/G. Schirmer
TANSMAN, ALEXANDRE (1897–1986)		
Concertino	fl, pf red	Eschig
Sonata	fl, pf	Salabert
TCHEREPNIN, ALEXANDER (1899–1977)		
Concerto da camera, D, op. 33	fl, vn, ch orch/pf red	Schott
Duo, op. 108	2fl	Belaieff
2 Esquisses, op. 45	fl, pf	Belaieff
Quartet, op. 60	4fl	Belaieff
Trio, op. 59	3fl	Belaieff
TCHEREPNIN, IVAN (1943–)		
Cadenzas in Transition	fl, cl, pf	Belaieff
Sombres lumieres	fl, gui, vc	Belaieff

THOMSON, VIRGIL (1896–1989)		
Concerto	fl, hp, str, perc/pf red	Belwin; Ricordi
Serenade	fl, vn	Peer
Sonata	fl	Elkan-Vogel
TOCH, ERNST (1887–1964)		
Sonatinetta, op. 84	fl, cl, bn	Mills
TOMASI, HENRI (1901–1971)		
Complainte Danse de Mowgli	fl, pf	Noël
Concertino, E	fl, orch/pf red	Leduc
Concerto, F	fl, orch/pf red	Leduc
Concerto de Printemps	fl, ch orch/pf red	Leduc
Les Cyclades	fl+optional afl	Leduc
Pastorale inca	fl, 2vn	Leduc
3 Pastorales	3fl	Leduc
Le Petit Chevrier Corse	fl, pf/hp	Leduc
Sonatine	fl	Leduc
Tombeau de Mireille	fl/picc, pf	Leduc
TOWER, JOAN (1938–)		
Concerto	fl, orch/pf red	AMP
Hexachords	fl	CFE/ACA
Snow Dreams	fl, guit	AMP
TULL, FISHER (1934–1994)		
Cyclorama I	2picc, 6fl, 2afl, bfl	Boosey
Erato	fl, pf	Southern
Fantasia on a Sonata of Scarlatti	fl/bfl, hpd/pf	Southern

VAN VACTOR, DAVID (1906–)		
Duettino	2fl	Roger Rhodes
Quintet	fl, 2vn, va, vc	G. Schirmer
Sonatina	fl, pf	Roger Rhodes
Suite	2fl	Roger Rhodes
VARÈSE, EDGARD (1383–1965)		
Density 21.5	fl	Belwin; Colfranc; Ricordi
VAUGHAN WILLIAMS, RALPH (1872–1958)		
The Bridal Day; A Masque by Ursula Wood, founded on Ephitamalion by Edmund Spenser	fl	Oxford
Suite de Ballet	fl, pf	Oxford (ed. Douglas)
VILLA-LOBOS, HEITOR (1887–1959)		
Assobio a Jato [The Jet Whistle]	fl, vc	Peer
Bachianas Brasilieras no. 6	fl, bn	AMP
Chôros no. 2	fl, cl	Eschig
Chôros No. 7	fl,cl,bn,vc	Eschig
Concerto Grosso	fl, ob, cl, bn, wind orch	Peters
Distribuicao de flores, op. post.	fl, gui	Eschig
Poema da Crianca	fl,cl,vc	Eschig
Poèmes Indiens	fl, guit	Eschig
Quatuor	fl,sx,hp,vc	Eschig
Quintet, op. post.	fl, vn, va, vc, hp	Eschig
Trio	fl, ob, cl	Eschig
WEINBERGER, JAROMIR (1896–1967)		
Sonatine	fl, pf	Fischer

WEISBERG, ARTHUR (1931–)		
Sonatina	fl	ACA
WESTERGAARD, PETER (1931–)		
Divertimento on Discobbolic Fragments	fl, pf	Continuo/A. Broude
Sonata, op. 30	fl	Hansen
WHEAR, PAUL W. (1925–)		
Five Haiku	fl	Ludwig
WIGGLESWORTH, FRANK (1918–)		
Lake Music	fl	Presser
Serenade	fl, va, guit	ACA
Trio	3fl	ACA
WILDER, ALEC (1907–1980)		
Air	fl, str/pf red	Bourne
4 Duets	2rec/2fl	Margun
Flute Suite	fl	Wilder
Movement for Flute Ensemble	picc, 2fl, 2afl, bfl	Wilder
Small Suite	fl/vn, pf	Wilder
Sonata no. 1	fl+picc+afl, pf	Wilder
Sonata no. 2	fl, pf	Margun; Wilder
Suite	fl	Margun
Suite	afl, bfl	Wilder
Suite for Flute Choir	2picc, 6fl, 3afl, bfl	Wilder
Suite	hpd, fl	Wilder
WOLPE, STEFAN (1902–1972)		
Piece in 2 Parts	fl, pf	McGinnis & Marx
2 Stücke	fl, pf	Tonos

WOOLLEN, RUSSELL (1923–)		
Fantasy	fl, hpd/pf	Armstrong
Quartet	fl, vn, va, vc	ACA
40 Variations on Au Claire de la Lune	2fl	Armstrong
WUORINEN, CHARLES (1938–)		
Bearbeitungen über das Glogauer Liederbuch	fl, cl, vn, db	Peters
Chamber Concerto	fl, 10 insts	McGinnis & Marx
Sonata	fl, pf	ACE
Trio	fl, vc, pf	ACE
2nd Trio	fl, vc, pf	Peters
3rd Trio	pf, fl, perc	Peters
Turetzky Pieces	fl, cl, ob	ACE
Variations	fl	McGinnis & Marx
Variations II	fl	Peters
ZANINELLI, LUIGI (1932–)		
3 Children's Dances	6fl	Zalo
3 Scenes	fl+afl+picc	Zalo
ZIMMERMANN, BERND ALOIS (1918–1970)		
Tempus loquendi, pezzi ellittici	fl+afl+bfl	Schott
ZWILICH, ELLEN TAAFFE (1939–)		
Chamber Symphony	fl/picc, cl/bcl,vn,va,vc, pf	Presser
Concerto	fl, orch/pf red	Presser

E. STUDY MATERIALS

Methods

ALTÈS, HENRI
Célèbre Méthode Complète, 2 vols. — Leduc (ed. Caratgé)
Method for the Boehm Flute, Part I — C. Fischer

ANDERSEN, MARK & IRENE MADDOX
An Artist's Guide to Alto and Bass Flute Playing — Pan

BARONE, CLEMENT
Learning the Piccolo — Edu-Tainment

BROOKE, ARTHUR
Method for Flute, 2 vols. — C. Fischer (ed. Pappoutsakis)

DEVIENNE, FRANÇOIS
Célèbre Méthode Complète de Flûte, 2 vols. — Leduc (rev. Gaubert)

DICK, ROBERT
The Other Flute — Oxford; Dick

ECK, EMIL
Method for Flute, Book I — Belwin

GARIBOLDI, GIUSEPPE
Complete Method, op. 128, 2 vols. — Leduc

GÜMBEL, MARTIN
Lern und Spielbuch für Flöte — Bärenreiter

HUGUES, LUIGI
School of the Flute, 3 vols. — Ricordi

KINCAID, WILLIAM & CLAIRE POLIN
The Advanced Flutist, 2 vols. — Elkan-Vogel
The Art and Practice of Modern Flute Technique, 3 vols. — MCA

KUJALA, WALFRID
The Flutist's Progress — Progress

LEJEUNE, HARRIET PEACOCK
A Flutist's Manual — Summy-Birchard

LE ROY, RENÉ
Traité de la Flûte — EMT

McCASKILL, MIZZY & DONA GILLIAM
The Flutist's Companion — Mel Bay

PAUBON, PIERRE
La Flûte Traversière — Leduc

SCHMITZ, HANS PETER
Flötenlehre, 2 vols. — Bärenreiter

SOUSSMAN, HEINRICH
Complete Method for Flute, 3 vols. — C. Fischer (ed. Popp)

STOKES, SHERIDON & RICHARD CONDON
Illustrated Method for Flute — Trio

TAFFANEL, PAUL & PHILIPPE GAUBERT
Méthode Complète, 2 vols. — Leduc

WYE, TREVOR
Proper Flute Playing — Novello

Technical Exercises and Études

Because études are generally referred to by their opus numbers and because the published titles differ widely, all exercises and études in this catalog are listed in opus number order, when applicable; otherwise, they are alphabetic.

ALTÈS, HENRI
26 Selected Studies — G. Schirmer (ed. Barrère)

ANDERSEN, JOACHIM
24 Études, op. 15 — Billaudot; Edu-Tainment (ed. Peck); C. Fischer; International (ed. Wummer); G. Schirmer (ed. Moyse); Southern (ed. Fenboque)
24 Études, op. 21 — Billaudot; Edu-Tainment (ed. Peck); International (ed. Wummer); G. Schirmer (ed. Barrère); Southern (ed. Ephross)

24 Instructive Études, op. 30	Billaudot; Edu-Tainment (ed. Peck); International (ed. Wummer); Southern (ed. Cavally)
24 Progressive Studies, op. 33	Berben; Billaudot; Edu-Tainment (ed. Peck); C. Fischer; International (ed. Wummer); Southern (ed. Cavally)
26 Small Caprices, op. 37	Billaudot (ed. Herich; Hansen; International (ed. Wummer); Southern (ed. Cavally)
18 Studies, op. 41	Billaudot (ed. Heriché); Edu-Tainment (ed. Thomas); International (ed. Wummer); G. Schirmer (ed. Barrère); Southern (ed. Cavally)
24 Grand Studies (The School of Virtuosity), op. 60	International (ed. Wummer); Kalmus; Southern (ed. Cavally); Zimmermann
24 Technical Studies, op. 63	Berben; Billaudot (ed. Heriché); Edu-Tainment (ed. Peck); Hansen; International (ed. Wummer); G. Schirmer
Southern (ed. Cavally)	
26 Selected Études	Southern

ARTAUD, PIERRE-YVES

Harmoniques	Billaudot

BAKER, JULIUS

Daily Exercises	Ludwig

BARRÈRE, GEORGES

The Flutist's Formulae	G. Schirmer

BERBIGUIER, TRANQUILLE

Great Characteristic Études	Leduc (ed. M. Moyse)
18 Studies in All Keys	Armstrong (ed. Thomas); Berben (ed. Altès); Billaudot (ed. Altès); C. Fischer (ed. Stringfield); Hansen; International (ed. Wummer); Kalmus; Leduc (ed. M. Moyse); Litolff; Reinhardt (ed. Bopp); G. Schirmer (ed. Barrère); Southern

BITSCH, MARCEL

12 Études	Leduc (ed. Rampal)

BOEHM, THEOBALD	
12 Études, op. 15	Amadeus; Armstrong (ed. Taylor); Billaudot; Costallat; C. Fischer (ed. Wummer); International (ed. Rampal); Kalmus; Leduc (ed. M. Moyse)
24 Caprices, op. 26	Amadeus; Armstrong (ed. Taylor); Billaudot (ed. LeRoy); Boosey; Chester (ed. Wye); Costallat; C. Fischer (ed. Wummer); International (ed. Rampal); Leduc (ed. M. Moyse); Schott
24 Melodious Studies, op. 37	C. Fischer (ed. Wummer); Leduc (ed. Caratgé); Schott
BOZZA, EUGÈNE	
10 Études sur des modes karnatiques	Leduc
14 Études Arabesques	Leduc
Graphismes	Leduc
BRICCIALDI, GIULIO	
Exercise indispensable	Billaudot; Costallat
18 Grand Studies, op. 31	Ricordi
24 Studies	Bongiovanni; Zimmermann
BROOKE, ARTHUR	
Harmonic Fingerings for the Flute	C. Fischer
CAMUS, PAUL	
12 Studies	Pan Educational
CASTÉRÈDE, JACQUES	
12 Studies	Leduc
CAVALLY, ROBERT	
Melodious and Progressive Studies, 4 vols.	Southern
COLQUHOUN, MICHAEL	
9 Études for the Contemporary Flutist	McGinnis & Marx
DE LORENZO, LEONARDO	
9 Great Studies	Zimmermann
Das "Non plus ultra" des Flötisten, op. 34	Zimmermann
18 Caprices, op. 35	Zimmermann
DEMERSSEMAN, JULES	
50 Études Melodiques, op. 4	Billaudot; Leduc (ed. M. Moyse)
DICK, ROBERT	
Flying Lessons, 2 vols.	Dick

DONJON, JOHANNES

8 Études de Salon	Amadeus; Jobert; Little Piper

DROUET, LOUIS

62 Etüden	Zimmermann
Étude Modulée	Heuwekemeijer
25 Études Célèbres	Broekmans (ed. De Reede); Leduc (ed. Fleury, Merry); Schott
18 Préludes et 6 Cadences	Heuwekemeijer
47 Studies	Broekmans

DUBOIS, PIERRE MAX

13 Études de Moyenne Difficulté	Leduc

ECK, EMIL

Tone Development for the Flute	Belwin

FILAS, THOMAS

Leger Domain—Top Register Studies	C. Fischer
52 Top Register Studies	C. Fischer
90 Top Register Studies	C. Fischer

FLOYD, ANGELEITA

The Gilbert Legacy: Methods, Exercises, and Techniques for the Flutist	Winzer

FÜRSTENAU, ANTON BERNHARD

Exercises or Études, op. 15	Billaudot; Leduc (ed. M. Moyse)
6 Grandes Études, op. 29	Leduc (ed. M. Moyse)
26 Exercises, op. 107	C. Fischer (ed. Hahn); Hofmeister (ed. List); Leduc (ed. M. Moyse); Peters
Bouquet de Tons [24 Übungen, Capricen und Präludien; Études de Bravoure], op. 125	Belwin (ed. Eck); Hofmeister (ed. List); Leduc (ed. M. Moyse); Lemoine; Peters
12 Grand Studies	C. Fischer

GARIBOLDI, GIUSEPPE

L'Indispensabile—Caprice Étude, op. 48	Ed. Musicus
20 Études chantantes, op. 88	Leduc (ed. Merry)
Exercises Journaliers, op. 89	Leduc (ed. Merry)
Étude Complète des Gammes, op. 127	Leduc (ed. Merry)
Études Mignones, op. 131	Leduc (ed. Merry)
20 Petites Études, op. 132	International; Kalmus; Leduc (ed. Merry)
Grandes Études de Style, op. 134	Leduc (ed. Merry)
Grands Exercises, op. 139	Leduc (ed. Merry)
30 Easy and Progressive Studies	Galaxy; Kalmus; Little Piper; Paterson
Die ersten Übungen [First Exercises]	Peters (ed. Prill)
15 Études (aux amateurs)	Broekmans
58 Exercises	Berben; Peters; Zerboni

GATES, EVERETT	
Odd Meter Études	Sam Fox
GENZMER, HARALD	
Modern Studies, 2 vols.	Schott
GILBERT, GEOFFREY	
Sequences	Southern
Technical Flexibility	Southern
HOTTETERRE, JACQUES	
L'Art de Préluder, sur la Flûte Traversière, op. 7	Zurfluh
48 Preludes from op. 7	Schott (ed. Doflein & Delius)
HUGUES, LUIGI	
30 Studies, op. 32	Ricordi
40 New Studies, op. 75	Ricordi
40 Studies, op. 101	Belwin; International (ed. M. Moyse); Ricordi (ed. Veggetti)
HUNT, SIMON	
Flute Gymnastics Workbook, Books 1-4	Pan Educational
JEANJEAN, PAUL	
16 Études Modernes	Leduc; Southern
KARG-ELERT, SIGFRID	
30 Caprices, op. 107	C. Fischer; International; Kalmus; Southern
KOEHLER, ERNESTO	
35 Exercises [The Flutist's Progress], op. 33, 3 vols.	C. Fischer; International (ed. Wummer); Peters (ed. Vegetto); Southern (ed. Cavally); Zimmermann
25 Romantic Etudies, op. 66	Kalmus; Southern; Zimmermann
30 Virtuoso Études in All Major & Minor Keys, op. 75, 3 vols.	Kalmus; Zimmermann
School of Velocity, op. 77	Billaudot (ed. Paubon); Zimmermann
22 Studies in Expression and Facility, op. 89	Southern; Zimmermann
20 Easy Melodic Progressive Exercises, op. 93, 2 vols.	Kalmus; Zimmermann
6 Preludes, op. 122, 2 vols.	McGinnis & Marx (ed. Marx)
24 Charakteristische Etüden	Zimmermann

KUMMER, KASPAR	
Melodic Études in All Major & Minor Keys, op. 110	Schott
LEJEUNE, HARRIET PEACOCK	
Pitch & Sound Search Studies for Flute	A. Broude
LENSKI, KARL	
18 Cells for Flute	Musica Rara
LINDPAINTNER, PETER J. VON	
50 Études, op. 126	Billaudot; Costallat
MAQUARRE, ANDRÉ	
Daily Exercises for the Flute	G. Schirmer
MATHER, BETTY BANG	
60 Favorite Airs in the Gallant Style	C. Fischer
30 Virtuosic Selections in the Galant Style	C. Fischer
MOYSE, LOUIS	
La Grande Velocité	Southern
MOYSE, MARCEL	
24 Caprice Studies	Leduc
Le Debutante Flûtiste	Leduc
De la Sonorité: Art et Technique	Leduc
100 Easy & Progressive Studies after Cramer	Leduc
École de l'Articulation	Leduc
20 Études d'après Kreutzer	Leduc
10 Études d'après Wieniawsky	Leduc
12 Études de Grande Virtuosité après Chopin	Leduc
48 Études de Virtuosité, 2 vols.	Leduc
25 Études de Virtuosité d'après Czerny	Leduc
Études et Exercises Techniques	Leduc
20 Exercises et Études sur les Grands Liaisons	Leduc
Exercises Journaliers	Leduc
Gammes et Arpèges	Leduc
Mecanisme—Chromatisme	Leduc
24 Petites Études Melodiques avec Variations	Leduc
12 Studies After Boehm	Leduc
10 Studies Based on Kessler	Leduc
Tone Development through Interpretation	MCA
50 Variations on the "Allemande" of Bach's Sonata for Flute Alone	McGinnis & Marx

NICOLET, AURÈLE	
Pro Musica Nova; Studies for Playing Avant-Garde Music	MCA
OFFERMANS, WIL	
For the Contemporary Flutist	Zimmermann
PRILL, EMIL	
30 Etüden in allen Tonarten, op. 6, 2 vols.	Zimmermann
Technischen Studien, op. 11	Zimmermann
24 Technical Studies, op. 12	Benjamin; Simrock
24 Etüden, op. 14	Zimmermann
24 Etüden, op. 15	Zimmermann
QUANTZ, JOHANN JOACHIM	
Solfeggi	Amadeus
REICHERT, MATHIEU	
7 Daily Exercises, op. 5	Little Piper; Schott
6 Études, op. 6	Cundy-Bettoney; Leduc
ROBISON, PAULA	
Flute Warmups Book	EAM
RYNEARSON, PAUL	
11 Contemporary Flute Études	WIM
SOUSSMAN, HEINRICH	
24 Daily Studies, op. 53	Billaudot (ed. Ehrmann); Edu-Tainment; Leduc (ed. M. Moyse)
24 Grand Studies	C. Fischer
30 Grand Études	Schott
TAFFANEL, PAUL & PHILIPPE GAUBERT	
17 Daily Exercises	Leduc
TERSCHAK, ADOLF	
64 Übungen, op. 67	Cranz
Daily Exercises, op. 71	Schott
12 Melodischen Studien, op. 127	Forberg
VESTER, FRANS	
50 Classical Studies	Universal
100 Classical Studies	Universal
125 Easy Classical Studies	Universal

VINCI, DOMENICO

12 Studies	Ricordi

WUMMER, JOHN

12 Daily Exercises	C. Fischer
6 Daily Exercises	International

WYE, TREVOR

Practice Book, Vol. 1: Tone	Novello
Practice Book, Vol. 2: Technique	Novello
Practice Book, Vol. 3: Articulation	Novello
Practice Book, Vol. 4: Intonation	Novello
Practice Book, Vol. 5: Breathing and Scales	Novello
Practice Book, Vol. 6: Advanced	Novello

WYE, TREVOR & PATRICIA MORRIS

Piccolo Practice Book	Novello

Orchestral and Operatic Excerpts

BACH, JOHANN SEBASTIAN

20 Concert Studies	Southern (ed. Mols)
24 Flute Concert Studies	Southern (ed. Schindler)
Flute Repertoire, 4 vols.	Peters (ed. Richter)
The Flute Solos from the Bach Cantatas, Passions and Oratorios	G. Schirmer (ed. Baker)
Flute Obbligatos from the Cantatas	Universal (ed. Vester)

BAXTRESSER, JEANNE & MARTHA REARICK

Orchestral Excerpts for Flute and Piano	Presser

BARGE, WILHELM

Orchesterstüdien, 6 vols.	Zimmermann
Orchesterstüdien, 16 vols.	Hofmeister

BARTUZAT, CARL

Orchesterstudien	Hofmeister

BROOKE, ARTHUR

Orchestral Studies	C. Fischer

DURICHEN, CHRISTOPH & SIEGFRIED KRATSCH

Flute/Piccolo Excerpts from the Operatic and Concert Repertoire	Peters

KRELL, JOHN C.
Twentieth Century Orchestra Studies — G. Schirmer

KUJALA, WALFRID
Flute Audition Book — EAM

PRILL, EMIL
Orchestral Studies for Flute — Spratt

RICHTER
Orchestral Studies, 6 vols. — Zimmermann

SMITH, WILFRED
Orchestral Studies for Flute, 4 vols. — Universal

VALADE, PIERRE ANDRÉ
La Flûte dans le repertoire du XXe siècle pour ensemble instrumental — Lemoine

WION, JOHN
Opera Excerpts for Flute, 10 vols. — Wion

WUMMER, JOHN
Orchestral Excerpts, 9 vols. — International

ZÖLLER, KARLHEINZ
Modern Orchestral Studies, 2 vols. — Schott

APPENDICES

Appendix A

FINGERING CHART FOR THE BOEHM FLUTE

The following chart illustrates the standard fingerings for the Boehm flute with closed G# and a B footjoint.

LEFT HAND	1st finger	●	●	●	●	●	●	●	●
	Thumb (B♭ lever)	○	○	○	○	○	○	○	○
	Thumb (B♮ lever)	●	●	●	●	●	●	●	●
	2nd finger	●	●	●	●	●	●	●	●
	3rd finger	●	●	●	●	●	●	●	●
	4th finger (G♯ lever)	○	○	○	○	○	○	○	○
RIGHT HAND	1st finger (side key)								
	1st finger	●	●	●	●	●	●	●	○
	2nd finger (D♮ trill lever)								
	2nd finger	●	●	●	●	●	●	○	○
	3rd finger (D♯ trill lever)								
	3rd finger	●	●	●	●	●	○	○	●
	4th finger (E♭ lever)	○	○	○	○	●	●	●	●
	4th finger (C♯ key)	●	●	●	○	○	○	○	○
	4th finger (C♮ key)	●	●	○	○	○	○	○	○
	4th finger (B key)	●	○	○	○	○	○	○	○
	4th finger (gizmo key)								

● indicates that the key or lever is depressed.

T = trill lever

G = gizmo key

LEFT HAND
1st finger
Thumb (B♭ lever)
Thumb (B♮ lever)
2nd finger
3rd finger
4th finger (G♯ lever)
RIGHT HAND
1st finger (side key)
1st finger
2nd finger (D♮ trill lever)
2nd finger
3rd finger (D♯ trill lever)
3rd finger
4th finger (E♭ lever)
4th finger (C♯ key)
4th finger (C♮ key)
4th finger (B key)
4th finger (gizmo key)
T

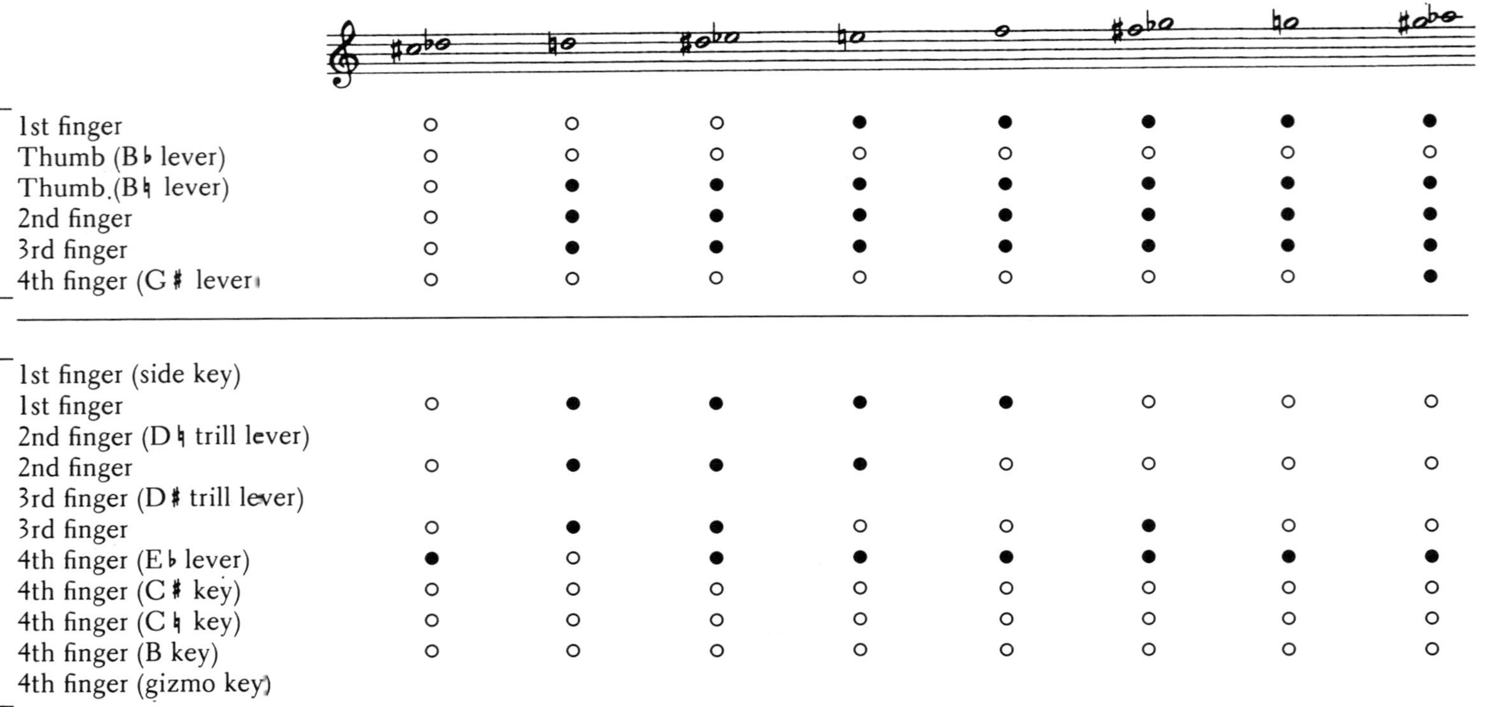
LEFT HAND
1st finger
Thumb (B♭ lever)
Thumb (B♮ lever)
2nd finger
3rd finger
4th finger (G♯ lever)
RIGHT HAND
1st finger (side key)
1st finger
2nd finger (D♮ trill lever)
2nd finger
3rd finger (D♯ trill lever)
3rd finger
4th finger (E♭ lever)
4th finger (C♯ key)
4th finger (C♮ key)
4th finger (B key)
4th finger (gizmo key)

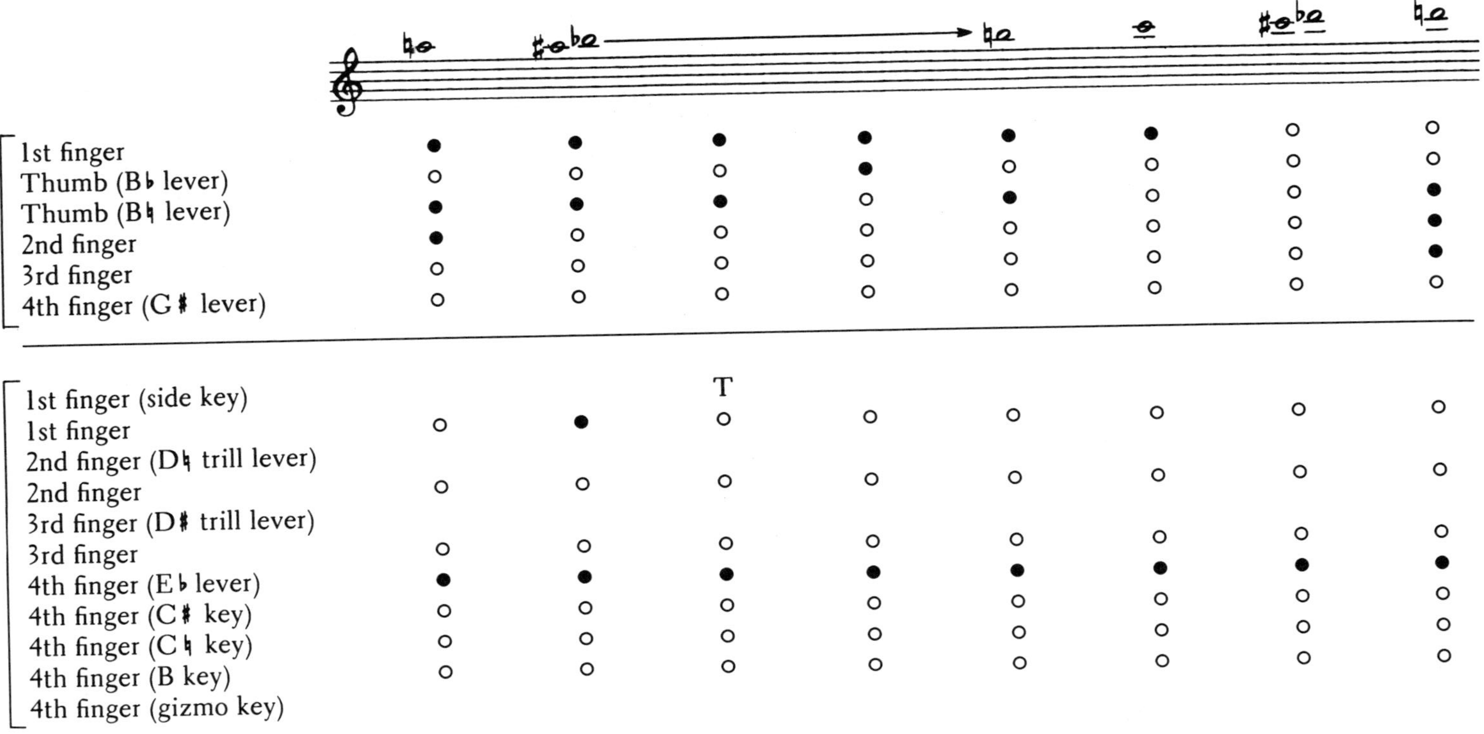
LEFT HAND
1st finger
Thumb (B♭ lever)
Thumb (B♮ lever)
2nd finger
3rd finger
4th finger (G♯ lever)
RIGHT HAND
1st finger (side key)
1st finger
2nd finger (D♮ trill lever)
2nd finger
3rd finger (D♯ trill lever)
3rd finger
4th finger (E♭ lever)
4th finger (C♯ key)
4th finger (C♮ key)
4th finger (B key)
4th finger (gizmo key)
T

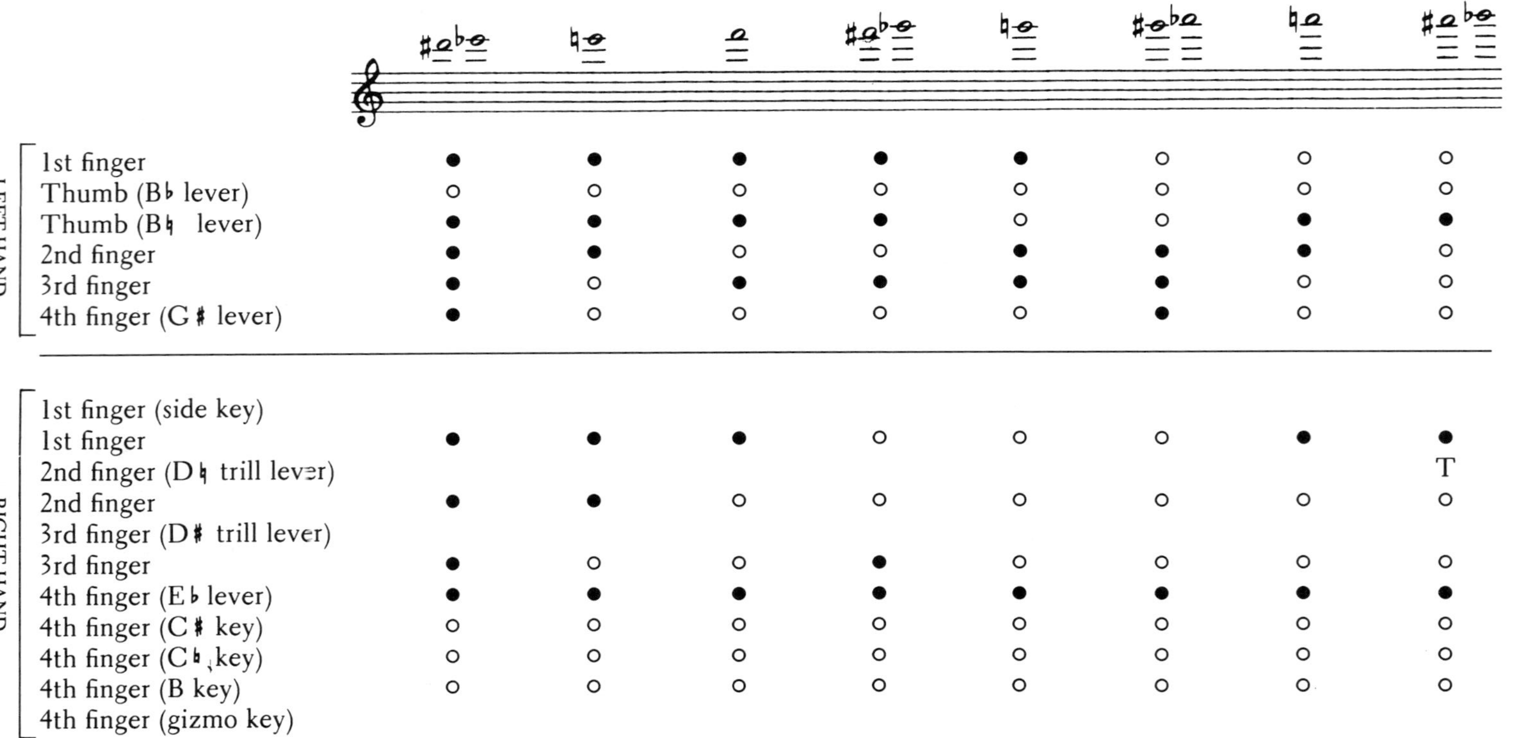
LEFT HAND
1st finger
Thumb (B♭ lever)
Thumb (B♮ lever)
2nd finger
3rd finger
4th finger (G♯ lever)
RIGHT HAND
1st finger (side key)
1st finger
2nd finger (D♮ trill lever)
2nd finger
3rd finger (D♯ trill lever)
3rd finger
4th finger (E♭ lever)
4th finger (C♯ key)
4th finger (C♮ key)
4th finger (B key)
4th finger (gizmo key)
T

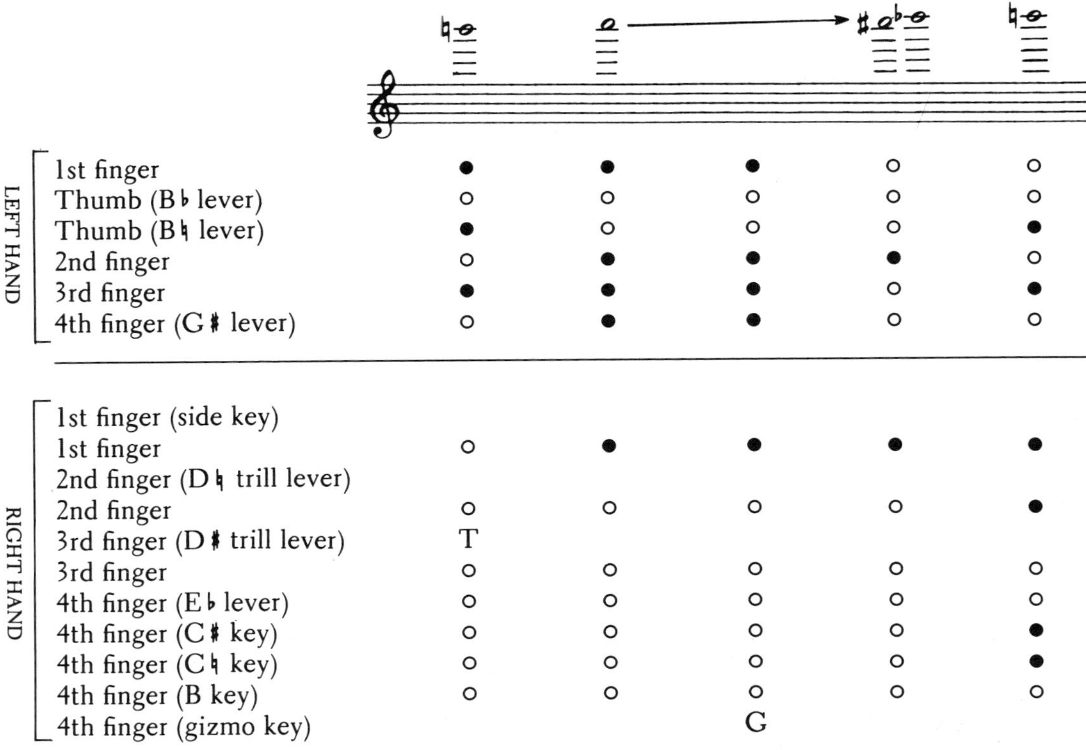
LEFT HAND
1st finger
Thumb (B♭ lever)
Thumb (B♮ lever)
2nd finger
3rd finger
4th finger (G♯ lever)
RIGHT HAND
1st finger (side key)
1st finger
2nd finger (D♮ trill lever)
2nd finger
3rd finger (D♯ trill lever)
3rd finger
4th finger (E♭ lever)
4th finger (C♯ key)
4th finger (C♮ key)
4th finger (B key)
4th finger (gizmo key)
T
G

Appendix B

FLUTE MANUFACTURERS

Abell Flute Company
111 Grovewood Road
Asheville, NC 28804
Phone/FAX (704) 254-1004
Wooden Boehm system flutes, headjoints, and whistles

Michael Allen
43 Rothbury Road
Rainham, Essex RM13 9HY England
(01708) 550039
Silver and gold flutes, headjoints

Altus/Jupiter Flutes
P.O.Box 90249
Austin, TX 78709-0249
(512) 288-7400 · FAX (512) 288-6445
Altus flutes, headjoints, alto flutes, bass flutes; Jupiter flutes and piccolos

Arista Flutes
15 Morningside Lane
Lincoln, MA 01773
(617) 275-8821

Armstrong Flutes
Artley Flutes
United Musical Instruments U.S.A., Inc.
P.O. Box 727
Elkhart, IN 46515
(219) 295-0079 · FAX (219) 295-8613
Flutes, headjoints, piccolos, alto flutes, bass flutes

Robert Bigio
1 Doveridge Gardens
London N13 5BJ, England
(0181) 882 2627
FAX (0181) 882 2728
Wood flutes, piccolos; wood, silver, gold headjoints

Boosey & Hawkes/Buffet Crampon
1925 Enterprise Court
P.O. Box 130
Libertyville, IL 60048
(708) 810-2500

Brannen Brothers Flutemakers, Inc.
58 Dragon Court
Woburn, MA 01801-1014
(617) 935-9522
Flutes, headjoints, piccolos

Burkart-Phelan, Inc.
41 Elm Street
Stoneham, MA 02180
(617) 438-7391 · (617) 279-4234
Burkart piccolos, piccolo headjoints

Albert Cooper
9 West Road, Clapham
London SW4 7DL
England
Phone/FAX (0171) 622 7863
Silver and gold flutes, headjoints

Nick Crabb
34 Pennybank Chambers
33-35 St. John's Square
Clerkenwell
London EC1M 4DS, England
(0171) 250 0727
Flutes, headjoints

Custom Music/Flutes Universal U.S.A.
1930 Hilton Road
Ferndale, MI 48220-1923
(800) 521-6380; (810) 546-4135
FAX (810) 546-8296
E.F. Dean, A.D. Geoffrey flutes, alto flutes

Del Rio Circular Flutes
800 S. Pacific Coast Highway
Suite 8-159
Redondo Beach, CA 90277
(310) 375-2799

Drelinger Headjoint Co.
P.O. Box 146
N. White Plains, NY 10603
(914) 946-1717; (800) 426-9832
Flute and piccolo headjoints

Emanuel Flutes Boston
1001 Great Pond Road
North Andover, MA 01845
(508) 686-6099 · FAX (508) 686-6066
Flutes, headjoints

Emerson Musical Instruments, Inc.
28135 West Hively Avenue
Elkhart, Indiana 46517
(219) 295-7118 · FAX (219) 522-1750
Flutes (regular, vertical, curved, or angled headjoint), piccolos, treble flutes in G, soprano flutes in E♭, tenor flutes in B♭, alto flutes in G, bass flutes in C

Flutemakers Guild Ltd.
10 Shacklewell Lane
London N16 7TA, England
(0171) 254 7175
Silver, gold, wood flutes, headjoints

La Flûte Traversiere
42, rue de Charenton
Paris 75012, France
011 1/48 44 42 35
Headjoints

Folkers & Powell
49 Route 25
Hudson, NY 12534
(518) 828-9779
Historical reproduction flutes

Gemeinhardt Co., Inc.
P.O. Box 788
Elkhart, IN 46515
(219) 295-5280; (800) 348-7461
FAX (219) 295-8323
Flutes, headjoints, piccolos, alto flutes, bass flutes

A. D. Geoffrey Flutemakers
1930 Hilton
Ferndale, MI 48220-1923
(800) 521-6380; (810) 546-4135
FAX (810) 546-8296
Flutes, headjoints

J. P. Goosman Flutes Ltd.
P.O. Box 13
Pickering, Ontario L1V 2R2
Canada
(905) 649-3687
Flutes, headjoints

Tom Green Flutes, Inc.
71266 Indiana Lake Drive
Union, MI 49130
(616) 641-7684
Flutes, headjoints

Philipp Hammig Piccolos
Westwind Musical Products
1214 Fifth Street
Coralville, IA 52241
(319) 351-2000
Piccolos

Wm. S. Haynes Co., Inc.
12 Piedmont Street
Boston, MA 02116
(617) 482-7456
Flutes, headjoints, piccolos

Kelischek Workshop for Historical Instruments
Rt. 1, Box 26
Brasstown, NC 28902
(704) 837-5833
Ocarinas, pennywhistles, tabor pipes, recorders, flutes

Eva Kingma
Hoofdstraat 10
9444 PB Grolloo, The Netherlands
05925 - 1659
Alto flutes, bass flutes, including quartertone models

Tom Lacy Flutes
56973 Pearl Ann Drive
Elkhart, IN 46516-5617
(219) 293-4800
Flutes, headjoints

Landell Flutes
RD 2, Box 277B
Richmond, VT 05477
Phone/FAX (802) 434-4317
Flutes, headjoints

Lopatin Flute Company
248 High Street
North Attleborough, MA 02760
(508) 699-5426
Flutes, headjoints

John Lunn Flutes
23 Fletcher Road
Newport, NH 03773
(603) 863-0035 · FAX (603) 863-3623
Flutes

David Lusk Flutes
2140 Laurel Woods Drive
Salem, VA 24153
(703) 387-4533
Flutes, headjoints

Mateki Flutes
Cincinnati Fluteworks
621 Clemmer Avenue #13
Cincinnati, OH 45219
(513) 579-8294 · FAX (513) 579-8305
Flutes, headjoints

Matit Flutebrothers
Matti Helin
Iso Roobertinkatu 39 F 52
00120 Helsinki, Finland
358 0 7001 9470
FAX 358 0 7001 9471
Carbon fiber flutes, headjoints

Alton McCanless Flutemaker
2596 Lincoln Avenue
Oskaloosa, IA 52577
(515) 673-8310
Flutes

Ewen McDougall
Holme Cottage, Ravensworth
Richmond, North Yorkshire
DL11 7EZ, England
(01325) 718368
Silver and gold flutes, headjoints

McKenna Flutes, Inc.
8 Raymond Road
Deerfield, NH 03037
(603) 463-4185
Flutes

Miyazawa Flutes, Ltd.
1214 Fifth Street
Coralville, IA 52241
(319) 351-2000
Flutes, headjoints, alto flutes

Jack Moore Flutes, Inc.
1218 Brentwood Avenue
Elkhart, IN 46514
(219) 262-4019
Flutes

Muramatsu Flutes
Muramatsu America
P.O. Box 344
Bloomfield Hills, MI 48303
(810) 540-6424 · FAX (810) 645-5446
Flutes, alto flutes

Nagahara Flutes/NNI, Inc.
197 Main Street
N. Reading, MA 01864
(508) 664-5939 · FAX (508) 664-5946
Flutes, headjoints

Northeast Winds
10 Gerry Road
Lynnfield, MA 01940
(617) 334-5798
Sakurai flutes, Takezawa flutes

Andrew Oxley
Rowan Cottage, Church Street
Castle Cary, Somerset
BA7 7EL, England
(01963) 350780
Silver and gold flutes, headjoints

Verne Q. Powell Flutes, Inc.
257 Crescent Street
Waltham, MA 02154
(617) 647-4111; (800) 824-9507
FAX (617) 647-4125
Flutes, headjoints, piccolos

Beverly Pugh Associates, Inc.
10 Manor Lane
Bridgeton, NJ 08302
(609) 455-1098
Pan flutes

Sagerman Flutes
P.O. Box 790
Waldoboro, ME 04572
(207) 529-5420
Alto flutes, headjoints

Sankyo Flutes USA
56 West 45th Street, Suite 605
New York, NY 10036
(212) 719-2917
Flutes, headjoints

R. Seaman Co.
5453 Saloma Avenue
Van Nuys, CA 91411
(818) 780-7791 · FAX (818) 780-4954
Roy Seaman and M. Zentner piccolos

The Selmer Company, Inc.
P.O. Box 310
Elkhart, IN 46515
(219) 522-1675
Flutes, piccolos

Sheridan Flute Company
Dana Sheridan
Neusserstr. 701
50737 Köln, Germany
Phone/FAX 0221 740 40 40
Flutes, headjoints

Straubinger Flutes
2521 East Southport Road
Indianapolis, IN 46227
(317) 784-3012 · FAX 317-784-1735
Flutes, headjoints

Sweetheart Flute Co.
32 South Maple Street
Enfield, CT 06082
(203) 749-4494
Reproduction Renaissance and baroque flutes, "Irish" style flutes, walking stick flutes, flageolettes and whistles, fifes; dealer in antique and used flutes

Tai Hei Shakuhachi
Monty H. Levenson
P.O. Box 294
Willits, CA 95490
(707) 459-3402 · FAX (707) 459-3434
Shakuhachis

Von Huene Workshop, Inc.
65 Boylston Street
Brookline, MA 02146
(617) 277-8690
Historical flutes, recorders

John Webb
Archway Cottage, Church Street
Mere, Wiltshire
BA12 6DS, England
(01747) 861472
Headjoints

J. B. Weissman Music Co.
196-62 67th Avenue
Fresh Meadows, NY 11365
(718) 454-9288
Flutes, piccolos

S. Wesley Co.
52 Alvarado Avenue
Pittsburg, CA 94565
(510) 439-5491
Vertical flutes

Stephen Wessel
Millbrook House, Alhampton
Shepton Mallet, Somerset
BA4 6PX, England
(01749) 860047
Silver flutes with stainless steel keys

Williams Flutes
1165R Massachusetts Avenue
Arlington, MA 02174
(617) 643-8839
Flutes, headjoints

David Wimberly Flutes
15 Schooner Cove Road
Head of St. Margaret's Bay
Nova Scotia BOJ 3JO, Canada
(902) 826-7846
Flutes, headjoints

Peter Worrell
11 Loxwood Avenue
Worthing, West Sussex
BN14 7QZ, England
(01903) 218599
Flutes, alto flutes

Yamaha Corporation of America
Band & Orchestral Division
3445 East Paris Avenue, S.W.
P.O. Box 899
Grand Rapids, MI 49512-0899
(616) 940-4900
Flutes, piccolos, alto flutes, bass flutes

Dean Yang Flutes
P.O. Box 9276
Rancho Santa Fe, CA 92067
(800) 60 FLUTE
Exclusive distributor (outside California):
Little Piper, P.O. Box 14038, Detroit, MI 48214
(800) 71 PIPER
FAX (810) 645-5446
Flutes

Appendix C

REPAIR SHOPS

UNITED STATES

Tim Burdick
Woodwind Workshop
2163 Lee Road
Cleveland Heights, OH 44118
(216) 371-0328

Cincinnati Fluteworks
621 Clemmer Avenue #13
Cincinnati, OH 45219
(513) 379-8294

Eugene S. Gordon Woodwinds
410 S. Michigan Avenue
Chicago, IL 60605
(312) 663-0414

Martin Gordon
48 Nagog Hill Road
Acton, MA 01720
Phone/FAX (508) 263-9019

House of Woodwinds
328 14th Street
Oakland, CA 94612
(510) 834-2425

Lagerquist Flute Service, Inc.
7006 Lovell Drive
Hyattsville, MD 20782
(301) 779-7674 · FAX (301) 927-9569

Denny Lawson
958 East 53rd Street
Davenport, IA 52807
(319) 391-9000
Modern flutes and restoration of old flutes

Chris McKenna
222 North Road
Deerfield, NH 03037
(603) 463-7251

Anne Pollack
301 West 108th Street
New York, NY 10025
(212) 459-4451

Jay Sleigh
5999 Cozzens Street
San Diego, CA 92122
(619) 457-5030

Elmer Suvegeas
24348 Loretta
Warren, MI 48901
(313) 754-5755

Ted Thiele
422 Dellbrook Avenue
San Francisco, CA 94131
(415) 759-1631

Albert Weatherly
56 West 45th Street #605
New York, NY 10036
(212) 719-2917

Woodwind Repair and Sales
Phil Unger
3 Joda Road
West Allenhurst, NJ 07711
(908) 77MUSIC · FAX (908) 531-5558

CANADA

Yutaka Chiba
362 Cedarvale Avenue
Toronto, Ontario M4C 4K6
(416) 421-1798

Mara Goosman
P.O. Box 13
Pickering, Ontario L1V 2R2
(905) 649-3687

Les Instruments de Musique Twigg
1230 St.-Hubert
Montreal, Quebec H2L 3Y7
(514) 843-3593
FAX (514) 843-3074

Russ Lewis
2404 9th Avenue NW
Calgary, Alberta T2N 1E7
(403) 289-9513

Ward Music
Bob MacDonald
412 West Hastings
Vancouver, British Columbia V6B 1L3
(604) 682-5288

Courtney Westcott
8 First Street
Ward's Island
Toronto, Ontario M5J 2A6
(416) 363-0397
historical keyed flutes

UNITED KINGDOM

All Flutes Plus
5 Dorset Street
London, W1H 3FE
(0171) 935 3339
FAX (0171) 224 2053

Helen Blore
Rushworths Music
31a Bridge Street
Chester CH1 1NG
(1244) 325252

Steve Butler
10 Gilbert Road
Bromley, Kent BR1 3QP
(0181) 464 5002

Brian Clover
54 Buckhurst Way, Buckhurst Hill
Essex IG9 6HP
(0181) 505 0557

Edward Kettlewell
56 Leabrooks Road
Somercotes, Derby
(01773) 603276

Peter Davies
The Woodwind Workshop
36 Byram Arcade
Westgate, Huddersfield HD1 1ND
Phone/FAX (1484) 533053

Lowes Woodwind
102 Greenwich South Street
London SE10 8UN
(0181) 691 6944
FAX (0181) 694 2503

Ewen McDougall
Holme Cottage, Ravensworth
Richmond, North Yorkshire
DL11 7EZ
(01325) 718368

Ian McLauchlan
36 Chipstead Valley Road
Coulsdon, Surrey CR5 2RA
(0181) 668 4444
FAX (0181) 668 7262

John Myatt Woodwind
57 Nightingale Road
Hitchin, Herts SG5 1RQ
(1462) 420057 • FAX (1462) 435464

John Packer Ltd.
1, Portland Street
Taunton, Somerset TA1 1UY
(01823) 282386 • FAX (01823) 337653

Sheehan's Music
50 London Road
Leicester LE2 0QD
(0116) 255 7492

Top Wind
2, Lower Marsh
London SE17RJ
(0171) 401 8787
FAX (0171) 401 8788

Michael White
11 Queens Parade
Queen's Drive
Ealing, London W5 3HU
(0181) 997 4088

Woodwind & Co.
208 Liverpool Road
Cadishead, Manchester M44 5DB
(0161) 775 1842

Wood, Wind and Reed (Daniel Bangham)
11 Homerton Street
Cambridge CB2 2NZ
(01223) 416131
FAX (01223) 416963

Appendix D

SOURCES FOR MUSIC AND BOOKS

UNITED STATES

Boulder Early Music Shop
2010 Fourteenth Street
Boulder, CO 80302
(303) 449-9231; (800) 499-1301
FAX (303) 449-3819
e-mail: rlh1939@aol.com

Early Music Shop of New England
65 Boylston Street
Brookline, MA 02146
(617) 277-8690
FAX (617) 277-7217
e-mail: vonhuene@world.std.com

Eble Music Company
P.O. Box 2570
Iowa City, IA 52244-2570
(319) 338-0313
FAX (319) 338-0108

Flute World Inc.
Shipping: 29920 Orchard Lake Road
Farmington Hills, MI 48334
Mailing: P.O. Box 250248
Franklin, MI 48025
(810) 855-0410
FAX (810) 855-2525
e-mail: flutes@rust.net
web site:
http://www.fluteworld.com/flutes

Kelischek Workshop for Historic Instruments
Route 1, Box 26
Brasstown, NC 28902
(704) 837-5833
FAX (704) 837-8755

Monty H. Levenson
P.O. Box 294
Willits, CA 95490
(707) 459-3402
FAX (707) 459-3434
web site:
http://www.mind.net/music/shakuhachi.html
Music, instructional materials for shakuhachi and other indigenous flutes

Joseph Patelson Music House
160 West 56th Street
New York, NY 10019
(212) JU2-5840

Sheet Music Service of Portland
34 N.W. 8th Ave.
Portland, OR 97209-3591
(503) 222-9607; (800) 452-1133

Stanton's Sheet Music, Inc.
330 South Fourth Street
Columbus, OH 43215
(614) 224-4257

CANADA

Hysen Music Co.
146 Dundas Street
London, Ontario N6A 1G1
(519) 433-6173

Royal Conservatory of Music
273 Bloor Street W.
Toronto, Ontario M5S 1W2
(416) 408-2824

UNITED KINGDOM

All Flutes Plus
5 Dorset Street
London W1H 3FE
(0171) 935-3339
FAX (0171) 224-2053

Blackwell's Music Shop
38 Holywell Street
Oxford OX1 3SW
(01865) 792792 · FAX (01865) 248833

Chappells
50 New Bond Street
London, W1Y 9HA
(0171) 491 2777
FAX (0171) 491 0133

Chimes Music Shop
65 Marylebone High Street
London W1
(0171) 935 1587

June Emerson
Windmill Farm, Ampleforth
North Yorkshire YO2 4HF
(01439) 788324
FAX (01439) 788715

Foyles
119-125 Charing Cross Road
London WC1
(0171) 437 5660

Just Flutes
36 Chipstead Valley Road
Coulsdon, Surrey CR5 2RA
(0181) 668 6969
FAX (0181) 668 7262

Top Wind
2 Lower Marsh
London SE17RJ
(0171) 401 8787
FAX (0171) 401 8788

Appendix E

USEFUL PERIODICALS

American Musical Instrument Society Journal and Newsletter
Journal:
Martha N. Clinkscale, Editor
Department of Music
University of California
Riverside, CA 92521-0325
Newsletter:
Harrison Powley, Editor
E-563 HFAC
Brigham Young University
Provo, UT 84602-6410
(801) 378-3279
FAX (801) 378-5973
e-mail:ehpowley@adml.byu.edu
Membership:
Albert R. Rice
6114 Corbin Avenue
Tarzana, CA 91356-1010
Phone/FAX (818) 776-9446
e-mail: al_rice@cucmail.claremont.edu

The American Recorder
Editorial:
Benjamin S. Dunham
472 Point Road
Marion, MA 02738
(508) 748-1750 · FAX (508) 748-1928
e-mail: amrec@aol.com
Subscriptions:
American Recorder Society
5554 S. Prince, Suite 128
Littleton, CO 81020
(303) 347-1120 · FAX (303) 347-1120
e-mail: 74363.3365@compuserve.com

Chamber Music
Chamber Music America
545 Eighth Avenue
New York, NY 10018-4385
(212) 244-2272 · FAX (212) 244-2776

Early Music
Editorial: Oxford University Press
3 Park Road
London NW1 6XN, England
Phone (0171) 724 1707
FAX (0171) 723 5033
e-mail: inl.early-music@oup.co.uk
UK Subscriptions:
Oxford University Press
Walton Street
Oxford OX2 6DP, England
Phone (01865) 267907
FAX (01865) 267773
U.S. subscriptions:
Oxford University Press
2001 Evans Road
Cary, NC 27513
(919) 677-0977 · FAX (919) 677-1714

Flute Network
P.O. Box 9472
San Bernardino, CA 92427
(909) 886-3101
Bulletin-board newsletter, primarily for instrument sales

Flute Talk
200 Northfield Road
Northfield, IL 60093-3390
(708) 446-5000; (800) 323-5559
FAX (708) 446-6263

Galpin Society Journal
Editor:
David Rycroft
Ashdown Cottage
Chapel Lane, Forest Row
East Sussex RH18 5BS,
England
Membership:
Galpin Society
2 Quinton Rise
Oadby, Leicestershire LE2 5PN, England

Historical Performance
Early Music America
11421 Bellflower Road
Cleveland, OH 44106
(216) 229-1685 · FAX (216) 229-1688
e-mail: bxs6@po.cwru.edu

The Instrumentalist
200 Northfield Road
Northfield, IL 60093-3390
(708) 446-5000; (800) 323-5559
FAX (708) 446-6263

Das Musikinstrument
Verlag Erwin Bochinsky
Münchenerstrasse 45
60329 Frankfurt am Main, Germany
(069) 239521

The Flutist Quarterly
Editor:
Sandra Schwoebel
2215 East Greenlee Road
Tucson, AZ 86719
Phone/FAX: (520) 321-4821
e-mail: flq@theriver.com
Membership: National Flute Association, Inc.
P.O. Box 800597
Santa Clarita, CA 91380-0597
(805) 297-5287 · FAX 805-297-0753
e-mail: 75322.324@compuserve.com

Instrumentenbau Zeitschrift-Musik International
Verlag Franz Schmitt
Kaiserstrasse 99-101
53721 Siegburg, Germany
(02241) 64039 · FAX (02241) 53891

Pan
British Flute Society
Editor: Judith Fitton
116 Woodwarde Road
Dulwich, London SE22 8UT, England
(0181) 693-8414 · FAX (0181) 693-1479
Membership:
Margaret Pether
82 Seagull Road
Strood, Rochester
Kent ME2 2RH, England

Recorder Magazine
Peacock Press
Scout Bottom Farms, Mytholmroyd
Hebden Bridge, W. Yorks. HX7 5JS
England
(01422) 882751 · FAX (01422) 886157

Tibia
Moeck Verlag
Postfach 3131
29231 Celle, Germany
(05141) 88530 · FAX (05141) 885342

Traverso
Folkers & Powell
49 Route 23
Hudson, NY 12534-9508
(518) 828-9779

Windplayer
P.O. Box 2666
Malibu, CA 90266
(310) 456-5813 · FAX (310) 456-5812
e-mail: dm@windplayer.com
web site: http://www.windplayer.com

Woodwind Quarterly
Northstar Publishing
1513 Old CC Road
Colville, WA 99114

Appendix F

FLUTE CLUBS AND RELATED ORGANIZATIONS

UNITED STATES

National Flute Association, Inc.
P.O. Box 800597
Santa Clarita, CA 91380-0597
(805) 297-5287 · FAX (805) 297-0753
e-mail: 75322.324@compuserve.com

Alabama

Montgomery Flute Society
1409 Buckingham Drive
Montgomery, AL 36116

Arizona

Tucson Flute Club
Sandy Schwoebel
2215 East Greenlee Road
Tucson, AZ 85719
(520) 321-4943

California

San Diego Flute Guild
Jane Masur
12222 Poway Road
Poway, CA 92064
(619) 578-4521

Ventura County Flute Association
Marianne Hinkle
2139 Millcreek Way
Palmdale, CA 93551
(805) 266-2543

Colorado

Colorado Flute Association
Christine Potter
2985 18th Street
Boulder, CO 80304
(303) 443-3330

Western Colorado Flute Association
Charlie Gaddy
P.O. Box 4395
Grand Junction, CO 81501
(303) 242-8017

Florida

Florida Flute Association
Grace Petree
P.O. Box 950818
Lake Mary, FL 32795
(407) 323-3639

Northwest Florida Flute Society
Jeanne Barber
1310½ North Carcelona Street
Pensacola, FL 32501
(904) 438-9762

Illinois

Chicago Flute Club
Susan Phelps
611 East Gartner Road
Naperville, IL 60540
(708) 961-0840

North Shore Flute Club
Frank Lestina
1701 Central Avenue
Wilmette, IL 60091
(708) 251-5131

Indiana

Flute Club of Southern Indiana
Bridget M. Whobrey
1409 Olympic Court
Evansville, IN 47715
(812) 473-2850

Kentucky

Louisville Flute Society
Sarah Fletcher
3507 Barclay Drive
Louisville, KY 40299
(502) 266-9137

Louisiana

Louisiana Flute Society
Judy Hand
2632 Edgewood Lane
Lake Charles, LA 70605
(318) 477-7948

Maryland
see also Washington, D.C.

Western Maryland Flute Club
Linda Kirkpatrick
Western Maryland College
Westminster, MD 21157
(301) 857-2550

Massachusetts

Greater Boston Flute Association
John Ranck
16 Tremlett Street
Boston, MA 021224
(617) 265-9176

Michigan

West Michigan Flute Association
Darlene Dugan
840 Parkway Drive NE
Grand Rapids, MI 49505
(616) 364-0076

Minnesota

Upper Midwest Flute Association
Judy Ranheim
P.O. Box 14741, University Station
Minneapolis, MN 55414
612) 825-6798

Mississippi

Mississipppi Flute Society
Subil Cheesman
3162 Adrienne Drive
Jackson, MS 39212
(601) 372-8304

Missouri

Flute Society of St. Louis
Anne Brickeen
1421 Venus Drive
St. Peters, MO 63376
(314) 256-8178

Kansas City Flute Association
Susan Murphy
P.O. Box 22308
Kansas City, MO 64113
(913) 339-6822

Montana

Bozeman Flute Club
Karen Leech
Department of Music
Montana State University
Bozeman, MT 59717
(406) 994-3561

Nevada

Las Vegas Flute Club
Marci Banks
138 Almendio
Henderson, NV 89014
(702) 361-0071

Sierra Flute Society
Kristin Slaughenhoupt
1625 Geary
Reno, NV 89503
(702) 746-1253

New Jersey

see New York, Pennsylvania

New Mexico

Albuquerque Flute Association
Carla Beauchamp
P.O. Box 3641
Albuquerque, NM 87190-3641
(505) 266-9869

Northern New Mexico Flute Association
Carol Redman
Route 10, Box 82E
Santa Fe, NM 87501
(505) 988-4863

New York

Central New York Flute Association
Rita Bongiovanni
6 Brattle Road
Syracuse, NY 13203
(315) 472-9756

Long Island Flute Club
Paul Gray
69 Marshall Avenue
Lynbrook, NY 1563
(516) 887-3712

New York Flute Club
Rie Schmidt
711 Amsterdam Avenue #10G
New York, NY 10025
(212) 662-8795

Niagara Frontier Flute Association
Michael Colquhoun
P.O. Box 151
Kenmore, NY 14217
(716) 874-0486

North Carolina

Raleigh Area Flute Association
Rosene Rohrer
3809 Midlakes Drive
Raleigh, NC 27612
(919) 781-3225

Ohio

Central Ohio Flute Association
Lori Akins
6024 Renfield Drive
Dublin, OH 43017
(614) 766-1838

Northeastern Ohio Flute Association
George Pope
School of Music, University of Akron
Akron, OH 44325-1002
(216) 972-6575

Southwest Ohio Flute Association
Mariam Wood
2295 Banyon Drive
Dayton, OH 54531
(513) 426-1787

Oregon

Greater Portland Flute Society
Becca Barlow
P.O. Box 3895
Portland, OR 97208-3895
(503) 295-5856

Pennsylvania

Allegheny Flute Association
Wendy Kumer
136 Fairfax Road
Pittsburgh, PA 15221
(412) 241-0209

Flute Society of Greater Philadelphia
Beverly Pugh
P.O. Box 321
Moorestown, NJ 08057
(609) 455-1098

Tennessee

Memphis Flute Society
Ruth McClain
6347 Egerton Circle
Memphis, TN 38119-5400
(901) 683-4110

Middle Tennessee Flute Society
MTSU Music Department, Box 47
Murfreesboro, TN 37132

Texas

Austin Flute Club
Leanne Morales
904 Deergrove Drive
Cedar Park, TX 78613
(512) 250-8534

Houston Flute Club
Natalie Syring
9 Mallard Glen Place
The Woodlands, TX 77381-4103
(713) 363-9855

San Antonio Flute Association
Cathy Clare
16334 Ross Oak
San Antonio, TX 78247
(210) 654-6826

Texas Flute Society
Ellen Kaner
P.O. Box 54202
Hurst, TX 76054
(817) 261-4425

Utah

Utah Flute Association
Kristen Gygi
1266 E. Bryan Avenue
Salt Lake City, UT 84105
(801) 485-7293

Virginia

James Madison University Flute Choir
Carol Kneibusch
Noe School of Music
James Madison University
Harrisonburg, VA 22807
(703) 568-6972

Washington

Inland Northwest Flute Society
S. 2319 University Road
Spokane, WA 99206

Seattle Flute Society
Francis Timlin
106 Sixteenth Avenue
Seattle, WA 98122
(206) 324-0572

Washington, D.C.

Flute Society of Washington, D.C.
Mary Jean Simpson
5106 Hesperus Drive
Columbia, MD 24044-1310
(410) 740-2971

Wisconsin

Flute Le Force
Christine Gagliano
7266 Highway 42
Egg Harbor, WI 54209
(414) 868-2081

Southside Flute Society
Grace La Rayne
3033 S. 55th Street
Milwaukee, WI 53219
(414) 327-0829

INTERNATIONAL

Argentina

Asociacion Argentina de Flautistas
E. Leon Brunner
Salmun Feijoo 730-DTO. 10
1274 Buenos Aires, Argentina

Australia

A.C.T. Flute Society
Jenny Stephenson
51 Rivett Street
Hackett, ACT 2602
06/249-6123

Alice Springs Flute Guild
Margaret Collins
22 Burke Street
Alice Springs, NT 0870
089/52-3464

Australian Flute Association, Ltd.
Robert Brown
P.O. Box 3208
Norwood, So. Australia 5067
08/379-1445

Darling Downs Flute Society
c/o Christine Kleidon
P.O. Box 85
Drayton North, QLD 4350

Darwin Flute Society
Claire Kilgariff
9 Westcombe Court
Malak, NT 0812
089/27-5352

Flute Society of N.S.W., Inc.
c/o Lisa Breckenridge
P.O. Box 248
Cammeray, N.S.W. 2062
phone/fax: 02/560-6226

Flute Society of South Australia
Sylvia Beare
P.O. Box 3208
Norwood, S.A. 5067
08/276-2750

Queensland Flute Guild, Inc.
c/o Frances Farmer
19 Franklin Street
Kelvin Grove, QLD 4059
07 356-8244

Tasmanian Flute Society, Inc.
c/o Jane Dickie
GPO Box 9994
Hobart, TAS 7001

Victorian Flute Guild, Inc.
Annette Sloan
P.O. Box 95
Malvern, Victoria 3144

Western Australia Flute Society
Helen Lampard
69 Watling Street
Lynwood, WA 6155
09 458-6964

Belgium

Belgium "Het Fiere Fluitertje"
Peter en Annemie Verhoyen
'T Kloosterhof 67
Sint-Michiels, B-8200
050/392627

Brazil

Asociacion Nationale do Flautistas
do Brasil
Celso Woltsenlogel
Rua Bulhoes de Carvalho 285, Ap 901
Copacabana 22081
Rio de Janeiro
267 0404

Clube dos Flautistas do Rio de Janeiro
Celso Woltsenlogel
Rua Bulhoes de Carvalho 285, Ap 901
Copacabana 22081
Rio de Janeiro
267 0404

Canada

Atlantic Flute Society
Elizabeth Du Bois
Site 8, Comp. 7, R.R. 1
Mount Uniacke, NS B0N 1Z0

Le Club de Flûte de Trois-Rivieres
Maurice Auger
3300 Calais
Trois-Rivieres-Ouest, QUE G8Y 3W5

Victoria Flute Circle
Austin A. Scott
3945 Shorn Cliff Road No.
Victoria, BC VSP2T5

China, People's Republic of

Shanghai Flute Association
Leon D.S. Ying
No. 4, Ln. 163, Mao-Ming Road
Shanghai

Finland

Finnish Flute Association
William Dyer
Minna Canthinkatu 4A 1
33230 Tampere 23
931-35 085

France

L'Association "Flûtes du Monde"
Charles Tripp
3 Rue de Brasse
90000 Belfort
84 21 57 38

Association Français des Flûtes
Traversières
Denis Verroust
16, Avenue Aubert
94300 Vincennes

Germany

Deutsche Gesellschaft für Flöte
Voelckerstrasse 9
D-60322 Frankfurt am Main
069/596 24 43

Friends of the German Flute
Kornerstrasse 51
D-5820 Gevelsberg

German Flute Association
Rudiger Jacobsen
Eschenheimer Anlage 30
D-6000 Frankfurt am Main 1
069 59 24 43

Ireland

Irish Flute Band League
Derek Greer
44 Suffolk Street
Ballymena, Co. Antrim BT43 7BD

Italy

Accademia Italiana del Flauto
Stefano Cioffi
V. Orti di Trastevere, 34
00153 Rome
06/5137036

Japan

Japan Flutists Association
Maso Yoshida
2-13-32-604 Kamiosaki
Shinagawa-ku, Tokyo 141

Korea

Seoul Flute Ensemble
Myng Ja Moon
P.O. Box Yungdong 531
Seoul
545-6840

Mexico

Mexican Flute Society
Elena Duran Emmerson
Santisimo 27, Col. San Angel
01000 Mexico DF
011-52-5-550-9449

Netherlands

Stichting Flutonicon
Academie voor Dwarsfluit
Postbus 85498
2508 CD Den Haag

New Zealand

New Zealand Flute Society
Kathryn Orbell
c/o 22 Strowan Avenue
Hamilton
09/ 4898887

Peru

Circulo Peruano de Flautistas
c/o Pablo Acosta, President
Assoc. Musical Renacimiento
Los Eucaliptos 245
San Isidro, Lima

South Africa

Flute Federation of South Africa
John Hinch
c/o Music Department
University of Pretoria
Pretoria 0001
Republic of South Africa
012 346-1639 (H)

Spain

Asociacion Espanola de Flautistas
Alfredo G. Matin-Cordova
C/. Esoejo, 4
28013 Madrid, Spain

Switzerland

National Flute Association of Switzerland
Urs Peter Salm
P.O. Box 252
CH-3000 Bern 25

Schweizer Flöten-Gesellschaft
Peter Lukas Graf
Postfach 252
CH-3000 Bern 25

Taiwan

Taipei Flute Ensemble Academy
Hsiao-Hwa Niu
7F No. 170 Sec. 1 Ta-an Road
Taipei, Taiwan
Republic of China
02/7025246

United Kingdom

British Flute Society
Jenny Wray, Membership Secretary
The White House
Hatton Green, Hatton CV35 7LA

International Shakuhachi Society
Wadhurst, Sussex TN5 6PN
Membership: P.O. Box 294, Willits, CA 95490

SELECTED BIBLIOGRAPHY

The Instrument

Agricola, Martin. "*Musica instrumentalis deudsch*": *A Treatise on Musical Instruments, 1529 and 1545*. Edited by William E. Hettrick New York: Cambridge University Press, 1994.

Artaud, Pierre-Yves. *La Flûte*. Paris: J.-C. Lattes/Salabert, 1986.

Baines, Anthony. *The Oxford Companion to Musical Instruments*. New York: Oxford University Press, 1992.

Baines, Anthony. *Woodwind Instruments and Their History*. New York: Norton, 1962.

The Bate Collection of Historical Wind Instruments. Oxford: Faculty of Music, University of Oxford, 1976.

Bate, Philip. *The Flute*. New York: Norton, 1969.

Benade, Arthur. "Analysis of the Flute Head Joint." Journal of the *Acoustical Society of America*, 37 (1965): 679-691.

———. *Fundamentals of Musical Acoustics*. New York: Oxford University Press, 1976.

———. *Horns, Strings, & Harmony*. 1960. Reprint. Westport, Conn.: Greenwood, 1979.

———. "The Physics of Wood Winds." *Scientific American*, October 1960, pp. 145-154.

Bevan, Clifford, ed. *Musical Instrument Collections in the British Isles*. Winchester: Piccolo Press, 1990.

Boehm, Theobald. *An Essay on the Construction of Flutes*. Edited by W.S. Broadwood. 1882. Reprint. Saint Clair Shores, Mich.: Scholarly, 1976.

———. *The Flute and Flute-Playing*. Translated and revised by Dayton C. Miller. 2nd ed., rev. 1922. Reprint. New York: Dover, 1964.

Bohm, Theobald. *Uber den Flötenbau und die neuesten Verbesserungen desselben/ On the construction of flutes* [English and German text]. 1847, 1882. Reprint. Introduction by Karl Ventzke. Buren: Frits Knuf, 1982.

Bowers, Jane, et al. *Concerning the flute: ten articles about flute literature, flute playing, flute making, and flutists*. Edited by Rien de Reede. Amsterdam: Broekmans & van Poppel, 1984.

Carse, Adam. *The History of Orchestration*. New York: E. P. Dutton, 1925.

———. *Musical Wind Instruments*. 1939. Reprint. New York: Da Capo Press, 1965.

Coltman, John. "The Acoustics of the Flute." *Physics Today*, November 1978, pp. 25-32.

———. "A New C♯ for the Boehm Flute." *The Instrumentalist*, May 1977), pp. 2, 64-65.

Cooper, Albert. *The Flute*. 2nd rev. ed. London: Albert Cooper, 1984.

Coover, James. *Musical Instruments Collections: Catalogs & Cognate Literature*. Detroit: Information Coordinators, 1981.

DeLorenzo, Leonardo De. *My Complete Story of the Flute*. Revised and expanded ed. Lubbock, TX: Texas Tech Press, 1992. Facsimile of the 1951 edition and three addenda (1954, 1955, and 1957), essays by Susan Berdahl and Nancy Toff, and index.

A Directory of Historical-Instrument Makers in North America. 2nd rev. ed. Cleveland, Ohio: Early Music America, 1995.

Engel, Hans. *The Concerto Grosso.* Translated by Robert Kolben.
Anthology of Music, vol. 23. Cologne: Arno Volk Verlag, 1964.

———. *The Solo Concerto.* Translated by Robert Kolben. *Anthology of Music,* vol. 25. Cologne: Arno Volk Verlag, 1964.

Estevan, Pilar. *Talking With Flutists.* 2 vols. New York: Edu-Tainment, 1976, 1978.

Fajardo, Raoul. "Flute Resonance and Projection." *The Instrumentalist,* March 1976, p. 62.

———. "The Wedged Cylindrical Headjoint." *Woodwind World Brass & Percussion,* 17 (1978): 10.

Farrell, Susan Caust. *Directory of Contemporary American Musical Instrument Makers.* Columbia: University of Missouri Press, 1981.

Fitzgibbon, H. Macauley. *The Story of the Flute.* 2nd ed., rev. New York: Scribners, 1928.

Fletcher, Neville. "Acoustical Correlates of Flute Performance Technique." *Journal of the Acoustical Society of America* 57 (1975): 233-237.

———. "Some Acoustical Principles of Flute Technique." *The Instrumentalist,* February 1974, pp. 57-61.

Galleras, Roger. *Histoire de la flûte.* Pau: Imprimerie moderne, 1977.

Geiringer, Karl. *Instruments in the History of Western Music.* 3rd ed. New York: Oxford University Press, 1978.

Giannini, Tula. *Great Flute Makers of France: The Lot and Godfroy Families, 1650-1900.* London: Tony Bingham, 1993.

Gilliam, Laura E., and William Lichtenwanger. *The Dayton C. Miller Collection: A Checklist of the Instruments.* Washington, D.C.: Library of Congress, 1961.

Girard, Adrien. *Histoire et Richesses de la Flûte.* Paris: Librairie Gründ, 1953.

Griscom, Richard, and David Lasocki. *The Recorder: A Guide to Writings About the Instrument for Players and Researchers.* New York: Garland, 1994.

Heyde, Herbert. *Flöten.* Leipzig: Deutscher Verlag für Musik, 1978. Catalog of Karl Marx University collection, Leipzig.

Jones, William J. "The Alto Flute." *The Instrumentalist,* December 1978, pp. 56-58; January 1979, pp. 38-41.

Landell, Jonathon. *The Landell Flute Tune-Up Manual.* Vergennes, Vt.: Vermont Guild of Flute Making, 1983.

Langwill, Lyndesay G. *An Index of Musical Wind-Instrument Makers.* 6th ed. Edinburgh: Lyndesay Langwill, 1980.

Lenski, Karl, and Karl Ventzke. *Das goldene Zeitalter der Flöte: Die Boehmflote in Frankreich, 1832-1932: Durchsetzung, Gestaltung, Wirkung.* Celle: Moeck, 1992.

MacGillivray, James A. "The Woodwind." In *Musical Instruments Through the Ages,* edited by Anthony Baines, pp. 216-50. London: Faber and Faber, 1961.

Mather, Roger. "Care and Repair of the Flute." *The Instrumentalist,* December 1972, pp. 40-43; January 1973, pp. 41-42, 44-45; March 1973, pp. 66-68; April 1973, pp. 54-57.

Merriman, Lyle. *Woodwind Research Guide.* Evanston, Ill.: The Instrumentalist, 1978.

Meyer, R. F. *The Band Director's Guide to Instrument Repair.* Edited by Willard I. Musser. Port Washington, N.Y.: Alfred Publishing, 1973.

Meylan, Raymond. *The Flute.* Translated by Alfred Clayton. Portland, Ore.: Amadeus, 1988.

Miller, Dayton C. "Modern Alto, Tenor, and Bass Flutes." *American Musicological Society Papers,* 1938, pp. 8-15.

Montagu, Jeremy. *The World of Baroque & Classical Musical Instruments.* New York: Overlook, 1979.

———. *The World of Medieval & Renaissance Musical Instruments.* New York: Overlook, 1976.

———. *The World of Romantic & Modern Musical Instruments.* New York: Overlook, 1981.

O'Kelly, Eve. *The Recorder Today.* New York: Cambridge University Press, 1990.

Phelan, James, and Mitchell D. Brody. *The Complete Guide to the Flute from Acoustics and Construction to Repair and Maintenance.* Boston: Conservatory Publications, 1980.

Praetorius, Michael. *Syntagma Musicum II. De Organographia Part I and II.* Translated and edited by David Z. Crookes. New York: Oxford University Press, 1986.

Rockstro, Richard Shepard. *A Treatise on the Construction the History and the Practice of the Flute.* 2nd ed., rev. 1928. Reprint. London: Musica Rara, 1967.

Rowen, Ruth Halle. *Early Chamber Music.* 1949. Reprint. New York: Da Capo, 1974.

Sachs, Curt. *The History of Musical Instruments.* New York: Norton, 1940.

Scheck, Gustav. *Die Flöte und ihre Musik.* Mainz: Schott, 1975.

Schmid, Manfred Hermann. *Theobald Boehm 1794-1881: Die Revolution der Flöte.* Tutzing: Hans Schneider, 1981.

Skei, Alan B. *Woodwind, Brass and Percussion Instruments of the Orchestra: A Bibliographic Guide.* New York: Garland, 1985.

Smith, Catherine P. "Changing use of the flute and its changing construction." *The American Recorder,* May 1979, pp. 4-8.

———. "Special Expressive Characteristics of the Pre-Boehm Transverse Flute." *Woodwind World Brass & Percussion.* Part I: Fall 1974, pp. 26-28, 34. Part II: January 1975, pp. 11-13, 24. Part III: September 1975, pp. 14-16, 31, 34, 50. Part IV: Holiday 1975, pp. 22, 50, 55.

Solum, John. *The Early Flute.* With a chapter on the Renaissance flute by Anne Smith. Oxford: Clarendon Press; New York: Oxford University Press, 1992.

Springer, George H. *Maintenance and Repair of Wind and Percussion Instruments.* Boston: Allyn and Bacon, 1976.

Thomson, John Mansfield, ed. *The Cambridge Companion to the Recorder.* Cambridge, New York: Cambridge University Press, 1995.

Tiede, Clayton H. *Practical Band Instrument Repair Manual.* Dubuque, Iowa: Wm. C. Brown, 1976.

Toff, Nancy. *The Development of the Modern Flute.* 1979. Reprint. Urbana: University of Illinois Press, 1986.

———. "Doctoral Dissertations on the Flute." *Flute Talk,* October 1986, pp. 24-25; November 1986, pp. 24-26; December 1986, pp. 31-32.

———. "Doctoral Dissertations on the Flute: 1991 Update." *The Flutist Quarterly,* Spring 1991, pp. 25-35.

———. "Doctoral Dissertations on the Flute: 1992 Update." *The Flutist Quarterly,* Fall 1992, pp. 44-46.

———. "Recent Developments in Flute Design." *The Instrumentalist,* June 1979, pp. 34-37.

———. "Technological Improvements of Woodwind Instruments: Woodwinds." In *The Orchestra: Origins and Transformations,* Joan Peyser, ed. New York: Scribners, 1986, pp. 137-51.

Tromlitz, J. G. *Über die Flöten mit mehreren Klappen: deren Anwendung und Nutzen; Nebst noch einigen ... Aufsätzen.* 1800. Reprint. Introduction and notes by Karl Ventzke. Buren: Frits Knuf, 1988.

Veinus, Abraham. *The Concerto.* New York: Dover, 1964.

Ventzke, Karl. *Die Boehmflöte.* Frankfurt: Verlag das Musikinstrument, 1966.

Ventzke, Karl, and Dietrich Hilkenbach. *Boehm-Instrumente : ein Handbuch uber Theobald Boehm und uber Klappenblasinstrumente seines Systems / Boehm woodwinds: a factbook on Theobald Boehm and woodwinds on his system.* Frankfurt am Main: Verlag Das Musikinstrument, 1982.

Virdung, Sebastian. *Musica Getuscht: A Treatise on Musical Instruments (1511)*. Edited and translated by Beth Bullard. New York: Cambridge University Press, 1993.

Voorhees, Jerry L. *The classification of flute fingering systems of the nineteenth and twentieth centuries*. Buren: F. Knuf, 1980.

Waterhouse, William. *The New Langwill Index. A Dictionary of Musical Wind-Instrument Makers and Inventors*. London: Tony Bingham, 1993.

Welch, Christopher. *History of the Boehm Flute*. 3rd ed., 1886. Reprint. Wakefield, N.H.: Longwood Press, 1977.

Young, Phillip T. *The Look of Music*. Seattle: University of Washington Press, 1980.

Young, Phillip T. *4900 Historical Woodwind Instruments: An Inventory of 200 Makers in International Collections*. London: Tony Bingham, 1993.

Biographies and Autobiographies

Dorgeuille, Claude. *The French Flute School 1860-1950*. Translated and edited by Edward Blakeman. London: Tony Bingham, 1986.

Floyd, Angeleita S. *The Gilbert Legacy: Methods, Exercises and Techniques for the Flutist*. Cedar Falls, Iowa: Winzer, 1990.

Galway, James. *An Autobiography*. New York: St. Martin's, 1979.

Goldberg, Adolph. *Biographieen zur Porträts-Sammlung hervorragender Flöten-Virtuosen, Dilettanten und Komponisten*. Edited by Karl Ventzke. Facsimile of 1906 edition, reduced. Celle: Moeck, 1987.

Mather, Roger. "The Flute Sound of Georges Laurent." *Woodwind World Brass & Percussion*, March 1976, pp. 12-14; May 1976, pp. 30-31, 47.

McCutchan, Ann. *Marcel Moyse: Voice of the Flute*. Portland, Ore.: Amadeus, 1994.

Rampal, Jean-Pierre, with Deborah Wise. *Music, My Love*. New York: Random House, 1989.

Toff, Nancy. *Georges Barrère and the Flute in America*. New York: New York Flute Club, 1994.

——. "Georges Barrère: Monarch of the Flute." *The Flutist Quarterly*, Fall 1994, pp.46-57.

Wye, Trevor. *Marcel Moyse: An Extraordinary Man*. Cedar Falls, Iowa: Winzer, 1993.

Performance and Technique

Artaud, Pierre-Yves. *Flûtes au present: traité des techniques contemporaines sur les flutes traversières à l'usage des compositeurs et des flutistes / Present day flutes: treatise on contemporary techniques of transverse flutes for the use of composers and performers*. Paris: Jobert, 1980.

Barnett, David. *The Performance of Music*. New York: Universe, 1972.

Barone, Clement. *Learning the Piccolo: A Treatise on the Subtleties and Problems of Playing the Piccolo in Relation to the Flute*. New York: EduTainment, 1975.

Brooke, Arthur. *Harmonic Fingerings for the Flute*. Boston: Cundy-Bettoney, 1925.

Bruderhans, Zdenek. "Circular Breathing and the Flute." *The Instrumentalist*, August 1981, pp. 34, 36-37.

Chapman, Frederick B. *Flute Technique*. 4th ed. New York: Oxford University Press, 1973.

Cone, Edward T. *Musical Form and Musical Performance*. New York: Norton, 1968.

Dart, Thurston. *The Interpretation of Music*. New York: Harper & Row, 1963.

Dick, Robert. *Circular Breathing for the Flutist*. New York: Multiple Breath, 1987.

Dorian, Frederick. *The History of Music in Performance*. New York: Norton, 1942.

Gärtner, Jochen. *The Vibrato*. Translated by Einar W. Anderson. Regensburg: Gustav Bosse, 1981.

Heriché, Robert. *A propos de la flûte*. Paris: Billaudot, 1985.

Jones, William J. "Some New Fingerings for Alto Flute." *The Instrumentalist*, May 1975, pp. 47-48.
Krell, John. *Kincaidiana: A Flute Player's Notebook*. Culver City, Calif.: Trio Associates, 1973.
Kynaston, Trent P. *Circular Breathing*. Hialeah, Fla.: Studio 224, 1978.
Lazarus, Annie. "Amplifying the Flute." *Woodwind World-Brass & Percussion*, January 1978, pp. 18-22.
LeRoy, René, with Claude Dorgeuille. *Traité de la flûte, historique, technique et pedagogique*. Paris: Editions musicales transatlantiques, 1966.
Mather, Roger. *The Art of Playing the Flute*. Volume I: *Breath Control*. Iowa City: Romney Press, 1980.
———. *The Art of Playing the Flute*. Volume II: *Embouchure*. Iowa City: Romney Press, 1981.
———. *The Art of Playing the Flute*. Volume III: *Posture, Fingering, Resonances, Tonguing, Vibrato*. Iowa City: Romney Press, 1989.
Montgomery, William. "Flute Tone Production." *The Instrumentalist*, September 1978, pp. 46, 48-49; October 1978, pp. 42, 44, 46-47.
Morris, Gareth. *Flute Technique*. New York: Oxford University Press, 1991.
Moyse, Marcel. *How I Stayed in Shape*. Translated by Paul M. Douglas. West Brattleboro, Vt.: Marcel Moyse, 1974.
Nyfenger, Thomas. *Music and the Flute*. Guilford, Conn.: Thomas Nyfenger, 1986.
Pellerite, James J. *A Modern Guide to Fingerings for the Flute*. 2nd ed., rev. and enl. Bloomington, Ind.: Zalo Publications, 1972.
Pincherle, Marc. *The World of the Virtuoso*. Translated by Lucile H. Brockway. New York: Norton, 1963.
Sachs, Curt. *Rhythm and Tempo*. New York: Norton, 1953.
Seashore, Carl E. *Psychology of the Vibrato in Voice and Instruments*. Iowa City: University Press, 1936.
Soldan, Robin, and Jeannie Mellersh. *Illustrated Fluteplaying*. London: Minstead Publications, 1986.
Stevens, Roger S. *Artistic Flute Technique and Study*. Edited by Ruth N. Zwissler. Culver City, Calif.: Trio Associates, 1970.
Tanzer, Stephen. *A Basic Guide to Fingerings for the Piccolo* Bala Cynwyd, Penn.: Sopranino Press, 1990.
Vinquist, Mary and Zaslaw, Neal. *Performance Practice: A Bibliography*. New York. Norton, 1971.
Weisberg, Arthur. *The Art of Wind Playing*. New York: Schirmer Books, 1975.
Wye, Trevor. *Proper Flute Playing: A Companion to the Practice Books*. London: Novello, 1988.

Repertoire Catalogues and Bibliographies

Baron, John H. *Chamber Music: A Research and Information Guide*. New York: Garland, 1993.
Boenke, Heidi M. *Flute Music by Women Composers: An Annotated Catalog*. New York: Greenwood, 1988.
Cobbett, Walter Willson. *Cobbett's Cyclopedia Survey of Chamber Music*. Supplementary volume edited by Colin Mason. 3 vols. New York: Oxford University Press, 1987.
Gronefeld, Ingo. *Die Flötenkonzerte bis 1850: Ein Thematisches Verzeichnis*. 3 vols. Tutzing: H. Schneider, 1992-93.
Helm, Sanford M. *Catalog of Chamber Music for Wind Instruments*. rev. ed., 1952. Reprint. New York: Da Capo, 1969.
Musik für Flöte. Hamburg: Musikbücherei, 1974.

Pellerite, James J. A *Handbook of Literature for the Flute*. 3rd ed. Bloomington, Ind.: Zalo Publications, 1978.

Pesek, Ursula, and Zeljko Pesek. *Flötenmusik aus drei Jahrhunderten: Komponisten, Werke, Anregungen*. 2nd ed. Kassel: Bärenreiter, 1993.

Pierreuse, Bernard. *Flute Litterature*. Paris: Jobert, 1982.

Rangel-Ribeiro, Victor, and Robert Markel. *Chamber Music: An International Guide to Works and their Instrumentation*. New York: Facts on File, 1992.

Rasmussen, Mary and Donald Mattran. *A Teacher's Guide to the Literature of Woodwind Instruments*. Durham, N.H.: Brass and Woodwind Quarterly, 1966.

Swanson, Philip J. "Avant-Garde Flute Music: A Partial Bibliography." *Woodwind World*, December 1972, pp. 19-20, 22; June 1973, pp. 6-8.

Vester, Frans, and Rien de Reede. *Catalogue of Dutch Flute Literature*. Buren: Frits Knuf, 1988.

Vester, Frans. *Flute Music of the 18th Century*. Monteux: Musica Rara, 1985.

——. *Flute Repertoire Catalogue*. London: Musica Rara, 1967.

Voxman, Himie, and Merriman, Lyle. *Woodwind Ensemble Music Guide*. Evanston, Ill.: Instrumentalist Co., 1974.

——. *Woodwind Solo and Study Material Guide*. Evanston, Ill.: The Instrumentalist Co., 1975.

Warner, Thomas E. *An Annotated Bibliography of Woodwind Instruction Books, 1600-1830*. Detroit: Information Coordinators, 1967.

Historical Flute Methods: Facsimiles and Translations

Corrette, Michel. *Méthode de la flûte traversière: 1735*. Paris, 1740. Reprint. Introduction and notes by Mirjam Nastasi. Buren: Frits Knuf, 1978.

Delusse, Charles. *L'Art de la Flûte Traversière*. 1760. Reprint. Introduction and notes by Greata Moens-Haenen. Buren: Frits Knuf, 1980.

Devienne, F. *(Nouvelle) Méthode de Flûte*. 1795 and 1800. Reprint. Buren: Frits Knuf, 1989.

Drouet, Louis. *Drouet's Method of Flute Playing*. 1830. Reprint. Marion, Iowa: Jan D. Boland, 1987.

Drouet, Louis. *The Method of Flute Playing*. 1830. Introduction by Stephen Preston and Rudolph Rasch. Buren: Frits Knuf, 1990.

Fürstenau, Anton Bernhard. *Die Kunst des Flötenspiels, op. 138*. 1844. Reprint. Foreword by Nikolaus Delius. Buren: Frits Knuf, 1991.

Gunn, John. *The Art of Playing the German-Flute*. ca. 1793. Reprint. Marion, Iowa: Janice Dockendorff Boland, 1992.

Hugot, Antoine, and Johann Georg Wunderlich. *Méthode de flûte*. 1804. Reprint. Introduction by David Jenkins. Buren: Frits Knuf, 1975.

Mahaut, Antoine. *A New Method for Learning to Play the Transverse Flute [Nieuwe manier om binnen korten tijd op de dwarsfluit te leeren speelen]*. Translated and edited by Eileen Hadidian. Bloomington: Indiana University Press, 1989.

Nicholson, Charles. *Nicholson's Complete Preceptor for the German flute*. 1816. Reprint. Buren: Frits Knuf, 1988.

Quantz, Johann Joachim. *On Playing the Flute*. 1752. Translated by Edward R. Reilly. 2nd ed. New York: Schirmer Books, 1985.

Ribock, J. J. H. *Bemerkungen über die Flöte, and Versuch einter kurzen Anleitung zuer bessem Einrichtung und Behandlung derselben*. 1782. Reprint. Introduction and notes by Karl Ventzke. Buren: Frits Knuf, 1980.

Tromlitz, J. G. *Ausführlicher und gründlicher Unterrich die Flöte zu spielen.* 1791. Reprint. Introduction and notes by Frans Vester. Buren: Frits Knuf, 1973.

Tromlitz, Johann George. *The virtuoso flute-player [Ausfuhrlicher und grundlicher Unterricht die Flote zu spielen].* Translated and edited by Ardal Powell, introduction by Eileen Hadidian. Cambridge: Cambridge University Press, 1991.

Tulou, Jean-Louis. *A Method for the Flute.* Translated by Janice Dockendorff Boland and Martha F. Cannon. Preface by Janice Dockendorff Boland. Bloomington: Indiana University Press, 1995.

The Baroque Era

Ambrose, Jane. "Authenticity in Performance: Where Do We Stand?" *The American Recorder,* August 1980, pp. 67-70.

Anthony, James R. *French Baroque Music from Beaujoyeulx to Rameau.* Rev. ed. New York: Norton, 1978.

Bach, Carl Philipp Emanuel. *Essay on the True Art of Playing Keyboard Instruments.* Translated and edited by William J. Mitchell. New York: Norton, 1949.

Baron, John H. *Baroque Music: A Research and Information Guide.* New York: Garland, 1993.

"Baroque Flute Performance Practice Bibliography." *Woodwind World Brass & Percussion,* 14, no. 4 (1975), pp. 23-25.

Best, Terence. "Handel's Solo Sonatas." *Music and Letters,* 58 (1977): 430-438.

Bowers, Jane. "New light on the development of the transverse flute between about 1650 and about 1770." *Journal of the American Musical Instrument Society* 3 (1977): 5-56.

Boyden, David. "Dynamics in Seventeenth- and Eighteenth-Century Music." In *Essays on Music in Honor of Archibald Thompson Davison.* Cambridge: Harvard University Press, 1957, pp. 185-194.

Bukofzer, Manfred F. *Music in the Baroque Era.* New York: Norton, 1947.

Castellani, Marcello. "The Italian Sonata for Transverse Flute and Basso Continuo." *Galpin Society Journal,* 19 (May 1976): 2-10.

Dolmetsch, Arnold. *The Interpretation of Music of the Seventeenth and Eighteenth Centuries.* Seattle: University of Washington Press, 1969.

Donington, Robert. *Baroque Music: Style and Performance.* New York: Norton, 1982.

———. *The Interpretation of Early Music.* New version. New York: St. Martin's, 1974.

———. *A Performer's Guide to Baroque Music.* New York: Scribners, 1973.

Farrar, Carol Reglin. *Michel Corrette and Flute-Playing in the Eighteenth Century.* Brooklyn, N.Y.: Institute of Mediaeval Music, 1970.

Fleury, Louis. "The Flute and Flutists in the French Art of the Seventeenth and Eighteenth Centuries." *Musical Quarterly,* 9 (1923): 515.

Helm, E. Eugene. *Music at the Court of Frederick the Great.* Norman: University of Oklahoma Press, 1960.

Higbee, Dale. "Michel Corrette on the piccolo and speculations regarding Vivaldi's 'Flautino.'" *Galpin Society Journal* 27 (February 1964): 115-16.

Hotteterre le Romain, Jacques. *Principles of the Flute Recorder and Oboe.* Translated and edited by David Lasocki. New York: Praeger, 1968.

Lasocki, David. "Baroque Flute and its role today." *Recorder and Music Magazine,* February 1967, pp. 99-100, 104.

Lasocki, David, ed. *Fluting and Dancing: Articles and Reminiscences for Betty Bang Mather on her 65th Birthday.* New York: McGinnis & Marx, 1992.

———. "New Light on Handel's Woodwind Sonatas." *The American Recorder,* February 1981, pp. 163-170.

——. "Vivaldi and the Recorder." *The American Recorder,* March 1969, pp. 22-27.
Mather, Betty Bang, with Dean M. Karns. *Dance Rhythms of the French Baroque: a Handbook for Performance.* Bloomington: Indiana University Press, 1987.
——. *Interpretation of French Music from 1675 to 1775 for Woodwind and Other Performers.* New York: McGinnis & Marx, 1973.
——. "Making Up Your Own Baroque Ornamentation." *The American Recorder,* August 1981, pp. 55-59.
Mather, Betty Bang, and David Lasocki. *The Art of Preluding, 1700-1830.* New York: McGinnis & Marx, 1984.
——. *Free Ornamentation in Woodwind Music.* New York: McGinnis & Marx, 1976.
Metcalfe, William. "Dolce or Traverso? The Flauto Problem in Vivaldi's Instrumental Music." *The American Recorder,* Summer 1965, pp. 3-6.
Neuhaus, Margaret N. *The Baroque Flute Fingering Book: a comprehensive guide to fingerings for the one-keyed flute, including trills, flattements, and battements, based on orginal sources from the eighteenth and nineteenth centuries.* Naperville, Ill.: Flute Studio Press, 1986.
Newman, William S. *The Sonata in the Baroque Era,* 2nd. ed. Chapel Hill: University of North Carolina Press, 1972.
Paillard, Jean-François. "Les Premiers concertos français pour instruments à vent." *Revue Musicale,* numero special 226 (1954-55): 448-451.
Priestman, Brian. "Catalogue thematique des oeuvres de Jean-Baptiste, John et Jacques Loeillet," *Revue Belge de Musicologie* 6 (1952): 219-274.
——. "An Introduction to the Loeillets." *The Consort,* July 1954, pp. 18-26.
Rangel-Ribeiro, Victor. *Baroque Music: A Practical Guide for the Performer.* New York: Schirmer Books, 1981.
Reilly, Edward R. "Further Musical Examples for Quantz's Versuch." *Journal of the American Musicological Society,* 17 (1964): 157.
——. *Quantz and his Versuch: Three Studies.* New York: American Musicological Society, 1971.
Schmitz, Hans-Peter. *Die Kunst der Verzierung im 18. Jahrhundert.* Kassel: Bärenreiter, 1955.
——. *Querflöte und Querflötenspiel in Deutschland während des Barockzeitalters.* Kassel: Bärenreiter, 1952.
Seyfrit, Michael. *Musical Instruments in the Dayton C. Miller Flute Collection at the Library of Congress, A Catalog.* Volume I: *Recorders, Fifes, and Simple System Transverse Flutes of One Key.* Washington, D.C.: Library of Congress, 1982.
Skempton, Alec. "The Instrumental Sonatas of the Loeillets." *Music and Letters* 43 (1962): 206-217.
Veilhan, Jean-Claude. *The Rules of Musical Interpretation in the Baroque Era.* Translated by John Lambert. Paris: Alphonse Leduc, 1982.
Waitzman, Daniel. "Historical Versus Musical Authenticity." *The American Recorder,* May 1980, pp. 11-13

The Classic Era

Badura-Skoda, Eva and Paul. *Interpreting Mozart on the Keyboard.* Translated by Leo Black. London: Barrie and Rockliff, 1962.
Brook, Barry S. "The Symphonie Concertante: An Interim Report." *The Musical Quarterly* 47 (1961): 493-516.
Carse, Adam. *The Orchestra in the XVIIIth Century.* New York: Broude Bros., 1969.
Cuming, Geoffrey. "Two Problems in Mozart's Letters." *The Music Review* 3 (1942): 124-129.

Gradenwitz, Peter. "Mid-Eighteenth Century Transformations of Style." *Music and Letters* 37 (1956): 107-117.

Lasocki, David, and Betty Bang Mather. *The Classical Woodwind Cadenza: A Workbook*. New York: McGinnis & Marx, 1978.

Leavis, Ralph. "Mozart's Flute Quartet in C, K. App. 171." *Music and Letters* 43 (1962): 48-52.

Mather, Betty Bang, and David Lasocki. *The Art of Preluding, 1700-1830*. New York: McGinnis & Marx, 1984.

Newman, William S. *The Sonata in the Classic Era*. Chapel Hill: University of North Carolina Press, 1963.

Ratner, Leonard G. *Classic Music: Expression, Form, and Style*. New York: Schirmer Books, 1980.

Schmitz, Hans-Peter. *Fürstenau Heute: Flötenspiel in Klassik und Romantik*. Kassel, New York: Bärenreiter, 1988.

Smith, Carleton Sprague. Haydn's Chamber Music and the Flute." *The Musical Quarterly* 19 (1933): 341-350, 434-455.

Smith, Catherine P. "The Woodwind Section in Haydn's Symphonies. *NACWPI Journal* 27 (1979): 4.

Souper, F. O. "Mozart's A Major Flute Quartet." *Monthly Musical Record* 70 (1940): 197-203.

Ward, Martha Kingdon. "Mozart and the Flute." *Music and Letters*, October 1954, pp. 294-308.

Warner, Thomas. "Tromlitz's flute treatise: a neglected source of eighteenth century performance practice." In *A Musical Offering: Essays in Honor of Martin Bernstein*. New York: Pendragon Press, 1977, pp. 261-271.

Wellesz, Egon and Sternfeld, Frederick, eds. *The Age of Enlightenment 1745-1790. New Oxford History of Music*, vol. 7. London: Oxford University Press, 1973.

The Romantic Era

Carse, Adam. *The Orchestra from Beethoven to Berlioz*. 1948. Reprint. Saint Clair Shores, Mich.: Scholarly Press, 1979.

Einstein, Alfred. *Music in the Romantic Era*. New York: Norton, 1947.

Hudson, Richard. *Stolen Time: The History of Tempo Rubato*. New York: Oxford University Press, 1995.

James, W. N. *A Word or Two on the Flute*. 3d. ed. 1826. Reprint. London: Tony Bingham, 1982.

Klaus, Kenneth B. *The Romantic Period in Music*. Boston: Allyn and Bacon, 1970.

Longyear, Rey M. *Nineteenth Century Romanticism in Music*. 2nd ed. Englewood Cliffs, N.J.: Prentice-Hall, 1973.

Schmitz, Hans-Peter. *Fürstenau Heute: Flötenspiel in Klassik und Romantik*. Kassel, New York: Bärenreiter, 1988.

The Modern Era

Austin, William H. *Music in the 20th Century*. New York: Norton, 1966.

Bartolozzi, Bruno. *New Sounds for Woodwind*. Translated and edited by Reginald Smith Brindle. New York: Oxford University Press, 1967.

Brindle, Reginald Smith. *The New Music*. New York: Oxford University Press, 1975.

Cooper, Martin. *French Music from the Death of Berlioz to the death of Fauré*. London: Oxford University Press, 1951.

Dick, Robert. *The Other Flute: A Performance Manual of Contemporary Techniques*. New York: Oxford University Press, 1975.

Gumbel, Martin. *Neue Spieltechniken in der Querflöten-Musik nach 1950*. Kassel: Bärenreiter, 1974.

Howell, Thomas. *The Avant-Garde Flute: A Handbook for Composers and Flutists.* Berkeley: University of California Press, 1974.

Nicolet, Aurèle, ed. *Pro Musica Nova: Studies for Playing Avant-garde Music for Flute.* New York: MCA Music, 1974.

Read, Gardner. *Compendium of Modern Instrumental Techniques.* Westport, Conn.: Greenwood, 1993.

———. *Contemporary Instrumental Techniques.* New York: Schirmer Books, 1976.

Stokes, Sheridon W., and Richard Congdon. *Special Effects for Flute.* Culver City, Calif.: Trio Associates, 1970.

Stone, Kurt. *Music Notation in the Twentieth Century: A Practical Guidebook.* New York: Norton, 1981.

Stuckenschmidt, H. H. *Twentieth Century Music.* New York: McGraw Hill, 1969.

Weisberg, Arthur. *Performing Twentieth-Century Music: A Handbook for Conductors and Instrumentalists.* New Haven: Yale University Press, 1993.

INDEX

References to illustrations and musical examples are in italics

Abel, Carl Friedrich, 233, 234–35
Accompaniment, recorded, 180–81
Accompanists, 167–68, 169–70, 174, 175
Acoustics: and baroque composition,190; of recital hall, 169, 172–73; of recording studio, 182; of tone, 90
Adjusting screws, 28, 29, 36, 38, 39, 40
Agréments, 191, 192. *See also* Embellishments; Ornamentation
Agricola, Martin: *Musica instrumentalis deudsch*, 43, 63, 71, 74, 109; on trembling breath, 109
Air varié, 245
Alain, Jehan, 261
Albinoni, Tommaso, 194, 196, 199, 202, 206
Albisi, Abelardo, 75
Albisiphone, 75
Albumblatt, 245
Aldrich, Putnam, 157, 158
Aleatory music, 276, 277, 278
Alternate fingerings, 99, 134–36; on alto flute, 73; on open-hole flute, 21, 99, 136; on piccolo, 66
Altès, Joseph Henri, 101, 132, 146, 252
Alto flute: Boehm's design, 71–73, 72; modern, 64, 70–74, *Plate 20*; music for, 73–74; of Praetorius, 43, 63
Amadio, John, 59, 73
Amateur Chamber Music Players, 162
American model, 21; pads, 22
American school/style: of flute playing, 102; of piano playing, 144–45
Analysis, 143, 147–149; of harmony, 151; of phrasing, 150–52; of technical problems, 133
Andersen, Joachim, 4, 253
Anderson, Marguerite de Forest, 249
Armstrong, W. T., Company, 12, 65, 74; Heritage division, 15, 19, 20, 60; Murray flute, 60; scale, 11, 61
Arnold, J. G., 246
Arnold, Malcolm, 265
Arpeggios, 130
L'art de préluder (Hotteterre), 194
Articulation, 116–23; in baroque music, 158; in ensemble, 147; exercises for, 131; front-of-the mouth, 103; in historical treatises, 153, 158; vocal model for, 150. *See also* Tonguing
Artley Flutes, 19, 65, 76
Ashe, Andrew, 4, 224
Assembling flute, 31, 32
Assisting artists, 167–68, 169–70
Attack. See Articulation; Tongueless attack; Tonguing
Audition tapes, 182–83
Authenticity, historical, 155–59
Avant-garde music, 273–81; performance practice, 154; tone color in, 149

Avant-garde techniques, 11, 102, 170, 255, 273–74, 275–80 passim; notation of, 154; on open-hole flute, 21. *See also* Circular breathing; Flutter-tonguing; Key percussion; Multiphonics

Babitz, Sol, 107–8
Bach, Carl Philipp Emanuel: compositions, 209, 210, 228–30; and *Empfindsamkeit*, 218; *Essay on Playing Keyboard Instruments*, 143, 228; and Frederick the Great, 214, 228; on virtuosity, 143
Bach, Johann Christian, 204, 234, 235
Bach, Johann Sebastian: *Brandenburg Concertos*, 202, 210; flute works, 87, 209–10; instrumentation, 189; ornamentation, 153; other works, 135, 153, 154, 155, 156, 157, 214; style, 153, 155, 191, 216
Bach, P. D. Q., 70
Bach, Wilhelm Friedemann, 233
Bach–Abel Concerts, 219, 234
Backus, John, 17
Baker, Julius, 104, 181
Barnett, David, 155
Baron, Samuel, 104, 279, 280
Baroque era: flute, 43–46; flute music, 187–215; instrumentation, 157, 158, 188–89; musical forms, 189–92; performance practice, 154
Barrère, Georges, xvii, 4–5, 20, 104, 258, 266; on B footjoint, 22; compositions, 256; *The Flutist's Formulae*, 131; and platinum flute, 102; on Taffanel, 253; on tone, 94, 96; on vibrato, 107, 112–13; works dedicated to, 270, 274–75
Bartok, Bela, 22, 267–68
Bartoli, Gino, 76
Bartolozzi, Bruno, 70
Bass flute: modern, 64, 74–76, *Plate 20*; of Praetorius, 43, 63
Basso continuo. *See* Continuo; Figured bass
Bate, Philip: *The Flute*, 90
Bax, Sir Arnold, 264
B-C trill key, 24
Beach, Amy Marcy Cheney (Mrs. H. H. A. Beach), 268–69
Bebung, 109
Beethoven, Ludwig van: flute music, 221, 239–40; other music, 68, 69, 73, 118, 156
Benade, Arthur, 11, 21, 27, 90
Benda, Franz, 214, 228
Ben-Haim, Paul, 268
Benker, Heinz, 69
Bennett, Richard Rodney, 266
Bennett, Robert Russell, 271
Bennett, William: scale, 11, 61; on tongueless attack, 121
Berbiguier, Benoit Tranquille, 248
Bergsma, William, 272
Berio, Luciano, 276
Berkeley, Sir Lennox, 265
Berlioz, Hector: influenced by Reicha, 227–28; instrumentation treatise, 243; works, 69
Best, Terence, 207
Beuker, J., 74, 75
B-flat shake key, 24
B-flat thumb keys: of Boehm, 26, 56; Briccialdi, 56, 139; modern flute, 140–41; Murray flute, 60
Bishop, Sir Henry, 64
Bizet, Georges, 121
Blacher, Boris, 267
Blanquart, Gaston, 261
Blavet, Michel: as composer, 196–97; as flutist, 4, 195, 199, 200, 201, 212, 223
Bliss, Sir Arthur, 265
Bloch, Ernest, 272
Blume, Friedrich, 216
Boccherini, Luigi, 223, 234
Bodinus, Sebastian, 210–11
Boehm, Theobald: alto flute of, 71–73, 72; D-flat key, 56; career of, 50–55; compositions, 73, 250; 1831 flute, 51–52, *Plate* 7; 1832 flute, 52–53, *Plate* 8; 1847 flute, 54–56, *Plate* 9; on expression, 174–75; *The Flute and Flute-Playing*, 71, 89, 150; and Molique, 248–49; as performer, 4, 50, 145, 244; on phrasing, 150; on tone, 89; vocal models of, 150
Boehm system, 6, 8–9, *10*, 23, 38, 50–57, *Plates* 8, 9, *18*, *19*, *20*; adoption of, 53–54, 57, 241; and alto flute, 72;

modifications to, 59–61; prizes won by, 57; *Schema*, 9, 55, 72
Bogner, Ferdinand, 248
Boismortier, Joseph Bodin de, 76, 195, 196, 197
Bona, Pasquale: *Rhythmical Articulation*, 146
Bononcini, Giovanni, 206
Boosey & Company, 59
Bore: Boehm's redesign, 54–55; cylindrical, 49, 54; Hotteterre's one-key flute, 44; of modern flute, 55
Borne, François, 60
Borne-Julliot flute, 60, *Plate 16*
Borouchoff, Israel, 17, 18, 19
Boston Classicists, 268–69
Boulanger, Lili, 263
Boulanger, Nadia, 148
Boulez, Pierre, 74, 275–76
Bowing and articulation, 116–17, 118, 119
Bozza, Eugène, 263
Bradley, Dr. George, 24
Brahms, Johannes, 69, 70, 247
Brannen Brothers-Cooper Flutes, 11, 20, 61
Brant, Henry, 77, 270
Breathing, 81–88; circular, 86–87, 116, 227; exercises, 83–85, 127; and phrasing, 81, 85–86
Breitkopf Thematic Catalogue, 222, 237, 238
Breval, Jean-Baptiste, 226
Breville, Pierre de, 281
Briccialdi, Giulio: B-flat thumb key, 56, 60, 251; compositions, 251
Brille, 57
British Flute Society, 6, 77
Britten, Benjamin, 265
Broadwood, Walter Stewart, 249
Brody, Mitchell: *Complete Guide to the Flute*, 41
Brögger Mekanik, 12
Brooke, Arthur: *Harmonic Fingerings for the Flute*, 139; on program planning, 164–65
Brooke, Paige, 113
Brossa, Jean Firmin, 59
Brossa F-sharp key, 25, 59
Brossard, Sebastien de, 194
Bruderhans, Zdenek, 87, 88
Brueggen, Frans, 100
Buffardin, Pierre Gabriel, 209, 212; register, 45, *Plate 2*
Buffet, Auguste, 53–54, 55, 59
Burghley, Dr., 58
Buzz flute (buzzing), 274, 279

Cadenzas: classic, 154, 219, 224, 225; for Mozart concertos, 154; romantic, 154, 246
Caldara, Antonio, 206
Cambini, Giovanni Giuseppe, 227
Campagnoli, Bartolomeo, 233
Camus, Paul, 53
Cannabich, Christian, 230, 232
Cannabich, M. F., 201
Cantabile style, 188, 205
Cantrick, Robert, 102
Card, William, 58
Carl Theodor, Elector Palatine, 230, 235
Carse, Adam, 74
Carte, Richard: adoption of Boehm flute, 54; 1850/51 flute, 58, *Plate 11*; 1867 flute (Guards' model), 57, 59, 76, *Plate 13*; on tremolo, 110
Carter, Elliott, 270
Case, for flute, 33
Casella, Alfred, 267
Castelnuovo-Tedesco, Mario, 267
Castérède, Jacques, 264
Castiglioni, Niccolò, 276
Chamber music, 162–63, 167–68; baroque, 190; classic, 220–23; romantic, 244–45; modern, 256; *See also* Ensemble playing
Chaminade, Cécile, 249
Character pieces, 192
Chédeville, Nicolas, 200
Cherubini, Luigi, 45–46, 222
Chevron, le, 110
Chevrotement, 106, 107
Childs, Barney, 278
Chopin, Fréderic, 150, 248
Chou Wen-Chung, 278
Cigarette paper, 36, 37, 39
Cimarosa, Domenico, 222, 224, 227
Circular breathing, 86–87, 116, 277

Classic era: flute, 6–47, 49, 217; flute music, 216–40; performance practice, 154
Cleaning flute, 31–32
Cleaning rod, 32; for headjoint calibration, 35
Clementi, Muzio, 4, 221
Clinton, John: and Boehm flute, 54, 58, 137; 1848 patent, 58; Equisonant flute (1863 patent), 58, *Plate 12*; on harmonics, 137; on vibration, 110
Closed G-sharp key, 54
Closed-hole flute, 21; pads, 22
Clutch, *11*, 53–54, 55
Coche, Victor, 54, 101, 110
Coltman, John: C-sharp mechanism, 11, 25–26
Comte de Guines, 237
Concerted symphony (J. C. Bach), 235
Concerto: baroque, 190, 195–96, 197; classic, 223–24, 234; romantic, 245. *See also* Cadenzas
Concert Spirituel, 195, 196, 199, 201, 219, 223–24, 226, 227
Condition of instrument, 27–28, 36–37, 39–40
Cone, Edward T., 148
Conical flutes: Hotteterre, 44; modern Boehm, 20–21; 19th century, 57–59; reform, 57
Conn, C. G., 12
Contests, 4, 77, 87
Continuo, 157, 158, 190, 218. *See also* Figured bass
Contra Bass FF flute, 76
Conversance with idiom, 143, 152–53, 155
Cooper, Albert, 20; on French model, 21; scale, 11, 61
Copland, Aaron, 270–71
Corelli, Arcangelo: concertos, 199, 209; sonatas, 190, 194, 204, 207, 209, 211
Corps de réchange, 45, 181, *Plate 3*
Corrette, Michel, 116, 196; compositions, 200, 223; on *flattement*, 109; treatise, 156, 195
Cortot, Alfred, 153
Couperin, François, 198–99
Cowell, Henry, 269, 270
Cramer, Johann Baptist, 246
Creuzberg, H.: *Partiturspiel (Score Playing)*, 147
Critical listening, 179–80
Cross-fingering, 43, 44, 46, 49, 158
Crunelle, Gaston, 101, 103
C-sharp trill key, 23, 24–25

Dahl, Ingolf, 272–73
Damase, Jean-Michel, 264
Dannhauser, A.: *Solfège des Solfèges*, 146
Dannreuther, Edward: *Musical Ornamentation*, 155
Danzi, Franz, 222, 223, 232
Dart, Thurston, 207
Davidovsky, Mario, 280
Dealers, flute, 14–15; repairs by, 29
Dean, E. F., Flutes, 12
Debussy, Claude, 69, 70, 101; flute music, 260–61; *Prélude à l'Après-midi d'un faune*, 96, 99, 114, 121
de Jong, Willem Britten, 236
De Lorenzo, Leonardo, 77
Delusse, Charles; bass flute, 75; on breath vibrato, 109, compositions, 226–27; treatise, 156, 226
Demersseman, Jules, 252
Descoteaux, René-Pignon, 192, 193
Deveau scale, 11, 61
Devienne, François, 101, 116; compositions, 225–26, 243, treatise, 156, 220, 225
Diaphragm, 82–83, 108, 109, 117
Diaphragm flexing, 83
Dick, Robert, 102
Diderot and d'Alembert: *Encyclopédie*, 71
Discographies, 179
Dittersdorf, Carl Ditters von, 223, 238
Divertimentos, 223
Dohnányi, Ernö, 268
Dolmetsch, Arnold, 155
Donington, Robert, 159
Donjon, Johannes, 252
Doppler, Franz, 4, 104, 138, 251–52
Doppler, Karl, 4, 251–52
Dorus, Vincent, 54, 101
Dorus G-sharp key, 54
Double concerto, 224. *See also* Symphonie concertante

Doublers, 21
Double-tonguing, 118, 119
Drouet, Louis, 4, 244, 248; compositions, 163, 251; slurred staccato, 118; style, 145; tone, 103
Dubois, Pierre-Max, 264
Dubois, Theodore, 258, 259
Duet, unaccompanied: baroque, 193, 196; classic, 222; romantic, 245
Dulon, Ludwig, 229, 237
Dureau, Th.: *Cours Théorique et Pratique d'Instrumentation et d'Orchestration*, 67
Dussek, Jan Ladislav, 246
Duverger, 101, 225
Dvorak, Antonin, 68
Dwyer, Doriot Anthony, 181, 270–71, 273
Dynamics: in Mannheim orchestra, 230; and melody, 149; in recital hall, 173, and vibrato, 106

Early Music Movement, 6, 145, 155–59
Ear training, 146–47
Eastman School of Music, 77, 271–72
Ebonite, 58
Edge-tone behavior system, 90
E-flat soprano flute, 64, *Plate 20*
Eggs, Leslie, 61
Egmont, Count, 195
Eight-key flute, 47, 48, *Plate 6*
Eisel, Johann Philipp: *Musicus*, 208
Electronic music, 273, 279–80
Embellishments: baroque, 191, 192; galant, 191, 192. *See also* Ornamentation
Embouchure: condition, 29; construction, 7–8, 36, 55; and edge tone, 90; offset, 91; and tone production, 91–93
Emerson Flutes, 26
Empfindsamkeit, 218, 228, 231, 232
Encores, recital, 176
Endings of notes, 121–22
Enesco, Georges, 96, 260
England. *See* Great Britain
Ensemble playing, 97, 113, 147, 163–64. *See also* Chamber music; Flute bands; Flute choir (ensemble)
Equal temperament, 46
Études, 131–33, 245, 422–28
Exercises: breathing, 83–85; circular breathing, 87–88; interval, 130–31; long tone, 127; matching tone, 95, 127–28, 131; tonguing, 122; vibrato, 109
Exhalation, 81, 82–83
Expression: baroque, 43, 191, 204, 216; classic, 218; modern, 256; romantic, 144, 241–42; theoretical basis for, 145–47. *See also* Interpretation; Style
Extended range, 44, 47

Fajardo Wedgehead, 11
"Fake" fingerings, 99, 135. *See also* Alternate fingerings
Fantasia, 245
Fasch, C. F. C., 214, 228
Fasch, Johann Friedrich, 214
Fauré, Gabriel, 259
Ferlendis, Giuseppe, 237
Fife, 49, 64, 76, 187
Figured bass, 154, 157, 158, 167; decline, 217, 218, 220
Filtz, Anton, 231–32
Finck, Henry T.: *Success in Music*, 166
Finger, Gottfried, 206
Fingering, 8–9, 134–36; charts, 99, 134, 139, *445–51*; harmonic, 136–39; thumb keys, 139–40; tricks, 140. *See also* Alternate fingerings; Technique
Finger position, 125–26
Fischer, Johann Christian, 214, 235
Flattement, 109
Flauto, 45
Fleury, Louis, 100, 103, 260, 261
Florio, Pietro, 46, 47
Flute bands, 64, 76–77
Flute choir (ensemble), 76–77, 270
Flute clubs, 4, 15, 162, 464–70
Flute construction and dimensions, 6–11, 16–17, 27–28, 35, 89
Flûte d'amour, 71, 72
Flute family, 42–43, 63–78, 162, *Plate 20*
Flute music: historical eras of, 256; publications, 4, 6, 156; sources for, 164, 460–61
Flute peg, 33

Flûtes Allemands, 43
Flutist, The, 59–60
Flutter-tonguing, 120, 265, 270, 274
Focus of tone, 94–95
Foote, Arthur, 268
Footjoint: baroque, 44, 45, *Plate 2*; construction, 7; C vs. B, 17, 22, 24, 102
Fork-fingering. *See* Cross fingering
Fortepiano, 221
Four-key flute, 46, 47, *Plate 4*
Fouse, Sarah Baird, 84
Françaix, Jean, 264
France: baroque era, 192–202; classic era, 225–28; modern era, 257–64; romantic era, 253; *See also* French school; Paris; Paris Conservatoire
Franck, César, 165, 258
Fransella, Albert, 103
Frederick the Great, 166, 209, 210, 212–14, 228
Fredersdorf, Michael, 209
French model, 21, 56, 101, 126, *Plate 18*; alternate fingerings on, 21, 99, 136; pads, 22
French school (style), 21, 100–3. *See also* Paris Conservatoire
Fukushima, Kazuo, 74, 277–78
Fürstenau, Anton Bernhard, 251
Fürstenau, Caspar, 234, 244
Fürstenau, Moritz, 251
Fürstenau family, 4

Gabrielski, Johann Wilhelm, 248
Gage Articulated B-F-sharp device, 12, 60
Galant style, 191–92, 214, 217
Galliard, Johann Ernst, 207
Galway, James, 5, 20, 103, 145, 165
Ganne, Louis, 259
Garsault, A. P.: *Notionnaire ou Memorial raisonné*, 189
Gaubert, Philippe, 4, 101, 103, 253, 261, 263, 264; career, 256; and French model flute, 101; *17 Daily Exercises*, 131; students, 101–2; on vibrato, 107, 111
Gaultier, Pierre [Gautier de Marseille], 193
Gazzelloni, Severino, 20, 22, 104, 275, 277, 278, 279
Gedney, Caleb, 46, 47
Gemeinhardt Company, 12, 18, 32, 65–66, 74
Geminiani, Francesco, 204, 205
Gentlemen's Concerts, 244
Genzmer, Harald, 266
German flute, 42, 47, 188. *See also* Old system flute; Simple system flute
Germany: baroque music, 208–14; Boehm flute in, 104; classic music, 228–34; 20th century music, 266–67; woodwind tone, 100, 104
Gerock and Wolf, 51
Gesensway, Louis, 275
Gianella, Luigi, 227
Giannetti, 75
Gilbert, David, 279
Gilbert, Geoffrey, 100, 103, 121
Gillet, Fernand, 111, 112
Giordani, Tommaso, 235
Giorgi, Carlo, 58
Giorgi flute, 58
Giuliani, Mauro, 239
Gizmo key, 23, 24
Glass flutes, 49, *Plate 4*
Glissando, 21, 274, 276, 279
Gluck, Christoph Willibald von, 68, 214, 236
Godard, Benjamin, 249
Godfroy, Clair, *ainé*, 21, 54, 55–56, 101
Goldberg, Bernard, 113
Gold flutes, 18, 19–20
Goossens, Sir Eugene, 265
Gossec, François-Joseph, 202, 226
Gounod, Charles, 253
Graaff, Artamano, 204
Graening, 245
Granom, Lew: *Plain and Easy Instructions for Playing on the German-Flute*, 46
Graun, Carl Heinrich, 213, 214, 228
Graun, Johann Gottlieb, 214, 228
Graupner, Christoph, 214
Great Britain: baroque music, 206–8; classic music, 234–35; flute bands, 64, 76–77; flute clubs, 470; flute playing style, 102–3; romantic music, 244;

20th century music, 264–66; wooden flutes, 20, 103; vibrato, 112
Grout, Donald, J., 157
Guards' model, 57, 59, 76, *Plate 13*
Guillemain, Louis-Gabriel, 202, 226
Guillemant, Benoit, 202
Guillou, 101

Haedrich, Walter, 11
Hahn, Reynaldo, 260
Half-holing, 99, 158
Handel, George Frideric, 156, 189, 207–8
Hand position, 8, 125–26
Hanson, Howard, 271
Harmonics, 24, 54, *90*, *93*, *136*–39; composed, 138–39, 273; fingering charts, 134, 139
Harmoniemusik, 223
Harmony, 149, 151; classic, 218; galant, 217; romantic, 242
Harrison, Lou, 272
Hasse, Johann Adolf, 213, 214
Haydn, Joseph, 46, 47, 73, 156, 176, 202, 214, 222; flute music, 223, 237–38
Haydn, Michael, 223, 238
Haynes, William S., 19
Haynes, Wm. S., Company, 11, 13, 15–16, 19, 29, 60, 65, 102
Headjoint: of baroque flute, 44–45; condition, 28; construction, 6, 7, 8; cork, 7, 35–36; Fajardo Wedgehead, 11; O-Ring, 7, 61; recurved, 75
Heinichen, Johann David, 208, 213
Hennebains, Adolphe, 100, 101, 249, 259; on vibrato, 111
Henze, Hans Werner, 266–67
Hiller, Johann Adam, 232
Hindemith, Paul, 266, 272; *Elementary Training for Musicians*, 146–47
Hipkins, Alfred, 155
Historical authenticity, 155–59
Historical editions, 6, 156
Hoffmeister, Franz Anton, 223, 239
Hofmann, Leopold, 238
Holliger, Heinz, 88, 277
Holst, Gustav, 74, 264–65
Holzbauer, Ignaz, 231
Honegger, Arthur, 70, 262
Hook, James, 221
Hotteterre, Jacques, *le Romain: L'art* de *préluder*, 194; compositions, 193–94; on *flattement*, 109; and French flute school, 101; one-key flute, 43–*44*, 45, 188; *Principes de la Flute Traversière*, 44, 45, 109, 194, 206
Hovhaness, Alan, 272
Howell, Thomas, 279
Hudson, Eli, 4, 103
Hugot, Antoine, 101, 220, 224, 225, 227
Hummel, Johann Nepomuk, 239

Ibert, Jacques, 137, 263–64
Impressionism, 260–61
Improvisation: in avant-garde music, 276, 277, 278; in classic music, 219
Inhalation, 82
Instruction books: Altès, 146, 252; C. P. E. Bach, 143, 228; Boismortier, 195; classic, 220; Corrette, 195; Delusse, 156, 226; Devienne, 156, 220, 225; Granom, 46; Hotteterre, 44, 45, 109, 194, 206; Lorenzoni, 204; Mahaut, 156; Majer, 208; Müller, 234; Prelleur, 206; Quantz, 44, 45, 109, 192, 208, 213, 220; 1740s French, 200; Stokes and Condon, 92; Taffanel and Gaubert, 91–93, 111, 146, 253; Tromlitz, 156, 200
Instrumentation: *Art of the Fugue* (Bach), 154; of baroque music, 157, 188–89, 256; treatises, 243, 258
Intensity, vibrato and, 106
International Style, 5, 100, 104, 180
Interpretation, 142–45, historical stereotypes, 153; listening for, 179–80; poetic context in, 153; and tone, 95–97
Interval exercises, 130–31
Intonation, 77, 97–100; of one-key flute, 44–45; of piccolo, 67; vibrato and, 106–7
Italy: baroque flute music, 202–6; modern flute music, 267
Ives, Charles, 266, 269

Jacob, Gordon, 69, 163, 265
Jambe de Ferre: *Epitome Musical*, 43

James, W. N.: on double-tonguing, 119; on footjoint keys, 47; on harmonics, 138; on musical context, 147–48; on Nicholson, 102, 144; on tone, 96; on vibration, 109–10
James Madison University flute club, 77
Japan, 12, 104, 277–78
Jarnach, Philipp, 261
Jaw: and tone production, 91, 93; and vibrato, 108–9
Jesperson, Holger Gilbert, 267
Jet whistle, 259
Jeune France, La, 275
Jolivet, André, 275
Jommelli, Niccolò, 230
Julliot, Djalma, 60
Junker, Carl Ludwig, 232

Kaplan, Phillip, 104
Karg-Elert, Sigfrid, 132
Kennan, Kent, 271
Key click, 274, 275
Keyless flutes, 58, 63
Key oil, 35
Key percussion, 116, 255, 274, 275
Keys: condition, 28; construction, 16, 27, 43, 49; lubrication, 35; open-hole, 21, 22; players' resistance to, 46–47; roller, 25, 28
Key slap, 116
Khachaturian, Aram, 165
Kincaid, William: *The Advanced Flutist*, 108; on B footjoint, 22; bracket system, 151–52; breathing exercises, 83–84; and Copland *Duo*, 271; on embouchure, 92; and Gesensway concerto, 275; on metal flute, 18; on phrasing, 151–52; platinum flute of, 20, 102; on sensitive fingerings, 134; tone of, 102; and vibrato, 108, 113, 114; and whistle and difference tones, xvii
Kingma, Eva, 12
Kirnberger, Johann Philipp, 209, 214, 228
Kitsch, 242
Klangarbenmelodie, 273
Kling, Henri, 245
Klosé, Friedrich, 75
Kniebusch, Carol, 77
Koch, Stephan, 71
Koechlin, Charles, 70, 259–60
Korte, Karl, 280
Kreisler, Fritz, 111
Krell, John, 66, 67, 117, 151
Krenek, Ernst, 276–77
Krommer [Krommer-Kramář], Franz, 239
Krumpholtz, Jean-Baptiste, 239
Kruspe, Friedrich, 57
Kubik, Gail, 271
Kuhlau, Friedrich, 22, 77, 247–48
Kujala, Walfrid, 66
Kummer, Caspar, 248, 251
Kupferman, Meyer, 280
Kytch, Jean Christian, 207

La Barre, Michel de, 193, 194
La Montaine, John, 272
Landell, Jonathon: *Flute Tune-Up Manual*, 41
Landowska, Wanda, 155
Lasocki, David, 207
Laubé, Mme. Cornélie Villedieu, 60
Laurent, Claude, 49, 71
Laurent, Georges, xvii, 4, 20, 22, 102, 280–81; on legato, 121; vibrato, 112
Lawson, Dennis, 11
Lax, Fred, 69
Learned style, 191
Le Cène, Michel-Charles, 208
Lechner, Konrad, 88
Leclair, Jean-Marie, 199–200
Lefebvre, Charles, 253
Left-hand levers, 25
Legato, 118, 121
Legato slur, 117–18, 119
Lemmone, John, 4
Lenski, Karl: *18 Cells for Flute*, 133
Le Roy, René, 103, 262
Levy, Burt, 279
Lindpaintner, Peter Joseph von, 132, 248
Lipatti, Dinu, 122
Liszt, Franz, 144
Locatelli, Pietro Antonio, 192, 205
Loeillet, Jacques [Jacob], 198
Loeillet, Jean Baptiste (John Loeillet of London), 198
Loeillet, Jean Baptiste (Loeillet de Gant), 198

Long tones, 127
Lora, Arthur, xvii, 22, 95, 104
Lorenzoni: *Saggio per ben sonare il flautotraverso*, 204
Lot, Louis, 21, 55–56, 101, 103
Lot, Thomas, 75
Lotti, Antonio, 206
Louis XIV, 192, 193, 198, 199
Louis XV, 195
Lubrication, 35, 39
Luening, Otto, 102, 278
Lully, Jean-Baptiste, 43–44, 192, 198, 199

MacGregor, Malcolm, 75
Mach, Antonin, 87
McKay, George: *Creative Orchestration*, 67
Maderna, Bruno, 276
Mahaut, Anton, 109, 156
Mahillon & Company, 58
Maintenance of flute, 31–41
Majer, Joseph: *Museum musicum*, 208
Mannheim, 224, 225; style, 211, 230–33
Manufacturing, 11–13
Maquarre, André, 101, 107
Maquarre, Daniel, 101
Marais, Marin, 188, 193
Marcello, Alessandro, 189, 204
Marcello, Benedetto, 204–5
Marshall, Robert, 209
Martellato, 118
Martin, Frank, 267
Martino, Donald, 74, 278
Martinů, Bohuslav, 268
Marx, Josef, 155–56
Mascagni, Pietro, 75
Mass production, 4, 12
Matching tone exercise: to test pads, 37; for tonal homogeneity, 95, 127–28, 130
Materials of construction, 12, 16, 17–21, 34, 50, 55, 65–66, 72. *See also* Gold flutes; Platinum flutes; Silver flutes; Wooden flutes
Mather, Betty Bang, 122, 132
Matsudaira, Yoritsune, 277
Mean-tone tuning, 45, 158
Mechanical options, 11, 17, 23, 24–26
Mechanism. *See* Boehm system; Keys
Melody, 149; classic, 218–19; galant, 191–92, 217; romantic, 242
Memorization: of scales and arpeggios, 131; for recitals, 175
Mendelssohn, Felix, 69, 114, 157, 248
Menuhin, Yehudi, 113
Mercadante, Saverio, 247
Mersenne, Marin, 43, 63, 74, 109
Messa di voce, 109
Messiaen, Olivier, 275
Methods. *See* Instruction books
Metronome, 85, 109, 122, 127, 130
Meyerbeer, Giacomo, 69
Meyer system, 47, 60. *See also* Old system flute; Simple system flute
Meysel, Anton: *Handbuch der musikalischen Literatur*, 220
Middle Ages, flute in, 42–43, 76
Milhaud, Darius, 262
Miller, Dayton, C., 21, 71, 74, 75; flute collection, 73, 250
Miller, George, 49
Minuet, 192
Miyazawa Flutes, 12
Modern Musick-Master, 206
Molique, Bernhard, 136, 248–49
Molter, Johann Melchior, 210, 211
Mondonville, Jean-Joseph Cassanea de, 200, 201
Mönnig family, 57
Montéclair, Michel Pignolet de, 194
Moore, Jack, 11, 12, 25, 26, 60, 61
Morceau characteristique, 245
Morris, Gareth, 103
Morris, R. O., and Ferguson, Howard: *Preparatory Exercises in Score Reading*, 147
Moscheles, Ignaz, 248
Motion and repose, 148, 150–51
Moyse, Louis, 124, 131
Moyse, Marcel, 12, 21, 22, 101, 102, 103, 104, 261, 262, 264; *De la Sonorité*, 91, 95; *Exercises Journaliers*, 131; on tone, 91, 93, 95; *Tone Development Through Interpretation*, xvii, 95; on vibrato, 107, 111, 112
Mozart, Wolfgang Amadeus, 46, 47, 154, 156, 202, 218, 225, 233; flute music, 73, 86, 136, 221, 222, 223, 224, 227, 236–37, 253; other music, 68, 69, 73, 150

Müller, August Eberhard, 233–34, 238, 248
Multiphonics, 21, 276, 279
Multiple option flute (Murray), 60
Muramatsu, Koichi, 104
Muramatsu Flutes, 11, 12, 15, 19, 20
Murchie, Robert, 103
Murray, Alexander, 60, 61
Murray flute, 60, *Plate 17*
Musgrave, Thea, 265–66
Musical instrument industry, 4
Music camps, 3
Music history, study of, 143, 258
Music Minus One, 181

National Flute Association, 4, 26, 77; library, 164; publications, 6, 15, 179
National styles: in baroque music, 190–91, 202, 204, 212; and materials of flute construction, 18; in romantic era, 243; and tone, 100–4
Naudot, Jacques Christophe, 195, 196, 197–98, 202
Needle springs, 27, 39–40, 58
Neni, Jacopo, 71
New York Flute Club, 4, 70, 271
Nicholson, Charles, 4, 50, 51, 143–45, 243–44; on double-tonguing, 119; flute of, 51, 103; on harmonics, 138, 139; *School for the Flute*, 119; tone of, 89, 102–3; use of vibration by, 110
Nicolet, Aurèle: *Pro Musica Nova*, 87, 88
Nielsen, Carl, 267
Nolan, Rev. Frederick, ring keys of, 49, 50, 51
Nono, Luigi, 276
Notation: avant-garde, 154; in 19th century, 242
Note endings, 121–22
Notes inégales, 192, 199

Octave key, 72
Okamura, Masao, 104
Old system flute, 42–50, *44*, *48*, 57–59, *Plates l*, *3*, *4*, *5*, *6*, *7*, *14*, *15*; in classic era, 217
One-key flute, 43–45, *44*, 47, 187, 192, *Plate l*
Open G-sharp key, 26, 54, 60
Open-hole model, 21, 56, 101, 126, *Plate 18*; alternate fingerings on, 21, 99, 136; half-holing on, 99; pads, 22
Open-key system, 9, 52, 58
Orchestra, alto flute in, 71, 74
Orchestra, flute in: baroque, 43–44, 202; classic, 49, 216, 217, 220, 224; romantic, 49, 241, 243
Orchestra, piccolo in, 68–70
Orchestral excerpts, 132, 441–42
Ordres, 192, 199
O-Ring, 7, 61
Ornamentation: baroque, 153, 154, 157–58, 191, 199, 204; classic, 218, 219–20; Dolmetsch and Dannreuther books on, 155; galant, 217
Ostroff-Sagerman Flutes, 74
Overtones, 19, 90, 137; and vibrato, 106. *See also* Harmonics

Pads, 9, 11, 21, 22, 55, 61; condition of, 28, 37; repair of, 36–37, 38–39
Paganini, Niccolò, 87, 143, 144
Panitz, Murray, 95, 96, 181
Pappoutsakis, James, xvii, 5, 280
Parabolic headjoint, 55
Paris, 225–28. *See also* Concert Spirituel; France; French school; Paris Conservatoire
Paris Conservatoire, 54, 101, 102, 225, 253
Peck, Donald, 20, 181
Pellerite, James, 61; *A Handbook of Literature for the Flute*, 132, 164; *A Modern Guide to Fingerings for the Flute*, 99, 134, 140
Pepusch, Johann Christoph, 206–7
Performance, 161–77
Performance practice, 143, 152–55
Pergolesi, Giovanni Battista, 204
Periodicals: on early music, 156; on flute, 6, 244, 445–46; on recordings, 178–79
Perle, George, 277
Perlé (pearled staccato), 118
Persichetti, Vincent, 74
Pessard, Emile, 249
Phelan, James: *Complete Guide to the Flute*, 41
Philidor, Anne Danican, 194, 195

Philippe d'Orleans, 195
Phrasing, 149–52; and breathing, 81, 85–86; and double-tonguing, 119
Piccolo, 12, 63–70, *Plates 19, 20*; music for, 68–70, 74, 164
Piccolo Society, 70
Pierné, Gabriel, 253, 259
Pillars, 50
Pincherle, Marc, 143
Piston, Walter, 270
Pitch: of leading tone, 99–100; modifying, 98–100; of recordings, 181; and vibrato, 106–7. *See also* Intonation
Pitch standards: 18th century, 45; 20th century, 97–98, 181
Pivot screws, 39, 40
Pizzicato, 116, 276
Plastic: pads, 11, 37; piccolo, 12
Plateau model, 21; pads, 22
Plated flutes, 12, 16, 18–19, 28; replating, 34–35
Platinum flutes, 12, 20, 102
Platti, Giovanni, 205–6
Playing position, 124–26
Pleyel, Ignace Joseph, 221, 226
Poetic context, 153
Polishing flute, 32–34
Popp, Wilhelm, 245–46, 252
Popularity of flute: in 18th century, 188–89, 192–93, 195, 200, 202–3, 206, 208, 220; in 19th century, 3, 244; in 20th century, 3–6
Popular music, transcriptions of, 165
Portato, 118
Porter, Andrew, 236
Porter, Quincy, 269
Position of flute, 124–26
Posture, 81–82, 91, 124–25
Potter, Richard, 46, 47
Pottgiesser, H. W., 51
Poulenc, Francis, 262
Pouplinière, Le Riche de la, 195
Powell, Verne Q., 12, 24, 89, 96
Powell, Verne Q., Flutes, 11, 13, 15–16, 19, 29, 60, 65
Practice, 127–34; articulation, 122, 132; breathing, 82, 83–85, 127; with recorded accompaniment, 180–81; warm-up, 127–28. *See also* Rehearsal
Praetorius, Michael: *Syntagma Musicum*, 43, 63; on vibrato, 109
Pratella, Balillo, 274
Pratten, Robert Sydney, 58
Pratten Perfected flute, 59, 76
Prelleur, Peter: *Modern Musick-Master*, 206
Prices: of flutes, 15–17, 18, 22, 24–26; of piccolos, 65–66; of reproduction antique woodwinds, 156–57
Prima Sankyo Flutes, 12
Primrose, William, 113
Principes de la Flute Traversière (Hotteterre), 44, 45, 109, 194, 206
Program, printed, 169–71
Program notes, 170–71
Programs, recital, 163–66
Projection of tone, 94–95
Prokofiev, Sergei, 268
Publicity for recitals, 171–72
Pulse, rhythmic, 149
Purcell, Daniel, 206
Purswell, Patrick, 279

Quantz, Johann Joachim, 116, 189, 202, 228; on audience, 163, 175; compositions, 212–14; on encores, 176; fingering chart of, 44, 46; on galant, 192; on *messa di* voce, 109; two-key flute of, 44, 45, *Plate* 3; *Versuch einer Anweisung zu spielen*, 44, 45, 109, 192, 208, 213, 220
Quarter-tone flute, 12
Quarter tones, 21, 274
Quartet, classic, 222–23
Quartet sonata, 201–2
Querflöten (*Querpfeiffen*), 63
Quintet, classic, 223
Quintet, wind, 223

Radcliff flute, 59, 76
Radcliff, John, 59
Raguenet, François: *Paralèle des italiens et des français*, 191
Rameau, Jean-Philippe, 188, 201, 214
Rampal, Jean-Pierre, 96, 101, 103; career, 5, 104, 262, 268, 275; flute of, 20, 22; recordings, 178, 180, 248, 264; style, 145, 179; transcriptions, 165

Range of flute, 43, 44, 47
Range of piccolo, 64, 67
Rateau, René, 101–2
Ravel, Maurice, 69, 259, 261; *Daphnis et Chloè*, 70, 74, 140; *L'Enfant et les Sortilèges*, 138–39
Read, Gardner, 271
Rebillé, Philbert, 192, 193
Recitals, 161–75; accompanists and assisting artists, 167–68; encores in, 176; lecture-, 162; location of, 168–69; planning program for, 163–68; protocol, 173–75; publicity for, 171–72; rehearsal for, 167, 172–73
Recorder, 43, 45, 63, 76, 188–89, 203
Recordings, 5, 103, 178–83; for auditions, 182–83; catalogs, 178–79; collecting, 178; and International Style, 11, 180; making, 182–83; of Moyse, 104; playing along with, 180–81; of Rampal, 178, 180, 248, 264; study of, 145, 147
Recurved headjoint, 75
Reform flute, 8, 57, *Plate 15*
Register, 45, *Plate 2*
Rehearsal, 147, 167, 172–73
Reicha, Antoine, 223, 227–28
Reichardt, J. F., 214, 228
Reinecke, Carl, 249
Renaissance, flute in, 42–43, 187
Rental instruments, 14–15
Repairs, 29, 36–37, 39–41
Repertoire: catalogs, 132, 164, 165; for recitals, 163–66
Response, tests for, 26–27
Reynolds, Roger, 279
Rhythm, 147, 148, 149; galant, 217; romantic, 242
Ribock, Dr. J. H., 47
Richardson, Joseph, 58
Richter, Franz Xaver, 223, 230–31
Riegger, Wallingford, 269–70
Riemann, Hugo, 190
Rieti, Vittorio, 262–63
Rimsky-Korsakov, Nicolai, 74
Ring keys, 9, 49, 50
Rivier, Jean, 263
Robison, Paula, 5, 104
Rockstro, Richard Shepard, 11, 58–59
Rococo, 202, 214, 217, 220; See *also* Classic era
Rod-axles, 9, *16*, 28
Roger, Estienne and Jeanne, 208, 209
Rogers, Bernard, 271
Roller keys, 25, 28, 57
Rolling flute, 94
Romantic era, 154, 157, 241–54
Rosetti, Antonio, 233
Rossini, Gioacchino, 22, 137–38
Rousseau, Jean-Jacques, 142, 149–50
Roussel, Albert, 261
Rubato, 144
Rudall, Carte & Co., 76
Rudall, George, 54
Rudall & Rose, 54, 55, 57
Ruge, Filippo, 227
Russia, 104
Russolo, Luigi: *The Art of Noise*, 274
Rynearson, Paul: *11 Contemporary Flute Etudes*, 133

Sachs, Curt, 148, 149
Saddles, keys on, *16*, 49
Saint-Saëns, Camille, 249–50, 257, 258, 259
Salieri, Antonio, 224, 227, 239
Sammartini, Giovanni Battista, 201, 202, 206, 234
Scale of flute, 11, 21, 61
Scales, practice of, 128–29
Scarlatti, Alessandro, 45, 202
Schafhäutl, Dr. Carl von, 54
Scheibe, Johann Adolf, 216, 222
Schickhardt, Johann Christian, 208–9
Schleifklappe, 72
Schmitt, Florent, 259, 260
Schmitt, Joseph, 224, 233
Schnietzhofer, 101, 225
Schoenberg, Arnold, 70, 273
Schonberg, Harold, 144
Schubart, C. F., 230
Schubert, Franz, 150, 156, 248
Schultze, Johann Christian, 208
Schwedler, Maximilian, 57
Schweizer Pfeiffen, 43, 63
Schwindl, Friedrich, 233
Score reading, 147
Seeger, Ruth Crawford, 269

Selmer, 12, 18, 65
Sensitive fingerings, 134. *See also* Alternate fingerings
Setzmanieren, 192
Shaffer, Elaine, 271
Siccama, Abel, 58
Siccama diatonic flute, 58, *Plate 14*
Silver flutes, 16, 18–19, 55, 101
Simple system flute, 47, 50–51; *See also* Old system flute
Single-tonguing, 117–19
Six, Les, 258, 262
Six-key flute, 47, *Plate 5*
Skinner, Harold, xvii, 18
Skowronek, Felix, 20
Société de musique de chambre pour instruments à vent, 253, 258
Société Musicale Indépendante, 259
Société Nationale de Musique, 249, 257, 258
Solfège, 146
Sollberger, Harvey, 102, 278–79
Solos, 132–33
Sonata: accompanied keyboard, 221, 245; baroque, 190, 191, 194, 196, 204–6; classic, 218, 220–22; da camera, 190; da chiesa, 190; quartet, 201–2; trio, 190, 196, 256
Sonata form, 216–17, 221
Soprano (E-flat) flute, 64, *Plate 20*
Sousa, John Philip, 69
Soussman, Heinrich, 251
Spain, 234
Spielmanieren, 192, 219
Split-E mechanism, 17, 23, 25, 60, 98
Split-G mechanism, 60
Sprenkle, Robert, 108
Springs, 16, 27, 28, 39–40, 50, 58
Staccato, 117–19
Stamitz, Anton, 231
Stamitz, Carl, 231
Stamitz, Johann, 204, 214, 223, 230, 231
Stanley, John, 208
Stevens, Roger, 114
Still, William Grant, 269
Stokes and Condon: *Illustrated Method for Flute*, 92
Stölzel, Gottfried Heinrich, 211
Storage of flute, 33
Straubinger, David, 61
Strauss, Johann, 69
Strauss, Richard, 74, 120, 243
Stravinsky, Igor, 74, 261, 262–63, 265, 272
Stringfield, Lamar, 269
Student flutes, 15, 16, 28, 36, 38
Sturm und Drang, 238, 239
Style, 132, 142–60
Subotnick, Morton, 70
Suite, baroque, 190, 192, 193, 194
Suspension (breathing), 82
Suzuki, Shin'ichi, 12
Suzuki flute method, 12
Symphonie concertante, 224–25. *See also* Concerted symphony

Tabuteau, Marcel, 112, 151, 152
Tacet, 201
Taffanel, Paul, 4, 84, 100, 101, 102, 250, 252–53, 258; on timbre and expression, 111; on vibrato, 107, 111
Taffanel and Gaubert: *Method*, 91–93, 111, 146, 253
Taillart, P. Evrard, *le cadet*, 200–1
Tailleferre, Germaine, 262
Takahashi, Takeo, 12
Takemitsu, Toru, 277
Tansman, Alexandre, 263
Tarnish, 31, 32, 33–34
Tartini, Giuseppe, 204
Tchaikovsky, Peter Ilyich, 69, 135
Tcherepnin, Alexandre, 263
Technique, 124–40; C. P. E. Bach on, 143; as expression, 144; and phrasing, 152; practice of, 127–33
Telemann, Georg Philipp, 201, 211–12, 213; *Methodical Sonatas*, 154, 170, 211
Temperature: effect on pitch, 98; of recital hall, 168
Tempo, 149, 173, 190
Tenons, 49
Tension and release, 148, 150–51
Tessarini, Carlo, 205, 206
Testing instruments, 15, 26–29, 37–38
Texture, compositional: baroque, 190, 191–92; classic, 216, 217, 218, 219–20, 221; galant, 191–92, 221; romantic, 243

Thibouville-Lamy, J., et Cie., 60
Thomson, Virgil, 270, 280
Thoreau, Henry David, 169
Throat, 83, 108, 109
Thumb keys: of Boehm, 26, 56; of Briccialdi, 56, 139; modern, 139–40; of Murray flute, 60
Timbral modification, 95–97, 256, 273–75, 276–80 passim
Toeschi, Carl Joseph, 204, 223, 232
Tomasi, Henri, 263
Tonal match, 95
Tone, 89–105; acoustical basis of, 90; of alto flute, 72–73; of baroque flute, 45; Boehm on, 72, 89; and breathing, 81, 82, 83; and expression, 95–97; focus and projection of, 94–95; harmonic content of, 24, 54, 90; homogeneity of, 95, 102; interpretation and, 95–97; intonation and, 97; national styles of, 100–4; of Nicholson, 102–3; pedagogy, 91–92; production of, 90–94
Tone color: of alto flute, 72–73; in composition, 49, 256–57; harmonics and, 136, 138–39; interpretation and, 95–97, 149; and musical structure, 149; notation of, 149, 154; of piccolo, 67–68, 69–70; in romantic music, 243; in 20th century music, 256–57, 273–74; and vibrato, 113–14
Tone holes, drawn vs. soldered, 28
Tongueless attack, 121
"Tongue out," 121
Tongue position, 91, 117, 121
Tonguing, 101, 116–120; double-, 118, 119; flutter-, 120, 265, 270, 274; single-, 117–19; triple-, 118, 120
Transcriptions, 165, 245, 251, 257
Transposition, 67, 146
Tremolo, 109, 110
Trill keys, 10, 23, 24–25, 28, 53, 54, 60, 72, 73
Trio, 196, 222
Trio sonata, 190, 196, 256
Triple-tonguing, 118, 120
Tromlitz, Johann Georg, 45, 156, 220, 244; on *Bebung*, 109; long F key of, 47
Trott, Laurence, 70
Tulou, Jean-Louis, 4, 101, 227, 244; compositions, 250, 253; 1851 flute, 57; tone, 103
Tuning, 98, 173, 174
Tuning slide, 6, 8, 45, 50
Tutors. *See* Instruction books

United States: flute playing in, 3–6, 102; French emigrés to, 101–2; 20th century flute music in, 268–73; 278–79
Ursillo, Fabio, 201
Urtext, 156
Used instruments, 15–16, 65

Valentine, Robert, 194
Vanhal [Wanhall], Johann Baptist, 204, 238
van Leeuwen, Ary, 75, 104
Varèse, Edgard, 97, 274–75
Vaughan Williams, Ralph, 264, 265
Veinus, Abraham, 143, 245, 246
Verdi, Giuseppe, 22, 71
Vermont Guild of Flute Making, 41
Versuch einer Anweisung die Flöte zu spielen (Quantz), 44, 45, 109, 192, 208, 213, 220
Vester, Frans, 100, 156; *Flute Repertoire Catalogue*, 164, 165
Vibration, 110–11
Vibrato, 91, 100, 102, 106–15; in avant-garde music, 270, 274; in baroque music, 109, 158–59; in France, 102, 111–12; history of, 109–13; speed of, 113–14; types of, 106–9; uses of, 113–14
Vienna, 104, 112, 235–40
Vigué, Louis-Fernand, 60
Villa-Lobos, Heitor, 258–59
Vinci, Leonardo, 206
Violin: bowing, 116–17, 118; music, 165; vibrato, 107, 111, 113
Virdung, Sebastian: *Musica getuscht und auszgezogen*, 42
Virtuosity, 143–45; Arthur Brooke on, 165; in classic era, 219; in 19th century, 243; in 20th century, 257, 270
Virtuosos, 143–45; and encores, 176; 19th century, 243–44, 245; 20th century, 4, 5. See *also* Concert Spirituel

Vivaldi, Antonio: concertos, 165, 196, 199, 203–4, 208; flautino concertos, 68, 69, 203; instrumentation, 68, 189; sonatas, 205
Vogler, Abbé Georg Johann, 221–22

Wagenseil, Georg Christoph, 223
Wagner, Richard, 69
Wanhall. See Vanhal, Johann Baptist
Ward, Cornelius, 54; 1842 flute of, 11, 58, *Plate 10*
Warm-up: of instrument, 98; for practice, 127–28; for recital, 173
Weber, Carl Maria von, 68, 246–47, 251
Weinberger, Jaromir, 268
Weiner, Eugene, 252
Weingartner, Felix, 74
Welch, Christopher, 59
Wendling, Johann Baptist, 201, 224, 225, 232–33, 235, 237
Wiedemann, Karl Friedrich, 189
Wilder, Alec, 271
Wilkins, Frederick, 92
Wilson, Ransom, 5
Wimberley, David, 12, 25
Wincenc, Carol, 5
Wind ensembles, 223
Wind quintet, 223
Wolf-Ferrari, 134
Wooden flutes, 18, 20–21, 28, 29, 98, *Plate 19*
Wummer, John, 22, 107, 113
Wunderlich, 101, 224, 225
Wuorinen, Charles, 278–79
Wye, Trevor, 11, 98, 103

Yamaha, 12, 19
Young, J. Harrington, 110–11

Zalo Publications and Services, 61
Zandonai, Riccardo, 75
Zelenka, Jan Dismas, 213
Ziegler, 71
Zukerman, Eugenia, 5
Zwerchpfeiff, 42